THE
INSIDERS'®
GUIDE
TO
NORTH CAROLINA'S
Triangle
CARY, CHAPEL HILL, DURHAM & RALEIGH

THE INSIDERS' GUIDE ®

TO NORTH CAROLINA'S

Triangle

CARY, CHAPEL HILL, DURHAM, RALEIGH

by
J. Barlow Herget
&
Janice Therese Mancuso

BCK Publishing Group

BCK
PUBLISHING GROUP

Published and distributed by:

BCK Publishing Group
P.O. Box 14154
Research Triangle Park, NC 27709
(919) 467-4035

•

NINTH EDITION
3rd Printing, Fall 1999

•

This publication is available from BCK
Publishing at special discounts for bulk
purchases by human resource and
relocation departments, Realtors®,
schools, libraries and companies.
Special editions, including
personalized covers, can be created
for large quantity orders. For more
information contact BCK Publishing.

•

ISBN 1-887717-03-X

BCK Publishing Group

President
Barbara King

Vice President
Tim Johnson

Editor
Rich Weidman

Copy Editor
David McNally

Art Directors
Judy Huyser
Evelyn Ward

Office Manager
Jim Harrop

Account Executives
Barbara Carr
Kate Lacey
Steve Laughman
Kerin Politis
Julia Teague

Administrative Assistants
Julie Pender
Gerry Pollard

Maps
Fraser Van Asch
Evelyn Ward

Staff Photographers
Tim Johnson
Robert Thomason

Cover Photo:
Kent Smith, Carolina Hurricanes

•

Produced under license of
The Insiders' Guide®
An imprint of Falcon® Publishing, Inc.
A Landmark Communications company.

P.O. Box 1718
Helena, MT 59624
(800) 582-2665
www.insiders.com

Preface

Welcome to the Triangle! If you're a newcomer, you made the right choice to come here. This book is your introduction to one of the most popular places in the country. If you're a Triangle resident, you already know why people keep coming here, so enjoy reading about what's new and what's changed.

You will enjoy the comprehensiveness that has always made this *the* guide to the Triangle. The guide has been painstakingly researched, completely revised in format and totally updated in content. However, things do change. By the time this edition is printed, some information will need updating. Your comments are always appreciated, so please drop us a note if you have any suggestions or find any factual discrepancies.

The core cities of the Triangle are the three that are home to the area's three large research universities—Chapel Hill, Durham and Raleigh. In the middle of the triangle formed by these three cities sat a lot of undeveloped red clay and piney woods that, according to the late George Watts Hill, "wasn't good for anything except holding the land together." It was here in the 1950s that the Research Triangle Park (RTP) was established as a nonprofit research park to attract research companies that would pay better wages than the state's traditional industries of textiles, apparel and furniture. It was a great idea and it worked. Today the Research Triangle Park is simply called "The Park" or RTP in general conversation and it has its own zip code.

The three original Triangle cities are bumping up against each other with over a million people now living in these cities and their environs, an area that residents abbreviate to "The Triangle." Cary, once a small, bedroom suburb of Raleigh, is larger than Chapel Hill and likely to have 100,000 people by the year 2000. The three universities, the University of North Carolina at Chapel Hill, Duke University in Durham and North Carolina State University in Raleigh, are celebrated as among the best in the country, and they continue to be a rich source of culture, research, sports and learning for Triangle residents.

The Triangle cities have won individually and together a string of awards and ratings during the 1990s. To brag about a few, you can cite *Money* magazine's 1998 ranking of the Triangle as the second-best metropolitan area in the South; other recent accolades include *U.S. News & World Report's* selection as one of the 50 Fabulous Places to Raise Your Family; *Money* and *PC World* magazines' titles as the No. 1 mid-size area in the country for people who work at home and telecommute; *Child* magazine's recognition of Raleigh as among the top five places to raise children in the U.S.; rankings as the No. 1 place in the country to live; the No. 1 place for business; a Top Hot Spot for starting a business; and as they say in *The King and I*, etceteras, etceteras, etceteras. See, we told you that you moved to the right place!

About the Authors

J. Barlow Herget

J. Barlow Herget is a writer who lives in Raleigh's Cameron Park neighborhood with his wife, Millie. They have two grown children. Barlow received his B.A. in English and history from the University of Arkansas and his M.A. in history from the University of Virginia. He was a Nieman Fellow ('70) at Harvard University. Barlow has worked for the *Daily Press* of Paragould, Arkansas, *The Detroit Free Press* and *The News and Observer*. His articles have appeared in *The Atlantic*, *The New York Times* and numerous other publications. He was special assistant to the N.C. Secretary of Commerce, '77-'79, and worked for Data General Corporation. Barlow is a commentator on public radio in the Triangle. He has been a resident of the Triangle since 1973 and served on the Raleigh City Council for two terms. Barlow was one of the champions in the 1992 Rex Tennis Classic and can be found hobbling around the racquetball courts at the Hillsborough Street YMCA. He operates a writing and media consulting business in Raleigh.

Janice Therese Mancuso

Janice Therese Mancuso is a freelance writer and editor who lives in Cary. She relocated from New York in the early '90s to pursue educational and business opportunities in the Triangle. Her interest in the region, community involvement and penchant for research led her to work on several local guidebooks. Her nationally published cookbook, *Herbed-Wine Cuisine, Creating and Cooking with Herb-Infused Wines*, was a featured selection of The Good Cook (a division of the Book-of-the-Month Club). Between writing, book signings, radio interviews and an appearance on the Food Network, Janice operates her own floral design and specialty food businesses. She even finds time to teach floral design and cooking classes. Janice received her MBA from Adelphi University and has taught college-level business courses locally. This year, she created and designed her own web site. She is also the publisher of several newsletters and a stationery line, "Almost All Raspberry," which features her cat "Raspberry."

ACKNOWLEDGMENTS

This book includes information and insight from our authors and dozens of individuals who offered encouragement, as well as their thoughts and ideas about the Triangle. We especially want to thank all the Chambers of Commerce, Convention and Visitors Bureaus, Boards of Realtors and many other companies, organizations and individuals who helped us compile and update this 9th edition.

YOUR COMMENTS

Please take a few moments to share your comments and suggestions on our "More Information" reply card and we will be happy to forward your requests for information.

Table of Contents

Directory of Close-ups

Directory of Maps

STATE OF NORTH CAROLINA
OFFICE OF THE GOVERNOR
RALEIGH 27603-8001

JAMES B. HUNT JR.
GOVERNOR

Dear Friends:

As Governor of the State of North Carolina, it is indeed my pleasure to welcome you to the Triangle, that vast metropolitan area that connects Raleigh, Cary, Durham, Chapel Hill and Carrboro.

This area is home to more than 50 corporate, academic and governmental research facilities. What sets it apart from other great research centers, however, is the superior quality of life. Unlike most metro areas, the Triangle consists of medium-sized cities which offer all the amenities of big-city living without the high costs. One can easily go from urban to suburban to rural settings within the area, experiencing Southern Hospitality at its very best all along the way.

Having been named America's best city for business by *Fortune* magazine, Raleigh/Durham continues to live up to its industrious reputation. Contributing to the area's top ranking is the presence of three top universities—Duke, UNC and N.C. State—and the 7,000-acre Research Triangle Park. We are extremely proud of this recognition and feel that it is well deserved.

On behalf of all our citizens, I again welcome you and invite you to enjoy all that the Triangle has to offer.

My warmest personal regards,

Sincerely,

James B. Hunt Jr.

Welcome Home!
to the Triangle

Photo courtesy of the Carolina Hurricanes

Check us out!

CitySearch
www.citysearch11.com

The News & Observer Online
www.news-observer.com

Cary Chamber of Commerce
www.carychamber.com

**Chapel Hill-Carrboro
Chamber of Commerce**
www.herald-sun.com/cchamber

Chapel Hill Visitors Bureau
www.chocvb.org

Durham Chamber of Commerce
www.durhamchamber.org

We just keep getting better!

Durham Convention & Visitors Bureau
www.Durham-NC.com

Raleigh Chamber of Commerce
www.raleighchamber.org

Raleigh Convention & Visitors Bureau
www.raleighcvb.org

Triangle Cities, Towns

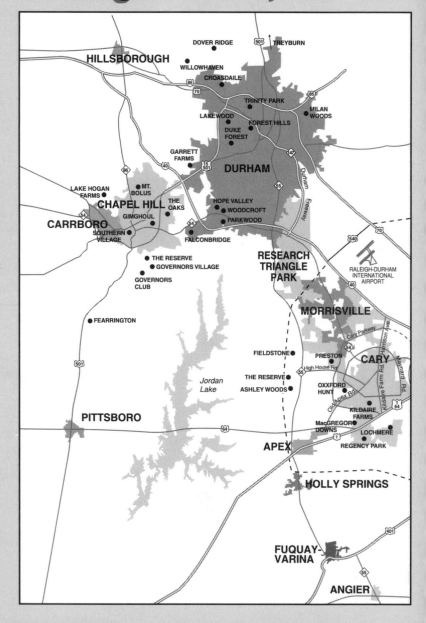

and Neighborhoods

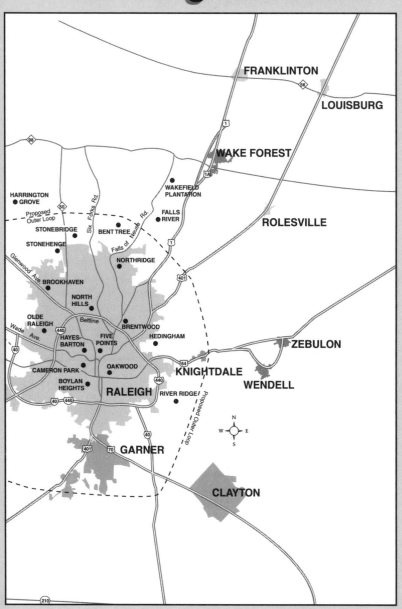

Cary

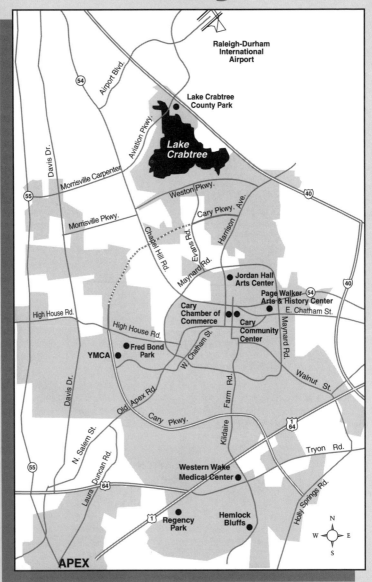

Raleigh-Durham
International
Airport

Lake Crabtree
County Park

*Lake
Crabtree*

54

Airport Blvd.

Aviation Pkwy.

Davis Dr.

55

Morrisville Carpenter

Weston Pkwy.

Cary Pkwy.

40

Morrisville Pkwy.

Chapel Hill Rd.

Evans Rd.

Harrison Ave.

Maynard Rd.

Jordan Hall
Arts Center

Page Walker
Arts & History Center

54

40

High House Rd.

High House Rd.

Cary
Chamber of
Commerce

E. Chatham St.

W. Chatham St.

Cary
Community
Center

Maynard Rd.

YMCA

Fred Bond
Park

Davis Dr.

Old Apex Rd.

Cary   Pkwy.

Farm   Rd.

Walnut   St.

N. Salem St.

Kildaire

1
64

55

Laura Duncan Rd.

Tryon   Rd.

64

Western Wake
Medical Center

Holly Springs Rd.

1

Regency
Park

Hemlock
Bluffs

N

W   E

S

APEX

Chapel Hill

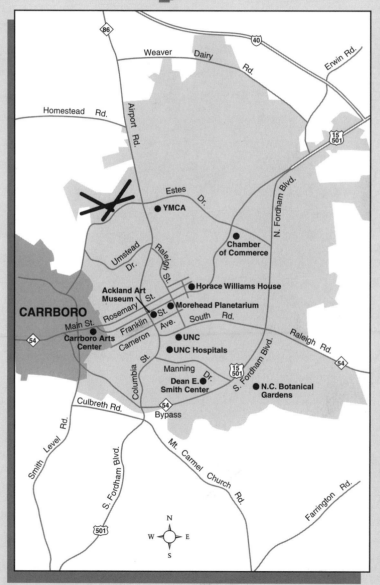

86

Weaver   Dairy   Rd.   40   Erwin Rd.

Homestead   Rd.   15 501

Airport   Rd.

Estes   Dr.   ● YMCA

N. Fordham Blvd.

Umstead   Dr.

Raleigh St.

● Chamber
of Commerce

**Ackland Art
Museum**   St.   ● Horace Williams House

CARRBORO   Rosemary   St.   ● Morehead Planetarium

Main St.   Franklin   Ave.   South   Rd.   Raleigh Rd.

54   **Carrboro Arts
Center**   Cameron   ● UNC   54

Columbia   St.   ● UNC Hospitals

Manning   Dr.   15 501

Dean E. ●
Smith Center   S. Fordham Blvd.   ● N.C. Botanical
Gardens

Culbreth Rd.   54
Bypass

Smith Level Rd.   S. Fordham Blvd.   Mt. Carmel Church Rd.   Farrington Rd.

501

N
W ✦ E
S

Durham

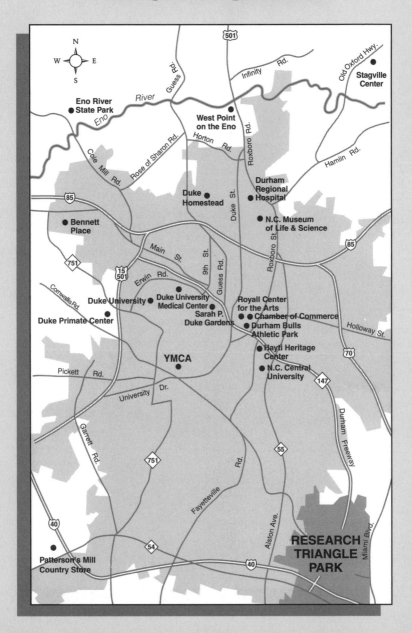

Raleigh

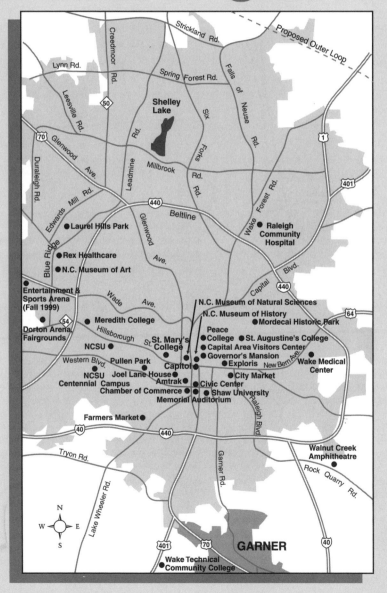

Strickland Rd.

Proposed Outer Loop

Lynn Rd.

Creedmoor Rd.

Spring Forest Rd.

Falls of Neuse Rd.

Shelley Lake

Leesville Rd.

50

70 Glenwood Ave.

Duraleigh Rd.

Leadmine Rd.

Six Forks Rd.

Millbrook Rd.

1

401

Edwards Mill Rd.

440

Beltline

Glenwood Ave.

Wake Forest Rd.

Blue Ridge

● Laurel Hills Park

● **Raleigh Community Hospital**

● Rex Healthcare

● N.C. Museum of Art

Capital Blvd.

440

●
Entertainment & Sports Arena (Fall 1999)

Wade Ave.

N.C. Museum of Natural Sciences

N.C. Museum of History

64

54

● Meredith College

Hillsborough St.

Peace ● College

● Mordecai Historic Park

Dorton Arena Fairgrounds

NCSU ●

St. Mary's College

● ● St. Augustine's College

● Capital Area Visitors Center

Western Blvd.

● Pullen Park

● Governor's Mansion

New Bern Ave.

● Wake Medical Center

NCSU **Centennial Campus**

● Joel Lane House

Capitol ●

● Exploris

● City Market

Amtrak ●

● Civic Center

Chamber of Commerce ●

● Shaw University

Memorial Auditorium

Raleigh Blvd.

● Farmers Market ●

40

440

Walnut Creek Amphitheatre ●

Tryon Rd.

Garner Rd.

Rock Quarry Rd.

Lake Wheeler Rd.

N
W E
S

401 70 **GARNER** 40

● **Wake Technical Community College**

Research Triangle Park

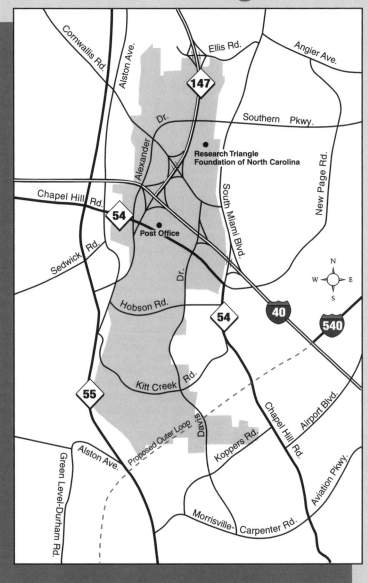

How to Use This Book

We're proud of the Triangle and our *Insiders' Guide* provides a one-stop source of information about this dynamic area. We designed the guide to be used by residents, newcomers, visitors and anyone else who wants a comprehensive overview of the Triangle. No matter where you travel throughout the area, take this guide with you. Keep it in your glove compartment, briefcase or backpack.

Newcomers will certainly find the chapter on the *History of the Triangle* insightful. Our *Triangle Overview* chapter highlights Cary, Chapel Hill and Carrboro, Durham and Raleigh. The *Triangle Towns* chapter includes information on the smaller neighboring towns of Angier, Apex, Clayton, Franklinton, Fuquay-Varina, Garner, Hillsborough, Holly Springs, Knightdale, Louisburg, Morrisville, Pittsboro, Rolesville, Wake Forest, Wendell and Zebulon.

If you're just getting to the area and want to know how to navigate our highways, our *Getting Around* chapter provides you with the information you'll need.

Visitors also will appreciate the chapters on *Accommodations, Annual Events, Arts and Culture, Attractions, Bed and Breakfasts, Night Life, Restaurants* and *Shopping.*

Our *Employment Opportunities* chapter is for those individuals considering relocating to the Triangle.

Newcomers will find the chapters on *Apartments and Temporary Housing, Real Estate and Neighborhoods* (with information on buying or building), *Colleges and Universities, Golf in the Carolinas, Health Care, Media, Retirement and Senior Services* and *Utilities and Services* especially helpful in making decisions associated with moving to a new area. Our *Spectator Sports* chapter gives you an Insider's view of the Wolfpack, Blue Devils, Tar Heels, Bulls, Mudcats, Hurricanes, Cougars, Capital Express, Wings, Dragons and local stock-car racing. We've even provided you with a variety of destinations in the mountains and along the coast in the *Daytrips and Weekend Vacations* chapter for those of you with a yearning to hit the road.

Parents will appreciate the chapters on *Kidstuff and Camps, Parks and Recreation* and *Schools and Child Care.*

Each chapter has Insider's tips to provide you with some of the secrets we've gleaned as longtime residents of the Triangle. In-depth "Close-ups" on such regional topics as North Carolina barbecue and March Madness are also included throughout the guide.

Please note that the area code for all phone numbers listed in this guide in 919, unless otherwise noted.

History of North Carolina

(Excerpted from an article by Dr. Jerry C. Cashion,
Research Branch, Division of Archives and History,
North Carolina Department of Cultural Resources)

Before the coming of European explorers, Native Americans inhabited the territory that is now North Carolina. Major tribes included the Tuscaroras, the Catawbas and the Cherokees. Beginning with Verrazzano in 1524, various French, Spanish and English explorers visited the area. In 1585 and 1587, English colonies were sponsored by Sir Walter Raleigh. These attempts at settlement failed. In 1629, Charles I of England declared all lands south of Virginia to be part of the British Empire. The first permanent settlement started in the 1660s when farmers settled the area around Albemarle Sound.

In 1677, economic and religious quarrels with the provisional governor in Virginia led to restrictions on shipping from North Carolina. These restrictions added to ill feelings in the state and hampered the growth of the state's significant tobacco crop. The settlers continued to resist the colonial rulings from England and Virginia and, in an attempt to restore order, the British formed the separate state of North Carolina in 1729 and sent a deputy governor to the area.

Meanwhile, the first town had been settled in 1700 and it was called Bath. After this, the population rose rapidly and settlements spread across the eastern and central (or Piedmont) part of the state.

Royal oppression mounted and American patriots talked, preached and fought for independence. Moores Creek, Halifax, Hillsborough and Fayetteville drew gatherings of North Carolinians who would be free to make their own laws and unite with the other American colonies to form the United States of America. With the famous Halifax Resolves, April 12, 1776, North Carolina became the first colony to instruct its delegates to the Continental Congress to vote for independence. General Cornwallis invaded the state in 1780 and was defeated soundly at the Battle of Guilford Courthouse. The weakened British army later surrendered in neighboring Virginia.

North Carolina representatives declined to ratify the new United States Constitution until assured that a Bill of Rights was to be added.

Development in the state after the American Revolution was very slow. The state's economy was unable to grow due to poor transportation and communication systems. A reawakening occurred after 1835 when constitutional revisions gave more power to the western half of the state. Plank roads, canals and railroads helped solve the problem of transportation. Improved access to markets stimulated agricultural and industrial growth.

Education proved to be the major key to the development of the state. The University of North Carolina, which opened in 1795, became one of the leading institutions in the nation. The state was the first in the South to establish a tax-supported system of public schools.

When the Civil War started, North Carolina was somewhat reluctant to leave the Union, but the state fought on the side of the Confederacy. The state supplied more troops and suffered more losses than any other in the Confederacy. The state's ports drew much Union fire, but the Port of Wilmington remained open until the fall of Fort Fisher in January 1865. Confederate General Joseph E. Johnston surrendered to the Federal army under General William T. Sherman in April 1865 at the Bennett House, near the present city of Durham.

Reconstruction saw much internal upheaval. Partisan discord marked much of the remainder of the century. Industrial development outpaced a resurgence of agriculture at this time.

During the early twentieth century the foundation was laid for the state's rapid progress. Dedication to public education and highway construction became hallmarks of generations of legislators.

North Carolina devoted its human, industrial and agricultural resources to engage in two World Wars. Gearing up for wartime production, the state became more educated, urban and internationally connected. Developments in agriculture made it possible for highly efficient farms to produce an abundance of food and fiber that found its way to the national and global market.

The Research Triangle Park was established in 1958 to boost growth in research-related fields. Located in close proximity to the University of North Carolina at Chapel Hill, Duke University in Durham and North Carolina State University in Raleigh, the Triangle contains the South's greatest concentrations of scientists, research sources, laboratory facilities and cultural resources. Industrial growth has followed the growth in research.

North Carolina is divided into 100 counties. The state has three distinct regions: Coastal, Piedmont and Mountains. The Coastal region comprises about 45 percent of the state's area. A long chain of islands called the Outer Banks is located on the northern coast. Kitty Hawk, located near Roanoke Island, is where the Wright brothers ushered in the age of flight in 1903. Other islands extend as far south as South Carolina.

The Piedmont, or central part of the state, is approximately 38 percent of the area of the state. It is the prime symbol of the "New South" in which modern industry and technology have replaced agriculture as the main source of income. Industry is prevalent in Raleigh, Chapel Hill, Durham, Greensboro and Charlotte.

The Mountain region of North Carolina is bounded by two ranges of the southern Appalachians, The Blue Ridge Mountains and the Great Smoky Mountains. The mountains are renowned for a variety of crafts including pottery, wood carving, basketry, needlework, handmade rugs and bedspreads. Today the mountains have become a well-known year-round resort and Asheville is the center of activity.

The Democratic party dominated state government for the first half of the twentieth century, but in 1972 both a Republican senator and governor were elected. Democrat James B. Hunt served as Governor from 1977-1985. Republican James G. Martin then served two terms. In 1992, Governor Hunt was elected to serve a third term and in 1996 was reelected to a record fourth term.

The Triangle is easily accessed off major interstate highways I-95, I-40 and I-85.

Getting Around

The Triangle is easily accessed off major interstate highways I-95, I-40 and I-85. The Raleigh-Durham International Airport and Amtrak service from Cary, Raleigh and Durham make getting to and from the Triangle a breeze. It's once you're here that you may have some difficulty maneuvering around. Although public transportation is limited, rental cars are readily available and most agencies provide road maps. Study road maps, observe the speed limits and ask for directions. The local folk are more than happy to help someone find their way around the Triangle.

Air Transportation

Raleigh-Durham International Airport

Located off Interstate 40 between Raleigh and Durham, the Raleigh-Durham International Airport (RDU) is a 20- to 30-minute drive from most points in the Triangle. We'd offer a word of caution, though. It helps to allow extra time, since traffic delays on I-40 can sometimes lengthen your trip en route to RDU. You also need to plan on a few extra minutes to park and ride to your terminal when you are leaving your vehicle for an extended trip. When the airport opened in what was an old U.S. Army barracks in 1943, its location was considered in the middle of nowhere. It remained out in the boondocks for a good 20 years. But those days are now a distant memory.

RDU has grown dramatically from its beginnings, with much of the growth coming in the last 15 years. In 1982, the airport added the $9.6 million Terminal A. In 1986, another $2.5 million was spent expanding the terminal's passenger waiting areas, gate space and aircraft parking, as well as building a new 10,000-foot runway. The $60 million Terminal C opened in 1987, after American Airlines made RDU one of its major north-south connecting hubs. Further renovations to Terminal A were completed in 1991 at a cost of about $2 million.

Today RDU International is served by more airlines than at any time in its history, offering service to both domestic and international destinations. In fact, over 6.7 million passengers passed through the airport's gates to their business and pleasure destinations in 1997, up nearly 5 percent from 1996. RDU's leading carrier, Midway, moved its headquarters from the Chicago area to Raleigh-Durham in 1995. Midway Airlines is Raleigh-Durham's hometown airline and now serves 20 major cities along the East Coast.

Some benefits for air travelers have emerged from the changes. The average price of a ticket has declined, due to more competition among the airlines for RDU's business. Passenger traffic continues to increase and that growth is expected to continue. An $18 million expansion of Terminal A has recently been completed that contains new aircraft gates for Continental and AirTran. Across the street from Terminal A, construction is underway on a $40 million, 2,700-space parking garage, which is scheduled for completion during the fall of 1999. Work has also begun on a $10 million, five-year program

Photo courtesy of Raleigh-Durham International Airport

The Raleigh-Durham International Airport, one of the country's fastest-growing airports, provides over 400 flights daily.

to overhaul its general aviation facilities. About 110,000 tons of cargo are shipped out of RDU each year, up from 90,000 tons a few years ago.

Thanks to this continuing growth and expansion of the airport, you can take your pick of a variety of flights—many nonstops—to most major U.S. metropolitan areas and direct flights to some international destinations, including London, Toronto and the Bahamas. Southwest, the country's fourth-largest airline, began flights out of RDU in June, 1999.

Airport Information

RDU Airport Information
• 840-2123
Airport Parking Information
• 840-2110

Airlines

Air Canada • (800) 776-3000
AirTran • (800) 247-8726
American Airlines • (800) 433-7300
Canadian Regional
• (800) 426-7000
Continental Airlines
• (800) 525-0280
Delta Air Lines • (800) 221-1212
Delta Express • (800) 325-5205
MetroJet • (800) 638-7653
Midway Airlines • (800) 446-4392
Midwest Express
• (800) 452-2022
Northwest Airlines
• (800) 225-2525
Southwest Airlines
• (800) 435-9792
TWA • (800) 221-2000
United Airlines • (800) 241-6522
USAirways • (800) 428-4322

Airlines (Commuter)

American Eagle • (800) 433-7300
Continental Express
• (800) 525-0280
Corporate Express
• (800) 555-6565
Delta Connection
• (800) 221-1212
United Express • (800) 241-6522
USAirways Express
• (800) 428-4322

Airport Parking

All lots charge $1 per hour with varying daily maximums, including $18 for hourly lots and $6 for daily lots. Park and Ride lots 1 and 2, which are located closer to the terminals, cost $4 per day. The overflow and Park and Ride 3 and 4 lots are $3 a day. Payment by cash, credit card or traveler's check is accepted. Allow at least an hour to park before your flight.

Airport Transportation

Bus service from the airport to major cities of the Triangle is available from Triangle Transit Authority (TTA) Monday through Friday. In addition, there are rental cars, taxis and limousine services. The airport limousine services (usually a van) will charge about $20 per person to get you to downtown Raleigh, Chapel Hill or Carrboro. That's cheaper than local taxis which will charge $25 to $30 for the same trip. But if you are sharing a ride to one location with one or more riders, you'll probably do better in a cab, since cabs charge by the trip and add only moderate surcharges for additional passengers. RDU is served by a number of cab companies and shuttle services to the cities of the Triangle. The major rental car companies also offer pick-up at the airport. Check with the airport information desk or in the Yellow Pages for cab companies offering service to and from RDU and for rental car information. Many hotels and motels offer free shuttle service to and from the

TRIANGLE RENTAL CAR AGENCIES

Alamo Rent A Car	800-327-9633
Raleigh-Durham International Airport	840-0132
Avis Rent A Car	800-331-1212
Raleigh-Durham International Airport	840-4750
Budget Car and Truck Rental	800-527-0700
Raleigh-Durham International Airport	876-8715
Dollar Rent A Car	800-800-4000
Raleigh-Durham International Airport	840-4850
Enterprise Rent-A-Car	800-325-8007
5105 Capital Blvd., Raleigh	790-1900
1859 N. Harrison Ave., Cary	677-1266
2501 University Dr., Durham	493-2683
110 N. Merritt Mill Rd., Chapel Hill	967-5128
Hertz	800-654-3131
Raleigh-Durham International Airport	840-4875
National Car Rental	800-227-7368
Raleigh-Durham International Airport	840-4350
Thrifty Car Rental	800-367-2277
Raleigh-Durham International Airport	832-9381
Triangle Rent-A-Car	
Raleigh-Durham International Airport	840-3400

Photo by Rich Weidman

Over 2,000 passengers a day take advantage of Triangle Transit Authority's regional bus service, which offers a comfortable commute at a reasonable rate.

airport, so check with them when you make your reservations.

General Aviation Services

North State Air Service, Inc.
• (800) 831-8208

North State provides air charter, air courier, aerial photography and scheduled weekend services to the Outer Banks.

Piedmont Charters
• 840-2700, (800) 548-1978

Piedmont offers air charter services from Raleigh-Durham International Airport using a variety of aircraft, from piston twins to intercontinental jets. Services are available 24 hours a day.

Southern Jet
• 840-4400

Formerly known as Raleigh Flying Service, Southern Jet offers air charters, aerial photography, sight-seeing flights, aircraft service and flight training.

Horace Williams Airport

The Horace Williams Airport, just north of downtown Chapel Hill, started out as a grass landing strip in the 1920s. The airport was constructed by the Navy just before World War II. Now owned by the University of North Carolina, it has a 4,000-foot paved and lighted runway. Pilots can give five signals on the 123.0 radio frequency to raise the intensity of the lights for landing. 100 octane, low-lead fuel and jet fuel are available. For more information on the airport, call 962-1337.

Ground Transportation
Bus Service

Carolina Trailways
Chapel Hill • 942-3356

Greyhound-Trailways Bus Lines
Raleigh • 834-8275
Durham • 687-4800

Triangle Transit Authority
• 549-9999

Regional Service

Triangle Transit Authority is a growing transportation catalyst that expedites service among and within the area's municipal bus systems. Monthly passes are available, as well as special rates for the elderly and handicapped. TTA has recently started offering evening and Saturday service via its hub in Research Triangle Park (near the intersection of Davis Drive and N.C. 54) to Chapel Hill, Durham and Raleigh. During the evenings, hourly service runs until 11:45 PM and on Saturdays buses run between 6:45 AM and 6:45 PM. TTA also offers fixed shuttle service between Raleigh-Durham International Airport and the RTP hub every half hour during peak times and every hour during other times.

Plans are in the works for TTA to expand service to RTP from South Cary, Apex and North Raleigh along Interstate 540, as well as routes from Raleigh to Garner and Durham to Hillsborough. TTA is also planning to start a commuter rail system within a couple of years. For TTA information, call 549-9999.

Raleigh

Raleigh's municipal bus system serves the city and some outlying areas such as Cary and Garner in peak hours and goes by the acronym of CAT (Capital Area Transit). The system doesn't make change, so have the exact fare of 75 cents. The buses are safe, clean and rarely crowded. There can be a long wait between rides and the routes are limited. Once a year, the system is jammed during State Fair week when every vehicle that rolls is used to ferry people to and from the Fairgrounds. CAT travel is a bargain and you escape the traffic jams. For CAT information, call 828-7228.

The Raleigh Trolley provides an easy and fun-filled way to see the sights in downtown. Call 828-7228 for schedules and information.

Durham

Durham is served by DATA (Durham Area Transit Authority), an intracity bus system that transports approximately 3 million passengers annually. Schedules are available at many locations, including municipal offices and public libraries. Call DATA at 688-4587 for route, rate and schedule information.

A special bus service is operated Monday through Friday to Duke University Medical Center. Call 684-2218.

For an educational and fun-filled overview of Durham's attractions and historical sites, consider taking an excursion with Bull City Sightseeing Tours. For more information, call 688-1230.

Chapel Hill

Chapel Hill Transit provides bus and shared-ride service throughout Chapel Hill. Buses run regularly from as early as 6 AM to as late as 11 PM on busy weekday routes, with less frequent service on

Photo by Tim Johnson

Amtrak's Piedmont and Carolinian trains stop daily at the Cary Depot, which doubles as a driver's license bureau.

weekends. Buses also run less often when the university is not in session. The fare is 75 cents. Annual and semiannual passes are available. Call 968-2769 for route and schedule information. The Triangle Transit Authority now runs weekdays year round from 6 AM to 7 PM between UNC and Chapel Hill to Durham and Duke University. The fare is $1. The Chapel Hill Trolley does not run on a regular basis but may be rented out for weddings and other events.

In some areas where buses do not run, residents can call Chapel Hill Transit at 968-2772 and request a ride to the nearest bus stop for the price of the regular bus fare. This service, called "shared-ride feeder service," is available in a number of areas in town. A special "E-Z Rider" service is provided for people who are unable to use regular bus service because of handicaps.

Trains

Amtrak
320 W. Cabarrus St., Raleigh
• 833-7594
211 N. Academy St., Cary (not staffed)
400 W. Chapel Hill St., Durham
• 956-7932
Information • (800) 872-7245

Amtrak offers a full schedule from its depot in Raleigh. Of special interest to many Triangle business people is the Carolinian—a daily train that runs between Charlotte and Raleigh. It then travels on to New York with stops in Virginia, Washington, D.C., and Philadelphia. The Piedmont departs daily from Raleigh, Cary and Durham to Greensboro, Charlotte and some cities in between. Call for schedules, as times are subject to change.

On the Road in the Triangle

Inside the Beltline, the Inner Beltline, the Outer Beltline, the Outer Loop, I-40, I-440, I-540. What does it all mean? Newcomers to the Triangle may be confused by the terms used to describe the roads they are traveling in the area. Let's start with Inside the Beltline. The Beltline, also known as I-440, encompasses downtown Raleigh and the surrounding vicinity within 1 mile of the State Capitol to the south and 3 miles to the north. This geographic area encircled by The Beltline (I-440) is known as "Inside the Beltline." This area is rich in history, containing the aforementioned State Capitol (circa 1840), the beautiful Governor's Mansion (built between 1883 and 1891), Historic Oakwood (established at the turn of the century), the State Legislative Building, City

Market (1914), the State Farmers Market, several colleges, and many other renovated buildings and homes. Many native Raleighites also live Inside the Beltline, as have generations of their families. Occasionally, you may hear a native refer to Inside the Beltline as "Old Raleigh." To the north, however, and still "inside the beltline" are many new subdivisions and shopping plazas. This is sometimes referred to as "New Raleigh."

The Beltline (I-440 that encircles downtown Raleigh and its environs) is divided into the Inner Beltline and the Outer Beltline. This can be confusing, especially when trying to figure out which way to go when you want to get on the Beltline as

I-40 and the Durham Freeway

you're traveling 60 miles an hour with traffic surrounding you. Just keep in mind—on the Inner Beltline, cars travel in a clockwise motion; on the Outer Beltline, cars travel in a counterclockwise motion.

The Outer Loop (also known as I-540) is relatively new and only partially completed. When it is finished, sometime around 2010, it will encompass almost all of the Wake County towns of Raleigh, Cary, Morrisville, Apex

Photo courtesy of N.C. Dept. of Transportation

and Garner. The completed portion currently extends from I-40, by RDU International Airport northeast to U.S. 70 (also known as Glenwood Avenue). I-40 extends from Wilmington at the coast and blends with I-440 southeast of downtown Raleigh. It winds west through Cary, becoming I-40 once again when it passes over U.S. 1 (also known as U.S. 64). I-40 then continues west to the North Carolina-Tennessee border.

So, now you should be able to navigate some of the highways and byways of the Triangle; but just to be on the safe side, it might be a good idea to keep a map handy.

The Triangle area is
rich in history.

History of The Triangle

The Triangle area is rich in history—from Raleigh, named after Sir Walter Raleigh; to Durham, known for its tobacco products and health care; to Chapel Hill, the home of the first state-owned university in the nation; to Cary, home of the first public school in the state. Each city is distinct, yet combined they form an area that has emerged as one of the fastest growing and most desirable places to live in the country.

Raleigh, the capital of North Carolina and home to North Carolina State University; Durham, home of Duke University; Chapel Hill, known for the University of North Carolina and its high concentration of Ph.D.'s; and Cary, known for its rapid growth, have come a long way, especially in the last 10 years. It's no wonder that right in the middle of all this activity is the Research Triangle Park, a world-renowned area of research and development rich in biotechnology and telecommunications.

A condensed version of the history of each town is given below. For more information on the history of each Triangle town, contact the Chamber of Commerce or Visitors Bureau for that town.

Cary

Unlike some ersatz post-World War II suburbs, Cary has a past. It's been around for more than 100 years on the state's legislative books. Citizens are especially proud of Cary's record for establishing the first public school in the state, the Cary Academy for which Academy Street is named.

Before Cary was a town, it was the busy home and gathering place for business friends and family of A. Francis (Frank) Page. He was founder of the town and father to five sons, one of whom was to become one of the state's famous sons—writer and diplomat Walter Hines Page. Indeed, some citizens then and later believed Cary should have been named Page, after Frank. It was he who, in the mid-1850s, set up a sawmill, store and inn along the main road between Raleigh and the university in Chapel Hill. He also ran the post office and began raising his family there. But it was the coming of the railroads in 1868 and the junction they formed at Page's place that literally put it on the map. That same year, he sold some of his lots: one 70-acre parcel went for $140 and a 10-acre piece sold for the grand sum of $50.

In 1871, the General Assembly incorporated the various enterprises and railroad crossing as the town of "Carey," a misspelling on the town clerk's part that was later corrected. The name was selected to honor one Samuel F. Cary, a famed Ohio temperance orator who reportedly stayed at Page's inn on one of his speaking tours in the South and greatly impressed his host. The selection must have been a brave choice for the times. Cary was not only a teetotaling Yankee outsider, he also had been a general in the Union Army, not a recommendation for honors in the South of 1871.

Cary began to make strides in the early 1900s. Cary High School became the first state-assisted public high school in North Carolina in 1907. In 1908, the Bank of Cary was chartered. By 1917, the "Western Wake Highway" (now East Chatham and Hillsborough streets) was paved between Cary and Raleigh, and the town received power from Carolina Power and Light Company the following year.

Cary's population grew by over 60 percent in the 1920s, but the Great Depression put an end to all of the prosperity. The Bank of Cary closed its doors in 1931 and the town defaulted on its bonds and declared bankruptcy the following year. Cary managed to bounce back after World War II, firmly establishing itself as a Raleigh bedroom community. However, few jobs were available, with the notable exception of the Taylor Biscuit Company (now known as Austin Foods), which opened in 1947. The development of Research Triangle Park in the late '50s changed everything, generating new industries and housing for Cary.

In 1960, Cary developed a comprehensive growth plan, which is updated annually. The town's first major housing development, MacGregor Downs, was incorporated in 1966. By the time Cary celebrated its Centennial in 1971, the town's population had reached 7,640 and it had begun to step outside of Raleigh's shadow and establish its own identity.

The success of MacGregor Downs led to the construction of other developments along Kildaire Farm Road, including Kildaire Farms (Cary's first planned unit development), Wimbledon and Lochmere. The arrival of industrial and business parks such as MacGregor Park, Regency Park and Weston brought in thousands of additional jobs. SAS Institute, which started in 1976 with less than a dozen employees, took off in the 1980s and currently employs approximately 3,100 people. Formerly known as Cary Village Mall, Cary Towne Center opened in 1979 and had tripled in size by 1991.

In the 1990s, Cary has become a favorite among many new Triangle residents who have moved here from the North. The population skyrocketed from 43,858 in 1990 to 85,000 in 1998.

Photo by Tim Johnson

Cary's oldest residence, The Nancy Jones House (ca. 1804), was often called the "White House" and, appropriately enough, President James Polk stopped here for lunch in 1847.

The cornerstone for the University of North Carolina's first building, Old East, was laid on October 12, 1793.

Chapel Hill and Carrboro

It's not clear just when UNC-CH and Chapel Hill picked up their reputations for being scandalously tolerant. Some would say it goes back to that fateful day in April 1865 when General Atkins of the Union forces then occupying Chapel Hill paid a visit to the home of University President Swain. It was there that the Yankee General met Swain's young daughter, Eleanor, and fell instantly in love. The two were married in August while students hung the General and the President in effigy. Later, someone recalling the disgrace scribbled on a classroom blackboard, "This old University ... has busted and gone to hell."

If Chapel Hill's identity is inescapably intertwined with UNC-CH's, it is because, like twins, their births occurred simultaneously. Legend has it that the location of both UNC-CH and Chapel Hill was sealed one warm summer day in 1792 when a committee entrusted with selecting a site for the first state university embarked on its search mission. They stopped to rest in the shade of a great tulip poplar, not far

from the New Hope Chapel. Refreshed by a picnic lunch and a few rounds of "exhilarating" spirits, the group agreed this was the perfect spot for their university. It was beautiful, served by pure water from a nearby spring and, most importantly, "inaccessible to vice" (or so they thought). More likely than not, the site was really chosen because the property had been donated to the cause by some wealthy benefactors. At any rate, on October 12, 1793, a formal ceremony was held for laying the cornerstone of Old East, the university's first building. That same day, taking advantage of the crowd that had assembled, an auctioneer offered 22 large lots for sale in what would soon become the surrounding town.

Prior to the opening of the university, Chapel Hill was nothing more than a muddy crossroads in the wilderness, a hamlet of Scottish and English families who had arrived in the mid-1700s. The community took its name from the New Hope Chapel located on a hill overlooking a valley to the east. The hamlet contained perhaps a half-dozen houses, a blacksmith shop and an inn. The town of less than 1,000

Photo courtesy of N.C. Travel & Tourism

Civil War soldiers created a demand for Durham's "Bright Leaf" tobacco, contributing to the fortunes of Washington Duke and his sons Brodie, Ben and James.

inhabitants was incorporated in 1851 and elected its first mayor in 1879.

Meanwhile, west of Chapel Hill, another community had sprung up around the only railroad station that served the university. One student, on a train he thought was destined for the UNC-CH campus, wrote of finding that he had been dropped off "in the middle of nowhere."

Eventually a settlement grew up around the railroad depot, consisting of a flour mill, a blacksmith shop and a cotton mill built in 1898 by Chapel Hillian Tom Lloyd. The community was known as West End, then West Chapel Hill and later Venable, for former UNC-CH President Francis P. Venable. Finally, after Lloyd's mill was purchased by the Julian Carr family of Durham, the town took the name of Carrboro, as it is still known today.

Although they grew up side by side, Chapel Hill and Carrboro were distinct communities for years. Chapel Hill evolved as a university village and a haven for liberal intellectuals, while Carrboro's population was made up of

blue-collar workers employed to service the university and the cotton mill. When Carr Mill shut down after the Great Depression, the town became more of a small bedroom community for people who worked at the university or its hospital. Right up through the 1970s, Chapel Hill and Carrboro maintained their distinct identities, one as the university village, the other as a small historic town. With the continuing surge of growth in the county, the two towns have grown together; however, merger of the two municipalities is not on the current agenda.

Durham

Back in the middle of the last century, Durham was not much more than a whistle-stop on North Carolina's east-west railroad line. Today the "City of Medicine" has become world renowned for its health-care facilities, cutting-edge research and development companies and educational institutions.

THOMAS KINKADE
Painter of Light™

Summer Gate

Available in three sizes

Please visit our galleries and discover why Thomas Kinkade has become the most collected artist in America!

THOMAS KINKADE
CRABTREE GALLERY
Second Level in front of Lord & Taylor
Closed Sundays
4325 Glenwood Avenue
Raleigh, NC 27612
(919) 781-2727
888-79-LIGHT

THOMAS KINKADE
Village of Pinehurst Gallery
#5 Market Square
Village of Pinehurst
North Carolina
(910) 235-5300

A Thomas Kinkade Signature Gallery

www.thomaskinkade.com

Coming Soon to a Bookstore Near You!

Daytrips & Weekend Vacations in

North Carolina

Great Money Saving Coupons Included!

The forces that built this town—tobacco, textiles, medicine and education—also shaped its uniquely diverse character. Once heavily populated by blue-collar tobacco and textile workers, it is as much a home today for doctors and dancers, high-tech execs and entrepreneurs.

It all started at the corner of Peabody and Corcoran streets where Bartlett Snipes Durham, a local physician, built his country estate and called it, some would say prophetically, "Pandora's Box." In 1852, Dr. Durham offered four acres of his homesite to the North Carolina Railroad Company for a depot along its Goldsboro-to-Charlotte line. Thus was born the hamlet known as Durham Station, Durham Depot, Durhamville and finally, just plain Durham. Durham's official birth date is April 26, 1853, when its first post office opened. By 1860, three stores, two saloons and a carpentry shop had sprung up on what was still an agricultural landscape inhabited by fewer than 100 persons. Dr. Durham's homesite was purchased by R. F. Morris, whose small tobacco factory nearby would add another significant chapter to the community's development.

Durham played a relatively minor role in the Civil War until the very end, when Confederate General Joseph Johnston surrendered to Union General William Sherman in 1865 at a nearby farm owned by James Bennett. The event marked the end of the Civil War in the Carolinas, Georgia and Florida. Ironically, it also launched the beginning of Durham's prosperity.

While Sherman and Johnston were taking care of business out on the Bennett farm, the boys in blue and gray were swapping war stories and smoking the peace pipe down at the Durham depot. Seems that soldiers from both sides had gotten a bit restless, broken into the nearby tobacco factory, then owned by John R. Green, and made off with what turned out to be the finest Bright Leaf weed any of them had ever smoked. When the honor-

able terms of surrender were finally consummated, the troops took their tobacco and went home.

It wasn't long before orders for Green's tobacco began pouring into the Durham post office from as far away as Maine and Texas. To meet the sudden demand, Green cranked up production on a brand of tobacco he named "Bull Durham" after the picture of a bull on the jar of Coleman's Mustard manufactured in Durham, England. Pretty soon the image of that bull was appearing in advertisements on walls and rooftops around the world, even on one of the Great Pyramids of Egypt. An ad painted behind the New York Yankees' dugout inspired a new baseball term— "bullpen." Durham was on the map and the "Bull City" shifted into high gear.

The demand for Durham tobacco prompted other entrepreneurs to get into the business, including Washington Duke and his sons Brodie, Ben and James. With the introduction of the cigarette rolling machine, the Dukes became the leading cigarette makers in the nation. Their powerful American Tobacco Co. was later broken up by antitrust legislation into Liggett & Myers, P. Lorillard and R. J. Reynolds.

Durham's population grew to more than 2,000 by the mid-1870s. Tobacco profits provided the capital for other ventures, including cotton and flour mills, banks, trucking firms and more railroads. Notable enterprises included Erwin Mills, the first mill in the South and one of the nation's largest manufacturers of denim, and Durham Hosiery, the world's largest maker of stockings.

In 1977, Durham became the first North Carolina city to have its downtown district placed on the National Register of Historic Places.

The tobacco that built the city also had a hand in shaping what would be Durham's next major industries: education and medicine. Tobacco magnate James Buchanan Duke thought it would be a good idea to endow Trinity College. With the aid of an $85,000 gift from James' father and land donated from tobacco-textile executive Julian Shakespeare Carr, Trinity College moved to Durham from Randolph County in 1892. In 1924, James B. Duke gave the college $40 million. As you might expect, it was warmly received; the college was promptly renamed Duke University. The Duke University Medical School opened in 1930.

There are many other success stories in Durham. While the Dukes were striking it rich in tobacco, Durham's black leaders were also thriving. Beginning around 1905, West Parrish Street turned from an industrial to a commercial district when the black-owned-and-operated North Carolina Mutual and Provident Association purchased several lots there. After the insurance company prospered and attracted other businesses, the block became known as the "Black Wall Street." The company, now known as North Carolina Mutual Life, remains the largest black-managed financial institution in the world.

Meanwhile, North Carolina Central University, founded in 1910 as a religious training school, went on to become the first state-funded liberal arts college for blacks and is now part of the University of North Carolina system. Little did Dr. Bartlett Durham realize when he opened "Pandora's Box" to the railroads and tobacco merchants, that a muddy, country whistle-stop would evolve into the eclectic "New South" city that it is today.

Raleigh

The city takes its name from the 16th-century English gentleman and explorer, Sir Walter Raleigh. It was Sir Walter, according to romantic lore, who spread his cloak before Queen Elizabeth to spare her feet from stepping in a mud puddle. Unfortunately for Sir Walter, Elizabeth was not around in 1618 to spare his head when James I asked for it. It was also Sir Walter

who lost a colony on North Carolina's coast in 1587 and, despite three years at Oxford, had trouble spelling his name, using Rawleyghe in his youth, then Ralegh and sometimes Raleigh. Such a checkered reputation, however, did not deter admiring North Carolinians in 1792 from naming their new capital after him.

The selection of the new capital city's site in Wake County was a political decision. Members of the state's General Assembly were tired of meeting in various cities and were anxious for an "unalterable seat of government." They purchased 1,000 acres of "woodland and old field" from Revolutionary War veteran and state Senator Joel Lane for 1,378 pounds (under $3,000). A planned city was mapped and lots were auctioned to raise money for the new Capitol building. The parcels sold for $60 to $263.

The city in its early years was dependent on the legislature for many of its public works and conduct. The city's commissioners, for instance, were instructed in 1801 to fine merchants who did business on the Sabbath; in 1803, city fathers were empowered to keep hogs from running at large; in 1820, they were given authority to establish a fire department; and in 1825, they were urged to keep infectious diseases from spreading. Members of today's General Assembly continue the tradition of giving advice to Raleigh and its residents. In turn, Raleigh residents are fond of the saying, "The legislature is in session; let us pray."

The city grew and shrank in spurts during the years before the Civil War. The first railroad puffed into town in 1840 and the city's population doubled during the decade, totaling 4,518 by 1850. Not surprisingly, its commerce centered around state government and one of its largest private businesses was based on the state's printing contract and book binding. The best beds in town for travelers were at the Yarborough House, sometimes called the legislature's "third house" because of the off-hours business conducted there. The city had adopted the slogan "City of Oaks" and it was under such a tree on North Street that Whig presidential candidate Henry Clay wrote the "Raleigh letter" opposing the annexation of Texas.

The Civil War left its mark on Raleigh as it did other Southern capitals. It was in Raleigh that "the scourge of the South," General William Tecumseh Sherman, was quartered with 60,000 restless Union troops when news of President Lincoln's assassination arrived. Luckily, the city escaped any vengeful wrath, thanks to Sherman's rein on his soldiers, but his good deed failed to improve his reputation among Raleigh residents. Indeed, the story persists to this day that Sherman's brief occupation of the governor's mansion so tainted the place that no respectable North Carolina governor would set foot in it. The empty house finally burned and in its place today stands the city's graceful Memorial Auditorium, home of the North Carolina Symphony.

By 1910, Raleigh's population was 19,218 and it had become a flourishing academic center as well as the seat of government. St. Mary's School for Girls, begun in 1842, had been joined by two of the nation's first colleges for blacks, Shaw University (1875) and St. Augustine's Normal and Collegiate Institute (1867), as well as by Peace College for women (1872). The Baptist Female Seminary, which is today's Meredith College, was founded in 1889, the same year as the North Carolina College of Agriculture and Mechanical Arts, now the renowned North Carolina State University (whose current enrollment is over 27,000).

The city turned on electric street lights in 1885 and at least 1,900 people were gossiping over the telephone by 1910. A count of manufacturers the same year produced a list of six cotton mills and 33 other manufacturing operations. Interestingly, it wasn't until the 1981-82 recession that Raleigh's last textile mills closed down.

Suburbia came early to Raleigh with the pre-World War I subdividing of the Boylan Plantation into Boylan Heights and

Photo by Tim Johnson

The Joel Lane House was built in 1760 by the Revolutionary War veteran and state senator who sold 1,000 acres of "woodland and old field" to the General Assembly, which selected it as the site of the new capital city.

the promotion of Cameron Park as a place to enjoy quiet country pleasures in the shadow of city lights. Both are considered downtown neighborhoods today.

In 1925, the state decided to sell its Raleigh fairgrounds and asked the newly formed Raleigh Board of Realtors to auction the property. The fairgrounds growth required a move further west of the city. The state, however, restricted the sales. For example, if you bought a lot on the city's main western boulevard, Hillsborough Street, you agreed to build a suitably grand home on the property—one that cost at least $7,500! The farther away from Hillsborough Street, the less demanding the restrictions. On Brooks Avenue, you could get by with a $5,000 home and east of Chamberlain Street, $2,500. The area is today called Fairmont after the fairgrounds. In its center is the Raleigh Little Theater and park grounds, which include the city's Rose Garden and amphitheater. If you look hard enough, you will see that they sit in what used to be the old fairgrounds racetrack.

By 1930, Raleigh's population reached 37,379, a 10-year increase of 53 percent. However, the city's prosperity came to an abrupt halt with the arrival of the Great Depression. Housing starts dwindled and no major commercial building was erected until 1942. Even fancy, new neighborhoods such as Hayes-Barton, named after Sir Walter's English home, did not escape foreclosures. A young real estate agent of the times recalled being offered by a banker friend the chance to live in one of Hayes-Barton's largest, newest homes rent free. He would have to pay only the utilities. The bank had foreclosed on the home, then had second thoughts when the vacant house began to deteriorate. The young real estate agent was sorely tempted until he discovered that the house's heating bill alone was more than his annual salary.

The New Deal brought public housing to town along with public works, among them Halifax Court, Chavis Heights and the Raleigh Little Theater. World War II brought the city a full employment economy and the city has grown ever since. FHA and VA loans financed whole neighborhoods following the war as Raleigh builders such as E. N. Richards and J. W. "Willie" York put up small, but affordable $6,000 homes with four percent mortgage rates. York went on to build the region's first shopping center, Cameron Village, about a mile from the downtown business district, which was thought of as a "crazy, wild" venture at the time.

In the 1960s, city government moved to meet new challenges, including the explosive issue of civil rights. Mayor W. G. Enloe used his office in 1963 to encourage better community relations and the shedding of institutional segregation. Amazingly, within a year of Enloe's initiative, most of Jim Crow's noxious feathers had been plucked and the era of separate black and white restaurants, hotels, parks, etc., faded. The city also moved to a city manager form of government as its population grew from 93,931 in 1960 to 122,830 in 1970. A highway Beltline across its northern half gave Raleigh a new profile on road maps and accelerated growth in North Raleigh.

Research Triangle Park

Insiders generally agree that the establishment of a vast research complex midway between the University of North Carolina at Chapel Hill, N.C. State University and Duke University was a good idea. But getting a consensus on just whose idea it was is another matter.

Our research leads us to conclude that the development of the now world-famous Research Triangle Park grew from the dreams of more than one creative individual.

There was the late Dr. Howard W. Odom, founder in 1924 of UNC's Institute

Photo courtesy of RTP Foundation

Established in 1959, Research Triangle Park has expanded rapidly and today contains 132 organizations that employ 39,500 people.

for Research in Social Science; he envisioned an academic center for research in the social sciences and human relations. Beginning in 1952, Odom wrote a series of proposals for the establishment of research institutes that would involve programs affiliated with the consolidated University of North Carolina.

About the same time that Odom was envisioning an academic center, Greensboro builder Romeo H. Guest was dreaming of ways to attract research and industrial development to the area. It was Guest who in 1953 coined the name "Research Triangle" to describe the triangular-shaped area lying among the state's three major research universities.

Guest was concerned that the influx of northern industries was slowing down. As a graduate of MIT in Cambridge, Massachusetts, he was familiar with the now famous research and industrial complex growing up along Boston's Route 128. Guest believed that the development of similar research facilities here would eventually spawn new industrial growth.

In 1955, Guest talked with Governor Luther H. Hodges about the idea. The Governor went for it and the rest is history. By the spring of that year, Hodges appointed a committee composed of prominent bankers, business executives, industrialists and university heavyweights. The committee eventually established a nonprofit organization known today as the Research Triangle Foundation.

The Foundation was entrusted with the task of acquiring land and finding appropriate tenants for the park. Its first executive director was Dr. George L. Simpson, a UNC sociology professor and former colleague of Dr. Odom.

Plans were soon made that forged the dreams of both Odom and Guest: there would be a vast research-industrial complex, including a separate Research Triangle Institute to be owned by the three universities.

By 1958, the Research Triangle Foundation had raised enough money to begin purchasing and developing the land that would soon be known as Research Triangle Park. The following year, the Chemstrand Corporation purchased a 100-acre site to build the Park's first research campus, now known as the Monsanto Triangle Park Development Center.

Things moved along slowly but steadily after that, with about one new tenant added each year until 1965 when both the National Institute of Environmental Health Sciences and IBM Corporation announced plans to construct major facilities here.

IBM put Research Triangle Park on the map. The number of organizations located here has grown since 1965 from six to 132.

This one metropolitan area is comprised of some very distinct cities that contribute their personality to the Triangle.

Triangle Overview

When you fly into Raleigh-Durham International Airport (RDU), you'll get an overview of the Triangle. But when you land, you'll find that this one metropolitan area is comprised of some very distinct cities and places and the differences contribute their personality to the Triangle. You'll discover areas soaked in history, art and politics; the country's top medical research, telecommunication and computer technology centers; the shady calm of college towns; and the bustle of retail establishments. It's all here, a myriad of lifestyles that makes the Triangle unique.

Cary

Cary is one of the nation's fastest growing cities. Its population rose from 7,640 in 1970 to 43,858 in 1990. In a special census taken in 1998 over 85,000 residents were counted. With an abundance of cultural, educational and recreational opportunities, as well as the lowest crime rate of the state's 10 largest cities, Cary has solidified its reputation as a great place to raise a family.

Today Cary shows off one planned community after another, many of them with their own golf courses, swimming pools, tennis courts and greenways. MacGregor Downs subdivision led the way in the 1960s, followed by such planned unit developments as Kildaire Farms, Lochmere and Preston, the Triangle's largest golf course community with over 20 neighborhoods.

Thanks to a forward looking Town Council in the 1970s, the city deliberately sought to increase its nonresidential tax base with businesses and industry. The policy has been stunningly successful. With beautiful research and business parks such as Weston, Regency Park and SAS Institute's serene, rolling campus, the city's job base makes the home-to-work drive a short commute for many Cary residents. SAS, one of the country's premier software developers, is the seventh largest private employer in the Triangle with 3,100 employees; MCI Telecommunications is 11th with 2,200 employees; American Airlines' Reservation Center is 12th with 2,000 people; and Austin Quality Foods is 20th largest with 1,300 workers. Many of the nation's big-name employers also have offices here: IBM, Union Carbide and Lucent Technologies, to name a few.

The town of Cary is governed by the Cary Town Council. Although Cary voters signaled they wanted slower growth in recent local elections, there's still plenty of action in Cary. A variety of new businesses and restaurants continue to open and prosper, such as Cool Mountain Creamery at Wellington Park, Backstage Restaurant at Waverly Place and Connolly's Irish Pub at Cornerstone Shopping Center.

New public school construction is on the top of Cary's agenda. Dillard Road

Photo by Tim Johnson

A rare snow blanketed downtown Cary during the winter of 1998.

elementary and middle schools opened their doors to students in August 1998 and plans for additional schools are in the works. Cary Academy, a private school founded by leaders of SAS Institute, opened in August 1997.

Health-care options in Cary also have increased to meet the growing demand. Western Wake Medical Center, an 80-bed community hospital located off Kildaire Farm Road, is the site of the new Women's Pavilion and Birthplace, Cary's only obstetrical center, and the state-of-the-art Wake Radiology Center. Rex Healthcare's new $8.5 million, 62,000-square-foot health and wellness center is located off Cary Parkway.

Cary's downtown includes a main street drugstore, a railroad station, antique stores, historic buildings and churches, a public library, one of the oldest elementary schools in the state and a modern Town Hall complex. Amtrak's Piedmont and Carolinian trains both make daily stops at the Cary Depot, which doubles as a

driver's license bureau. Ashworth Village Center, located on the corner of Chatham and Academy streets, recently expanded by 12,000 feet, adding new shops and a restaurant. Cary Parkway shows off some of the city's prime residential real estate and its shopping centers, such as Cary Towne Center and Crossroads Plaza, rival Raleigh's malls and discount power centers in retail revenue.

Currently, Cary has over a dozen city parks, including the 310-acre Fred G. Bond Metro Park, which is the largest municipal park in Wake County, and the 150-acre Hemlock Bluffs Nature Preserve, which features a grove of Canadian hemlocks. Cary's expanding network of greenway trails now extends over 10 miles. The Cary YMCA, located off Cary Parkway, opened its doors in 1992 and has proven extremely popular with the fitness crowd. The $2.1 million Cary Community Center on North Academy Street offers classes and special events for all ages. A Kids Together Playground is being constructed at Wellington Park, near the corner of Tryon Road and Cary Parkway.

Town officials have developed a $40 million plan to expand recreation facilities by the year 2010. Recommendations include 25 new parks, six new community centers, a tennis center, an aquatic center and additional greenways and bike paths.

For the artistically inclined, Jordan Hall Arts Center offers visual and performing arts classes. The Page-Walker Arts and History Center, built in 1868 as a hotel to serve train passengers, contains a fine arts gallery featuring the works of local and regional artists, and sponsors a Starlight Concert series each summer. It also houses the Cary Museum.

Downtown Cary is the site of the annual Lazy Daze Arts and Crafts Festival, which takes place the last Saturday in August, featuring approximately 400 craftspeople and artisans from all over the region. Other popular events include the Cary Road Race and Spring Daze Arts and Crafts Festival in April, Summerfest at Regency Park in June and July, the Jimmy V Celebrity Golf Classic in August, the Gourd Festival in September and Cary Band Day in November.

There's also plenty of activity with Cary's award-winning high school band, high school sports teams (it's a wrestling powerhouse) and some of the finest golf courses in the Triangle.

It's not brag but fact when Cary leaders declare: Cary, it's a great place to live.

For More Information

Cary Chamber of Commerce
307 N. Academy St., Cary, NC 27513
• 800-919-CARY or 467-1016

Chapel Hill

Chapel Hill is not your ordinary small Southern town. First of all, there is nothing ordinary about the people who live here: there are more Ph.D.'s per capita living in Chapel Hill than just about any other place on the planet.

Secondly, it's not all that Southern. Believe it or not, a higher percentage of the population here reads *The New Yorker* magazine than in the Big Apple. That's not to say that everyone who lives here comes from New York; they come from everywhere, many of them to study or teach at the University of North Carolina, to work in the Research Triangle Park or to retire in the hospitable climate.

Come to think of it, Chapel Hill is not really very small as North Carolina towns go. While the downtown still feels like a village, the town's population and borders have expanded considerably. Today there are about 45,000 residents, with another 24,000 or so students when the university is in session.

Finally, although Chapel Hill is geographically situated in the conservative Bible Belt, it has long been considered an oasis for liberals and one of the most tolerant communities in the state. Perhaps that's why our notoriously conservative U.S. Senator Jesse Helms is said to have once suggested that instead of wasting tax dollars on a state zoo, we simply build a fence around Chapel Hill.

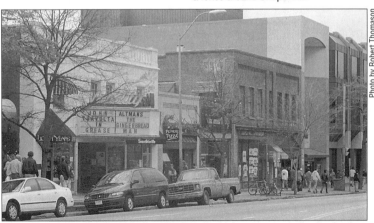

Photo by Robert Thomason

Downtown Chapel Hill's hub, Franklin Street, which was named after Benjamin Franklin, offers an abundance of shopping, dining and entertainment options.

So it is that the "Southern part of heaven" has grown into a most unusual and appealing community. Chapel Hill is the home of UNC-CH—the oldest state university in the nation, which first opened its doors in 1795. In fact, in most parts of North Carolina, the words Chapel Hill and UNC-CH are synonymous and, therefore, used interchangeably. For instance, if you sit at a lunch counter in any small town around the state and loudly express your fondness for the politics of Ted Kennedy, someone will undoubtedly raise an eyebrow and observe that you "must have gone to Chapel Hill." That doesn't mean they think you went shopping here; it means they are assuming you must have picked up your liberal views while attending the University of North Carolina in Chapel Hill.

State and county elections are held every even year, with city and school board elections every odd year. Primaries are held in May. The mayors of Chapel Hill and Carrboro are elected for two-year terms; the council members of each town, members of the Chapel Hill-Carrboro school board and County Commissioners hold four-year overlapping terms. Members of the Orange County school board are elected to six-year overlapping terms.

Chapel Hill is governed by the Chapel Hill Town Council. Rosemary Waldorf is the Mayor. Mike Nelson is the Mayor of Carrboro.

Downtown Chapel Hill still has a "village" feel, but a boom in residential construction in the last decade has brought many new citizens to the community. Meanwhile, Carrboro has become one of the fastest-growing municipalities in the Triangle and one of the most densely developed communities in the state. Its population of about 15,000 is expected to increase by several thousand by the end of the century. Vacant farmland and mill houses are rapidly being replaced by apartments and condominiums. The old cotton mill has been converted into Carr Mill Mall, a quaint shopping mall housing local businesses.

The interest in Chapel Hill and Carrboro can be linked to several factors. First, they offer the charm of small-town life with the sophistication of a university community tied

Triangle Names You Should Know

Frank Porter Graham. Charles Brantley Aycock. Bill Friday. Asa Spaulding. Mary Duke Biddle Seamans. If you're a long-time Triangle resident and haven't been living in a refrigerator, you will recognize these names. They are names that Triangle citizens know or will need to know at some point in their stay. These names belong to people in all walks of life, some living, some not. Their names, however, all live on, and they are important entries in the Triangle's  vocabulary. This is not a Who's Who list, but rather a useful primer for newcomers. If you're already an Insider, you, no doubt, may add to the names below, but no subtractions are allowed!

Frank Porter Graham, for example, is deceased but his name is invoked at almost every University of North Carolina function and often appears in any noteworthy political commentary. He was the happy president of UNC in the years before and after WWII, and his race for the U.S. Senate was one of the great watersheds in North Carolina politics. (That race also launched the political career of Jesse Helms, who opposed Graham.)

Aycock was elected governor in 1900 and is remembered annually by state Democrats at the Vance-Aycock gathering as the state's father of public education. Bill Friday is not a detective; he is the respected and wise builder of today's unified University of North Carolina System. Asa Spaulding founded one of American's most successful black-owned businesses during the early part of the century, and his name lives on in several of Durham's current leaders. Okay, you got a clue on Mary Duke Biddle Seamans. She is a Triangle philanthropist, former Durham City Councillor and the only Duke living in town.

Here are some other need-to-know names: J.W. and Smedes York are father and son who have long records in Raleigh business and politics. J.W. shaped Raleigh's future after WWII, and Smedes, a former mayor, airport authority chairman, chamber chairman, etc., continues J.W.'s tradition. The Kenans, as in Kenan Transport, are known for UNC's Kenan Institute and the many endowed Kenan Chairs at

Photo by Tinka Deal, courtesy of UNC-TV

William Friday

universities across the country. The late Frank Kenan was one of the state's most generous benefactors. And the Daniels, Frank Jr. and Frank III, are the latest in Josephus Daniels' line of newspaper barons. No longer owners of *The News & Observer,* Frank Jr. can still afford to speak the truth and often does. John Caldwell is the Yazoo, Mississippi, transplant who transformed NCSU into a premier research university and for whom the Caldwell Scholarships are named.

Which leads us to John Motley Morehead, the famed chemist whose largess lingers in the coveted Morehead Scholarships and UNC's Morehead Planetarium. Jim Goodnight is founder of Cary's SAS Institute and is the Triangle's top billionaire. Don't confuse him with Jim Goodmon, head of Capital Broadcasting (WRAL-TV and radio) among other businesses, and one of the Triangle's Fletcher family who run the Fletcher Foundation. Jeannette Hyde, that's Ambassador Hyde to you, translates to "fundraising fairy godmother" to Democratic politicians. In the Triangle's black business and political community, you will hear these names: Clarence Lightner, former Raleigh mayor; Mickey Michaux, veteran House member from Durham; and Daniel Blue, Raleigh lawyer and first black Speaker of the House.

At some point, you will be asked, "Did you see Powell this morning?" That's Dwane Powell, the *N&O's* wickedly accurate cartoonist. Similarly, you will be asked if you've read Crowther, as in Hal Crowther, the unarmed but dangerous commentator for the weekly *Independent.*

There are some names that even people outside the Triangle recognize, so we don't include them. You know—Jesse Helms, Dean Smith, Billy Graham and Michael (that's Jordan, of course).

to a booming metropolis. Second, they are accessible to a number of desirable jobs nearby in Research Triangle Park. Finally, Interstate 40 puts Chapel Hill and Carrboro within convenient commuting distances to Raleigh. It's impossible to maintain the charm of village life while attracting thousands of newcomers each year. And that is the challenge facing local officials today.

Residents of Chapel Hill and Carrboro, like their counterparts in the other cities of the Triangle, worry that runaway development will destroy what is unique about their communities. These folks may have a reputation for tolerance, but one thing they will not accept is unsightly development, hence some rather restrictive zoning laws. Today citizens and elected officials are continuing to work together to ensure the preservation of those qualities that make their towns such attractive places to live and work.

For More Information

Chapel Hill-Carrboro
Chamber of Commerce
104 S. Estes Dr.
Chapel Hill, NC 27514 • 967-7075

Chapel Hill-Orange County Visitors Bureau
501 W. Franklin St., Ste. 104
Chapel Hill, NC 27516 • 968-2060

Durham

Durham offers something for everyone: excellent cultural and recreational opportunities, quality health-care facilities, superb educational institutions, eclectic restaurants, a Triple-A baseball team and a prime location near Research Triangle Park.

With the influx of new businesses and industries have come changes in the nature of Durham's work force. Tobacco and textiles were once the leading industries.

Not so today, as the top employers include Duke University and its Medical Center, as well as some of the new large research facilities in and around Research Triangle Park.

So it is that tobacco warehouses and cotton mills downtown have been converted into chic shops, restaurants, condominiums and office spaces. Plans are in the works for others to accommodate apartments for senior citizens and studios for artists, dancers and craftspersons.

But sudden changes have also meant growing pains. A part of Durham's black community was razed to make way for a crosstown expressway. Some downtown businesses have lost out to the competition of nearby suburban malls. Local leaders, however, are hoping downtown attractions—such as the Royall Center for the Arts; the 10,000-seat, state-of-the-art Durham Bulls Athletic Park (DBAP); and the $9 million, 46,000-square-foot YMCA—will bring businesses back downtown.

New developments are already in the works. The recently constructed $9.6 million Diamond View office building lies adjacent to DBAP. West Village, a complex of apartments, specialty shops and restaurants, has begun construction between downtown and Brightleaf Square.

At the same time, rapid growth throughout the county has meant that roads have become snarled, strip development is transforming the rural landscape and real estate speculation is fast driving the price of a home out of reach for many who grew up here. Like their counterparts in the other cities of the Triangle, Durhamites are determined that this surge in growth does not destroy the very characteristics that have brought so many people here.

The city of Durham, with a population of about 172,000, is the only municipality in the county. The city operates on a council-manager form of government with an elected mayor and 6 council members. The county is governed by a

Photo courtesy of N.C. Travel and Tourism

The future looks bright for downtown Durham, where old tobacco warehouses are being converted into apartments, offices, specialty shops and restaurants.

five-member board of commissioners and administered by a county manager. Durham is governed by the Durham City Council. Nicholas Tennyson is the Mayor.

State and county elections are held every even year. City elections are held every odd year. Primaries are held in May. The Mayor is elected to a two-year term; city council members to four-year staggered terms. County commissioners hold office for two years at a time. State senators and representatives serve two-year terms. Today Duke University is Durham's largest private employer and one of the top private colleges and medical research facilities in the nation. Duke's reputation, as well as its proximity to three other universities and Research Triangle Park, helped to eventually establish Durham as an ideal location for high-tech research companies.

For More Information

Durham Chamber of Commerce
300 W. Morgan St.
Durham, NC 27701 • 682-2133

Durham Convention & Visitors Bureau
101 E. Morgan St.
Durham, NC 27701 • 687-0288

Raleigh

Raleigh makes a perfect capital city. It's in the middle of the state. It's connected to a major east-west Interstate freeway, I-40, and it's less than an hour from the East Coast's major north-south roadway, I-95. It's served by an international airport, Raleigh-Durham International. Amtrak stops here. Eastern North Carolina shops here. The North Carolina Symphony and the North Carolina Art Museum play and show here. While North Carolina history wasn't started here, this is where we keep it—in the state's Archives and History Museum. And where we make a lot of it, thanks to the Governor, the General Assembly, Council of State members and the Supreme Court. It's home to 298,003 people in 1998.

Photo courtesy of N.C. Travel and Tourism

Downtown Raleigh contains some of the state's most valuable cultural assets, such as the State Capitol, the Executive Mansion and the North Carolina Museum of History.

There are some names and phrases that you need to know in your education as an Insider. For example, Beltline is a proper noun here. It is the circumferential highway that splits Raleigh into two real estate markets—Inside the Beltline and the rest of Raleigh. It has other, official highway names such as I-440, but most directions you will hear for getting around town will include the word, "Beltline." The new road around North Raleigh that is under construction is called the Northern Wake Expressway or "Outer Loop." When people say they're going to Crabtree, that's not a suburb. It's Raleigh's biggest and second-oldest mall. You may also hear the term "old Raleigh" and it has to do more with genealogy than geography as in "his family is 'old Raleigh'." The designation North Raleigh (that part of the city north of the Beltline) covers a range of things such as neighborhoods and shopping centers, as well as a state of mind and the intimation

that you may have ties north of the Mason Dixon Line. The *N&O* refers to the city's venerable newspaper, *The News and Observer*, just as RDU is the airport and the ACC is the Atlantic Coast Conference, whose college sports provide approximately half of all Raleigh conversation topics. The Creek is the popular outdoor amphitheater at Walnut Creek where you can see the latest touring bands from country to rock. When friends offer you barbecue, they mean pork, soaked in distinctive eastern North Carolina vinegar based sauce, and if you're invited to a 'pig pickin,' go. If you're going to Jones Street, it's a polite way of saying you're going to seek the company of ... legislators at the General Assembly on Jones Street.

Raleigh's established neighborhoods reflect the city's history as a place of moderate and broad affluence. Real estate has been one of the strongest segments of the Raleigh economy during the '90s. Homes, which were selling in Raleigh and Wake County for an average of $170,820 at the start of 1998, are very likely to appreciate. The demand for houses and nonresidential projects, however, means builders struggle to find skilled craftsmen in all construction sectors.

Unemployment in the Triangle repeatedly falls under 3 percent and many shops and restaurants display faded "Help Wanted" signs. It is not uncommon to find people who, having heard about the comfortable living and strong economy, move here without first finding a job. A word of caution: Trailing spouses sometimes have to wait a while to find a job that fits and may be "underemployed" at first.

Activities abound as the other chapters of this book spell out. An overview of Raleigh will show a lively city that legitimately claims itself the cultural as well as the political capital of the state. Sparked by a youthful population that includes students from six colleges and universities, Raleigh bubbles with art shows and shops, music and museums, flea markets and the Farmers Market, tournaments and concerts. There is enough music that the city sings all year. There are classical and pops performances at the Symphony and free rock and jazz music downtown in the summer. The city has earned a reputation as a popular waystation for bands and performers working toward the Big Time. The Connells and Corrosion of Conformity both have roots in a single Raleigh neighborhood, and country western stars and blue grass bands enjoy strong followings in Raleigh.

Like big cities that rally around professional teams and players, Raleigh loves its college and amateur sports. Ah, to be in Raleigh when North Carolina State wins a national basketball championship (twice since 1974) is to rise toward Rapture! In 1987, Raleigh was the center for the Summer Olympic Festival, and in 1999, it hosted the International Special Olympics. The city has built a new sports and entertainment arena that is home to NCSU's men's basketball team and the National Hockey League franchise, the Carolina Hurricanes.

For political junkies, Raleigh is their fix. It's a rite of spring to watch school children from all over the state parade between the Capitol and the Legislature, observing their elected representatives at work. (If you are really tall, you can peek in the windows on the southwest corner of the Capitol and see the Governor at work.) Raleigh's government complex also includes its most popular museums, Natural Science (a new one's on the way), History and the state Archives and Library. Raleigh's Exploris, a children's museum of the world, opened in Moore Square downtown on October 9, 1999.

We could go on ... and on some more, but you get the picture. Raleigh is a city that's not too provincial. Not too sophisticated. Not too busy. Not too slow. Not too hot. Not too cold. Not too big. Not too small. For many, it's just right.

For More Information

Raleigh Chamber of Commerce
800 S. Salisbury St.
Raleigh, NC 27601 • 664-7000

Raleigh Convention & Visitors Bureau
421 Fayetteville St. Mall, Ste. 1505,
Raleigh, NC 27603 • 834-5900

Research Triangle Park

The Research Triangle Park or RTP is the engine that drives the Triangle's economy. The Park's founding is one of those select examples of public-private partnership at its best. RTP was established in the 1950s, the result of visionaries and practical politicians. Credit is due a number of people: Dr. Howard Odom, founder of UNC's Institute for Research in Social Science; Romeo H. Guest, a Greensboro builder and developer; and the man who made it happen, Gov. Luther Hodges. They all wanted to develop an industrial or business park that would attract good paying research jobs and provide employment for the state's best and brightest students who were leaving home to go elsewhere. RTP, contrary to some notions, is not a government project; it is a private, nonprofit research park—that has good government connections. By 1958, the Research Triangle Foundation was in business buying land.

Today RTP is 6,900 acres and the site for some 137 organizations that employ about 42,000 people. Foundation directors no longer have to take their show on the road to trade shows and industry fairs. Companies come to RTP looking for land where they can build research and science-oriented manufacturing facilities. States and countries send delegations to learn

Photo by Tim Johnson

NORTH CAROLINA BIOTECHNOLOGY CENTER

Research Triangle Park is teeming with innovative research facilities, including N.C. Biotechnology Center, a nonprofit corporation dedicated toward strengthening the state's leadership in biotechnology development.

how RTP works. The late Executive Director Ned Huffman, for instance, told of one week's worth of visitors that included representatives from Kansas, Texas, Indiana, Germany, Netherlands, Japan and Singapore.

RTP is located almost in the middle of the triangle formed by Raleigh, Durham and Chapel Hill. Most of the land is in Durham County and it abuts Raleigh-Durham International Airport. Interstate 40 bisects the Park and is the principal commute artery. A drive through the park reveals jogging paths, landscaped sites and glimpses of facilities among the pine trees. There are some architectural standouts, the most famous of which is the Glaxo Wellcome building, which was a film location for the movie, *Brainstorm*. Other show stoppers include the National Humanities Center, the National Institute of Environmental Health Sciences and the fortress-like U.S. Environmental Protection Agency's research center.

Restaurants, gas stations and shops are prohibited in RTP. There are, however, many businesses and shopping centers on the Park's edges and many companies

operate their own cafeterias. But you don't go to the Park for fine dining or shopping. The jobs and the work are the featured attractions here. It was at the former Burroughs Wellcome laboratories in the Park, for instance, that scientists won Nobel Prizes in chemistry. The virtual reality, computer-created, special effects in today's Hollywood movies were spawned here and Northern Telecom, the Canadian telecommunication powerhouse, and Sweden's mobile telephone giant, Ericsson, work here and in offices close by. The biggest presence is IBM's site where 13,000 people work in one million square feet of building space. One of the nation's 24 supercomputers lives here at MCNC, and the Supercomputing Center and Foreign Trade Zone No. 93 are also here. Other tenants include such familiar names as BASF, Cisco Systems, Corning Labs, Data General, DuPont, GTE, Kobe Steel, Lucent Technologies, Research Triangle Institute and Sumitomo.

If you're going to live in the Triangle and you don't work at the Park, take a Sunday drive to inspect the region's namesake. Do not, we repeat, do not go during

Downtown Angier is evolving into a trendy commercial district.

morning or evening drive time on weekdays. It's about 20 minutes from Raleigh, 10 minutes from Durham and 15 minutes from Chapel Hill. RTP's payrolls put over a billion dollars into the Triangle economy, so most residents endure the traffic jams.

For More Information

Research Triangle Foundation
2 Hanes Dr., P.O. Box 12255
RTP, NC 27709 • 549-8181

Triangle Towns

When you move to a new neighborhood, you like to know that you have nice neighbors. Well, the Triangle is filled with good neighbors in the smaller towns that make up Wake, Durham and Orange counties as well as those in adjacent counties. These places enjoy a growing popularity among newcomers and with those who like a small-town pace of life— and lower real estate prices!

Companies are locating their facilities there and you might be closer to work living in Wake Forest or Hillsborough than Raleigh or Durham. Some, like Garner, border on Raleigh's southern city limits, while others, such as Fuquay-Varina, are farther out. No matter, none are more than 30 to 40 minutes away from Research Triangle Park. Each has its own identity: Hillsborough, for example, offers a colonial past; Wake Forest (one-time home of Wake Forest University) is a college town; and Wendell and Zebulon grew up with railroads and tobacco.

They're great places to visit on a weekend drive. They offer the pleasant rhythm of small-town living and easy access to the cultural offerings of the larger Triangle cities. The towns are listed alphabetically.

Angier

Population: 2,800
Commute to Raleigh: 20 mi.
Commute to RTP: 18 mi.
Chamber of Commerce: 639-2500

For years, Angier was a quiet crossroads town; however, strip shopping centers have recently sprouted in former

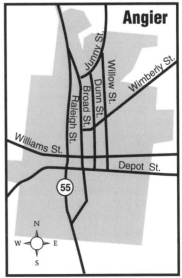

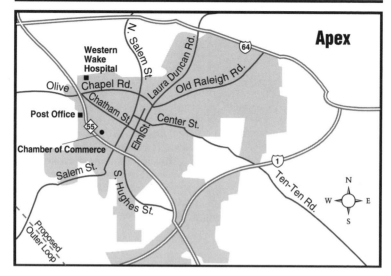

tobacco fields. Angier is located off N.C. 55 in Harnett County about 2 miles south of the Wake County line. Town leaders are currently working toward turning the downtown area along Broad Street into a trendy commercial district with restaurants and specialty shops.

The old town depot, built around 1900, has been renovated and is the site of festivals and other town get-togethers. Angier's friendly small-town charm is demonstrated at the annual Crape Myrtle Festival in September, featuring arts and crafts, food and entertainment.

Apex

> **Population: 15,000**
> **Commute to Raleigh: 12 mi.**
> **Commute to RTP: 10 mi.**
> **Chamber of Commerce: 362-6456**

If recent years are indicators, Apex is definitely poised for continued strong growth. In 1998, the population stands at approximately 15,000, compared to 4,789 in the 1990 census.

Apex is adjacent to Cary and particularly close to Regency and MacGregor office parks, only minutes from the Raleigh Beltline and a 15-minute commute to RTP. In addition to the "small-town" feel, what has caught the eye of many new homebuyers is Apex's proximity to Jordan Lake on U.S. 64. To find Apex, go south on U.S. 1 or take Old Apex Road (which turns into N. Salem Street) coming out of Cary. Located at the crossroads of N.C. 55, U.S. 1 and U.S. 64 and near Interstate 40, Apex offers residents easy access to Raleigh, Cary, Chapel Hill, Durham and Research Triangle Park.

Apex's history is tied to the growth of the railroads, in this case, the Chatham Railroad Company. The rail tracks still run through the city, but they're now the CSX line. The land on which the tracks ran was one of the highest points along the line at 504 feet above sea level, hence the town's name, Apex, and its motto, "The Peak of Good Living." The community was incorporated in 1873.

Locals believe Apex was the obvious choice of *Business North Carolina* when the magazine named it "The Best Small

Town in North Carolina" in 1994. Townspeople and those nearby have taken to the ambience evident in Apex's historic downtown. The Town Depot, the downtown centerpiece, has been renovated to reflect its 1914 origins. Now on the National Register of Historic Places, it houses the Apex Chamber of Commerce. During the spring, summer and fall, the Depot is the site of concerts sponsored by the Apex Chamber and Apex Department of Parks, Recreation and Cultural Resources.

Neighborhoods have quickly sprouted in Apex over the past few years. Popular new developments include Walden Woods, Amherst, Holly Glen and Haddon Hall.

Apex High School is one of the largest high schools in the state. A new high school, Green Hope, is set to open in 1999, followed by Green Hope Elementary in 2000.

Leisure activities are important to Apex residents. Residents approved a $6 million bond referendum to renovate existing parks and build new ones. The Eva Perry Regional Library, which opened in 1996 to serve southwest Wake County, leads the state in circulation with over 1 million books checked out annually.

Some popular Apex restaurants include House of China and Daniel's Pizza Pasta Cafe on N.C. 55 North. Salem Street is still the center of town with its small retail shops, offices and restaurants. The town celebrates an annual downtown festival during the first week of May. It's called "Peak Week," offering arts and crafts, musical entertainment, food concessions, children's activities, road races, historic home tours and other events. Apex's "Today and Yesteryear Festival," which celebrates the town's history, takes place each September.

Clayton

Population: 14,000
Commute to Raleigh: 15 mi.
Commute to RTP: 35 mi.
Chamber of Commerce: 553-6352

Just a few miles beyond Garner on U.S. 70 lies Clayton. A small town with friendly people and affordable housing, Clayton is just beginning to feel the Triangle's boom in population and economic growth. In 1996 it was named to *Money* magazine's list of top 50 suburban growth towns.

To reach Clayton in Johnston County, travel east on U.S. Highway 70. It's convenient to N.C. Highway 42, U.S. 70 and Interstate 40. For Clayton, the growth spurt began in the 1980s when the town experienced a 40 percent increase in population.

Clayton has a quality school system, excellent roads, a low crime rate and a good mix of newcomers and residents whose families have lived in the area for generations. New home communities abound with reasonable prices. The

Photo by Robert Thomason

Apex derived its name from being the highest point on the Chatham Railroad.

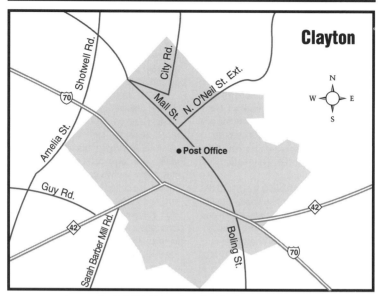

Clayton

average new home price is $133,000 and the average resale home price is $137,000. No longer is Clayton simply "that little town on the way to the beach." Officials have good reason to use the slogan, "Clayton — the Complete Community."

Commercial growth is on the rise. Winn-Dixie is building a distribution center that will contain over 1 million square feet. The new Rockin' Comet diner on U.S. 70 has already become a favorite among locals.

Clayton also boasts a vital downtown where older business buildings are getting a face-lift for use as retail space and offices. The Chamber of Commerce renovated its headquarters in the First Citizens Bank building, which is on the National Register of Historic Places. This vibrant

Photo by Robert Thomason

Many older homes and buildings are undergoing renovation in downtown Clayton, a burgeoning community just 15 minutes southeast of Raleigh.

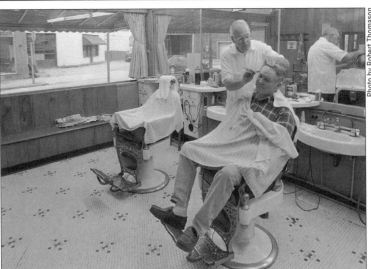

Triangle commuters seeking small-town ambience need look
no further than Franklinton in Franklin County.

downtown features antique shops and specialty boutiques selling everything from drapes to vitamins and herbs. Someone even wanted to open a soda fountain downtown, but space wasn't available. Downtown is abuzz with activity. In the long term, many envision old-fashioned street lamps, buried power lines and park benches in the downtown area.

Clayton is home to four golf courses: The Neuse Golf Course, which is part of the upscale Glen Laurel subdivision; Pine Hollow Golf Club and Riverwood Golf Course, both championship courses with Bermuda fairways and bent grass greens; and Plantation Golf Course, a nine-hole course with a driving range and practice green.

The annual Steeplechase at Brookhill Farm and Clemmons Educational State Forest are major draws from across the region and the state. The Steeplechase runs each May and offers a purse of $60,000, with proceeds benefitting the Raleigh Jaycees. The Clemmons Forest functions as a living environmental

education center. A 42-acre town park is slated for completion in early 1999.

Franklinton

Population: 2,200
Commute to Raleigh: 25 mi.
Commute to RTP: 35 mi.
Chamber of Commerce: 496-3056

Located about 25 miles northeast of Raleigh off U.S. 1 in Franklin County, Franklinton was built around a cotton mill and rail line during the early 1800s. Franklinton is becoming popular with commuters who want to enjoy some small-town ambience.

Locals flock to the antique auction downtown Tuesday and Thursday nights. The popular Fun in the Sun Festival, which is held each May, draws people from all over the Triangle. However, growth is definitely making its way to Franklinton. New developments in the planning or

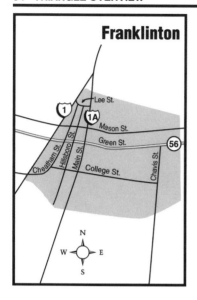

Franklinton

construction stages include a shopping center with a Food Lion along U.S. 1, a satellite campus of Vance-Granville Community College and a new middle school between Franklinton and Louisburg.

Fuquay-Varina

Population: 7,500
Commute to Raleigh: 17 mi.
Commute to RTP: 20 mi.
Chamber of Commerce: 552-4947

Fuquay-Varina is a southern Wake County town of 7,500, located on U.S. 401 about 17 miles from Raleigh's Beltline. It not only has a double name, but two main streets since the town grew up as two communities—Fuquay Springs and Varina, after the pen name of the postmaster's wife.

The area was long famous for its mineral springs, discovered in 1852, and developed in the earlier part of the 20th century as a tourist destination and health spa. The town was first incorporated in

1909 as Fuquay Springs. The two communities joined names in 1963.

City leaders believe that Fuquay-Varina's future is linked to the growth of Research Triangle Park and the town boasts of its proximity to Raleigh and Research Triangle Park. The town's hospitality impressed the likes of such large employers as Turfcare and Guilford Fibers. Other businesses that have found homes here are Berk-Tek, a maker of fiber optics; Bob Barker Company, which specializes in institutional supplies; John Deere, a producer of commercial equipment for residential and golf course use; Johnson Concrete; Raychem, a manufacturer of telecommunications cable accessories; SDM International, a computer software developer; and Tomsed Corp., a manufacturer of turnstiles. The town has a 50-50 split between residential and commercial/industrial growth, what many consider "an ideal situation."

There is a comfortable feel about Fuquay-Varina. Local folks gather along South Main Street, which has several restaurants, a busy drug store, a hardware store and the historic Ben-Wiley Hotel, which is under renovation to celebrate Fuquay-Varina's past. The town is bringing the park around the springs back to life. New subdivisions such as Crofts at Brackenridge, Crooked Creek Country Club, Marcom Place, Northwyck, Sandy Springs and the Village of Sippihaw lure homeowners from all over, from the chill of northern latitudes and from the bustle of Raleigh. Residential properties range from starter homes at $90,000 to a golf community house at $600,000. Occasionally, homes are available in the Jones-Johnson-Ballentine Historic District.

People find the relaxed pace in places like The Golden Leaf Tea Room, a popular lunch spot located on Main Street. China, crystal, silver and antiques are only part of this tea room's charm. The local newspaper, *The Fuquay-Varina Independent*, keeps track of town events such as the Tourna-

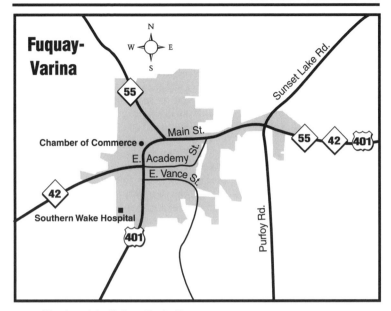

ment of Bands and the Heritage Festival in October, the Annual Draw Down for Autos in the spring, the Celebration of the Outdoors in May and the annual Christmas Parade and Christmas Tree Lighting.

For the outdoor enthusiast, Carroll Howard Johnson Environmental Education Park offers a variety of nature programs. Golfers have a choice of four local courses: Crooked Creek County Club, Devil's Ridge Country Club, Bentwinds Country Club and Hidden Valley Country Club.

Garner

Population: 19,200
Commute to Raleigh: Adjacent
Commute to RTP: 12 mi
Town of Garner 772-4688
Chamber of Commerce: 772-6440

The town billed as the "Most Promising Corner In The Triangle," was founded in

Photo by Tim Johnson

The bustling community of Fuquay-Varina has adopted an ideal 50-50 split between residential and commercial growth.

1883 as "Garner's Station" and rechartered in 1905 as Garner.

Garner is located immediately south of Raleigh and shares some of its southern city limits with Raleigh at the fork of U.S. 401 South and U.S. 70. Garner is the third-largest town in Wake County behind Raleigh and Cary; its current population is a little over 19,000. For years it was a stopping point for eastern North Carolinians who were drawn to jobs in Raleigh, but wanted to live in a smaller town. Today Garner is home to many families from other states.

Perhaps because of its proximity to Raleigh, Garner is diversifying as shopping, entertainment and employment opportunities grow at a rapid pace. The town's recent commercial growth began with North Station and South Station shopping centers. Stores include Hudson Belk with 46,000 square feet; Fashion Ave. of New York, a family-owned clothing store; and Staples, a discount office supply store. Combined, the two power centers are the largest retail draw on the southern side of metro-Raleigh. The town's newest shopping center, the 475,000-square-foot Garner Towne Square, is anchored by a Kroger grocery store and also includes the 10-screen United Artists Theater.

The completion of the southern link of the Raleigh Beltline and the extension of Interstate 40 also have spurred Garner's growth. The I-40 and U.S. 70 Interchange has become a prime industrial location, known as Greenfield Industrial Park, which is an 850-acre business and office park. Perstorp Flooring Inc.'s $20 million North American Headquarters and Manufacturing Plant is located here. Perstorp expects to add 300 new employees by decade's end. Just north along I-40 is the recent $28-million expansion of Goodmark Foods,

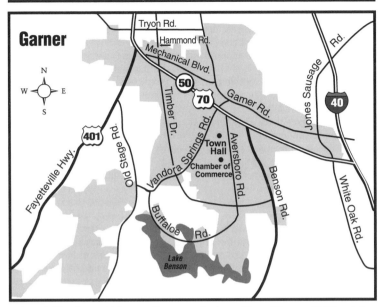

maker of Slim Jims, which currently employs 650 workers.

Garner business and town officials have forged a favorable business climate, underscored by their lapel buttons saying "Garner is a Great Place to do Business." Officials have identified a goal of a 60 percent residential to 40 percent nonresidential tax base. The split is now 66-34 and closing, due largely to the boom in commercial development of manufacturing and distribution firms in the industrial corridor. Notable additions or improvements include: approval of a new 30-acre business park off U.S. 70 East; the attraction of new businesses such as Sigma Electric to White Oak

Photo by Robert Thomason

Founded in 1883 as "Garner's Station," Garner has evolved into Wake County's third-largest town with over 19,000 residents.

Business Park; the additions of Target and Applebee's at Garner Towne Square; and the 115,000-square-foot Super-Lowe's at Garner Station at the intersection of U.S. 401 and U.S. 70.

Through a unique public-private partnership, Olde School Commons, formerly Garner Elementary School, has become a 45-unit residential apartment building for senior citizens in the heart of town. The old auditorium will be maintained by the town and used for community events organized by the Garner Arts Association. Olde School Commons, the 19th-century Banks House and the recently restored Garner Depot constitute portions of the Garner Historic District, which in 1989 was listed on the National Register of Historic Places.

Part of the Wake County School System, Garner is a "Community Involved In Its Schools." Community leadership through the Garner Educational Foundation has resulted in one of the strongest high school science programs in North Carolina. The town proudly rallies around its high school academics as well as its sports programs. Friday night football is a town ritual. At one time the girls' softball team went to the state playoffs for 11 straight seasons.

As the commercial development spreads south along U.S. 401 and U.S. 70, the residential growth is also increasing in prestigious areas, such as Avery Park, Heather Springs, Heather Woods, Lee's Plantation, Wynds of Lakemoor, Kenwood Meadows, Kenland Trails, South Meadow, Hampton Ridge, Highland Ridge and Holland Farms. Home sales range from the low $100,000s to more than $300,000. Homes on 3/4-acre lots in Turner Farms, one of the town's newest subdivisions, average around $215,000. The 18-hole River Ridge Golf Community has opened along Auburn-Knightdale Road. And the 530-acre site of Eagle Ridge, the largest residential development in Garner, will be developed for high-end homes—about

FYI

Unless otherwise noted, the area code for all phone numbers listed in this guide is 919.

Photo by Robert Thomason

Hillsborough's Orange County Museum, housed in the Confederate Memorial Building, contains a variety of unique exhibits, including Occoneechee Indian artifacts and Civil War items such as the battle flag of the Orange Guard.

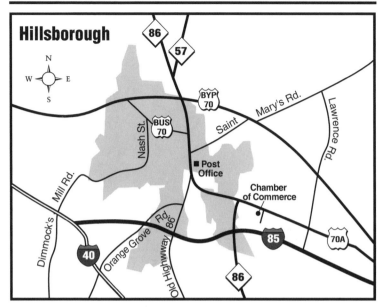

600—with prices ranging from $130,000 to $400,000. The road system expansion, including Timber Drive, Garner's garden parkway that goes past five public schools, also provides greater accessibility to the town's growing neighborhoods. The Hammond Road extension at Timber Drive will create a new exit for Garner from I-440.

Townspeople say their family-oriented tradition has met and mingled with new ideas and technology. That harmony and diversity has drawn thousands to Garner and with its convenient access to Research Triangle Park, area colleges and universities, the trend continues.

Hillsborough

Population: 5,000
Commute to Chapel Hill: 12 mi.
Commute to Durham: 15 mi.
Commute to RTP: 22 mi.
Chamber of Commerce: 732-8156

Founded in 1754, Hillsborough was the site of both the Regulator tax revolt and the most successful Tory raid on Colonial forces during the Revolutionary War. The town functioned as the Colonial Capital of North Carolina and as the Capital during the Revolutionary Period. Several royal governors and elected governors lived here as did William Hooper, a signer of the Declaration of Independence. The War of the Regulation ended here in 1771. Hillsborough hosted the Third Provincial Congress in 1775 and the state's Constitutional Convention of 1778, which demanded the inclusion of a Bill of Rights in the U.S. Constitution. It is also said to have been the starting point of Daniel Boone's journey west to Kentucky. The town was laid out by William Churton, a surveyor and Earl of Granville, near a village once inhabited by the Occoneechee Indians.

Today residents find a pleasing mixture of modern convenience and rural ambience and, despite the phenomenal growth taking place all around it, this bustling county seat has retained much of its historic charm. Buildings of Colonial, Antebellum, Victorian and other architectural styles dot the landscape with gardens that

Photo by Robert Thomason

Although it's one of the fastest-growing communities in Wake County, Holly Springs continues to maintain its small-town atmosphere.

enhance the town's visual history. Wood-frame homes dating back hundreds of years line the town's narrow streets. More than 75 buildings date to the 1700s, 1800s or early 1900s. Over a dozen are found on the National Register of Historic Places and one, the Nash-Hooper House, is a National Historic Landmark. The downtown area has been designated a National Historic District.

Antique stores, small shops and a 19th-century courthouse frame the central business district, with nearby bed and breakfast inns. Dozens of antique shops are found in town—in downtown and in the Daniel Boone Village antique mall, a few blocks south. The Triangle SportsPlex on U.S. 70-A East in the Meadowlands business park offers a fitness center, ice skating and indoor swimming pools. The annual Hog Day festival in June reflects local tastes in music and pork; it draws folks from all over to eat barbecue, listen to music and buy local crafts. Art galleries reflect a burgeoning artist community.

Novelists Lee Smith and Allan Gurganus make Hillsborough their home.

Hillsborough is about a 15-minute drive north of Chapel Hill, along N.C. 86, and 20 minutes from Durham via I-40 or I-85. While Hillsborough has managed to preserve its small-town character, it is perhaps more receptive to growth today than ever before. This former rural outpost is only about a 20-minute commute to the heart of the Triangle via I-40. Some developers are already looking at Hillsborough as the next suburban frontier.

Holly Springs

Population: 6,500
Commute to Raleigh: 13 mi.
Commute to RTP: 15 mi.
Chamber of Commerce: 557-3925

Before the Civil War, Holly Springs was a promising little town on one of the main roads to Raleigh. The Chatham Railroad changed that when the tracks were laid north of Holly Springs through Apex and Cary. Holly Springs is now one of the hottest residential communities in Wake County as its population continues to skyrocket, from 900 in 1992 to approximately 6,500 today. The formula is simple: small-town atmosphere, better utility and road systems, and reasonably priced homes, all within driving distance of RTP and Raleigh.

The Holly Springs Methodist Church and the First Baptist Church (founded by freed slaves) are two of the oldest churches in town. The town had a general store, a liquor store, two turpentine distilleries and four flour and grist mills during its early years. In keeping with the need to retain the "small-town" feel, plans are in the works to turn a 38-room mansion that was built in the 1840s into a museum.

Today the town has its own Chamber of Commerce, a weekly newspaper, *The Holly Spring Sun*, and one of the most popular golf course communities in Wake County, Sunset Ridge, home to Devil's Ridge Golf Club. The largest employer in town is yarn manufacturer Warp Technology with 145 workers. Much of Holly Springs' work force is found in service-oriented businesses.

Town leaders are striving to maintain the town's traditional Southern image by developing building and landscaping guidelines. Revitalization of the downtown area, including plans for a new town hall, shops, office and amphitheatre, as well as construction of Holly Springs Elementary School and a new middle school, are included in the town's plans for growth. Holly Springs' newest park will incorporate the freshwater springs that gave the community its name.

Holly Springs is located southwest of Raleigh on N.C. 55 between U.S. Highways 1, 64 and 401. Harris Lake and Jordan Lake, located nearby, provide water activities including boating, fishing and swimming and the town's parks have baseball fields, basketball courts and tennis courts.

The single-family neighborhood Somerset Farms offers homes from $107,000 to more than $165,000, and custom homes in Arbor Creek start at $110,000. Homes at Holly Glen are priced from $140,000 to the mid $200,000s, and at Sunset Ridge from $160,000 to

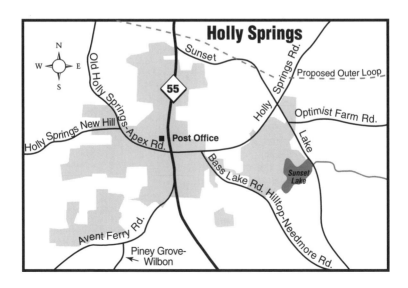

Knightdale

complete with three elementary schools, a public library and national retail stores and eateries. A 21,000-square-foot regional library is set to open in 1999, and Wake Technical Community College is planning to locate a campus nearby.

About 6 miles east of Raleigh on U.S. Highway 64, the town of Knightdale is evolving from a rural farming community into one of the fastest growing communities in the Triangle. In fact, its population more than tripled between 1983 and 1994. In 1994 Knightdale was the sixth fastest growing community, in both residential and commercial growth, for towns over 2,500 people in North Carolina. Knightdale is close to Raleigh and RTP, has the lowest tax rate in the Triangle at 52 cents per 100 dollars of property valuation and offers quality housing at reasonable prices.

Two limited access roads planned for the area—the Northern Wake Expressway and the U.S. 64 Bypass—will improve access to Knightdale from other parts of the

$700,000. Sunset Lake is in the final phase of development and has lots available for custom-built homes.

Knightdale

Population: 4,450
Commute to Raleigh: 6 mi.
Commute to RTP: 20 mi.
Chamber of Commerce: 266-4603

The history of the community dates back to 1701 when the Tuscarora Indians inhabited the Knightdale-Marks Creek area. The development of the downtown area began in 1907 when Henry Haywood Knight donated land for a depot for the newly completed Norfolk and Southern Railroad, and in 1927 the town of Knightdale was incorporated. In 1989, the town moved a caboose to the downtown area and constructed a park to serve as a constant reminder of the town's heritage.

Since then, Knightdale has experienced a great deal of growth, from one bank and little else to a thriving community,

Photo by Robert Thomason

Knightdale has grown from a country crossroads into a thriving residential community.

Photo by Robert Thomason

The Franklin County Courthouse in Louisburg has been renovated
and expanded extensively since it was built in 1850.

Triangle and open up a variety of opportunities for additional development.

Recent redevelopment activities have included private and public ventures such as roadway improvements that will result in new sidewalks and improved on-street parking. Other development includes the construction of an urban forest-environmental park next to the new town hall.

The average price of a new house in Knightdale is $125,000. Construction continues on hundreds of single-family and multifamily homes. Major developments include Planters Walk, Parkside, Emerald Pointe and Carrington Woods.

Louisburg

Population: 3,500
Commute to Raleigh: 45 mi.
Commute to RTP: 55 mi.
Chamber of Commerce: 496-3056

Founded as the Franklin County seat in 1779, Louisburg was named for

France's King Louis XVI. The town contains a number of quaint Greek revival and Victorian houses along its shady avenues as well as Louisburg College, the nation's oldest two-year college, which

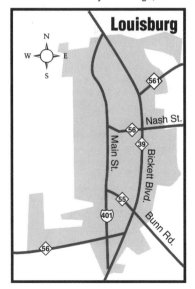

was chartered in 1789. It is also home to the 85-bed Franklin Medical Center.

Louisburg hosts two popular annual events: the Tar River Festival at River Bend Park and the National Whistler's Convention. The popular Murphy House restaurant, which opened in 1951, is famous for its authentic North Carolina pork barbecue.

Morrisville

Population: 2,500
Commute to Raleigh: 8 mi.
Commute to RTP: Adjacent borders
Chamber of Commerce: 380-9026

History records show that Gov. Tryon's army camped "at Jones on Crabtree Creek" on May 7, 1771, on the way to fight the Regulators in Hillsborough.

Nathanial and Tingnall Jones were landowners and plantation operators where the town of Morrisville is now situated. In 1852, Jeremiah Morris, then a landowner, gave the railroad a right-of-way and three acres of land for a "water station, woodshed and other buildings and a yard." In return, the railroad named the town Morrisville.

Morrisville, another "railroad" town that began as a depot on what is now the Norfolk Southern Railroad, lies between Cary and Research Triangle Park, about 8 miles from Raleigh. Its population has grown from 251 in 1980 to 2,265 in 1998. While people have relocated from all parts of the country to live or work in Morrisville, the town has pride in its roots: the Shiloh community was founded by freed men and women after the abolition of slavery. The community began in 1867 when Rev. Ed Cole organized the congregation of Shiloh. In 1925 Rev. James Dunston divided 2,000 acres into farms for the 12

Photo by Rich Weidman

Nestled between Research Triangle Park and Cary, Morrisville continues to develop at a rapid pace.

The Art of Living

At North Creek you'll find amenities usually reserved for upscale homes.

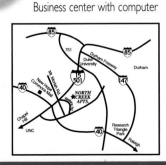

Private detached garages

Elegant decorative molding

Vaulted ceilings

Ceiling fans

Full sprinkler systems

Garden tubs with glass

Woodburning fireplaces

Aerobics room with TV & VCR

Fully equipped fitness center

Custom built bookshelves

Patios & Balconies

Lovely Wooded Views

Swimming pool & Spa

Business center with computer

NORTH CREEK

919/490-6013

100 Northcreek Drive
Durham, NC 27707
email: nrthcreek@aol.com

Come Home to The Hamptons

*P*erfectly situated on Highway 54, one mile west of RTP, this location offers easy access to RDU, Duke, UNC and downtown Durham. It is close to retail shops, movie theaters and many fine restaurants.

Interior Features

- Crown Molding
- Nine Foot Ceilings
- Computer Desks
- Fireplaces
- Microwaves
- Berber Carpet
- Garden Tubs
- Tiled Entries
- Washers & Dryers
- Patios/Balconies

Amenities

- Club Room
- Swimming Pool
- Business Center
- Fitness Center
- Cinema Room
- Detached Garages
- Carports
- Mountain Bikes

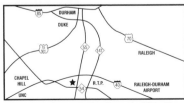

Directions: From I-40 take exit 278. Turn south on Hwy. 55. Turn right at the light onto Hwy. 54. We're 1/4 mile on the right.

300 Seaforth Drive, Durham
(919) 484-1321

Developed and Managed by The Hanover Company

BRAND NEW LUXURY APARTMENTS AT RTP

Edinborough
AT THE PARK

A Renaissance
IN APARTMENT HOME LIVING

This beautiful premier apartment community offers one, two, and three bedroom apartments featuring:

* *Gas Fireplace*
* *Energy efficient gas heat/cooking*
* *Individual Monitored Alarm System*
* *Breathtaking views*
* *Dens and Sunrooms (select units)*
* *Garden tubs/separate showers*
* *Sprinkler system*
* *9-foot ceilings*
* *20 elegantly appointed floor plans*
* *24-hour emergency maintenance*
* *Attached and detached garages*
* *Covered parking available*
* *Playground*
* *Complimentary airport service*
* *Corporate apartments available*

TIRED OF THE DAILY COMMUTE?
CALL (919) 941-9635

200 Edinborough Dr., Durham, NC 27703
From the I-440 Beltline, exit I-40 west. Exit Miami Blvd., take the first right on Guardian Drive and our Clubhouse is located on the left.

RENT TO OWN — While We Build Your New Home!
While you rent at Edinborough at the Park, you are eligible to have 25% of your monthly rent credited toward the purchase of one of Country Lane Development's new homes in Somerset Farm or Somerset Place (up to 2.5% of the total purchase price).

www.edinboroughpark.citysearch.com

Edinborough

AT THE PARK

RESORT STYLE LIVING AT IT'S FINEST
The 8,000 sq. ft. clubhouse has swimming pools, indoor lap pool, tennis court, fitness center, putting green, business center and conference center.

More Plans To Choose From, Call For Our
Floor Plan Booklet: **919.941.9635**

MONET
852 SQ FT STANDARD
OPTIONAL SUNROOM
AND DEN AVAILABLE

Plan

DA VINCI
1174 SQ FT-STANDARD
OPTIONAL SUNROOM
AND DENS AVAILABLE

Plan

VAN GOGH
1444 SQ FT

Plan

Take I 40 to RTP/Miami Blvd Exit. Edinborough
is just across from the Marriot on Guardian Rd.

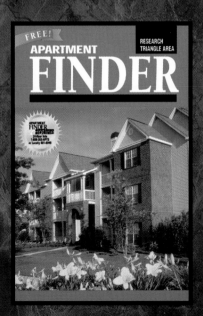

GTE Wireless For Families

"I need more than just talk time"

Feeling a little overwhelmed by all the wireless hype? Want a wireless provider that understands your family's mobile lifestyle and your desire for simplified wireless service? Welcome to GTE Wireless for Families. We've developed an array of rate plans and packages with your needs in mind. Like FamilyNet[SM] to help you stay in touch simply and affordably. And important advantages like simplified pricing and billing. The flexibility to change rate plans. Personalized customer service. Automatic credit for dropped calls. And the most reliable digital service in the region. We are family. GTE Wireless. People Moving Ideas.

GTE

WIRELESS

1-800-868-2355

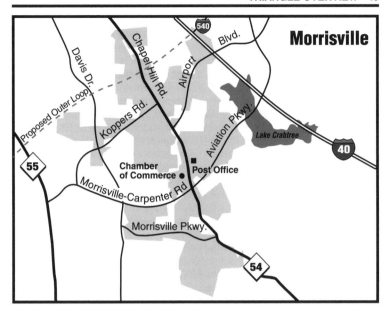

original major church members, the descendants of whom developed the community. More than 150 descendants still live in the community.

In comparison to its neighbors, Morrisville's growth has been nonresidential and has resulted in a healthy tax base. The town has changed from a sleepy country village straddling N.C. 54 to a community with industrial parks, planned neighborhoods and even a lovely community center and park. While other communities, especially Cary, attracted residential newcomers, this little town near the big airport busied itself attracting businesses such as EDS, Kaiser Permanente, AT&T, Radian and MCI. Along the roads linking downtown to Interstate 40, one finds office parks, with innumerable tenants. Morrisville recently added the Carolina Hurricanes to its stable of businesses headquartered in town.

Just off I-40, Morrisville's commercial growth includes Prime Outlets at Morrisville (formerly known as Triangle Factory Shops), a mall of more than 40 manufacturer-owned outlet stores. The Northern Wake Expressway, a new highway that will pass through the northern portion of the town and move traffic from the Airport around the capital faster, will create two exits within the town limits and add further polish to Morrisville's image as a hub for business.

This view of Morrisville's landscape and prospects led *The New York Times* to call the town an "entrepreneurial hot spot" and one of the best places in America to start and grow a company. *Expansion Management* magazine concluded "Morrisville has all the answers" when assessing its attributes — skilled labor, local training programs for workers, a high quality of life, world-class research and development facilities, advanced telecommunications capacity and a key location.

The town's tax base has grown from $85 million in 1987 to $430 million in 1997. Its land use plan, revised in 1990, envisions an ultimate tax base that has roughly a mix of 20 percent residential and 80 percent commercial/industrial growth. Its residential population, although small, is expected to continue to grow due to its proximity to Research Triangle Park and RDU International Airport. About 70 percent of the land within the town limits remains undeveloped.

Development of Huntington, the 680-acre planned community, doubled the town's population and companies such as Bristol-Myers, which has a plant near Huntington's industrial park, have added to the town's job market. Satellite parks in Morrisville include Perimeter Park off I-40 and Airport Road (200 acres and 500,000 square feet), Perimeter Park West off I-40 (six buildings totaling 413,320 square feet), and Gateway Center off I-40 and Aviation Parkway (154,000 square feet with flex space).

With the airport a nearby neighbor, Morrisville occupies about 13.2 square miles; it has five parks on 51 acres, allowing the townspeople the opportunity to enjoy outdoor activities. A greenhouse in the downtown area boasts poinsettias that bloom year round, and the newly renovated Town Hall houses Civil War artifacts.

The town even purchased a health club and converted it into a community center complete with municipal pool, tennis courts and exercise facility. Morrisville also has the distinct honor of having one of the largest year-round elementary schools in the country located within its boundaries.

With the opening of the 16-screen Park Place Cinema on Chapel Hill Road, the small town nestled near the airport has become a small pocket of night life, attracting people from across the Triangle, especially on weekends. The cinema will soon be joined by Park Place Shopping Center, which will include a Food Lion grocery store and Golden Corral restaurant.

Pittsboro

Population: 2,050
Commute to Chapel Hill: 16 mi.
Commute to RTP: 30 mi.
Chamber of Commerce: 742-3333

When you arrive in Pittsboro, located along U.S. 15-501, the first thing you'll

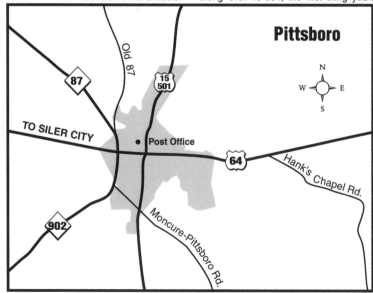

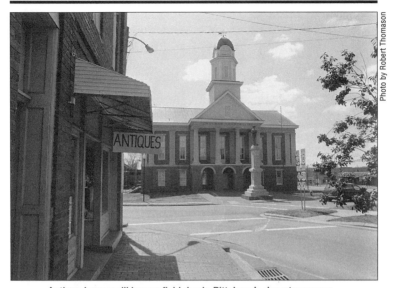

Photo by Robert Thomason

Antique lovers will have a field day in Pittsboro's downtown area.

notice is the courthouse situated squarely in the middle of a traffic circle. Nearby, you'll find the Pittsboro General Store, a good place to stop for natural foods, wine and cheese. Here you can also pick up a handy map to the many craft and antique shops in the area.

Like Hillsborough, this Chatham County seat, 16 miles south of Chapel Hill, still feels like a small Southern town. Historic homes line its streets. Town inhabitants include a blend of longtime natives and newcomers drawn to the area because of its charm, proximity to UNC-CH and Research Triangle Park, and, of course, lower land prices and property taxes.

Pittsboro is also becoming a mecca for antique and crafts hunters. If you're driving from Chapel Hill, you'll pass the Fearrington Market, a good place to stop for a casual lunch. Also located at Fearrington Village is Pringle's, a shop featuring hand-thrown stoneware, jewelry and fine crafts. As you cross the Haw River at Bynum, you'll see Stone Crow Pottery,

located in a rebuilt log cabin and Cooper-Mays Pottery just across the road. Bynum is home to the famed Clyde Jones, who fashions rustic wood art.

Key industries in this agricultural county are textiles and poultry production. Perdue Farms with 800 workers and Townsends, Inc., with 1,350 workers, are major poultry producers in the area. Among textile producers, Glendale Hosiery employs 700 people, CharlesCraft Inc. employs 240 people and Collins & Aikman employs 650 people,

Pittsboro, like the other small towns on the edges of the Triangle, faces the challenge of balancing growth pressures against the desire to preserve the qualities that make this such a pleasant place to live. Nearby is Jordan Lake, a state recreational area with 150 miles of shoreline. Take a boat out on the lake, fish, water-ski or just enjoy the scenery. Camping enthusiasts trek en masse to the many campsites at the lake. They join bird-watchers trying to spot a bald eagle in their largest summertime home in the Eastern United States.

Photo by Robert Thomason

Rolesville must face the challenge
of encouraging growth while preserving its rural charm.

The lake is home to many varieties of wildlife, including birds of prey, deer, songbirds, flying squirrels and beavers. Don't miss the Talking Tree Trail with recorded messages about the lake's history and surroundings.

Pittsboro residents find hours of relaxation in the Pittsboro Memorial Library and at area festivals such as the Pittsboro Fall Festival, which celebrates the area's strong agricultural roots.

Rolesville

**Population: 850
Commute to Raleigh: 14 mi.
Commute to RTP: 24 mi.
Chamber of Commerce: 556-6471**

Located about 14 miles northeast of Raleigh, Rolesville is the second-oldest town in Wake County. Incorporated in 1837, the town was named for William (Billy) Roles, a landowner, merchant, cotton broker and cotton gin owner, postmaster, deacon and trustee of the Baptist church. He also founded the first local school, Rolesville Academy, in 1832.

A fire destroyed part of the original downtown in 1913. The downtown area was reconstructed and today a variety of businesses operate there, including a dance studio, flea market, furniture store, sandwich shop, antique store and grocery store. The Senior Citizens Building, which formerly housed a jewelry store and shoe shop, is now available for group meetings.

Rolesville's Parks and Recreation department offers children and adult athletic and art programs. A joint venture between the town and Rolesville Elementary School has produced a 20-acre park with a picnic shelter, two ball fields, a new concession stand and a running track. Plans are underway to add a tennis court, walking

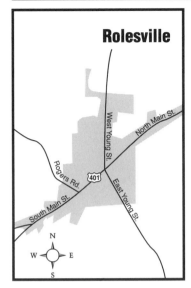

Rolesville

U.S. 401 South. Due to its proximity to Raleigh, the town is in the process of expanding its residential, commercial and industrial sectors. Town planners are currently preparing a comprehensive land use plan to encourage growth while preserving Roleville's rural charm.

Wake Forest

Population: 10,284
Commute to Raleigh: 12 mi.
Commute to RTP: 30 mi.
Chamber of Commerce: 556-1519

This lovely old college town, which was established in 1838, sits about 12 miles northeast of Raleigh's outskirts off U.S. 1. Its small-town charm and its proximity to the Triangle has been enhanced by the development of Falls Lake a few miles to the west. The challenge to city leaders is to keep Wake Forest's small-town pace and grace while accommodating growth.

The town's history is intertwined with education, beginning with three private academies that operated nearby in the early 1800s and the founding of Wake

trails and an open play area. The town's annual Recreation Day is a popular event held in April.

Rolesville's population is expected to double within the next five years. It already contains several residential subdivisions, including Olde Towne, located to the north of town, and Wall Creek on

Although surrounded by sprawling suburban developments, Wake Forest's beautiful historic district retains a strong sense of community.

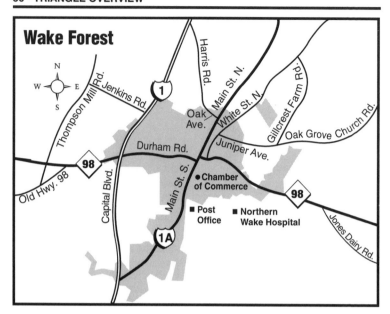

Wake Forest

Forest College in 1834 by the state's Baptist Convention.

When the college moved to Winston-Salem in 1956, its buildings were occupied by an older crowd of Southeastern Baptist Theological Seminary students. Wake Forest, in the words of one town historian, became "a much quieter and more sedate place." It also became an attractive residential town.

The average sales price of a new home is about $159,000. Starter homes at The Village of the Olde Mill Stream sell for $100,000 to $130,000; Tarlton Park lists homes from $200,000 to $300,000; and The Oaks at Waterfall Plantation, from $280,000 to more than $600,000. A two-story Victorian home in the historic district might sell for considerably less than homes in a nearby, newer neighborhood.

Ligon Mills Business Center, an office and retail center, is located a couple miles outside the downtown area. The town has six parks, including a baseball park and one swimming pool. The beautiful Wake Forest Country Club offers graceful amenities to its members. Kids will love ZooFauna, a nature park with more than 200 animals from around the world.

Wake Forest offers a variety of community activities, the largest of which is the Fourth of July celebration at the Wake Forest-Rolesville High School stadium.

With the completion of Interstate 540 (the Northern Wake Expressway or Outer Loop) over the next couple of years and Wakefield Plantation, a 2,260-acre housing and commercial development in North Raleigh, Wake Forest will undergo significant growth, providing a host of new challenges for town planners.

Wendell

Population: 3,926
Commute to Raleigh: 13 mi.
Commute to RTP: 25 mi.
Chamber of Commerce: 365-6318

Wendell, located about 13 miles east of Raleigh, off U.S. 64, is named after poet Oliver Wendell Holmes. Residents pronounce the name Wen-DELL, since that's the way the train conductor called out the stop during the town's early years.

Incorporated in 1903, Wendell's economy was tied to tobacco. Today Wendell has prospered from the Triangle's explosive growth and the town has refurbished its downtown with a small, municipal park with a gazebo. The town's first store still stands, although it was moved to a different location and is now the home of the Wendell Historical Society. The heart of Wendell's downtown business district is located at the intersection of Main and Third streets. Town officials are in the process of applying to have the area listed in the National Register of Historic Places.

Wendell still has a tobacco market, one of the few left in Wake County. Several manufacturing operations, such as Siemans Energy & Automation, have located close by, bringing jobs and demands for housing. There is a solid core of professional services whose practitioners have deep roots in the community.

Photo by Robert Thomason

Incorporated in 1903, Wendell is applying to have its downtown listed in the National Register of Historic Places.

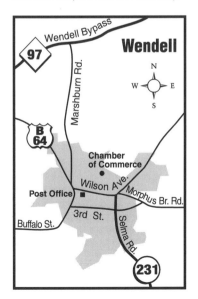

Eastern Wake Senior Center, a joint public and private venture, provides a unique social and cultural facility for older adults in the community. It shares space on its two-acre site with a branch of the Wake County Public Library. A favorite attraction in Wendell is St. Eugene's Catholic Church, one of the few in mostly protestant eastern Wake County. The church has been there for years and until recently was the parish for Catholics from surrounding counties, too. The annual Bright Leaf Folk Festival, held the first weekend in October, celebrates Wendell's rich heritage surrounding the flue-cured tobacco leaf. Family-centered activities and entertainment fill the two-day event.

Wendell's residential growth has been steady rather than spectacular. Some folks like it that way because the older homes that surround the business district show off Victorian and Craftsman-style

Photo by Robert Thomason

Zebulon has been discovered by Triangle commuters for its wide range of affordable housing options.

architecture and are a good buy. Subdivisions such as Meadows of Northwinds and Hollypointe are currently being developed with home prices starting at $80,000.

Zebulon

Population: 4,800
Commute to Raleigh: 17 mi.
Commute to RTP: 42 mi.
Chamber of Commerce: 269-6320

A short distance from Wendell, Zebulon serves as a hub for those commuting to Johnston, Wilson, Nash and Franklin counties. Its central location near Raleigh and Rocky Mount, its affordable housing and industrial growth mark the town as an outstanding relocation choice for professionals and families moving to the Triangle area from both in-state and out-of-state.

In 1907, the town was chartered and laid out into "lots, blocks, streets, alleys, avenues and parks" by the Zebulon Company, which took its name from North Carolina Governor Zebulon B. Vance. According to the *Historic Architecture of Wake County*, Zebulon's core business district of two blocks between Arendell and Gannon avenues is one of the "largest intact historic commercial districts among Wake County's 11 small towns."

The town recently embarked on a downtown revitalization project, complete with banners proclaiming "Discover Downtown Zebulon." The first phase of the project involved planting trees, burying power lines and replacing light poles. Town officials hope the revitalization efforts will draw more specialty shops and restaurants to the business district.

Glaxo Wellcome, the pharmaceutical giant; Nomaco, a foam manufacturing company; PYA/Monarch, one of the Southeast's largest food distributors; and

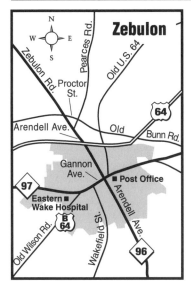

Blount Industries have operations in Zebulon, spurring more growth and drawing interest by other companies.

Developers boast a wide range of housing options and costs. Homes can be built bigger here for less and on more acreage than people may spend elsewhere. The older residential homes sit among tree-lined streets and display Victorian, Craftsman and Colonial Revival styles, many of them are still occupied by longtime Zebulon families.

Zebulon's Five County Stadium is home to the Carolina Mudcats, a minor league AA affiliate of the Colorado Rockies. Zebulon's other big draw for Triangle homeowners is Whitley's Furniture Gallery near downtown. Wedgewood and Triangle East shopping centers also combine to provide an unusual choice of fine merchandise for shoppers. For the growing number of Hispanic residents, the Mexico Store sells Spanish-language magazines, videos and clothing.

At the turn of the century, there was a large pine forest, a one-room school and three houses where Zebulon stands today. Today, it's a thriving community. The new town motto—"The town of friendly people"—says it all.

The Triangle's hotel business has been very strong in recent years, both for the innkeepers as well as travelers.

Accommodations

The Triangle's hotel business has been very strong in recent years, both for the innkeepers as well as travelers. While the industry here has a record for boom or bust markets, right now the availability of rooms is about right. The area has a good selection, from economy chains to mid-priced hotels aimed at the business traveler to convention-sized name brands such as Holiday Inn, Marriott, Embassy Suites and Hilton. Also, there are long-term temporary accommodations as well as bed and breakfast inns, each of which have their own respective chapters in this book.

The Accommodations Chapter is straightforward in listing a variety of Triangle hotels and amenities. It is by no means complete. If you want something other than a chain, we've included some locally owned hotels such as the Plantation Inn and Washington Duke Inn. We've also provided you with pricing information so you won't have any surprises when your travel budget is an issue. Most, if not all, accept major credit cards. Keep in mind that many of the more expensive hotels often have weekend rates that are almost half the price of weekday rates. By the way, one of the country's fastest growing hotel franchisers, Winston Hotels, is based in Raleigh. Check out our "Restaurants" chapter for hotels that have distinguished themselves in the dining room.

Under state law, pets are not allowed in hotels, so call ahead, if possible, about arrangements for Snoopy or Garfield. Also, because the Triangle is loaded with colleges and universities, there are some weekends when you really need to make reservations ahead—like a year to six months in advance for graduation weekends in May. Rooms are also scarce during big football weekends in the fall.

Price Code

We have categorized accommodations with one to four dollar signs ($), based on the typical daily rates charged for a standard room with two double beds:

$	Under $50
$$	$51-$75
$$$	$76-$100
$$$$	$101-up

Keep in mind that this is a guide and rates may change. What doesn't change is the Southern hospitality for y'all.

Raleigh

Brownestone Hotel
$$$ • 1707 Hillsborough St. • 828-0811

Once Raleigh's Hilton Hotel, the Brownestone is locally owned by veteran hoteliers who know their market. It is downtown, about one mile from the Capitol, and is popular with politicians and legislators and lobbyists when the General Assembly is in session. It is also next to the NCSU campus and contains banquet facilities for moderate-sized conventions and meetings. It has a restaurant and pool. A color TV with HBO is in each of its 192 rooms. The Hillsborough Street YMCA is just next door.

Club Hotel by Doubletree
$$$-$$$$ • 2815 Capital Blvd.
• 872-7666

The Club Hotel, which recently completed $3.5 million in renovations, is located minutes from downtown. It features 200 rooms, a new restaurant, a heated indoor pool, exercise facility and 4,300 square feet of meeting space.

Embassy Suites Raleigh's restaurant, Nicola's, features authentic Italian cuisine.

Country Inn & Suites by Carlson
$$ • 2715 Capital Blvd. (U.S. 1 N. & I-440 Beltline) • 872-5000

The Country Inn replaced the Holiday Inn Highwoods in mid-1995 with $1 million of renovations. Like its predecessor, this hotel has maintained its clean and efficient service. Still popular with traveling business people because of its reasonable rates, it is close to a number of restaurants as well as the Highwoods business park. It has a pool and 156 rooms, complimentary breakfast and an open bar Monday through Thursday evenings. It sits across the highway from the Parker Lincoln office building.

Courtyard by Marriott
$$-$$$ • 1041 Wake Towne Dr.
(Wake Forest Rd. and the I-440 Beltline)
• 821-3400

This is one of the Marriott chain's four Courtyards in the Triangle and if you've seen one Courtyard, you know to expect a high level of service. The location—near Raleigh Community Hospital—gives it excellent access to all parts of the city. It has 153 rooms and is very popular with business travelers who want more than a light left on for them.

Crabtree Summit Hotel
$$-$$$ • 3908 Arrow Dr. • 782-6868

Formerly the Comfort Suites at Crabtree, the Crabtree Summit offers 88 rooms, all with coffee makers and other amenities to make your stay a comfortable one. Some suites are equipped with refrigerators and whirlpool baths. A weekday stay in any room gets you a full breakfast buffet and free van service to and from the airport. Every Monday through Thursday from 5 to 7 PM, this establishment offers The Manager's Reception with complimentary drinks and hors d'oeuvres to all guests and their guests. An outdoor pool provides a means for exercise and relaxation while away from home.

Embassy Suites Raleigh/ Crabtree Valley
$$$$ • 4700 Creedmoor Rd. • 881-0000

Embassy Suites Raleigh, which was named the best Embassy Suites in the world in 1995, offers spacious, two-room suites; a complimentary breakfast and manager's reception; and an indoor pool and sauna. Guests can also enjoy authentic Italian cuisine at the hotel's new restaurant, Nicola's.

Four Points Hotel by Sheraton
$$$$ • 4501 Creedmoor Rd. • 787-7111

Upgraded from a Sheraton Inn to hotel status, the Four Points provides several amenities, including an indoor pool, fitness room and upscale restaurant. With 317 rooms, this is one of the largest hotels in the city, located adjacent to Crabtree Valley Mall. It caters to business clients with convention-size facilities.

Holiday Inn Crabtree
$$$ • 4100 Glenwood Ave. • 782-8600

After more than $4 million in renovations, the Holiday Inn Crabtree re-opened recently, featuring an outdoor heated pool, saunas, a fitness center, Carolina Jacks Steakhouse and state-of-the-art meeting and banquet facilities. It is conveniently located off the I-440 Beltline.

Holiday Inn State Capital
$$$ • 320 Hillsborough St. • 832-0501

Part of the Raleigh skyline since the 1970s, this renovated Holiday Inn tower is in the round and is one of the more convenient places to downtown and the state government complex, both within walking distance. From The Top of the Tower restaurant, you have a grand view of the city and its byways. It has 201 rooms and the amenities one expects at a Holiday Inn, including a pool on the second floor.

Homewood Suites
$$$$ • 5400 Edwards Mill Rd. • 785-1131

Located in Crabtree Valley within walking distance from the mall, Homewood Suites features 137 two-bedroom suites with spacious bedrooms, living rooms and fully equipped kitchens.

FYI

Unless otherwise noted, the area code for all phone numbers listed in this guide is 919.

Marriott at Crabtree Valley
$$$$ • 4500 Marriott Dr. • 781-7000

One of Raleigh's national chain hotels, this 375-room Marriott sits off Glenwood Avenue, across from Crabtree Shopping Mall and is the largest hotel in the city. It quickly established itself as a popular gathering-place for the party and sports crowd. The hotel's central location to growing northwest Raleigh has made it a popular business meeting place. It's also only 18 minutes from RTP and RDU. When there's a seminar on a big party night, parking can present a challenge. Amenities include an indoor-outdoor pool, tennis courts, a fitness room and a restaurant, the Crabtree Grill. Also check out the Marriott's less expensive Courtyard, at the intersection of the I-440 Beltline and Wake Forest Road. Newer still is the Fairfield Inn, Marriott's least expensive chain, located at the I-440 Beltline and U.S. 1 North.

North Raleigh Hilton
$$$$ • 3415 Wake Forest Rd. • 872-2323

Built by one of Raleigh's premier hotel-motel building families, Seby and Roddy Jones, this has been a growing hotel, located right off the I-440 Beltline and across the road from Raleigh Community Hospital. It is Raleigh's biggest convention center

Located within walking distance of Crabtree Valley Mall, Homewood Suites features 137 spacious two-bedroom suites.

Photo by Tim Johnson

The Plantation Inn Resort has the appearance of a grand old Southern mansion.

hotel and contains an indoor pool with sun deck, restaurant and an upscale night spot, Bowties. Politicians are moving their election night parties here as are many charity balls. The large convention and meeting facilities accommodate up to 1,500 people—one of the largest such centers on the East Coast—and its 338 rooms lodge plenty of guests.

Plantation Inn Resort
$$ • 6401 Capital Blvd. • 876-1411

This is one of the city's grand old motels, about 50 years old, and the place to stay when it offered travelers the luxuries of a swimming pool, playground, putting green and even a fishing pond! The Inn has seen Raleigh grow past its doorstep, yet it retains its green landscape and serene, Southern plantation motif. The buffet at Jacqueline's restaurant has been popular for years. The inn has 93 rooms and offers bargain rates for travelers as well as meetings and/or private dining.

Quality Suites
$$$-$$$$ • 4400 Capital Blvd. • 876-2211

Located in North Raleigh, Quality Suites offers 114 two-room suites, complete with refrigerator, microwave cven, coffee maker, cable TV and VCR. Other amenities include a complimentary full buffet breakfast and newspaper, outdoor pool and fitness room.

Ramada Inn, Crabtree
$$-$$$ • 3920 Arrow Dr. • 782-7525

This locally owned Ramada Inn is one of the best and has the awards to prove it. The Colonnade Restaurant has a great reputation and serves many homemade specialties. Stay alert when nearing this inn, since the entrance is somewhat obscured by the traffic jamming the I-440 Beltline and Glenwood Avenue interchange. (The entrance is off the eastbound lane of Glenwood Avenue, immediately before the I-440 Beltline interchange.) It has 174 rooms, a pool and outdoor exercise stations and satellite access for television.

Another Ramada Inn is located at 1520 Blue Ridge Road, 832-4100.

Residence Inn
$$$-$$$$ • 1000 Navaho Dr. • 878-6100

Another establishment in the Marriott Hotel group, this one is aimed at the person who wants more than the usual motel room and is planning to stay longer than a single night. The rates vary according to stay and it's popular with corporate visitors. There are 144 units, including suites with fireplaces, free continental breakfasts, heated pool, whirlpool and sports courts.

Sheraton Capital Center Hotel
$$$ • 421 S. Salisbury St. • 834-9900

Formerly known as the Raleigh Plaza Hotel, the new Sheraton Capital Center recently underwent $7 million in renovations, which include a new restaurant, The Grove Cafe. The 17-story downtown hotel is located next to and is connected through the underground parking lot with the city's Civic Center and the BB&T York-Hannover skyscraper and is a block from Memorial Auditorium and the City Market. The Sheraton Capital Center offers business meeting facilities for groups ranging

from 15 to 700 and its indoor pool features a whirlpool.

Velvet Cloak Inn
$$-$$$ • 1505 Hillsborough St. • 828-0333

Built during the 1960s, the Velvet Cloak has been a fixture in the city's hotel life ever since. The Velvet Cloak and its restaurants set the standard for many years. The 172-room inn has an indoor pool and atrium and is next to the YMCA where visiting members can play racquetball and work out. Its location near NCSU and downtown makes it popular both with academic and government leaders and rock stars performing at Walnut Creek.

Cary

Best Western
$$-$$$ • 1722 Walnut St. (near South Hills Mall exit off U.S. 1 & U.S. 64 S.) • 481-1200

Like all units in the Best Western chain, this one is independently owned and the chain gives it a top rating. It is located at one of Cary's busiest exits off I-440 and if you're coming from the airport, you will exit I-40 at

Photo by Tim Johnson

The Velvet Cloak Inn is named after Sir Walter Raleigh's gallant gesture of placing his velvet cloak over a mud puddle so Queen Elizabeth wouldn't dim the shine on her shoes.

Exit 293. Many of Cary's motels are clustered at this exit. The Best Western has suites, mini-suites and standard rooms. It has two conference rooms, a satellite dish receiver and a swimming pool. Complimentary breakfast is served daily and complimentary transportation for business guests is provided to and from RDU airport and to some local business parks.

Courtyard by Marriott
$$$ • 102 Edinburgh Dr. • 481-9666

This is one of Cary's upscale accommodations, offering 149 rooms. Like other Courtyards, it's designed for business travelers and is conveniently located in southwest Cary, where U.S. 1 intersects U.S. 64 at MacGregor Village Shopping Center. It opened in 1987 and offers a pool, laundry, exercise room and whirlpool.

Embassy Suites Hotel And Convention Center
$$$$ • 201 Harrison Oaks Blvd. • 677-1840

The hotel offers 273 residential suites and 7 hospitality suites. Meeting space totals 21,000 square feet in gracious, flexible ballrooms and break-out areas. Two-room suites include kitchen appliances. Full restaurant service, a gift shop, indoor pool, sauna, Jacuzzi, fitness room and access to a business center with audiovisual equipment are also available. The hotel offers guests a complimentary full breakfast and airport shuttle service.

Fairfield Inn by Marriott
$$ • 1716 Walnut St. • 481-4011

A member of the Marriott chain, the 125-room Fairfield Inn features cable TV in every room, a complimentary continental breakfast and an outdoor pool and sun deck.

Other Fairfield Inn locations in the Triangle include Crabtree Valley at 2201 Summit Park Lane, Raleigh, 881-9800; Durham/RTP at 4507 Hwy. 55, Durham, 361-2656; 3710 Hillsborough Road, Durham, 382-3388; and Raleigh Northeast, 2641 Appliance Court, Raleigh, 856-9800.

Hampton Inn
$$ • 201 Ashville Ave. • 859-5559

This affiliate of the popular chain caters to the mid-range customer. Like most of the town's other accommodations, the Hampton is located in southwest Cary, near the Western Wake Medical Center and has 131 rooms. It offers a free continental breakfast, nonsmoking rooms, pool and exercise room. Children stay free.

Photo by Tim Johnson

The new La Quinta Inn & Suites is conveniently located next to Regency Park, Cary's largest research and business park.

Homewood Suites
$$$-$$$$ • 100 MacAlyson Ct. • 467-4444

Homewood Suites is what the proprietor calls an "all suites hotel" located near MacGregor Village off U.S. 1. It opened in 1994 and offers 120 suites in three sizes. The typical tenant stays a week and all suites include bedrooms and living rooms with daily maid service and breakfast. Guests are invited to a reception in the late afternoon every Monday through Thursday.

Durham

Brookwood Inn at Duke
$$-$$$ • 2306 Elba St. • 286-3111

An eight-story high rise near Duke University and area hospitals, Brookwood Inn at Duke has 149 rooms with double or king-size beds, color satellite TV and the University Grille restaurant. Kids stay free.

Brownstone Inn
$$-$$$ • 2424 Erwin Rd. • 286-7761, N.C. (800) 872-9009, Outside N.C. (800) 367-0293

The Brownstone is conveniently located next to the Duke Medical Center and Duke University. Complimentary shuttle service to and from the Medical Center is available. The Inn has 140 rooms with double or king-size beds and color cable TV with HBO. Upscale amenities are available on the Executive level, a floor with its own limited-access elevator and special services such as a complimentary morning newspaper and a continental breakfast.

Other services and facilities include a heated indoor pool, Jacuzzi and sauna, handicap-access rooms, nonsmoking rooms, self-service laundry and same-day dry cleaning and complimentary afternoon tea in the Williamsburg-style lobby. A full-service restaurant and a pub feature daily lunch, dinner and drink specials.

FYI
Unless otherwise noted, the area code for all phone numbers listed in this guide is 919.

Carolina Duke Motor Inn
$ • 2517 Guess Rd. (off I-85) • 286-0771, N.C. (800) 672-7578, Outside N.C. (800) 438-1158

The Inn provides a free shuttle to Duke University Hospital and the Veterans Administration Hospital. There are 181 rooms, each with a color TV and HBO, and your choice of queen- and king-size beds. There's a swimming pool as well as two conference rooms for meetings that accommodate up to 30 persons.

Comfort Inn University
$$-$$$ • 3508 Mt. Moriah Rd. I-40 at U.S. 15-501 • 490-4949, (800) 221-2222

Conveniently located to Duke University and UNC-Chapel Hill, Comfort Inn has 138 rooms (including 18 suites with whirlpools and VCRs) that are carefully planned for business and leisure travelers. Facilities include an outdoor pool, an exercise room, a guest laundry and valet services, handicap-access and nonsmoking rooms. Meeting space is available to accommodate up to 160.

Durham Hilton
$$$-$$$$ • 3800 Hillsborough Rd. (off I-85) • 383-8033, (800) 445-8667

This six-story facility has 154 rooms, 10 suites, an outdoor pool and complete healthclub facilities, including a sauna, a Jacuzzi, a VCR for Jazzercise tapes and lots of exercise equipment. Tipton's offers regional and New American cuisine, a piano bar and can accommodate private parties and banquets. Blue Chips lounge has two bars. With 19 meeting rooms, the Hilton can also accommodate conferences of more than 500.

Photo by Tim Johnson

Conveniently located at the edge of Duke University's West Campus, the Washington Duke Inn and Golf Club features an 18-hole, Robert Trent Jones-designed championship golf course.

Durham Marriott at the Civic Center
$$$$ • 201 Foster St. • 683-6664

Located downtown, the former Omni Durham recently completed $2 million in renovations and became a part of the Marriott chain in spring 1998. The hotel complex includes the Durham Civic and Convention Center, which contains 40,000 square feet of meeting space. It offers 187 beautifully refurbished rooms and three suites. A restaurant, lounge and new exercise room are on the premises. It is a great place to stay when you have business downtown or at Duke University.

Forest Inn
$-$$ • 3460 Hillsborough Rd.
• 383-1551, (800) 238-8000

Located just off I-85 at the U.S. 15-501 Bypass, the Forest Inn is convenient to the Durham Expressway. It has a restaurant, lounge and meeting rooms that accommodate up to 200 people. Other amenities include a swimming pool and a rose garden courtyard.

Regal University Hotel
$$$$ • 2800 Campus Walk Ave.
• 383-8575, (800) 633-5379

Each of the hotel's 315 rooms has cable TV with pay-per-view movies. Guests on the VIP floor receive complimentary hors d'oeuvres, a continental breakfast and a morning newspaper. Discount rates are available on holidays, during summer months and for extended stays. Special rate plans are offered for hospital patients and their families.

Praline's Cafe has an all-you-can-eat breakfast and lunch buffet seven days a week, plus a la carte dining. The Executive Club offers the traveling business person a place to work (personal computers, printers and desks are provided), network or just unwind and relax. The Varsity Lounge in the lobby is a handy place for a drink or a bite to eat.

Travel Time Inn
$ • 4145 Garrett Rd. • 489-9146

Travel Time is just across the street from Darryl's restaurant and adjacent to the Oak Creek Shopping Village. The Inn has 80 rooms and offers color satellite TV and an outdoor pool. It is convenient to UNC-Chapel Hill and Duke University.

Washington Duke Inn and Golf Club
$$$$ • 3001 Cameron Blvd.
• 490-0999, (800) 443-3853

This $16-million luxury hotel is located at the edge of Duke's west campus, facing the Robert Trent Jones-designed 18-hole golf course, which was recently redesigned by the architect's son, Rees Jones. It has 171 rooms and suites and many amenities that include an outdoor pool and jogging trails. For fine dining, guests enjoy the Fairview Restaurant. Terrace-on-the-Green features more casual alfresco dining and the Bull Durham Bar serves cocktails. Meeting facilities include the Duke University Room for small conferences and the Ambassador Ballroom for groups up to 600.

Chapel Hill

Best Western University Inn
$$$ • N.C. 54 E. • 932-3000

The University Inn has been a Chapel Hill landmark since 1952. Located minutes from downtown, the UNC campus, UNC Hospitals, the Friday Center and Finley Golf Course, it is an excellent choice for those who are traveling for business or for pleasure. The 80-room Inn offers a pool, complimentary breakfast and cable television with HBO.

The Carolina Inn
$$$$ • 211 Pittsboro St.
• 933-2001, (800) 962-8519

A lot of history lives in this building, which underwent a $14.5 million renovation and addition in 1995. The old New Hope Chapel, from which Chapel Hill derives its name, once stood about where the Inn's parking lot is today. The original Inn was built in 1924 by John Sprunt Hill, an industrialist, financier and graduate of the UNC class of 1889. His family deeded it to the university in 1935. It has been enlarged twice prior to the recently completed project.

The Inn, which contains 184 rooms, is located on the UNC-CH campus and is one block from the town center. Many upgrades in services and facilities have been added to the natural charm and tradition of the Inn. Rooms have two telephone jacks, allowing use of modems. There is a gift shop and exercise room. Meals are a delightful experience.

Hampton Inn
$$$ • 1740 U.S. 15-501 Bypass
• 968-3000, 800-HAMPTON

A two-story, 122-room hotel, this Hampton Inn is part of a national chain offering comfortable accommodations at lower-than-average prices. The Inn eliminates a few "frills" such as restaurants, lounges and meeting spaces—a minor concession to economy given its location near the many eateries and shops at Eastgate and along U.S. 15-501. You still get a swimming pool, television, movie channels, free local calls and a complimentary breakfast and newspaper. Eighty percent of the rooms are nonsmoking.

Holiday Inn of Chapel Hill
$$-$$$$ • 1301 N. Fordham Blvd.
(U.S. 15-501 Bypass) • 929-2171

This Holiday Inn has 135 comfortable rooms with color cable TV and an outdoor pool. It is convenient to downtown Chapel Hill, the UNC campus and close to the Interstate 40 interchange. Teddy's Grill & Pub serves three meals daily.

Sheraton Chapel Hill Hotel
$$$$ • 1 Europa Dr. (U.S. 15-501 Bypass)
• 968-4900, N.C. (800) 672-4240,
Outside N.C. (800) 334-4280

As soon as you walk in the door you'll see the highlight of the well-appointed lobby, a wall-sized bas-relief sculpture called "The Dream," commissioned for this location. The 172-room Sheraton Chapel Hill Hotel, formerly the Omni, sits on 6 rolling acres with lighted tennis courts and a pool.

You can enjoy an elegant dinner in Ruben's Restaurant or more casual fare in the Lobby Lounge. Take the glass elevator to the King's Club lounge on the top floor for late night entertainment.

The Siena Hotel
$$$$ • 1505 E. Franklin St. • 929-4000

Named for a small Italian city, this luxurious addition to Chapel Hill was designed to recall the intimate hotels of Europe. The

---

INSIDERS' TIP

The Carolina Inn is about as close as you can get to UNC's famed Business School, and its meeting rooms have been frequented by many distinguished visitors.

TRIANGLE ACCOMMODATIONS

Hotel/Motel	Address	$-$$$$	Shuttle	Phone
RALEIGH				
Best Western Crabtree	6619 Glenwood Ave.	$$-$$$	N	782-8650
Best Western Hospitality Inn	2800 Brentwood Rd.	$$	N	872-8600
Brownestone Hotel	1707 Hillsborough St.	$$$	Y	828-0811
Club Hotel by Doubletree	2815 Capital Blvd.	$$$-$$$$	N	872-7666
Comfort Inn North Raleigh	2910 Capital Blvd.	$-$$	N	878-9550
Comfort Inn Six Forks	4220 Six Forks Rd.	$$	N	787-2300
Country Inn & Suites by Carlson	2715 Capital Blvd.	$$	N	872-5000
Courtyard by Marriott	1041 Wake Towne Dr.	$$-$$$	N	821-3400
Crabtree Summit Hotel	3908 Arrow Dr.	$$-$$$	Y	782-6868
Days Inn-Crabtree	6329 Glenwood Ave.	$$	N	781-7904
Embassy Suites, Crabtree	4700 Creedmoor Rd.	$$$$	Y	881-0000
Fairfax Inn	2813 Capital Blvd.	$	N	850-9986
Fairfield Inn Crabtree	2201 Summit Park Ln.	$$	N	881-9800
Fairfield Inn N. Raleigh	2641 Appliance Ct.	$$	N	856-9800
Four Points Hotel by Sheraton	4501 Creedmoor Rd.	$$$$	Y	787-7111
Hampton Inn Crabtree	6209 Glenwood Ave.	$$-$$$	Y	782-1112
Hampton Inn N. Raleigh	1001 Wake Towne Dr.	$$	N	828-1813
Hampton Inn Raleigh/Cary	111 Hampton Woods Ln.	$$-$$$	Y	233-1798
Holiday Inn Crabtree	4100 Glenwood Ave.	$$$	Y	782-8600
Holiday Inn State Capital	320 Hillsborough St.	$$$	N	832-0501
Homewood Suites	5400 Edwards Mill Rd.	$$$$	Y	785-1131
La Quinta Crabtree	2211 Summit Park Ln.	$$$	N	785-0071
Marriott Crabtree Valley	4500 Marriott Dr.	$$$$	Y	781-7000
North Raleigh Hilton	3415 Wake Forest Rd.	$$$$	Y	872-2323
Plantation Inn Resort	6401 Capital Blvd.	$$	Y	876-1411
Quality Suites	4400 Capital Blvd.	$$$$	N	876-2211
Ramada Inn Blue Ridge	1520 Blue Ridge Rd.	$$$	Y	832-4100
Ramada Inn Crabtree	3920 Arrow Dr.	$$-$$$	Y	782-7525
Red Roof Inn	3201 Old Wake Forest Rd.	$-$$	N	878-9310
Residence Inn	1000 Navaho Dr.	$$$-$$$$	N	878-6100
Sheraton Capital Center	421 S. Salisbury St.	$$$$	Y	834-9900
Sundown Inn	3801 Capital Blvd.	$$	N	790-8480
Velvet Cloak Inn	1505 Hillsborough St.	$$-$$$	Y	828-0333
CARY				
Best Western	1722 Walnut St.	$$-$$$	N	481-1200
Courtyard by Marriott	102 Edinburgh Dr.	$$$	N	481-9666
Embassy Suites	201 Harrison Oaks Blvd.	$$$$	Y	677-1840
Fairfield Inn by Marriott	1716 Walnut St.	$$	N	481-4011
Hampton Inn-Cary	201 Ashville Ave.	$$	N	859-5559
Homewood Suites	100 MacAlyson Ct.	$$$-$$$$	N	467-4444
La Quinta Inn & Suites	191 Crescent Commons	$$$-$$$$	N	851-2850
Ramada Inn	U.S. 1 & Hwy. 55, Apex	$-$$	N	362-8621
Red Roof Inn	1800 Walnut St.	$$	N	469-3400

TRIANGLE ACCOMMODATIONS

Hotel/Motel	Address	$-$$$$	Shuttle	Phone
DURHAM				
Best Western Skyland Inn	5400 Hillsborough Rd.	$$	N	383-2508
Brookwood Inn at Duke	2306 Elba St.	$$-$$$	N	286-3111
Brownestone Inn	2424 Erwin Rd.	$$-$$$	N	286-7761
Carolina Duke Motor Inn	2517 Guess Rd. at I-85	$	N	286-0771
Comfort Inn University	3508 Mt. Moriah Rd.	$$-$$$	N	490-4949
Courtyard by Marriott	1815 Front St.	$$$-$$$$	N	309-1500
Durham Hilton	3800 Hillsborough Rd.	$$$-$$$$	Y	383-8033
Durham Marriott	201 Foster St.	$$$$	N	683-6664
Fairfield Inn	3710 Hillsborough Rd.	$$	N	382-3388
Forest Inn	3460 Hillsborough Rd.	$-$$	N	383-1551
Ramada Inn	600 Willard St.	$$-$$$	N	956-9444
Red Roof Inn	1915 North Pointe Dr.	$$	N	471-9882
Regal University Hotel	2800 Campus Walk Ave.	$$$$	Y	383-8575
Travel Time Inn	4145 Garrett Rd.	$	N	489-9146
University Inn	502 Elf St.	$$	N	286-4421
Washington Duke Inn	3001 Cameron Blvd.	$$$$	Y	490-0999
CHAPEL HILL				
Best Western University Inn	N.C. 54 E.	$$$	N	932-3000
The Carolina Inn	211 Pittsboro St.	$$$$	N	933-2001
Hampton Inn	1740 U.S. 15-501	$$$	N	968-3000
Holiday Inn of Chapel Hill	1301 N. Fordham Blvd.	$$-$$$$	N	929-2171
Sheraton Chapel Hill	1 Europa Dr.	$$$$	N	968-4900
The Siena Hotel	1505 E. Franklin St.	$$$$	Y	929-4000
RESEARCH TRIANGLE PARK				
Budgetel	1001 Aerial Center Pkwy.	$$	Y	481-3600
Courtyard by Marriott	2001 Hospitality Ct.	$$-$$$	Y	467-9444
Days Inn Airport	1000 Airport Blvd.	$$$	Y	469-8688
Doubletree Guest Suites Hotel	2515 Meridian Pkwy.	$$$-$$$$	Y	361-4660
Fairfield Inn by Marriott	4507 Hwy. 55	$$	N	361-2656
Fairfield Inn RDU Airport	2750 Slater Rd.	$$-$$$	Y	468-2660
Hampton Inn	1010 Airport Blvd.	$$$	Y	462-1620
Hawthorn Suites	300 Meredith Dr.	$$$$	Y	361-1234
Hilton Garden Inn	1500 RDU Center Dr.	$$-$$$$	Y	840-8088
Holiday Inn	4810 Page Rd.	$$$$	Y	941-6000
La Quinta Inn and Suites	1001 Hospitality Ct.	$$$	Y	461-1771
Marriott at RTP	4700 Guardian Dr.	$$-$$$$	Y	941-6200
Microtel Inn	104 Factory Shops Rd.	$$	N	462-0061
Radisson Governors Inn	N.C. 54 & I-40 at Davis Dr.	$$$-$$$$	Y	549-8631
Sheraton Imperial	I-40 & Page Rd.	$$$-$$$$	Y	941-5050
Wyndham Garden Hotel	I-40 & Miami Blvd.	$$-$$$$	Y	941-6066

80 rooms range from doubles with king-size beds to the two-bedroom Presidential Suite and feature traditional furnishings, spacious marble-tiled baths (including whirlpools) and 9-foot ceilings.

Il Palio, the Siena's restaurant, features Northern Italian and Mediterranean cuisine. A complimentary continental breakfast, daily newspaper and even limousine service round out the hotel's special amenities.

Research Triangle Park/Airport

Doubletree Guest Suites Hotel
$$$-$$$$ • 2515 Meridian Pkwy.
• 361-4660, (800) 222-8733

Well situated in the Research Triangle Park, the 203-suite Guest Quarters Suite Hotel offers travelers spacious accommodations in a conveniently located, first-class hotel. The hotel offers three flexible meeting and banquet rooms, a health club, an indoor/outdoor pool, a tennis court and jogging trails. The guest library is equipped with personal computers or visitors can read the regional and national newspapers and periodicals. The Piney Point Grill & Seafood Bar is a comfortable place to enjoy good food.

Hawthorn Suites
$$$$ • 300 Meredith Dr. off N.C. 55
• 361-1234, (800) 527-1133

These luxury accommodations include 100 fully furnished and equipped suites geared to business travelers, visitors planning an extended stay or people relocating to the area. Each suite contains a

kitchenette, living room and one or two bedrooms. The hotel has an outdoor lap pool, meeting and conference rooms and audio/visual equipment. A complimentary breakfast is served, and catered lunches, dinners and bar services are available.

Holiday Inn/RDU Airport
$$$$ • 4810 Page Rd. at I-40
• 941-6000

The Holiday Inn in the Research Triangle Park—rated one of the Top 20 in the chain—has 249 rooms, all with TVs and VCRs. The hotel has a fine restaurant, Remington's, as well as the more casual Cafe, a lobby bar and a popular area night spot, Horsefeathers. An upgraded concierge floor, the fifth offers special amenities for the business traveler.

La Quinta Inn & Suites
$$$ • 1001 Hospitality Crt. • 461-1771,
(800) 531-5900

Opened in the fall of 1996, La Quinta has 135 rooms, an exercise room and a pool. Continental breakfast, free local calls, laundry service and a shuttle service are offered to guests. The hotel is near the airport and is just across the street from Prime Outlets of Morrisville.

La Quinta has two other locations in the Triangle: Raleigh Crabtree at 2211 Summit Park Lane, 785-0071; and Raleigh/Cary at Hwy. 1/64 and Tryon Road, 851-2850.

Marriott Research Triangle Park
$$-$$$$ • 4700 Guardian Dr.
(South Miami Blvd. at I-40) • 941-6200,
(800) 228-9290

This $7-million, six-story Marriott is just off I-40, a few miles from RDU International Airport. Features include 224 rooms,

INSIDERS' TIP
There is only one hotel located in Research Triangle Park itself, the Radisson Governors Inn, and up until the 1980s, it had little competition. Since then, there's been a boom in hotel building on land surrounding the Park, including the 10-story Sheraton Imperial Hotel and Convention Center.

Photo by Tim Johnson

The Holiday Inn/RDU Airport, which has 249 rooms,
offers special amenities for the business traveler.

nearly 4,000 square feet of meeting and banquet space and a 2,600-square-foot conference center. The hotel also offers two executive boardrooms, the Garden Court restaurant and lounge, a lobby bar, gift shop, indoor pool, health club and sauna.

Radisson Governors Inn
$$$-$$$$ • N.C. 54 & I-40 at Davis Dr.
• 549-8631

Adjacent to Research Triangle Park and convenient to RDU International Airport, the Radisson Governors Inn is one of the nicer accommodations in the Triangle. It offers 193 rooms with queen-size beds and color satellite TV. The Radisson Governors Inn also features the elegant Galeria Restaurant, Quorum Lounge and 7,000 square feet of meeting space and banquet facilities. A swimming pool, tennis courts and exercise trails are some of the amenities.

Sheraton Imperial Hotel
$$$-$$$$ • 4700 Emperor Blvd.
(I-40 at Page Rd.)
• 941-5050, N.C. (800) 222-6503,
Outside N.C. (800) 325-3535

This 10-story, 330-room hotel offers luxurious accommodations for tourists and traveling business executives. The 19-acre hotel and convention center complex includes two restaurants and a nightclub/ lounge. Tennis courts, a 2.5-mile-long jogging trail, an outdoor pool and a Jacuzzi round out the amenities. It also offers plenty of space for meetings, conferences, and private parties, from an intimate boardroom to the Imperial Ballroom that accommodates up to 2,000. The 30,000-square-foot Imperial Athletic Club offers a gym, 25-meter lap pool, aerobics, basketball, racquetball and Nautilus equipment for a daily guest fee.

Wyndham Garden Hotel
$$-$$$$ • 4620 South Miami Blvd.
• 941-6066

The Wyndham Garden Hotel features 172 rooms, two suites and many excellent amenities. The Wyndham has an outdoor heated lap pool, a weight room, sauna and whirlpool. There is a full-service restaurant on the premises. Other features geared to the business traveler include a library in the hotel and a club room with a large-screen television for relaxing when your business day is done.

For the traveler who wants more than a clean, well-lighted hotel, there are bed and breakfast inns.

Bed and Breakfasts

For the traveler who wants more than a clean, well-lighted hotel, there are bed and breakfast inns. The Triangle may not have as many as other parts of the country such as New England, but the area has some unique and lovely offerings, including the historic Colonial Inn in Hillsborough, which claims the distinction of being one of the 10 oldest inns still in operation in the United States—since 1759. You definitely get more than a bed and breakfast when you stay here. The visit usually includes a short course history lesson, Insider's tips from the innkeepers and a flavorful taste of local breakfast fare like cheese grits. Umm, good!

Raleigh

Oakwood Inn Bed & Breakfast
$$$ • 411 N. Bloodworth St.
• 832-9712

Opened in 1984, this bed and breakfast is located in historic Oakwood, a neighborhood behind the Governor's Mansion in downtown Raleigh. Business travelers with appointments in North Carolina's capital city will find the Oakwood Inn a welcome respite. Built in 1871 as the Raynor Stronach House, the Inn is listed on the National Register of Historic Places and has six rooms, all with private baths and telephones. The rooms are exquisitely furnished, entirely in Victorian decor. Guests get the "chef's choice" breakfast and afternoon refreshments.

Each room has a TV and fireplace. Fax and copy machines are also available.

William Thomas House
$$$-$$$$ • 530 North Blount St.
• 755-9400

This bed and breakfast is operated by former Secretary of Administration Jim Lofton and wife Sarah, who know government and state history from an Insider's view. The house was built around 1881 as an office and home for attorney William Thomas on Raleigh's finest residential row, Blount Street.

Today its Victorian elegance offers four guest rooms named after the Thomas' family members. Rooms come with private baths, cable TV and refrigerators. The porch has rocking chairs and a swing. A full breakfast and turndown service are also included. The Inn offers a library and business amenities such as fax and copy machines. Guests are in walking distance to downtown attractions.

Cary

Park Street Inn
$$$ • 107 W. Park St. • 469-3303

Located across the street from the First Baptist Church in downtown Cary, this is Cary's first and only bed and breakfast. Innkeepers Pat and Ed Haley are original "Caryites" and can certainly make you feel at home. Plan ahead and make reservations, since only two rooms are available.

The five-foot-high arrowhead marker that sits in front of the Arrowhead Inn commemorates the site of the Great Trading Path to the Smoky Mountains.

Apex

B&B's Country Garden Inn
$$-$$$$ • 1041 Kelly Rd. • 303-8003

Located in a secluded country setting, this three-room Inn is surrounded by beautiful ponds and gardens. Innkeepers Bud and Beth McKinney opened the Inn in 1997. Guests can enjoy the cozy family room, complete with TV and games. Other amenities include a home-cooked breakfast, large sun deck with grill and picnic table and a hot tub. The Inn is also available for small weddings, bridal showers, church groups and meetings.

Pearson Place Bed & Breakfast
$$-$$$ • 1009 North Salem St.
• 362-4290

Opened by innkeepers Jeanne and David Floyd in 1997, this elegantly decorated Victorian farmhouse offers two guest rooms. The Inn sits on two acres of land and is a popular spot for indoor and outdoor weddings, parties, luncheons and teas.

Durham

Arrowhead Inn
$$-$$$$ • 106 Mason Rd. • 477-8430

Located on 3.5 acres north of town, the Inn is an elegant plantation home built in 1774. It features eight guest rooms, all furnished in antiques and country primitives. Downstairs in the parlor, guests can watch TV or relax with an assortment of games. New innkeepers Philip and Gloria Teber are happy to direct you to the best local restaurants and interesting sites.

Included in the price of a room is a hearty gourmet breakfast. Children are welcome. The Inn can also accommodate small meetings.

The Blooming Garden Inn
$$$-$$$$ • 513 Holloway St. • 687-0801

This 1892 yellow Victorian Inn features leaded, beveled and stained-glass windows, a custom picket fence, a wraparound porch and lots of blooms in season. There are four beautifully appointed rooms, including two luxury suites with whirlpool baths, lace curtains, antiques and artwork set in a tasteful mix of warm colors. In addition, the popular "Holly House" across the street from the Inn, is available for a minimum stay of one week.

The Southern hospitality of innkeepers Dolly and Frank Pokrass makes this place a special treat. Guests enjoy a full gourmet breakfast on a relaxed schedule. Children are also welcome.

Convenient to Duke University, Ninth Street and Brightleaf Square, The Blooming Garden Inn is a comfortable and pleasant place to spend a few days.

Morehead Manor Bed & Breakfast
$$$-$$$$ • 914 Vickers Ave. • 687-4366

Morehead Manor, which opened in 1997, offers elegant accommodations in a splendidly decorated 8,000-square-foot, 1910 Colonial Revival style home. The Inn provides four common areas and four large guest rooms with private baths, including a honeymoon suite with a fireplace and sitting area.

The Inn is conveniently located within walking distance to the Durham Bulls Athletic Park, Brightleaf Square and downtown Durham. Innkeepers Daniel and Monica Edwards can assist guests with their sightseeing, shopping and dinner plans, if asked. The Inn is also available for weddings, private parties, corporate retreats and receptions.

Old North Durham Inn
$$$-$$$$ • 922 N. Mangum St. • 683-1885

An intimate bed and breakfast located in the heart of Durham less than a mile from Duke University, the Old North Durham Inn offers turn-of-the-century charm. In addition to the lovely four guest rooms with private baths, a family suite with two rooms is available. Amenities

include fireplaces, televisions, VCRs, a whirlpool tub and complimentary refreshments. Innkeepers Debbie and Jim Vickery truly make visitors "welcome" by offering a full complimentary breakfast and free tickets to Durham Bulls home games.

Chapel Hill

Fearrington House Country Inn
$$$$ • Fearrington Village, Pittsboro • 542-2121

This luxurious 31-unit Inn evokes images of an 18th-century country retreat, complete with cozy suites, exquisitely landscaped gardens and Belted Galloway cows grazing in the pasture.

Each room is uniquely decorated with antiques. In addition to the country charm, there are plenty of civilized touches: stereo music, modern baths, a full breakfast and a complimentary afternoon tea. The Country Inn is located at Fearrington Village, a 100-acre planned residential development located on a former dairy farm about 6 miles south of Chapel Hill.

In addition to the Inn and restaurant, there is the Fearrington Market, where you'll find fresh bagels and breads, gourmet coffee, wines, cheeses and a wide assortment of gifts. You may spend time strolling through the gardens or shopping at The Fearrington Village Shops.

The Inn at Bingham School
$$-$$$$ • 6720 Mebane Oaks Rd., Orange Cty. • 563-5583, (800) 566-5583

Located in the countryside on the site of the old Bingham Preparatory School 10 miles west of Chapel Hill, the Inn offers a convenient and comfortable retreat. Meticulously restored, the former headmaster's home (listed on the National Historic Registry) is now a cozy bed and

Photo by Tim Johnson

Located in the rolling countryside of Chatham County, Fearrington House offers luxurious quarters in the tradition of the 18th-century country retreat.

breakfast getaway. The owners received an award from Preservation North Carolina for the restoration.

Furnished in 19th-century antiques, the Inn offers five spacious guest rooms with fireplaces and private baths, including one with a whirlpool. One room is located away from the main house in a building called The Milk House.

During your stay, you'll be invited to relax by the fire, roam the surrounding farm and woodlands, enjoy complimentary wine and cheese or join in a game of croquet. A complete gourmet breakfast is served in either the formal dining room or the outside patio.

Windy Oaks Inn
$$ • The Paul Green Homeplace, Old Lystra Church Rd., Chatham Cty. • 942-1001

This century-old farmhouse, once occupied by noted playwright Paul Green,

has been lovingly renovated. Located on 25 oak-shaded acres about 4 miles south of Chapel Hill, Windy Oaks Inn has four guest rooms, including one with a shared bath. Full country breakfasts, featuring delicious homemade biscuits, are included in the price of the room. The Inn can also accommodate weddings, parties and luncheon meetings.

Hillsborough

Colonial Inn
$$ • 153 W. King St. • 732-2461

Built in 1759, this is one of the 10 oldest inns in continuous operation in the United States. It has provided lodging for the likes of Aaron Burr and Lord Cornwallis from our Colonial Period. It welcomes today's guests with quality service and Southern charm.

INSIDERS' TIP

General Sherman made a bed and breakfast out of the Governor's Mansion in Raleigh in 1865, and when he departed, no respectable North Carolina governor would stay there. Finally, it burned and Memorial Auditorium stands on the site today.

Located in historic Hillsborough about 10 miles north of Chapel Hill, the Inn, operated by Carlton and Sara McKee, has eight guest rooms. Throughout the building you'll see many antiques, including some of the original furnishings.

Guests will enjoy dining on Southern-style food in the Inn's restaurant, antique hunting in downtown Hillsborough or just sitting on rocking chairs on one of the porches overlooking this historic town.

FYI

Unless otherwise noted, the area code for all phone numbers listed in this guide is 919.

drinks in the library. Children over 10 are welcome. Pets may be boarded at a nearby kennel if prior arrangements are made.

The Inn at Teardrop
$$-$$$$ • 175 W. King St. • 732-1120

Located in the historic district of Hillsborough, this 18th-century Inn offers a charming retreat within a 15- to 20-minute drive of Durham and Chapel Hill. Proprietor Tom Roberts—who opened the six-room Inn in 1987—invites guests to stroll in his gardens and relax in the elegantly furnished parlor or on the back veranda.

This lovely 2 1/2-story home, which has been occupied alternately as a residence and an inn since 1767, is furnished in antiques and features reproductions by local craftsman Stephen Jones. Rates include a deluxe continental breakfast.

Hillsborough House Inn
$$$-$$$$ • 209 E. Tryon St. • 644-1600

The Hillsborough House Inn, owned and operated by descendants of the families that have owned the house since the 1850s, has six charming guest rooms. One is a suite in a renovated 1790's kitchen building, perfect for a romantic getaway. Guests may enjoy a pool, a complimentary full breakfast, and tea or afternoon

Photo by Robert Thomason

Insiders believe that in addition to Aaron Burr and Lord Cornwallis, George Washington also slept at Hillsborough's Colonial Inn. He had black-eyed peas and country ham for dinner. Really.

National magazines such as *Fortune* and *Money* consistently list the Triangle among the best places to work.

Employment Opportunities

In the 1980s, the Triangle posted one of the nation's lowest unemployment rates in the nation for the decade. The '90s is continuing this tradition. The Research Triangle Park is the hive for scientific, technical and executive jobs, but a recent job survey also showed a desperate demand for skilled tradespeople throughout the Triangle. National magazines such as *Fortune* and *Money* consistently list the area among the best places to work, especially for "knowledge" industries such as electronics, software development, pharmaceuticals and bio-tech. A number of employees who moved here with such companies have turned entrepreneur and started their own dreamworks. The jobs are here and if they're not exactly what you want, wait a year or two and they will be!

Employment Resources

Useful resources and publications you should explore when seeking employment in the Triangle are listed below. A number of these publications describe the major employers in the area.

Major Employers in Wake County
Greater Raleigh Chamber of Commerce
P.O. Box 2978, Raleigh, NC 27602
• (919) 664-7004 • Order by mail or phone. $18 (Visa/MC accepted)

Organizations Employing Over 100
Greater Durham Chamber of Commerce
P.O. Box 3829, Durham, NC 27702
• (919) 682-2133
Order by mail or phone.
$15.50 (Visa/MC accepted)

RTP Owners and Tenants
Research Triangle Foundation
• (919) 549-8181
Order by phone—no charge.

The classified section of a local newspaper is a cheap and easy source of many job listings and is an excellent place to begin your job hunt. The Sunday edition of the major local newspapers will provide the largest selection of opportunities and can also help you identify personnel agencies that may specialize in your field or give you access to small companies that don't use agencies. If you live in a large city, there may be a retailer near you that sells newspapers from across the country. Otherwise, a subscription to one of the area's largest papers might be a good investment.

The Raleigh *News & Observer* offers the largest classified section in the region. To order a subscription, call 829-4700 or (800) 522-4205. *The Herald-Sun* covers Durham; you can order a subscription by calling 419-6900. Each of these papers has a Chapel Hill edition: *The Chapel Hill Herald*, 967-6581, is a product of *The Herald-Sun* and *The Chapel Hill News*,

967-7045, is owned by *The News & Observer*. The *N&O* also offers *Employment Weekly* (available by special subscription).

The *Carolina Job Finder* is a biweekly employment newspaper that is available free at locations throughout the Triangle or by subscription, 319-6816.

Check our "Media" chapter for online sites with current job listings.

Temporary Placement

One of the best ways to explore career options is with the help of temporary or permanent staffing agencies. For the newcomer, a temporary position has the advantage of providing an opportunity to become more familiar with the area and with employment options before settling on a permanent position. In addition to placement, many agencies offer training and some even offer skill and personality testing to determine the best working situation for each individual.

Research Triangle Park Companies

Research Triangle Park, the area's high-tech centerpiece, is home to 132 private, governmental and nonprofit companies, employing over 39,500 people. It is estimated that by the year 2010, more than 50,000 people will be employed in the Park. Here's a list and brief description of some of the major employers located in RTP today.

BASF Corporation
Agricultural Products
400 Employees
26 Davis Dr. • 547-2000
RTP is the Agricultural Products Headquarters and Research Center for BASF.

Becton Dickinson
Research Center
120 Employees
21 Davis Dr. • 549-8641
B-D conducts basic and applied research related to medical devices and health-care products.

CIIT (Chemical Industry Institute of Toxicology)
150 Employees
6 Davis Dr. • 558-1200
CIIT is an independent, not-for-profit research laboratory dedicated to developing an improved scientific basis for understanding and assessing potential adverse effects of chemicals, pharmaceuticals and consumer products on human health.

Cisco Systems, Inc.
820 Employees
7025 Kit Creek Rd. • 472-2000
RTP is the headquarters for Cisco's InterWorks Business Unit. The company is a leading global supplier of enterprise networking equipment and software.

Data General Corporation
575 Employees
62 T.W. Alexander Dr. • 549-8421
Data General houses its Systems Software Development, the Software

INSIDERS' TIP

The Triangle is the entrepreneurial capital of North Carolina, a fact reflected by the presence of the Council for Entrepreneurial Development, the Kenan Institute for the Study of Private Enterprise at the University of North Carolina and Duke's Fuqua School of Business' annual Venture Fair that tries to match new businesses with venture capitalists.

IBM Corporation

Company:
IBM Corporation
3039 Cornwallis Road
RTP, NC

Business:
Computer
Manufacturer

Triangle Employees:
14,000

Human Resources:
(800) 964-4473

NYSE:
IBM

Headquarters:
1 New Orchard Road
Armonk, NY, 10504
(914) 499-1900

Internet Address:
www.ibm.com

IBM in the Triangle Area…
A Crossroads on the Information Superhighway

In 1965, IBM became one of Research Triangle Park's first major tenants to buy land. It set the stage for a rapid period of investment by a "who's who" of the world's research and development community. Over the years, we have grown to become IBM's largest site with 14,000 employees and seven million square feet of floor space in 50 buildings in RTP, Cary, Raleigh and Morrisville.

IBM's Triangle Area products are found in every industry in virtually every country in the world. We're worldwide headquarters for IBM's Networking Hardware, Retail Store Systems, National Human Resources Service Center and Personal Systems Group. Our industry-leading software is a multi-billion dollar business. These products help run banks, airlines, governments, the credit/debit card industry, as well as large and small businesses and the Internet. IBM's Triangle Area facility is home to more than 100,000 square feet of software testing area, accommodating the largest and most diverse programming skill base in the industry.

More than 50 percent of our employees are involved in the development, refinement and manufacture of computer hardware and software solutions. An IBM Personal Computer is produced every 10 seconds on more than half a dozen state-of-the-art manufacturing lines. IBM HelpCenters here handle millions of calls a year, linking with other IBM facilities around the world to provide continuous customer support. IBM in the Triangle Area is noted for its long history of community leadership and support. In 1997 and 1998, employees pledged more than $4 million to IBM's charitable contribution campaigns and volunteered for thousands of hours of community service.

MAJOR TRIANGLE EMPLOYERS

Name	Type of Business	# of Employees
Raleigh		
State of North Carolina	State Government	23,200
N.C. State University	Education	10,400
Wake County Schools	Public Education	9,200
City of Raleigh	City Government	5,500
Wake Medical Center	Health Care	4,600
Winn-Dixie Stores	Groceries	4,500
Rex Healthcare	Health Care	3,500
Carolina Power & Light	Utilities	3,000
Wake County Government	County Government	2,620
United Parcel Service	Package Delivery	1,500
Cary		
SAS Institute, Inc.	Computer Software	3,100
MCI Telecommunications	Telecommunications	2,200
American Airlines	Reservation Center	2,000
Austin Quality Foods	Snack Foods	1,300
IBM Corporation	Computers and Software	750
Town of Cary	Town Government	570
Bristol-Myers Products	Pharmaceuticals	450
Holiday Inn Reservation Center	National Reservation Center	450
Imonics Corporation	System Integration Software	450
Western Wake Medical Center	Health Care	400
Durham & RTP		
Duke University	Education, Medical Center	23,000
IBM Corporation	Computers and Software	14,000
Nortel Networks	Digital Switching Equipment	7,500
Glaxo Wellcome, Inc.	Pharmaceuticals	4,500
Durham Public Schools	Public Education	4,000
Blue Cross & Blue Shield/NC	Health Insurance	2,450
Durham Hospital Corporation	Health Care	2,000
VA Medical Center	Health Care	1,900
Durham City Government	City Government	1,720
Research Triangle Institute	Contract Research	1,450
Chapel Hill		
UNC-Chapel Hill	Education	9,500
UNC Hospitals	Health Care	4,850
Blue Cross/Blue Shield	Insurance	2,260
Chapel Hill/Carrboro Schools	Public Education	1,200
General Electric Co., Inc.	Electrical Components	1,100
Orange Cnty Bd. of Education	Public Education	850
Orange County Government	Government	580
Town of Chapel Hill	Town Government	550
Marriott Education Services	Institutional Food	445
Home Health Agency/CH	Home Health Care	425

Research Triangle Park, which is set in 6,900 acres of North Carolina pinelands, contains such innovative research and development facilities as Rhone-Poulenc.

Qualifications and Support and the Customer Documentation divisions at RTP.

Delta Products Corporation
50 Employees
5101 Davis Dr. • 767-3800
Delta Products designs and develops data communication products and switching power supplies.

DuPont Electronic Technology Center
280 Employees
14 T. W. Alexander Dr. • 248-5000
Research, development, applications engineering and sales support associated with materials and systems for the electronics industry are the focus here.

Eisai Inc.
54 Employees
900 Davis Dr. • 941-6920
Eisai performs pharmaceutical formulation research and manufacturing at its RTP facility.

Ericsson, Inc.
1,200 Employees
7001 Development Dr. • 472-7000
Digital cellular telecommunications, microcell base station research and development are conducted here.

Glaxo Wellcome, Inc.
4,500 Employees
5 Moore Dr. • 483-2100 • Job Line 483-2565
The U.S. corporate headquarters and research facilities of this pharmaceutical company are located in RTP. A manufacturing plant is located in nearby Zebulon. Basic research is in cancer, as well as viral and metabolic disorders.

GTE Government Systems
275 Employees
400 Park Plaza • 549-1111
GTE Government Systems maintains an engineering organization at RTP responsible for the development of telecommunications for the government. Engineering disciplines are software development and systems integration.

TRIANGLE EMPLOYMENT AGENCIES

Company	Type	Phone
Ablest Staffing Solutions	Clerical, Light Industrial	388-0633
Accountants On Call	Financial Services	403-3330
Accountemps, Robert Half, Inc.	Financial Services	787-8226
Accounting Solutions	Financial Services	828-3940
Action Staffmasters	Manufacturing, Clerical, Technical	873-0567
Adecco	Clerical, Light Industrial	572-2662
Bullington Associates	Medical, Industrial	781-1350
Capital Temporaries, Inc.	Administrative, Clerical, Light Industrial	833-8367
Duke Temporary Service	Clerical, Technical, Service	286-4889
Executive Staffing Solutions	Administrative, Technical	481-0093
Express Personnel Services	Administrative, Clerical, Light Industrial	875-1268
Five Star Staffing	Administrative, Accounting	854-4488
Fortune Personnel Consultants	Executive, Manufacturing	848-9929
Global Software	Data Processing	872-7800
Greer Personnel Consultants	Administrative	571-0051
Griffin Staffing Services	Clerical, Technical	554-3811
Headway Corporate Staffing	Office, Technical	544-2600
Healthcare Recruiters	Medical Sales, Administration	319-6306
Information Systems Professionals	Computer Systems	954-9100
Interim Personnel	Technical, Medical	420-0026
Kelly Temporary Services	Technical, Light Industrial	781-8667
Legal Personnel Services	Legal Secretaries, Paralegals	787-0049
Longistics	Administrative, Industrial	872-2167
Manpower	General	755-5800
Monarch Services	Professionals, Health Care	490-0000
Norrell	Administrative, Clerical	850-0046
Office Specialists	Clerical, Office Support	676-0068
Office Team	Administrative Staffing	787-6970
Olsten	General Office, Production	847-9999
Pat Licata Associates	Medical, Pharmaceutical	859-0511
Personal Communications	Secretarial, Light Industrial	544-4575
Piedmont Staffing	Administrative, Clerical, Light Industrial	833-0407
Quality Staffing Specialists	Medical, Accounting, Clerical	481-4114
Radeco Technical Services	Technical	851-7630
Remedy Staffing Services	Administrative, Accounting	783-6300
Renaissance Worldwide	Technical, Systems	678-1001
Sales Consultants	Sales, Sales Management	460-9595
Smither and Associates	Administrative, Office Support	493-5444
Snelling Personnel Services	Engineering, Medical Sales	876-0660
Staffmark	Clerical, Light Industrial	493-8367
Tandem	Industrial	828-4110
TRC Staffing Services	Administrative, Technical	481-2525
Triangle Temporaries	Administrative, Technical	876-0009
USA Staffing	Clerical, Light Industrial	479-8471
Westaff Services	Office, Industrial, Technical	781-7998
Volt Services Group	Technical, Administrative	829-1660
State of North Carolina Job Service		733-3941

IBM

(International Business Machines Corp.)
14,000 Employees
3039 Cornwallis Rd. • 543-5221
• Job Line (800) 964-4473

IBM undertakes development, assembly and programming for its networking business products division at RTP. The facility is also the headquarters for its personal computers division.

ISA

(International Society for Measurement and Control) 120 Employees
67 T.W. Alexander Dr. • 549-8411

RTP is the headquarters of an international society of engineers, scientists, technicians, managers and educators. The Society develops publications, standards and educational programs in instrumentation, control and automation.

Larscom Incorporated

100 Employees
77030 Kit Creek Rd. • 991-9000

Larscom manufactures telecommunications equipment, particularly equipment that provides access to wide area networks.

Litespec, Inc.

162 Employees
76 T.W. Alexander Dr. • 541-8411

Litespec develops and manufactures optical fiber. It is a subsidiary of AT&T and Sumitomo Electric.

Lockheed Martin

365 Employees
79 T.W. Alexander Dr. • 541-3351

Lockheed Martin's office provides support for the U.S. EPA's National Data Processing Center.

MCNC

225 Employees
3021 Cornwallis Rd. • 248-1800

MCNC is a private, nonprofit corporation that supports advanced education, research and technology programs in partnership with the state's universities, research institutes and industry. The N.C. Supercomputing Center and the N.C. Research and Education Network are based here.

Southern Hospitality: Alive and Well

Southern hospitality is a deeply rooted and real tradition, and the Triangle is no exception, no matter how many non-Southerners move here. That tradition continues today in the region's growing number of philanthropic foundations and charities. Getting involved in a community's philanthropy is a well-traveled avenue toward a community's heart.

North Carolina has perhaps one foundation with the clout of a Rockefeller, Ford or Kresge, the Duke Endowment, based in Charlotte with over $1.2 billion in assets in 1995. The state also is home to several foundations that have a long history in supporting North Carolina programs and causes. They are the Smith Richardson, Kate B. Reynolds, Burroughs Wellcome Fund, the William Kenan Trust, Z. Smith Reynolds and the Mary Reynolds Babcock Foundations.

The Triangle has a multitude of charities and good works. A good source for information is the *Philanthropy Journal of North Carolina,* based in Raleigh and edited by Todd Cohen. The monthly periodical tracks news in the nonprofit community, publishes a classified advertising section targeting the philanthropy business and serves as a clearinghouse for events. There is also an indispensable statewide directory of philanthropies, *North Carolina Giving*, that you can usually find at the local library. The directory is a product of John Bennett's Capitol Consortium in Raleigh, and it lists groups alphabetically, by their location and by their interests, i.e., the kinds of projects they typically fund.

Photo courtesy of Triangle United Way

If you want to have a hands-on experience, contact the United Way. The three city campaigns combined in recent years to form a Triangle United Way and that's always a good place to start if you're interested in getting involved. The United Way can also provide information on other charitable organizations if you have a specific interest such as the homeless or the hungry, children's issues or the arts.

There are special nonprofits in all three Triangle counties that target the public schools. Wake Education Part-

Triangle United Way volunteer

nership, for instance, is a nonprofit that raises money from the private sector to fund groups such as Community in Schools and the Literacy Council. Durham has its own group, the Durham Public Education Network. In the Triangle, some names to remember are the William Kenan Trust ($258 million in '95) of Chapel Hill, The Burroughs Wellcome Fund ($318 million in '95) of Morrisville, the Triangle Community Foundation in the Research Triangle Park and the Fletcher Foundation in Raleigh. The Triangle Community was established by one of Burroughs Wellcome's (now Glaxo Wellcome) Nobel laureates, George Hitchings, and it has pooled resources from other groups such as the Josephus Daniels Trust and has assets of $55 million in 1998. It, along with the Fletcher Foundation, offer workshops and programs for nonprofits on such subjects as grant-writing. The Fletcher is another home-grown philanthropy; it was started by the heirs of Raleigh broadcasting pioneer and insurance businessman A.J. Fletcher. Most large businesses in the Triangle also set aside money for nonprofit work. BellSouth, Glaxo Wellcome and Northern Telecom, for example, each have a formal process by which they evaluate grant requests and make awards. And many of these same companies also operate their own foundations, which target certain areas of interest such as communication, family planning, child issues or health care.

In North Carolina, most of the foundations' interest, 42 percent, is in education, which received $109 million in 1994, the last year for which figures are available. Other major recipients include health and hospitals, $57 million or 22 percent and social services, $50 million or 19 percent. As noted above, getting involved in a charity or nonprofit organization is a quick way to establish roots in the Triangle community and you can almost always count on a warm welcome. So, come on down and sign up!

Photo courtesy of Research Triangle Foundation

Underwriters Laboratories, which employs over 500 people, conducts product tests for public safety.

ManTech Environmental Technology, Inc.
130 Employees
2 Triangle Dr. • 549-0611

ManTech provides technical support services to various agencies of the U.S. government and to industry.

Mobius Group, Inc.
60 Employees
68 T.W. Alexander Dr. • 549-0444

Mobius is a leading developer and provider of information and software in the investment management, consulting and financial planning industry.

National Center For Health Statistics
80 Employees
12 Davis Dr. • 541-4873

The Center prepares health data and undertakes computer operations and data processing research.

National Institute of Environmental Health Sciences
900 Employees
Headquarters • 541-3863
South Campus
111 T. W. Alexander Dr.
East Campus
9 T. W. Alexander Dr.
North Campus
104 T. W. Alexander Dr.

NIEHS conducts biomedical research on the effects of chemical, physical and biological environmental agents on human health and well being.

Nortel Networks
7,500 Employees
4001 E. Chapel Hill/Nelson Hwy.
Morrisville • 992-5000

RTP is the world headquarters for Public Carrier Networks. The company designs, develops, manufactures and supplies one of the industry's most complete lines of fully digital switching and transmission systems for the public telephone network.

Novartis Biotechnology
180 Employees
3054 Cornwallis Rd. • 541-8500

Novartis conducts research and development using biotechnology for more efficient crop production.

Reichhold Chemicals, Inc.
600 Employees
2400 Ellis Rd. • 990-7500

RTP is the corporate headquarters and home for the research and development laboratories for Reichhold, a leading manufacturer of coating resins, emulsion polymers, polyesters and adhesives.

Research Triangle Institute
1,450 Employees
3040 Cornwallis Rd.
• 541-6000

The Institute is an independent, applied research institute serving government and industry in the U.S. and abroad. Disciplines at RTI include applied statistics, social engineering, chemistry and life sciences.

Rhone-Poulenc AG Company
560 Employees
2 T.W. Alexander Dr. • 549-2000

This company conducts research and development, engineering and marketing of agricultural products.

Sphinx Pharmaceuticals
150 Employees
20 T.W. Alexander Dr.
• 489-0909

A division of Eli Lilly and Company, Sphinx Pharmaceuticals conducts research to identify new drug leads for various disease areas.

Sumitomo Electric Lightwave Corporation
580 Employees
78 T.W. Alexander Dr.
• 541-8100

Sumitomo Corporation develops and manufactures fiber optic cable and sells fiber optics apparatus and video products to other manufacturers.

Troxler Electronic Laboratories, Inc.
140 Employees
3008 Cornwallis Rd. • 549-8661

Troxler develops, manufactures and distributes instruments and systems for measuring physical properties and characteristics of engineering materials through the use of radioactive isotopes.

Underwriters Laboratories, Inc.
510 Employees
12 Laboratory Dr. • 549-1400

Underwriters Laboratories conducts product testing for public safety.

U.S. Environmental Protection Agency
1,400 Employees
Public Affairs • 541-4577

The EPA conducts research on the health effects of exposure to air pollutants, pesticides and toxic substances and develops and evaluates techniques for monitoring and controlling air pollutants.

University of North Carolina Center For Public Television
192 Employees
10 T.W. Alexander Dr. • 549-7000

North Carolina's 11-station statewide public television network maintains its headquarters here.

FYI

Unless otherwise noted, the area code for all phone numbers listed in this guide is 919.

YOU WANT HOME COOKING? STAY HOME

WE COOK THE WORLD

BRIGHTLEAF 905

WORLD FOOD - WORLD BEVERAGE - WORLD MUSIC

BRIGHTLEAF SQUARE, 905 WEST MAIN STREET
DURHAM 919.680.8848

PRIVATE DINING ROOM
AVAILABLE

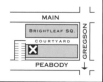

Restaurants and Caterers

Restaurants

Triangle area restaurants are in a constant state of change—from trendy, innovative restaurants opening to local favorites closing. Owners change, chefs change, some restaurants expand, some branch out, but even with all the changes, you can be sure to find just about any type of food you desire.

The Triangle has its fast-food and chain restaurants, which offer convenience, comfort and familiar dishes to residents and travelers alike. In addition to the usual fast-food places, you'll find chains such as Golden Corral (which started in Raleigh), Applebee's, Bennigan's, Chili's, Houlihan's and Red Lobster, to name just a few.

There is, however, a new breed of upscale chain restaurants that open in highly marketable areas. The Triangle is appealing to this type of restaurant, with Ruth's Chris Steak House opening in the summer of 1997 and several other restaurants planning to open soon.

For regional and ethnic cuisine, the chef- or proprietor-owned restaurants in the Triangle can fulfill just about any whim. The best fried chicken, shrimp and grits, Indian curry, dim sum, pasta served family-style or countless other dishes can be found within easy driving distance.

Price Code

The dollar signs ($) beside a restaurant entry are an indication as to what your bill for dinner for two might be, assuming that you don't order a bottle of Chateau Lafite-Rothschild with your meal. Lunch at many of the fancier places will be about half the cost of evening fare. If a restaurant has all ABC permits, it means the place serves mixed drinks as well as beer and wine. The cost code dollar signs ($) can be deciphered as follows:

$	Under $20
$$	$21 to $35
$$$	$36 to $50
$$$$	$51 and up

AMERICAN

23
$-$$$ • 200 W. Franklin St., Chapel Hill • 960-9623

Legendary basketball star Michael Jordan recently opened a trendy restaurant within strolling distance from his alma mater, the University of North Carolina. 23 is named after the lucky number Jordan wore on his jersey throughout most of his career as a member of the Tar Heels (1982 NCAA national champs) and Chicago Bulls (winners

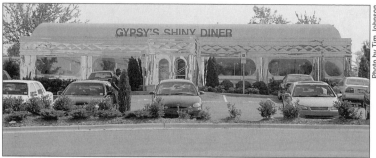

Photo by Tim Johnson

Because of its unique stainless steel decor, Gypsy's Shiny Diner ran afoul of zoning codes, but finally opened in 1997 to rave reviews from Cary residents.

of six NBA championships). The 9,000-square-foot restaurant, located in the Pavilion building, specializes in American cuisine, featuring local ingredients. 23 is decorated with memorabilia from Jordan's playing days. Lunch and dinner are served daily. Arrive early or be prepared to wait.

Carolina Coffee Shop
$$ • 138 E. Franklin St., Chapel Hill • 942-6875

Conveniently located on the edge of the UNC-CH, this is a traditional Southern restaurant and coffee shop that is reminiscent of the coffee shops in Europe. Try the delicious Breakfast Egg Sardou, stop in for a lunch of burgers or other sandwiches or wait for dinner and order the acclaimed crab cakes. It has all ABC permits.

Darryl's Restaurant & Bar
$$ • Hwy. 70 W., Raleigh • 782-1849
$$ • 4603 Chapel Hill Blvd., Durham • 489-1890
$$ • 1906 Hillsborough St., Raleigh • 833-1906
$$ • 4309 Old Wake Forest Rd., Raleigh • 872-1840

Darryl's expansive menu includes steaks, chicken, seafood, ribs, burgers, sandwiches, salad bar and late-night snacks. Darryl's draws a large lunch crowd and is popular in the evenings with students and families.

Gypsy's Shiny Diner
$ • 1550 Buck Jones Rd., Cary • 469-3663

Area residents have packed Gypsy's ever since it opened in 1997. Open from early morning until late at night through the week and 24 hours on the weekend, Gypsy's offers traditional diner fare.

Houlihan's
$-$$ • 2007 Walnut St., Cary • 859-0668
$-$$ • 6004 Falls of Neuse Rd., Raleigh • 874-0505
$-$$ • 6711 Glenwood Ave. • 783-0700

Houlihan's is a lively eatery that specializes in a diverse selection of American cuisine. Enjoy chicken and shrimp platters, pasta dishes, fajitas, steaks, baby back ribs, seafood, classic sandwiches, burgers, salads and soups. Each location is open for lunch and dinner daily.

Jasper's American Eatery
$$ • 4300 NW. Cary Pkwy., Cary • 319-3400

Jasper's menu changes every six weeks, highlighting regional cuisines. Lunch and dinner is served seven days a week, and brunch is served on Sunday.

Jillian's
$$ • 117 S. West St., Raleigh • 821-7887

Jillian's is a unique dining and entertainment complex. The Sports Video Cafe & Bar features classic American favorites including steak, salmon and barbecue ribs. It is open for lunch and dinner daily.

Lucky 32
$$-$$$ • 832 Spring Forest Rd., Raleigh • 876-9932

The art deco interior, grill room and bar offer several dining options. The menu changes monthly and offers innovative appetizers, salads, sandwiches, grilled fresh seafood and meats, gourmet pizzas, pastas and burgers. Lucky 32 has all ABC permits.

Michael Dean's Wood Oven & Bar
$$$-$$$$ • 1705 E. Millbrook Rd., Raleigh • 790-9992

A popular North Raleigh eatery, Michael Dean's features the best of new American cuisine, with entrees such as Shrimp Pizza with Spinach and Basil Pesto, Grilled Beef Tenderloin, Roasted Lobster Tail and Pistachio-Crushed Salmon. Michael Dean's offers dinner Monday through Saturday and live music Friday and Saturday.

Mo's Diner
$$-$$$ • 306 E. Hargett St., Raleigh • 856-9938

Located in a 112-year-old house in the Moore Square Arts District, Mo's Diner serves new American cuisine, including such dishes as Garlic and Herbed Shrimp on Angel Hair Pasta, Pan Seared Beef Tenderloin and Spicy Jambalaya. It is open for dinner Tuesday through Saturday. Call ahead for reservations.

Owen's 501 Diner
$$ • 1500 N. Fordham Blvd., Chapel Hill • 933-3505
Owen's Broad Street Diner
$$ • 1802 Main St., Durham • 416-6102

Owen's two restaurants serve traditional diner fare offering hamburgers, meatloaf and mashed potatoes and other "blue plate specials," as well as house specialties such as Pan-Seared Salmon, Brie and Chicken Fettuccini and Grilled Eggplant. Daily specials and homemade desserts round out the menu. Both are open for breakfast, lunch and dinner Tuesday through Saturday and for brunch on Sunday, and have all ABC permits.

Pantana Bob's
$-$$ • 300 W. Rosemary St., Chapel Hill • 942-7575

Pantana Bob's specializes in casual dining, featuring fajitas, gourmet burgers and sandwiches and late-night snacks. Eat inside or out on the patio. Live music is an occasional treat.

Piney Point Grill and Seafood Bar
$$$ • Doubletree Guest Suites I-40 at N.C. 55 (Exit 278), RTP • 361-4660

Piney Point Grill offers ribeye steak, North Carolina mountain trout, Shrimp and Salsa, seafood pasta, fresh oysters and a variety of fresh North Carolina coastal seafood. Be sure to ask about the daily blue-plate special. Piney Point Grill is open for lunch and dinner seven days a week. It has all ABC permits.

The Rathskeller
$-$$ • 157-A Franklin St., Chapel Hill • 942-5158

Since 1946, "The Rat" has been a major hangout for students, faculty, sports fans and alumni. It's always packed on home football weekends. The Rat features a selection of steaks, sandwiches, its famous lasagna, pizza, salads and daily specials. Scrumptious desserts include apple pie and cheesecake. The Rat is open daily for lunch and dinner. Beer, wine and mixed drinks are available.

The Rathskeller
$-$$ • 2412 Hillsborough St., Raleigh • 821-5342

The Rathskeller sits across the street from NCSU and is popular with students, faculty and local business people.

Conveniently located at the corner of Franklin and Columbia streets, Spanky's has evolved into a casual meeting place for college students, locals and visitors alike.

Despite its name, the menu is not the same as "The Rat" in Chapel Hill. The menu offers an excellent selection of vegetarian entrees, an extensive soup and sandwich selection and homemade daily specials.

Spanky's Uptown
$-$$ • 101 E. Franklin St., Chapel Hill • 967-2678

A downtown landmark, the recently renovated Spanky's is open daily and most noted for its wide variety of menu selections such as weekly pasta, steak and seafood specials, burgers, grilled chicken, quiche and homemade desserts.

Top of the Hill
$$-$$$ • 100 E. Franklin St., Chapel Hill • 929-8676

The floor-to-ceiling windows of this third-floor restaurant provide a spectacular view of Chapel Hill on one side and a view of the copper and stainless steel brew tanks on the other. The food is American, featuring pasta, chicken, beef, pork loin and cedar-roasted salmon.

Winston's Grille
$$-$$$ • 6401 Falls of the Neuse Rd., Raleigh • 790-0700

This restaurant and bar is one of "the" places for a power lunch or special dinner. The bar is packed on weekends as the young and single crowd checks out the scene and the "grazing menu," which features crab dip and popcorn shrimp. The dinner menu offers steaks, live Maine lobster and fresh seafood and pasta.

BAKERY

Big Sky Bread Company
$ • Cameron Village, Raleigh • 828-8389

This incredible bakery makes the best rolls, croissants, muffins, cookies and breads you can imagine. The bakery mills its organic whole wheat flour every day, adding only the finest natural ingredients. A variety of sandwiches is served at lunch, all delicious. It is open seven days a week.

The Croissant Cafe and Bakery
$ • 3901 Capital Blvd., Ste. 177, Raleigh • 981-0032

C'est bon! This is a pleasant surprise in northeast Raleigh. The owner and baker takes his pastries—the best chocolate eclairs in town— and breads seriously. The Cafe offers lunch only. The quiche has a flaky, tasty crust and the salads and soups could be served on the Left Bank, while the sandwiches are more American in style.

The Mad Hatter's Bake Shop
$ • 2200 W. Main St., Durham • 286-1987

The Mad Hatter is a great breakfast and lunch spot. Come for cappuccino and fresh-baked muffins or pastries, for a mid-day meal or a late night snack. It is also a great source for delicious custom cakes for birthdays and other special occasions. While you're waiting for your food, marvel at the incredible hats on display.

BARBECUE

Bullock's Bar-B-Cue
$-$$ • 3330 Wortham St., Durham
• 383-3211 • No Credit Cards

Bullock's offers a no-nonsense decor, veteran waitresses and the most extensive barbecue menu in town. You can get it chopped or sliced, plain or spiced, with the usual sides of hushpuppies, slaw, South-ern-style vegetables, French fries and, of course, a big glass of sweet tea. If you've still got room, there's plenty of home-style desserts. Takeout and catering are available. Bullock's is closed on Sunday and Monday.

Cooper's BBQ & Catering
$ • 109 E. Davie St., Raleigh • 832-7614

This downtown restaurant serves some of Raleigh's best Eastern Carolina pork barbecue. You can get your pork chopped or sliced, and it comes with fried hushpuppies, crisp pork skin and cole-slaw. Eastern Carolina barbecue has a vinegar, not tomato-based, sauce. You can sit at the counter or at one of the booths and mingle with blue collar work-ers or politicians.

Dillard's Bar-B-Que
$ • 3921 Fayetteville St., Durham
• 544-1587

Enjoy authentic barbecue smothered in a homemade spicy sauce at this popular southern Durham eatery. It is open for breakfast, lunch and dinner Tuesday through Saturday.

Don Murray's Barbecue
$ • 2751 Capital Blvd., Raleigh • 872-6270

Open for lunch and dinner seven days a week, Don Murray's serves authentic North Carolina barbecue. Catering and Pig Pickin's are available.

Ole Time Barbecue
6309 Hillsborough St., Raleigh • 859-2544

For delicious Eastern-style barbecue at an economical price, look no further than Ole Time. Owner Jerry Hart jokes with all the regulars to keep the atmo-sphere lively. It is open for breakfast, lunch and dinner Monday through Friday and for breakfast and lunch on Saturday. Ole Time also offers catering.

Red Hot & Blue
$$ • 100 Colonades Way, Cary • 851-2282
$$ • 115 S. Elliott Rd., Chapel Hill
• 942-7427
$$ • 6615 Falls of Neuse Rd., Raleigh
• 846-7427

Red Hot & Blue is the local home of Memphis barbecue, whether it's ribs, wet or dry, a tasty barbecue sandwich, delicious chili, authentic hickory smoked chicken, ribs, pulled pork or beef brisket. It's worth a trip just to try the homemade desserts. Blues memorabilia cover almost every inch of wall space and there is nonstop back-ground blues music that ranges from upbeat and sassy to downright moody. A good place to bring the kids or meet for a casual business lunch, each Red Hot & Blue is open daily for lunch and dinner and has all ABC permits. Catering is also available.

BREAKFAST, BRUNCH & LUNCH

Breadmen's
$ • 324 W. Rosemary St., Chapel Hill
• 967-7110

Breadmen's, long an Insiders' favorite, has good food and character. It's the

Southern Durham residents flock to Dillard's Bar-B-Que for authentic North Carolina barbecue doused in a homemade spicy sauce.

kind of place where, no matter what time of the day it is, you can order breakfast and take your time reading the newspaper while you drink a bottomless cup of coffee. Besides breakfast anytime, Breadmen's offers the basics: cheeseburgers, sandwiches, salads, and meat and vegetable plates. After a movie, it's a good place to get a piece of pie. Beer and wine are also available.

Brigs

$-$$ • 1225 N.W. Maynard Rd., Cary • 481-9300

$-$$ • 4900 Hwy. 55, Durham • 544-7473

$-$$ • 8111 Creedmoor Rd., Raleigh • 870-0994

$-$$ • 1303 Fifth Ave., Garner • 779-0003

Billed as "The Ultimate Brunch and a whole lot more," Brigs features brunch items, sandwiches and salad platters. Since the full menu is served day and night, it's one of the few places you can order breakfast for dinner.

Welcome to Pig Pickin' Paradise

Food often marks a region's personality. If you're in Louisiana, for example, you will get invited more than once to a party or political function that serves crab boil, a steaming pot of crawfish. In Virginia, every traditional wedding reception serves thinly sliced and super salty Virginia ham biscuits. Boston bakes beans and the catfish fry is popular in Arkansas and Mississippi. In North Carolina, it's barbecue and pig pickin's. More specifically, it's barbecue pork, cole slaw and hushpuppies.

Close-up

State authors write books on barbecue, and UNC's public TV airs documentaries on the subject. One of the ritual tests for every new, local newspaper columnist, for instance, is the treatise on North Carolina barbecue. Family reunions serve it; political rallies entice crowds with it; neighborhood picnics spread it; and churches celebrate homecomings with it. This is a serious cultural subject.

Start with the fundamentals. When you say barbecue, just plain, simple barbecue, you're talking about pork. Not chicken. Not beef. Not fish. Pig. If someone says, "We're having a barbecue in the backyard. Come on over," it is understood that he or she is cooking pork.

Next, and you need to underline this, there are two basic types of barbecue in North Carolina, and it remains unsettled as to which is better. Families have divided over this argument and debates have been argued over it. And when the talking stops, fights have been fought over it. In short, there is Eastern Barbecue and Western Barbecue. Note that these are proper nouns.

• Western Barbecue uses a red, tomato-based sauce. It's not bad. Some is downright tasty. Even excellent, depending on the family recipe. But, tomato-based barbecue sauce is what you get in the 49 other states.

Eastern-style barbecue

• Eastern Barbecue is basted with a distinctive vinegar-based sauce. It is truly a North Carolina creation, found nowhere else except in enclaves where transplanted eastern North Carolinians have settled. Some claim that it is an "acquired taste." It is sharp and tangy and brings out the flavor of the pork.

While the dividing line between these two barbecue sauces is unclear, you should be aware that the Triangle, for the most part, is considered Eastern Barbecue territory. For the full barbecue experience, you must attend a pig pickin'. Some families still put on their own pickin' but most people hire out the cookers. The best ones seem to come from outlying Triangle towns such as Dunn, Benson or Bunn. These fellows have their own rigs and they will start cooking before dawn. The pig is split down the middle and basted throughout the day. By late afternoon, the pig will be ready (sometimes, the cooking team is pretty basted, too, if they're sippin' along with the basting). The side dishes include coleslaw, hushpuppies, boiled potatoes and Brunswick stew. Coleslaw is another item that is subject to special treatment and the best tasting hushpuppies are the fat short ones. Brunswick stew is a meal unto itself, but it has been sanitized and modernized in that chicken now replaces squirrel as the meat of choice.

The cooking team usually carves off chunks of the best meat and chops them into shreds, which are served from a platter. But do not deny yourself the succulent pleasure of actually picking morsels directly off the pig with your fingers. The ribs are especially prized.

Are we getting hungry, yet?

Cary Cafe

$ • 904 N.E. Maynard Rd., Cary • 469-9415

This unassuming, family-operated cafe, located in a corner of the Reedy Creek Plaza, serves delicious freshly made food. Omelettes, quiches, soups, salads and baked goods are among its specialties. It is open for breakfast and lunch Monday through Saturday. The Cary Cafe Market offers delicious and healthy take-home entrees, sides, sauces, breads, soups, quiches and appetizers. Cary Cafe is also an excellent caterer.

Courtney's

$ • 685 Cary Towne Blvd., Cary • 469-8410

$ • 407 Six Forks Rd., Raleigh • 834-3613

$ • 2300 Gorman St., Raleigh • 859-3830

Courtney's offers breakfast, brunch and lunch. Omelettes, waffles and sandwiches are its specialties.

Gregory's Grand Occasions

$-$$ • Waverly Place, Cary
852-3694

Decorated with a casual elegance, this popular restaurant is a great place for brunch and lunch. Insiders like Gregory's for family parties. It's also a place where you can visit over a cup of coffee and croissant for as long as you want. Gregory's contains a two-story main dining room with a separate club room available. It is open for breakfast, brunch and lunch seven days a week. Gregory's is also an excellent caterer for Christmas, corporate and theme parties.

Honey's

$ • 2700 Guess Rd., Durham • 477-2181

Honey's serves breakfast and country cooking 24 hours a day, seven days a week. It is conveniently located off I-85, northwest of downtown Durham.

Mecca
$ • 13 E. Martin St., Raleigh • 832-5714

The Mecca has been an American success story for three generations of the Dombalis family. It is a downtown lunchtime restaurant, with fading photographs on the wall and room upstairs when the wooden booths downstairs are full. The food is solid, good fare—the lightly fried trout is excellent. John buys his produce fresh at the Farmers Market. The rice pudding, when available, is one of the best in the Triangle.

Sunflower's Sandwich Shop
$ • 315 Glenwood Ave., Raleigh
• 833-4676

This is a bright, corner sandwich shop that serves what may be the best chunky chicken salad sandwiches in town. It's small and open only for lunch, but the noon crowd knows one another, so waiting usually turns into a time to visit. The shop also provides catering.

CAFE

The Cafe at Weaver Street Market
$ • 101 E. Weaver St., Carrboro • 929-0010

The Cafe at Weaver Street Market features fresh house-baked breads, ethnic and regional vegetarian food, fresh seafood and meat entrees, and a large selection of fine wines and beers. You can dine indoors, outside on the lawn or choose from the extensive takeout menu. Lunch and dinner are served Monday through Saturday and a wholesome brunch is served on Sunday, complete with live jazz.

Fearrington Market & Cafe
$-$$ • Fearrington Village Ctr.,
Pittsboro • 542-5505

Homemade entrees, delicious breads (best bran muffins around), fresh salad platters and deli-style sandwiches are served in a quaint setting of Fearrington Village. In warm weather, you can sit outdoors, admire the flower beds and enjoy your food. Lunch and dinner are served Monday through Friday, and brunch is served weekends.

Golden Leaf Tea Room
$-$$ • 105 South Main St.,
Fuquay-Varina • 557-5355

The Golden Leaf Tea Room provides delightful elegance in a hometown atmosphere. Specialties include Broccoli Salad, Creamy Chicken Puff, Quiche of the Day and sandwiches such as baked ham, pepperjack turkey, roast beef with provolone and tuna melt. Make room for the savory desserts like Chocolate Raspberry Indulgence. The Tea Room is open for lunch Tuesday through Saturday and brunch on Sunday. Catering services are also available.

Irregardless Cafe
$$-$$$ • 901 W. Morgan St., Raleigh
• 833-9920, 833-8898

Chef and owner Arthur Gordon has never been afraid to test convention since he opened the restaurant in the '70s with a vegetarian menu. The changing menu

Photo by Evelyn Ward

Chef and owner Arthur Gordon has served up savory and healthful entrees at Irregardless Cafe since 1975.

now offers delicious fish, poultry, and beef along with vegetarian and vegan dishes. The produce arrives fresh from the State Farmers Market. The homemade desserts are wonderful, and if the Chocolate Kahlua Fantasy Cake is on the menu, be sure to order it. The ambience is metropolitan and live entertainment is provided nightly. The Irregardless Cafe serves lunch Monday through Friday, dinner Monday through Saturday, and brunch on Sunday. The Cafe is planning a 25th Birthday Celebration from February 28 through March 5, 2000, complete with reunions, original dishes at original prices and great music from the '70s.

Second Nature Cafe
$-$$ • Olde Raleigh Shopping Ctr., Raleigh • 571-3447

The Second Nature Cafe is known for healthy delicious dishes made with no preservatives, artificial ingredients or red meat. It is open for breakfast, lunch and dinner every day except Sunday.

Simple Pleasures Market & Cafe
$-$$ • Glenwood Village, Raleigh • 782-9227

Located off Glenwood Avenue, in one of Raleigh's favorite specialty food stores, Simple Pleasures offers sandwiches, salads, daily specials and homemade zesty soups in a smoke-free environment. Lunch is served daily, and brunch is provided on weekends. Catering is also available.

The Weathervane Cafe At A Southern Season
$$-$$$ • Eastgate Shopping Ctr., Chapel Hill • 929-9466

The Weathervane offers a delightful place to sit down and sample some of the delicious homemade fare turned out by the kitchen. The Cafe serves entrees like paella, grilled chili-rubbed ribeye, great sandwiches and salads and luscious desserts. Try the Blueberry and Lemon Trifle or the old-fashioned pecan pie. During nice weather, an outdoor patio offers a special dining experience. The Weathervane is open for lunch and dinner and has all ABC permits.

CAFETERIA

K & S Cafeteria
$ • 1177 Buck Jones Rd., Cary • 462-8404
$ • 3620 Bastion Ln., Raleigh • 231-8040
$ • 3101 Edwards Mill Rd., Raleigh • 783-7791
$ • 9420 Forum Dr., Raleigh • 676-7781

These local cafeterias offer a wide variety of Southern food and are well known for their turkey and dressing, fried chicken, fresh vegetables, salads and delicious homemade desserts.

K & W Cafeteria
$ • University Mall, Chapel Hill • 942-7809
$ • Cameron Village, Raleigh • 832-7505

A Triangle mainstay for over 30 years, K & W Cafeteria is very popular with local residents, especially senior citizens.

Picadilly Cafeteria
$ • South Square Mall, Durham • 489-1041

Another excellent cafeteria, Picadilly is a wonderful place to eat after a busy day of shopping at South Square Mall.

CARIBBEAN

Bahama Breeze
$-$$ • 3409 Wake Forest Rd., Raleigh • 872-6330

New to the Triangle dining scene, Bahama Breeze offers a taste of the tropics at this lively and colorful Caribbean-themed chain restaurant. Unique appetizers and entrees range from pan-seared salmon pasta to tropical pizzas and coconut curry chicken. The wait staff is dressed in shorts and colorful island shirts adding to the ambience. The outdoor patio and bar serve island drinks such as the frozen Bahamarita and the Bananaberry Daiquiri. It is open for dinner daily.

Ben's Jamaican
$-$$ • 8306 Chapel Hill Rd., Cary • 380-1818

This restaurant, whose layout conforms to the shape of Jamaica, does not compromise when it comes to the preparation of its authentic cuisine. Jerk chicken and pork, patties and curried chicken and goat keep Ben's food lovers coming back for more. Ben's has all ABC permits.

Jamaica Jamaica
$-$$ • 4853 Hwy. 55, Durham • 544-1532

Jamaica Jamaica is the place to go for authentic West Indian cuisine in Durham. Among the offerings are curried chicken and goat, jerk chicken, jerk pork and Caribbean shrimp. Live jazz takes place Thursday nights.

Rum Runners
$-$$ • 6413 Falls of Neuse Rd., Raleigh • 878-1959

The dueling piano players at this popular tropical night spot keep the crowd entertained with rock 'n roll singalongs Wednesday through Saturday. Lunch and dinner are served daily.

Enjoy fresh meats and vegetables cooked on Main Garden's Mongolian stove.

CHINESE

35 Chinese
$$ • University Square, Chapel Hill
• 968-3488
$$ • 1135 Kildaire Farm Rd., Cary
• 467-4262

35 Chinese is best known for its extensive lunch and dinner buffet offering 60 to 70 items, including vegetables, shrimp, chicken, pork, soups and desserts. It is open seven days a week.

China Chef
$-$$ • Eastgate Shopping Ctr., Chapel Hill • 942-2688

Cozy and attractively decorated, China Chef serves well-prepared Chinese food at reasonable prices. Some house specialties include Ivory Shrimp and Chicken with Black Bean Sauce. There is a daily special including soup and an egg roll with an entree. Lunch and dinner are served seven days a week, and takeout is available. Wine and beer are offered.

China Inn, Durham
$-$$ • 2701 Hillsborough Rd., Durham
• 286-2444

Located close to Duke University and the medical center, this restaurant gladly prepares food for people with special dietary requirements. For health conscious diners, this restaurant never uses MSG. It is open for lunch and dinner seven days a week.

China One
$-$$ • 4325 Hwy. 55, Durham • 361-3388

Convenient for RTP workers, this popular restaurant offers a fabulous weekday lunch buffet. For a weekend brunch, China One is the place for dim sum. Carts wheeled throughout the dining area allow you to preview the appetizer-sized entrees of dumplings, buns and noodle rolls filled with shrimp, pork and other Chinese delicacies. It is open seven days a week for lunch and dinner.

China Pearl
$$ • Waverly Place, Cary • 851-0358

China Pearl serves Hunan, Szechuan, Mandarin and Cantonese dishes, and it's a family place, so don't hesitate to take the kids. Open for lunch Sunday through Friday and dinner every night, it also has all ABC permits.

Crystal Palace
$$ • 4011-161 Capital Blvd., Raleigh
• 878-9699

Fortunately, almost every section of town has its own favorite Chinese restaurant. This popular, inexpensive spot is located in Tarrymore Square. The buffet is one of the best, including General Tso's chicken, vegetable lo mein, chicken teriyaki and steamed crab legs. Crystal Palace serves lunch and dinner daily. A take-out menu, catering and banquet facilities are available.

FYI

Unless otherwise noted, the area code for all phone numbers listed in this guide is 919.

Main Garden
$-$$ • 1353 Kildaire Farm Rd., Cary
• 481-9009

Main Garden features a diverse buffet with over 100 items and a Mongolian Stove. Lunch and dinner are served seven days a week.

Neo-China
$$ • 6602-1 Glenwood Ave., Raleigh
• 783-8383
$$ • 4015 University Dr., Durham • 489-2828

Authentic Chinese cuisine is served in an upscale, contemporary setting. You may even order takeout from the extensive menu of this elegant restaurant. Neo-China is open for lunch Monday through Friday and for dinner seven days a week. A Sunday lunch buffet is available.

Shanghai
$$ • 3433 Hillsborough Rd., Durham
• 383-7581

Shanghai has a relaxed atmosphere where you can enjoy tasty Chinese cuisine prepared with the freshest ingredients. This established restaurant takes pride in the dishes it serves, and has all ABC permits.

CONTINENTAL

The Fairview at
The Washington Duke
$$$-$$$$ • 3001 Cameron Blvd., Durham • 493-6699

The Fairview, in the elegant Washington Duke Inn, is a wonderful place to entertain friends or out-of-town guests. The menu features Continental cuisine and regional specialties. Salads, fresh homemade soups, steaks and seafood specialties highlight the menu. It is open for breakfast daily, lunch Monday through Saturday, brunch on Sunday and dinner nightly. Reservations are highly recommended on weekends.

Foster's
$$-$$$ • Cameron Village, Raleigh
• 832-9815

Foster's features an American Continental menu with fresh fish, choice beef, pastas and daily specials. The wine bar, open kitchen, architectural details and outdoor patio add to the atmosphere. Foster's is open for lunch, dinner and late night Monday through Saturday. Reservations are suggested. It has all ABC permits, and it is a popular late night spot.

Galeria
$$$$ • Radisson Governors Inn, I-40 at Davis Dr., RTP (Exit 280) • 549-8631

The Galeria's noontime buffet is generous and varied, but it has made its reputation as an evening dining spot. The menu offers some of the best fish, veal and pasta in the Triangle. The Galeria has all ABC permits. Reservations are recommended.

The Melting Pot
$$$-$$$$ • 3100 Wake Forest Rd., Raleigh • 878-0477

Enjoy sizzling beef, chicken and seafood at Raleigh's original fondue restaurant. For dessert, try one of the spectacular Chocolate Fondue delights. It is open seven days a week and reservations are suggested.

Rubens
$$-$$$ • Sheraton Chapel Hill, Europa Dr. and U.S. 15-501 Bypass, Chapel Hill • 968-4900

Located in the luxurious Sheraton Chapel Hill Hotel, Rubens is named for the famous Flemish painter. Here you'll find nicely prepared regional American cuisine as well as a wide variety of seafood dishes. Rubens is open daily for breakfast, lunch and dinner, and reservations are recommended. It has all ABC permits.

DELICATESSEN

Hotpoint Deli
$ • 1284 Buck Jones Rd., Cary
• 460-6299

After Maximillian's Restaurant was damaged by fire, the owners decided to repair and renovate the building, turning it into an eclectic deli. The menu features cold and hot subs, focaccia and grilled panini sandwiches, pasta dishes, salads and an array of pizzas, from Buffalo Chicken to Voodoo Chile. Hotpoint is open for lunch and dinner Monday through Saturday.

Piper's Deli
$ • 3219 Old Chapel Hill Rd., Durham
• 489-2481

Popular with students, professors, and employees at Duke University, this deli has the atmosphere of a neighborhood tavern. The prices are modest and the food is homemade.

Serendipity Gourmet-Deli
$ • 118 S. Academy St., Cary
• 469-1655 • No Credit Cards

Serendipity offers creative and unusual sandwiches and a deli counter for takeout. It is open for lunch Monday through Saturday and dinner Tuesday through Friday.

The Upstairs
$ • Upstairs over Heilig-Levine Furniture, 135 S. Wilmington St., Raleigh • 833-9734

The Upstairs restaurant and delicatessen has been a fixture in Raleigh's cultural and political life for decades. The art crowd, journalists, bureaucrats and politicians continue to swap news and see who's eating with whom. Daily specials such as Brisket of Beef with Fried Potato Cakes and blintzes are offered. The desserts are scrumptious, especially the Bishop's Pie—five layers of sin, according to author-hostess Nell Styron.

ECLECTIC

Acme Food & Beverage Co.
$$-$$$$ • 110 E. Main St., Carrboro
• 929-2263

Enjoy regional cuisine at Acme, which offers a seasonal menu full of diverse entrees such as soft shell crabs, barbecued baby back ribs, angel hair pasta with shrimp, oven-roasted chicken, jambalaya and vegetarian curry. Located in downtown Carrboro, Acme is open for lunch Monday through Friday and for dinner nightly. A brunch is served on Saturday and Sunday. It has all ABC permits. Reservations are not accepted.

Anotherthyme Restaurant
109 N. Gregson St., Durham
• 682-5225

A local landmark since 1982, Anotherthyme offers a tantalizing array of delicious Mediterranean and Southwestern entrees in an elegant atmosphere. Diners will also enjoy creative appetizers, a 150-item wine list, homemade desserts and a friendly neighborhood bar that serves a variety of frozen drinks, imports and microbrewed beers. The walls are decorated with artwork from local artists. Anotherthyme is open for dinner seven nights a week. Reservations are recommended.

INSIDERS' TIP

If you plan to visit the area in late May, keep in mind that many restaurants are booked solid. With three major universities and numerous colleges, graduation ceremonies are a major event with many families celebrating by going out to eat.

Backstage Restaurant
$$-$$$ • Waverly Place Shopping
Center, Cary • 858-5041

One of Cary's hottest new eateries, Backstage serves casual American cuisine in a series of unique, multilevel dining rooms decorated with show business memorabilia. Backstage also boasts an espresso and smoothie bar, an extensive specialty drink menu, live entertainment on weekends, a dessert market and private rooms for large parties. It serves lunch and dinner Monday through Saturday and brunch on Sunday.

The Grill at Glen Lennox
$$-$$$$ • 1201 Raleigh Rd.,
Chapel Hill • 942-1963

Located in the Glen Lennox Shopping Center, The Grill serves delicious cuisine with California and Mediterranean influences. The menu changes seasonally. Enjoy hearty portions of fire-grilled fish and meats, thin-crust pizza cooked in a wood-fired oven, pasta specialties and a wide selection of wines. Try one of the delicious homemade desserts. The Grill at Glen Lennox serves lunch Monday through Friday and dinner Monday through Saturday. It has all ABC permits.

Henry's Bistro
$$-$$$ • 403 W. Rosemary St., Chapel
Hill • 967-4720

Henry's Bistro features an eclectic selection of bistro fare in a relaxed atmosphere. Chef Henry Samelson, a veteran of the kitchen at Crook's Corner, offers creative cuisine—often with a Mediterranean or Caribbean influence—at very reasonable prices. Dinner is served nightly and a late-night menu is available.

Pyewacket
$$$ • 431 W. Franklin St., Chapel Hill
• 929-0297

Pyewacket has been a mainstay of the Chapel Hill restaurant scene since 1977 and was remodeled in 1995. It is known for its vegetarian, pasta and fresh seafood specialties. Original homemade dressings and freshly baked breads complement Pyewacket's seasonal menus. Desserts are not to be missed.

Zest Cafe and Home Art
$$-$$$ • 8831 Six Forks Rd., Raleigh
• 848-4792

Zest features light New American cuisine and a home furnishings boutique in a

Photo courtesy of Pyewacket

The outdoor veranda at Pyewacket is a great spot to enjoy the restaurant's acclaimed vegetarian, pasta and fresh seafood specialties.

contemporary setting. Roasted chicken, herbed salmon fillet, tacos, quesadillas and "pizzestas" are offered on a menu that changes weekly to take advantage of the freshest ingredients. It is open Tuesday through Saturday for lunch, Wednesday through Saturday for dinner and Sunday for brunch.

ETHIOPIAN

Blue Nile
$$-$$$ • 2300 Chapel Hill Rd., Durham • 490-0462

For an exotic culinary adventure, nothing beats a visit to Blue Nile where diners sit at woven "basket" tables and sample traditional Ethiopian dishes with a spongy bread called injera. Live music and Ethiopian dance are performed occasionally. Blue Nile serves lunch and dinner daily.

FINE DINING

Bloomsbury Bistro
$$$$ • 509 Whitaker Mill Rd., Raleigh • 834-9011

Located in the heart of Raleigh's Five Points neighborhood, Bloomsbury Bistro was named for Bloomsbury Park, an early 20th-century amusement park. It offers a creative menu that changes seasonally and an extensive wine selection. Dinner is served Monday through Saturday.

Brightleaf 905
$$$-$$$$ • Brightleaf Square, Durham • 680-8848

Brightleaf 905 features exciting international cuisine in a casually elegant atmosphere. Dinner entrees include such delicacies as Fire Roasted Black Sirloin, Cherry Wood Smoked Pork Chop and Herb Crusted Halibut. Enjoy the famous 905 Bacon Cheeseburger or the Grilled Picadillo Quesadilla for lunch. Brightleaf 905 serves lunch Tuesday through Friday and dinner Monday through Saturday and has all ABC permits.

The Fearrington House
$$$$ • Fearrington Village Center, Pittsboro • 542-2121

This charming restaurant lies about 6 miles south of Chapel Hill in Fearrington Village. The Fearrington House has been noted in *Food and Wine* and *Gourmet* magazines for its "new cuisine of the South."

Dinner is served as a five-course fixed price meal (excluding wine). It's served in elegant surroundings by an attentive and professional waitstaff. Desserts are a specialty and include chocolate souffle with warm chocolate sauce and whipped cream, fruit tarts and incredible homemade ice creams. The menu changes daily, depending on the availability of ingredients. It has all ABC permits. Reservations are required.

Four Square
$$$-$$$$ • 2701 Chapel Hill Rd., Durham • 401-9877

Located in the beautifully restored 1908 Bartlett-Mangum House, Four Square specializes in globally influenced contemporary American cuisine. It was named for the unique "four-square" style architecture of the house, which is listed on the National Register of Historic Places. The menu changes monthly, offering the freshest seasonal and local ingredients. Start with a tantalizing array of appetizers such as Grilled Duck and Duck Foie Gras on Sticky Rice Cakes with Cranberry Compote. Entrees include such innovative culinary creations as Rock Crabmeat-laced Grouper, Grilled Rosemary-scented Lamb, and Herb Crusted Salmon with Fried Green Tomatoes. Save room for one of the delicious homemade desserts.

Four Square also boasts a cozy bar, extensive wine list, eclectic selection of beers, seasonal outdoor dining and private dining facilities. Dinner is served Monday through Saturday. Reservations are recommended.

Photo by Tim Johnson

Experience contemporary American cuisine at Second Empire.

Il Palio Ristorante

$$$$ • Siena Hotel,
1505 E. Franklin St., Chapel Hill
• 929-4000

The Siena Hotel's gracious restaurant, Il Palio, serves Northern Italian and Mediterranean preparations of fresh pasta, seafood, veal, lamb, poultry and beef. Enjoy after-hours cappuccino on the private, glassed-in terrace. Breakfast, lunch and dinner are served daily. There is also a Sunday brunch. Reservations are recommended. Il Palio has all ABC permits.

La Residence Restaurant & Bar

$$$-$$$$ • 202 W. Rosemary St.,
Chapel Hill • 967-2506

La Residence has a long tradition of offering fine, innovative cuisine in the Triangle. This charming, elegant restaurant is located in the heart of Chapel Hill. The menu changes monthly and has included such items as seared tuna, filet mignon and lobster, all creatively prepared. The restaurant uses the freshest local produce for the seasonal vegetable side dishes and salads. Desserts include Kaluga—a divine

chocolate creation—sorbets and fresh fruit, and berry specialties.

In warm weather, you may dine on the patio overlooking colorful gardens. It's no wonder the restaurant has won accolades through the years from *Food and Wine, Bon Appetit, Gourmet* and *The New York Times.* Private parties are a specialty. Dinner is served Monday through Saturday. Reservations are advised. It has all ABC permits.

Magnolia Grill

$$$$ • 1002 Ninth St., Durham
• 286-3609

The Magnolia Grill is one of the Triangle's FINEST places to dine, with its commitment to innovative and absolutely delicious food. It features a daily menu composed of the freshest ingredients of the season. That means you're likely to find anything from Moroccan eggplant soup to Brunswick strudel—tantalizing, eclectic fare that defies labels. Each menu features six to nine appetizers (like watercress and watermelon salad in raspberry vinaigrette), just as many entrees and incredible desserts (blueberry gingerbread with lemon ice cream, anyone?).

Reservations are essential, especially during American Dance Festival season. It is closed on Sundays and Mondays.

Margaux's

$$$$ • 8111 Creedmoor Rd., Brennan Station, Raleigh • 846-9846

Be prepared for a special dining experience. From the cozy and eclectic atmosphere to the excellent service to the innovative menu, a meal at Margaux's is one you won't forget. The menu changes frequently and offers a variety of daily and seasonal specials with an emphasis on seafood. If you are a fan of crabcakes, order them as an appetizer or as part of the seafood grille. The desserts are among the best in the Triangle, with many seasonal fresh fruit offerings. It has all ABC permits.

Nana's

$$$-$$$$ • 2514 University Dr.,
Durham • 493-8545

Nana's, named for chef Scott Howell's grandmother, has gained national acclaim for its new American cuisine. The changing menu features entrees like Tomato Consomme with Smoked Salmon Ravioli and Grilled Veal Chop over a Risotto Cake. Nana's reopened in fall 1999 after extensive renovations that included an expansion of the dining room. Reservations are requested. It has all ABC permits.

Second Empire
Restaurant and Tavern

$$$$ • 330 Hillsborough St., Raleigh
• 829-3663

One of the hottest restaurants in Raleigh, Second Empire features fine dining in the elegant but relaxed surroundings of the historic Dodd-Hinsdale House, which has a Second Empire-style Mansard-roofed tower. Chef Daniel Schurr dishes up contemporary American cuisine, such as Striped Bass and Roasted Guinea Hen Breast. Every Thursday is Rib Night. A separate menu is available in the Tavern. The wine cellar features 150 varieties. Private dining rooms are available for large and small groups. Dinner reservations are strongly recommended.

The Warehouse

$$$-$$$$ • Dawson & Cabarrus Sts.,
Raleigh • 836-9966

Enjoy innovative American cuisine in this popular combination restaurant and dance club, which is located in downtown Raleigh's bustling warehouse district. Start your culinary adventure with one of over 50 tapas—tantalizing appetizers such as Coconut Shrimp, Lobster Ravioli and Grilled Japanese Eggplant. Then choose from a variety of delectable entrees, including Pistachio Crusted Salmon, and Giant Sea Scallops. Cap it all off with one of The Warehouse's spectacular desserts.

The Wine Cellar at Angus Barn

$$$$ • 9401 Glenwood Ave., Raleigh
• 787-3505

Enjoy French country cuisine in an elegant atmosphere surrounded by nearly 35,000 bottles of wine offering over 1,100 selections. Each of the five to six courses is matched with the appropriate wine selection. This unique culinary experience was designed for parties of 12-28. Call ahead for reservations.

FRENCH

Butterflies

$$$-$$$$ • 6325 Falls of Neuse Rd.,
Raleigh • 878-2020

Butterflies specializes in innovative French cuisine with a Mediterranean influence. The seasonal menu features such delicacies as acorn squash ravioli, grilled tuna and roasted chicken. Dinner is served Monday through Saturday.

Gaulart & Maliclet French Cafe

$$ • 957 N. Harrison Ave., Cary
• 469-2288

This cafe has been a hit with its food, wine and atmosphere. The food is not always French, but it is enthusiastically recommended by the customers.

Jean-Claude's French Cafe

$$ • North Ridge Shopping Ctr.,
Raleigh • 872-6224

Jean-Claude's offers a varied French menu in a cafe atmosphere. If you look over the counter, you might see the owner, Therese Freeman, at work fixing soft-shell crab or the daily special, which might be duck or fresh salmon, or a special crepe. The Beef Stroganof Crepe is highly recommended and the caramel flan is the best in town. A wine-tasting is held nearly every month. It's popular and relaxed, so get there on time or you may have to wait outside. Banquet facilities are available.

Tartines Bistro Provencal
$$$-$$$$ • 1110 Navaho Dr., Raleigh
• 790-0091

Experience French Provencale cuisine in Tartines' intimate and comfortably elegant dining room. The traditional menu offers such entrees as Roasted Rack of Spring Lamb and Pan-Seared Tuna. Tartine's is open for dinner Monday through Saturday.

GREEK

Mariakakis Gourmet Market and Deli
$-$$ • U.S. 15-501 Bypass, Chapel Hill
• 942-1453

This deli offers stuffed sandwiches, salads and appetizers, as well as other Greek favorites such as stuffed grape leaves and baklava. It is open Monday through Saturday for lunch. The market features an extensive wine selection.

Papa's Grill
$$-$$$ • 1821 Hillandale Rd., Durham
• 383-8502

Papa's Grill specializes in Greek cuisine, and offers a wide assortment of Greek appetizers such as Kalamari Saluta and Tiri a la Mikonos. It also serves delicious steaks, seafood and pasta dishes. Try the chocolate mousse cake for dessert. Papa's is open for lunch and dinner Monday through Friday and only for dinner on Saturday.

Spartacus
$$ • 4139 Chapel Hill Blvd., Durham
• 489-2848
$$ • Waverly Place, Cary • 852-5050

Spartacus offers Greek, Middle Eastern, vegetarian and seafood specialties, and

Photo by Julia Teague

Since the 1970s, Mildred "Dip" Council and her family have been dishing up down-home Southern cooking at Dip's Country Kitchen.

we heartily recommend the homemade rice pudding. This spacious restaurant and bar is decorated with hand-painted murals and an outdoor dining deck is open when weather permits. It is closed on Mondays.

Taverna Nikos
$$-$$$ • Brightleaf Square, Durham
• 682-0043

Taverna Nikos offers some of the most delicious and authentic Greek food to be found in the Triangle. Moussaka, Souvlaki and other favorite Greek dishes fill the menu, along with huge salads and hearty soups. The atmosphere is friendly and it's a great place to go with a group of friends, when you can share platters heaped with food. It has all ABC permits and is open for lunch and dinner Monday through Saturday.

Zorba's
$$ • 105 S. Elliott Rd., Village Plaza, Chapel Hill • 967-5517

Zorba's features deliciously authentic Greek dishes, huge portions and reasonable prices. The lemon chicken is especially good and the pastitsio and moussaka melt in your mouth. The appetizer platter is a good way to sample some of the specialties; it features stuffed grape leaves, spanakopita, gyros and souvlaki to share. Zorba's is open for lunch Monday through Friday and nightly for dinner. Beer and wine are available.

GRILL- 50's Style

The Char-Grill
$ • 618 Hillsborough St., Raleigh
• 821-7636
$ • 3211 Edwards Mill Rd., Raleigh
• 781-2945
$ • 4617 Atlantic Ave., Raleigh
• 954-9556
$ • 9601 Strickland Rd., Raleigh
• 845-8994

The Char-Grill is an enduring '50s-style, drive-in fixture that keeps the lunchtime and late-night crowd standing in line for burgers, fries and shakes.

Grill '57
$ • 4202 Fayetteville Rd., Raleigh
• 779-5757
$ • Wellington Park, Cary • 852-5557

Grill '57 specializes in hamburgers, chicken sandwiches and hot dogs grilled over an open flame. BBQ sandwiches, salads, fries and onion rings are also available.

HOME COOKING

Big Ed's City Market
$ • City Market, Raleigh • 836-9909

Fresh vegetables from the Farmers Market make this restaurant's country cooking truly down-home. Surplus food is donated to the Raleigh Rescue Mission daily. Breakfast is served Monday through Saturday and lunch is served Monday through Friday.

Dip's Country Kitchen
$-$$ • 408 W. Rosemary St., Chapel Hill • 942-5837

If you've been looking for The Real Thing Southern-style, this is it. Started well over 20 years ago by Mildred "Dip" Council, this is the place to get fried chicken, smothered pork chops, chicken dumplings or even (if you can handle it) real chitlins, served up with okra, black-eyed peas, collards and cornbread. Dip's slogan is "put a little South in your mouth," and, boy, does she! Mama Dip makes up her daily specials with seasonal ingredients, so they are always fresh. Dip's serves breakfast, lunch and dinner daily. Beer and wine are available.

Elmo's Diner
$-$$ • 200 N. Greensboro St., Carrboro • 929-2909
$-$$ • 776 Ninth St., Durham • 416-3823

Elmo's Diner serves freshly prepared traditional food with family-friendly customer service. The menu features "Square Meals" such as meatloaf, salmon cakes and roast turkey as well as "Daily Specials" ranging from stir-fry to Italian entrees. A wide variety of sandwiches, burgers and salads is also available.

Joe's Place
$ • 301 W. Martin St., Raleigh • 832-5260

Joe offers his mom's cooking and it's popular with the downtown noontime crowd. Joe's provides home-cooked entrees, big sandwiches and vegetables. Joe's place is open Monday through Friday for lunch and dinner.

Melba's Country Kitchen
$ • 121 E. Chatham St., Cary
• 467-0929 • No Credit Cards

Melba has been working here since 1978. It's a downtown Cary restaurant for working folks and a good place for newcomers to get a taste of small town Southern cooking. Specialties are barbecue, hushpuppies, chicken-fried steak, and black-eyed peas and onions.

Toot-N-Tell Family Restaurant and Catering
$ • 903 W. Garner Rd., Garner • 772-2616

Originally a drive-in, this country-cooking restaurant has been packing customers in for over 50 years. It still has a drive-up window for orders to go. The buffet lunch has a variety of meats and country vegetables, along with homemade desserts. The most unbelievable thing about this all-you-can-eat extravaganza is the price, just $4.95 for lunch. Lunch and dinner are served every day and and there is a Sunday brunch.

Village Diner
$ • 600 W. King St., Hillsborough
• 732-7032

Located west of Hillsborough's historic downtown, the Village Diner features an extensive buffet lunch.

INDIAN

Darbar Indian Restaurant
$-$$ • 423 W. Franklin St., Chapel Hill
• 968-8706

Authentic Indian appetizers, breads, vegetarian, chicken, lamb and seafood dishes are served in an unpretentious setting. The menu is large and diverse and the dishes range from mild to spicy. Darbar is open for lunch and dinner.

INSIDERS' TIP

Many Triangle restaurants are closed between the hours of 2 PM and 5 PM, and some are closed on Sundays. It's always best to call ahead to make sure the restaurant is open.

India Garden

$-$$ • Cary Towne Center • 319-3722

Cary residents flock to India Garden for its famous lunch buffet, which features authentic Indian specialties. It is also open for lunch and dinner seven days a week.

India Mahal

$$ • 3212 Hillsborough St., Raleigh • 836-9742

Serving delicious North Indian food in an informal setting, India Mahal is close to N.C. State University. It specializes in vegetarian, lamb and tandoori entrees and offers a variety of Indian beers to go with your meal.

ITALIAN

411 West

$$-$$$ • 411 W. Franklin St., Chapel Hill • 967-2782

411 West is consistently good and consistently crowded. We recommend that you go early or be prepared to wait in the bar, but it is worth the wait. The restaurant's wood-burning pizza oven gives an authentic touch to the four cheese or prosciutto and peppers "prizzettes." Homemade pasta dishes like lemon linguini, and fresh seafood are offered. Lunch is served Monday through Saturday and dinner is served seven nights a week. Catering is available.

518 West

$$-$$$$ • 518 W. Jones St., Raleigh • 829-2518

This culinary addition to downtown Raleigh opened with the established reputation of its sister restaurant, 411 West in Chapel Hill preceding it. The renovated warehouse has been beautifully redecorated to resemble a Roman piazza with terrazzo floors, wrought iron balconies and a trompe l'oeil sky ceiling. The menu offers Italian contemporary cuisine with fresh seasonal pastas, seafood, vegetarian dishes and pizzettes, individual pizzas cooked in a wood-fired oven. Try the Grilled Shrimp Polenta or the Vegetarian Steak.

Photo by Julia Teague

Delicious Northern Italian cuisine is the specialty at Aurora in Chapel Hill.

In-house desserts are made daily and weekly specials are available. Lunch is served Monday through Saturday and dinner is served nightly.

Amedeo's Italian Restaurant
$ • 3905 Western Blvd., Raleigh
• 851-0473

This inside-the-Beltline restaurant has been serving homemade lasagna, pizza and veal since the early '60s. Located close to N.C. State, the TV in the sports bar is tuned to the Wolfpack. Amedeo's is open for lunch and dinner daily.

Aurora
$$$ • N.C. 54, Chapel Hill • 942-2400

Aurora, which had been a fixture at Carr Mill Mall since 1981, recently moved to its new location on N.C. 54 in the former Slug's on the Pines building, which can accommodate about 250 diners. Here you can enjoy superb Northern Italian cuisine. Select tender veal, lamb, poultry or fresh seafood for the entree, then complement it with one of many handmade pastas. Appetizers, fresh salads, irresistible desserts and a fine wine will complete your delightful meal. The new location also offers a wood-fired oven. Dinner reservations are advised. It has all ABC permits.

Cafe Roma
$$$-$$$$ • 7361 Six Forks Rd.,
Raleigh • 846-6080

Traditional Italian multi-regional dishes are the specialty at Cafe Roma. Cafe Roma also has an impressive wine list and offers live blues and jazz most nights of the week, as well as a dance floor. It has all ABC permits and is open for lunch Monday through Friday and dinner is served nightly.

Cafe Tiramisu
$$ • 6196 Falls of the Neuse Rd.,
Raleigh • 981-0305

Northern Italian cuisine is the speciality of this North Raleigh restaurant

named for the dessert. It is open for dinner Tuesday through Sunday. Reservations are recommended.

Caffe Luna
$$-$$$$ • 136 E. Hargett St.,
Raleigh • 832-6090

Enjoy superb Italian cuisine at this New York-style eatery, which offers a seasonally changing menu with such entrees as Pasta Primavera, Linguini Pescatore, Farfalle al Salmone and Parmigiana di Vitella. Choose from a wide selection of wines to accompany your entrée. Caffe Luna is open for lunch Monday through Friday and dinner Wednesday through Saturday. Dinner reservations are recommended.

Casa Carbone
Ristorante Italiano
$$ • U.S. 70 W., Oak Park Shopping Ctr.
Raleigh • 781-8750

The Carbones have been in the business for a long time. For years their cooking was the standard by which Raleigh measured its Italian food. Casa Carbone specializes in veal and pasta entrees, sauces and homemade bread. This is a family place, so don't worry about taking the little ones. It has all ABC permits.

Casalinga Ristorante Italiano
$ • 4538 Capital Blvd., Raleigh
• 873-1334

This cozy restaurant is perfect for a romantic evening. It serves homemade dishes made to order. Vegetarians will delight in the options. It is open daily for lunch and dinner.

Daniel's
$$ • 1430 Hwy. 55, Apex • 303-1006

Daniel's is not just another pizza restaurant. Creative Italian specialties, such as Mushroom Ravioli and Penne Ala Casa, keep customers waiting in line. Daniel's homemade desserts are incredible. The

Photo by Tim Johnson

Tokyo House offers delicacies such as sushi, shabu shabu and katsu-don.

Cafe is located near the intersection of N.C. 55 and U.S. 64, and is open for dinner daily.

Nina's Ristorante
$$$-$$$$ • 8801 Lead Mine Rd., Ste. 113, Raleigh • 845-1122

Nina's is a warm and inviting Italian ristorante that promises a memorable dining experience. The restaurant, which specializes in Tuscan and Sicilian cuisine, was opened in the fall of 1999 by Nina and Chris Psarros. A native of Palermo, Sicily, Nina is a member of the Italian Culinary Institute and also serves as Food Master for the Italian Table in the Triangle. Specialties include Osso Bucco, Gnocchi, Cannelloni Fiorentina and Chicken Scarpariello. The menu also offers seafood, chicken and veal. The extensive wine list is exclusively Italian. Nina's is open for dinner Monday through Saturday.

Piccola Italia
$$-$$$ • Cameron Village, Raleigh • 833-6888

This restaurant specializes in fresh Italian dishes prepared in an authentic Italian kitchen. It serves lunch Monday through Saturday and dinner daily.

Pop's
$$-$$$ • 810 West Peabody St., Durham • 956-7677

If you think that a casual restaurant owned by Scott Howell (of Nana's)

sounds intriguing, you're right. Pop's features exotic pizzas and homemade breads straight from the wood-burning brick oven and simple, delicious Italian fare. Prices are reasonable, the atmosphere is pleasantly bustling and the food is as good as you'd hoped for.

Pulcinella's Ristorante
$$-$$$ • 4711 Hope Valley Rd., Durham • 490-1172

Located in Woodcroft Shopping Center, this cozy Italian restaurant is very popular with local residents. The restaurant features Northern Italian cuisine and gourmet pizza.

Sorrento
$$-$$$ • Prime Outlets at Morrisville Morrisville • 380-0990

The food is rich, Northern Italian cuisine. Pasta, seafood and creative treatments of vegetables highlight the menu. Lunch and dinner are served Monday through Saturday.

Vincenzo's
$-$$$ • 8111-137 Creedmoor Rd. Raleigh • 847-4440

Vincenzo's, a new Italian restaurant from the owners of Vincent's, serves authentic Italian dishes such as eggplant, veal, mussels and a variety of homemade pasta and seafood dishes. You can dine on the outdoor enclosed patio or reserve the private room for large parties. Lunch is served Monday through Friday and dinner is served daily.

JAPANESE

Kanki Japanese House of Steaks
$$ • Crabtree Valley Mall, Raleigh • 782-9708
$$ • 4500 Old Wake Forest Rd., North Market Square, Raleigh • 876-4157

It may not be traditional "live entertainment," but the chefs put on quite a

Wine Cellar Dining at the Angus Barn

The Ultimate Culinary Experience

For parties of 12-28, reserve an elegant five or six course French Country Cuisine wine dinner with classic white glove service.

Upon descending the winding staircase, you will experience not only the rare Bordeaux wines of France and the signed, oversized bottles from California's greatest wine makers, but also the antiques, the artwork and the other unique appointments that make our wine cellar the finest dining room in the Triangle area.

You will dine surrounded by nearly 35,000 bottles of wine, offering over 1,100 selections. The Angus Barn is recognized as having one of the top 100 wine lists in the world. Our classically trained Chef will spend days preparing the courses of your choice and, if you so desire, you are invited to join the Cellarmaster in the pairing of the evening's wines.

the **ANGUS BARN** ltd.®

Hwy. 70 at Aviation Parkway, Raleigh

919-787-3505 • www.angusbarn.com

*T*he Angus Barn is a fine dining restaurant with a casual atmosphere. Whether you are out for a nice, quiet meal, a business dinner or an elegant evening on the town, the Angus Barn's goal is to make the dinner one that will be long remembered. We feature three separate dining rooms and luxurious accommodations in the Wine Cellar. We also offer spacious banquet facilities for any occasion. Whenever dining at the Angus Barn, we encourage you to look around and tour our kitchen and wine cellar.

Monday-Saturday 5-11pm • Sunday 5-10pm
The Wild Turkey Lounge opens at 4pm

For Reservations Call 919-787-3505

Reservations are not required, but are recommended. No reservations are taken on Saturdays or holidays.

the **ANGUS BARN** ltd.®
9401 Glenwood Avenue (US Hwy. 70), Raleigh
www.angusbarn.com

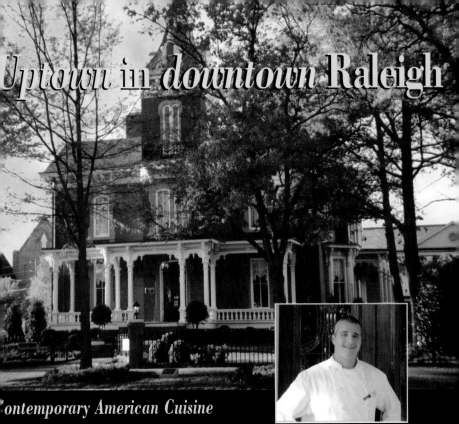

Casual Elegance

- Globally influenced Contemporary American Cuisine

- Menu changes monthly, offering the freshest seasonal ingredients

- Located in the Bartlett Mangum House which is currently on the National Register of Historic Places

- Eclectic beer & wine list
- Spacious dining rooms
- Seasonal patio dining
- Ample parking
- Cozy bar
- Reservations are suggested
- Private rooms for large parties and corporate functions

Owners Elizabeth Woodhouse & Shane Ingram

FOUR SQUARE RESTAURANT

Serving Dinner
Mon.-Thurs. 5:30-10pm
Fri. & Sat. 5:30-11pm

2701 Chapel Hill Road
Durham
919-401-9877

THE AREA'S PREMIERE GREEK RESTAURANT.

BRIGHTLEAF SQUARE • DURHAM, NC • (919) 682-0043

www.citysearch.com/rdu/tavernanikos

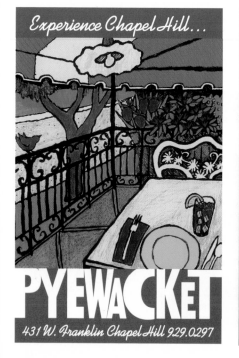
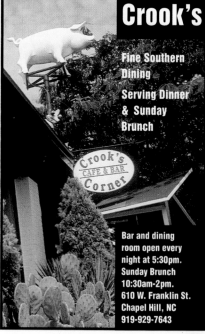

BACKSTAGE
Restaurant

Waverly Place Shopping Center, Cary
Corner of Tryon Rd. & Kildaire Farm Rd.

919-858-5041

Casual American Cuisine

Spacious Dining Rooms

Live Entertainment on Weekends

Private Rooms Available
for Large Parties

Espresso & Smoothie Bar

Extensive Speciality
Drink Menu

Kids Menu Available

On-site Parking

Reservations Accepted

Local Owners
Greg & Paula Papadopoulos

Open 7 Days a Week

Monday-Thursday 11am-9pm
Friday & Saturday 11am-10pm
Sunday 11am-3pm
Lounge 5pm-until

Dessert Market
We are proud of all our delicious
baked goods and pastries, which
are made fresh daily on premises.

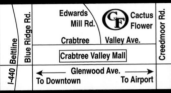

EAT! DRINK! PLAY!

FEATURING
CLASSIC AMERICAN FAVORITES

Entrees Include: Steak, Salmon, BBQ Ribs...
Plus Salads, Sandwiches, Pizza & More!

Open 7 days a week, 11:30am - 2am
117 S West St • Raleigh • 919.821.7887

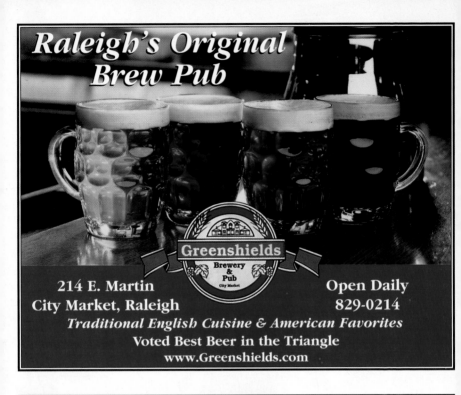

Do you want to increase sales to new homeowners?

Please accept our invitation to join the area's most prominent merchants and professional service providers in welcoming new homeowners to your area.

Welcome Home! the area's premier community-oriented welcoming service provides one of the most effective direct marketing opportunities available. Your business will reach new homeowners in your local area *before* they establish new buying patterns and professional loyalties.

Our sponsorships are exclusive and your business will be the only sponsor in its category.

A full page, 2-sided ad placed in the *Welcome Home!* gift certificate book will introduce your business to the new family.

You will be supplied with a list of families welcomed each month for your follow-up.

Call 919-467-4035 to reserve your exclusive category and begin attracting new homeowners to your business.

Welcome Home
8085 Chapel Hill Road, Cary
919-467-4035 • 800-777-4843

show. The menu features beef, pork and seafood, and the dishes are all prepared tableside with great flair. A Sushi Bar is available at both locations.

Kurama Fantasy Japanese Steak & Seafood House & Sushi Bar
$$ • 3644 Durham-Chapel Hill Blvd. Durham • 489-2669

Meals are prepared with a flash of a knife right before your eyes at Kurama (formerly known as Kyoto), which also features sushi. It is open for dinner nightly.

Tokyo House
$$-$$$$ • 7439 Six Forks Rd., Raleigh • 848-3350

In addition to traditional offerings, Tokyo House serves eclectic dishes that include tempura-battered oysters and stir-fried giant clams. It is open for lunch and dinner Monday through Saturday. The Tatami private party room is also available.

Yamazushi
$$ • Hope Valley Rd. Woodcroft Shopping Ctr., Durham • 493-7748

Enjoy sushi, as well as Japanese cuisine such as seafood teriyaki, shrimp tempura and stir-fried vegetable dishes at Yamazushi. Wine and beer are offered, and catering is also available.

MEDITERRANEAN

Cafe Parizade
$$$ • 2200 W. Main St., Durham • 286-9712

Seasonal Mediterranean cuisine is served in a contemporary setting at Parizade. There is an extensive wine list and Cafe Parizade has all ABC permits.

George's Garage
$$$-$$$$ • 737 Ninth St., Durham • 286-4131

George Bakatsias' latest restaurant has some unusual big-city features,

including a casual dining atmosphere with an upscale menu offering many seafood entrees, a fun, late-night bar and a take-out market and bakery. Breakfast and lunch are self-serve from a hot and cold buffet. It is open seven days a week for breakfast, lunch and dinner.

Saladelia Cafe
$ • 105 N. Columbia St., Chapel Hill • 932-1020
$ • 4201 University Dr., Durham • 489-5776

Saladelia is a unique Greek and Lebanese cafe offering specialties such as Hummus, Tabbouleh and Falafel pockets, along with salads, soups and quiche. Catering is also available.

MEXICAN

Bandido's Mexican Cafe
$-$$ • East Franklin St., Chapel Hill • 967-5048
$-$$ • Woodcroft Shopping Ctr., Durham • 403-6285
$-$$ • 122 S. Churton St., Hillsborough • 732-8662

The original Bandido's in Chapel Hill proved to be so popular that owners Tony and Maria Sustaita opened a second in Durham and a third in Hillsborough. These restaurants all offer standard Mexican fare in addition to a variety of vegetarian and low-fat dishes. Bandido's is open for lunch Monday through Friday and for dinner nightly, except for the Hillsborough location, which is closed Sundays.

Carrburritos Taqueria
$-$$ • 711 W. Rosemary St., Carrboro • 933-8226

This popular spot features tacos, tostadas, burritos and quesadillas with a variety of meat and vegetarian fillings. Top them off with distinctive salsas and the best guacamole in town. All menu items are available to go. Carrburritos is open for lunch and dinner Monday through Saturday.

The Cosmic Cantina

$$ • 1920 Perry St., Durham • 286-1875

Durham's first burrito bar features mostly organic and all natural Mexi-Cali food. The food is made fresh daily and low-fat items are available. Fresh fruit smoothies, margaritas and a large variety of Mexican and microbrewery beers are available. Eat in or take out. Cosmic Cantina is open daily for lunch and dinner. It has all ABC permits.

El Dorado

$ • 990 High House Rd., Cary
• 461-4900
$ • 1404 E. Franklin St., Chapel Hill
• 929-6566
$ • 4900 Hwy. 55, Durham/RTP
• 361-0302
$ • 2811 Brentwood Rd., Raleigh
• 872-8440
$ • 8111 Creedmoor Rd., Raleigh
• 848-0788

El Dorado is a local Triangle restaurant chain that offers a true Mexican experience. Delicious fajitas, burritos, tacos, enchiladas, vegetarian selections and Corona beer are served. Each site is open for lunch and dinner daily.

El Rodeo Mexican Restaurant

$ • Brightleaf Sq., Durham • 683-2417
$ • University Dr., Durham • 402-9190
$ • 1404 E. Franklin St., Chapel Hill
• 929-6566
$ • 4112 Pleasant Valley Rd., Raleigh
• 571-1188
$ • 2400 Hillsborough St., Raleigh
• 755-9697
$ • 2402 Wake Forest Rd., Raleigh
• 833-1460

El Rodeo is another authentic Mexican restaurant chain in the Triangle. Vegetarian dishes and traditional Mexican foods such as enchiladas, tacos, burritos, quesadillas and nachos can all be found on their menu. Each site is open seven days a week for lunch and dinner.

Photo by Tim Johnson

The Cosmic Cantina, Durham's first burrito bar, features fresh, locally grown rice, beans and salsa.

The Flying Burrito

$ • Town and Country Shopping Ctr., 746 Airport Rd., Chapel Hill
• 967-7744 • No Credit Cards

Some of the finest Mexican/Southwestern cuisine in the area , with the best smothered burritos and the hottest burrito in North Carolina (the Ultimate Raging Bull), and fresh seafood specialties await you at the Flying Burrito. The restaurant is open daily for lunch and dinner. It has all ABC permits.

Margaret's Cantina

$-$$ • Timberlyne Shopping Ctr., Chapel Hill • 942-4745

This artfully decorated Southwestern cuisine cafe dishes up unique and tasty dishes with a Mexican flavor. Check out the impressive imported beer selection and the scrumptious desserts. Margaret's is open for lunch and dinner Monday through Saturday.

Tippy's Mexican Restaurant
$ • 808 W. Hodges St., Raleigh
• 828-0797

Tippy's was the first Mexican restaurant to open in Raleigh in 1968. To veterans, it's still Tippy's Taco Hut. The restaurant is bigger and fancier with bullfight scenes on the wall, but the refried beans, chili, tacos and hot enchiladas are as good as when it was a taco hut. It is open for lunch and dinner Monday through Saturday.

Torero's
$-$$ • 800 W. Main St., Durham
• 682-4197
$-$$ • 3808 Guess Rd., Durham
• 477-3939
$-$$ • 4125 Chapel Hill Blvd., Durham
• 489-6468
$-$$ • 1207 Kildaire Farm Rd., Cary
• 468-8711

Torero's serves authentic Mexican food in a relaxed atmosphere. The menu offers a wide array of freshly made tacos, enchiladas, burritos and sizzling fajitas. A variety of Mexican beer is available and the margaritas are enormous. The west Main Street location has a mariachi band on the first Thursday of the month and the Guess Road location features a mariachi band on the first Wednesday of each month. Each site is open daily for lunch and dinner.

PIZZA

Brothers Pizza Restaurant
$ • Kildaire Farm Rd., Cary • 481-0883
$ • 2508 Hillsborough St., Raleigh
• 832-3664

A family-owned, friendly neighborhood restaurant, Brothers serves homemade, hand-tossed pizzeria-style pizza and other hearty Italian dishes. The Raleigh location is open for lunch and dinner daily. The Cary location is open for lunch Monday through Saturday and for dinner seven nights a week.

CiCi's Pizza
$ • Cary Village Square, Cary
• 469-9988

One of the best meal deals in the Triangle, CiCi's features a $2.99 all-you-can-eat pizza buffet. It is open for lunch and dinner seven days a week.

Italian Pizzeria
$ • 508 W. Franklin St., Chapel Hill
• 968-4671 • No Checks

This is an honest-to-goodness, no frills, family-owned New York-style pizza joint. If you are particularly fond of deep-dish Sicilian pizza, you can't go wrong. You can get freshly made slices with exactly the toppings you want.

This pizzeria also has Greek salads and great hot sandwiches like the Italian sausage and cheese on a submarine roll. The Pizzeria is open daily.

J.S. New York Pizza
$ • 540 East Williams St., Apex
• 363-0071

The owners of this popular pizza restaurant operated Silvio in Brooklyn for 20 years before moving to Apex in 1995. Although known for its delicious pizzas, J.S. New York Pizza also offers pasta, calzoni, hot and cold subs and salads. It is open seven days a week.

Lilly's Pizza
$ • 1813 Glenwood Ave., Raleigh
• 833-0226

Lilly's is in the Five Points area on Glenwood Avenue and it's one of the hip places to go. The pizzas are as unconventional as the crowd who will sit at the sidewalk tables outside in 30-degree weather, eating and talking. The pizza is among the best in town.

The Fox & Hound, an authentic version of a British public house, specializes in traditional English fare, wild game and fresh seafood.

The Loop
$ • Eastgate Shopping Center, Chapel Hill • 969-7112

Although the Loop specializes in California- and Chicago-style pizza, diners can also enjoy fabulous burgers, sandwiches, hot dogs, soups and salads. It is open for lunch and dinner daily.

Pepper's Pizza
$ • 127 E. Franklin St., Chapel Hill • 967-7766

You haven't been to Chapel Hill without a visit to Pepper's. A favorite among students, Pepper's offers some of the best pizza and Italian dishes around. It's also one of the best places in town to people-watch. Pepper's is open for lunch and dinner daily.

PieWorks
$$ • 201 Colonades Way, Cary • 233-8008
$$ • 607 Broad St., Durham • 286-6670
$$ • 5610 Atlantic Ave., Raleigh • 878-5111

PieWorks is a popular contemporary pizza restaurant that allows customers to design their own pizzas or order from the extensive menu of unusual pizzas. Each site is open daily for lunch and dinner.

Pizza Pasta Cafe
$-$$ • 8314 Chapel Hill Rd., Cary • 460-1772

This cafe is known for great pizzas and a wonderful pizza buffet lunch and serves creative dinner specialties such as Mushroom Ravioli.

Satisfaction
$ • Brightleaf Square, Durham • 682-7397

Located in Brightleaf Square, this restaurant is a favorite among Duke students. Gourmet pizza and sandwiches are featured as well as an extensive selection of beer. There are three wide-screen TVs so the place is packed during Duke sporting events.

Vincent's
$ • 3911 Capital Blvd., Raleigh • 876-6700
3500 N. Roxboro Rd., Durham • 471-3700
1305 Kildaire Farm Rd., Cary • 461-3799

Established in 1990, Vincent's features authentic New York-style pizza, as well as calzones, stromboli, homemade pasta dishes, hot and cold subs, salads and desserts. Vincent's is open for lunch and dinner daily.

PRIVATE DINING

Capital City Club
$$$-$$$$ • 411 Fayetteville St., Raleigh • 832-5526

Associated with Club Corporation of America, this is the Triangle's original private dining club. Located in downtown Raleigh at the top of the CP&L Building, the club offers an American menu served with a distinctive touch of class.

The Cardinal Club
$$$-$$$$ • 150 Fayetteville St. Mall, Ste. 2800, Raleigh • 834-8829

This luxurious dining club is on the top two floors of the First Union Capitol Center, providing a breathtaking view of Raleigh and an elegant atmosphere for its members. Members and their guests can enjoy superior cuisine, vintage wines and reciprocal privileges with private clubs worldwide.

Prestonwood Country Club
$$$-$$$$ • 300 Prestonwood Pkwy., Cary • 467-2566

The service, atmosphere and cuisine are unequaled in Cary. Special dining events are planned monthly. A dining membership to Preston is not only affordable, it's considered a necessity in Cary.

The University Club
$$$-$$$$ • 3100 Tower Blvd., Durham • 493-8099

Located on the top floor of University Tower, this club provides a lounge, a dining room and many private rooms for conducting business while enjoying a meal. Members have reciprocal privileges at more than 150 clubs across the country, including the Cardinal Club in Raleigh.

PUBS & TAVERNS

Carolina Brewery
$$ • 460 W. Franklin St., Chapel Hill • 942-1800

Chapel Hill's first microbrewery is also a fine place to dine for lunch or dinner. Try the Artichoke and Beer Cheese Rarebit, the Hickory Smoked Chicken Pasta or the Fish and Chips. A surprising number of desserts are made with beer brewed on the premises! You may be tempted by the Stout Cheesecake to complete your meal. This attractively decorated restaurant has all ABC permits.

The Fox and Hound
$$-$$$ • MacGregor Village, Cary • 380-0080

Owner Dane Johnston provides good English fare and suggestions on which wine goes with which dish. If you have a favorite wine, he'll special order it for your next meal. He also has a great selection of draught and bottled beer. The menu is full of John Bull's favorites: Roast Beef with Yorkshire Pudding, Shepherd's Pie, Beefsteak and Kidney Pie, Roasted Lamb Chops, and Fish and Chips. Cheerio! This is a bully handsome pub. It is open for lunch Monday through Saturday and dinner nightly.

Greenshield's Brewery & Pub
$$-$$$ • City Market, Raleigh • 829-0214

For the best beer in town, this is the place. It brews its own and has light and dark varieties. The centerpiece restaurant in the old City Market building, Greenshield's has earned a following among the Anglophiles of the Triangle. The location is superb and the fare reasonably priced. It is open for lunch and dinner daily.

FYI
Unless otherwise noted, the area code for all phone numbers listed in this guide is 919.

RiRa

$-$$ • 126 N. West St., Raleigh
• 833-5535

RiRa means a place "where exuberance and revelry prevail," according to the owners of this cozy pub that features traditional and eclectic Irish fare. RiRa is open Monday through Saturday for lunch and for dinner daily.

Southend Brewery & Smokehouse

$$-$$$$ • 505 W. Jones St., Raleigh
• 832-4604

Housed in a renovated warehouse in downtown Raleigh, Southend Brewery offers a good selection of house-brewed drafts. The menu includes such entrees as smoked chicken and baby back ribs as well as pizza cooked in a wood-burning oven. It is open for lunch and dinner daily.

W.B. Yeats

$$ • 306 W. Franklin St., Chapel Hill
• 968-6224

The recently opened W.B. Yeats pub, named after the famous 20th-century Irish poet, offers the same menu as its sister restaurant in Durham, The Kelt. The walls and tables are full of sayings and quotes from the author.

SEAFOOD

Cappers

$$$-$$$$ • 4421 Six Forks Rd., Raleigh
• 787-8963

Cappers is located across from North Hills Mall and has become a popular lunch stop for North Raleigh business people. You will find an excellent selection of seafood, and it's one of the best places in the city for those who like jazz with their food. Cappers seats about 135 and has all ABC permits. It is open for lunch Monday through Friday and for dinner Monday through Saturday.

Captain Stanley's Seafood

$-$$ • 3333 S. Wilmington St., Raleigh
• 779-7878

If you're willing to wait in line, sometimes a very long line, this is the place for inexpensive seafood. Calabash seafood, named for a North Carolina coastal town, is dipped in batter and then deep fried. Lunch is served Tuesday through Friday and dinner is served Tuesday through Saturday.

Fins

$$$-$$$$ • 7713-39 Lead Mine Rd.,
Raleigh • 847-4119

Owner and chef William D'Auvray offers quintessential fusion cuisine, specializing in seafood with Californian and Asian flavors in a casual atmosphere. The menu, which changes monthly, features such entrees as Slate-Roasted Salmon and Sea Scallops, as well as beef and pork dishes. Fins was voted "Best New Restaurant" in the 1998 *Spectator* reader survey. Reservations are recommended on the weekends. Catering is also available. Fins is open for dinner Monday through Saturday.

Fishmonger's Restaurant and Oyster Bar

$$ • 806 W. Main St., Durham • 682-0128

Once primarily a fresh seafood market, Fishmonger's now serves lunch offering seafood salads, fish sandwiches and chowders, and dinner, featuring fresh steamed crabs, oysters, shrimp and lobster; broiled fish in season and daily specials. Beer and wine are available. It's open seven days a week and is the closest you can get to the beach without leaving home.

42nd Street Oyster Bar

$$$-$$$$ • 508 W. Jones St., Raleigh
• 831-2811

The grilled swordfish and tuna are as good as you will get anywhere and the shrimp salad is a meal by itself. The meat dishes rival the city's best and the menu has Cajun specials and children's portions. It's also a great

Photo by Evelyn Ward

Fishmonger's offers a variety of fresh seafood and chowders that will keep you coming back for more.

late night place to be seen and meet people. 42nd Street Oyster Bar is open for lunch Monday through Friday and for dinner nightly, and has all ABC permits.

Squid's Restaurant, Market & Oyster Bar
$$ • 1201 N. Fordham Blvd., U.S. 15-501 Bypass, Chapel Hill • 942-8757

Squid's offers freshly shucked oysters, peel-your-own shrimp, and littleneck clams. A main menu of fresh seafood features specialties such as Broiled Scrod, Roasted Garlic Mussels and Tuna Burritos. You'll also find steak, lobster, salads and chowder on the menu, and a variety of special desserts. Squid's also has a seafood market and oyster bar. Squid's is open for dinner nightly and has all ABC permits.

Tony's Bourbon Street Oyster Bar
$$$-$$$$ • MacGregor Village, Cary • 462-6226

In addition to the oyster bar, which features crawfish, oysters, clams, mussels and shrimp, Tony's offers fresh seafood, Cajun-style entrees, steaks, pasta and chicken—all in a Mardi Gras atmosphere. Live entertainment is

available Thursday, Friday and Saturday nights. Tony's Bourbon Street Oyster Bar is open for dinner Monday through Saturday.

SOUTHERN CUISINE

Carolina Crossroads
$$$-$$$$ • 211 Pittsboro St., Chapel Hill • 918-2777

Carolina Crossroads is an elegant restaurant located in the Carolina Inn. Chef Brian Stapleton, who was formerly the executive chef at Il Palio, dishes up innovative Southern-style cuisine with an Italian influence. The seasonal menu offers specialties like catfish encrusted in smoked pecans, grilled Georgia quail, cherry-wood smoked beef tenderloin and oven-roasted red snapper jambalaya. Save some room for the homemade desserts. Breakfast, lunch and dinner are served every day. A Sunday brunch is served from 11 AM to 2 PM. Reservations are recommended.

Crook's Corner
$$$ • 610 W. Franklin St., Chapel Hill • 929-7643

It is safe to say that there is no restaurant like Crook's anywhere else in the Triangle. The first thing you notice is the pig on the roof, the work of sculptor Bob Gaston, surrounded by a herd of wooden animal figures, made by Chatham County folk artist Clyde Jones. A changing menu features a wide choice of seasonal entrees along with ethnically and regionally authentic dishes. It's always crowded and fun. Dinner is served nightly and brunch is served on Sunday. Reservations are accepted but not required. It has all ABC permits.

Glenwood Grill
$$$ • 2929 Essex Cr., Glenwood Village Shopping Ctr., Raleigh
• 782-3102

Glenwood Grill has a flair for presentation and an innovative new Southern cuisine menu. Specialities range from Vidalia Onion Pancakes to prime filets and shrimp and grits. Glenwood Grill is open for lunch Monday through Friday, dinner Monday through Saturday and brunch on Sunday. The Grill has all ABC permits.

SOUTHWESTERN

Cactus Flower
$$-$$$ • 5300 Edward's Mill Rd. • 789-0125

Located behind Crabtree Valley Mall, Cactus Flower features specialties such as Red Chile Chicken Enchiladas, Southwestern wraps, and seafood, steaks and pasta dishes. It is open daily for lunch and dinner.

Coyote Cafe
$$ • Cary Village Square, Cary • 469-5253

Coyote Cafe offers such specialties as Blue Corn Tacquitos and chimichangas, salads, and white chili, made with northern white beans, and served with jack cheese and sour cream. Popular with the business bunch, Coyote Cafe is open Tuesday through Friday for lunch and seven nights a week for dinner. Weather permitting, the Coyote Cafe presents live acoustic music on its 3,500-square-foot patio Friday and Saturday. If it's raining, the low-key party moves inside.

Newton's Southwest Restaurant & Bar
$$-$$$ • 1837 N. Harrison Ave., Cary
• 677-1777

This Cary restaurant is hot off the Texas grill. Certified Angus steaks, barbecued beef ribs, brisket, chili and fresh fish are some of its specialties. The restaurant caters to groups. It has all ABC permits and a bar called The Trophy Room. Newton's is open Monday through Saturday for lunch and dinner.

SPORTS BAR

Blinco's Sports Restaurant
$$ • 5009 Falls of Neuse Rd., Raleigh
• 790-3882

Twelve satellite dishes and 17 TVs make this a sports enthusiast's place to be in Raleigh. It serves terrific wings, pasta dishes, steaks and seafood. Blinco's has all ABC permits and is open for lunch and dinner daily.

Damon's Clubhouse
$$ • 3019 Auto Dr., Durham • 493-2574

Four 100-inch TV screens allow sport lovers to eat delicious food and enjoy their favorite game at the same time. Lunch and dinner is served every day.

Devine's Restaurant & Sports Bar
$ • 904 West Main St., Durham • 682-0228

Open since 1978, you can relax and enjoy great food and company inside or out on the patio seven days a week for lunch, dinner or late night.

Upper Deck Sports Pub
$ • 329 N. Harrison Ave., Cary
• 460-9977
$ • 2235 Avent Ferry Rd., Raleigh
• 755-3880

No matter what the sport, you can find it televised at either location, with a variety of appetizers and sandwiches served on the side. Both sports pubs are popular

The most popular steakhouse in the Triangle since 1963, Angus Barn features certified Angus beef, a cigar-friendly lounge and a 35,000-bottle wine cellar.

with many of the area's fan clubs, and both are open for lunch and dinner seven days a week.

Woody's Sports Bar
$ • 8322 Chapel Hill Rd., Cary
• 380-7737

You can enjoy good food and friends while you watch your favorite game on state-of-the-art TV screens. It is open for lunch, dinner and late night daily.

STEAK HOUSE

Angus Barn
$$$$ • 9401 Glenwood Ave., Raleigh
• 781-2444

Angus Barn is "THE" steak house in town and has been for over 40 years. Located near the airport, it has always been popular with business travelers. The dining room is decorated in classic Americana with antiques, quilts, farm equipment, artwork and even a gun collection. Popular specialties include steak, prime rib, filet mignon and lobster. For the ultimate culinary experience, groups can reserve the wine cellar dining room, surrounded by nearly 35,000 bottles of wine. After dinner, enjoy a drink in the Wild Turkey Lounge. Open seven nights a week for dinner, Angus Barn has all ABC permits. Reservations are recommended but no reservations are accepted on Saturday.

The Farm House
$$-$$$ • N.C. 86, Chapel Hill
• 929-5727

Set off the beaten path between Chapel Hill and Hillsborough, The Farm House is a welcome discovery for newcomers and longtime residents alike. Enjoy superb steaks, seafood and chicken entrees at this rustic eatery. Don't miss an opportunity to sample the homemade cheesecake or apple pie for dessert. The Farm House is open for dinner Wednesday through Saturday.

Hartman's Steak House
$$-$$$ • 1703 E. Geer St., Durham
• 688-7639

Hartman's opened in 1940 and operated by the same family until the summer of 1998. The new owners do not plan to make any major changes, although they did convert one of the rooms into a bar, the Bull City Tavern. Hartman's serves grain-fed beef and fine seafood. Prime Rib is a specialty Tuesday through Thursday. It is open for dinner Tuesday through Saturday. You can even get a table with a view of the backyard lake. Private dining rooms are available for your special event. It has all ABC permits.

It's Prime Only
$$$-$$$$ • 5509 Edwards Mill Rd., Raleigh • 420-0224

Overlooking Crabtree Valley, It's Prime Only offers a panoramic view. Choose from filet mignon, New York strip and prime rib. The menu also includes grilled seafood, chicken and pasta dishes. It has all ABC permits and is open for dinner Monday through Saturday. Banquet facilities are available for up to 200 guests.

J. Gilbert's Wood-Fired Grill
$$$-$$$$ • 6464 Tryon Rd., Cary • 852-2300

A recent addition to the Cary dining scene, J. Gilbert's specializes in fresh, certified Angus steaks and features pasta and seafood, such as Herbed Marinated Swordfish, Sauteed Crab Cakes and Grilled Barbecue Salmon. Located in Wellington Park Shopping Center, the restaurant is open seven days a week and has all ABC permits.

Jimmy V's Steakhouse & Tavern
$$$-$$$$ • MacGregor Village, Cary • 380-8210

Catering to business clientele, this steakhouse serves certified Angus beef, fresh seafood, Southern Italian specialties and homemade desserts. Dinner is served Monday through Saturday.

Outback Steakhouse
$$-$$$ • 1289 Kildaire Farm Rd., Cary • 460-1770
$$-$$$ • 7500 Creedmoor Rd., Raleigh • 846-3848
$$-$$$ • 3500 Mount Moriah Rd., Durham • 493-2202

The Outback has been one of the most popular chains in the Triangle. Try its "blooming onion." The Outback is open for lunch and dinner daily and has all ABC permits.

The Peddler Steak House
$$$ • 6005 Glenwood Ave., Raleigh • 787-6980

Small, candlelit and cozy, The Peddler opened in 1969. If you're a steak lover, you can choose your cut of meat right at your table. Lobster, seafood and chicken are other entrees. The restaurant is open

Simpson's Beef and Seafood serves some of the best steaks in the Triangle.

Monday through Saturday and has two private dining rooms available for meetings.

The Prime Exchange Steakhouse
$$$-$$$$ • 1742 Fordham Blvd.
at 15/501, Chapel Hill • 929-1518

The Prime Exchange serves Midwestern grain-fed beef. Dine in the smoke-free dining room or relax in the smoke-friendly lounge. It features an extensive wine list, has all ABC permits and is open for dinner Monday through Saturday. Banquet facilities are available for up to 160 guests.

Ruth's Chris Steak House
$$$-$$$$ • 1130 Buck Jones Rd., Cary
• 468-1133

This upscale chain, which opened here in 1997, is known as the "home of serious steaks." It specializes in custom-aged, corn-fed U.S. Prime beef. Banquet facilities are available for up to 100 people.

Simpson's Beef and Seafood
$$-$$$ • 5625 Creedmoor Rd.,
Raleigh • 783-8818

Simpson's serves some of the best steaks in the Triangle. The diverse menu also includes chicken and seafood dishes such as lemon chicken fettucine and chargrilled salmon. Simpson's has live piano music during the week and jazz on the weekends. Reservations are suggested. It has all ABC permits.

Sullivan's Steakhouse
$$$$ • 414 Glenwood Ave., Raleigh
• 833-2888

Sullivan's is an upscale steakhouse named for the last bare-knuckle boxing champ, John L. Sullivan. Choose from the 20-ounce Kansas City strip, the 24-ounce porterhouse, the filet mignon or the New York strip. Seafood dishes are also available such as the salmon steak and the tequila-lime shrimp. Sullivan's is open Monday through Saturday. It boasts an extensive wine list and has all ABC permits. Reservations are strongly suggested.

Vinnie's Steakhouse & Tavern
$$$$ • 7440 Six Forks Rd., Raleigh
• 847-7319
3210 Yonkers Rd. • 231-9030

Vinnie's has a loyal following for its pleasant atmosphere and well-prepared food. It features Italian specialties but grills some of the best steaks and chops in town. Watch out for the legislators when they're in town; it's a lobbyist's favorite. It is open nightly and has all ABC permits.

THAI

Thai Garden
$$ • 1408 Hardimont Rd., Raleigh
• 872-6811

Located off Wake Forest Road, Thai Garden is North Raleigh's finest Thai restaurant. Many vegetarian choices are available. It is open for lunch Monday through Friday and for dinner every day.

Thai Palace
$$ • N.C. 54 E., Glenwood Village,
Chapel Hill • 967-5805

Thai Palace serves authentic Thai food and offers many vegetarian dishes. It's a pleasant place for a good meal and is open for dinner daily except Monday.

VIETNAMESE

Dalat Oriental Restaurant
$ • 2109 Avent Ferry Rd., Mission Valley
Shopping Ctr., Raleigh • 832-7449

Dalat seats about 40 and its prices are popular with North Carolina State University students. The unfried vegetable Dalat roll, pork dishes and pasta salad are excellent. Lunch is served Monday through Friday and dinner is served Monday through Saturday.

Caterers

Caterers provide everything from picnics and pig pickin's to private parties, banquets and weddings. Many of the restaurants mentioned in these pages also cater.

The Catering Company
2 Mariakakis Plaza, U.S. 15-501 Bypass, Chapel Hill • 929-4775

One of Chapel Hill's most established caterers, this company offers imaginative and delicious cuisine for any occasion.

Chefs Unlimited
1818 St. Albans Dr., Raleigh • 873-9500

Chefs Unlimited caters weddings, parties, corporate gatherings and also provides holiday meals. It also offers delicious and healthy food in a dinner service that includes delivery to your home.

Durham Catering Company
2510 University Dr., Durham • 489-9535

A joint venture between Nana's and Pop's restaurants, Durham Catering Company offers full-service catering, including corporate events, pig pickings, private parties, receptions and weddings.

Foster's Market & Catering Company
2694 Chapel Hill Blvd., Durham • 489-3944

The market has become a popular source for everything from homegrown fresh vegetables to delicious dinners and desserts to go. It's also a good spot for lunch, a light snack, espresso or afternoon tea. On weekends, brunch is served. Foster's catering service offers creative cuisine for both private and corporate affairs.

Gregory's
Waverly Place, Cary • 852-3694

Gregory's is available seven days a week for private parties or business functions. It specializes in wedding receptions and intimate rehearsal dinners.

Grill '57
S. Station Shopping Ctr., Garner • 779-5757
Wellington Park, Cary • 852-5557

If you're looking for Beach Music and great hot dogs and hamburgers for your next corporate or special event, give owners John Bradley or Mark Taylor a call.

Horwitz's Delicatessen
MacGregor Village, Cary • 467-2007

Horwitz's is one of Cary's most reliable caterers. The same quality that makes Horwitz's one of the best deli's in the Triangle also holds true for its catering platters from smoked fish, vegetables, gourmet desserts, sandwiches and, of course, Jewish delicacies. This deli works with corporate customers as well as mothers-of-the-bride.

LadyFingers
627 E. Whitaker Mill Rd. • Northside Shopping Ctr., Raleigh • 828-2270

LadyFingers has been catering since 1980 and has developed a large corporate following. Located in Northside Shopping Center, the storefront offers salads, sandwiches and oven-ready gourmet entrees to go, as well as full-service catering. The staff will oversee the preparation and make sure your guests have fresh drinks and full plates.

Marcia & Friends
Apex • 362-8936

Marcia & Friends has been serving the area since 1983 and specializes in corporate meetings, weddings, receptions and special events.

Marlin Events, Inc.
Cameron Village • 874-0370

Marlin Events specializes in corporate events, weddings, cigar and wine dinners, and semiprivate and private parties.

Grill '57 caters everything from family reunions to corporate events. In addition to hamburgers and hot dogs, the Grill can serve steaks, chicken and seafood.

Mitchell's Catering & Events
6633 Falls of Neuse Rd., Raleigh
• 847-0135

Mitchell's is big-time catering, featuring smoked fish, shrimp, roast pig, fowl and more. Mitchell's is known throughout the Triangle for its ice sculptures.

Sandi's Catering
817 Bradley Rd., Fuquay-Varina
• 552-8964

Whether it's a corporate event, wedding reception or theme party, Sandi's Catering offers full-service catering to make yours a memorable occasion.

Savory Fare
908 W. Main St., Durham • 683-2185

Savory Fare proprietor Gary Wein started at the top when he was a Duke University student and offered to cook for then-Duke-President Terry Sanford and his wife. The Sanfords encouraged him to start a catering business and Gary is still at it,

offering everything from simple box lunches to cocktail buffets to elegant six-course dinners, for any number from 10 to 500.

Sisters' Catering Company
2400 East Millbrook Rd., Raleigh
• 782-2837
3300 Woman's Club Dr., Raleigh
• 782-0985

Established in 1976, Sisters' has become one of the largest privately owned catering companies in the state. Sisters' main facility is located on Millbrook Road and it is the exclusive caterer for The Woman's Club. Sisters' caters to the N.C. film industry and corporate events and is also a wedding reception specialist.

Tripodi's
Terrace at Calvander, Chapel Hill
• 933-9407

Tripodi's offers full-service catering for weddings, luncheons, cocktail parties and corporate entertaining.

A RARE FIND

Night Life

It's the weekend and you want to party or it's a weekday evening and you want to make it something special. Either way, the Triangle has clubs, pubs, cafes and restaurants that can provide great evening excitement.

You can learn how to dance the Texas two-step, listen to the latest in alternative music, visit an art gallery, experience an authentic Irish pub or watch a movie and catch a bite at the same time. Speaking of movies, there are several movie houses in the area, including the state-of-the-art Raleigh Grand 16 that features stadium-type seating.

All of the places listed offer a chance for you to meet other people and most are a good place to take a date. Some have a cover charge, so call ahead for details. For more information on what's happening in the Triangle, see our chapters on "Attractions," "Annual Events" and "The Arts."

Raleigh

Raleigh has a reputation as a waystation for bands, solo artists and comedians working toward the big time. You can see these people at places like The Ritz, Berkeley Cafe, The Longbranch, The Brewery and Charlie Goodnight's Comedy Club. Singers Mike Cross and Carole King were regulars at the long-gone Underground in Cameron Village and Jimmy Buffett once played to sold-out crowds at the old Pier. Raleigh itself attracts big-name performers to the ALLTEL Pavilion at Walnut Creek, including Jimmy Buffett, James Taylor, Stevie Nicks, Rod Stewart, Tom Petty and LeAnn Rimes.

Raleigh also has been touted as a city with everything but a night life. Not true. The West End, a developed section of old warehouse space downtown, might change some minds. Here you'll find retail establishments, restaurants and clubs popping up around and between Hargett and Cabarrus streets. Individual new business owners here are hoping to enliven the downtown area and offer the city a variety of places to be seen after dark. The West End is home to the night club WickedSmile, the hip retro Vertigo Diner, Jillian's Billiards Cafe, Humble Pie, The Warehouse and its newest addition, The Cellar. Keep your eye on this area. The West End still has a lot more in store for Raleigh night life.

Alive After Five
Fayetteville Street Mall, Civic Center Plaza • 831-6011

This is an after-work event sponsored by the city and others to get people downtown. Surprise ... it works! It happens only in the summer and only on Thursdays, but it has become popular with the younger professionals and working crowd as a place to hear free live music and mingle. The bands are rock 'n' roll and R&B.

ALLTEL Pavilion at Walnut Creek
Rock Quarry and Sunnybrook Rds. • 834-4000

When there's a hot concert in town, this is the night life for the Triangle and eastern North Carolina. It is the latest in multimillion-dollar outdoor amphitheaters built with public and private funds. Built in 1991, the $13.5 million amphitheater has a capacity of about 20,000, 7,000 under the roof.

Photo by Tim Johnson

ComedySportz at City Market features live competitive improvisational comedy.

Walnut Creek has seen tremendous sell-out performances over the years, including the Dave Matthews Band, Pearl Jam and perennial favorite Jimmy Buffett, a hit with Triangle "parrotheads."

The Berkeley Cafe
217 W. Martin St. • 821-0777

No, this is not where expatriate Californians sip coffee and get down. However, poetry is read here and an open mike night takes place on Mondays and an acoustic jam occurs on Tuesdays. It is a small cafe and club facing Nash Square downtown and the live music won't blow you out in the street. Good bands on the rise as well as local folks play here. Because of its R&B and local grass roots rock acts, one critic described the cafe as "a little bit of Memphis in downtown Raleigh." The Berkeley also features Southern Championship Wrestling once a month.

Bowties
North Raleigh Hilton, 3415 Wake Forest Rd. • 872-2323

Bowties draws some of the yuppie crowd and has survived the "bar wars," in which one hotel was competing with another to attract the singles flock. It features high-energy dance music. The big screen and four TV monitors for music videos or ACC basketball make this a popular place on game nights. It offers half-price appetizers and has all ABC permits.

The Brewery
3009 Hillsborough St. • 834-7018

If your heart is in alternative rock and rock and roll, this is the place for you. It brings in the best of the original rock groups and features good local and regional bands. Its proximity to NCSU gives the crowd a student flavor. Beer is served and the cover charge is usually modest. The crowd—300 is the limit—likes music. It's one of the more popular stops on the rock tour for working bands.

Cappers
4421 Six Forks Rd. • 787-8963

Located across the street from North Hills Mall, this North Raleigh restaurant is a hit among Triangle jazz buffs. Cappers often leads *The Spectator* magazine's annual "Best List" as the best place for jazz. Musicians such as Lindsay Rosebrock, Joshua Bland and Norb Bleau are featured most of the week.

The Cellar
Dawson & Cabarrus Sts. • 836-9966

After enjoying a relaxing gourmet meal at The Warehouse Restaurant, head downstairs to The Cellar. This lively nightclub contains video gaming machines (winners receive gift certificates), pool tables and snooker tables. Catch sports action on The Cellar's mega screen TVs, and enjoy music and dancing at this late-night hotspot.

Charlie Goodnight's Comedy Club
861 W. Morgan St. • 828-5233

Charlie Goodnight's is big-time comedy. It's the city's first comedy club and is considered one of the best on the East Coast. It's been a stop for familiar acts and now features famous names like Jay Leno and Richard Jeni.

Charlie Goodnight's restaurant downstairs serves Mexican fare and the club serves drinks and snacks. It has all ABC permits. Shows run Tuesday through Saturday with one show a night during the week, two on Friday and three on Saturday.

ComedySportz
City Market, Raleigh • 829-0822

ComedySportz offers live competitive improv comedy every Friday and Saturday night. Two teams of comedians battle against each other for points and laughs. A second ComedySportz location is at 128 East Franklin Street in Chapel Hill, 968-3922.

Crowley's Old Favorites Restaurant & Lounge
3071 Medlin Dr. • 787-3431

There are three Crowley's and this was the first one. It attracts some of the young and beautiful and boisterous bunch, and the food is good, too. The other two locations are Crowley's Courtyard at 3201 Edwards Mill Road, 783-5447, and Crowley's of Stonehenge at 7330 Creedmoor Road, 676-3431—the latter which offers live music on weekends.

East Village Grill and Bar
Hillsborough St. and Dixie Tr. • 821-9985

East Village's outside deck, with its laid-back atmosphere, is the perfect spot to mingle. It was voted the "Best Hangout on Hillsborough Street" in *The Spectator* magazine's annual reader survey.

42nd Street Oyster Bar
508 W. Jones St. • 831-2811

This downtown restaurant and bar is a place to be seen among the single's set. It has all ABC permits and live music on special days—and an interesting decor, including a bar mural that celebrates the late restaurateur Thad Eure Jr. and friends. If you're interested in meeting people, then go on Friday or Saturday night. You will definitely meet people—waiting to get in!

Goodnight Lounge
7112 Sandy Forks Rd. • 847-3869

Goodnight Lounge is the place to go in North Raleigh for dancing, live music, billiards and stand-up comedy acts.

Have A Nice Day Cafe
901 Tryon St. • 831-2555

Have A Nice Day Cafe is located off Morgan Street in the Charlie Goodnight's Entertainment Complex. In an energetic atmosphere with a two-level lighted dance floor, DJs play disco hits from the '70s.

Hillsborough Street Hangouts
NCSU strip along Hillsborough St.

This is no combat zone, but with the 40+ bars and clubs that line Hillsborough Street between Oberlin Road and Gorman Street, it's a busy part of the city for night life. Some of the hottest spots where you will find the young, beautiful and generally impoverished student crowd are the Comet Lounge, the Five-O Cafe, the Cantina and Pantana's Pool Hall and Saloon. The Comet Lounge serves liquor, so it's a private club. It starts rockin' late and has DJs and a dance floor. The Five-O Cafe is above Studio I Theater, serves only beer and is a popular dance bar. The Cantina crowd is younger and sits on the porch outside in good weather. An upstairs dance floor also features live bands. Cup A Joe is a coffee house that features live music some nights. Across the street is Pantana's, a membership club that serves mixed drinks. It's crowd is a little older but still mostly under 30. It features live music, what one patron calls "Southern rock," alternative, hard rock and Top 40.

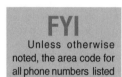

FYI

Unless otherwise noted, the area code for all phone numbers listed in this guide is 919.

Humble Pie
317 S. Harrington St. • 829-9222

Billed as "Downtown Raleigh's Oldest Fine Dining Restaurant," Humble Pie also hosts live entertainment on the weekends, featuring local and regional rock 'n' roll acts. Shows take place Friday and Saturday from 11 PM to 2 AM. Dinner is served Tuesday through Saturday from 6 to 10 PM and there is also a Sunday brunch.

Irregardless Cafe
901 W. Morgan St. • 790-4304

This popular restaurant offers live jazz, classical and acoustic music most nights of the week. Except for special performances, there is usually no cover charge. Call for details.

Jillian's
117 S. West St. • 821-7887

Billed as "Your Food and Entertainment Universe," Jillian's entertainment complex contains a sports cafe, Hibachi Grill, dance floor, 14 pool tables, outdoor volleyball court and video games. An outdoor beach party is held most Sundays.

Jillian's entertainment complex has something for everyone, including pool tables, electronic games, an outdoor volleyball court and a dance floor.

Photo by Tim Johnson

The Longbranch
600 Creekside Dr. • 829-1125

This is one of the three or four places in town where you can find name entertainment. It's a membership club with all ABC permits. Despite its name, it features Top 40 acts, some "beach music" and rock. The Longbranch also offers a room for country and western and country rock groups, so you won't feel out of place in your cowboy boots and hat. You can meet and mingle and even take line dancing and country dance lessons.

O'Malley's Tavern
5228 Holly Ridge Dr. • 787-1234

Open seven days a week until 2:30 AM, O'Malley's is a friendly neighborhood pub that features live bands Thursday through Sunday and open mike night on Wednesdays. It also offers wide-screen TVs, pool tables and dart boards.

Players Retreat
105 Oberlin Rd. • 755-9589

A Raleigh institution, the PR is a true-blue neighborhood pub or tavern that is rumored to be the oldest of its kind between Washington and Atlanta. Near the NCSU campus, many a State student has grown wise watching the fish behind the bar and debating the finer points of ACC basketball. Pool, darts and video games are available. The Bernie Burger is one of the best hamburgers in town. If you plan to live in Raleigh, you need to visit the PR at least once to appreciate the culture.

Plum Crazy
2215 New Hope Church Rd. • 790-0017

Plum Crazy is a dance club popular with the young set. It also hosts comedy shows and live jazz and R&B concerts.

Raleighwood Cinema Grill
6609 Falls of the Neuse Rd. • 847-8370
24-Hour Movie Hotline • 847-0326

Raleighwood's logo says it all, "Great Movies, Food & Spirits!" Basically, the idea is to combine great food, a fun atmosphere and Hollywood's newest movies to create an enjoyable and affordable evening out. The contemporary decor is upbeat and the wide beverage selection and tempting food is served by a friendly and hospitable staff. The menu features pizza, burgers and salads, as well as beverages, including beer, wine and soft drinks.

Red's Beach Music
4400 Craftsman Dr. • 876-7337

If you live in North Carolina, you should know about beach music—easy moving rock 'n' roll/soul of the late 1950s and early '60s. It took root on the Carolina campuses and is an institution now. Red's capitalizes on the nostalgia and the crowd there will reflect the age of the music. It's relaxed and a good place to take the spouse to shake up the metabolism. Red's is a private club and has all ABC permits. Shag lessons are offered every Monday and Tuesday.

The Ritz
2820 Industrial Dr. • 836-8535

The Ritz has had many lives and the latest incarnation may be its liveliest. It has the best in tour music, from country to rock, and there's plenty of room and lively dancing. The Ritz features Latino music Friday nights.

Tir na nOg
218 South Blount St. • 833-7795

Tir na nOg is Gaelic for "land of eternal youth." An authentic Irish pub and restaurant located at Moore Square, it features delicious food and live music Tuesday through Saturday. Tir na nOg also has a Sunday brunch with a make-your-own Bloody Mary Bar.

The Warehouse After Five
Dawson and Cabarrus Sts. • 836-9966

The Warehouse complex is located in the former Button South building in downtown Raleigh. The Warehouse Restaurant

The multimillion-dollar ALLTEL Pavilion at Walnut Creek is the place to catch the hottest national acts during the summer.

serves innovative American cuisine, while The Warehouse After Five features a sports bar, music and dancing, widescreen TVs and pool tables.

WickedSmile
51 W. Hargett St. • 828-2223

Located in a restored West End Warehouse space, WickedSmile is a former restaurant that has been transformed into a trendy bar.

Cary

While most night life in suburbia remains G-rated, there are places where you can kick up some excitement. Here's where Cary Insiders go.

Backstage Restaurant
Waverly Place Shopping Center
• 858-5041

An eclectic restaurant that serves casual American cuisine, Backstage also offers live entertainment on weekends, as well as an espresso and smoothie bar, and an extensive specialty drink menu.

Cary Tavern and Grill
928 West Chatham St. • 467-1816

Formerly known as Wivi & Me, this eclectic pub and grill features Karaoke Thursday and Saturday nights, and live entertainment

every Friday. It also offers four pool tables, eight TVs and pinball and video games.

Coyote Cafe
1014 Ryan Rd. • 469-5253

Coyote Cafe serves up Southwestern fare and features classic rock, jazz, blues or acoustic music on Friday and Saturday nights. Local favorite Kim Hale usually takes the stage on Friday nights.

The Fox and Hound
MacGregor Village • 380-0080

On Thursdays and Saturdays, musicians play blues, jazz or acoustic music as the good English fare is served.

Newton's Southwest
1837 N. Harrison Ave. • 677-1777

The Newtons made a hit with a bit of Texas in north Cary. At the Southwest, the music gets loud and from March 'til October, the feet kick out on a heated, outdoor dance floor called The Pepper Patio. Thursday night is reserved for beach music.

Woody's Sports Tavern & Grill
8322 Chapel Hill Rd. • 380-7737

Woody's has two oak bars and 11 satellite systems that feed 25 TV screens. The menu features burgers, sandwiches and late-night munchies. On Friday and Saturday nights, bands perform blues, rock and classic rock. During the week,

TRIANGLE COFFEEHOUSES

Raleigh

Barnes & Noble Cafe	Crabtree Valley Mall	782-0030
Caribou Coffee Company		
Sutton Square	6511 Falls of the Neuse	790-5397
Hillsborough	2428 Hillsborough St.	821-1801
Classic Coffees	Six Forks Rd. and Saw Mill Rd.	848-9878
Cream & Bean	2010 Hillsborough St.	828-2663
Cup A Joe		
Hillsborough	3100 Hillsborough St.	828-9665
Mission Valley	2109 Avent Ferry Rd.	828-9886
Keagan's Coffee House	2522 Hillsborough St.	834-1366
New World Music Cafe	4112 Pleasant Valley Rd.	786-0091
Starbucks Coffee		
University Grille	2500 Hillsborough St.	836-0814
Falls of the Neuse	900-101 Spring Forest Rd.	873-9615
Pleasant Valley Promenade	6282-104 Glenwood Ave.	785-0111
Cameron Village	501 Oberlin Rd.	856-9444
Olde Raleigh Village	3101 Edwards Mill Rd.	789-4422
Stonehenge Market	7498 Creedmoor Rd.	846-0633
Third Place Coffee House	1811 Glenwood Ave.	834-6566

Cary

Barnes & Noble Cafe	760 S.E. Maynard Rd.	467-3866
Caffe Piazza	107 Edinburgh South	460-7177
Caribou Coffee Company		
Preston Corners	4214 N.W. Cary Pkwy.	462-0690
Maynard & Kildaire	109 S.W. Maynard Rd.	319-6265
The Ground Finalé	1287 N.W. Maynard Rd.	460-4747
Jitters Gourmet Coffee	976 High House Rd.	462-3320
Paradigm Coffee House		
Waverly Place	105-D Colonnades Way	859-8099
Northwoods	919 N. Harrison Ave.	481-3838

Durham

Barnes & Noble Cafe	New Hope Commons	489-3012
Francesca's Dessert Caffe	706 Ninth St.	286-4177
Java Republic Coffee House	4900 N.C. 55	361-0055
Starbucks	1817 Martin Luther King Pkwy.	403-6676

Chapel Hill

A Southern Season	Eastgate Shopping Center	929-7133
Caffe Driade	1215-A E. Franklin St.	942-2333
Caribou Coffee	110 W. Franklin St.	933-5404
Carolina Coffee Shop	138 E. Franklin St.	942-6875
Cup A Joe	1129 Weaver Dairy Rd.	967-2002
Java Cafe	231 S. Elliott Rd.	967-4888
P.J.'s Coffee & Tea Cafe	1289 N. Fordham Blvd.	967-5411
Provisions of Chapel Hill	University Mall	968-1722
Starbucks	103 E. Franklin St.	932-3824

Photo by Evelyn Ward

The cozy Irish pub atmosphere of James Joyce would have made the author of *Finnegans Wake* proud.

dart leagues compete and tournaments are held on a regular basis.

Durham

If you're looking for late night music, Durham has several night spots, where you'll find mostly jazz, folk or reggae-rock, for a modest cover charge.

Devine's Restaurant and Sports Bar
904 W. Main St. • 682-0228

Devine's offers live rock 'n' roll, R&B or blues music a couple of nights a week during the winter and about five nights a week during the summer. Wide-screened TVs are tuned to the day's sporting events.

Down Under Pub
802 W. Main St. • 682-0039

A popular hangout for Duke students, the Down Under Pub offers occasional live music, from folk to alternative. It has a pool table and two dartboards. Enjoy pub fare and choose from a wide selection of beer.

Duke Coffeehouse
Duke University, East Campus
• 684-4069

Popular with Duke students and locals alike, Duke Coffeehouse features live bands playing everything from acoustic to alternative rock.

George's Garage
737 Ninth St. • 286-4131

George's Garage is a popular upscale restaurant on Ninth Street that contains a 40-foot bar, wide-screened TVs and a dance floor. It features live music Thursday through Saturday. Duke students flock to the Garage on Thursday nights.

The Green Room
1108 Broad St. • 286-2359

One of the best billiard spots in the Triangle, The Green Room features nine regulation size pool tables, as well as dartboards, shuffleboards, video poker and a foosball table.

James Joyce
912 West Main St. • 688-6189

The author of *Ulysses* himself would have felt right at home in this cozy Irish pub, billed as "A Little Bit of Ireland in Durham." It is located across the street from Brightleaf Square.

The Kelt
744 Ninth St., Durham • 416-3337

The owners of James Joyce opened up this charming pub on bustling Ninth Street. Inside, The Kelt has the appearance of a castle and there is a large outdoor deck. Live bands perform here regularly. Wednesday is college night.

The Lounge
1920 Perry St. • 286-9414

Located downstairs from the Cosmic Cantina, The Lounge is a classy establishment that offers jazz on Wednesdays and rock and blues on weekends.

Talk of the Town
108 E. Main St. • 682-7747

Talk of the Town specializes in jazz and rhythm and blues Thursday through Saturday night. There is a cover charge.

Tobacco Roadhouse
115 North Duke St. • 688-4505

Located in a converted warehouse near Brightleaf Square, Tobacco Roadhouse Restaurant and Brewpub features live entertainment on its outside deck Wednesday through Saturday, a large dance floor, a late-night menu and pool tables.

Chapel Hill

Although Chapel Hill is a small town, there's always been a large interest in music here. It's a regular stop for young and alternative bands on tour. The live music in night spots in town is often innovative and occasionally astounding. Here's our guide to a few places that regularly

TRIANGLE CINEMAS

Cary & Morrisville

Imperial 6	Cary Village Shopping Ctr.	467-0009
Park Place 16	9525 Chapel Hill Rd., Morrisville	481-9686
Waverly Place 6	2001 Kildaire Farm Rd., Cary	851-9713

Chapel Hill

Carolina Theatre	108-B E. Franklin St.	933-8464
Chelsea Theater	1129 Weaver Dairy Rd.	968-3005
Movies at Timberlyne	Timberlyne Shopping Ctr.	933-8600
Plaza Theatres	Village Plaza Shopping Ctr.	967-4737
Ram Triple	NCNB Plaza	967-8284
Varsity Theatres	E. Franklin St.	967-8665

Durham & RTP

Carmike 7	2000 Avondale Dr.	220-3393
Carolina Theatre Cinemas	309 Morgan St.	560-3060
Starlite Drive-In	2325 E. Club Blvd.	688-1037
Willowdaile Cinema 8	Willowdaile Shopping Ctr.	477-4681
Wynnsong 10	1800 Martin Luther King Blvd.	489-9020

Raleigh & Garner

Blue Ridge 14	600 Blue Ridge Rd.	828-9003
Carmike Cinema 7	5501 Atlantic Springs Rd.	878-8778
Colony Twin Theatre	5438 Six Forks Rd.	847-5677
Garner Towne Square 10	2600 Timber Dr.	779-2201
Mission Valley Cinemas	Mission Valley Shopping Ctr.	834-8520
Pleasant Valley 7	U.S. 70 at Pleasant Valley Rd.	783-0074
Raleigh Grand 16	U.S. 70 and Lynn Rd.	788-8000
Raleighwood Cinema Grill	Falls Village Shopping Ctr.	847-0326
Rialto	1620 Glenwood Ave.	856-0111
Sixforks 6	9600 Forum Dr.	846-2120
Studio I & II	Electric Co. Mall, Hillsborough St.	856-0111
Tower Merchants 6	Tower Merchants Village	231-6477
Tower Twin	Tower Shopping Ctr.	834-8592

Photo by Rich Weidman

Locals and UNC students alike gather at Local 506, one of the best places in the Triangle to hear live rock bands.

feature live music, usually for a modest cover charge.

The ArtsCenter
300-G East Main St., Carrboro • 929-ARTS

The ArtsCenter often sponsors jazz shows, including a Sunday night open jam once a month. You can also catch scheduled performances by well-known musicians and singers like David Wilcox, Guy Clark, Livingston Taylor and Ian Tyson. The ArtsCenter offers table seating for some shows and refreshments are available. You're in for a treat at a reasonable admission price.

Cat's Cradle
300 E. Main St., Carrboro • 967-9053

The old favorite, Cat's Cradle keeps on keepin' on, tucked away behind The ArtsCenter in Carrboro. Popular with the twenty- and thirty-somethings for the past few decades, the Cradle is open seven nights a week, with the best of new local and touring bands. Advance tickets are available for some shows at local independent music stores. If you call the Cradle, a recorded message will give you current information on hours and upcoming bands and musicians. Shows usually begin at 10 PM.

The Cave
452 1/2 W. Franklin St. • 968-9308

The Cave is a basement pub below Franklin Street that has been around forever. It features everything from folk to rock 'n' roll, blues, alternative and acoustic. Music begins nightly at 9:30 PM. The Cave is a great place for a cold beer and a game of pool.

He's Not Here
112 1/2 W. Franklin St. • 942-7939

The name comes from an old cartoon, in which the bartender answering the phone says, "He's not here," while all the customers shake their heads. A Chapel Hill landmark well known to Insiders, He's Not Here features bands at 9 PM on Friday and Saturday nights and Karaoke Night for would-be stars on Sunday at 9:30 PM.

Local 506
506 W. Franklin St. • 942-5506

Local 506 is becoming an institution among local music fans for providing a great place to see great bands. In August, Local 506 hosts *Sleazefest*, an annual multi-night extravaganza of questionable taste. National and regional touring bands as well as the best local artists ply their trade here. Local 506 has all ABC permits and a membership is required. There is almost always a cover charge.

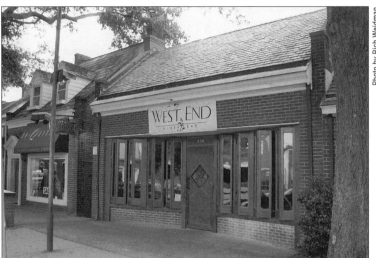

The West End Wine Bar offers 50 wines by the glass in a relaxing environment, complete with live jazz Wednesday and Thursday nights.

Skylight Exchange
405 1/2 W. Rosemary St. • 933-5550

The Skylight Exchange is a coffeehouse/music club/restaurant and a used book and record store business. There is music Thursday through Saturday and open mike nights on Monday and Wednesday, most often without a cover. During the day and on non-music nights, the Skylight Exchange is always good for a sandwich or light snack, cup of coffee and several hours of browsing through old paperbacks, records and tapes.

Top of the Hill
Corner of Franklin & Columbia Sts.
• 929-8676

Top of the Hill is a popular downtown restaurant that offers live music on Thursday nights from 8 to 11 PM. In good weather, the music moves out to the third-floor heated patio. Even on nights without music, this is definitely a "hot" night spot for Chapel Hill.

West End Wine Bar
450 West Franklin St. • 967-7599

The West End Wine Bar, which opened in the fall of 1997, offers a reprieve from the typical noisy and rowdy Chapel Hill bar environment. It features 50 wines by the glass and 200 bottle selections. Live jazz takes place on Wednesday and Thursday nights.

Shopping

Years ago, shopping in the Triangle was limited to a few malls and some local shopping centers. In the past several years, the malls have been renovated and expanded and shopping centers have sprouted at almost every major intersection. Today the Triangle area is the largest regional shopping district between Washington, DC, and Atlanta, Georgia.

Although each of the larger Triangle towns has a variety of stores, there are a number of specialty stores and shopping districts that are worth a special trip. Brightleaf Square in Durham, Cameron Village and City Market in Raleigh, Franklin Street and A Southern Season in Chapel Hill and Waverly Place in Cary offer unique shopping experiences.

This chapter provides information on regional malls, shopping centers listed by town and stores by category of goods.

Regional Malls

Cary Towne Center
Maynard and Walnut Sts., Cary
• 460-1053

Cary Towne Center is Cary's largest enclosed mall. It opened in 1979 and was expanded in 1991 by its present owners, the Richard E. Jacobs Group of Cleveland, Ohio. As the second largest enclosed mall in Wake County, it truly is a regional shopping center. Anchor tenants include: Hudson Belk, Sears, JCPenney, Hecht's and Dillard's. National apparel and shoe stores include Lerner of New York, The Gap and GapKids, The Limited and Limited Too, Casual Corner, Eddie Bauer, Lane Bryant, Talbot's, Victoria's Secret,

Frederick's of Hollywood, Foot Locker and Lady Foot Locker. There are specialty stores such as Bath and Body Works, Learning Smith, Cyber Station, Logo Joe's, Kay-bee Toys, Great Outdoor Provision Company, The Disney Store, Candleman, Kirklands, Butterfields, Etc., a specialty kitchen store , Gypsy's Candies, The Allen Montague's Collectors Gallery, North Carolina Remembered, Aggie's Gifts and Collectibles and Mitchum Optometry. Select Comfort Air Bed Company even has a store in the mall so you can try out their famous mattresses that are always being advertised. In addition to the food court, Ragazzi's, India Garden and Spinnakers restaurants are located here. Across the street you'll find a large Barnes & Noble, complete with coffee shop.

Crabtree Valley Mall
U.S. 70 at I-440, Raleigh • 787-8993

Crabtree Valley Mall is Raleigh's largest enclosed mall with over 240 stores, restaurants and services. The mall opened in 1972 and underwent an extensive renovation and expansion program in 1992. Anchor stores include Lord & Taylor, Hudson Belk, Hecht's and Sears. It has a number of national, name-brand stores such as Pottery Barn, Smith and Hawkens, Brooks Brothers, Laura Ashley, J. Crew, Ann Taylor, Banana Republic, Abercrombie and Fitch, Williams Sonoma, The Disney Store, The Museum Company and Godiva Chocolatier.

A few of the specialty stores you will find here include: This End Up, Garibaldi & Bruns jewelry store, Maternité by Mothers Work, Gymboree, Successories, North Carolina Remembered, The Great Train Store, Sam Goody, Sharon

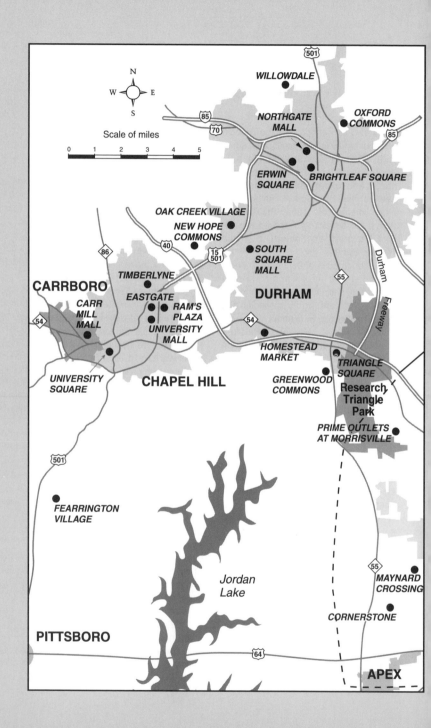

Triangle Shopping

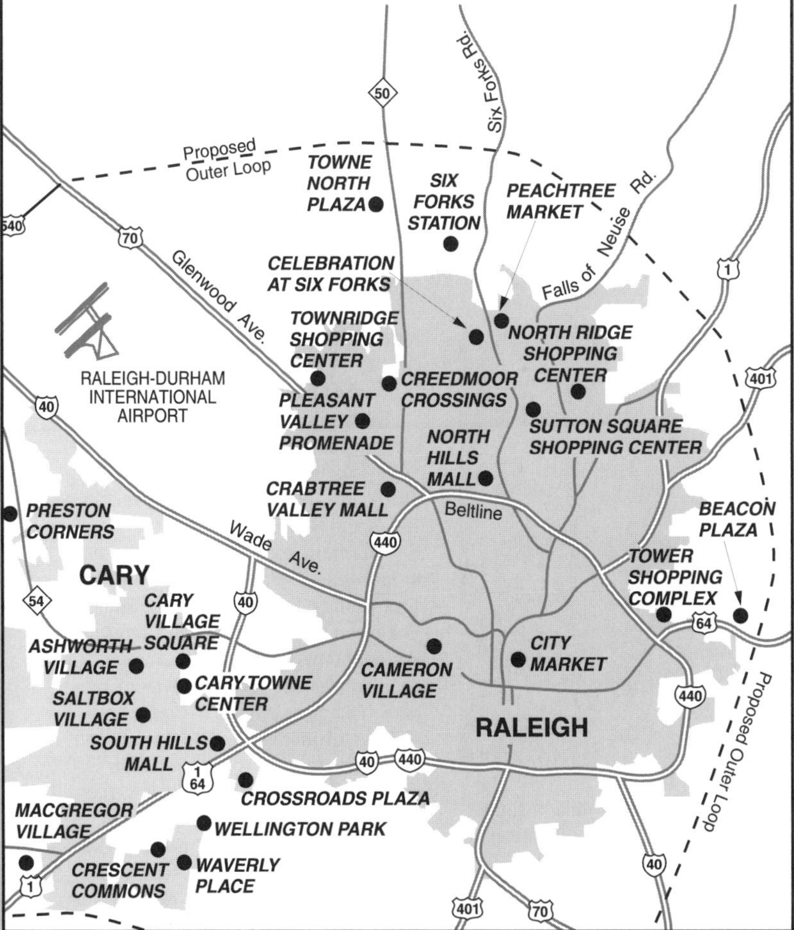

Six Forks Rd.
50
Proposed Outer Loop
TOWNE NORTH PLAZA
SIX FORKS STATION
PEACHTREE MARKET
Falls of Neuse Rd.
540
70
Glenwood Ave.
CELEBRATION AT SIX FORKS
1
TOWNRIDGE SHOPPING CENTER
NORTH RIDGE SHOPPING CENTER
RALEIGH-DURHAM INTERNATIONAL AIRPORT
CREEDMOOR CROSSINGS
401
40
PLEASANT VALLEY PROMENADE
SUTTON SQUARE SHOPPING CENTER
NORTH HILLS MALL
CRABTREE VALLEY MALL
Beltline
PRESTON CORNERS
BEACON PLAZA
Wade Ave.
440
TOWER SHOPPING COMPLEX
CARY
54
CARY VILLAGE SQUARE
40
64
ASHWORTH VILLAGE
CITY MARKET
CAMERON VILLAGE
CARY TOWNE CENTER
SALTBOX VILLAGE
440
RALEIGH
SOUTH HILLS MALL
40
440
1
64
CROSSROADS PLAZA
MACGREGOR VILLAGE
WELLINGTON PARK
CRESCENT COMMONS
WAVERLY PLACE
1
40
401
70
Proposed Outer Loop

Luggage & Gifts, Suncoast Motion Pictures, Ross-Simons, Nine West, Pacific Sunwear, The Body Shop, Crabtree and Evelyn, Luggage and Leather, Victoria's Secret, Papyrus (fine stationery), Great Outdoor Provision Company, Brookstone, Wolf Camera, Babbage's, Electronics Boutique, Restoration Hardware and Pier 1 Imports. Popular apparel stores include: Cache, Casual Corner, The Gap, Eddie Bauer, The Limited, The Limited Too and Banana Republic. Barnes & Noble's bookstore serves lifestyle along with the titles. Thomas Kinkade Art Gallery is truly worth visiting to see why Thomas Kinkade has become the most collected artist in America. Deck the Walls is a locally owned frame shop and gallery that provides beautiful custom framing.

Crabtree Valley Mall is also home to several popular eateries: the Capital Room at Hudson Belk, Ruby Tuesday's, Mr. Dunderbak's, Kanki Japanese House of Steaks, P.F. Chang's China Bistro and Panera Bread.

Photo by Tim Johnson

With 130 stores and 1 million square feet of space, Cary Towne Center is the second largest enclosed mall in Wake County.

Crossroads Plaza
U.S. 1 and I-440, Cary

This regional shopping complex offers the convenience of front door parking since it is not a traditional enclosed mall. The anchor tenants are OfficeMax, Marshalls and Stein Mart. Of interest to readers is Bookstar, a book superstore that carries over 100,000 titles at a discount. Crossroads Plaza has some specialty discounters such as Just for Feet, Dick's Sporting Goods, REI, the membership store for outdoorsmen, Toys 'R Us, Pet Depot Superstore, Classical Clocks, Linens 'n' Things and Bed Bath & Beyond. There are restaurant chains, too, such as Ryan's Family Steakhouse, Red Lobster, Olive Garden and Chick-Fil-A.

Walnut Plaza is adjacent to Crossroads and includes Target, Home Depot, Office Depot, National Tire & Battery and the popular Houlihan's restaurant franchise. Located across the street is Lowe's Plaza, a home building supplies and hardware megastore.

Northgate Mall
Off I-85 at Gregson on W. Club Blvd.
Durham • 286-4400

Durham's first large shopping mall, which celebrated its 35th anniversary in 1998, boasts over 160 stores and services. Its anchor stores are Hecht's, Sears and Hudson Belk.

The many specialty shops in the mall include Ann Taylor, Talbot's, The Gap, The Disney Store, Victoria's Secret, Sharon Luggage, The Bombay Company, Waldenbooks, Footlocker, Aerosole's shoe store, Great Outdoor Provision Company, Hungates Arts and Crafts and a number of unique, locally owned and managed stores such as The Scrap Exchange. A full-size Italian Carousel is a permanent fixture and a favorite of children.

Northgate recently underwent renovations, adding 40,000 square feet, including the construction of Shops at Northgate, a shopping strip located north of the mall.

North Hills Mall
Six Forks Rd. and I-440, Raleigh
• 787-8896

Built in 1967, North Hills is Raleigh's original enclosed mall. Since that time, it has been updated and currently offers a diverse range of shops where you can find just about everything. The mall is anchored by two department stores, Dillard's and JCPenney, but it has found a niche by providing smaller specialty shops and national name shops such as Structure, The Limited Too, The Gap, Express and Victoria's Secret.

Other stores include Globetrotter Luggage, Added Dimensions Fashions, Zales jewelry, Storehouse Furniture, Gallery and Gifts, Little Art Gallery and the N.C. Museum of History Shop. There are numerous eating establishments, including Chick-Fil-A. North Hills Plaza is a small shopping center across Lassiter Mill Road from the mall. It is geared strongly toward service with merchants such as a U.S. Post Office, Blockbuster Video and the N.C. Division of Motor Vehicles. It has specialty shops as well, such as Dan Howard's Maternity Factory Outlet, Audio Book World and Hickory Hams.

Prime Outlets at Morrisville
1001 Airport Blvd., Morrisville • 380-8700

Conveniently located near the airport and directly off I-40, the former Triangle Factory Shops recently changed its name to Prime Outlets at Morrisville, reflecting owner Prime Retail's recent merger with the Horizon Group. The mall features beautiful hardwood floors and upscale shops offering off-retail prices. About 40 retail stores such as Off 5th (Saks Fifth Avenue Outlet), Corning Revere Factory Store, Nine West Outlet and Samsonite Company Store sell clothing, housewares, jewelry and more.

Photo by Tim Johnson

South Square Mall, one of Durham's two mega-malls, contains over 120 specialty shops, restaurants and department stores.

Fine dining can be enjoyed at Sorrento, which features Italian cuisine.

South Square Mall
U.S. 15-501 N./Bus., Durham • 493-2451

The other of Durham's two mega-malls, South Square is anchored by Hudson Belk, JCPenney and Dillard's. Popular national chains include: The Limited, Abercrombie & Fitch, Eddie Bauer, The Gap, Paul Harris, Ashley Stewart, Structure and Express. Visit The White House for women's fashions and Moondance Gallery for gifts and jewelry. Shop Deck the Walls for frames and prints and Lechter's for household goods and gadgets. Both B. Dalton and Waldenbooks are also located in the mall. Picadilly Cafeteria is a great place to eat.

South Square is located adjacent to Toys 'R Us store. Next door is Circuit City, the discount stereo, TV and appliance chain.

INSIDERS' TIP

The combined regional malls contain almost 800 stores with over 5,437,000 square feet of shopping space.

University Mall & Plaza
U.S. 15-501 and Estes Dr.
Chapel Hill • 967-6934

Featuring over 65 stores, restaurants and services, University Mall and Plaza offers Chapel Hill its most varied array of shopping possibilities. This mall is anchored by Dillard's and Hudson Belk. A host of apparel and specialty shops ranging from athletic apparel to maps to electronic equipment add to the diversity of University Mall.

Some Insiders' favorites are Pleasing Mona, a women's wear shop; Kitchenworks, an eclectic mix of anything you'd ever want for your kitchen; Cameron's, filled with wonderful gifts, jewelry and things that defy description; and The Children's Store and The Toy Corner for quality clothing, toys and games. Other special shops are Minata, a jewelry and gift shop, Storehouse Furniture and De Gustibus (fine cigars, wines and other delicacies). There's a K & W Cafeteria in addition to several fast-food restaurants, including Chick-Fil-A.

University Mall is currently undergoing renovations and additions that will include a food court, among other improvements.

Shopping Centers

Raleigh

Raleigh has long served as a regional shopping area for eastern North Carolina and it continues to hold that reputation. It is where people come to buy the fancy shoes and special dress or the delicate dessert and dry wine they can't find in Smalltown, NC. Raleigh is also where many people come for their "big ticket" items at discount prices. The trend of off-pricing or discount buying of brand names has made it a more competitive market.

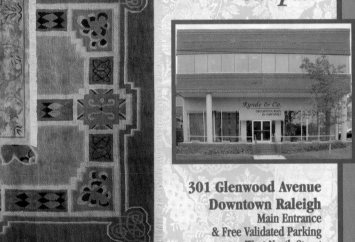
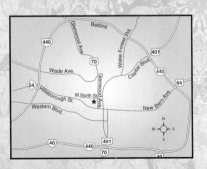

Apex...
The Peak of Good Living

DESIGN GROUP SOUTH

Interior Design Services and Home Furnishings

118 N. Salem Street
Apex

919-363-9951

Basket Tree Florist

We Deliver Happiness
Over 35 Years of Experience

100 N. Salem St.
Apex

919-362-7680

dare to be
Different
gift shoppe

Home Decor • Florals
Garden Accents • Espresso Bar

122 N. Salem Street
Apex

919-362-6207

Ashworth Village...

Fashion,
Gifts
Accessories

107 W. Chatham Street
919-388-8446

**A Fine Consignment Shop
For Women**

200 S. Academy Street
Upper Level
919-481-1151

DANIELLE HUNTER
LIMITED

Inspired Design, Meticulous
Craftsmanship, Designer Line
Jewelry in Platinum, Eighteen
Karat and Sterling Silver

200 S. Academy Street
919-460-2500

the Heart of Cary

Historic
Brightleaf Square

Yesterday's Charm
Today's Place to Be

Cameron Village

Tyler House

Fashion To Fit
Your Lifestyle

432 Daniels St.
Cameron Village, Raleigh
919-833-2979

The Globetrotter
LUGGAGE, LEATHERGOODS AND GIFTS

Our Customers Are
Going Places

417 Daniels St.
Cameron Village, Raleigh
919-828-1226

The Beltline at Six Forks Rd.
North Hills Mall, Raleigh
919-782-6936
www.theglobetrotter.com

Lavender and Lace

The Finest Selection of Linen,
Lingerie, Toiletries and Baby Gifts.

400 Daniels St.
Cameron Village, Raleigh
919-828-6007
www.lavenderlace.citysearch.com

Cameron Village

THOMPSON·LYNCH COMPANY

Fine Lamps, Shades, Repairs,
Accessories, Antiques

439 Daniels St.
Cameron Village, Raleigh
919-821-3599

Falls of the Neuse Rd.
Northridge Shopping Center, Raleigh
919-872-7253

The Athlete's Foot®

For straight laced comfort
see our expert shoe fitters.
We carry all major brands.
Locally owned.

419-B Daniels St.
Cameron Village, Raleigh
919-828-3487

THE COOK'S CHOICE

The cook's store with
so much more!

2028 Cameron St.
Cameron Village, Raleigh
919-821-8450
www.cookschoice.citysearch.com

Shop in the Village...

Follow the Cobblestones to City Market

Sally Huss Gallery

For Gifts That Touch The Heart
This Upbeat Gallery Has
Something For Everyone

309 Blake Street, Raleigh
919-833-0809

Magnolia Marketplace, Cary
651 Cary Towne Blvd.
919-319-0505

Sweet Tea & Grits, Inc.

Southern Pottery At Its Best…
And Other Neat Stuff!
Specializing in Regional Art
Pottery • Jewelry • Art
Coffee and Dessert Bar

307 Blake Street, Raleigh

919-834-7752
www.sweetteaandgrits.com

The Brass Key Inc.

Baldwin Brass 30% Off
The Triangle's Best Selection
of Home Accessories,
Collectibles and Fine Gifts

317 Blake Street, Raleigh

919-828-9126

Discover...

Golden Leaf Tea Room

Unique Atmosphere, Exceptional
Service, Delicious Food

Serving Lunch Tuesday through
Saturday and Sunday Brunch

105 S. Main St.
919-557-5355

BOSTIC *and* WILSON

Purveyors of Fine
Antiques and Collectibles

12,000 Square Feet Showroom

105 S. Main St.
919-552-3248

Ann's DIAMOND CENTER

Small Town Service and
Values on a Grand Scale

201 S. Main St.
919-552-3548

Fuquay~Varina

GIFT *Selections* LTD.

Extraordinary Home Decor, Gifts and Collectibles!

Authorized Bradford Exchange and Ashton -Drake Galleries Dealer

301 S. Main St.
919-552-3742

Hoke Powell Interiors

Shop with Hoke Powell Interiors for complete one-on-one customer service and design!

101 S. Main St.
919-552-2004

Sandi's Catering of Fuquay

Simple Elegance…
Simple Excellence…
Simply the Best!

817 Bradley Rd.
919-552-8964

Directory of
Stores, Services & Eateries

MAJOR STORES
Bed, Bath & Beyond
Dick's Sporting Goods
Linens 'N Things
Marshalls
Office Max/Copy Max
REI
Service Merchandise
Stein Mart
Toys 'R' Us

EATERIES
Atlanta Bread Company
Chick-fil-A
China King
HoneyBaked Ham Company
Juice It Up
Kashin Restaurant
Olive Garden
Red Lobster
Remington Grill
Ruby Tuesday
Ryan's Family Steakhouse
Sbarro
Subway
Steak N' Hoagie Shop

SPORTING GOODS & APPAREL
Omega Sports
Play It Again Sports
TSI Soccer

ELECTRONICS, MUSIC & ENTERTAINMENT
Coconuts Music & Movies
The Computer Exchange, Inc.
Music Go Round
Radio Shack
TopLine Cellular

HOME FURNISHINGS & DECOR
Art & Frame Gala
Classical Clocks
Leather Center
My Room
Pier 1 Imports
Twist & Turns
Woodwise Interiors

BOOKS & CARDS
Bookstar
Lynn's Hallmark

FITNESS & BEAUTY
General Nutrition Center
Jenny Craig Weight Loss Center
Mitchell's Hair Styling
Nail Time
Trade Secrets

SHOES
Just For Feet
Pic 'n Pay Shoes
Rack Room Shoes

SERVICES
American Airlines Ticket Office
Children's Discovery Center
Countrywide Home Loans
Crossroads Chiropractic
Crossroads Travel & Cruise Centre
Dental Works
East Coast Cleaners
Nationwide Insurance
Optometric Eye Care

SPECIALTY MERCHANDISE
Barbeques Galore
Kid to Kid
Party City
Pet Depot Superstore
Tinder Box

MEN'S APPAREL & ACCESSORIES
Gingiss Formalwear
Men's Wearhouse
S & K Famous Brands Menswear

WOMEN'S APPAREL & ACCESSORIES
Catherine's
Dress Barn
Paul Harris
Sizes Unlimited
USA Designer Discounts

crossroads
plaza

**Located on Walnut Street
off US 1/64 in Cary**

Olde Raleigh Village

The Bare Wall

Where framing becomes an art and quality is essential.

3201-131 Edwards Mill Rd.
Raleigh

919-787-5528

Serotta's

Designer Furs, Storage on Premises, Cashmere Coats, Cocktail Dresses, Sportswear and Fine Leathers

3201-139 Edwards Mill Rd.
Raleigh
919-789-9535

Waverly Place, Cary
919-859-3600

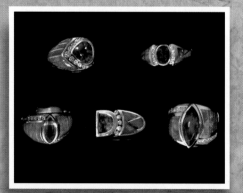

Sparrowood
JEWELERS

Full Service Jeweler
Contemporary and
Designer Styles
Jewelry and Watch Repair

3201-137 Edwards Mill Rd.
Raleigh

919-781-0212

The adventurous shopper will not be disappointed with Raleigh.

A new regional mall, the 1.4 million-square-foot Triangle Tower Center, is under development at the intersection of Capital Boulevard and Old Wake Forest Road. It is scheduled to open in late 2001 and will feature five anchor department stores, 160 specialty shops and a food court. Another regional mall over one million square feet, Brier Creek, has been proposed for west Raleigh near Research Triangle Park. Plans are also in the works for a 226,000-square-foot cinema and retail entertainment complex off Capital Boulevard called the MARQ.E. It is set to open in fall 1999.

Cameron Village Shopping Center
Oberlin Rd. and Clark Ave.

Cameron Village is the city's third largest shopping center, celebrating its 50th anniversary in 1999. When it opened on November 17, 1949, Cameron Village was the Southeast's first outdoor shopping center. One of the most popular shopping destinations in the Triangle, the Village underwent extensive renovation in the '90s.

Cameron Village is known for its large number of locally owned, family stores and shops. Some families have been affiliated with the Village since the '50s, such as Nowell's and Burton's, both fine clothing stores; Thompson-Lynch Company, which in addition to selling fine lamps, shades and accessories can make your old lamp new again; The Hobby Shop; Village Book & Stationery, and Medlin-Davis, cleaners of distinction. Dina Porter offers fine crafts and women's fashions. Tyler House offers some of the smartest styles for women of all ages. Other specialty women's clothing stores include Beanie & Cecil, Cameron Clothing, Christian's, Galatea, Pea in the Pod, Razooks, SoHo, Talbot's and Uniquities. Georgiano's shoe salon carries the finest European ladies shoes, handbags and accessories. The expert shoe fitters at The Athlete's Foot will help you find the perfect fit. Lavender and Lace carries an incredible selection of fine linens, lingerie, toiletries and baby gifts. Nowell's and Joseph A. Bank Clothiers offers a wide selection of quality men's suits and apparel for all occasions. Gentleman's Choice offers an extensive line of formal wear.

For estate and one-of-a-kind fine jewelry, the Elaine Miller Collection is unsurpassed. Other Village jewelers include:

Photo by Tim Johnson

Cameron Village, one of the Southeast's first shopping centers, is known for its large number of locally owned, family shops.

Jolly's Jewelers, Monte Cristo's, Bailey's Fine Jewelry and Charlotte's Jewelry & Gifts.

Cook's Choice is literally a dream store for the home chef, where you can find just about anything for the kitchen from unique utensils and gadgets to designer dinnerware. Discover solutions to home organization and storage problems at Hold Your Own.

Antiques Emporium offers a wide array of traditional antiques. Together with Carolina Antique Mall and George McNeil Antiques, the Village is a popular stop for antique shoppers looking for something different.

Accipiter is the place to find eclectic gifts and custom made furniture. The Globetrotter will meet all your luggage and leathergoods needs. Jill Flink Fine Art features contemporary and original local artists, as well as framing, photo developing and hard to find art supplies. Other Village favorites include: Frances T. King, Stationery, Past and Presents, Ten Thousand Villages, Quintessentials, Danneburg Galleries, Pine Box, Dolls Plus, Party Shop, Junior League Bargain Box, CEO's Executive Gifts and Parsley, Sage & Rosemary.

Big Sky Bread Company bakes fresh specialty breads, muffins and cookies and is a great place to have lunch in the Village. The Fresh Market is a specialty food store. Foster's, The Village Deli, Leon's Deli, Piccola Italia, Second City Grill and K & W Cafeteria are some of the favorite eating places located in Cameron Village. It has the city's most popular library branch, too. Check it out.

City Market
Downtown, Moore Square

Two blocks east of the Fayetteville Street Mall in the Moore Square Art District is the City Market complex that is attracting artists and craftspeople as well as new customers

Photo by Tim Johnson

Billed as "a family adventure," the State Farmers Market at Lake Wheeler Road and I-440 provides shoppers with an abundance of fresh fruit and vegetables.

to downtown. Historic old buildings house unique establishments with collectible antiques. Artspace offers artisans both a place to work and to sell their goods. For adult fun, laugh it up at ComedySportz. Also don't miss The Brass Key for unique gifts, The American Indian Company, Sweet Tea & Grits for Southern pottery, Sally Huss Gallery, Maximilian Home Accents and Amazing Glaze Ceramics. Some of the most popular restaurants in the Triangle are located in City Market, such as Big Ed's City Market Restaurant, Greenshield's, The Aussie Pub and Restaurant and Vic's Italian Cafe.

The Falls Centre
Old Wake Forest and Falls of Neuse Rds.

The Falls Centre offers a variety of stores to meet your family's shopping needs, including Stein Mart, Office Depot, Party City, GNC, The Cosmetic Center and Jo-Ann Fabrics.

State Farmers Market
Lake Wheeler Rd. & I-440, Raleigh
• 733-7417

This state-operated market is located near the southern half of the Beltline interchange and Lake Wheeler Road and provides shoppers from across the state with the garden bounty of area farmers as well as seasonal produce, such as citrus fruits, trucked in from neighboring states. It's open year round every day except Christmas. Saturday is usually the busiest day. It's the place to go in season to get fresh produce, often from the person who grew it: strawberries, blueberries, shelled black-eyed peas, sweet corn, tomatoes, yams, watermelon, you name it. Here you will find your Halloween pumpkin or that perfectly shaped Christmas tree.

In April, Buildings One and Two are in full bloom with flowers and bedding plants. The Garden Center features Family Home & Garden, which has stores in Apex and Raleigh.

In the market specialty shops you'll find Ford's Fancy Fruits "The North Carolina Store" and The Fudge Master's Factory and Candy Garden. For those who want their fresh produce or seafood already prepared, The Farmers Market Restaurant serves breakfast and lunch and N.C. Seafood, famous for its fried shrimp, serves lunch and dinner.

As the sign leading into the Farmers Market proclaims, it's "more than fresh vegetables, it's a family adventure." Indeed, for some, Saturday morning at the Farmers Market is a family tradition.

Photo by Tim Johnson

Centered around a restored 1914 marketplace, City Market features offbeat shops and art galleries, as well as eclectic restaurants.

Greystone Village
Leadmine and Sawmill Rds.

The quaint stone architecture makes this center remarkable. Greystone Village is the home to several popular restaurants such as Imperial Garden and Fins.

North Ridge
Falls of Neuse and Spring Forest Rds.

Built in 1980 at a key intersection, near North Ridge Country Club, this strip shopping center includes a locally owned French restaurant, Jean-Claude's, and the popular China Inn restaurant, which serves the best lunch buffet in this part of town. Thompson-Lynch Company has a fine selection of lamps, shades and accessories.

Oak Park
U.S. 70 W. and Holly Ridge Rd.

A vintage, late '50s shopping center, Oak Park was built to accommodate its namesake residential development nearby. For shoppers, it has a diverse lineup including Bernina's World of Sewing, Heirlooms and Accents fine furniture, an auto parts store and Hertzberg Furs. Maus Piano, which sells Baldwins and provides tuning, has been around since 1934. Oak Park also has a friendly tavern with the atmosphere of a neighborhood pub. The Peddler steakhouse and Casa Carbone, one of the oldest Italian restaurants in town, are both located here.

Olde Raleigh Village
Edwards Mill and Duraleigh Rds.

Anchored by a Harris Teeter supermarket, Olde Raleigh Village contains over 25 stores, including Serotta's, women's fine fashions; Sparrowood Jewelers; The Bare Wall, frame shop and gallery; Trillium gift shop and art gallery; The French Knot, a unique needlepoint shop; K & S Cafeteria; Crowley's Courtyard restaurant; Second Nature Cafe; and an Eckerd Drug store.

Pleasant Valley Promenade
Glenwood Ave.

Best Buy, Marshall's, Office Max, Michael's, Pleasant Valley Cinema, Zany Brainy, Bikes USA and a host of specialty shops and restaurants can all be found at Pleasant Valley Promenade.

Six Forks Station
Strickland and Six Forks Rds.

This neighborhood shopping center includes a Food Lion, Eckerd Drug and K-mart as major tenants. Big attractions are Waccamaw pottery and Sixforks 6, a six-screen movie complex in the southwest corner. You won't go hungry here either with the K & S Cafeteria and O'Charley's.

Stonehenge Market
Creedmoor Rd.

This shopping center, located along Creedmoor Road, contains 39 retail and service stores, including Harris Teeter, Eckerd Drug, Stein Mart, Discount Pet Supply and a post office. A Crowley's restaurant is located here.

Tower Shopping Complex
U.S. 64 and I-440

Built at Raleigh's main gateway to the east, this strip center quickly established itself in the late '50s as a shopping place for east Raleigh residents as well as commuters from suburbs such as Knightdale and Wendell. Behind the Tower center is another discount shopping center. Together, they contain eight theaters, two in the shopping center strip, Tower Twin, and another six in a complex around back, Tower Merchants 6, and fast-food restaurants proliferate in and around the strip. It has service operations like dry cleaners, animal clinics and shoe repair shops, as well as name-brand stores like Advance Auto Parts, The Finish Line and The Rack Room.

FYI

Unless otherwise noted, the area code for all phone numbers listed in this guide is 919.

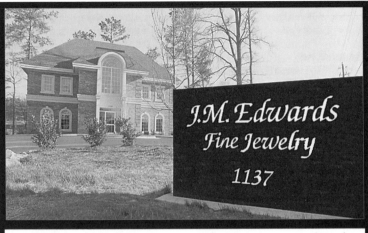

Cary

Cary's record-breaking residential growth is driving its retail growth. The biggest attractions are the Cary Towne Center, an enclosed mall that rivals Raleigh's Crabtree Valley Mall in space, and Crossroads Plaza, a collection of large, mostly discount, national chains. Park Place Shopping Center on N.C. 54 in Morrisville is currently under development with a 16-screen movie theatre complex, Park Place 16, and Golden Corral, which will soon be joined by a Food Lion, other restaurants and specialty shops.

Ashworth Village Center
115 W. Chatham St.

Located in downtown Cary, this village center is a collection of specialty shops. Some of our favorite shops include Chocolate Smiles, a candy lover's paradise; Ordinary and Extraordinary; Suzanne's gift shop; and Adria's fashion, gifts and accessories. Also check out Ashworth Drugs, an old-fashioned corner drugstore. Serendipity Gourmet Deli serves creative sandwiches, soups and salads. Ashworth Village recently expanded by 12,000 feet, adding a variety of new retail establishments, including Once Upon a Time children's boutique, Danielle Hunter Limited jewelry and Annie's Attic, a fine consignment shop. Also located downtown is Little Squash, an exclusive children's clothing store.

Cary Village Square
Cary Towne Blvd. and Walnut St.

Cary Village Square includes a consignment marketplace that contains about 150 showspaces featuring art, furniture, fine antiques, pottery, garden accessories and more. Other stores include T.J. Maxx, Real

Wood Furniture, and The Frame Up Gallery. For dining, you'll find Coyote Cafe, CiCis Pizza, Courtney's, Jersey Mike's and others.

Cornerstone
Corner of High House Rd. and Davis Dr.

The primary anchor here is a Lowes Foods superstore. Locally owned Carbonated Video, Rudino's Pizza, Connolly's Irish Pub, Art Connection Art Gallery, Goodberry's and PostNet postal and business services are also located here.

Crescent Commons
Kildaire Farm Rd. at Tryon Rd.

Across the street from Waverly Place is one of the area's most attractive shopping centers. Here you'll find a Harris Teeter superstore and Cary's first Wal-Mart, with a brick front. The center also has many locally owned businesses, including Wild Birds Unlimited, The Paper Company, Affinity Gifts, Frame Masters & Awards, specializing in unique framing of family treasures, MailBoxes, Etc., TGI Fridays, Blockbuster Video and Tudor Rose Tea Room.

Kroger Plaza
Kilmayne Dr.

This neighborhood shopping center is located off Kildaire Farm Road and features a Kroger supermarket, open 24 hours. The center also includes Brother's Pizza, Sewing Solutions and Zero's Subs.

MacGregor Village Shopping Center
Near U.S. 64 and U.S. 1

MacGregor Village is a neighborhood shopping center best known for its restaurants. Along with established favorites, Jimmy V's Steakhouse, Fox and Hound, Horwitz's Deli and Hickory Honey Glazed

Bargain hunters head to the State Fairgrounds Flea Market on weekends searching for a diamond in the rough.

Hams and Cafe, you will find Tony's Bourbon Street Oyster Bar, Canton Buffet and Caffe Piazza. It also has an Eckerd Drug, Artistic Hair Designers and Spa Health Club. Renovations and additions that include a new gourmet grocery store are planned for the near future.

Maynard Crossing
Maynard Rd. and High House Rd.

Anchored by a Kroger superstore, Maynard Crossing also includes Bayleaf Peddler, Jerry Miller Art Gallery, Blockbuster Video. Restaurants include The Ground Finale coffee shop and cafe, Philly Steak Factory, Il Sogno and Brigs.

Preston Corners
Corner of Cary Pkwy. and High House Rd.

Made up of four corners of retail shops and professional buildings, Preston Corners also offers branches of BB&T, CCB, First Citizens, First Union and Wachovia. For dining, you'll find McDonald's, Jersey Mike's Subs, China Gate, El Dorado, Jasper's, The Bermuda Room Sports Pub and Roly Poly rolled sandwiches, among others. Hannaford's grocery store is one of the anchors, and you'll also find an ABC Store, a Pet Mania, a Howard Perry & Walston office, The Flower Basket, Manhattan Bagel and Bruegger's Bagels, Jitter's and Caribou Coffee Company, and a Carolina Pharmacy.

Saltbox Village
Kildaire Farm Rd.

Saltbox Village is home to some of Cary's unique shops. Cary Insiders soon find out about The Fresh Market, Possibilities, a women's clothing boutique, Pattywhacks, an upscale children's boutique, Advanced Audio, Science Safari, D'Nardy's, The Spin Cycle, Write Image specialty stationery and Saltbox Valet, a very popular local dry cleaner. Outback Steakhouse is also located here.

South Hills Mall and Plaza
U.S. 1 and Buck Jones Rd.

South Hills is a community mall and adjacent service plaza that features several unique stores, specialty shops, services and eateries. This shopping center is anchored by the newly remodeled and expanded Burlington Coat Factory and Michael's—The Arts and Crafts Store. Country Sonshine offers a wide variety of home decor choices. South Hills also has a host of locally owned businesses such as Carroll's Office Supply, George Bryant's Florist & Gifts, American Nostalgia collectibles and Sew-N-Vac, to name a few. Two of the newest speciality shops are Carolina Custom Golf and Grand Asia Market. The mall also includes Kerr Drug, Mitchell's Hairstyling and United Fabrics. A branch office of the N.C. License and Title Agency also makes South Hills its home. A K&S Cafeteria opened here in the fall of 1998.

Waverly Place
Kildaire Farm and Tryon Rds.

This uniquely designed bi-level shopping plaza with an outside escalator, fountain and outdoor sculpture is conveniently located near Lochmere and Regency Park. Here you'll find Merle Norman, Eckerd Drug, Amazing Glaze, Workbench, Sundram Rug Gallery and several restaurants such as China Pearl, PieWorks, Red Hot and Blue, Paradigm Coffee House and Gregory's. You'll also find a movie complex, Waverly Place 6, and Cary Travel.

Wellington Park
Cary Parkway and Tryon Rd.

One of Cary's newest strip shopping centers, Wellington Park, is anchored by Lowes Foods and also includes Bedroom and Sofa Emporium, Carbonated Video, Learning Express, Discount Pet Supply, The Bermuda Room Sports Pub, Grill '57, J. Gilbert's Wood-Fired Grill, among others.

Durham

With several dozen shopping centers and malls in and around Durham, it's a shopper's paradise. The area offers hundreds of retail outlets, from major department stores, like Dillard's, Hecht's and Belk's

to discount houses, and specialty boutiques. In addition, a Chicago developer has proposed a regional mall of over one million square feet at Fayetteville Road and I-40 in south Durham. The mall, tentatively called Southpoint Center, is scheduled to open in 2000, featuring five anchor department stores including Nordstrom, 120 specialty shops, five restaurants and a movie theater.

Here's our guide to the major malls as well as some other special places to browse and shop in Durham.

Brightleaf Square
Gregson and West Main Sts.

In 1980 a couple of local businessmen saw potential beauty in the twin giant American Tobacco Company warehouses at the corner of Gregson and West Main streets. They worked painstakingly to preserve and display the all-heart-pine beams, 20-inch-thick brick walls and ornate chimneys. Several years later, what had become a symbol of economic decline was resurrected as an upscale shopping center called Brightleaf Square.

Here, you'll find Millennium Music and Collections, an upscale woman's clothing boutique. The Glassworks Gallery at Goldworks, Horizon and Tyndall galleries offer fine art and crafts. Antique stores include LaFayette Antiques and James Kennedy Antiques, don't miss Wentworth & Leggett Old Rare Books and Goldworks jewelry. Food is plentiful as well with El Rodeo, Satisfaction, Taverna Nikos, one of the best Greek restaurants in the Triangle, and Brightleaf 905, Brightleaf's newest restaurant serving world cuisine. Across the street in the Brightleaf Shopping District you will find Fowler's Market and Morgan Imports.

Erwin Square
Ninth St.

Located adjacent to historic Ninth Street, the Erwin Square complex occupies the former Burlington Industries textile plant.

Shops here include Jewelsmith, K. Peterson for leathergoods and Jos. A. Banks, a men's clothier. Restaurants are The Market Place, Cafe Parizade and The Mad Hatter's Bake Shop.

Homestead Market
N.C. 54 and Fayetteville Rd.

This shopping center is anchored by a Harris Teeter supermarket, Kerr Drug and Rose's. Other stores and shops include David Michael jewelers and Optometric Eye Care Center. You can also take your driver's license exam or get your license renewed at the N.C. Driver's License Examiners office here.

Loehmann's Plaza
1821 Hillandale Rd.

The Plaza is home to the anchor store Loehmann's, offering great discounts on women's designer clothes, and a number of small shops, including Michelle's Fine Jewelry and Gifts. Loehmann's Plaza also features Papa's Grill, a casual cafe.

New Hope Commons
U.S. 15-501 and I-40, Durham

A long-awaited shopping center for both Chapel Hill and Durham, New Hope Commons provides shoppers of both cities with quite a choice of discount shops. Anchor tenants Wal-Mart, Best Buy, Marshall's and Office Max offer low prices and huge selections. Other stores include Barnes & Noble bookstore, Uptons department store, the Old Navy Clothing Company, Chesapeake Bagel Bakery, Michael's, craft supply store, Zany Brainy, Bikes USA and Linens 'n Things. There's ample parking and the shops offer something for everyone.

Ninth Street
West Durham

Ninth Street is neither a shopping center nor a mall. It is a charming commercial block in west Durham that grew up around the Erwin Cotton Mill, a neighborhood that in the past decade has made a comeback. Mosey on down to the two blocks of Ninth Street running

Staff Photo

Spend a day at historic Brightleaf Square, a shopping center housed in a cluster of restored tobacco warehouses in downtown Durham.

between Hillsborough Road and West Main Street, within walking distance of Duke University's East Campus. Here's a sample of what you'll find.

Shops include Earth & Spirit, with gifts from the earth, Vaguely Reminiscent, a boutique featuring stylish natural-fiber garments and fun accessories and Look Out!, with catalog clothing for men and women at outlet prices. An Insiders' favorite is The Regulator Bookshop, offering a great selection of books and the best assortment in town of left-liberal newspapers, magazines, bizarre postcards and more. Check out One World Market (on Perry Street) and Zola for art, crafts and jewelry. Keep on walking and you'll find an exotic ice cream, pastry and chocolate shop called Francesca's Dessert Caffe. In the old Wachovia Bank Building, you'll now find Bruegger's Bagel Bakery. Nearby is Schoolkids Records, Eno Traders, Sandy Creek Children's Bookstore (just off Ninth on Perry Street), The Play House, a wonderful toy store and The Duck Store for Duke memorabilia. Be sure to stop at McDonald's Drug Store, which one local writer called "the beating heart of Ninth Street." Here you can ask for an old-fashioned soda (or even an egg cream, if you please) while you wait for your prescription to be filled. Popular restaurants include George's Garage and Blue Corn Cafe.

Two blocks away on Broad Street is Owen's Broad Street Diner and Wellspring, a market of natural, organic and gourmet foods, including naturally grown meats and whole-grain baked goods.

Oak Creek Village
U.S. 15-501 and Garrett Rd.

Oak Creek features T.J. Maxx, the designer-label discount clothing and housewares store, Rack Room Shoes and Hit or Miss. Other stores include a Pet Depot, waterbed store and cellular phone outlet. Restaurants at Oak Creek include Chili's Grill & Bar, Panda Inn, CiCi's Pizza and Subway sandwiches.

Woodcroft Shopping Center
Hope Valley Rd. and N.C. 54

There are many shopping centers in Durham about the size of Woodcroft: 20 stores anchored by a chain supermarket, a bank and a fast-food eatery. We're making a fuss over this one because it was done with style and sensitivity to its location. The entire mall is done in earth-toned brick. The awnings are uniform evergreen. Even the McDonald's has class and, by the way, no golden arches.

The reason may be that Woodcroft has a captive shopping audience located conveniently next door in the planned residential development by the same name. Shops include The Little Professor Book Center, Woodcroft Optical and Kerr Drug. Restaurants include Bandido's, Pulcinellas and Yamazushi.

Chapel Hill

From boutiques to malls, Chapel Hill offers the range of shopping choices you might expect to find in any growing, university community. Here's a quick guide to Franklin Street, the major shopping centers and malls.

Downtown Franklin Street

This is Chapel Hill's main thoroughfare, the first place UNC students and visitors hit when they wander off campus or drive through town. As a result, Franklin Street has its fair share of places for cheap eats, Carolina paraphernalia and basic collegiate clothing. Though many Franklin Street businesses are designed with the college community in mind, they also have plenty to offer the over 25 crowd.

Favorite clothing stores on East Franklin include Anjana's, Mia and Barr-Ee Station, which specializes in catalog clothing (J. Crew and Tweeds among them), and Julian's for top-quality menswear. Designer Alexander Julian has also opened Julian's Home an upscale furnish-

Photo by Robert Thomason

A variety of new retail establishments are sprouting all over downtown Carrboro, a former cluster of textile mills.

ings store. If you need a special gift or a fine new watch, try longtime jewelers Wentworth & Sloan.

The downtown area also has three cinema houses with six screens: The Varsity I and II, which offer first runs and foreign films, The Ram Triple on Rosemary Street and the Carolina Theatre on the corner of Franklin and Columbia streets. Ice cream and frozen yogurt aficionados can choose from Swensen's, Ben and Jerry's and The Yogurt Pump. Restaurants include Spanky's, Top of the Tower, Carolina Coffee Shop, Rathskellar and Bandido's.

The west end of Franklin Street features specialty shops like Time After Time, which sells vintage clothing, small decorative items and jewelry. Close by is Modern Times, where local clothing designer Lisa Heyward purveys her creations. Further down the block is Uniquities, featuring Betsy Johnson and Nicole Miller fashions. Another shop you'll want to visit is Hill Country Woodworks, where you will find handmade contemporary furniture. For authentic Middle-Eastern food like stuffed grape leaves and tabouli, The Mediterranean Deli is delicious, fast and friendly. Other favorites include 411 West and The Wicked Burrito.

West Franklin is also home to a number of secondhand bookstores. They're all great places for an hour's browse.

Further down East Franklin, heading toward Durham, there is Photo Quick, a good place for black and white film developing and Dickinson Garden Center.

Carrboro's Main Street

If you continue west on Franklin Street, you will eventually run into Carrboro's Main Street. Just as you enter Carrboro, you'll see Nice Price Books in the white and hot pink little house. On the right, a block or so before you cross the railroad tracks, you'll find Surplus Sids, a good source for military gear, rain slickers and old jeans. Further down is Carr Mill Mall.

Keep heading west and at the corner of Main Street and Greensboro you'll find Cliff's Meat Market, an independently owned butcher shop offering an assortment of quality meats and fresh seafood.

Continuing west, don't miss one of our favorite shops, the PTA Thrift Shop, where you'll find unbelievable bargains among the castoffs of Chapel Hill's well-dressed contributors. Proceeds go to the Chapel Hill-Carrboro schools via the PTA.

Just up Main Street from the PTA, look for the North Carolina Crafts Gallery, showcasing ceramic pieces, jewelry, woodwork and more, all made in the Tar Heel state.

Carr Mill Mall
Downtown Carrboro

Some year's ago, Julian Carr's old cotton mill was converted into an upscale shopping village. A group of local citizens and businesses banded together to preserve and transform the dormant mill into one of the area's most unique shopping centers, the Carr Mill Mall. The careful restoration of the original brick exterior, heart-pine interior and other fine architectural details highlight the original structure. It now houses more than two dozen businesses including the fashionable Talbot's clothing store and other fine specialty shops like The Clock Works Again (antique and contemporary clocks and clock repairs) Benchmark Furnishings, Mandarin Gazebo (a gift shop), Monire's Jewelers, Mulberry Silks, O'Neill's (for menswear), Ali Cat Toys, Animation and Fine Art Galleries, Gallery Americas furniture and A New Attitude a women's clothing boutique. The mall is anchored by a Harris Teeter supermarket and CVS, a drug store on one side and Weaver Street Market on the other. The Carr Mill Mall is currently undergoing a 4,000-square-foot expansion.

The Courtyard
W. Franklin St., Chapel Hill

You won't believe that this office and retail complex tucked into Chapel Hill's West Franklin Street was once a milk processing plant. Today, The Courtyard features Pyewacket restaurant, The Stock Exchange, an upscale consignment clothing store for women, Pipes by George, a hair salon, and a number of offices.

Eastgate Shopping Center
E. Franklin St. and U.S. 15-501

Eastgate has many noteworthy features setting it apart from the run-of-the-mill shopping center. First, there's A Southern Season, offering a dazzling assortment of fine wines, coffees, nuts, cheeses, crackers, chocolates and other gourmet goodies, as well as The Weathervane cafe. Other Eastgate attractions are the Potted Plant, for a wide array of house plants; Workbench, a locally owned store belonging to the largest contemporary furniture chain in the country; and Eastgate BP.

There's also The Bentwood, for contemporary furniture and accessories for the home; Steinway Gallery, offering everything from art prints to oil paintings; Joe Rowand's Somerhill Art Gallery; and Black Mountain, for handwrought gold and silver jewelry. The Wild Bird Center and Womancraft are great for gifts, and Hold Your Own or Minta Bell Interior Design can help with furnishing and decorating your home. Blockbuster Video, Eckerd Drug, Food Lion and Lynn's Hallmark are some other tenants. Good places to eat at Eastgate include The Loop, a casual place with something for the whole family, Sal's N.Y. Pizza (for family dining) and China Chef.

Fearrington Village
Chatham County

Six miles south of Chapel Hill, in rural Chatham County, lies a village complete with its own quaint post office, a pasture with grazing Belted Galloway cows, a market/cafe and an elegant inn and restaurant. Amidst this pastoral setting, you'll find a collection of unique shops, including Pringle's for pottery and gifts, A Stone's Throw for jewelry and gemstones,

INSIDERS' TIP

While you're in Carrboro, don't miss the Carrboro Farmers Market. In fact it's worth scheduling your Saturday shopping around it. It's open Wednesdays from 5-7 PM and Saturdays 7 AM-noon and is located at 301 W. Main Street in Carrboro. For more information call 732-6223.

Dovecote garden shop and McIntyre's Fine Books and Bookends.

Glen Lennox Shopping Center
N.C. 54 E., Chapel Hill

Located across from Glenwood Square, Glen Lennox Shopping Center is home to The Grill at Glen Lennox, one of Chapel Hill's most popular new restaurants. Other stores include Pace Gift Shop, Traditions Bridal Store and All Things Good gourmet take-out. At Glenwood Square is a Harris Teeter, Eckerd Drugs and the Thai Palace restaurant.

Ram's Plaza
U.S. 15-501, Chapel Hill

Across U.S. 15-501 from Eastgate, Ram's Plaza features several interesting places to shop. Dance Design is the place to go for dancewear and for costumes for parties and Halloween. There's also a florist, a women's fitness center, a tanning salon and Serenity Day Spa. Other businesses include a Sav-A-Center grocery store, Fred's Beds and a CVS drugstore. Just behind Ram's Plaza is Yarnell-Hoffer, a locally owned hardware store that stocks or will special order almost anything you need to fix up your home.

Timberlyne
Weaver Dairy Rd., Chapel Hill

This growing shopping center on Weaver Dairy Road includes Tsing Tao restaurant, Timberlyne Hardware and the Chelsea Theatres. Other shops and businesses include Framemakers, Small World Travel, Cup A Joe, Margaret's Cantina, Bud and Eb's Grill and J & J Deli. The U.S. Post Office also has a branch here. Movies at Timberlyne, a seven-theatre complex, plays first-run features.

University Square
W. Franklin St., Chapel Hill

University Square is a small shopping center located on West Franklin Street, just a few steps away from the UNC campus. It offers a diverse mix of shops and restaurants, geared to a wide range of tastes and budgets. You can find quick fried chicken and biscuits at Time Out, open 24 hours, or designer clothes at Fine Feathers, with a lot in between. There's The Painted Bird that sells imported clothing for women and children and Central and South American crafts, Shoes at the Square with fine footwear for women, Peacock Alley, purveyor of fine gifts and accessories for the home, and Peacock's Nest, a garden shop. Browse at T'boli imports and The Whistlestop, both great sources for inexpensive and always unusual gift ideas. Stop at the Looking Glass Cafe or 35 Chinese restaurant for a bite to eat.

Village Plaza
Elliott Rd., Chapel Hill

The Village Plaza, located on Elliott Road, is anchored by Wellspring Grocery. Penguin's Cafe is located inside the store. There is a mini-mall here with The Cotton Boll for fine fabrics, the Design Workshop offering upholstery fabrics and design services, Lacock's Shoe Repair (also selling clogs and other shoes), Shaw Business Machines and other shops and services. Viking Travel and the Plaza Theatres are here, as well as Red Hot & Blue and Zorba's restaurants. You'll also find Knit-A-Bit, which provides a full selection of knitting and crochet yarns.

Across the street is the Galleria with specialty shops such as the Purple Puddle I and II, Plum Gardens, The World Traveller, Silk Quarters, Way Cool! for children's books and clothing, Baum Diamonds, Plaza Dry Cleaners and Mina's, a salon for women and men. The Chapel Hill Senior Center is adjacent to the Galleria shops. Located close by on Elliot Road is the Vacuum Cleaner Hospital.

Attractions

This is the chapter that needs to be in bright lights—Attractions!—because the entries here are places and events that you have to visit or attend before you can become an Insider. There's enough to keep you busy year round. And when friends or relatives visit, sit them down and get them to read this chapter first. Where else, for example, can they sample in one building—the General Assembly in Raleigh—all of North Carolina's wonderful accents?

For our sporting attractions such as the world-famous Durham Bulls, see our "Spectator Sports" section. For area events and festivals, such as the serendipitous July 4th Festival for the Eno, see our "Annual Events" section.

Raleigh

ALLTEL Pavilion at Walnut Creek
Sunnybrook and Rock Quarry Rds.
Concert Line: 831-6666
Ticketmaster: 834-4000

Built in 1991, the $13.5 million amphitheater holds about 20,000 people, 7,000 under the roof. Other patrons are seated on a great, green sloping hill from which they can view and hear the stage via giant video screens and a state-of-the-art digital sound system.

The amphitheater is part of the city's 240-acre Walnut Creek Park that also features the city's largest softball complex. Walnut Creek is one of the top spots for national tours. Recent acts include Shania Twain, Bob Dylan, Jimmy Buffett, Dixie Chicks, Tom Petty, Reba McEntire, Dave Matthews Band and Lenny Kravitz.

You can't bring cameras, lawn chairs, food or drink, so bring money for food and refreshments when you go. Parking is extra. Be sure to take a moment and stand on the top of the hill and soak up the glittering scene below you—it's where the stars come to shine!

Capital Area Visitor Center
301 N. Blount St. • 733-3456

You may want to start your downtown tour here because you'll sample our warm Southern hospitality along with generous helpings of information about the Capital City from the award-winning staff. The recently renovated Center, which is located in the 1918 Andrews-London House, welcomes more than 100,000 walk-in visitors annually and provides maps, brochures, a 15-minute orientation film about Raleigh and true Insider tips on gifts, artwork, restaurants, accommodations and history.

City Market
Management Office • 303 Blake St.
• 828-4555

The 1914 City Market, located on the south side of Moore Square in downtown, began an exciting rebirth in 1988. Today, the cobblestone streets are home to a tantalizing array of restaurants, shops and art galleries. Try the homemade brew at Greenshields, visit galleries displaying crafts by local and regional artisans, shop for fresh produce or eat a power breakfast at Big Ed's with local and state politicians and big-time lobbyists. Mounted police and old-fashioned trolley cars, complete with bells and finished with brass and mahogany, recall the elegance and pace of days gone by.

College Attractions

All of the colleges and universities draw big-name entertainment and speakers to the Triangle. NCSU's Reynold's Coliseum, the new Raleigh Entertainment and Sports Arena and UNC's Dean E. Smith Center ("The Dean Dome") are where the biggest entertainers show up during the winter months.

Exploris
201 E. Hargett St. • 834-4040

The world's first global learning center opened its doors downtown in October 1999, featuring hands-on exhibits, daily performances and programs for all ages. Exploris' attractions are brought to life by an expert program staff, a host of interactive computer activities, video and videoconferencing, the Internet, and art, sculpture and artifacts from around the globe. Plans for the center include a state-of-the-art IMAX Theater. It is open Tuesday through Saturday from 9 AM to 5 PM and Sunday from 12 to 5 PM.

The General Assembly
16 W. Jones St., Downtown • 733-4111

Some consider this the best attraction in town. The General Assembly used to officially meet on a biannual basis; however, the legislators come to town every year now, for what's called a Short or Long Session. Sessions of the House and Senate begin at 1:30 PM with the ringing of bells to alert stray legislators.

Sitting in the comfortable, red plush seats in the galleries, you can watch legislation being made. There is drama; there is comedy; there is tragedy; there is intrigue; and there is oratory, vintage Southern style. You can hear the Elizabethan accents of the state's Outer Banks, the rounded drawls of the coastal plains and the distinct twang of mountain vernacular. In one seat may sit the state's next governor and in another may sit the next subject of an FBI investigation. Where else in the state can you see a show that costs millions and spends billions and charges no admission? The General Assembly, up close and personal in Raleigh.

Historic Trolley Tours
Downtown • 834-4844

Narrated trolley tours begin at Mordecai Historical Park and wind through the heart

Photo by Tim Johnson

Watch the General Assembly in action at the North Carolina State Legislative Building, which was designed in the early 1960s by Edward Durell Stone, the renowned architect who also planned the John F. Kennedy Center for the Performing Arts in Washington, D.C.

of the Capital City, with stops at historical sites, art galleries, museums and City Market. The trolley runs every Saturday (except in January and February) from noon to 3:45 PM (the last trolley departs at 3 PM). The admission is $5 for adults, $2 for ages 7 to 17 and free for children 6 and under.

N.C. Museum of Art

(See "Visual Arts" section of our "Arts" chapter.)

N.C. State Fairgrounds
Hillsborough St. & Blue Ridge Rd.
• 733-2145

Events occur throughout the year at the N.C. State Fairgrounds. The most popular attraction of the year is the N.C. State Fair. The fair starts on the third Friday in October and runs for 10 days. Other popular attractions at the fairgrounds include the Ringling Brothers' Circus in February, the Southern Women's Show in April and numerous animal shows and civic events throughout the year. A Flea Market is held every weekend.

Raleigh City Museum
Briggs Building, Fayetteville St. Mall
• 832-3775

The 10,000-square-foot museum features fascinating exhibits, which change regularly, relating to the history of the Capital City. It is open 10 AM to 4 PM Tuesday through Friday and 1 to 4 PM Saturday and Sunday. The museum's gift store contains a variety of fascinating items. Admission is free and group tours are available.

Raleigh Convention & Conference Center
500 Fayetteville Street Mall • 831-6011

The $18 million Civic Center, which offers 100,000 square feet of interior space and can seat up to 4,000 concertgoers, is home to a number of special shows each year, including the Raleigh Antiques Extravaganza, the Southern Women's Show and the Home, Garden and Flower Show.

Raleigh Entertainment & Sports Arena
1400 Edwards Mill Rd. • 829-8132

Completed in the fall of 1999, this $158 million, 20,500-seat multipurpose arena serves as the home of the National Hockey League Carolina Hurricanes and the North Carolina State University Wolfpack men's basketball team. The arena also functions as a regional entertainment showcase, hosting such diverse acts as Disney on Ice, Limp Bizkit, World Wrestling Federation, TLC, James Taylor and Royal Lippizzaner Stallions.

Gardens

Beautiful gardens abound in and around Raleigh, and some consider Fayetteville Street Mall and the adjoining Government Mall two of the best landscapes in the state. Three area gardens are of special interest: the Raleigh Rose Garden, WRAL-TV's gardens and NCSU's J.C. Raulston Arboretum located on Beryl Road, near the Fairgrounds. The first two gardens are very popular for spring and summer weddings.

J.C. Raulston Arboretum
4301 Beryl Rd. • 515-7641

This is an Insiders' place and part of North Carolina State University's Horticulture Sciences Department. It is on Beryl Road, which runs parallel to Hillsborough Street just past Meredith College, toward the State Fairgrounds. Call first to check on the hours. The Arboretum is a wonderful collection of gardens and plants. Master gardener classes are offered and each spring you may take advantage of the Arboretum's plant sale.

Raleigh Rose Garden
301 Pogue St. • 821-4579

The Raleigh Rose Garden is on Pogue Street, two blocks off Hillsborough Street

Mordecai Historic Park contains the modest cabin where Andrew Johnson, the 17th president of the United States, was born in 1808.

where it runs in front of the NCSU campus. The garden is maintained by some of the city's garden clubs and includes an outdoor amphitheater.

WRAL Gardens
2619 Western Blvd. • 821-8576

On the other side of the NCSU campus are the WRAL gardens. They are open to the public most of the year and are a favorite location for intimate weddings.

Historic Homes

Four historic Raleigh homes are on any Insiders' list: The Governor's Mansion, the Joel Lane House (he's the fellow who sold the land that became Raleigh), the Mordecai House at Mordecai Park and Oak View.

Governor's Mansion
200 N. Blount St. • 733-3456

Call the number above for planning your tour, not for chatting with the Governor. The Mansion, officially called the

Executive Mansion, is where the Governor and his family live. The ground floors are open to the public. One of the most popular times for tours is during the December holiday season.

The Mansion is a classic example of Queen Anne Cottage-Style Victorian architecture, known as gingerbread style. The building was started in 1883 and completed in 1891, using mostly native North Carolina materials. The 40,000-square-foot house is filled with antiques and crystal chandeliers, many manufactured in North Carolina. It is a "working" mansion in that Governor Jim Hunt's family not only lives there but he also conducts much of the state's business and entertaining in the mansion and on the grounds. Tours take about 30 minutes and are open to the public in the fall and spring.

Joel Lane House
Hargett and St. Mary's Sts. • 833-3431

This renovated home and grounds was once part of a 1,000-acre plantation and considered the finest house within a

Photo by Tim Johnson

100-mile radius in the late 18th century. Built in 1760 by the man who later sold the state the property on which the capital city grew, the house is now maintained by volunteers. It is open to the public each Tuesday, Thursday and Friday from 10 AM until 2 PM and is available for receptions and meetings.

Mordecai House
1 Mimosa St. • 834-4844

Part of the city's parks system, the Mordecai House and grounds is a quiet spot downtown. Built in 1785, the house remained in the same family until the 1960s. Its furnishings span two centuries of styles. When the city acquired the home, officials were amazed at the treasure trove of antiques found in the dilapidated barn out back. The country's Bicentennial Celebration spurred interest and contributions and with the city's acquisition, the home has been preserved.

The grounds also contain the cabin in which Andrew Johnson, 17th president of the U.S., was born. There is a charming plantation chapel that can be reserved for small weddings. Hours are 10 AM to 4 PM Monday through Saturday and Sunday from 1 to 4 PM (the last tour each day starts at 3 PM). The Mordecai House is closed Tuesdays. Tours begin on the half hour and last one hour.

Oak View
The Beltline & Poole Road • 212-7248

Through the persistence of former Wake County Commissioner Merrie Hedrick, the county acquired this onetime farmstead and it is being restored as a historic site. Some of the buildings date back to before the Civil War and the complex contains the farmhouse, plank kitchen, carriage house, cotton gin house, gazebo,

family cemetery and a still-productive pecan grove. It's open 8:30 AM until 5 PM Monday through Saturday. Tours are available daily. Oak View can be rented for special events.

Government Buildings

As the capital city, Raleigh's most enduring attractions, perhaps, are its capital buildings near the Government Mall. Several can be seen in a day's walking tour and all are deserving of closer inspection. They are not only attractions; they're the state's heritage.

N.C. Museum of History
5 E. Edenton St. • 715-0200

This elegant building opened in 1994 across the street from the Capitol. It contains four grand display areas for North Carolina historical collections. You can visit the state's Sports Hall of Fame, a collection on folk life, a chronological history of the state and temporary exhibits detailing North Carolina's storied past. Recent exhibits included "Carolina Quilts" and "Health & Healing Experiences in North Carolina." The museum also offers a gift shop filled with items from North Carolina, most of them made in the state. The museum's open, spacious rooms make popular spots for government receptions. The collections include over 350,000 artifacts, photographs and videos and offer hands-on activities for children. Admission is free. The museum is closed on Mondays.

N.C. Museum of Natural Sciences
Bicentennial Plaza • 733-7450

Probably the most popular place in the capital among North Carolina's children, this aging museum is in the process of building

---

INSIDERS' TIP

You can take a free tour of a fully furnished solar-operated house at North Carolina State University's Solar Center, located at Western Boulevard and Gorman Street. Call 515-3799 for information.

Photo courtesy of N.C. Museum of Natural Sciences

When completed in the spring of 2000, the $60 million, 200,000-square-foot State Museum of Natural Sciences will be the largest natural history museum in the Southeast.

a new $60 million, 200,000-square-foot museum to be completed in spring 2000. The present museum sits between the Capitol and the Legislative Building and is home to thousands of preserved and living creatures. One emphasis is on the modern environment. Living creatures of all epochs are studied and presented. The Museum has a long list of classes for children and adults such as "The Killer Bees," "Indians of Eastern North America" and "Meet the Mammals." The new museum will house all 600,000 specimens, an auditorium, new classrooms and will include new exhibits such as the Fossil Hall, an animal conservatory, a hands-on science experiment center and Marine Hall. Admission is free. The Museum is open Monday through Saturday 9 AM to 5 PM, and Sunday 1 PM to 5 PM.

N.C. State Archives and Library
109 E. Jones St. • 733-3952

This shining white building serves several purposes: it holds the offices of the Secretary of Cultural Resources, the state's archives and the state library. The building also displays the original Carolina Charter of 1663. You will also find many people here researching their family trees. The Federation of North Carolina Historical Societies has its office here and there is a special section in the Library for genealogical research.

N.C. State Capitol
Capitol Square, Downtown • 733-4994

The recently renovated State Capitol building is the center of downtown, a landmark from the day it was built in 1840. The current structure is considered one of the best-preserved examples of Greek Revival architecture in the country with its columns, moldings and the honeysuckle crown atop the dome carefully patterned after certain Greek temples. It cost $532,682 to build which, at the time, was three times the state's annual income.

Looking around the Government Mall today, it's hard to believe that until the 1880s, the Capitol housed all of state government! The Capitol, which attracts over

250,000 visitors a year, is still in use. The Governor and his press office work here as does the Lieutenant Governor. Several legends surround the building, including one involving an escape tunnel and secret rooms. You can walk through between 8 AM and 5 PM during the week and 1 PM to 5 PM on Sunday. Tours may be scheduled through the Capital Area Visitor Center, 733-3456.

N.C. State Legislative Building
Corner of Jones and Halifax Sts.
• 733-7928

When the General Assembly outgrew the Capitol, the state employed famed Arkansas architect Edward Durrell Stone to design a new home for the legislators. The 206,000-square-foot building that resulted is every bit as classic as the Capitol. It has Stone's trademark colonnade of columns outside and soothing garden fountains inside. The building's native granite and its marble facing give it a sense of public majesty. Inside, the House and Senate chambers are within view of public galleries overhead. Weekdays, the building is open to the public. Unlike legislators, children must be accompanied by an adult.

N.C. State Supreme Court
Justice Building • Corner of Morgan and Fayetteville Sts.

This is not one of your tourist hot spots, but as the third branch of state government standing quietly across Morgan Street from the Capitol, it's worth notice. Ask the security guard at the entrance for instructions and go take a look at the court chambers where even the most aggressive lawyers mind their manners when arguing before the seven-member court.

Durham

Bennett Place
4409 Bennett Memorial Rd. • 383-4345

You don't have to be a Civil War buff to appreciate the significance of what occurred on the farm of James and Nancy Bennett in April 1865. It was in the Bennett's home that two battle-fatigued adversaries—generals Joseph E. Johnston and William T. Sherman—met to work out a peaceful settlement. Their original agreement was nixed in the wake of hostilities surrounding Abraham Lincoln's assassination, but their talks continued and eventually resulted in Johnston's surrender. It was the largest troop surrender of the Civil War, ending the fighting in the Carolinas, Georgia and Florida.

The Bennett grandchildren lived on the farm until 1890. A fire destroyed the farmhouse and kitchen in 1921. The present buildings were reconstructed in the 1960s from Civil War sketches and early photos. To get to Bennett Place, take the Hillsborough Road exit off U.S. 15-501 Bypass or Interstate 85 and follow the signs. It's open from 10 AM to 4 PM Tuesday through Saturday and from 1 AM to 4 PM Sunday. Call about extended summer hours. Admission is free and you can picnic on the grounds.

Downtown Historic District

Thanks to the Historic Preservation Society of Durham, in 1977 downtown Durham became the first solely commercial district to be placed on the prestigious National Register of Historic Places. Take a walk in and around the downtown loop and just look up: You'll be amazed at the

---

INSIDERS' TIP

A reconstructed 17th-century Occaneechi Indian village can be found on the banks of the Eno River within walking distance of downtown Hillsborough. It is the site of a Spring Cultural Festival held annually in June.

A replica of Antonio Canova's 1820 marble statue of George Washington, which was destroyed during the State House fire of 1831, stands in the center of the State Capitol's four-story rotunda.

exquisite facades and cornices of buildings dating back to the late 19th century. Begin your tour at the NationsBank building at the intersection of Main and Corcoran streets. The 1914 building sits on the property once owned by the city's founder, Dr. Bartlett Snipes Durham. Proceeding up Main Street you'll take in the Kress Building, a 1932 art deco jewel featuring a facade of polychromed terracotta ornaments. Further up the street, you'll see the lovely arched pedimented doorway of a white marble, Beaux Arts-era building. The district also includes the beautifully restored Carolina Theatre (formerly the Durham Auditorium). A detailed brochure and map of the district is available from the Greater Durham Chamber of Commerce by calling 682-2133, it is also available at the Visitor's Center.

Duke Homestead and Tobacco Museum
2828 Duke Homestead Rd. • 477-5498

You can't fully appreciate Durham until you understand how tobacco figured into the city's growth and development. The Duke Homestead and Tobacco Museum is where you go for a quick course in how the local industry began. Every year on the last weekend in July, you can attend the Tobacco Harvest Festival and see how tobacco was tied on sticks and cured over wood fires. The Homestead hosts a Christmas by Candlelight Tour each December. The museum is open free of charge April through October from 9 AM to 5 PM Tuesday through Saturday and 1 to 5 PM Sunday, and November through March from 10 AM to 4 PM Tuesday through Saturday and 1 to 4 PM Sunday.

Duke Primate Center
3705 Erwin Rd. • 489-3364

The world-renowned Duke Primate Center was established to promote the preservation of some endangered species of primates, including lemurs and bush babies. The Center is open for tours, which must be scheduled by appointment. It's a fascinating place full of nearly 400 primates—a bit of the wild right in the heart

Photo courtesy of N.C. Travel and Tourism

of the Triangle. Admission is charged. Call for more information or to schedule a tour.

Museum of Life and Science
433 Murray Ave. • 220-5429

The Museum of Life and Science, a 70-acre regional science-technology center, features two floors of hands-on exhibits and an outdoor Nature Park. Kids will be fascinated with the 15-foot tornado in the ABC News Channel 11 Weather exhibit, the models of pumping hearts and demonstrations in BodyTech and the native animals in Carolina Wildlife. Explore the Science Arcade, the Tree House discovery room, the outdoor Loblolly Park complete with wind chimes and water play or lose yourself in the MegaMaze. The Ellerbee Creek Railway winds through Nature Park with views of black bears, red wolves and hawks. Other exhibits include Aerospace, Small Science (for the little ones), Geology, Data Earth and Discovery Rooms. Nationally touring exhibits, such as the popular "Turbulent Landscapes," stop here. The Museum also has originated exhibits that have gone on tour. The Magic Wings Butterfly House, one of only 10 permanent butterfly houses in the United States, opened in spring 1999, featuring about 1,000 exotic butterflies. Seasonal annual events include a moonlight train ride to the North Pole. School programs, community classes, summer camps and teacher workshops are also offered at the Museum. Annual memberships may be purchased that provide admission to the museum and discounts on classes. Group rates are available with reservations. Hours are 10 AM to 5 PM Monday through Saturday and noon to 5 PM on Sunday. Call for extended summer hours. The museum is wheelchair-accessible.

Patterson's Mill Country Store
5109 Farrington Rd. • 493-8149

In a rural setting, tucked on a wedge of land between highways and housing developments, John and Elsie Booker have built a tribute to a simpler time. Elsie, a pharmacist with a fascination for old-time medicines, and John, a retired tobacco company employee, have scoured the state, collecting the paraphernalia they might have encountered in their respective professions if they had lived in an earlier era. The result is a replica of a mom-and-pop country store, drugstore, doctor's office and tobacco shop all rolled into one. While the Bookers also sell antiques and North Carolina crafts from the store, 90 percent of what you'll see there is not for sale at any price. Considered one of the best collections of mercantile Americana, the Patterson's Mill Country Store is open from 10 AM to 5:30 PM Tuesday through Saturday and from 2 to 5:30 PM Sunday. It's on Farrington Road, about 2 miles north of N.C. 54 between Durham and Chapel Hill.

Photo by David Haring, courtesy of Duke Primate Center

The Duke Primate Center houses nearly 400 endangered primates, including the black and white ruffed lemur from Madagascar.

Photo by Mark Dolejs, courtesy of Museum of Life and Science

The Museum of Life and Science's Ellerbee Creek Railway winds through Nature Park, offering views of red wolves, black bears and hawks.

Sarah P. Duke Memorial Gardens
Duke University West Campus
• 684-3698

You'll want to keep going back to this spectacular spot on the edge of Duke's West Campus to catch each dazzling display of flowers and shrubs in season. Twenty acres of landscaped gardens and 35 acres of pine forest are open daily to the public. Seasonal blooms include pansies, tulips, daffodils, azaleas, wisteria, roses, daylilies and chrysanthemums as well as flowering dogwood, magnolia, redbud, crab apple and cherry trees. Sunday afternoon concerts and programs are held in the late spring and summer. This is a great place to picnic and spend a peaceful afternoon.

Stagville Center For Preservation
Old Oxford Hwy. • 620-0120

Several historic 18th- and 19th-century plantation buildings set on 71 acres make up the Stagville Center. This is the nation's first state-owned research center for the study of historic and archaeological preservation. Workshops and demonstrations are scheduled throughout the year. The center is located 7 miles northeast of Durham on the Old Oxford Highway (S.R. 1004). It's open from 9 AM to 4 PM Monday through Friday.

Chapel Hill

Ackland Art Museum
Columbia St. at Franklin St. • 966-5736
(See our "Arts" chapter.)

Morehead Planetarium and Sundial Gardens
UNC, 250 E. Franklin St. • 962-1236

From watching the universe spin above your head to visiting the rare walk-in Copernican Orrery, to enjoying the beautifully cultivated sundial rose gardens, the Morehead Planetarium offers a day full of activities for the whole family. This Triangle treasure offers both traveling and original shows about moon landings, UFOs, space voyages and more. The staff also presents special children's shows. Friday evenings, catch *Sky Rambles*, a live narrated show.

The Morehead Planetarium is open every day except December 24 and 25. There is a sky show nightly except Mondays. Call for more information about show times, prices, group rates and special events.

N.C. Botanical Garden
U.S. 15-501 • 962-0522

Located on 600 acres, this is the largest natural botanical garden in the Southeast. As part of UNC's Totten Center, the Botanical Garden is set up for research and conservation of plants native to the Southeastern U.S. The main visitor area features displays of native plants arranged by habitats and more than

Photo by Tim Johnson

Visitors who stroll through the North Carolina Botanical Gardens' display collections will view about 2,500 of the 4,700 plant species known to be native or naturalized in North and South Carolina.

2 miles of trails through the woods. Throughout the year, special programs and workshops are offered in the Totten Center. The Botanical Garden also hosts a Labor Day Open House featuring free entertainment, educational exhibits and a scavenger hunt. It is open from 8 AM to 5 PM daily except on winter weekends. The nature trail is open dawn to dusk year round.

UNC Walking Tour
Visitors Center • 962-1630

You can take a half-hour "Walkman" tour of the historic University of North Carolina, the nation's first state university. You'll see and hear about the Old Well, the Davie Poplar and the 5-acre Coker Arboretum, among other sights. The tours begin at the Rotunda of the Morehead Building Monday through Friday from 10 AM to 4 PM. A driver's license or credit card is needed as a deposit to ensure return of the equipment used on the free tour. The Rotunda is well supplied with informative brochures and pamphlets and is staffed at most times by volunteers. Call to arrange special tours.

Kidstuff and Camps

Talk about a great area for kids! The Triangle is definitely a family-friendly place. Throughout the year you'll find wonderful indoor and outdoor attractions, programs and events that will entertain and captivate your children.

During the summer, each town holds a variety of classes and camps directed toward keeping kids active and happy. In the fall and spring, many locations plan their activities as after-school programs. The winter months offer a wide scope of holiday events to educate and delight your children.

One very informative and useful publication is *Kidsville News, The Triangle's Fun Family Newspaper*, a free monthly tabloid available at local libraries. *Carolina Parent* is another good source for information and local newspapers also publish kids' events.

See our chapters on "Attractions," "Annual Events," "Arts and Culture," "Daytrips and Weekends," "Spectator Sports" and "Parks and Recreation" for many more interesting and fun things for kids to do in the Triangle.

Clubs

Boy Scouts
3231 Atlantic Ave., Raleigh • 872-4884
Girl Scouts
6901 Pinecrest Dr., Raleigh • 782-3021

Educational Explorations

Raleigh and Cary

Cary Cultural Resources
318 N. Academy St. • 469-4061
Call for information on lessons and special summer activities on arts and crafts.

Exploris
201 E. Hargett St. • 834-4040
The $37.5 million Exploris interactive global learning center opened its doors in downtown Raleigh on October 9, 1999. It is open Tuesday through Saturday from 9 AM to 5 PM and Sunday from 12 PM to 5 PM.

N.C. State Museum of Natural Sciences
102 N. Salisbury St. • 733-7450
This state-supported museum has lots for kids to see, touch and experience, as well as special programs and activities, including the Discovery Room, the Children's Saturday Series and Nature Fun for the Very Young. The museum also hosts special events on weekends several times a year, such as Reptile and Amphibian Day (usually in March). The museum is undergoing a major renovation that will be completed in spring 2000. The new $60 million, 200,000-square-foot

facility will be four times larger than the current museum and will contain exciting interactive exhibits and dioramas showcasing North Carolina's rich natural history, new research labs, a Special Exhibits Gallery, a Rooftop Cafe, expanded classroom space and much more. Admission is free.

N.C. Museum of History
5 E. Edenton St. • 715-0200

Children will enjoy the over 250,000 items in the museum's collection, including Indian artifacts, folk art and crafts, old-time transportation and the N.C. Sports Hall of Fame, which boasts a race car originally owned by Richard Petty. This free museum hosts classes, films, concerts and lectures and holds a Family Night quarterly.

N.C. Museum of Art
2110 Blue Ridge Rd. • 839-6262

The North Carolina Museum of Art has several collections that fascinate children—among them the Egyptian mummies and the shimmering silver of the Judaica exhibit. There are also changing special shows that often appeal to younger ones. The museum offers classes, movies, concerts and puppet shows for kids some weekdays and Saturdays each month. The museum also has several Family Festivals each year. There is a charge for special classes.

Playspace
400 Glenwood Ave. • 832-1212

A magical place for budding imaginations, Playspace is a nonprofit, educational organization staffed by volunteers. Housed here are a pretend hospital, a grocery store, a cafe, a dress-up area and a stage, as well as an exploration area designed for infants and toddlers. Play sessions begin on the hour and last for 50 minutes. It's a good idea to arrive a few minutes before the hour in case there's a crowd. Playspace is appropriate for children ages 7 and younger and their adult care-givers. Admission is $2 for a 50-minute session. It is closed on Sunday and Monday afternoons.

Raleigh Arts Commission
• 890-3477

Call for information on year-round and summer classes, camps and activities.

Wake County Public Libraries
Cameron Village Regional Library, Raleigh • 856-6710
Eva Perry Regional Library, Apex
• 387-2113
North Regional Library, Raleigh
• 870-4000
Southeast Regional Library, Garner
• 662-2250

Libraries are our favorite recommendation and offer a lot more than just books. There are branches located throughout Wake County in addition to the regional branches. Each library has a variety of children's programs and activities.

Durham

Bennett Place
4409 Bennett Memorial Rd.
• 383-4345

Bennett Place is the site of negotiations that led to the largest troop surrender of the Civil War, when Confederate General Joseph Johnston surrendered his troops to General William Tecumseh Sherman. Now a state historic site, Bennett Place offers exhibits, historic buildings and a video presentation for visitors.

INSIDERS' TIP

Hands on Nature is a nonprofit organization designed to teach children about the wonders of nature through exploration and creative experiences. For more information, call 676-1615.

A highlight of the site's annual calendar is the April Civil War reenactment, complete with period costumes and replicas of Civil War era weapons. Admission is free.

Duke Homestead & Tobacco Museum
2828 Duke Homestead Rd. • 477-5498

Duke Homestead, another state historic site, is the restored home and tobacco farm of Washington Duke. The house, curing barn, pack house and other outbuildings on the grounds are all part of the living history program offered here. Staff members re-create late 19th-century farm life with special programs each fall and spring. The Homestead hosts a Tobacco Harvest Festival in July and a Christmas by Candlelight tour each December. Admission is free.

Duke University Museum of Art
East Campus • 684-5135

This museum houses several art collections of interest to children. While downstairs exhibits periodically, the upstairs displays statues of Classical heroes. It is open daily, except Monday. Admission is free.

Durham Arts Council
120 Morris St. • 560-ARTS

DAC sponsors year-round classes in all art disciplines, with special classes for children. In the summer, DAC sponsors longer classes, or "camps" for kids. Check out the Young People's Performing Company, a theater troupe for younger people.

Durham County Library System
300 North Roxboro St.
• 560-0100

Again this is our favorite recommendation for a children's activity. Libraries now offer a lot more than just books. There are branches located throughout Durham County and they even have bookmobiles that bring books to you. Each library has a variety of children's programs and activities. Call your closest branch to obtain current information.

Hayti Heritage Center
804 Old Fayetteville St. • 683-1709

Hayti Heritage Center is housed in a historic church building. It has a gallery featuring African-American art and hosts concerts, plays, programs and events for

THEME PARKS & DAYTRIPS FOR CHILDREN

Battleship North Carolina	Wilmington	910-251-5797
Busch Gardens	Williamsburg, VA	757-253-3350
Carolina Renaissance Festival	Huntersville	704-896-5555
Discovery Place	Charlotte	704-372-6261
Emerald Pointe Water Park	Greensboro	336-852-9721
Ghost Town in the Sky	Maggie Valley	828-926-1140
Grandfather Mountain	Linville	828-733-4337
Kings Dominion	Doswell, VA	804-876-5000
North Carolina Aquariums	Pine Knoll Shores	252-247-4003
	Manteo	252-473-3493
	Fort Fisher	910-458-8257
North Carolina Zoo	Asheboro	800-488-0444
Old Salem	Winston-Salem	800-441-5305
Paramount's Carowinds	Charlotte	704-588-2606
Tweetsie Railroad	Boone	800-526-5740

Photo by G. W. Willis, Museum of Life and Science

About 1,000 exotic butterflies, such as the Zebra Longwing, are featured at the Magic Wings Butterfly House, which opened in spring 1999.

children and adults. The First Saturday (of most months) family program is a free arts, crafts and activity program designed for school-aged children. Call for information on upcoming events.

Museum of Life and Science
433 Murray Ave. • 220-5429

The Museum of Life & Science is a great place for science exploration and fun. The 70-acre regional science-technology center, with two floors of hands-on exhibits, is located in the heart of Durham, off I-85. Exhibits include Aerospace, ABC News Channel 11 Weather Exhibit, Small Science (for the little ones), Geology, Carolina Wildlife, Data Earth and Discovery Rooms. Outdoor exhibits include Loblolly Park, Water Play, Farmyard Animals and an outdoor Nature Park with black bears, endangered red wolves and hawks.

The outdoor MegaMaze is filled with delighted kids and adults in warm weather and the Ellerbee Creek Railway ride around the grounds is a perennial favorite. Special exhibits rotate through the Duke Power Gallery—such as "Turbulent Landscapes," a fascinating exhibit about natural forces that shape our world. Outside on the grounds, there are climbing structures, wind chimes, water play and farmyard.

The Museum's three-story Magic Wings Butterfly House, one of 10 permanent year-round butterfly houses in the United States and the largest butterfly house east of the Mississippi, opened in spring 1999. A state-of-the-art insectarium is set to open at the museum in 2000.

Museum hours are 10 AM to 5 PM Monday through Saturday and noon to 5 PM on Sunday. Call for extended summer hours.

A family membership gives unlimited admission for a year and may be used for admission at other science museums around the country.

Chapel Hill

Ackland Art Museum
South Columbia St. at East Franklin St., UNC Campus • 966-5736

The Ackland's small but very fine collection spans the ages, from ancient Greek and Roman sculptures to modern paintings, and the variety will keep children interested. In recent years, the museum has hosted a display of a lovely hand-built Victorian doll house during November and December. Admission is free.

ArtsCenter
300-G East Main St., Carrboro
• 929-ARTS

The ArtsCenter offers classes, Saturday morning "Kids Cabaret" performances, family concerts and summer day camp programs. It is a great resource, providing almost limitless entertainment and educational services for children and parents. Call for a current schedule of classes and upcoming events.

Chapel Hill Public Library
Estes Drive • 968-2777
Children's Room • 968-2778

This library opened in 1994 and is truly a delight for children. One of their special programs for children is the "Dial-a-story" service (968-0222).

Horace Williams House
610 East Rosemary St. • 942-7818

The Horace Williams House, the restored home of a former UNC professor, occasionally hosts exhibits of interest to children. Shows change monthly. The house is located on a big lawn, perfect for rambling. The huge magnolia tree is an ideal hideout for little ones. The Chapel Hill Preservation Society maintains the house and sometimes sponsors events such as an afternoon of storytelling. Admission to the house is free.

Morehead Planetarium
250 E. Franklin St. • 962-1236
For show times: 549-6863

The Morehead Planetarium offers a changing schedule of shows throughout the year, from the popular Star of Bethlehem program that runs from November to early January to shows on UFOs, the age of the dinosaurs, black holes and much more. The planetarium runs three shows concurrently, one for younger children and two for school-aged children and adults. On Friday afternoon and evenings,

BIRTHDAY PARTY IDEAS

ENTERTAINMENT

Abracadabra the Magic Clown	Durham	544-6770
Androgeena (puppeteer)	Durham	286-0002
Art N' Soul/Sky Blue: A Clown From Cloud 9	Carrboro	968-8704
Ba Tumbler's Tumblebus (gymnastics in a bus)	Raleigh	847-7215
Best Wishes (theme parties)	Cary	468-0684
Bruce Stevenson (draws caricatures & sings)	Raleigh	872-3609
Calvin Klown and Tutu (comedy magic show)	Raleigh	782-8841
Comedy Magic	Cary	233-1005
F & M Entertainment (costumed characters & clowns)	Raleigh	787-7742
Grimbo the Clown	Durham	361-3000
Jelly Bean the Clown	Durham	286-9431
Karate International	Durham	489-6100
Kinderfeste (music, stories & activities)	Raleigh	783-7341
Mr. Rainbow the Clown	Durham	489-7040
Musicaleigh Inclined (games & sing along music)	Chapel Hill	933-1683
Party Pros (clowns, magicians, face painting & puppeteers)	Durham	361-3000
Tate the Great (magic show)	Cary	469-2441

PARTY PLACES

Adventure Landing (miniature golf, video games, food)	Raleigh	872-1688
AMF South Hills Lanes	Cary	467-2411
Amazing Glaze (ceramics studio)	Cary	851-2500
Amazing Glaze (ceramics studio)	Raleigh	856-1234
Capital Skating Center (rollerskating parties)	Raleigh	875-1994
Cary Family YMCA (summer swimming party)	Cary	469-9622
Cary Parks & Rec. (rooms & picnic shelters for rent)	Cary	460-4965
Chapel Hill Parks & Rec. (gyms, ball fields, pool, tennis cts.)	Chapel Hill	968-2784
Durham Bulls Baseball Club	Durham	687-6500
Durham Parks & Rec. (picnic shelters, ball fields & more)	Durham	560-4358
Funtasia Family Fun Center (mini golf & bumper boats)	Durham	493-8973
Funtasia North (roller skating, go-carts, video)	Durham	598-1944
GymCarolina (gymnastics parties)	Cary	467-0946
GymCarolina (gymnastics parties)	Raleigh	848-7988
Ice House, The (ice skating parties)	Cary	467-6000
Kids' Town (theme parties)	Cary	468-1080
Kindermusik Kids of Cary (participatory music)	Cary	467-4398
Little Gym of Durham (gymnastics parties)	Durham	403-5437
Little Gym of Raleigh/Cary (gymnastics parties)	Cary	481-6701
Mardi Gras, The (bowling, party room)	Chapel Hill	489-1230
Morehead Planetarium	Chapel Hill	962-1236
Museum of Life and Science (super science parties)	Durham	220-5429
North Raleigh Gymnastics (trampoline & obstacle course)	Raleigh	790-9400
Paint the Earth (ceramics)	Chapel Hill	968-0400
Panner's Creek Gem Lines (hunt for gem stones)	Apex	303-3400
Party Machine, Ltd. (video games, dancing room, hostess)	Cary	461-0800
Playspace (educational, creative parties)	Raleigh	832-1212
Putt-Putt (miniature golf, video games, food)	Durham	479-5773
Raleigh IcePlex (ice skating parties)	Raleigh	878-9002
Raleigh Little Theatre (discounted group tickets)	Raleigh	821-3111
Raleigh Parks & Rec. (comm. ctrs., pools, picnic shelters)	Raleigh	890-3285
Raleighwood Cinema Grill (special party packages)	Raleigh	847-8370
Raleigh YWCA (gym or swimming pool & party room)	Raleigh	828-3205
Science Safari (electricity, safari & chemistry parties)	Cary	460-6051
Scrap Exchange (pick a theme & make a project)	Durham	286-2559
Soccer Dome America (rent field, referee avail.)	Raleigh	859-2997
Swensen's (birthday parties in the "Greenhouse" room)	Chapel Hill	929-3121
Take Ten (video games & pinball)	Chapel Hill	968-3040
Village Lanes (bowling)	Durham	560-4358
Wood's Hole Miniature Golf (golf & pizza)	Cary	233-7189

CAPITAL AREA SOCCER LEAGUE

Meeting the Needs of All Players!

3344 Hillsborough St.
Raleigh, NC 27607
(919) 834-3951
(919) 834-4369

Sky Rambles gives a look at the current night sky. A small gift shop has a nice selection of astronomy and science-related toys, most less than a couple of dollars. There are also Saturday classes (like model rocket launching) and summer day camp programs for kids.

Entertainment

Raleigh and Cary

Adventure Landing
3311 Capital Blvd., Raleigh • 872-1688
Miniature golf, go-karts, laser tag, a human slingshot, video games and fast-food are offered at this location.

Chuck E. Cheese's
3501 Capital Blvd., Raleigh • 850-9922
This national chain serves pizza and provides rides and video games for entertainment while you wait.

Grand Slam U.S.A.
4500 Western Blvd., Raleigh • 233-7522
Four indoor batting cages and two basketball courts make this a children's year-round sports center.

Ice House
1410 Buck Jones Rd., Cary • 467-6000
This is the coolest entertainment in the Triangle. The Ice House features skating, lessons and team sports.

Jellybeans
1120 Buck Jones Rd., Cary • 467-5283
This skating rink is very popular with both in-line and regular skaters. It provides well-supervised, family fun.

Panners' Creek Gem Lines
1930 N. Salem St., Apex • 303-3400
Located between Cary and Apex, this back to nature, hands-on experience allows children to pan for gemstones and keep what they find.

Putt-Putt Golf & Games
4020 Tryon Rd., Raleigh • 832-0600
Experience over seven acres of fun and excitement at the Triangle's newest entertainment park. Attractions include two 18-hole miniature golf courses, the Swiftcreek Speedway with three go-kart tracks and a large video arcade.

Raleigh IcePlex
2601 Raleigh Blvd., Raleigh • 878-9002
The Raleigh IcePlex offers ice hockey, figure skating and a birthday party room.

Science Safari
Saltbox Village, Cary • 460-6051

This quality toy store offers both classes in science as well as birthday parties with science themes. There is usually a waiting list, so sign up early.

Silver Lake
5300 Tryon Rd., Raleigh • 851-1683

Silver Lake, near Swift Creek, is one of the area's most popular swimming parks. Admission is charged.

Twin Towers Stables
319 Green Level Rd., Apex • 303-5020

Twin Towers is a full-service equestrian facility that offers quality instruction for beginning and advanced riders and a Pony Club for kids ages 8-15.

Wood's Hole Miniature Golf Club
5815 Holly Springs Rd., Cary
• 233-7189

Experience miniature golf in a family setting. Wood's specializes in birthday parties.

Durham

Funtasia
4350 Garrett Rd. • 493-8973

Funtasia is a commercial family fun center that offers a 36-hole miniature golf course, bumper boats, video arcade, go carts, batting cages, two-story maze and a 14-acre paintball field.

Funtasia North
715 N. Hoover Rd. • 598-1944

Formerly Wheels Family Fun Park, Funtasia North offers go-carts, bumper

Photo by Evelyn Ward

Vertical Edge Climbing Center sponsored a climbing demonstration at the Festival for the Eno.

cars, batting cages, mini-golf, a three-story jumbo gym, arcades and a roller rink.

Mardi Gras
N.C. 54 at I-40 • 489-1230

This 24-lane bowling alley and video arcade is a good venue for entertainment for southwest Durhamites and Chapel Hillians. Food is available and birthday parties and group outings are welcome by reservation. Bowling fees are lower during certain weekday hours.

Pleasure Horse Farm
8311 Fayetteville Rd. • 544-5867

If you want your child to learn the

INSIDERS' TIP

The Town of Cary has donated 17 acres for the Kids Together Playground, which was conceived by two industrious eight year olds. This public playground, located at the corner of Cary Parkway and Tryon Road, is designed for all children, including those with physical disabilities.

basics of how to care for a horse as well how to ride, this is the place.

The Scrap Exchange
Northgate Mall • 286-2559

This nonprofit organization recycles cloth, ribbons, lace, paper, foam, tubing and plastic squirls and industrial materials donated from area companies. Creative workshops are available as well as bags of scraps for craft and school projects.

Triangle SportsPlex
One Dan Kidd Dr., Hillsborough • 644-0339

Ice skating, hockey, and kiddie, lap and recreational swimming pools are available in this facility, which opened in 1995.

Vertical Edge Climbing Center
2422 U.S. Hwy 70 • 596-6910

Indoor rock climbing center teaches team building and self reliance.

Outdoor Recreation

Raleigh and Cary

All Children's Playground
Laurel Hills Park

Designed with the help of many children, 1,500 volunteers built this playground in 4 days. Discovery, adventure and fun are available to all children. Children with disabilities will find sights, sounds and textures to excite their senses.

Bond Park
801 High House Rd., Cary • 469-4100

The largest park in Wake County offers a playground, boat rentals, fitness trail, and over five miles of hiking trails. The park is home to several annual kid's events such as a "haunted house" at Halloween and a community Easter Egg Hunt.

Durant Nature Park
8305 Camp Durant Rd. • 870-2871

Durant Nature Park is a little gem in the Raleigh Parks and Recreation Department's crown. There are trails to explore, a butterfly and bird garden (best in spring and summer) and many wonderful weekend nature programs for children and families. Durant has picnic facilities, too, if you want to make a day of it. One highlight of the park's yearly schedule of programs and events is the Halloween Trail each October. Call for more information about the park and its classes and activities.

J. C. Raulston Arboretum
4301 Beryl Rd. • 515-7641

The J. C. Raulston Arboretum at North Carolina State University is small and worth discovering. It is near Meredith College and the N.C. State Fairgrounds and covers about 8 acres. It is a delightful place for a quiet stroll through Japanese and English-style gardens. If you and the kids need a respite from the high-tech world,

the Arboretum may be a solution. There are places to picnic. Admission is free.

Pullen Park
408 Ashe Ave. • 831-6468

The highlight of Pullen Park (at least to this Insider) is the carousel. One of only 25 hand-carved Dentzel carousels still in operation, it was restored in 1982. You can ride a horse, an ostrich, a cat or a rabbit—or perhaps all of them, since you'll undoubtedly ride it more than once. The park also has a train and a boat ride for little ones, a large playground, picnic areas, paddle boats on the small man-made lake and an outdoor pool for summertime swimming. Admission to the park is free. There are charges for rides and the pool.

Shelley Lake and Sertoma Park
1400 West Millbrook Rd. • 420-2331

One of the best playgrounds in the Triangle is Sertoma Park. Shelley Lake is just located down the hill from the playground where paddle boats, sailboats, canoes and rowboats are available for rent from April through September.

William B. Umstead State Park
8801 Glenwood Ave. • 571-4170

William B. Umstead and adjoining Reedy Creek State Parks offer 5,000-plus acres of trails, fishing, picnic sites, campgrounds and woodlands to explore right in the middle of the Triangle (just minutes from RDU International Airport). The parks contain bridle trails, a self-guided nature trail, a lake with boat rentals in warm weather, camping and picnic sites and more. It's worth a stop, especially if you need a place to let the kids run loose on a sunny afternoon. The new Umstead State Park Visitors Center, which opened in June 1998, features a museum and other educational exhibits relating to the park. Admission is free.

> **FYI**
> Unless otherwise noted, the area code for all phone numbers listed in this guide is 919.

Photo by Robert Thomason

A miniature train takes kids for a spin around Raleigh's 65-acre Pullen Park.

SUMMER DAY CAMPS

Academic & Cultural

Carolina Friends School	Durham	Coed	4-15	919-383-6602
Durham Academy	Durham	Coed	4-18	919-489-9118
Hill Learning Development Ctr.	Durham	Coed	K-6th Gr.	919-489-7464
Imagineering Center	Pittsboro	Coed	8-15	919-932-1215
Jr. Statesman (Politics & Gov.)	Various	Coed	14-17	800-334-5353
Kantner School	Hillsborough	Coed	K-4th Gr.	919-732-7200
Meredith's Computer Camp	Raleigh	Coed	7-12	919-829-8353
N.C. Museum of Life & Science	Durham	Coed	4-14	919-220-5429
Saint Mary's Summer Odyssey	Raleigh	Coed	3-7 Gr.	919-676-8927
Schoolhouse of Wonder	Durham	Coed	7-15	919-471-1623
Summer Peace Camps	Carrboro	Coed	6-12	919-929-9821
Ravenscroft	Raleigh	Coed	5-16	919-847-0900

Arts & Music

American Dance Festival	Durham	Coed	12-16	919-684-6402
Arts Together	Raleigh	Coed	4-18	919-828-1713
Artspace Summer Arts Program	Raleigh	Coed	8 & up	919-821-2787
Brightleaf Music Workshop	Durham	Coed	7-12 Gr.	919-493-0385
Chapel Hll Arts & Music	Chapel Hill	Coed	6-12	919-933-7278
Durham Arts Council	Durham	Coed	5-16	919-560-2726
Expressions! Duke's Fine Arts Camp	Durham	Coed	10-13	919-684-6259
Jordan Hall Arts Center	Cary	Coed	6-14	919-469-4069
Maple Meadows Art Camp	Chapel Hill	Coed	12-18	919-942-6696
Meredith's (Art, Music, Theatre)	Raleigh	Coed	6 & up	919-829-8536
Raleigh Little Theatre	Raleigh	Coed	6-18	919-821-4579
Raleigh School of Ballet	Raleigh	Coed	7-18	919-834-9261
Raleigh School of Dance	Raleigh	Coed	5-11	919-850-9030
The Scrap Exchange	Durham	Coed	6-11	919-286-2559

Gymnastics & Cheerleading

Artistic Gymnastics	Raleigh	Coed	3-18	919-772-9463
Carolina Gymnastics Academy	Raleigh	Coed	5-16	919-848-7988
Champion Cheer Gym	Raleigh	Coed	5-12	919-859-1511
North Raleigh Gymnastics	Raleigh	Coed	3-12	919-790-9400

Horsemanship Camp

Ballentine Farm Riding Academy	Fuquay-Varina	Coed	5-18	919-552-7869
Brasswood Summer Horse Camp	Durham	Coed	7-13	919-403-0758
Camp Cheval (MacNair's)	Raleigh	Coed	6-16	919-851-1118
Pleasure Horse Farms	Durham	Coed	6 & up	919-544-5867
Quail Roost Stables	Rougemont	Coed	6 & up	919-477-8932
Tamryss Farms	Raleigh	Coed	6 & up	919-847-3080
Triton Stables	Raleigh	Coed	6 & up	919-847-4123

Summer Day Camp

A.E. Finley YMCA	N. Raleigh	Coed	4-13	919-848-9622
Cary Parks & Recreation	Cary	Coed	3-18	919-469-4061
Cary YMCA	Cary	Coed	5-13	919-469-9622
Central YMCA	Ral. & Garner	Coed	7-13	919-832-9622
Chapel Hill/Carrboro YMCA	Chapel Hill	Coed	6-15	919-942-5156
Chapel Hill Parks & Recreation	Chapel Hill	Coed	6-12	919-968-2784
Durham Parks & Recreation	Durham	Coed	5-18	919-560-4355
Durham YMCA	Durham	Coed	4-17	919-493-4502
Garner YMCA	Garner	Coed	5-14	919-833-1256
Raleigh Parks & Recreation	Raleigh	Coed	6-12	919-831-6640
Triangle SportsPlex	Hillsborough	Coed	7-13	919-644-0339

SUMMER SPORTS CAMPS

Duke, N.C. State and UNC offer over 20 different sports camps. Call their Sports Information Offices for information on individual camps.
Duke: 684-2633   N.C. State: 515-2102   UNC: 962-2123

Baseball

Duke Baseball Camp	Durham	Boys	13-18	684-2358
Duke Youth Baseball Camp	Durham	Coed	7-14	687-6500
Durham Bulls Youth Baseball	Durham	Coed	7-14	687-6500
N.C. State Baseball Camp	Raleigh	Boys	9-18	515-3613
UNC Baseball Camp	Chapel Hill	Boys	6-18	962-2351

Basketball

Campbell University Basketball	Buies Creek	Boys/Girls	8-18	800-760-8962
Dave Odom Basketball Camp	Winston-Salem	Boys	7-18	336-759-5622
Duke Univ. Basketball Camp	Durham	Girls	9-17	613-7527
Duke Univ. Basketball Camp	Durham	Boys	9-17	684-8515
N.C. State Basketball Camp	Raleigh	Boys	8-17	828-7100
N.C. State Basketball Camp	Raleigh	Girls	7-18	859-1511
UNC Basketball Camp	Chapel Hill	Boys	10-17	962-1154
UNC Basketball Camp	Chapel Hill	Girls	9-18	408-0221

Football

Duke University Football Camp	Durham	Boys	13-18	684-2635
Gerald Williams Football Camp	Charlotte	Boys	8-18	800-555-0801
N.C. State Football Camp	Raleigh	Boys	13-18	515-2114
UNC Football Camp	Chapel Hill	Boys	9-18	966-2575

Golf

Duke Golf School (Residential)	Durham	Coed	11-17	681-2494
Duke University Golf Club (Day)	Durham	Coed	9-18	681-2288
N.C. State Golf Camp (Residential)	Raleigh	Coed	6-18	846-1536

Soccer

Blue Devil Day Camp	Durham	Coed	6-12	471-9655
Capital Area Soccer League	Raleigh	Coed	5-18	834-3951
N.C. State Soccer Camp	Raleigh	Boys	6-12	851-1627
Soccer Dome	Raleigh	Coed	6-15	859-2997
UNC Soccer Camp	Chapel Hill	Boys	10-18	408-0770
UNC Soccer Camp	Chapel Hill	Girls	13-17	962-4100

Tennis

Duke Tennis Camp	Durham	Coed	8-18	479-0854
Mary Lou Jones (St. Mary's)	Raleigh	Coed	5-18	839-4015

Miscellaneous

Campbell U. Sports Camp	Buies Creek	Coed	8-18	336-893-1325
Duke Field Hockey Camp	Durham	Girls	13-18	684-4116
NC Track & Field/Cross Country	Chapel Hill	Coed	8 & up	962-5210
North Raleigh Sports Camp	Raleigh	Coed	6-14	790-0596
Pembroke State All-Sports Camp	Pembroke	Coed	6-12	910-521-6343
Outward Bound, USA	Various	Coed	14-up	800-243-8520
Carolina Friends School	Durham	Coed	4-15	383-6602

Durham

Duke Forest
For Information: 613-8013

Duke Forest is over 8,000 acres of woods, part of the research lab for the School of Environmental Sciences (formerly the School of Forestry) at Duke. There are trails to hike and bike, picnic areas, streams and fishing holes in the forest, which straddles Durham and Orange counties. Duke Forest has a number of entrances. The most widely used are along N.C. 751 and Erwin and Whitfield roads. The forest is a great spot for a family walk (bring the dog along!) or a solo stroll when you need to clear your mind. Admission is free.

Duke Gardens
Anderson St., Duke Campus

The Sarah P. Duke Memorial Gardens are glorious in the springtime, but worth a visit any time of the year. There are over 20 acres of lawn, flowers and foliage. It's a prime place for families, Duke students and others to picnic or just hang out. The gardens contain ponds with goldfish, paths to follow and woodlands to explore. There are concerts in the spring and fall. Admission is free.

Eno River State Park
6101 Cole Mill Rd. • 383-1686

The Eno River State Park was established in 1973 and runs along a 14-mile stretch of the river. There are a number of access points to the park, including Cole Mill and Few's Ford, where the park office is located. There are hiking and bridle trails, creeks to fish and picnic spots. Admission is free.

West Point on the Eno
5101 N. Roxboro Rd. • 471-1623

West Point on the Eno is part of the Durham City Parks and Recreation system. There is a reconstructed mill, the 1880's Greek Revival McCown-Mangum house and the Tobacco Barn and Pack House. West Point has trails to hike, a picnic area and a blacksmith shop. The park hosts the annual Fourth of July Festival for the Eno, Hallow-Eno, a special Halloween celebration for families, and other special programs like nature classes for children throughout the year. Admission to the park is free.

Chapel Hill and Carrboro

N.C. Botanical Garden
Fordham Blvd. (U.S. 15-501 Bypass)
• 962-0522

The Botanical Garden's 600-plus acres are a part of the University of North Carolina. There are collections of native plants, grouped in coastal plain, piedmont and mountain sections, herb and wildflower gardens, goldfish ponds and a series of trails to walk throughout the garden property. The annual Labor Day Open House, featuring fresh apple cider and a botanical scavenger hunt is a favorite for kids. Admission is free.

Summer Camps

There is so much to be considered that picking a summer camp is difficult, at best. A good resource is the *North Carolina Resident and Sports Camp Directory* published each year by NCSU College of Forest Resources. Call to order a copy at 515-7118. There is a charge. *"How to Choose a Summer Camp"* is available at no charge from the National Camp Association's Camp Advisory Service by calling 800-966-CAMP. If you are looking for camps throughout the United States, pick up a copy of Peterson's *Summer Opportunities for Kids and Teenagers*.

Although certainly not a complete listing of available camps, we have tried to give you a variety of day, sports and resident camps convenient to the Triangle.

SUMMER RESIDENT CAMPS

Piedmont

All-Arts & Sciences Camp (UNCG)	Greensboro	Coed	7-15	800-306-9033
Betsy-Jeff Penn 4-H Center (4-H)	Reidsville	Coed	8-12	910-349-9445
Camp Cheerio (YMCA)	Glade Valley	Coed	7-16	910-869-0195
Camp Chestnut Ridge (Methodist)	Efland	Coed	7-17	919-304-3900
Camp Graham (Girl Scout)	Henderson	Girls	6-17	919-782-3021
Camp Kanata (YMCA)	Wake Forest	Coed	6-15	919-556-2661
Camp Mary Atkinson (Girl Scout)	Selma	Girls	6-17	919-782-3021
Camp New Hope (Presbyterian)	Chapel Hill	Coed	6-15	919-942-4716
Camp Oak Hill (Christian)	Oxford	Coed	7-17	919-782-2888
Camp Thunderbird (YMCA)	Lake Wylie, S.C.	Coed	7-16	803-831-2121
Camp Willow Run (Christian)	Littleton	Coed	8-18	919-586-4665
Duke Action: Science-Forestry	Durham	Girls	10-12	919-684-6259
Duke Creative Writers' Workshop	Durham	Coed	16-18	919-684-2827
Duke Drama Workshop	Durham	Coed	15-17	919-684-6259
Duke Young Writers Camp	Durham	Coed	11-17	919-684-6259
Gifted and Talented Develop. Ctr.	Charlotte	Coed	11-15	704-366-6052
Keyauwee Program Ctr. (G.Scouts)	Sophia	Girls	7-17	910-861-1198
Lutheran Outdoor Ministries	Fuquay-Varina	Coed	5-12	919-552-9421
Millstone 4-H Center (4-H)	Ellerbee	Coed	6-18	919-515-3244
Mount Shepherd (Methodist)	Asheboro	Coed	6-18	910-629-4085
Mountain Top Camp(Christian)	Pinnacle	Coed	8-20	910-767-7158
New Life Camp (Christian)	Raleigh	Coed	8-18	919-847-0764
N.C. School of the Arts	Winston-Salem	Coed	12-adult	336-770-3204
NCSU (Challenge & Champions)	Raleigh	Coed	10-13	919-515-7061
NCSU (Math & Science-Gifted)	Raleigh	Coed	15-18	919-515-6118
Payne Woodmen Camp	Greensboro	Coed	8-15	910-275-5949
Rockfish (Christian)	Parkton	Coed	6-16	910-425-3529
Sertoma 4-H Center (4-H)	Westfield	Coed	9-18	336-593-8057
Summer Ventures (Science & Math)	Durham	Coed Jrs. & Srs.		919-286-3366
Talent Identification Program (TIPS)	Durham (Duke)	Coed	12-16	919-684-3847
The Summit (Episcopal)	Brown Summit	Coed	7-18	800-448-8775
The Vineyard (Christian)	Westfield	Coed	6-16	910-351-2070
YMCA Camp Hanes	King	Coed	7-15	910-983-3131

Coast

Camp Albemarle (Presbyterian)	Newport	Coed	7-18	252-726-4848
Camp Hardee (Girl Scout)	Blounts Creek	Girls	6-16	800-558-9297
Camp Morehead	Morehead City	Coed	6-15	252-726-3960
Camp Seafarer (YMCA)	Arapahoe	Girls	7-16	252-249-1212
Camp Sea Gull (YMCA)	Arapahoe	Boys	7-16	252-249-1111
Camp Pretty Pond (Girl Scout)	Winnabow	Girls	7-17	800-558-9297
Don Lee (Methodist)	Arapahoe	Coed	7-17	800-535-5475
Duke Action: Science-Coast	Pine Knoll Shores	Girls	10-12	252-684-6259
Lutheran Outdoor Ministries	Kure Beach	Coed	5-18	252-552-9421
Mitchell 4-H Center (4-H)	Swansboro	Coed	6-18	252-515-3244
Roanoke Christian (Church of Christ)	Washington	Coed	5-18	252-946-2203

Mountains

Brevard Music Center (Audition req.)	Brevard	Coed	13-35	828-884-2975
Camp Arrowhead	Tuxedo	Boys	7-15	828-692-1123

SUMMER RESIDENT CAMPS

Mountains cont.

Camp Broadstone (ASU/Gifted Prog.)	Boone	Coed	9-14	828-262-3045
Camp Carolina Backcountry	Brevard	Boys	7-17	828-884-2414
Camp Celo	Burnsville	Coed	7-12	828-675-4323
Camp Chosatonga	Brevard	Boys	8-17	828-884-6834
Camp Ginger Cascades (Girl Scouts)	Lenoir	Girls	5-17	800-328-8388
Camp Green Cove	Tuxedo	Girls	7-17	828-692-6355
Camp Greystone (Christian)	Tuxedo	Girls	7-17	828-693-3182
Camp Grier (Presbyterian)	Old Fort	Coed	7-18	828-668-7793
Camp High Rocks	Cedar Mt.	Boys	8-16	828-885-2153
Camp Hollymont	Black Mountain	Girls	6-16	828-686-5343
Camp Illahee	Brevard	Girls	6-16	828-883-2181
Camp Kahdalea	Brevard	Girls	8-17	828-884-6834
Camp Kanuga (Episcopal)	Hendersonville	Coed	7-15	828-692-9136
Camp Living Water (Christian)	Bryson City	Coed	7-16	828-488-6012
Camp Merri-Mac	Black Mountain	Girls	6-16	828-669-8766
Camp Mishemokwa	Bat Cave	Coed	6-16	828-625-9051
Camp Mondamin	Tuxedo	Boys	7-17	828-693-7446
Camp Pinnacle	Hendersonville	Boys	7-16	828-692-3591
Camp Pisgah (Girl Scout)	Brevard	Girls	7-17	828-252-4442
Camp Rockbrook	Brevard	Girls	6-16	828-884-6151
Camp Rockmont	Black Mountain	Boys	7-16	828-686-3885
Camp Sky Ranch	Blowing Rock	Coed	6-17	828-264-8600
Camp Tekoa (Methodist)	Hendersonville	Coed	6-17	828-692-6516
Camp Timberlake	Black Mountain	Boys	6-15	828-669-8766
Camp Ton-A-Wandah	Flat Rock	Girls	6-15	800-322-0178
Camp Winding Gap	Lake Toxaway	Coed	7-16	828-966-4520
Christ School's Center (Episcopalian)	Arden	Coed	13-17	828-684-6232
Cullowhee Experience (A. Gifted)	Cullowhee	Coed	9-15	828-227-7249
Deep Woods Camp	Brevard	Boys	10-17	828-885-2268
Eagle's Nest Camp	Pisgah Forest	Coed	6-17	336-761-1040
Falling Creek Camp	Tuxedo	Boys	7-16	828-692-0262
Green River Preserve	Cedar Mtn.	Coed	9-13	828-885-2250
Gwynn Valley	Brevard	Coed	5-12	828-885-2900
Hickory Cove Bible Camp	Taylorsville	Coed	8-21	828-635-0858
Holston Presbytery (Presbyterian)	Banner Elk	Coed	8-18	828-898-6611
Johns River Valley (Church of Christ)	Blowing Rock	Coed	8-18	828-264-1516
Keystone Camp	Brevard	Girls	7-17	828-884-9125
Laurel Ridge (Moravian)	Laurel Springs	Coed	6-18	336-359-2951
Lutheridge (Lutheran)	Arden	Coed	6-18	828-684-2361
Lutherock (Lutheran)	Newland	Coed	8-18	828-733-3309
Merriwood	Sapphire Valley	Girls	6-16	828-743-3300
Mountaincamp	Highlands	Coed	6-18	828-526-4505
N.C. Outward Bound School	Asheville	Coed	14-18	828-299-3366
Oak Ridge Military Academy	Oak Ridge	Coed	10-17	336-643-4131
Occoneechee (Girl Scouts)	Mill Spring	Girls	7-17	828-537-7974
Ridgecrest (Southern Baptist)	Ridgecrest	Coed	7-16	828-669-8051
Skyland Camp	Clyde	Girls	7-15	828-627-2470
South Mountain Baptist Camp	Connelly Springs	Coed	6-17	828-437-9475
South Mountain Christian Camp	Bostic	Coed	7-15	828-247-1168
Talisman Summer Camp	Black Mountain	Coed	9-17	828-669-8639
TVR Christian Camp	Plumtree	Coed	8-18	828-765-7860

Each year, the Triangle
hosts hundreds of events that
have become part of the lifestyle
and culture of the area.

Annual Events

Each year, the Triangle hosts hundreds of events that have become part of the lifestyle and culture of the area. During the warmer months, it seems that hardly a weekend will go by without some sort of ethnic feast, seasonal street fair or musical performance. During the cooler months, there are harvest festivals and holiday celebrations.

Want a taste of the South? Plan to spend some time in Hillsborough for Hog Day. Looking for something with a Latin flavor? Celebrate Cinco de Mayo. Need an original piece of artwork? Browse through Artsplosure in Raleigh, Lazy Daze in Cary, Centerfest in Durham or Apple Chill in Chapel Hill, just to name a few. From the minute you greet the new year at First Night in downtown Raleigh to the end of the year when you bid it adieu, the diversity of events in the area will keep you busy throughout the year.

January

Raleigh Antiques Extravaganza
Raleigh Convention and Conference Center, Fayetteville Street Mall
• (336) 924-8337

This three-day event features over 175 exhibitors from all over the East Coast offering the finest in country and Americana, Victorian, wicker, dolls, toys, clothing and much more. Admission fee is $4.50 for one day and weekend passes are available for $5.50. The Antiques Extravaganza is also held in July.

February

Carnaval Brasileiro
The ArtsCenter, Carrboro • 929-ARTS

A Brazilian version of Mardi Gras, this event features traditional and new Carnaval and Samba sounds. Costumed and masked participants contribute to the festivities. Tickets are $8 and include a complimentary sampling of Brazilian food.

Home, Garden & Flower Show
Raleigh Convention and Conference Center, Fayetteville Street Mall
• 831-6011

Each year, local and regional garden centers, garden clubs, landscapers, contractors and remodelers turn the Raleigh Convention and Conference Center into an indoor wonderland of gardens, featuring water gardens and thousands of plants and flowers. Decks, spas and many other related garden and home products are also on display.

Ringling Brother's Circus
Dorton Arena, Raleigh • 733-2145

Mark your calendar for the annual return of the "Greatest Show on Earth" to Dorton Arena at the State Fairgrounds.

March

ACC Tournament

Okay, we're cheating. This event does not take place in Raleigh, Durham or Chapel Hill. But it is still very much a Triangle attraction because when tournament time arrives in March, the Atlantic Coast Conference basketball tournament is THE event. As Tournament week begins, the local media will run stories and features; there will be private parties to watch the games; bars and clubs will host special ACC TV nights; and it becomes difficult to get your business phone calls returned during game times.

The Tournament was once held at NCSU's Reynolds Coliseum but these days, the playing sites—supposedly neutral arenas—have been in larger coliseums, such as the Greensboro Coliseum, Atlanta's Omni and the Charlotte Coliseum. The tournament was expanded to four days with the addition of Florida State to the ACC. In 1998, the format was again changed to eliminate the dreaded "play-in" game that paired the two teams with the worst season records in the opening round. Now the 1st and 9th seeds battle on opening night. Tickets are sometimes available and the trip is worth their cost.

FYI

Unless otherwise noted, the area code for all phone numbers listed in this guide is 919.

North Carolina International Jazz Festival
Baldwin Auditorium, Duke University
• 684-4444

North Carolina International Jazz Festival, which celebrated its 15th anniversary in 1998, features musicians from such countries as Italy, Monaco, Portugal and The Netherlands. The festival runs from late March through April at Duke University's Baldwin Auditorium. Tickets for the 1998 festival were general admission, $15; students, $12.

St. Patrick's Day Parade
Downtown Raleigh
• 571-7869

This Irish-style celebration, which takes place in the Moore Square Arts District in downtown Raleigh, offers activities for all ages. After the parade be sure to head over to Tir na nOg for a green beer.

Staff Photo

The Spring Daze Arts and Crafts Festival features the works of local artists, great food and live entertainment.

April

Apple Chill
Franklin St., Chapel Hill • 968-2784

Thousands of residents from all over the Triangle converge on Chapel Hill for this famous street fair, which offers a variety of arts and crafts, music, clogging, magicians, puppet shows, jugglers, potters, incredible edibles and more.

Cary Road Race
Cary High School, Cary • 469-4062

Sponsored by the *Cary News,* Cary Parks, Recreation and Cultural Resources and Hannaford Foods, the Cary Road Race attracts hundreds of runners each year. The event features a 5K (3.1 miles) race, a 10K (6.2 miles) run and a one-mile fun run. All of the courses wind through Cary. Proceeds from the race benefit the Kids Together playground at the corner of Cary Parkway and Tryon Road.

DoubleTake Documentary Film Festival
Carolina Theatre, Durham • 660-3699

DoubleTake celebrates the power and artistry of documentary cinema with four days of film screenings. The festival also features seminars led by acclaimed documentary directors such as Ken Burns, Albert Maysles, Michael Apted and Ross McElwee. Call ahead for ticket prices.

Outdoor and Sports Show
Raleigh Convention and Conference Center, Fayetteville Street Mall
• 831-6011

Here's where you can see the latest in camping, hunting and hiking gear.

Southern Ideal Home and Garden Show
State Fairgrounds, Raleigh • 851-2911

If you want to remodel your home or just get some ideas for a future project, this is the place to visit. You'll find many of the area's home improvement specialists, home decorators and specialty vendors at the show, which is sponsored by the Home Builder's Association. The Home Show is also held the last week in September.

Southern Women's Show
Raleigh Convention & Conference Center, Fayetteville Street Mall
• 831-6011

This very popular event has become a traditional outing for many women in the area. Exhibits include jewelry, clothing, fashion accessories, cosmetics, books, food and decorative items.

Spring Daze
Cary Community Center • 469-4061

Handmade crafts from dolls' clothes to stained glass are sold at this outdoor event, which features local artists and craftspeople.

May

Artsplosure Spring Jazz & Art Festival
Downtown Raleigh • 832-8699

More than 200 artists and craftspeople combine with over 30 musicians to mix art, international jazz and regional blues into a spectacular celebration of the arts. Artsplosure also features 150 juried art exhibits and children's exhibits. The 1998 event drew approximately 80,000 people.

INSIDERS' TIP

Don't miss your opportunity to apply for admission to Wake County Magnet Schools. You have a one-week window in February for mailing your application. Don't be early or late!

Photo by Tim Johnson

Approximately 80,000 people turn out for Artsplosure
Spring Jazz & Art Festival annually.

Bimbe Cultural Arts Festival
Durham Athletic Park, Durham
• 560-4355

Bimbe Festival celebrates the traditional West African end of harvest and the spirit of hope with music, dance, rides, children's events and much more.

Brookhill Steeplechase
Clayton • 510-7915

We're so uptown in the Triangle that we started a nationally sanctioned steeplechase in 1992. Brookhill, which is sponsored by the Raleigh Jaycees, started in 1993 and is held the first Saturday in May on Brookhill Farm outside of the Johnston County town of Clayton, east of Raleigh. Brookhill is offered as the Triangle's answer to the older, more famous Stonybrook race near Southern Pines. This race draws thousands of spectators.

Celebration of the Outdoors
Falcon Park, Fuquay-Varina • 552-1410

Fuquay-Varina's four-acre Falcon Park comes alive for this celebration, which includes crafts, food, music, carnival rides and a petting zoo.

Duke Children's Classic
Duke University Golf Club • 419-5400

This event, which has become one of the Triangle's biggest spectator attractions, celebrated its 25th anniversary in 1998. It raises money for the Duke Children's Hospital and Health Center.

In addition to golf, the Classic also includes tennis, entertainment and a sumptuous banquet. In 1998, the Classic concluded with a "Dream Round" of golf, featuring Arnold Palmer, Lee Trevino, Fred Couples and Michelle McGann. It is held in late May and tickets for participants usually are sold out before Christmas. Celebrities at past events have included the late Frank Sinatra, former President Gerald Ford, Michael Jordan, Dinah Shore, Bill Murray and, of course, Perry Como, the founding chairman. Comedian Jeff Foxworthy is the current tournament chairman.

Great Raleigh Road Race
Downtown Raleigh • 831-6011

Sponsored by Mix 101.5 and WRAL-TV, this is Raleigh's largest single participant sporting event with as many as 2,000 runners and joggers lining up for the starting gun on Wilmington Street next to Memorial Auditorium. Two races, 10K (about 6.2 miles) and 5K (about 3.1 miles), are some of the highlights of a whole weekend of activities, including the city's Artsplosure. The course winds its way through downtown and then up Hillsborough Street—and that's UP, too, folks—past NCSU and then back downtown, finishing at the Civic Center. Although it is a sanctioned event, the participants are those same men, women, boys and girls you see plugging along the Triangle's byways and sidewalks year round. The registration fee is $7 or $15 if you would like to receive a commemorative T-shirt.

Landmark Tours
Downtown Raleigh • 833-6404

Spend the day exploring some of the most interesting historic homes and buildings in Raleigh on this self-guided tour. From Mordecai Historic Park (1785) to Montfort Hall (1858) to Nordon Grocery Store (1917), you'll find a variety of architectural styles that are sure to educate and enlighten you. Individual tickets are $20 and family tickets are $40. Ticket price includes a one year introductory membership in Capital Area Preservation, Inc.

Meet in the Street
Downtown Wake Forest • 556-1519

Hosted by the Wake Forest Chamber of Commerce, this street fair offers arts and crafts, food, entertainment and exhibits.

NIKE Carolina Classic
Raleigh • 380-0011

The Carolina Classic, which celebrated its fifth year in 1998, features some of the PGA Tour's up-and-coming pros as well as some older players who are trying to get back on the tour. The 1998 event included a number of recent NIKE Tour winners, including Casey Martin, Eric Johnson, Michael Allen, Joe Ogilvie and John Wilson. The event was played at Raleigh Country Club and will eventually reside at the Wakefield Plantation TPC course. The Classic, one of 30 events on the Nike Tour, features a $225,000 purse. All net proceeds are donated to the Boys and Girls clubs of Wake County.

Old Durham Home Tour
Durham • 682-3036

The Historic Preservation Society of Durham Houses in downtown Durham sponsors a self-guided tour of historic houses in the Forest Hills and Fayetteville Street areas. Tickets cost $12 in advance; $15 the day of the tour.

Peak Week Festival
Apex • 362-6456

This entertaining, day-long festival, sponsored by the Apex Chamber of Commerce, offers arts and crafts, food concessions, children's activities and musical groups. In 1998, the festival added a new event, "Motorsports '98: A Day of Speed," which featured NASCAR drivers and race cars.

June

American Dance Festival
Page Auditorium, Duke University • 684-6402 (See "Dance" section in our "Arts" chapter.)

INSIDERS' TIP

Many events provide shuttle service from parking lots throughout the area. Check local listings for parking arrangements.

Day At The Park Festival
Lumley Community Park, Morrisville
• 469-9760

Music, arts and crafts, food, clowns, pony rides, a children's stage and much more make up this entertaining festival. You'll even find a dunk tank, with local officials volunteering to get wet. Free admission, free rides and fireworks make this a very popular event.

Edible Arts Festival
Durham Arts Council, Durham
• 560-2787

This festival of food and art features a wide assortment of delectable food from the Triangle's restaurants and cafes. Past festivals have included Cafe Parizade, Magnolia Grill, 411 West Italian Cafe, George's Garage and Il Palio Ristorante.

A silent auction includes travel and dining packages, artwork, wine and gifts. All proceeds benefit the Durham Arts Council's Arts Education Program. Tickets are $35 in advance; $40 at the door.

Hillsborough Hog Day
Hillsborough • 732-8156

This unusual event takes place every June in Hillsborough, north of Chapel Hill and Carrboro. If you like to eat pork, you'll feel at home here. Hog Day features a highly competitive barbecue cook-off, with the results to be enjoyed by those attending this event. In addition to Carolina barbecue, other foods are there for you to enjoy. A best-dressed pot-belly pig contest, arts and crafts, music and dance, an antique car show, games and activities for kids round out the offerings of the festival.

Photo by Rich Weidman

The best-dressed pot-belly pig contest is always a popular event at Hillsborough Hog Day, which is held the third week of June every year.

Spring Cultural Festival
Hillsborough • 304-3723

The Occaneechi-Saponi Tribe share their culture with all on the banks of the Eno River in downtown Hillsborough. The festival features traditional dancing, music, samples of native foods, primitive weapon demonstrations and arts and crafts from tribes such as Abanaki, Cherokee, Coharie, Haliwa and Lumbee. A reconstructed 17th-century Occaneechi village opened recently, enabling visitors to learn more about the lifestyle of this Piedmont tribe.

Summerfest at Regency Park
Regency Park, Cary
• 733-2750, ext. 260

The North Carolina Symphony's Summerfest at Regency Park in Cary has become the informal, fun, family event all the Triangle looks forward to every Saturday night in June (7:30 PM), two June Thursday nights (6:30 PM) and the Fourth of July (8 PM). You can picnic on the lawn with food you've brought or purchased. If you're not a grass and blanket fan, some seats are available under a tent where you can sit at a table with friends and enjoy the concert in comfort. The venue will boast a new $8.5 million pavilion for the year 2000. Recent highlights have included Dixieland jazz from the New Reformation Band, R&B singer Ben E. King, Red Clay Ramblers, and folk singers Arlo Guthrie and Mike Cross. Adult tickets are $10 when purchased in advance and $12 at the gate. Children under 12 are admitted free of charge. Single tickets are available at the gate or call 831-6060 or (800) 292-7469.

Sunday in the Park
Fletcher Park, Raleigh • 831-6640

This popular, laid-back and free concert series is held every Sunday at 6 PM from early June until mid-September, featuring such area talent as the Steel Creek Bluegrass Band, the Raleigh Concert Band and the Blues in the Night Jazz Orchestra. It's the perfect chance to picnic with the whole family.

Tar Heel Regatta
Lake Wheeler Park, Raleigh • 662-5704

The Tar Heel Regatta offers national competition boat races at Lake Wheeler, the largest of Raleigh's city parks. Tickets for the Regatta run about $5 per person; $20 per carload.

July

Carrboro Community Fourth of July Celebration
Carrboro • 968-7703

This old-fashioned July 4th celebration is presented each year by the Carrboro Recreation and Parks Department. It features a kid's parade, food, games, face painting and many more activities.

Durham Fireworks Celebration
Wallace Wade Stadium • 560-4355

Held at the football stadium on Duke's West Campus, this popular free event features a classical pops concert followed by fireworks at 9 PM.

Family Fourth at Kenan Stadium
Kenan Stadium, UNC-CH • 968-2784

If you like fireworks, live music and big crowds, this is where you ought to celebrate Independence Day in Chapel Hill. In recent years, it has been jointly sponsored by the towns of Chapel Hill and Carrboro and Orange County.

Garner Independence Day Festival
Lake Benson Park, Garner • 772-4688

Get a jump on the Fourth of July crowd by attending this fun-filled extravaganza, which consists of a pops concert starring the North Carolina Symphony and an impressive fireworks display.

July 4th Celebration
State Fairgrounds, Raleigh • 831-6640

Raleigh celebrates the Fourth in a big way, starting about 3 PM at the State Fairgrounds at the intersection of Hillsborough Street and Blue Ridge Road. Admission is free. It's a relaxed day in which you can toss horseshoes, test your basketball free throws or football passes in contests sponsored by the city's Parks and Recreation Department, WRAL 101.5 FM radio and the North Carolina State Fairgrounds. Entertainment has featured popular bands such as Celebration, Casablanca, the Breeze and some country and bluegrass music from Windy Creek. Games and rides are throughout the grounds. Concession stands sell Fourth of July specials such as hot dogs and soft drinks. Cold watermelon is usually free.

The big show—and the one that draws 40,000 people to the Fairgrounds and another 100,000 spectators parked all along Interstate 40, Meredith College and any street, road or highway within sight of the Fairgrounds—is the fireworks display. The city spends over $7,500 to light up the sky with the rockets' red glare. It's a show that would make Francis Scott Key proud and brings thrills to contemporary patriots.

July 4th Celebration with N.C. Symphony
Regency Park, Cary • 469-4061

Everything about the free Fourth of July concert and fireworks extravaganza is Americana at its best—American pops favorites, flags waving, families and friends together and a sky exploding with spectacular sights and sounds.

July 4th Festival for the Eno
West Point on the Eno • 477-4549

Every year the Eno River Association sponsors a Fourth of July extravaganza at West Point on the Eno city park. It's three days jam-packed with crafts, exhibits, food, fun and most of all, music. Styles include big-name gospel, folk and bluegrass. There's an admission charge ($8 in advance, $10 at the gate and

Photo by Evelyn Ward

All proceeds from the Festival for the Eno go toward the purchase of natural parklands on the Eno River.

children 12 and under free) and proceeds go to preservation of the park and the Eno River. A detailed schedule of events is published in the local newspapers in advance of the event.

Kroger Senior Expo
Raleigh Convention and Conference Center, Fayetteville Street Mall • (888) 367-8878

Demonstrations, seminars, free samples and health screenings provide seniors with information and products geared toward their health and well being. Entertainment and prizes are also available at this free event.

Tobacco Harvest Festival
Duke Homestead • 477-5498

This festival highlights the tradition of tobacco harvesting and curing and other related activities.

August

Photo by Julia Teague

Michael Jordan brought his famous competitive drive to Prestonwood for the Jimmy V Celebrity Golf Classic.

Italian Festival
Siena Hotel, Chapel Hill • 929-4000

Inspiration for the Siena Hotel's Italian Festival, begun in 1994, came from the pageantry of the medieval horse race held twice each summer in Siena, Italy. The festival features a culinary journey through Italy, including a Murder Mystery Dinner, a Lessons in Italian Class, a Tuscan Table dinner, an Italian Wine Tasting Class, a Cooking Demonstration, a Kid's Day and more.

Jimmy "V" Celebrity Golf Classic
Prestonwood Golf Club, Cary • 319-0441

The Classic honors former N.C. State basketball coach Jim Valvano, who died of cancer. His family started the Classic in 1994 to raise money for the "V" Foundation, which sponsors cancer research. In 1997, the tournament generated $900,000 for cancer research. It attracts big name

sports and entertainment celebrities such as Michael Jordan, Charles Barkley, Meatloaf and Kevin Costner to the Triangle for two days of parties and golf. Expect 30,000 fans to attend. Spectators park at Carter-Finley Stadium and receive shuttle service to Prestonwood. Pay $5 in advance or $8 on tournament day to stroll the links with the celebrities. Tickets can be ordered through Ticketmaster at 834-4000.

Lazy Daze Arts & Crafts Festival
Downtown Cary • 469-4061

Lazy Daze, which has become a real Triangle attraction, is held the last Saturday in August in downtown Cary. The festival draws approximately 400 craftspeople and artisans from all over the region. They show their wares and paintings from booths set up along Academy and Chatham streets. It's a great place to look for handmade items, some of them at very good prices. Live entertainment from mountain cloggers to bluegrass music is featured on a bandstand set up near the intersection.

September

Bull Durham Blues Festival
Durham Athletic Park, Durham • 683-1709

Some of the country's best-known blues artists descend on historic Durham Athletic Park for two days of blues standards and new blues variations.

Centerfest
Downtown Durham • 560-2787

The Durham Arts Council and the City Parks and Recreation Department co-sponsor this two-day street festival, which celebrated its 25th anniversary in 1998. It draws thousands of participants downtown for high-quality, beautiful arts-and-crafts exhibits, kids' activities, theatre, dancing, music, all kinds of food and more. It's fun for all ages.

La Fiesta del Pueblo
Chapel Hill High School • 929-7174

Started in 1994, this two-day festival celebrating Latino culture continues to grow in popularity. Traditional dancing, music, food and crafts are enjoyed annually by close to 20,000. A soccer tournament, which features teams from the state's Latino leagues, adds to the excitement and festivities.

Gourd Festival
Cary Community Center, Cary • 362-4357

This two-day event, co-sponsored by the Cary Gourd Village Garden Club and Cary's Parks, Recreation and Cultural Resources Department was first held in 1941. The festival showcases dried gourds made into a variety of jewelry and decorative accessories, including bowls, birdhouses, pitchers, lamps, clocks, masks and three-dimensional puzzles.

Grecian Festival
State Fairgrounds, Raleigh • 781-4548

Greek dancing and entertainment, food, pastries and coffee, cooking demos

Photo by Evelyn Ward

Wilson Pickett thrills the crowd "Till the Midnight Hour" at the Bull Durham Blues Festival.

and a gift shop are all part of the fun at this three-day event sponsored by the Holy Trinity Greek Orthodox Church.

Labor Day Weekend Pops In The Park
N.C. Symphony • 733-9536

"Pops in the Park" is the Labor Day Weekend Concert that's the Triangle's unofficial salute to the end of summer. Thanks to the graciousness of Meredith College in Raleigh, the concert is held on the college's beautiful front campus and is televised by WRAL-TV.

Families and friends start gathering about 4 PM Sunday to spread their blankets, set up tables and partake of the biggest community picnic (25,000 picnickers) of the summer. It's a great time for people who have been away on vacations or off to summer camp to get back together and swap news or gossip and listen to beautiful music. Meanwhile, you can watch the orchestra set up, tune its instruments and then hear light classical and show tunes with a rousing finale of the "1812 Overture," punctuated with booming fireworks. What follows is Raleigh's most mellow traffic jam of the year as thousands patiently load up their cars and station wagons and slip into the night and into the start of another autumn.

Oktoberfest
North Hills Mall, Raleigh • 828-6399

Despite its name, Oktoberfest is held in late September. German beer, food and entertainment become part of North Hills Mall for four days to raise funds for Hospice of Wake County.

Today & Yesteryear Festival
Downtown Apex • 387-9550

Historic downtown Apex comes alive for two days of good old-fashioned fun at the Today & Yesteryear Festival, which features arts and crafts, entertainment, food, a Civil War reenactment and more. Sponsored by the Apex Downtown Merchant's Association, the festival draws over 10,000 people each year.

The Umstead Festival
Reedy Creek Road, Raleigh • 833-6067

A 5K run/walk kicks off the festivities at this two-day event. Music, entertainment and crafts attract the crowds to help raise funds for the preservation and protection of William B. Umstead Park and other park-related programs. A shuttle runs from the N.C. State Fairgrounds.

FYI

Unless otherwise noted, the area code for all phone numbers listed in this guide is 919.

October

Bright Leaf Folk Festival
Downtown Wendell • 365-6318

Held the first weekend in October, this festival features family-centered activities and entertainment, including arts and crafts, children's games, a parade, food and face painting.

Festifall
Franklin St., Chapel Hill • 968-2784

This street fair celebrates fall with arts and crafts, music, dancing, magicians, puppet shows, jugglers, potters, food and more.

Five Points Festival
Glenwood Ave. & Fairview Rd., Raleigh

Arts, crafts, music, food, and plenty of activities for children are all part of this neighborhood event.

International Festival
Raleigh Convention & Conference Center, Fayettevillle Street Mall • 832-4331

This is a celebration of all the different nationalities that now call the Triangle home. The food is the tastiest part of the

The North Carolina State Fair, held for 10 days in October, features carnival rides, crafts, food, agricultural expositions, fireworks, music and much more.

festival, but dancing, singing and native crafts are also on display. A $6 admission fee is charged; $3 for children 3-12.

N.C. State Fair
Hillsborough St. & Blue Ridge Rd.
• 733-2145

The fair lasts 10 days, starting on the third Friday of the month. For first timers, it's a great place to taste, touch, see and smell all those things that reveal the richness of North Carolina's people and culture. Check at fair time for admission prices, which are under $10 for adults, less for children 6 to 12 and free for children under 6 and adults over 65. Each ticket is good for the entire day, including the Dorton Arena's evening performances of popular stars.

It's the kind of fair where judges still hand out blue ribbons for the best cakes, pies, preserves, pigs and cows. If you're looking for really good down-home food at the fair, try the restaurants across from the Dorton Arena staffed by volunteers from local organizations. The big attractions are the rides and tents on the midway that arrive by rail. A fireworks display brings every fair night to an end—with a BANG.

Gates open at 9 AM. Expect a crowd, even if it rains. Avoid the traffic jam if you can by taking a CAT bus from several outlying locations. Buses run regularly down Hillsborough Street every 15 minutes.

A Shopping Spree
Raleigh Convention and Conference Center, Fayetteville Street Mall
• 787-7480

Organized by the Junior League of Raleigh, this four-day event offers the perfect opportunity to start your holiday shopping. Food and entertainment are also provided. Admission is $5 in advance; $6 at the door.

November

Carolina Christmas Show
Raleigh Convention and Conference Center, Fayetteville Street Mall
• (800) 232-4936

A wonderful shopping experience, the Christmas Show features many of the state's craftspeople and their wares.

Cary Band Day
Downtown Cary • 481-0949

This all-day event starts with a parade of high school bands through downtown Cary and winds up at the Cary High School for competition among participating bands. Since 1958, Cary Band Day has drawn high school bands from throughout the United States.

N.C. Film & Video Festival
Rialto Theater, Raleigh • 212-0690

This five-day event features seminars, panel discussions, viewings of independent films and an awards ceremony. Filmmakers such as Victor Nunez (*Ulee's Gold*) and Robert Young (*Caught*) have participated. A festival pass or individual tickets are available. Ticket prices vary.

Raleigh Christmas Parade
Downtown Raleigh • 420-0120

Sponsored by the Greater Raleigh Merchants Association, this is the city's biggest parade of the year. Starting at the intersection of Hillsborough and St. Mary's streets, 40 floats, 20 bands and a cast of thousands march down Hillsborough Street toward the Capitol. If you're used to attending Thanksgiving parades in New York City or Detroit, you're in for a Sunbelt treat—no mittens, woolen underwear, thermal socks or pocket handwarmers are needed down here. Just find a good place along the street before the 10 AM starting time.

Photo by Tim Johnson

The Executive Mansion, an 1891 Queen Anne Cottage-style Victorian house, opens its doors each December for a Holiday Open House.

Several traditions keep the crowds—estimated at 150,000—coming back. One of them is the competition between children marchers in costume. Another competition is held for children with costumed pets. Reflecting the city's more cosmopolitan makeup, recent years have seen floats from differing nationalities, including Scandinavian, Indian and Latin American. You'll see some of the country's best baton twirlers and in the last float, guess who? Santa Claus himself, who always gets the biggest cheer of the day.

December

Dickens Fair
Raleigh Convention & Conference Center, Fayetteville Street Mall • 497-0169

The brainchild of former City Council member Mary Cates, the fair began in 1992 as an annual celebration of Charles Dickens' vision of Christmas. A costume competition and readings by Dickens' scholar Dr. Elliott Engel or other literary guests are a part of the fair. Of course, there is authentic Victorian England food, music and games. There are modest fees for some of the activities.

Executive Mansion Holiday Open House
200 N. Blount St., Raleigh • 733-3456

In early December, Governor and Mrs. James B. Hunt invite Triangle residents over for a tour of the 1891 Queen Anne Cottage-style Victorian house.

First Night Raleigh
Downtown Raleigh • 832-8699

Held in downtown Raleigh, First Night is an artistic and alcohol-free community celebration of New Year's Eve that keeps getting bigger each year. You will especially want to be part of the crowd of thousands in front of the Civic Center when the famous copper Raleigh Acorn drops to bring in the New Year.

Historic Oakwood Candlelight Tour
Historic Oakwood Association
• 821-7276

A walking tour of Oakwood, the Victorian neighborhood near the Governor's Mansion, organized in 1972, has turned into an annual public event. The two-day Historic Oakwood Christmas Tour, one of the capital city's showplaces, usually begins on the first or second weekend of December, starting at 1 PM and ending at 7 PM each day. Advance tour tickets cost $8 for adults; $10 on the day of the tour. It's free for children under 12 and group discounts are available.

The Christmas Tour lets you inside the wonderful old homes, many of them decorated in period greenery. There are from six to 11 homes on the tour (it changes each year) and the homeowners will usually greet you and give you the history of the house. Refreshments, tea and homemade cookies may be offered. The hosts and hostesses need rest and refreshment too, since 2,000 to 3,000 people usually make the tour. This is great entertainment for your visiting grandmother or mother-in-law or the cousin who is renovating an older home. A walking garden tour of the neighborhood is offered in September.

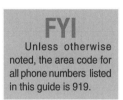

FYI

Unless otherwise noted, the area code for all phone numbers listed in this guide is 919.

Holly Days Parade & Festival
Holly Springs • 557-3925

Held on the second Saturday of December, the event begins with a community parade, followed by live entertainment ranging from beach music to rock 'n' roll, food and the traditional lighting of the Town Christmas Tree.

New Year's Eve Concert
N.C. Symphony • 733-9536

The North Carolina Symphony's New Year's Eve concert is one of the Triangle's most pleasant ways to ring in the new year. The concert is billed as a "Viennese evening" of light music and waltzes. Those who want the full treatment (about $110 per ticket), can begin the evening with a pre-concert sip of champagne at a local hotel and end it with a post-concert dinner and dancing. The concert begins about 8 PM and lasts for about two hours. Conductor Gerhardt Zimmerman leads the fun with commentary along with the music. After the concert, the crowd is bused to the hotel and guests dine sumptuously while a dance band picks up the beat and continues the mood with waltzes and other rhythms. Many merrymakers choose to spend the night at the hotel, thus avoiding the anxiety of being on the road late New Year's Eve. Check with the Symphony's box office for ticket prices. Make reservations through the hotel.

It seems with each passing year, the Triangle has more to offer in dance, music, theater and visual arts.

Arts and Culture

It seems with each passing year, the Triangle has more to offer in dance, music, theater and visual arts. Not only is the area abundant with professionals who perform and provide exhibits, but each college also has a cornucopia of performers and exhibits that offer interesting entertainment.

In 1998, one of the biggest events was *The Phantom of the Opera* at Raleigh Memorial Auditorium. For almost five weeks, the downtown Raleigh theater district was alive with loyal fans of *Opera* and the theater. Almost 90,000 people attended, with ticket sales of $5.4 million.

An event of international renown takes place every year in June and July in Durham. The multidimensional American Dance Festival provides extraordinary modern dance performances that will entertain and delight you. In its 65th year, the "World's Greatest Dance Festival" (as billed by *The New York Post)* presented 13 world premieres.

If it's music you want, Raleigh is home to the North Carolina Symphony, which performs throughout the state; however, when it is in the Triangle, the Symphony provides an extensive series of music from classical to pop.

As for visual arts, one of the state's most treasured art museums is located in Raleigh. The North Carolina Museum of Art offers permanent displays of Egyptian statues, European paintings and everything in between, plus several touring exhibits each year.

In the past several years, documentary and independent film festivals have become part of the Triangle art scene. These events include panel discussions and award ceremonies and provide the opportunity to view a variety of films by some of the brightest emerging filmmakers in the industry.

Theater

Raleigh and Cary

The Raleigh-Cary area is a stage full of theater. If the stage is your world, you will find parts aplenty. If you like the critic's seat, we have a variety of venues. You want to start, however, with the basic arts organizations. They are the Raleigh Arts Commission, 890-3477, the Raleigh Fine Arts Society (which is more social), the Cary Parks, Recreation & Cultural Resources, 469-4061, Visual Art Exchange, 828-7834, and the United Arts Council, 839-1498, a private, nonprofit agency founded in the 1980s to provide financial support to the arts much the way the United Way supports human services agencies. The United Arts Council publishes a quarterly calendar and the news weeklies, *The Spectator* and *The Independent,* publish weekly calendars; these publications and *The News and Observer* are the best sources for information on

Photo by Robert Thomason

Nearly 90,000 people attended *The Phantom of the Opera* during its run at Raleigh Memorial Auditorium in 1998.

Raleigh and Cary cultural activities. The Wake County Public Library also maintains a list of clubs, many of which are involved in the arts. The associations and organizations listed here are major and minor groups, but ones that Insiders will know.

Best of Broadway Series
Memorial Auditorium • 831-6060

Through the Best of Broadway Series at Memorial Auditorium, the City of Raleigh offers national tours of current hits such as *Les Miserables*, *Cats* and 1998's phenomenally successful Broadway smash, *The Phantom of the Opera*. 1999-2000 productions in the Best of Broadway Series include *Ragtime*, *Sunset Boulevard* and *Titanic*.

The Memorial Auditorium complex is currently undergoing a $38 million expansion that will include a 1,700-seat symphony hall for the North Carolina Symphony and a 600-seat multipurpose theater. The new complex, which will be called the BTI Center for the Performing Arts, is set to open in the year 2000.

Burning Coal Theatre Company
7308 Bryn Athyn Way, #278 • 388-0066

Since debuting in 1997 with the intense and disturbing drama, *Rat in the Skull*, the Burning Coal Theatre Company has taken the independent theater scene by storm with its innovative productions. Formed by the husband and wife team of Jerome Davis and Simmie Kastner, Burning Coal was voted "Best New Ensemble in Raleigh" by *The News and Observer*. It concluded its inaugural season with a production of David Edgar's *Pentecost*.

North Carolina Theatre
Memorial Auditorium • 831-6948

The North Carolina Theatre is located in the beautiful 2,300-seat Memorial Auditorium. It is sponsored in part by the City of Raleigh and produces professional theater for the capital city. Auditions are held for each production in New York and Raleigh. The group traces its roots back to 1972 and Chapel Hill; but in 1983 with partial funding offered by the City of Raleigh, it made its home in Memorial

Auditorium downtown. Since then, it has produced well-known musicals, including recent hits *Big River: The Adventures of Huckleberry Finn* and *The Secret Garden*. 1999 productions include *Grease, South Pacific, La Cage Aux Folles* and *The Music Man*. Season tickets are available.

Raleigh Ensemble Players
201 E. Davie St. • 832-9607

The Ensemble Players began in 1980 and is a community theater group that specializes in contemporary plays and musicals in a second-floor gallery at Artspace in downtown Raleigh. Four to five "Mainstage" productions are performed each season. Recent productions included *Love! Valour! Compassion!*, Sam Shepard's *True West* and *A View from the Bridge*. The group sponsors acting classes and has plans for voice, technical theater classes and movement. For a schedule, tickets or information, give the Ensemble Players a call.

Raleigh Little Theatre
301 Pogue St. • 821-3111

This is one of the country's oldest community theaters, born in the Great Depression, and the building is vintage WPA architecture. The theater, known to Insiders as RLT, is comprised of volunteer performers, with a paid artistic director, managing director and technical staff. RLT's productions range from comedies to musicals to dramas. Each season, the Main Stage Series includes five well-known Broadway shows, the City Stage Series presents four contemporary works and the Youth Series includes five shows for family audiences. Recent productions have included *Oklahoma, Man of La Mancha, The Lion in Winter* and *Godspell*. For individual ticket prices at the door, call the box office.

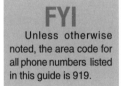

FYI

Unless otherwise noted, the area code for all phone numbers listed in this guide is 919.

Theatre in the Park
107 Pullen Rd. • 831-6058

Theatre In The Park has earned a reputation as one of the state's most exciting and innovative community theater centers since its start in the early '70s. TIP annually presents a wide range of productions in its intimate and totally flexible performance space. The best in comedy, musicals, Shakespeare, contemporary drama and children's theater are offered as mainstage productions. Recent productions have included *Julius Caesar* and *Of Mice and Men*. TIP also offers theater classes and workshops for all ages.

A Christmas Carol has been a traditional sellout at Raleigh's Memorial Auditorium. Sign up or become a season member of TIP if you want to be guaranteed a seat!

University Theatre
NCSU • 515-2405

North Carolina State University's Theatre consists of the student-run University Players and the Center Stage professional series. Performances are held at the 200-seat Thompson Theatre and the 816-seat Stewart Theatre.

University Players productions are student-oriented, with an emphasis on experimentation. Each production is open to all NCSU students, whether experienced or not, as actors, technicians, crew members and directors. Student Studio Series productions are completely student run, and African-American and children's theater are also available for all students. The tickets are among the best value in the Triangle: $10 for adults and $9 for senior citizens. Recent productions included William Inge's *Bus Stop* and Noel Coward's *Blithe Spirit*.

The Center Stage series offers over 30 professional events each year. Every season includes music, modern dance, comedy, mime, children's theater, jazz, international events, drama and more. Recent performers have included The Flying Karamazov Brothers, the Kronos Quartet, David Dorfman Dance Company, jazz vocalist Carol Sloane and the Reduced Shakespeare Company. Ticket prices range from $5 to $22. Call 515-1100 for tickets.

Durham

Duke University
Page Box Office • 684-4444

Of course we don't always get the big plays before they hit Broadway, but we can always catch them when they come this way on tour—and for usually about half the price—thanks to the Broadway at Duke series. One of the nicest places to enjoy that level of theater, as well as music and dance, is at Duke's $16 million Bryan Center. Performances take place in the 600-seat Reynolds Theater or the 150-seat Sheafer Laboratory Theater.

Duke Drama, 660-3343, is a group of drama students at Duke who produce theater for the university, the community and the state. It stages close to a dozen plays a year in the Bryan Center theaters. The Duke Institute of the Arts, 660-3356, is breaking the boundaries of convention with its new directions in performance art. Hoof 'N' Horn is a Duke student organization that produces one to three musicals a year. Duke also offers dramatic productions and dance, music and film during its annual Summer Festival of Arts.

Durham Arts Council
120 Morris St. • 560-ARTS

The Durham Arts Council makes grants to and houses a number of outstanding local arts organizations, including community theater groups such as the Durham Savoyards, the Little Big Theatre Company and the Young People's Performing Company. It also helps with art programs in the Durham Public Schools, produces the annual CenterFest and Edible Arts Festival and provides over 350 classes in the arts for the community. Call the council for more information or a schedule of upcoming events.

Durham Savoyards
120 Morris St. • 309-9059

If you like Gilbert and Sullivan, you'll love the Durham Savoyards. This community theater group has devoted itself to presenting at least one major G&S production a year for more than two decades. Call for more information.

Manbites Dog Theater
P.O. Box 402, Durham, NC 27702
• 220-6779

As the name suggests, the establishment of this innovative local group in 1988 was exciting news for downtown arts patrons seeking something different. Having outgrown its Roxboro Road theater location in 1995, Manbites Dog recently opened a new performance space at 703 Foster Street in downtown Durham. This offbeat laboratory focuses on timely and controversial subjects that otherwise might not be dramatically addressed in our neck of the woods. Manbites Dog produces four to five shows a season. Recent productions have included Nicky Silver's comedy *The Food Chain*. Call or write for performance information or to make donations for its new theater.

INSIDERS' TIP

When attending an opening night, dress is usually more formal than for other performances. Otherwise, dress may vary from very casual to very formal at the same event.

Come Soar with Us

Handel's Messiah
December 22-23, 26-28, 1999
A holiday event of lyric reverence and majesty, Handel's Messiah combines dance, music, song, costumes, and effects to create a sensory masterpiece. Accompanied by members of The North Carolina Symphony.
Raleigh Memorial Auditorium

Carmen
May 18-21, 2000
The passionate tale of love, seduction, betrayal, and jealousy comes to life with all-new choreography by Robert Weiss. Accompanied by The North Carolina Symphony.
Raleigh Memorial Auditorium

Cabaret & Variations
June 1-4, 2000
Internationally acclaimed talents combine as cabaret singer Andrea Marcovicci and choreographer Lynne Taylor-Corbett collaborate to bring you new ballets you won't want to miss!
Raleigh Memorial Auditorium

World Premieres with Ciompi Quartet
February 25-27, 2000
Music, dance, and theatre are entwined in the world premiere of Tolstoy's novella, The Kreutzer Sonata, performed with live orchestration by the Ciompi Quartet.
Duke University, R.J. Reynolds Theatre

Subscribe and Save 20%

Carolina **Ballet**
Robert Weiss, Artistic Director

1999-2000 Season

For Tickets Call the *Ballet line* **303-6303**
Some Locations Already SOLD OUT

The North Carolina Theatre's
2000 Season

The Shows You've Always Wanted to See!

Drama League recently voted Best Musical of all time.

March 24 - April 2, 2000

Come to the wide-open skies of Oklahoma! for Rodgers and Hammerstein's first and arguably best musical ever.

July 14 - 23, 2000

A satirical look at sex and politics in the lone star state. "A fun musical full of gusto and a wealth of comic details and music with a bustle." -NY Post

September 8 - 17, 2000

A Big Band era musical by the creators of Cabaret and Chicago about a dance marathon in Atlantic City in 1933 and two people who fall in love - there and then.

November 3 - 12, 2000

The timeless enchantment of a magical fairytale is reborn with Rodgers and Hammerstein's hallmarks of originality, charm and elegance.

ALL PERFORMANCES AT RALEIGH MEMORIAL AUDITORIUM

Call Now For Tickets & Information

The North Carolina Theatre: (919) 831-6950

The North Carolina Theatre • One East South Street, Raleigh, NC 27601
www.nctheatre.com • Box Office Hours are Monday - Friday, 10:00am - 5:00pm

Funded in part by the City of Raleigh, based on recommendations of the Raleigh Arts Commission

North Carolina Central University
Fayetteville St. • 560-6242

North Carolina Central University's Department of Dramatic Art sponsors the Ivan-Dixon Players, a student group that puts on at least four major productions a year. NCCU also has featured appearances by guest artists such as James Earl Jones.

The Triangle Performance Ensemble focuses on works by black playwrights. Performances are at the University Theatre in the Farrison-Newton Building at North Carolina Central University.

Royall Center for the Arts
120 Morris St. • 560-ARTS

Royall Center for the Arts, named for State Senator Kenneth Royall, is actually a plot of land in downtown Durham, bounded by Morris, Chapel Hill, Foster and Morgan streets, on which stand the Durham Arts Council Building, the Carolina Theatre and the Civic Center Plaza. Thanks to the fund-raising efforts of the Council itself, the persistence of several leaders in the local arts community and the passage of a bond referendum in the 1980s, the theater and adjoining building were renovated into a vast multipurpose complex.

The Durham Arts Council Building opened in September 1988. And in 1994, the restored Carolina Theatre reopened after five-plus years of design and construction work. The Carolina Theatre, built in 1926, holds a 1,016-seat main hall for films and live performances and a 3,700 title video rental shop. The Carolina Theatre screens films and hosts concerts, opera, dramatic productions and other special events. The box office number is 560-3030.

Young People's Performing Company
120 Morris St. • 560-2745

As the name suggests, this community theater group offers classes and performance opportunities for young people from ages 5 to 18.

Chapel Hill and Carrboro

ArtsCenter
300-G E. Main St., Carrboro
• 929-ARTS

Formerly known as The ArtSchool, the ArtsCenter started in 1974 as a modest community venture located in a one-room loft in Carrboro. It has since outgrown its second home—in the restored Carr Mill

Volunteering in the Triangle

Do you have some free time? Would you like to meet some of your Triangle neighbors? Would you like to contribute in some way to a local group or spend some time one-on-one with an individual? With almost 200 agencies and organizations in the area, it's easy to get involved in the community. Wake, Durham and Orange counties each have group hotlines that provide a vast assortment of possibilities. If you would like to volunteer and aren't sure where you fit in, they'll even match something to your schedule and interest.

Close-up

The Wake County Voluntary Action Center's mission is to "mobilize people and resources to deliver creative solutions to community problems." Through this agency, you'll connect to some of the larger organizations such as the American Red Cross, to transport clients to and from clinics; the Boy Scouts of America, to be a scout leader; Habitat for Humanity, to help with construction needs; Hospice of Wake County, to be a family support volunteer; the Inter-Faith Food Shuttle, to deliver food to nonprofit agencies or Meals on Wheels, to deliver meals at lunch time; and the Salvation Army, to be a kitchen stockroom volunteer. On a more personal level, you can become an advocate for a child through Guardian Ad Litem or become a mentor to a child at the YMCA. On a more creative note, if you can play the piano and conduct sing-a-longs, you can participate in the Play Piano for Senior Program; at Helping Horse, your skills can be used to teach horseback riding as therapy; and at Cherish the Earth, you can put your gardening skills to good use. Call 460-8687 to volunteer or for more information.

The Junior League of Raleigh is a nonprofit organization with more than 1,500 women who promote volunteerism through many programs. SAFE*child*, created by the League in 1992, is a community-based, nonprofit, child abuse prevention agency that helps Wake County adults and children create nurturing environments. Contact the League at 787-7480 or SAFE*child* at 231-5800.

The Volunteer Center of Greater Durham provides a wide choice of volunteer opportunities for local citizens and businesses to serve the community. One of the largest is in early July, when the Festival for the Eno needs volunteers to help set up for the festival, paint children's faces, staff booths, park cars or provide other services. Other opportunities during the summer include matching readers with books at local libraries, supporting children under five who have been victims of abuse, translating for Spanish-speaking clients and ushering at performances of international artists. The Center also matches employees with volunteer opportunities and coordinates group projects. Call 688-8977 to learn more about how you can volunteer.

A service of the Triangle United Way, Volunteer Orange! recruits and refers

Photo by Evelyn Ward

Habitat for Humanity home

volunteers to many nonprofits and public organizations for ongoing projects and for special events. Among the services needed during the summer are volunteers to provide transportation to the clinic for cancer treatment patients, to assist in providing hot meals to seniors, to tutor teenagers and to teach English. Volunteer Orange! also has an Advisor who will match your interests and time availability with a volunteer need. For more information, call 929-9837.

Are you looking for a more specific volunteer experience? If you're interested in arts and history, call the Historic Preservation Society of Durham at 682-3036 and volunteer to help out at Stagville Plantation, Duke Homestead or other historic sites in Durham. Or volunteer to work behind the scene at UNC-TV, 549-7126, in research, for general administrative work or in production. If you want to contribute to the field of education, you can tutor an algebra class, or if you are a law student or lawyer, you can help with law-related education classes, both in Chapel Hill. If you want to work with seniors, you can staff a crisis line for the elderly or support caregivers of the very ill throughout the Triangle, or even join a sewing group at Cary Senior Center. Are you interested in contributing your time to animal services or environmental, literacy or outreach programs? You'll find those causes and a lot more throughout the area seeking volunteers. For online information about volunteer opportunities visit the Community Volunteers page at www.citysearch11.com/The-Triangle/Community/Volunteers/.

shopping village—and is presently located in a much larger, renovated space nearby. Its home on East Main Street in Carrboro includes an intimate 350-seat theater, six classrooms, a gallery with skylights, offices and studios for ceramics, dance, television and recording.

Among the many activities that take place at the ArtsCenter are theatrical events geared to participants of all ages, interests and levels of experience. In addition to offering performances and events, the ArtsCenter occasionally sponsors theater classes for students of all levels and ages. Adults can learn about scenes, play writing and improvisational techniques. There are classes for children from ages 6 to 17 in creative drama, improvisation and fantasy. Two drama groups housed at the ArtsCenter are the Transactors and New Plays Rising.

Classes and performances are offered to the public at very reasonable prices, with discounts available to Friends of the ArtsCenter.

Community Youth Theatre

Each summer the Community Youth Theatre offers four weeks of classes in all phases of drama to talented 9- to 13-year-olds in Orange County. Classes focus on movement, speech, pantomime, acting and technical theater, and culminate in a public performance.

University of North Carolina

Whether it's a production by the PlayMakers Repertory Company or an experimental piece by the Drama Department, UNC provides Triangle audiences with an array of theatrical possibilities and facilities.

The PlayMakers Repertory Company, 962-7529, is the state's only year-round professional resident theater. Since joining the national League of Resident Theatres in 1976, PlayMakers has been committed to preserving the classics, as well as performing more modern works. The company also presents a special holiday show each year: The Nutcracker was performed in 1997 and A Christmas Carol was the 1998 production. All shows are produced in the modern Paul Green Theater, named in honor of the late Pulitzer Prize-winning playwright and UNC alumnus. The theatre seats 500 people on three sides of its thrust stage.

In addition to working with the PlayMakers company, UNC's drama department also stages plays six times a semester in its Laboratory Theatre, 962-1132. "The Lab's" productions range from classic modern drama (Tennessee Williams, Neil Simon) to original works written and directed by the undergraduate drama students themselves.

Music

Whether you like the jazz sounds of Jim Ketch and his compatriots, the rousing folk ballads of troubadour Mike Cross, the sassy lyrics of The Red Clay Ramblers, the croons of Nnenna Freelon or the harmonic strains of the North Carolina Symphony, you can hear them and other musical notes regularly in Triangle clubs and music halls. For more information on the night life scene, see our chapter on "Night Life." Here's a look at what other kinds of live musical presentations are available in Raleigh and Cary, Durham, Chapel Hill and Carrboro.

Raleigh and Cary

Cary School of Music
127 W. Chatham St. • 460-0052

Instructor Pam Mole saw her lifetime dream come true when the doors of the Cary School of Music opened in May of 1993. The school offers private lessons for strings, guitar, piano, orchestra and flute choirs, brass and woodwinds, voice and percussion. The school draws its 35 instructors from such organizations as the North Carolina Symphony, the North Carolina School of the Arts and others. Student ensembles perform every other Friday night at Glenaire retirement complex. The school plans performances with the Raleigh Symphony and a series of music camps.

Concert Singers of Cary
P.O. Box 1921, Cary, NC 27512 • 481-3745

This Cary group of singers, formed in 1991, now has about 150 singers and performs three or four concerts each year. Auditions are held each August. The chorus is directed by Lawrence Speakman and meets at the Cary Community Center at 404 N. Academy Street, behind the Town Hall Annex on Monday nights from 7:30 until 9:30 PM. Concerts are exciting events. An ensemble is available for performances at civic and corporate functions. Projects include additional community outreach and development of a children's chorus. The group has recorded an album of classical and popular music.

Little German Band
Contact: Doug Walker • 571-9080

Raleigh residents knew the city had attained a cosmopolitan status when the Little German Band began to play in 1971. Many of its members were raised around such ethnic music and the band members even put on lederhosen and feathered hats when they perform. The band has become a featured attraction at local Oktoberfest celebrations and plays "at any opportunity" according to one member.

National Opera Company
P.O. Box 12800, Raleigh, NC 27605 • 890-6082

H. L. Mencken's ghost would be surprised to find that, yes, Raleigh does have its own opera company. Started in 1948, it has survived and prospered. The company's mission is threefold: to introduce opera to public school students; to give experience to young singers; and to perform opera in a language the audience understands, namely English. The company has proven to be a good training ground and its alumni include such stars as Samuel

FYI

Unless otherwise noted, the area code for all phone numbers listed in this guide is 919.

Formed in 1933, the North Carolina Symphony performs nearly 200 concerts a year throughout the state.

Photo courtesy of N.C. Symphony

Ramey, Jeannette Scovotti and Arlene Saunders. The company conducts about 90 to 100 performances a season and two or three of those are operas in Raleigh. The group usually will make about 20 appearances in Wake County schools in a season.

North Carolina Symphony
Memorial Auditorium
• Box Office: 831-6060

The North Carolina Symphony is one of the state's treasures, dating from 1933. It was the first continuously state-supported symphony in the country and it lives up to that acclaim by performing nearly 200 concerts a year, including 65 in admission-free school performances. It truly is a "people's orchestra" and a special bonus for Triangle residents because many performances are in this area. It employs about 65 full-time musicians and is conducted by Gerhardt Zimmermann, former Associate Conductor of the St. Louis Symphony.

Most Raleigh performances are in Memorial Auditorium which, with its crystal chandeliers and improved acoustics, rivals any facility in the Southeast. The Memorial Auditorium complex is currently undergoing renovations that will add a new 1,700-seat symphony hall, which will be completed in the year 2000. The Symphony, which also offers series in Chapel Hill and Durham, has performed at Carnegie Hall, the Kennedy Center and Chicago's Orchestra Hall.

The Symphony offers several series, including a classical group; a pops series for the Chablis and brie bunch; a children's series for the young and restless; a ballet series that features well-known ballet companies such as St. Petersburg, Pittsburgh and Washington; and an outdoor "Summerfest" concert series at Cary's Regency Park. There is also an "Open Rehearsal" series for those who want a peek at stars and players before the curtain goes up. The Durham Series of five concerts takes place in the Carolina Theatre. The Chapel Hill Classical Series of five concerts takes place in Memorial Hall on the UNC Campus. Guest performers have included Andre Watts, Henry Mancini, Nadja Salerno-Sonnenberg, Susan Starr, Horacio Gutierrez and Doc Severinsen.

You can sign up for season tickets or buy single tickets; call the box office for price ranges for the different series.

Pinecone
P.O. Box 28534, Raleigh, NC 27611
Contact: Susan Newberry • 990-1900

The Piedmont Council for Traditional Music has brought a heaping helping of traditional North Carolina grassroots music, dance and singing to Raleigh and Cary residents. Along with the city's Parks and Recreation Department, this nonprofit organization produces monthly concerts and sessions of traditional music and song. It also sponsors a monthly contra dance.

PineCone started the Fiddlers' Convention in 1990, which is now called the

Eno River Old Time Fiddler and Bluegrass Convention, and it performs at Durham's West Point on the Eno Amphitheater. Admission is charged for some events; others, especially the outdoor shows, are free.

Raleigh Boychoir
1329 Ridge Rd. • 881-9259

This choir was started in 1968 by Thomas E. Sibley, who has developed the choir into one of the finest boys' choirs in the region. In 1998, it toured the United Kingdom where it gave three performances. There are 45 boys in the performing choir and 85 total in the larger singing group, ranging in age from 8 to 14. There is a monthly membership charge and singers must supply their own concert clothes. In Raleigh, the group is perhaps best known for its annual Carols of Christmas concert at Edenton Street United Methodist Church.

Raleigh Chamber Music Guild
Ravenscroft School • 821-2030

The Raleigh Chamber Music Guild started in 1941, and it brings to the Triangle a season of chamber groups. Guest artists have included the Eastman Brass Quintet, Emerson String Quartet, the Guarneri String Quartet, the Boston Camerata, which specializes in music of the Middle Ages, and the Bach Ensemble. Adult season tickets cost about $50; call for the location of upcoming performances. Another chamber series of note is the Smedes Parlor performances at St. Mary's School. These concerts attract the devoted chamber music fan and are held Monday evenings, once a month. Call St. Mary's at 839-4045 for more information.

Raleigh Civic Symphony
Price Music Center, NCSU • 515-8279

For those who are not content to sit in their seats and listen, there is the Civic Symphony that is less a city group than an outgrowth of the NCSU Music Department. The orchestra is a combination of "town and gown" performers and meets weekly at NCSU's Price Music Center. It is a full symphony with 70 members and it performs two or three times each semester. The orchestra is the parent group for several other orchestras; for more information about where you and your flute might fit in, contact Professor Randy Foy.

Raleigh Concert Band
Contact: Mark Gloden • 881-9328

The Concert Band is another nonprofit, all-volunteer group. It is often asked to play at major civic functions where a little horn blowing and a few drum rolls are in order. Many of the 60 members are former high school and college band players who can't put their instruments away. The band performs regularly throughout the Raleigh area.

Raleigh Conservatory of Music
3636 Capital Blvd. • 790-1533

The Raleigh Conservatory of Music was established in 1986 as a nonprofit organization dedicated to enriching the lives of individuals through music. Programs include "Kindermusik," the exposure of infants and preschool children to musical experiences; childhood through adult music instruction; special programs for the handicapped on an individual basis; community performances and accompanying; and outreach programs to expose all segments of the community to the joys of music.

Raleigh Oratorio Society
Contact: Michelle Hile • 856-9700

The Society, which is under the direction of Alfred E. Sturgis, consists of a volunteer symphonic choir and a professional chamber choir. These are serious singers and they can hold a note with the best, including annual performances with the North Carolina Symphony and other visiting orchestras. The Society recently celebrated its 57th anniversary and is considered to be perhaps the best of the Triangle's choral groups. It has performed at Memorial Auditorium and in some of the city's larger churches, and a sample of its work includes its rousing performances of *Carmina Burana,* as well as *The Messiah* and Mendelssohn's *Elijah.*

Raleigh Symphony Orchestra
336 Fayetteville Street Mall
• 832-5120

The Raleigh Symphony Orchestra is not to be confused—although many do—with the Civic Symphony even though some of its members began there and left to form their own orchestra. Over half of the orchestra is comprised of volunteer musicians with a portion of paid players. It is a full, 65-member orchestra that performs 12 to 15 concerts annually, including one of its annual favorites, *The Messiah.* It is not afraid to tackle Beethoven, Brahms, Mozart or Mussorgsky.

Sunday in the Park
Fletcher Park • 831-6854

Sponsored by the City of Raleigh Parks and Recreation Department, this laid-back concert series is held every Sunday at 6 PM from early June to mid-September. It features such bands as Raleigh Concert Band, Steel Creek Bluegrass Band and the Blues in the Night Jazz Orchestra.

Youth Orchestras
N.C. Symphony • 733-9536
Wake County Schools • 850-1700

Raleigh and Cary children can play in several orchestras, and to find which one best suits their talents, they should contact the North Carolina Symphony or the Wake County Public School system. All the orchestras give concerts and provide young musicians the experience of ensemble playing. The Symphony sponsors the Triangle Youth Philharmonic, which draws from the Triangle area. The group performs five concerts annually and young musicians receive coaching and advice from musicians in the North Carolina Symphony. The public schools sponsor the Raleigh Preparatory String Orchestra (K through 6th grade), the Capital Area Youth Orchestra (middle school grades) and the Raleigh Youth Symphony Orchestra (high school students).

Photo by Tim Johnson

The Durham Arts Council building houses such innovative community theater groups as the Durham Savoyards, the Little Big Theatre Company and the Young People's Performing Company.

Durham

In addition to clubs and restaurants (see "Durham" section of "Night Life"), you can regularly find live music at a number of other locations in Durham, including Duke University and North Carolina Central University. In the summer, there's Jazz in the Parks, a series of concerts in community parks sponsored by the Durham Recreation Department, 560-4355. There's always live music at the July 4th Festival for the Eno, the Bull Durham Blues Festival and CenterFest, the downtown street festival. And throughout the year, you can attend concerts at St. Joseph's Performing Arts Center, a concert auditorium located on Fayetteville Street.

Here's a guide to the musical groups and events you are likely to find in Durham.

Choral Society of Durham
120 Morris St. • 560-2733

Formerly known as the Durham Civic Choral Society, which was founded in 1949, the Choral Society of Durham gives local residents an opportunity to perform large and small works accompanied by an orchestra. The Society usually presents at least two concerts a year, including the annual Christmas concert in Duke Chapel.

Duke University

The quantity, quality and diversity of musical offerings on the Duke University campus is enough to keep anyone busy. Here's a quick look at some of what is available. Except where noted, additional information on any of the following may be obtained by writing the Duke University Music Department, P.O. Box 90665, Durham, NC 27708-0665, or by calling 660-3300.

The Duke University Artists' Series brings to campus a string of nationally and internationally renowned musical artists and performances.

Photo courtesy of N.C. Travel and Tourism

The immense Benjamin N. Duke Memorial Organ, which contains 5,000 speaking pipes with five keyboards, is located in the Duke University Chapel.

Since 1965, the Ciompi Quartet, a resident chamber music quartet, has provided classes and concerts at Duke as well as worldwide. It emphasizes variety, offering pieces from Mozart to Ward to Brahms to Copeland, in four formal concerts a year.

The Chamber Arts Music Society brings to Duke internationally acclaimed artists, such as the Beaux Arts Trio, the Guarneri String Quartet and the Tokyo String Quartet.

The 65-piece Duke Symphony Orchestra is composed of Duke students, faculty and local residents. Led by conductor Lorenzo Muti, it performs about four concerts during the academic year. Individual members often perform with Duke choral groups such as the Duke Chorale that performs several concerts each year.

Lovers of vocal and instrumental music from the Medieval, Renaissance and

Baroque periods will enjoy performances by the Duke University Collegium Musicum, a select group of Duke students, faculty and local residents. It gives at least one concert each semester.

The 20-member Duke Jazz Ensemble is composed of students and performs several times during the academic year with a repertoire that includes big band, jazz-rock and swing.

And if that's not enough, each year the Duke University Wind Symphony selects a group of about 60 musicians who perform two formal concerts and several informal concerts held outdoors in the Sarah P. Duke Gardens.

Durham Symphony
120 Morris St. • 560-2736

This 65-member, community orchestra annually presents a classical concert series, a Holiday Pops concert and a Lollipops Family Concert in the spring. The Symphony also sponsors a Young Artists' Competition and a concert featuring the winners. It has collaborated with other Durham Arts Council beneficiaries on such elaborate opera productions as *Carmen* and *Pagliacci*.

Mallarme Chamber Players
120 Morris St. • 560-2788

Last season, the Mallarme Chamber Players performed its Music Series of five Sunday afternoon concerts at the Peoples Security Insurance Theatre in the Durham Arts Council Building on Morris Street. The group, which is currently in its 15th season, draws mostly from early 20th-century, classical and Romantic pieces not typically performed by other groups in this area. The Mallarme Players also presents two Family Concerts during the fall and spring.

North Carolina Boys Choir
Contact: Bill Graham • 489-0291

This choir of more than 40 musically talented boys between the ages of 9 and 14 performs about 50 concerts a year, including major Christmas and spring concerts in Duke Chapel, television appearances and programs for local nursing homes, hospitals, schools, churches and other groups. The choir takes an annual two-week tour of the United States and Canada. It also offers workshops, scholarships and summer camps. The choir features a training choir for beginning singers and a choir of high-school-aged tenors and basses.

North Carolina Central University

NCCU's Department of Music sponsors several groups and concerts each year. They include New Central Connections, a contemporary jazz ensemble that performs on campus and on tour, the Piano Trio, a faculty chamber group, and the NCCU Choir. For additional information, contact the Department of Music, North Carolina Central University, Durham, NC 27707.

Chapel Hill and Carrboro

If you've read the "Chapel Hill" section of "Night Life," you know that you can find great music at lots of clubs and restaurants in this town. But those aren't the only places you should look. A variety of musical performances are regularly scheduled on the UNC campus and at the ArtsCenter in Carrboro. And there are several community groups you may want to join yourself. Here's a guide to what you can expect.

ArtsCenter
300-G E. Main St., Carrboro
• 929-ARTS

Most weekends, the ArtsCenter sponsors one or more musical concerts at reasonable admission prices. Recent

Photo courtesy of N.C. Museum of Art

The North Carolina Museum of Art's outdoor amphitheater has evolved into one of the premier performing arts facilities in the region, offering music, drama, dance and film.

concerts have included jazz, folk, zydeco, Cajun, country, Irish, big band, rock, reggae and new wave groups. What's more, the ArtsCenter has an ongoing Sunday jazz series, featuring popular local artists and groups like Tony Galiani and the ArtsCenter Rhythm Section. In addition, a Swing Big Band Jazz Concert featuring such bands as the Gregg Gelb Swing Band takes place on the third Thursday of the month. Ticket prices are in the $3 to $15 range for local performers, more for national performers on tour. Friends of the ArtsCenter receive a discount on ticket prices.

Chapel Hill-Carrboro Community Chorus
• 968-7944

This group is made up of individuals at all levels of musical achievement who share a common interest in choral music. The Chorus practices at 7:30 PM on Tuesdays at Binkley Baptist Church. The group performs public concerts twice a year.

Piedmont Youth Orchestra
229 S. Elliott Rd. • 968-8099

The Piedmont Youth Orchestra offers experience in playing standard orchestral pieces for students from elementary through high school grades. The orchestra rehearses weekly.

University of North Carolina

UNC's Student Union sponsors a slew of music acts each year. All concerts are open to the public. Major concerts are held at the Dean Smith Center, Memorial Hall or Hill Hall for faculty and student concerts. Occasionally, there are concerts outdoors on campus, like the annual North Carolina Symphony Pops performance in June. For information, call the Carolina Union at 962-1449.

During the school year, the Department of Music presents dozens of free concerts by students, faculty and occasional guest artists. Student music groups sponsored by the department include the following: Carolina Choir, Jazz Lab, Wind Ensembles, Men's and Women's Glee Clubs, Mixed Chorus, Chamber Singers, Symphony and Chamber Orchestra, and others. For more information, contact the Department of Music, University of North Carolina, Chapel Hill, NC 27514.

In addition, the Black Student Movement sponsors a Gospel Choir that performs on campus. For more information, contact the Black Student Movement, UNC, Chapel Hill, NC 27514.

Village Symphony Orchestra
• 929-5487, 489-1587

The Village Symphony Orchestra is a private, nonprofit group for adults who get together to play and further the tradition of community music. The orchestra rehearses Thursdays at 7:30 PM at Hill Hall (the music building) on the UNC campus.

Visual Arts

There must be over 50 galleries and museums in the Triangle displaying the works of locally and nationally known painters, sculptors, photographers and craftspeople. But you definitely need a guide to help you find them all. Unlike some major urban centers, the cities of the Triangle don't have well-defined art districts. Instead you'll find worthwhile exhibits all over the place: from the North Carolina Museum of Art in Raleigh and college campuses in Durham and Chapel Hill, to displays at banks, restaurants and, of course, private galleries tucked into business districts and shopping centers throughout the area. Following is a brief synopsis of some of the best visual arts venues in the Triangle, plus some class listings.

Raleigh and Cary

Ant Farm
303 Kinsey St. • 828-2514

The Ant Farm is a true Insiders' place, located in a fading, downtown neighborhood, Boylan Heights, off Dupont Circle in an old warehouse. It is a private 2,200-square-foot studio for young artists and artisans who display their works from time to time in public showings. About 10 artists work out of the studio. The works vary from sculpture to jewelry to painting to furniture to ceramics. If you are an art collector looking for new talent, take in the Ant Farm, but call first. It's by appointment only.

Arts Together
114 St. Mary's St. • 828-1713

Arts Together is a nonprofit community arts school and performance center that has developed a devoted following over the years, especially among young dancers. It has classes in visual arts, too, for 2-year-olds up to adults.

Artspace
201 E. Davie St. • 821-ARTS

Artspace is a very special part of Raleigh's downtown renovation. It was conceived to be a community of artists with studios and performance areas housed under one roof. Today, it has become the heart of the city's Art District, located in the old Sanders Ford building in the City Market block across from Moore Square. Artspace has a gallery on the first floor and a small auditorium upstairs used for lectures, receptions and even political forums! You can stroll through the building and see the artisans at work on jewelry or crafts and some will sell you their wares on the spot. Artspace also offers a variety of summer arts programs for youths and adults.

Artspace is unique in North Carolina and draws residents as well as visitors who find a lively hub of art and entertainment, including a comedy club, antiques and the city's first brewery at Greenshield's. For a taste of this part of the city, take a Gallery Walk in the spring or fall when seven galleries, all near Artspace and Moore Square, put on a show.

Contemporary Art Museum
409 W. Martin St. • 836-0088

Formerly the City Gallery of Contemporary Art, the Contemporary Art Museum will contain a variety of galleries, a museum and a small theater. It is scheduled to open in a warehouse in downtown Raleigh in late

1999. It will be the only Triangle museum devoted to contemporary art and design.

Gallery A
1637 Glenwood Ave. • 546-9011

Gallery A, which is part of Dr. Steven Andreaus' dental office, offers mostly contemporary painting, pottery, sculpture and photography. A different artist is featured every six to eight weeks.

Gallery C
Ridgewood Shopping Center • 828-3165

Owner Charlene Newsom opened Gallery C in the 1980s. It contains three exhibition rooms and offers about eight major shows a year. The emphasis is on contemporary art, mostly from Southeastern artists, and there is also a selection of vintage animation art. Don't miss the annual Holiday Crafts Exhibition. It is open Monday through Friday 10 AM to 6 PM, Saturday 10 AM to 5 PM and Sunday 1 to 5 PM.

Jordan Hall Arts Center
908 North Harrison Ave. • 469-4069

Jordan Hall offers visual and performing arts classes. The Cary Cultural Arts Association meets here at 7:30 PM on the fourth Thursday of the month.

Little Art Gallery
North Hills Mall • 787-6317

Little Art Gallery, which is co-owned by Ruth Green and Rosanne Minick, has been a fixture on the Raleigh art scene for over two decades. It features original artwork and contemporary crafts. The owners are usually there, and like many of those from whom they buy, they have definite opinions about art. Don't be afraid to get their advice.

Lump Gallery
505 S. Blount St. • 821-9999

Owners Bill Thelan and Med Byrd opened Lump in 1996 as a showcase for emerging local artists creating cutting-edge art. Half of the gallery consists of three studios and the other half is reserved

Photo by Tim Johnson

Dianne Rodwell is one of nearly 50 artists who have studios at Artspace, which has become the heart of Raleigh's Art District.

for a variety of shows from one-person exhibits to group displays to complex installations. Gallery hours are 1 to 5 PM Saturday and Sunday and by appointment.

NCSU Crafts Center
Lower level, Thompson Theater, NCSU • 515-2457

NCSU Crafts Center provides opportunities for hands-on experience in beginning through advanced crafts courses such as woodworking, pottery, weaving and photography. Special interest classes range from flower arranging to telescope making—over 150 multi-session courses in 30 disciplines each year. The Center's Gallery features local and national exhibitions and is open to the public afternoons and evenings.

North Carolina Museum of Art
2110 Blue Ridge Rd. • 839-6262

The Museum of Art is the premier art museum in the state and has become one of North Carolina's treasure houses for the visual arts. Much of the state's fine art activities are centered here. Like the North

Carolina Symphony, this is a tax-supported museum, and it reaches out to its people with a wide variety of free or inexpensive programs.

In 1983, the museum opened at its current address on Blue Ridge Road. It has over 181,000 square feet, displaying its permanent collections in American, ancient and European art to maximum advantage. The European paintings are considered the museum's finest, particularly in Italian and Dutch and Flemish artists. Its American collection has a number of lush landscapes from the Hudson River School.

The museum organizes between 12 and 15 special exhibitions a year, many from other museums. Four galleries are set aside for these shows, including the Mary Duke Biddle Gallery, which provides changing educational exhibitions designed particularly for the handicapped. Another gallery is reserved primarily for work by North Carolina artists. A popular recent exhibition was "It's Only Rock and Roll: Rock and Roll Currents in Contemporary Art."

The museum offers lectures, adult classes, children's workshops and film festivals. It also features an outdoor amphitheater for films and live entertainment.

The museum also operates a gift shop and The Museum Cafe. Admission to the museum is free; hours are 9 AM to 5 PM Tuesday through Saturday (Friday, it's 9 to 9) and 11 AM to 6 PM Sunday. It's closed Mondays.

Page Walker Arts & History Center
119 Ambassador Loop, Cary • 460-4963

Built in 1868 as a hotel, the Page Walker Arts & History Center contains a fine arts gallery featuring the works of local and regional artists. It also sponsors a summer Starlight Concert Series. A Cary Town museum is also being developed here.

Pullen Park Arts Center
Hillsborough St. & Pullen Rd. • 831-6126

Pullen Park Arts Center offers a variety of art exhibits and classes for adults and children. It is open Monday through Thursday 9 AM to 10 PM, Friday 9 AM to 1 PM and Saturday 10 AM to 3 PM.

Raleigh Contemporary Gallery
323 Blake St. • 828-6500

This eye-catching gallery shows original paintings, sculpture, fiber art and limited edition graphics by local and national artists. It also features custom

Photo by Tim Johnson

The former Page-Walker Hotel, built in 1868, fell into disrepair during the early 1980s, but was restored as the Page Walker Arts & History Center in 1991.

conservation frames and provides consulting services for individuals as well as for corporate clients.

Sertoma Arts Center
1400 W. Millbrook Rd. • 420-2329

The Sertoma Arts Center is part of Raleigh's Shelley Park and has become the center for most of the city-sponsored art activities, including a multitude of children's programs. It is listed under the visual arts because it's probably best known for art classes, programs and shows, but the Sertoma Center is equally a hub of interest for dance, music, drama, pottery, quilt making, photography and literature.

If you want to learn about the art scene in Raleigh and Cary at the grassroots level, this is a good place to start. Hours are Monday through Thursday, 9 AM to 10 PM; Friday 9 AM to 3 PM; and Saturday 10 AM to 3 PM (during the school year). The Center is also available Sundays for nonalcoholic private receptions for weddings, anniversaries, etc.

Sweet Tea & Grits
City Market • 834-7752

Sweet Tea & Grits is a small studio in City Market that offers Southern pottery at its best. It is open Monday through Thursday 8:30 AM to 6 PM, Friday and Saturday 8:30 AM to 11 PM and Sunday 1 to 5 PM.

Trillium
Olde Raleigh Village, Raleigh
• 783-0030

Trillium, which contains a gallery and gift store, attracts a strong market among the upscale buyer and big city newcomers. It started as an art gallery and gift shop but added a clothing boutique in 1994. For the young working woman, it is one of the Triangle's special places for dressy or career fashions. The gifts include jewelry and ceramic pieces and it maintains a bridal registry when you want to give someone a piece of her "best china."

Visual Arts Center
NCSU Student Center • 515-3503

The Visual Arts Center was added to the University Student Center on Cates Avenue in 1991 and opened in 1992. Exhibitions of contemporary art and design that are related to the University's various curricula are featured in the Cannon and Foundations galleries. Exhibitions are sometimes derived from the University's substantial research collections, which are also available for study by appointment.

The gallery hours are from noon to 8 PM Wednesday through Friday and 2 PM to 8 PM Saturday and Sunday.

West Side Furnishings
200 S. West St., Raleigh • 829-0770

Owner Nancy Kitchner offers artistically designed furniture, accessories, antiques, oriental rugs and brocades at this popular West End gallery. The designs are classic, yet modern, and the shop features local artists in a variety of mediums. This is the spot to find some not-so-usual pieces for your home and a beautiful place if you just want to browse. The shop is open Monday through Saturday 10:30 AM to 6 PM, Sunday noon to 5 PM and by appointment.

Durham

Thanks to the Durham Arts Council and Art Guild, Duke and North Carolina Central universities and several impressive private galleries, there are plenty of places to explore the visual arts, if you just know where to look. In addition, you'll discover original works by local artists regularly on display at many Durham restaurants.

Cedar Creek Gallery
Interstate 85 at Creedmoor Rd.
• 528-1041

If you like pottery and crafts, you'll enjoy the short trek out to Cedar Creek, which celebrated its 30th anniversary in 1998. Drive 9 miles north of Durham on I-85 to

Photo by Tim Johnson

Art galleries in the Moore Square Art District open their doors from 6 to 9 PM during the First Friday Gallery Walk.

Exit 186-A (Creedmoor Road and N.C. 50) and follow the signs. Featuring the works of more than 200 craftspeople, it is open daily from 10 AM to 6 PM.

Duke Campus Galleries
East and West campuses • 684-2911

In addition to the Duke Museum of Art, there are two galleries on the East Campus and two more on the West (main) Campus, featuring rotating exhibits of paintings and photography. They are open to the public free of charge. The Hanks Gallery and the Brown Gallery are located in the Bryan Center on the West Campus. They are open daily from 8 AM to 5 PM when school is in session.

The Bivins Gallery on the East Campus is open from 8 AM to 5 PM Monday through Friday. Exhibits by area artists change monthly. The East Campus Gallery is located in the East Campus Library and is open daily from 8 AM to 6 PM. It features exhibits of artworks by Duke faculty, staff and employees.

Duke University Museum of Art
East Campus, Main Street Entrance
• 684-5135

This fine museum boasts a permanent collection of Medieval and Renaissance sculpture and decorative arts, Chinese porcelain and jade, Peruvian weavings and other textiles, and African and pre-Columbian works. In addition, there's usually a visiting or temporary exhibit. On Thursday evenings, the museum is open from 5 to 7 PM for tours and a "mix-and-mingle" hour for adults. Admission is free. Hours are 9 AM to 5 PM Tuesday through Friday, 11 AM to 2 PM Saturday and 2 PM to 5 PM Sunday.

Durham Arts Council
120 Morris St. • 560-ARTS

The Arts Council sponsors classes in painting, graphic design, fiber art, photography and video for students of all ages and experience levels, at various locations in the city. Recent classes have been basic drawing and portraiture, graphic design and composition, drama, dance, performing arts, writing, sculpture, photography, quilting, weaving and spinning. Call for a current schedule.

Horizon Gallery
Brightleaf Square • 688-0313

In its new and expanded gallery space, Horizon offers functional and wearable art: ceramic pieces, pottery by North Carolinian as well as national craftsmen, jewelry, blown glass, wooden bowls and cutting boards, mirrors and woven items. Hours are 11 AM to 7 PM Monday through Friday, 10 AM to 8 PM Saturday and 1 PM to 6 PM on Sunday.

North Carolina Central University Museum of Art
1801 Fayetteville St. • 560-6211

Located on the campus of North Carolina Central University, this museum features exhibits of the works of students and African-American artists. During the school year, it's open to the public free of charge from 9 AM to 5 PM Tuesday through Friday and 2 to 5 PM Sunday. In the summer, it's open from 9 AM to 5 PM Monday through Friday.

Semans Gallery
120 Morris St. • 560-ARTS

The gallery offers a series of exhibits throughout the year that are open to the public free of charge. Exhibitions usually change monthly. The gallery is in the Royall Center for the Arts in the Durham Arts Council Building. Hours are Monday through Saturday 9 AM to 9 PM and Sunday 1 PM to 6 PM.

Tyndall Galleries
Brightleaf Square • 683-8489

Jane Tyndall's gallery showcases painting, sculpture, prints and wearable art, primarily by local and regional artists. The gallery also offers framing and art consultation services for corporate and individual clients and is open from 11 AM to 6 PM Monday through Saturday and 1 to 4 PM on Sunday.

Chapel Hill and Carrboro

Like other parts of the Triangle, the art exhibits in Chapel Hill and Carrboro are scattered about. But since Chapel Hill and

Photo by Robert Thomason

Local and regional artists exhibit at the Carrboro Arts Center, which also offers a variety of visual arts classes for all ages and all levels of experience.

Carrboro are relatively small towns, it's easy to find the museums and galleries.

Ackland Art Museum
UNC, Columbia St. • 966-5736

UNC's Ackland Art Museum's permanent collection features Greek and Roman art, Renaissance paintings, works by Flemish masters and a fine collection of prints. Special exhibits change periodically. Hours are Wednesday through Saturday 10 AM to 5 PM and Sunday 1 PM to 5 PM.

ArtsCenter Galleries
300-G E. Main St., Carrboro • 929-ARTS

The ArtsCenter Galleries features exhibits by local and regional artists. It's open from 10 AM to 5 PM Monday through Friday and on Saturday from 10 AM to 4 PM. In addition to providing exhibit space for emerging artists, the ArtsCenter offers a variety of classes in the visual arts for all ages and all levels of experience. A recent schedule included classes in graphic design, illustration, printmaking, drawing, Chinese painting, photography and video technique. The ArtsCenter also sponsors summer art classes for kids ages 6 and older. Call for a current class schedule.

Cameron's
University Mall • 942-5554

If you're looking for pottery and other functional craft items, you'll want to check out Cameron's 5,000-square-foot gallery and shop in University Mall. Danny Cameron chooses works from North Carolina and across the United States, focusing often on the whimsical or eccentric. Cameron's is open from 10 AM to 9 PM Monday through Saturday and 1 to 6 PM on Sunday.

Carolina Union Galleries
UNC, Carolina Union • Info: 962-2285

The galleries are located in the Student Union building on campus, where you'll find exhibits of student artists. The galleries are open from 8 AM to 11 PM when school is in session.

Green Tara Gallery
118 E. Main St., Carrboro • 932-6400

Green Tara Gallery hosts monthly exhibits and poetry readings, and has a coffee cafe. It is open Tuesday through Saturday from 11 AM to 7 PM and Sunday from 12-5 PM.

Hanes Art Center
**UNC Art Classroom Studio Bldg.
(next to the Ackland) • 962-2015**

The Hanes Art Center features exhibits by students and emerging local artists. Admission is free. The gallery is open Monday through Friday from 8 AM to 5 PM.

Horace Williams House
610 E. Rosemary St. • 942-7818

One of Chapel Hill's oldest homes, the Horace Williams House has been maintained by the Chapel Hill Preservation Society and today is a cultural arts center and a place for wedding receptions, private parties, small dance ensembles, concerts and rotating art exhibits. Here you'll find paintings, sculptures and crafts by local and regional artists. Other special events include Historic Trolley Tours every Wednesday at 2 PM, a Chamber Concert series and an annual 4th of July band concert. The house is open from 10 AM to 5 PM Monday through Saturday and 1 to 5 PM on Sunday.

North Carolina Crafts Gallery
North Carolina Arts Gallery
212 W. Main St., Carrboro • 942-4048

These two back-to-back galleries were originally opened by Sherri Ontjes as a means to encourage and support North Carolinal craftsmen; her mission has expanded to include painting and other fine arts They sell quilts, pottery, jewelry, stained glass, blown glass, baskets, toys, knitting and weavings, and handmade wooden objects and paintings, drawings and other artwork.

Somerhill Gallery
Eastgate Shopping Center • 968-8868

Open since 1973, Sommerhill Gallery has been bringing together emerging regional artists and enthusiastic collectors. Here you'll find paintings, sculptures and tapestries.

Toktumee European Art Gallery
200 W. Franklin St., Ste. 280
• 960-4004

The Triangle's own showcase for exciting new European art, Toktumee, opened its doors in downtown Chapel Hill in the fall of 1999. The innovative, 1,500-square-foot gallery is the creation of Evanne and Jean-Claude Solvinto, two Parisian art lovers and collectors who have made their home in the Triangle for the past several years. The gallery features the works of such talented artists as Yarek Godfrey.ow, Sibylle de Monneron, Christine Vidil, Francoise Denis

and Barbara Goraczko. The owners plan to eventually expand the gallery's selections to include promising new artists from America and other parts of the world. Toktumee European Art Gallery is located on the second floor of the new Pavillion II building on West Franklin Street.

Womancraft
Eastgate Shopping Center • 929-8362

Womancraft offers all kinds of functional items by area craftswomen, including splendid pottery, woven clothing and quilts. It is a co-op of artists and periodically juries new pieces for membership.

Dance

If you think you can only really find dance in the Big Apple, think again. Believe it or not, little ole' Durham is where you'll find the acclaimed American Dance Festival.

But the ADF is only part of the Triangle dance scene. If you really want to

get a taste of Southern culture, you'll want to see the Apple Chill Cloggers and the Cane Creek Cloggers, both based in Chapel Hill.

Raleigh and Cary

Arts Together
114 St. Mary's St. • 828-1713

While Durham is the recognized dance mecca in the Triangle, a number of teaching and community dance organizations serve Raleigh and Cary. Arts Together is one, and it is home to one of the city's better known groups, The Rainbow Dance Company.

Carolina Ballet
336 Fayetteville St. Mall • 303-6303

The total sensory experience of ballet is exploding in the Triangle with the creation of Carolina Ballet. This dynamic professional company under the direction of Robert Weiss will capture your imagination like no other form of entertainment, presenting the full range of ballet from the finest classics to fresh, contemporary new works.

Cary Ballet Conservatory
3791 N.W. Cary Pkwy., Cary • 481-6509

The conservatory provides instruction in classical ballet for ages 3 1/2 years to adult and hosts many local benefits. It is also home to the semiprofessional Cary Ballet Company, which presents local and regional performances. The 18-member professional faculty also offers instruction in jazz, modern dance and tap dancing. The conservatory recently moved into a new 14,000-square-foot facility, which contains a retail dancewear store.

The Dancers Studio
6124 St. Giles St. • 782-0622

Started in 1974 by director Karen Edwards, this 20-member ballet includes apprentice, senior and concert dancers. It is the home of the Concert Dancers of Raleigh. It occasionally performs ballets in Triangle schools; the studio has classes in ballet tap and jazz as well.

Raleigh School of Dance Arts
608 North Market Drive • 850-9030

The school offers lessons in ballet, jazz and tap dancing for ages 3 to adult. It is also home to the Raleigh Civic Ballet, which holds performances at such locales as the Raleigh Little Theatre.

Triangle Academy of Dance
2918 Kildaire Farm Rd. • 387-1298

Cary's classical ballet academy offers some of the finest instruction, facilities and programs in the Triangle. The professional staff includes guest teachers from the neighboring Carolina Ballet. Specialized programs are available for the very young such as tap, jazz and tumbling. The Academy also schedules master classes, summer workshops and multiple opportunities for students to perform.

Durham

American Dance Festival
Duke University • 684-6402

You could spend six weeks in New York City and still not catch as many internationally renowned modern dance performances as you can get right here in Durham every June and July as part of the six-week American Dance Festival.

Established in 1932 in Bennington, Vermont, the ADF chose Durham as its home in 1978, and has been thrilling local audiences ever since with the best modern dancers from the world over. Over the years, the ADF has featured such dance greats as Merce Cunningham and Martha Graham, and notable companies including those of Paul Taylor, Pilobolus, Cleo Parker Robinson and Chuck Davis, Parsons Dance Company and The Next Ice Age.

For six weeks, the ADF offers classes, workshops and nightly performances,

Photo courtesy of ADF

The Parsons Dance Company performs *Step Into My Dream* at the American Dance Festival.

many to sellout audiences. Performances are in Page Auditorium and Reynolds Theatre. Single tickets range from $17 to $35, with a few less expensive seats for special performances. Season tickets covering more than a dozen events range from about $60 to over $100.

Chapel Hill and Carrboro

Chapel Hill has become another local mecca for American folk dance. Clogging, and more recently, international folk dancing, seem to be the favorite forms of dance activities taking place.

The Apple Chill Cloggers
P.O. Box 119, Carrboro, NC 27510

The Apple Chill Cloggers is a nonprofit group dedicated to preserving and promoting the art of clogging. This group performs and holds workshops all over the South and, occasionally, abroad. For a schedule of dances and appearances, write the Cloggers at the above address.

The ArtsCenter for Visual, Performing and Literary Arts
300-G E. Main St., Carrboro • 929-ARTS

The ArtsCenter periodically offers classes in both the appreciation and performance of a variety of dance styles.

The Cane Creek Cloggers
• 933-2440

Like The Apple Chill Cloggers, this troupe specializes in preserving and performing traditional Appalachian folk dance. The Cane Creek Cloggers appear regularly at square dances throughout the Triangle.

Carolina Song & Dance Association
• 967-9948

The Carolina Song & Dance Association sponsors dances and instruction in contra dance regularly at various local elementary schools. These popular dances are usually held once a month on Friday night. The association features instruction for beginners at 7:30 PM and dancing (with live music) at 8 PM.

The Chapel Hill Ballet Co.
P.O. Box 3233, Chapel Hill, NC 27514
• 942-1339

The Chapel Hill Ballet Company is committed to developing the potential of area dance students through classes, while bringing an appreciation of ballet to the community through dance concerts and demonstrations. The Company sponsors two performances a year that are open to the public.

INSIDERS' TIP

Throughout the year, bookstores regularly feature readings by Southern writers such as Reynolds Price, Doris Betts, Kaye Gibbons and Tim McLaurin to name a few.

North Carolina Youth Tap Ensemble
The Ballet School, Chapel Hill
• 967-9624

Founded in 1983, the North Carolina Youth Tap Ensemble, formerly the Children's Tap Company, was created to offer young dancers an opportunity to perform and refine their skills, and to offer audiences a chance to enjoy tap dancing entertainment. The company includes about 45 dancers ages 7 to 23, who perform approximately 35 times a year.

Writing

The Triangle is home to a number of excellent writers, among the best in the land. An Insider knows that you can meet Doris Betts, the author of *Souls Raised from the Dead* and other stories, at the University of North Carolina at Chapel Hill where she teaches in the English Department. Lee Smith, named as one of the South's best writers and author of *Saving Grace*, used to teach writing at NCSU; her husband Hal Crowther writes a syndicated column in *The Independent.* Kaye Gibbons, whose books *Ellen Foster, A Virtuous Woman, On the Occasion of My Last Afternoon* and others have all gotten rave reviews, lives in Raleigh, and novelist Tim McLaurin lives outside of Chapel Hill. Clyde Edgerton, the floatplane pilot and author of *Raney, Killer Diller* and *RedEye: A Western* and others, lives in Orange County with his writer/editor spouse, Susan Ketchin.

Creedmoor is home to Charles Frazier, the author of *Cold Mountain*, which won the National Book Award and spent over a year on the bestseller list.

The dean of Triangle fiction writers, Reynolds Price, teaches at Duke University and seems to have produced almost a book a year lately. Durham is also home to poets Michael McFee and Jaki Shelton Green.

The North Carolina Writers Series is a literary showcase featuring guest author readings and discussions spread over four nights during the winter and spring at North Carolina State University's Thompson Theatre. Recent participants include such regionally acclaimed writers as Kaye Gibbons, Allan Gurganus, Jaki Shelton Green, Alan Shapiro, Sarah Lindsey and G. D. Gearino.

Outside of the college campuses and places such as the local arts centers, you can pursue the art of writing through the North Carolina Writer's Network. Contact information for the Network is listed below, along with some Triangle publishers.

Algonquin Books of Chapel Hill
P.O. Box 2225, Chapel Hill, NC 27515
• 933-2113

Algonquin Books, founded by UNC professor Louis Rubin, is affiliated with New York's Workman Publishers. This house has published notable books, such as novels by acclaimed Southern contemporary novelists Clyde Edgerton, Jill McCorkle, Larry Brown, Lewis Nordan and Julia Alvarez.

Carolina Wren Press
120 Morris St., Durham • 560-2738

Supported by the Durham Arts Council, Carolina Wren Press publishes fiction, poetry and drama of writers, says the brochure, "who are working at the cultural edge." The press is nonprofit and dedicated to the cause of "meaningful contemporary literature."

N.C. Writers' Network
P.O. Box 954, Carrboro, NC 27510
• 967-9540

The N.C. Writers' Network is a statewide organization that publishes a bimonthly newsletter, sponsors an annual conference and offers a wide variety of information and support for fiction and nonfiction writers and poets.

Triangle cities win blue
ribbons and gold medals
for their parks and recreation
facilities and activities.

Parks and Recreation

Triangle cities win blue ribbons and gold medals for their parks and recreation facilities and activities. These prize-winning programs help explain why the Triangle always scores high on "livability" ratings, whether conducted by national magazines or that visiting cousin.

Remember that the Triangle is located in the North Carolina Piedmont, not too hot and not too cold, not too far from the mountains and not too far from the ocean. There are greenways along river banks and sailboats in the lakes. Softball or soccer, dancing or diving, here's where you get started, and all cities operate full schedules of activities for young and old alike. In some cases, cities and counties each have their own programs, not to mention the state's park system. Indeed, the state's venerable Umstead Park sits almost at the center of the Triangle, offering a quiet respite to the hustle and bustle next door at Raleigh-Durham International Airport.

This chapter also lists some of the established private and nonprofit recreation places and organizations like Durham's Hillandale Golf Course or Raleigh's Central YMCA, where you can find one of the co-authors struggling to improve his racquetball game. For the soccer moms, there is the mom of all soccer leagues, the 12,000 plus member Capital Area Soccer League. If you want an active life or, equally important, if you would like to wear out your kids with wholesome activities, read this chapter and get started.

Recreation Areas

With numerous bodies of water in the vicinity, swimming, boating, sailing, fishing, picnicking and camping are popular activities throughout the year. Jordan Lake, Falls Lake and the Eno River are among the best known of these recreation areas and are maintained by the state. But there are numerous accessible sites for those who enjoy water sports, camping or just being outdoors. Here's an overview of a few of the most popular locations.

Eno River State Park
6101 Cole Mill Rd., Durham • 383-1686
Main access: Northern end of Cole Mill Rd.

The Eno River State Park was established in 1973 and runs along a 14-mile stretch of the river. There are a number of access points to the park, including Cole Mill (off the road by the same name) and Fews Ford (at the end of Cole Mill Road), where the park office is located. There are hiking trails, creeks to fish, picnic spots, primitive camping and, of course, the river itself (for experienced canoeists only).

Photo by Rich Weidman

The peaceful waters of the Eno River meander through 14 miles of the Eno River State Park.

Falls Lake
13304 Creedmoor Rd.,Wake Forest • 676-1027
Access: N.C. 50 north of N.C. 98; Rollingview Marina, S.R. 1807; Sandling Beach, 3.5 miles north of N.C. 50 and N.C. 98 intersection.

The 22-mile-long Falls Lake is one of Raleigh's reservoirs, formed when the Neuse River was dammed at the tiny village of Falls, north of the city. Since it opened in 1983, Triangle residents have streamed to its shores and waters for swimming, picnicking, fishing, water skiing and camping. It is one of the area's biggest attractions with 12,490 acres of water and 230 miles of shoreline.

There are four boat ramps with free access. And one of the park's impoundments, Beaver Lake, is restricted to non-motor-driven boats and is reserved for fishing.

The state maintains several wildlife resources at Falls Lake, including Falls Lake Trail on Falls of the Neuse Road, Ledge Rock Boat Access on Cheek Road

and Upper Bartons Creek Access on North Six Forks Road.

Jordan Lake
U.S. 64 and Fearrington Rd., Chatham County • 362-0586
Access: Crosswinds Boat Ramp off U.S. 64 E. at B. Everett Jordan Bridge; Ebenezer Church on S.R. 1008 S.; Crosswinds Marina off U.S. 64 E. on S.R. 1008; Parkers Creek west of B. Everett Jordan Bridge; Vista Point west of B. Everett Jordan Bridge on S.R. 1700.

On summer weekends, rural Chatham County south of Durham draws thousands of visitors from all over the Triangle to the 14,000-acre lake and recreation area built by the U.S. Army Corps of Engineers. Jordan Lake offers hiking, boating, windsurfing, fishing, swimming, picnicking and camping opportunities. There are several beaches, boat ramps and campgrounds available to users for a modest fee. Backcountry camping is not permitted. Call for a detailed map and more information about boat ramps and beaches.

Lake Crabtree County Park
Off Aviation Parkway • 460-3390

This is a Wake County park located in Cary. It's a popular, 71-acre park surrounding 520-acre Lake Crabtree, which you can see off I-40. The lake is not deep—from 3 to 10 feet—but it is stocked with bass, bluegill and catfish. Sailboats are available for rent at $8 an hour—there's a $10 deposit, too. Canoes and rowboats cost less. There are picnic shelters for rent, a playground and hiking and biking trails. Enter off Aviation Parkway.

Lake Michie
Roxboro Rd.
Boating and fishing: 477-3906
Spruce Pine Lodge: 560-4358

Lake Michie (pronounced like the Mouse), a small lake located 10 miles north of Durham on Roxboro Road, is a great getaway spot. Here you can rent boats, fish or just spend the day hiking or picnicking. Spruce Pine Lodge, a 1940's vintage log building, may be reserved for parties and meetings. The official address is Bahama, but the area is easily accessible from Durham.

Lake Wheeler
6404 Lake Wheeler Rd. • 662-5704

The biggest of Raleigh's city parks, Lake Wheeler lies just south of the city limits. In June 1998, the park opened a new Waterfront Program Center, which includes a park office, classroom, concession stand, restrooms and large outdoor deck. Lake Wheeler is aimed at the water-sports crowd and offers boating, water skiing and fishing. It is the base of the NCSU Sailing Club and is also home to the annual Tar Heel Regatta in June when powerboats from all over come to race.

Parks

City, county and state authorities often overlap in matters of park jurisdiction. Under normal circumstances, this makes little difference to those of us who enjoy them. However, reservations are needed to utilize some park facilities, so you need to know who to call.

Raleigh City Parks

Raleigh takes particular pride in its parks system, which helped it earn the nickname "a park with a city in it." The city regularly wins national awards for its parks and recreation programs and recognition in publications such as *National Geographic* for its greenway program that connects neighborhoods, parks and streams in a network that stretches over 39 miles. There is a weekly update on the city's recreational programs on cable television. Access to local and statewide information is available on the Internet.

Raleigh residents have voted consistently for bond issues that have increased parklands to over 4,050 acres, 156 parks and open spaces, and thousands of recreational activities. If you want to plan a special event for a city park, you will need to call for specific dates and a reservation permit. Also check with the staff concerning availability of water, restrooms and electricity. A fee is charged to reserve city picnic facilities—$30 for all-day.

Raleigh offers several parks with special attractions, such as Pullen Park (see the "Parks of Special Interest" section in this chapter)—home to both a celebrated Dentzel Carousel and a miniature passenger train. Of special note, Laurel Hills Park in west Raleigh (Glen Eden Drive and Edwards Mill Road) opened in 1992 and offers a unique playground for all children, including those with special needs. Jaycee Park is the site of Raleigh Beach, home of the city's outdoor volleyball addicts and there is a BMX bicycle course at Lions Park. The Sertoma Arts Center at Shelley-Sertoma Park is the de facto arts center in the city's park system and hosts a number of study programs and summer concerts. Durant Nature Park is home for the city's popular summer day camp, Ranoca, as well as Camp Friendly, a special day camp for children with special needs.

Also part of the city's park system are both the entertainment jewel, Walnut Creek Amphitheatre (see our "Attractions" chapter), with 20,000 seats and a five-field softball complex and Lake Wheeler (see "Recreation Areas" section in this chapter), which caters mainly to water-sports enthusiasts.

Cary Parks

Cary has 13 public parks with more on the planning board. Many Cary residents

Photo by Rich Weidman

Lake Crabtree's 520 acres are stocked with large-mouth bass, bluegill, red-eared sunfish and channel catfish.

are closer to some Raleigh parks than some Raleigh residents—Lake Wheeler for example.

The showpiece of Cary's parks, with picnic shelters, athletic fields, a lake for fishing, hiking trails and an amphitheater, is the 310-acre Fred Bond Park. The park also offers—for a fee—a D.A.R.E. ropes course. Hemlock Bluffs nature preserve (see "Parks of Special Interest" section in this chapter) is also maintained by the town of Cary and Lake Crabtree County Park (see "Recreation Areas" section in this chapter) is located here.

Cary officials recently developed a $40 million plan to expand recreation facilities by the year 2010. Recommendations include 25 new parks, six new community centers, a tennis center, an aquatic center and additional greenways and bike paths.

Durham Parks

With a more than $4 million annual budget, the Durham Parks and Recreation Department oversees more than 1,300 acres of park land throughout the county, including 53 parks within the city limits. Durham offers 18 lighted athletic fields. A dozen parks provide 72 hard-surfaced tennis courts, 68 of them with lights, and there are four public swimming pools. What's more, there are plenty of hiking, biking, jogging and horse trails as well as fishing and boating opportunities.

Two of Durham's most popular parks are the Lake Michie Recreational Area (see "Recreation Areas" section in this chapter) and the unique, historic West Point on the Eno (see "Parks of Special Interest" section in this chapter).

Chapel Hill-Carrboro Parks

Both Chapel Hill and neighboring Carrboro have their own separate parks and recreation departments, providing acres of park land and a wide variety of activities for Orange County residents of all ages. Together the two towns provide 10 ball fields, 21 lighted tennis courts, three gymnasiums and two swimming pools.

Parks of Special Interest

There are a few parks in the Triangle area that you should make a special point of visiting. Each has a unique characteristic and offers special features or activities that are worth the short drive that may be involved.

Hemlock Bluffs
Kildaire Farm Rd., Cary • 387-5980

This is a nature preserve in southern Cary, located between Tryon and Penny roads. It covers about 150 acres and features a grove of Canadian hemlocks, which are viewed from a series of trails winding around the distinctive 90-foot bluffs. The preserve is not for picnicking or camping, but for walking and observing.

Park tours are available on weekends and guides will tell you that 10,000 years ago hemlocks used to be common in this part of the country. But time flies and so did the hemlocks, except in special places like Hemlock Bluffs, which the good citizens of Cary and North Carolina have preserved for your hiking pleasure. The Stevens Nature Center offers exhibits, classes and lectures.

Pullen Park
408 Ashe Ave., Raleigh • 831-6468

This is the grandaddy of Raleigh's parks with 65 acres that lie between the NCSU campus and the state's School for the Blind off Western Boulevard. A train ride through the park and over its lake offers a great view of the amenities, including children's boat rides and even pedal boats on the lake as well as the region's top indoor aquatics center.

The crown jewel of the park is the 1911 Dentzel Carousel, which has been restored to its original grandeur with great skill and hundreds of thousands of dollars. Put your child on a carved masterpiece and watch him or her go round and round. It's also a great place to picnic and has several covered pavilions that may be reserved for large groups.

A $4 million indoor aquatics center opened in 1992. It is connected to a Special Programs Center that offers classes and activities such as senior citizen dancing. A concession stand offers the usual hot dogs, sodas and cotton candy. Six tennis courts and, across the railroad tracks, two ball fields and the city's Theatre in the Park are located here. The park also includes the Pullen Art Center, which offers a variety of art classes—even weaving on traditional overshot colonial-patterned warped looms.

Umstead State Park
8801 Glenwood Ave., Raleigh • 571-4170

Right in the heart of the Triangle, next to the Raleigh-Durham International Airport, William B. Umstead State Park offers visitors an opportunity to trade the bustle of everyday life for the beauty and serenity of nature. The park has two sections and two entrances. The Reedy Creek section can be accessed from Harrison Avenue off I-40 in Cary and the Crabtree section from U.S. 70 in Raleigh. Although the sections are connected, you cannot drive across the park.

The 5,381-acre park has nature trails, fishing and rental boats, 11.5 miles of horseback riding and bicycling trails, 28 campsites and three large group campsites that are available to nonprofit organizations. In the spring, go for a Sunday walk in the Reedy Creek section down by the creek where you will see a spectacular display of the rhododendron blossoming throughout the park. A new Umstead State Park Visitor Center, which opened at the Crabtree section in June 1998, houses a museum and nature exhibits related to the park.

INSIDERS' TIP

At one point, the cities of Cary and Raleigh spent more on their parks and recreation budgets combined than North Carolina spent on state parks.

Photo by Rich Weidman

The new Umstead State Park Visitor Center opened its doors in June 1998, featuring a variety of nature exhibits related to the park.

West Point On The Eno
5101 N. Roxboro Rd., Durham • 471-1623

West Point on the Eno is unique among Durham's city parks. This 371-acre setting represents the joint efforts of a group of citizens (The Friends of West Point) and the city to restore and preserve a part of the 19th-century community that existed before Durham.

West Point was a thriving community of about 300 families with a post office, general store, blacksmith shop, saw mill and cotton gin. Its inhabitants depended on water power generated by the West Point Mill, which operated continuously along the river from 1778 to 1942. Today you can visit the park and see corn and wheat grinding demonstrations. The cornmeal and flour produced are bagged and sold in the park's mill country store.

You will also see a traditional timber-frame blacksmith shop, a tobacco barn typical of the sort used to cure brightleaf tobacco and the restored Greek Revival country house of longtime mill owner John Cabe McCown.

Every year, West Point on the Eno is the site of a Fourth of July Festival for the Eno, which attracts musicians, artists and craftspersons from all over North Carolina. There are also annual events at Halloween and Christmas.

Recreational Activities

Raleigh

The city maintains an active recreation program for all ages and sizes. There are also some programs—the most notable being the Capital Area Soccer League (CASL)—that are independent of municipal administration but an integral part of metropolitan recreation.

Because of the favorable climate, recreational programs are active year round—the city even sponsors a Frostbite Doubles Tennis Tournament in December. In addition to the city's eight public swimming pools, the Aquatic Center in Pullen Park is one of the finest indoor swimming pools on the East Coast. Optimist Park Swimming Pool wears an inflatable dome during winter to accommodate competitive swimmers.

The city has 17 staffed community centers that offer everything from indoor basketball courts to handcrafts. Following is a list—by activity—of some of the recreational programs available. For more information about city programs, call 831-6640.

The Parks and Recreation Department also offers an integrated package of fitness and recreational services to area businesses called Corporate Leisure Services, which includes fitness classes, company picnics, corporate team sports, outdoor adventure programs and meeting sites. For more information, call 890-3298.

Baseball

There are five youth leagues operated by the city Parks and Recreation Department, starting with T-ball for 6- to 8-year-olds and including Little League. The senior league is for students ages 15 to 16. A midsummer city tournament ends each season. Games are played on 14 fields throughout the city and local businesses underwrite team expenses for uniforms. Contact Raleigh Parks and Recreation, Athletics Department, 2401 Wade Avenue, 831-6836.

The Salvation Army, 902 Wake Forest Road, 832-6918, operates its own youth athletic program, including baseball, where the emphasis is on fundamentals. There's no tournament and each participant—boys and girls—must play during the games. Registration begins in March and the season ends before school is out in June. The registration fee for one sport is $45; each additional sport costs $30. There are 30 teams in the 5 to 10 age group (T-ball, coach-pitch and machine pitch) and five teams for Little League-age children. Games for the 5 to 10 age group are played on the three fields at the Salvation Army Center on Wake Forest Road. The Little League teams play at the nearby Peace College field.

Basketball

The Raleigh Parks and Recreation Department runs an active youth league 12-game schedule in the fall, plus a tournament for city champions. It's a competitive league with lots of teams. Players, ages 10 to 18 in the youth programs, sign up at their respective neighborhood recreation centers.

FYI

Unless otherwise noted, the area code for all phone numbers listed in this guide is 919.

Call the Athletics Department, 2401 Wade Avenue, 831-6836, for the center nearest you. Registration is in October, practice in November and play starts in late December. Most facilities also have free time for pickup games, but call first.

The city also operates an adult league that follows a 16-game schedule with registration starting in October. Play begins in November.

The Salvation Army's 9-week basketball league fields 32 teams for ages 5 to 10, which are divided into three leagues. Every child gets to play and parents are recruited as coaches. The $45 registration fee is good for baseball and soccer also. Sign-up begins around November with December practices and leagues play in January on Friday nights and Saturday mornings at the Army's center at 902 Wake Forest Road. Call the Salvation Army at 832-6918.

The Hillsborough Street YMCA, 832-6601, and the North Raleigh "Finley" YMCA at 9216 Baileywick Road, 848-9622, sponsor youth leagues in the fall and members-only adult leagues. It's open registration for the youth league and costs about $55 for members; $75 for nonmembers. About 500 kids from kindergarten to grade 12 participate in the Hillsborough Street league and a comparable number at Finley, which serves the tribes of North Raleigh suburbanites. Each child gets to play, with much emphasis on the fundamentals. Sign-ups start in early fall, practice in December and play begins in January and runs through March. Most games are played at the Y, but some have moved to public and private school gyms.

The adult leagues are competitive and sometimes include past ACC stars. Eight teams play in the summer and 12 teams in winter at the Hillsborough Street and Finley YMCAs. Cost is about $25 over and above membership fees.

Photo by Evelyn Ward

West Point on the Eno was once the site of a thriving community, complete with a mill, general store, blacksmith shop, post office, cotton gin and still.

Biking

The city adopted a comprehensive bicycle plan in 1991 and has an active bicycle lobby pushing for designated bikeways. There are about 39 miles of greenways currently available to bikers. For an excellent $1 bikeway map, contact the Planning Department in City Hall, 890-3125.

Lions Park at 516 Dennis Avenue is the center for BMX racing. Teams compete there on Sundays most of the year and on Wednesdays during the summer. Bikers come from all over and races are organized through the Capital City BMX Association. For information and race times, call 790-4BMX or Lions Park at 831-6995.

Football

The city operates a league with three divisions for ages 7 to 12. There are weight limitations to make things even. About 21 teams or about seven per division compete over five fields in the Parks system. Registration starts in July and games run from September through mid-November, when a Superbowl champion in each division is crowned. Call Raleigh Parks and Recreation, Athletics, 831-6836.

Golf and Disc Golf

In a state known for world-class golfers and courses, its Capital City has no publicly owned golf course. Shame! It does have a number of excellent private club courses (described in our chapter on "Golf in the Carolinas") as well as private courses open to the public. The private courses open to the public are Hedingham, part of the Hedingham planned community and Raleigh Golf Association at 1527 Tryon Road, 772-9987, one of the older courses and a favorite among NCSU students. The other courses open to the public are all out of the city and include: Wil-Mar Golf Club on Route 5, Knightdale, 266-1800; Eagle Crest Golf Course near Garner, 772-6104; and Pine Hollow near Clayton, 553-4554. The city maintains two disc golf (Frisbee golf) courses at Kentwood and Cedar Hills parks.

Health Clubs

Like the rest of the country, health and fitness centers boomed in Raleigh during the '80s. There are plenty still around, including franchise operations like Gold's Gym or Spa Health Club and established local operations such as the Pulse Athletic Club at Celebration at Six Forks and Research Triangle Park and The Club For Women Only with locations in Raleigh and Cary. Both the YMCA and the YWCA have extensive programs, including indoor pools.

The face of the YWCA has changed and it's not just for women anymore. The YWCA at 1012 Oberlin Road, 828-3205, has a pool, Nautilus equipment and aerobics classes, as well as other fitness and recreation programs. The basic membership fee is $25. An additional monthly or annual fee gives you access to the use of the particular facilities in which you are interested. Call for more information and a copy of the YWCA's schedule. The location at 554 East Hargett Street, 834-7386, has no pool or gym and its programs focus on southeast Raleigh community needs such as day care, summer camp, adolescent pregnancy issues and activities for older citizens.

Horseback Riding

There is no publicly owned riding stable in Raleigh, although the State Fairgrounds maintains one of the best show-horse arenas and schedules in the state. MacNair's Country Acres Stables probably is the best known of the private stables and offers lessons and boarding. Call 851-1118 for information. Other stables include Raleigh Riding Academy in North Raleigh, 847-3080, and Triton Stables, 847-4123.

Ice Hockey & Ice Skating

After years of sharing Cary's successful Ice House, 467-6000, Raleigh residents finally got their own ice skating rink in 1996. Raleigh IcePlex, 878-9002, is located at the corner of Brentwood Road and Raleigh Boulevard.

Jogging, Running, Walking

If you're a jogger, you probably will want to map out your own course, but you'll have company because Raleigh is a running town. Its premier Great Raleigh Road Race, for instance, draws up to 5,000 runners and joggers annually. The city also has worked with the Raleigh Roadrunners Association to build a course near Lake Johnson.

Two of the more popular courses are the paths around Shelley Lake in northwest Raleigh and NCSU's track stadium on the main campus near Pullen Road. The city's award-winning Capital Area Greenway system is one of the best in the country and it laces the city like a spider's web, generally running beside the city's creeks and streams. The master plan shows a 200-plus-mile system of which over 39 miles are complete. The Shelley Lake to Sawmill Road Trail is the most popular, followed by the Lake Johnson and Buckeye paths. A pedestrian bridge was completed in 1994 across Lake Johnson so walkers and joggers can now make a 3.5-mile circular course around the lake. The Lake Lynn trail, completed in 1994, won a Sir Walter Raleigh Award for Community Appearance in 1995. The trail's five boardwalk sections are its most unusual and costly feature. Motorized vehicles are not allowed. Some of the trails are paved and are shared by bicyclists, but other parts are strictly for walking or jogging. Greenway maps with a description of the system are available

INSIDERS' TIP

You can rent many of the facilities in Triangle parks and recreation systems for reasonable rates. Wedding receptions, anniversary parties and company picnics are some of the events that are held in area parks. Call your local parks and recreation department for more information.

TRIANGLE LAKES & RECREATION AREAS

NAME/AUTHORITY	ACTIVITIES AVAILABLE
Eno River (State of N.C.) *Three miles northwest of Durham,* *off S.R. 1569.*	Boating, sailing, fishing, hiking, picnicking, rock hounding, bird watching.
Falls Lake (State of N.C.) *Seven miles north of Raleigh, off* *N.C. 50 and N.C. 98.*	Beaches, boating, swimming, water skiing, picnicking, fishing, bird watching. Boat rentals available.
Flat River *Bahama Rd. at Veasey Rd., Durham.*	Boating, sailing, fishing, hiking, rock hounding.
Harris Lake (CP&L) *6 mi. south of Apex off S.R. 1130* *nr. Shearon Harris Nuclear Power Plant.*	Two boat ramps.
Jordan Lake (State of N.C.) *Twenty miles southwest of* *Raleigh off U.S. 1/64.*	Boating, swimming, sailing, picnicking, camping and full-service marina.
Kerr Lake (State of N.C.) *Eleven miles north of Henderson off* *I-85 to S.R. 1319.*	Camping, swimming, fishing, boating, sailing, water skiing.
Lake Benson (City of Raleigh) *Off Buffaloe Road in southwest Raleigh.*	Fishing only. No swimming.
Lake Crabtree (Wake County) *Aviation Parkway in Wake County*	Boating, camping, hiking, picnicking, fishing, nature trails.
Lake Johnson (City of Raleigh) *Off Avent Ferry Rd. in southwest* *Raleigh.*	Jonboats, paddle boats, paved greenway trails, boardwalk across lake. No swimming.
Lake Lynn (City of Raleigh) *Off Lynn Road in north Raleigh.*	Biking, inline skating, jogging, paved greenway trail. No swimming.
Lake Michie *Off U.S. 501, 10 miles north of Durham.*	Boating, fishing, hiking, picnicking. No swimming.
Lake Wheeler (City of Raleigh) *Off Lake Wheeler Road in Raleigh.*	Fishing, sailing, canoeing, rowing, kayaking, picnicking. No swimming. Rental boats.
Little River *Johnson's Mill Road off U.S. 501 N.*	Boating, sailing, hiking.
New Hope Creek *Duke Forest in Durham.*	Canoeing, hiking.
Shelley Lake (City of Raleigh) *W. Millbrook Road in Raleigh.*	Fishing, canoeing, sailing, rowboating, pedal boating, hiking, biking. No swimming.
Silver Lake (Private) *5300 Tryon Road in Raleigh.*	Paddle boat rides, swimming, picnicking, water slide.
University Lake *Off Jones Ferry Road,* *one mile west of Carrboro.*	Non-engine boating, canoeing, fishing. No swimming. Boat rentals available.

through Raleigh Parks and Recreation for a small fee. Call 890-3285.

The city's Parks and Recreation Department also co-sponsors the 5K Run for the Oaks in early March as well as other youth races. It also can put you in touch with the people who coach the city's formidable Junior Striders, which are comprised of boys and girls ages 8 to 18. For information, call 890-3285. Finally, a number of the newer planned communities have met the demand for jogging and walking by installing their own trails.

Racquetball

Despite the interest in racquetball, the city still has no public courts. If you want to play, you'll have to join a club or the YMCA on Hillsborough Street. The YMCA has the best courts; they're solid and give you a lively bounce, but you have to share them with handball players. Other places where you will find strong racquetball crowds are Pulse Athletic Club at Celebration at Six Forks, 847-8189, and the Pulse Athletic Club at 4700 Emperor Boulevard in RTP, 941-9010.

Soccer

The Capital Area Soccer League, 3344 Hillsborough Street, 834-3951, is known as the league for soccer players of all ages, sizes and sexes. Last season, over 12,000 youth and adults participated as active players and CASL expects approximately 13,000 players in 1999. It is a nonprofit organization built on volunteers within the Raleigh/Cary community and has been the training program for some of the area's best players and coaches. It sponsors over 800 classic, challenge, recreational and adult teams. Micro soccer (3 v 3) begins with 4-year-olds and the youth league goes up to age 19. An adult league consisting of Women's Open, Men's Open, Men's Over 30 and Men's Over 40 is available for all outside the youth league. The 118-acre WRAL Soccer Complex located on Perry Creek Road off U.S. 1 N. has

25 heavily used fields. The Cedar Fork Park Complex, located in Morrisville off Aviation Parkway, has 10 active fields.

CASL has two playing seasons—fall and spring—each consisting of nine scheduled weekly games. Tournaments highlight the beginning and end of each season. The prestigious and highly competitive Raleigh Shootout is in December and the CASL Cup (one of the largest recreational tournaments in the country with over 300 participating teams) is in May. Soccer camps are available in the summer for children ages 5 to 17.

The Salvation Army, 832-6918, sponsors soccer in its athletic program and it organizes teams for boys and girls ages 5 to 10. There's a $45 registration fee (and then you can add baseball and basketball for $30 each). Sign-ups begin in July. The season runs from August to October.

The new Triangle Soccer Academy was created to enhance the development of the classic level players in the Triangle. Tryouts are held in early June and teams begin competing in August. Raleigh tryouts are held at Method Road Soccer Stadium and Durham tryouts take place at Duke Soccer Stadium. For more information, call 684-5180 (boys' soccer) and 681-3456 (girls' soccer).

Soccer Dome America, an indoor soccer facility at 5600 Hillsborough Street, offers leagues for players of all ages and skill levels. Call 859-2997 for more information.

Softball

The city has fields for about 265 teams. City officials can put you in touch with the Raleigh Amateur Softball Association and, among others, a very active church league and some company team leagues. Altogether, the city coordinates play among a variety of leagues, including medium pitch, slow pitch, coed and 40-and-older leagues. It also sponsors a slow-pitch softball league for girls ages 12 and under and a girls' fast-pitch softball league for ages 9 to 18. Registration

Staff Photo

Soccer has become the most popular recreational sport among kids in the Triangle.

for most leagues begins in mid-February and play starts in April. Call the city's Athletic Office, 831-6836, for information.

Swimming

There are a number of private clubs in Raleigh, but Candler Swim & Gym Club at 1013 Jones Franklin Road, 851-3935, is one of the oldest and best known. You can learn about competitive teams here. Its founder is a former Olympian and the quality of his diving program and swim teams has won the club national attention. It has an Olympic-size diving tower and a 25-meter pool. It was the site for the very successful 1987 Olympic Festival diving competition.

The city runs an active aquatics program, from teaching babies how to swim to hosting some of the region's top swimming competitions. The centerpieces of its swim program are the $4 million indoor Pullen Park Aquatic Center, which opened in 1992 and the Optimist Park pools, which are open year round, too. The Pullen Center is home to a number of area swim

clubs and has a diving board. Optimist includes a diving pool, a shallow baby's pool and a competitive, 50-meter Olympic-size swimming pool. The city also has pools at the following locations: Biltmore Hills, Chavis Park, Lake Johnson, Longview, Millbrook Exchange and Ridge Road. The city offers season passes if you plan to swim often; otherwise, there is an admission charge for everyone over the age of six. Diving lessons are taught as well as American Red Cross courses. For information on swim clubs and teams, call 831-6852.

A favorite swimming hole for Cary and Raleigh residents is Silver Lake, east of Cary and south of Raleigh, at 5300 Tryon Road, 851-1683. It has developed into one of the area's popular privately operated swimming parks open to the public. It features a 400-foot-long waterslide, white sand beach, pedal and motorized boats, snack bar and picnic areas. Call 851-7782 for special group rates.

All three Raleigh YMCAs sponsor competitive coed swim teams and also have pools for instructional and lap swimming for members. The Finley YMCA in North Raleigh at 9216 Baileywick Road, 848-9622, has the largest program for children and like the Hillsborough Street YMCA, 832-6601, competitive swimming is a year-long program but can be taken on a month-by-month basis. Swim classes are available for toddlers, too. The third YMCA location is on Garner Road, 833-1256.

The YWCA at 1012 Oberlin Road, 828-3205, offers swimming programs and classes for children and adults. The pool is available for members' use for lap swimming and recreational swimming. The basic membership fee at the YWCA is $25; call for additional information on fees and types of memberships that include the use of the pool.

Tennis

Raleigh was caught napping when the tennis boom hit in the mid '70s, but it has recovered since then and maintains 100 courts today—95 of which are lighted. Operation Central for city tennis programs is the Millbrook Exchange Park at 1905 Spring Forest Road, 872-4129, which has 23 courts and hosts city tournaments. The old clay courts have been converted and all courts today are hard surface. There is plenty of league play and tournaments run into December. The famed Raleigh Mojo Tournament is played every Labor Day at Pullen Park.

Play at all parks is free unless you sign up for a tournament or league or reserve courts at Millbrook Exchange. League play, by the way, is a good way to meet people.

Raleigh Racquet Club at 5516 Falls of the Neuse Road, 876-0565, is a private membership club with clubhouse and swimming pool attached. It is also home to some of the best tennis in town and features composition (soft surface) as well as hard-surface courts, 29 total, including eight indoor courts. It also has a stadium court and its tournaments attract some of

the stars of tomorrow—John McEnroe passed this way as a youngster. In addition, the club hosts a number of charity tournaments, such as the BTI Champions Tournament, which was won by Jimmy Connors in June 1998.

Volleyball

The city sponsors several leagues at different park centers and co-sponsors, with the Inland Beach Volleyball Association, tournaments at Raleigh Beach in Jaycee Park on Wade Avenue. Lions Park has a power volleyball league with six-person teams that begins registration in August. Other centers with volleyball programs include Millbrook Exchange, Biltmore Hills, Chavis Center, Robert Park and Jaycee Park. For a taste of California, two-man ball under the sun or under the lights, stop by Jaycee Park's Raleigh Beach on the weekend or during warm summer nights. It's where some of the East Coast's championship teams work out. For more information, check with Raleigh Parks and Recreation at 831-6836.

Cary

Cary is getting bigger and its recreational programs are growing as well. The town currently has over 20 Planned Unit Developments that offer their own recreational amenities to residents. Kildaire Farms, for example, has its own swimming pool with team swimming, a tennis complex and a nearby private racquetball club. The community is laced with jogging and walking trails that connect neighborhoods and include exercise stations along the way. Lochmere and Preston offer a similar menu of activities and have championship golf courses in the middle of their neighborhoods.

Because Cary is so close to Raleigh, many of its residents belong to Raleigh clubs and organizations, such as the

Photo by Tim Johnson

At 310 acres, Fred G. Bond Metro Park is the largest municipal park in Wake County, offering fishing, boating, picnic shelters, athletic fields, an amphitheatre, a large playground and a D.A.R.E. Ropes Course.

famed YMCA on Hillsborough Street or the Raleigh Racquet Club (swimming and serious tennis). Many of Raleigh's recreation programs are open to Cary residents, too, for a slight fee, such as the Pullen Park Aquatic Center. Cary has no public swimming pool.

The Town of Cary has made every reasonable effort to make facilities accessible to individuals with disabilities and accommodation can be made for most programs. A Kids Together Playground is being developed at the corner of Cary Parkway and Tryon Road. If you have questions about a facility or need special assistance, contact Cary's Parks, Recreation and Cultural Resources located at the Town Hall, 318 N. Academy Street, 469-4061. The administrative office hours are 8 AM to 5 PM.

Baseball and Softball

Cary operates seven different leagues of youth baseball, starting with T-ball for 6- to 7-year-olds and going up to senior

league players ages 17 to 18. The coaches are volunteers and the emphasis is on sportsmanship. Registration is held in February. Fees are determined annually, so call for information, 469-4062.

The girls' softball program has four leagues: ponytail (ages 8 to 10) through senior league (16 to 19). Registration times, places and fees are the same as for the baseball leagues.

In addition to the youth leagues, the town operates adult softball leagues for women and men. It also coordinates a slow-pitch church league and a coed league in the fall. There is also a men's fall league. For information on registration times and places, call 469-4063. Games are played in one of 12 town parks with baseball/softball fields. For older leagues and more competitive play, check with the Cary Softball Club at 467-4223.

Basketball

The town sponsors boys and girls leagues, starting at age 7 and going through age 18. Registration for ages 7 to 10 is held in July with games starting in mid-September. Registration for ages 11 to 18 is held in October with games beginning in November. Costs are usually the same as in youth baseball. There are two adult basketball leagues, one in the fall and one in the winter for men ages 35 or older. Call 469-4063 for more information.

The Cary YMCA on Cary Parkway, 469-9622, offers seven basketball leagues for children in kindergarten through grade 12 and adult men. They play at the YMCA and at Kingswood Elementary.

Dancing

There are a number of dance groups in the Triangle area. To get more information, consult the Wake County Library's referral services or the ARTS chapter of this book. In Cary, there is a Plus Level square dance group, the TNT Twirlers, which meets weekly on Mondays at 7 PM. While it is not a town-sponsored group, The Parks and Recreation Department, 469-4065, provides contact information. Shag, Two-Step, line dancing, ballroom dancing and jive/swing adult dance lessons are offered on a continuing basis at the Cary Community Center, 460-4965. Clogging and tap dancing are offered at Jordan Hall Arts Center, 469-4069.

Day Camps

The town offers a summer day camp for children ages 6 through 11. It meets weekdays from 7:30 AM until 5:30 PM. Activities include arts and crafts, drama, field trips, games, music and sports. There are four 1-week sessions, starting in mid-June and going through the first week in August. The Athletics Division offers several youth instructional camps throughout the summer in baseball, volleyball, basketball, tennis and golf. Camps are structured to develop the young athlete's skills. For more information, call 469-4062.

The Cary YMCA on Cary Parkway, 469-9622, has two summer day camps for children in kindergarten through grade 5. Camp Rising Sun meets at the Y and Camp Outer Limits meets at the West Cary Middle School. Kindercamp for ages 3 to 5 meets at the Y two half days a week.

Football

The town can provide you with information on the youth football program, but it is operated by the Cary Booster Club, 376-3558. It has three different divisions separated by age and weight. Youths can begin play as young as 7 or as old as 14, provided they don't weigh more than 125 pounds. Registration is on the first two Saturdays in August at the Booster Club office at 411 W. Chatham Street. Fees are determined annually.

Golf

Like Raleigh, Cary has no municipally owned golf course. Shame! Golfers do not want for courses, however. There are reportedly 18 courses open to the public in and around Raleigh and Cary. For a short list, see the "Raleigh" section in our "Golf in the Carolinas" chapter.

Ice Hockey & Ice Skating

The Ice House, located at 1410 Buck Jones Road behind Borders bookstore, has been a big hit since it first opened. Admission includes skate rental and the Ice House has open skating as well as lessons. The rink has a well-stocked snack bar and a game room. The Ice House is open to the public seven days a week. To check for specific hours and for information on lessons, call the information line at 467-6000. For information on the Raleigh Youth Hockey which practices at the Ice House, call 233-8210.

A new 128,000-square-foot facility, N.C. Ice Tri-Plex, is being constructed off Davis Drive, featuring two NHL regulation rinks and one Olympic-size rink.

Racquetball

Cary Athletic Club at 302-A Pebble Creek Drive, 467-5405, offers four racquetball courts, a Nautilus room, free weights, wallyball, volleyball, basketball court and exercise and aerobics classes. It is conveniently located near the Kildaire Farms tennis and swimming pool complex. Memberships are open to the public and it also has corporate memberships.

The Cary YMCA on Cary Parkway also has racquetball courts. Call 469-9622 for more information.

Running, Jogging

As noted earlier, many of the PUDs have their own jogging and running trails. The town has its own greenway network, designed to connect existing facilities such as schools with parks, churches and lakes. Existing trails total about 10 miles and include the Tarbert-Gatehouse Trail, Pirate's Cove, Hinshaw, Swift Creek, Parkway, White Oak, Black Creek, Oxxford Hunt, Coatbridge, Lake Pine, McCloud and Higgins Greenway. Cary is home to the Cary Road Race, sponsored by *The Cary News*. The race usually is scheduled in April and features a 5K and 10K course. It is one of the early races in the year and serves as a good warm-up for some of the longer runs.

Soccer

The Capital Area Soccer League (CASL) is the largest recreational soccer program in the Southeast. With over 800 youth and adult teams (over 12,000 participants) CASL runs fall and spring seasons for boys' and girls' teams. Children can begin playing in the 3 v 3 Micro League as early as age 4. Applications are available at local sports stores or the CASL office in Raleigh (one block from Meredith College). There is a fee per individual participant. Children under 8 years of age receive uniform shirts; all older children must purchase their uniforms. Volunteer coaches are offered free training clinics semiannually, and soccer camps are scheduled in Raleigh and Cary every summer for children 12 years old and younger.

The 136-acre CP&L Soccer Training Center, which opened in the summer of 1998 between Apex and Holly Springs, includes 13 soccer fields that will be used mostly by CASL players. For more information, call 546-6189.

The Capital Park Soccer Complex, a new 20,000-seat stadium that will be managed by CASL, is scheduled to open in late 1999 near Cary Towne Parkway and I-40. The complex will include 15 additional soccer fields and six baseball fields as well as other recreational areas. CASL's office is at 3344 Hillsborough Street in Raleigh, 834-3951.

Swimming

Cary has no municipal swimming pool, so most of the swimming is done at the many private swimming clubs connected to residential developments. Many of these clubs will accept members from outside their particular development. Some to check are Kildaire Farms, 467-4314, and Scottish Hills Recreation Club, 469-8109.

The Cary YMCA offers an extensive summer swimming program. Swimming privileges are included in Y Memberships, but you can also join just for summer swimming. Call 469-9622 for further information. Silver Lake, 851-1683, near Swift Creek Elementary School on Tryon Road, is a favorite swimming hole for Cary and Raleigh residents.

Tennis

In addition to the many private tennis clubs in Cary's planned communities, the town maintains many lighted tennis courts. The town is also developing a tennis center beside the new Green Hope High School. It will feature 32 courts, including a championship court, as well as meeting space and a pro shop. Reservations are permitted during certain times of the year by calling the recreation office, 469-4062. The department sponsors tennis lessons for a fee from March through October. There are four seasons for team tennis with four levels of play. The town sponsors two tournaments: the Polar Doubles in February and Cary Town Championships in September. A popular league is the "Ladies Morning Tennis Team" play.

Volleyball

Cary offers three seasons of adult volleyball. The Spring league registration is held in March with matches beginning in April. Summer league registration takes place in June with play in July. Fall league registration is held in August and play

begins in September. Men's, women's and coed leagues are offered.

Walking

You can go walking around the town's parks or along the town's 10-mile greenway network, but there's a special walking tour and architectural guide of Cary's historical places. You can pick up a tour folder from the Chamber of Commerce on Academy Street or at the Page-Walker Arts and History Center.

Durham

Though some folks think Durham's a little too quiet at night, there's an abundance of daytime activities available at public and private facilities all over town.

The Parks and Recreation Department's 12 recreation centers offer a full range of individual and team sports for children and adults, including baseball, basketball, boxing, soccer, softball, racquetball, handball, swimming, tennis and volleyball. Four regional recreation centers

Photo by Tim Johnson

Future Olympic hopefuls take the plunge at Cary's Lochmere Swimming Complex.

offer expanded programs: Edison Johnson District Arts & Athletics Center, 600 W. Murray Avenue, 560-4270; Irwin R. Holmes, Sr. Recreation Center at Campus Hills, 2000 S. Alston Avenue, 560-4444; W.D. Hill Community Center, 1308 Fayetteville Street, 560-4292; and Weaver Street Recreation Center, 3000 Weaver Street, 560-4294. These and other centers sponsor a variety of arts, dance and crafts classes and other special programs for all ages, including senior citizens and the handicapped.

Here's a handy guide to how and where you can participate in some of these activities. Those facilities operated by the Parks and Recreation Department are noted. For more information, contact the City of Durham Parks and Recreation Department at their office located at the Durham Bulls Athletic Park on Blackwell Street, 560-4355.

Baseball

Little League Baseball is played at five city parks: Lakeview, Red Maple, Long Meadow, Oval Drive and Lake Michie Recreation Area. Baseball is also offered at Woodcroft, and Pony and Colt Baseball for 13- to 16-year-olds at the Southern Boundaries ballfield. Contact the Parks and Recreation Department at 560-4355 for more information.

Basketball

You can probably find a good pickup game at any one of the 50 full-size outdoor courts (30 of them lighted) located at city parks or at the gyms at the Edison Johnson or W.D. Hill recreation centers. Courts are located at the following city parks: Old Farm, Lakeview, Red Maple, Sherwood, East Main Street, Lyon/Ramseur, East End, Long Meadow, East Durham, Birchwood, C.R. Wood, Burton, Hillside, Elmira Avenue, Unity Village, Southern Boundaries, White Oak, Rockwood, Forest Hills, Lyon, Morreene, Crest Street, West Durham, Oval Drive and Whippoorwill. There is a lighted court at Walltown Center. There are half-courts at Rocky Creek, Carroll Street and Albany/Sovereign parks.

For youth and adult league play, contact the Parks and Recreation Department, 560-4355.

The new Downtown YMCA also offers youth and adult leagues. Call 667-9622 for more information.

Biking

Durham's Trails and Greenways Commission is working on providing hiking, biking and jogging trails throughout the city.

Bike trails marked with green and white signs will run from Durham Academy to Duke University to North Carolina Central University. There are plenty of paved secondary roads ideal for biking through the surrounding countryside. For more information, contact the Durham Trails and Greenways Commission, 101 City Hall Plaza, 560-4137.

DEPARTMENTS OF PARKS AND RECREATION

N.C. State Parks and Recreation	733-7275
Raleigh Parks and Recreation	831-6640
Cary Parks, Recreation and Cultural Resources	469-4061
Durham Parks and Recreation	560-4355
Chapel Hill Parks and Recreation	968-2784
Carrboro Recreation and Parks	968-7703
Orange County Parks and Recreation	732-8181

Join the Carolina Tarwheels Bicycling Club for weekend recreational rides, 467-8457.

Eagle Watching

The northern section of Jordan Lake is home to the largest population of bald eagles in the eastern United States. You can spot them from several bridges passing over the water, but the best vantage point is from a special observation deck built by the New Hope Audubon Society. This site is located along N.C. 751 south of Durham, 6 miles south of I-40. Turn right after the "Wildlife Observation Site" sign, park your car and enjoy a pleasant 15-minute walk through the woods to the deck. Best observation times are dawn and dusk.

Golf

There are four public golf courses and four private ones in Durham—all of them 18 holes. The public facilities are: Duke University Golf Club at N.C. 751 and Washington Duke Inn, 681-2288; Hillandale Golf Course at Hillandale Road, 286-4211; Lake Shore Golf Course at Lumley Road, 596-2401; and semiprivate Lake Winds Golf Course at U.S. 501 N., 471-4653.

Championship courses are available to members and their guests at the country clubs serving some of Durham's most prestigious neighborhoods: Croasdaile, Willowhaven and Treyburn north of town and Hope Valley to the southwest.

Every spring Croasdaile, the Washington Duke Golf Course and Perry Como host the Duke Children's Classic, a golf/tennis benefit for Duke University Medical Center's pediatric facilities. Celebrities abound, often drawing more than 20,000 spectators during the three-day event, which celebrated its 25th anniversary in 1998.

Health and Fitness

The Lakewood YMCA at 2119 Chapel Hill Road, 493-4502, is a complete fitness center, offering separate men's and women's free-weight rooms, Nautilus, saunas and steam rooms. The Y features an indoor 25-meter pool, two full-size indoor basketball courts and four indoor racquetball courts. Behind the main facility is a 1/5-mile graded outdoor track. The Y offers men's, women's, coed and senior aerobic classes for all levels. Child care is available for those exercising or taking classes. Call for more information.

The Irwin R. Holmes, Sr. Recreation Center at 2000 S. Alston Avenue, 560-4444, has a weight and exercise room with free weights, stairclimbers, Airdyne bikes, a treadmill and a rotary torsion hip machine. There is also a heated, indoor pool, two racquetball/handball courts, a lighted softball field, a pond, playground and picnic shelters.

The new $9 million, 46,000-square-foot Downtown YMCA, 667-9622, contains state-of-the-art exercise equipment, two swimming pools, regulation-size basketball court, indoor running track, aerobics/dance studio and day-care center.

Hiking and Jogging

The Durham Trails and Greenways Commission has plans for 170 miles of hiking, jogging and biking trails throughout the city.

A portion of the North/South Greenway Trail is open from Trinity Avenue to Club Boulevard through Northgate Park into Rock Quarry Park. The 3.5-mile Quarry Trail will eventually join at its southern end with the Pearl Mill Trail, providing a connection to downtown and eventually a network of trails and greenways throughout Durham.

Meanwhile, some local developers have been persuaded to set aside land for hiking and jogging trails through their new residential neighborhoods. Woodcroft in southwest Durham already has a network of paved trails in place.

For getting away from it all, the best hiking opportunities are at Duke Forest, 613-8013; Lake Michie, 477-3906; Eno

River State Park, 383-1686; and West Point on the Eno city park, 471-1623.

Horseback Riding

You may go horseback riding in some of the same places recommended for hiking. In addition, riding and stables are available at the following private facilities: Pleasure Horse Farm on Fayetteville Rd., 544-5867; B-Bar Farms on Bivins Rd., which also has public riding, 477-3750; Longwood Farm on N.C. 751, 387-9400; and Quail Roost Stables on U.S. 501 N., 477-8932.

Ice Hockey and Ice Skating

Triangle SportsPlex located between Durham and Hillsborough has a beautiful rink offering open skating and lessons. This rink is where Triangle Youth Hockey, 644-0339, is based.

Racquet Sports

Racquetball and handball can be played at two facilities run by the city's Parks and Recreation Department: the Edison Johnson Center at 600 West Murray Avenue and Duke Park at 1530 Acadia Street. Courts for racquet sports are also available at the following private facilities: MetroSport, 501 Douglas Street, 286-7529, and the YMCA, 2119 Chapel Hill Road, 493-4502.

Scuba Diving

Water World in Durham, 596-8185, rents and sells scuba equipment, organizes trips and offers certification courses. Basic scuba classes are held two nights a week for three weeks. Open water tests are taken at Rolesville Quarry or the Florida Springs, depending on the season. The shop organizes trips to exotic dive spots like Curacao, Bonaire and Cozumel.

Soccer

The city's Parks and Recreation Department oversees youth and adult soccer teams. Seven playing fields (five of them lighted) are available at the following parks: Old Farm, Rock Quarry, Northgate, C.R. Wood, Southern Boundaries, Weaver Meadow and Erwin. Call 560-4355 for information on registration and schedules.

The new Downtown YMCA offers a youth soccer league. Call 493-4502 for more information.

Softball

The city Parks and Recreation folks supervise about 300 youth and adult softball teams playing at the following parks: Old Farm, Rock Quarry, Sherwood, Long Meadow, Edgemont, East Durham, Birchwood, Hillside, Elmira Avenue, Campus Hills, Southern Boundaries, Lyon, Wrightwood, Morreene, Walltown and Whippoorwill. There are also neighborhood and teen softball in some city parks. Call the Parks and Recreation Department for registration information, 560-4355.

The new Downtown YMCA offers an Adult Softball League. Call 493-4502 for more information,

Swimming

Public outdoor pools are open in the summer at these city parks: Forest Hills (outdoor) at 1639 University Drive, 560-4782; Hillside (outdoor) at 1300 South Roxboro Road, 560-4783; and Long

---

INSIDERS' TIP

Wake County Parks and Recreation, along with Yates Mill Associates and North Carolina State University, are working to restore historic Yates Mill in southern Wake County and develop an educational park around the mill site.

Photo by Tim Johnson

Lake Johnson in southwest Raleigh features a boardwalk and 5.5 miles of paved greenway trails.

Meadow at 917 Liberty Street, 560-4202. I.R. Holmes Center at Campus Hills, 2000 S. Alston Avenue, 560-4781, and Rock Quarry Park at 600 W. Murray Avenue, 560-4265, have indoor pools that are open year round. In addition, there are several private membership clubs available only to members and their guests.

A growing number of residential developments have private swimming facilities for residents and, if you're brave, check out the swimming holes on the Eno River.

Tennis

Finding a place to play tennis in Durham is easy to swing. There are 72 hard-surface courts (all but four are lighted) at these city parks: Rock Quarry, Northgate, Sherwood, East End, W. D. Hill, Elmira Avenue, Southern Boundaries, Garrett Road, Forest Hills, Morreene, Oval Drive and Whippoorwill. The main facilities are at Garrett Road, 489-6873; Rock Quarry, 471-2681; and Morreene Road parks, 560-4405.

Or you may want to join one of the following private facilities: Croasdaile Country Club, 383-1591; Eno Valley Swim and Racquet Club, 477-9042; Hollow Rock Racquet and Swim Club, 489-1550; Hope Valley Country Club, 489-6565; and Willowhaven Country Club, 383-5511.

Tennis classes are available through the Parks and Recreation Department, 560-4355. Under a city program, instructors have also provided classes at some public housing complexes.

Volleyball

There are over 100 volleyball teams for youth and adults competing through the Parks and Recreation Department. For times and registration information, contact the department at 560-4355.

Windsurfing

Thanks to Durham's proximity to both Falls and Jordan Lakes, windsurfing has become very popular in the area. For more information, contact the Triangle Boardsailing Club at 596-8185.

Chapel Hill-Carrboro

The Chapel Hill Parks and Recreation Department oversees 15 parks or playgrounds, including four community centers (two with pools), fitness and nature trails, two small play areas and one separate athletic field. It also offers an amazing assortment of activities, including adult volleyball as well as youth and adult tennis, swimming, basketball, baseball, softball and lacrosse. You can sign up for outdoor programs and trips involving rock climbing, kayaking or skiing, or take classes in everything from martial arts to pottery. The department sponsors special activities for senior citizens and handicapped persons.

In addition, Carrboro's own Recreation and Parks Department has a number of recreation facilities and activities. It maintains more than 72 acres of park land at six locations, providing ball fields, basketball courts, playgrounds, tennis courts, picnic shelters, nature trails and a lake. Like Chapel Hill's recreation department, it offers a wide range of athletic programs for both youth and adults including basketball, softball, baseball, volleyball and football. You can sign up for classes and workshops on all sorts of activities, like aerobics, tumbling, tennis, basketry and craft classes, or you may participate in the annual fishing rodeo or kite-flying field day. In Chapel Hill and Carrboro, some activities are free but most require a nominal charge or registration fee.

Here's a handy guide to help you sort it all out. For a schedule of activities and more information, contact the Chapel Hill Parks and Recreation Department at 968-2784 or the Carrboro Recreation and Parks Department at 968-7703.

Triangle SportsPlex is at the intersection of N.C. 86 and Business 70 in historic Hillsborough, creating a multitude of activities for the area's enjoyment. This $11 million multisports center is a partnership between Orange County and a private, nonprofit group and offers ice skating, swimming, camps for kids and ice hockey on its official NHL-sized rink. For more information about hours and activities, call 644-0339.

Baseball and Softball

Both Chapel Hill and Carrboro sponsor youth and adult baseball and softball leagues. Girls ages 8 through 15 play in softball leagues. Boys have baseball leagues for Pee Wees (ages 6 to 7) and ages 8 to 16. In addition to its Spring program, Carrboro offers a Fall baseball program for youth ages 9 to 18. There is a coed softball league for high school students, and for Chapel Hill adults, there are separate competitive and recreational co-rec softball leagues. There is co-rec (coed) softball in Carrboro. For further information, call the parks and recreation departments in either location.

Basketball

Newcomers may find it difficult adjusting to the basketball fever that suddenly strikes otherwise perfectly healthy adults here sometime after Thanksgiving. One way to get involved is to go down to the gym and shoot a few hoops.

The Chapel Hill Parks and Recreation Department offers two men's basketball leagues. The "recreational" league is for men 18 years old and older; but don't worry, former college players are not allowed. Then there's the "competitive open" league for the same age group in which the action is a bit more fierce. Carrboro also offers a men's league and some open gym playing times for men and women.

There are also youth leagues in both Chapel Hill and Carrboro. For information on teams and registration, call the parks and recreation department in the appropriate town.

If you just want to practice your jump shot or play a few pickup games, there are basketball hoops and willing participants available all over town. You can play at any one of the following locations in Chapel Hill: Hargraves, Umstead, North Forest Hills and Ephesus parks and the Lincoln and Community Center sites—some are indoors and some are outdoors. In Carrboro there are basketball courts at the following sites: Community Park, Brewer Lane Mini-Park and Carrboro Elementary School Park.

Biking

Bicycle enthusiasts may be interested in meeting fellow cyclists for weekend rides. For information, contact one of the local bicycle shops or the Carolina Tarwheels Bicycle Club at 467-8457.

Bocce

Believe it or not, they've been playing this Italian game of lawn bowling in the Chapel Hill area for a great while. Bocce is played on a court next to the Community Center on Plant Road every Tuesday and Friday morning starting around 9:00 AM. You can start pickup games anytime. Balls are available at the Community Center. There are two more bocce courts located at the Fearrington development, about 8 miles south of Chapel Hill on U.S. 15-501.

Canoeing And Kayaking

The Haw River, about 10 minutes south of Chapel Hill, is a great place to put in a canoe or kayak and spend a day shooting rapids or dodging rocks, depending on the level of the water and your skill level. The Haw is best in the early spring or after a good rain. Take care—any river at flood stage can be a deadly adversary.

The Chapel Hill Parks and Recreation Department usually cosponsors a couple of trips a year. For information, call the department at 968-2784.

Golf

There are four places to play golf in Chapel Hill: the (private) Chapel Hill Country Club, the (private) Governors Club, the (public) Finley Golf Course (which is currently closed for renovations) and the (public) Twin Lakes Golf Course, just south of town in Chatham County. You can take private lessons at Finley; call 962-2349 for details. Twin Lakes Golf course,

Staff Photo

Built by the U.S. Army Corps of Engineers, Jordan Lake in Chatham County provides a host of recreational activities.

933-1024, is located on Willow Way, off of Manns Chapel Road from U.S. 15-501 S.

Health Clubs

The YMCA and three private health clubs provide a range of exercise facilities for residents of Chapel Hill and Carrboro.

The Club for Women Only in Rams Plaza, 929-8860, offers equipment, sauna and steam, whirlpool, aerobics and a pool. The Chapel Hill-Carrboro YMCA on Airport Road, 942-5156, offers Nautilus equipment, racquet sports, sauna, whirlpool, a gym, aerobic classes, a pool and massage. The Spa Health Club on Elliott Road, 942-1182, has Nautilus, sauna, whirlpool, aerobic classes and a pool. There are also several places that offer step, toning and low impact aerobic exercise classes, including The Body Shop, 933-9281.

Horseshoes

That most Southern of sports, horseshoes, still thrives in small towns, including Carrboro. Carrboro's Recreation and Parks Department sponsors horseshoe tournaments with men's, women's and youth divisions, several times a year. Call 968-7703 for information.

Ice Hockey and Ice Skating

Triangle SportsPlex located near Hillsborough has a beautiful rink offering open skating and lessons. This rink is where Triangle Youth Hockey, 644-0339, is based.

Lacrosse

Lacrosse has seen an increase in popularity in Chapel Hill in the last several years, due in part to the successful record of the UNC lacrosse team. Culbreth, McDougle and Phillips Middle Schools and Chapel Hill High field competitive teams.

The Chapel Hill Parks and Recreation offers junior and senior Lacrosse.

Soccer

The Chapel Hill area has a thriving coed soccer program with activities for all ages and skill levels. In 1972, Rainbow Soccer was founded as a private, nonprofit organization. If you or your child want to play in a Rainbow Soccer league, all you have to do is sign up and pay the registration fee. This is a "noncompetitive" league. Everybody gets to play and everyone receives plenty of encouragement. Coed leagues—divided by age in two-year increments—are available for preschoolers (ages 3 and 4) all the way through 9th graders. The adult league, from high school age on up through adults, is called Sunset Soccer. There are also two all-girls leagues, for grades 1 through 4 and 5 through 9. Rainbow Soccer leagues play during the fall and spring seasons. Practice is twice a week and games are on Saturdays. Rainbow Soccer also sponsors special summer day camps for youths up to age 15 and for coaches and goalkeepers. For more information, call 967-8797.

If your kids are interested in highly competitive play, they should try out for the Central Carolina Youth Soccer Association teams.

The Carolina United Soccer Club was created to provide an atmosphere where children can receive soccer instruction from its experienced staff. Call 644-6800, ext. 1150, for more information.

Swimming

In Chapel Hill, you can swim year round in the indoor pool at the Community Center. The phone number is 968-2790. Since open swim times vary, call the pool hours hotline at 685-8316. There are special times for aquacize, senior swim, masters swimming and lessons. Fees range from $1.25 for children 6 to 13, to $1.75 for 14 to 17 and $2.50 for ages 18 and up; kids 5 and under swim free. Annual passes are available for $75 for children up to age 13, $115 for youth and $165 for adults 18 and up. Family passes ($250 and up) area also available. Twenty punch passes are also available ($18 to $40).

There is an outdoor pool open during the summer at Hargraves Park. Pool passes are valid at either pool.

Indoor pools are also available at three private membership facilities: the YMCA on Airport Road, 942-5156; the Spa Health Club on Elliott Road, 942-1182; and The Club for Women Only at Rams Plaza, 929-8860.

Tennis

Tennis lessons are available for youths ages 8 to 17 and for adults through Chapel Hill's Parks and Recreation Department. Chapel Hill also has a youth tennis league and a men's and women's singles league. Further information is available from the Chapel Hill Parks and Recreation Department at 968-2784. Tennis may be played at public courts at the following locations: in Chapel Hill—Hargraves, Umstead, Oakwood, Cedar Falls, Ephesus Park and Phillips Parks; in Carrboro—Community and Wilson parks. Carrboro offers instructional tennis classes for youth and adults.

Members and guests can play at the Chapel Hill Tennis Club, 929-5248. There are also private courts at the Stoneridge Racquet and Swim Club, the Chapel Hill Country Club, the Faculty-Staff Recreation Association facility (owned by UNC with membership open to permanent UNC faculty and staff) and several other private tennis clubs.

Volleyball

Coed volleyball leagues are open to players at all competitive levels, ages 18 and up. Teams play regularly at Culbreth Middle School from August to November. Registration is on a team basis. Call the Chapel Hill Parks and Recreation Department at 968-2784 for more information.

Carrboro offers Fall and Spring leagues.

Windsurfing

A few years ago the U.S. Army Corps of Engineers dammed up the Haw River to form Jordan Lake. In doing so, the Corps inadvertently created an inland windsurfer's paradise.

There are so many wide open spaces on the lake that just about anywhere is a good place to practice windsurfing. You can rent a sailboard and get information about lessons at Water World in Durham, 596-8185.

If you enjoy driving,
chipping and putting,
you're in the right place.

Golf In The Carolinas

We're stretching this chapter to include some places way outside the Triangle, but golfers deserve the information. We provide you an Insider's critique on Triangle courses and as a bonus, you also get tips on some of the best courses elsewhere in the state. There are many courses to choose from, about 500, and more are being built every year. In the Triangle alone, for instance, there have been about 10 new courses built since 1980 and two older ones have undergone major renovations. If you enjoy driving, chipping and putting, you're in the right place and will become part of the 11 percent of the population in North Carolina who play the game.

Golf, of course, is not just a sport. Golfers understand this and so do the state's industrial recruiters, who use the state's celebrated links to lure business here. Major events such as the PGA Tournament, which came to Pinehurst in June 1999, also bring in tourist dollars. Pinehurst, home of the elegant Pinehurst Resort and Country Club, features eight courses alone!

This chapter is not written for the professionals but for the amateur who occasionally shoots an 80 and enjoys the 19th hole as much as the other 18. Golfers can play the game year round, thanks to the state's temperate climate. They have a good selection between public and private links from which to choose. (If you don't belong to a private club, find a friend who does. Some of the best courses such as Treyburn in Durham and Prestonwood in Cary are attached to splendid private country clubs.) Typical green fees for most of the public courses range from $12 to $17 during the week and between $18 to $25 on weekends. Some require that you use a cart, which is an extra fee.

If you're really picky about golf courses, go to your local public library and dig up a copy of the March issue of *North Carolina* magazine published by the business lobby N.C. Citizens for Business and Industry in Raleigh. The magazine ranks the top 40 courses in the state annually, according to a group of 50 or so golfers who were told to rank only those courses they had played and had "bragged about" afterwards. So check out the courses here and start your own brag list.

Triangle Courses

Cheviot Hills Golf Course
7301 Capital Blvd., Raleigh
• 876-9920

Cheviot Hills is a veteran course that used to be on the outskirts of North Raleigh but has the city at its clubhouse door today. Rated near the middle for area courses, it's one of the better bargains and won't embarrass a beginner. Total yardage: 6475.

The Gene Hamm-designed course at Lochmere Golf Club offers golfers a fun and challenging round in a picturesque setting.

Crooked Creek Golf Course
4621 Shady Greens Dr., Fuquay-Varina
• 557-7529

Chuck Smith designed Crooked Creek, which opened in 1994 as a nice addition to golf in the Triangle. Hole No. 12 is waiting for you. Total yardage : 6329.

Devil's Ridge Golf Club
5107 Linksland Dr., Holly Springs • 557-6100

This semiprivate course is rated among the best. It was built in 1991 as part of a residential real estate development located south of Cary in Holly Springs. Says one golfer, "I like the layout; it has some water and some interesting holes. You have to think about shot placement, but it's not going to kill you." Hole No. 17, a 388-yard par 4, is the signature hole. Total yardage: 7002.

Eagle Crest Golf Course
4400 Auburn Church Rd., Garner
• 772-6104

John Baucom designed this course that's been serving Triangle golfers for more than 25 years. Total yardage: 6514.

Finley Golf Club
Old Mason Farm Rd., Chapel Hill
• 962-2349

Finley Golf Club, which is the University of North Carolina's backyard course, has been extensively renovated at a cost of approximately $8.5 million. It reopened in November 1999. Internationally renowned golf architect Tom Fazio redesigned the course, which is a par 72 with 7100 total yardage. Finley Golf Club has already been acclaimed as one of the top college facilities in the United States. It provides plenty of challenges for all skill levels.

Hedingham Golf Club
4801 Harbour Towne Dr., Raleigh
• 250-3030

This course is part of the attractive Hedingham planned community in east Raleigh, north of U.S. 64. It was completed in 1993, has a well-equipped pro shop and offers a driving range. It is rated above average among the public courses and is a good place to find other newcomers. Total yardage: 6675.

Hillandale Golf Course
Hillandale Rd., Durham
• 286-4211

Hillandale is the grandaddy of the public courses in the Triangle. The crowd that hangs out here doesn't put on any social airs. There's no charge for the philosophy or golf tales. You might even find a few golfers who will put a friendly wager on a friendly match. The course is kept in excellent condition and has some challenging holes. According to some, the pro shop is the best in the Triangle. Total yardage: 6435.

Knight's Play Golf Center
2512 Ten Ten Rd., Apex
• 303-4653

Knight's Play opened in May 1998 and features a state-of-the-art, fully lit 18-hole course and driving range open from 8 AM until midnight. David Postlethwait designed the course, which provides a variety of challenges for all skill levels. Knight's Play offers a fully stocked pro shop and sandwich grill. Total yardage: 2601.

Lochmere Golf Club
2511 Kildaire Farm Rd.,
Cary • 851-0611

Lochmere is a favorite in Cary and was a hit when it opened in 1985. It is part of a very popular residential community and offers a beautiful, scenic landscape that includes two lakes. The course has more that 40 bunkers and 10 water holes. It was the first home for the One Club World Championships. The clubhouse includes a pro shop and a bar and grill. It has a driving range and it ranks above average in play. Total yardage: 6876.

The Neuse Golf Club
918 Birkdale Dr., Clayton • 550-0550

Running parallel to the Neuse River, this scenic golf course opened in 1993 in the Clayton development of Glen Laurel. One golf magazine rated it the best new public course in the state in 1994. It's about 15 to 20 minutes from the east side of Raleigh. The course's signature hole is No. 14, with rocks on the left and water on the right. A well placed tee shot is critical on this 176-yard par-3 hole. Total yardage: 7010.

Occoneechee Golf Club
1500 Lawrence Rd., Hillsborough
• 732-3435

Marvin Ray designed this course, which opened in 1963. Although you can walk this course anytime, carts are very affordable. Total yardage: 6062.

Pine Hollow Golf Club
3300 Garner Rd., Clayton • 553-4554

This course has been around for a long time, and is located east of Raleigh amid rolling fields and tall pines. It has an informal, relaxed air and you can find industrial league players here during the week. It's also a great escape from household or weekend chores. The latter is reflected by $26 green fees on the weekend. The course is kept in good shape and offers a putting green, a driving range and a pro shop with a snack bar. Total yardage: 6266.

Raleigh Golf Association
1527 Tryon Rd., Raleigh • 772-9987

Raleigh Golf Association is another veteran course, perhaps one of the oldest in the Triangle. It was built in the country, south of Raleigh off Tryon Road, but is now within the city limits. Described by one player as a "nice member's course," it is unpretentious and plays fast. The fairways and greens are well-tended, especially Hole No. 13, which is a challenging 434 yard par 4. Total yardage: 6276.

FYI

Unless otherwise noted, the area code for all phone numbers listed in this guide is 919.

Wake Forest Golf Club
13239 Capital Blvd., Wake Forest
• 556-3416

Gene Hamm designed this course, which opened in 1968. This very challenging course starts with an incredible 711 yard par 5. Total yardage: 6956.

Washington Duke Inn and Golf Club
N.C. 751 at Science Dr., Durham
• 681-2288

This classic championship course was designed by Robert Trent Jones in the 1960s and recently redesigned by his son Rees Jones. In the 1998 *North Carolina* magazine survey, it ranked highly among the state's best courses. It has the most accommodations, including a pro shop, hotel, driving range and 19th-hole restaurant. If you're coming to visit Duke University, stay here and work in a round. Hole No. 12 is considered one of the most beautiful in the area. Total yardage: 7054.

Wildwood Green Golf Club
3000 Ballybunion Way, Raleigh
• 846-8376

Wildwood Green was one of the city's older public courses that underwent major renovations during the '80s and emerged as part of a golf course community. It is locally owned and managed, offering a number of membership options, including weekday plans for older golfers and junior cards for those under age 21. Hole No. 2, a 377-yard par 4, is a special challenge—short and scenic. Wildwood Green is rated among the average courses in play and is one of the shorter courses. Total yardage: 6218.

Other Area Courses

Cedar Grove Golf Course
619 McDade Store Rd., Cedar Grove
• 732-8397

Lakeshore Golf Course
4621 Lumley Rd., Durham • 596-2401

Photo courtesy of Washington Duke Inn and Golf Club

The championship golf course at Washington Duke Inn and Golf Club will host the 2001 NCAA Men's Championship.

Mill Creek Golf Club
1700 St. Andrews Dr., Mebane
• 563-4653

Twin Lakes Golf Course
Mann's Chapel Rd., Chapel Hill
• 933-1024

Wil-Mar Golf Club
2300 Old Milburnie Rd., Raleigh
• 266-1800

Willowhaven Country Club
253 Country Club Dr., Durham
• 383-1022

Private Club Courses

The Triangle also has some of the best private country club courses in the state. While these courses are not open to the public, they should be part of every golfer's education about Triangle golf.

There are seven courses that rise to the top: Treyburn in Durham; Governors Club in Chapel Hill; Raleigh, North Ridge and Carolina in Raleigh; and MacGregor Downs and Prestonwood in Cary.

Treyburn, a vast real estate community north of Durham's downtown, is a spectacular course, which was designed by Tom Fazio and opened in 1988 to rave reviews by the golf press. It is one of the top-rated courses in the Triangle and across the state. The clubhouse is warm, beautiful and ranked by *Southern Links* as among the region's top five. It also has one of the finest croquet greens around. A number of Duke's and UNC's famous athletes are club members, including Mike Gminski and Michael Jordan. It features a super finishing hole, No. 18, a par 4.

Governors Club is a Jack Nicklaus design that opened in 1990 as part of a planned community. It's ranked very high among the state's best courses. The setting is against Edwards Mountain and from the ninth tee, you get a spectacular view

of the neighborhood. There are five sets of tees, so the course ranges from over 7085 yards to just under 6000 yards.

Among the private clubs in Raleigh, North Ridge usually gets top honors, although the venerable Raleigh Country Club over by Wake Medical Center gets good reviews and is notable as one of the last courses designed by golfing legend Donald J. Ross. It features a 6700-yard, par-70 course. Raleigh Country Club celebrated its 50th anniversary in 1998 and hosted the annual Nike Carolina Classic.

Today North Ridge, which opened in 1970, has 36 holes—the original 18 holes were designed by George Cobb, who left his mark on courses at Linville Ridge and Bald Head Island, other courses in North Carolina. Its members are often connected to the Triangle's corporate establishment.

Surrounded by the Country Club Hills neighborhood on Glenwood Avenue, which was developed mostly in the 1950s, Carolina Country Club is the hub of the Old Raleigh Establishment. It features a 5502-yard, par-71 course.

Cary's MacGregor Downs dates back to 1968. It is considered a great "member's course" and was designed by Willard Byrd.

Prestonwood opened in the mid-'80s as part of Preston, one of Cary's trademark planned unit developments and the Triangle's largest golf course community. The clubhouse is elegant and the course is surrounded by some of the most attractive real estate in the county. The Nike Tour made its Triangle debut here in June '94 and the club pro is former PGA great Vance Heafner. Prestonwood is also home to the annual Jimmy V Celebrity Golf Classic. The course has 54 holes.

Other notable private country club courses in the Triangle include Chapel Hill, Hope Valley and Croasdaile. Chapel Hill Country Club, located northeast of downtown, features a 6752-yard, par-72 course. Hope Valley's 6148-yard, par-70 course is surrounded by some of the most colossal older homes in Durham. Built in

1966, Croasdaile's 6797-yard, par-72 course is located about 5 minutes from Duke University.

Courses Elsewhere

Triangle residents may prefer to travel a relatively short distance to tee-up on some of the state's other great fairways. This is like jumping from Cloud Nine to Golfer's Heaven.

For instance, it's only an hour's drive to the village of Pinehurst, home of Pinehurst Resort and Country Club, (800) 487-4653. The town dates back to 1895 when James W. Tufts bought 5,000 acres of North Carolina piney woods and hired Frederick Olmsted, the designer of New York's Central Park, to plan a private village. Tufts then hired Scotsman Donald Ross to build a course in 1899. Olmsted's concentric city plan continues today as the core of a town that Ross developed into the state's acknowledged golf capital and the first home of the PGA's World Golf Hall of Fame.

Queen of the eight courses at the resort is Pinehurst No. 2, which will be home to the 1999 U.S. Open Tournament. It easily captured the title as No. 1 course in the state in the 1998 *North Carolina* magazine survey. Guests at the resort can play here and entire articles have been written just about this one course. If you make the trip, just remember that as you line up your first shot you're playing the same course where Ben Hogan won his first pro tournament in 1940, and where golf legends Sam Snead, Byron Nelson and Jack Nicklaus played and won. Makes you want to go right for the flag, doesn't it?

The eight courses at the resort are just the beginning of the feast. Pinehurst No. 7 is also among the top-rated courses, listed at No. 23 out of the Top 40. Tom Fazio designed Pinehurst No. 8, which was voted the year's best new course in

the 1997 *North Carolina* magazine survey and placed 10th overall in the 1998 survey. There are many more courses in and around the towns of Pinehurst and Southern Pines. Most of them wear designer labels with names like Jack Nicklaus, Arnold Palmer, Tom and George Fazio, Dan Maples and Rees Jones.

Another Insider's favorite is Mid Pines Resort, (800) 323-2114, in Southern Pines. This resort has a Donald Ross course that opened in 1921 and was ranked 17th in the 1998 *North Carolina* poll. The greens are small and the fairways are narrow.

Pine Needles Resort, (910) 692-7111, in Southern Pines is a 1927 Ross course. It is a challenging par 71 and was host to the 1996 Ladies U.S. Open. It's among the state's top courses and is operated by three generations of the same family.

Country Club of North Carolina has two private courses, but guests at Pinehurst Resort may play here. Insiders claim it is among the best in the state— with a notable membership. It's kept in immaculate condition, which helps explain why it's so highly rated.

Rees Jones designed the championship course Talamore, (910) 692-5884, which was nominated for best new public course in the nation in its debut. It offers a truly unique feature—llama caddies.

Carolina Trace Country Club, (919) 499-5611, which is in a private retirement community, features two 18-hole courses designed by Robert Trent Jones. Tournament group play is welcome.

When you travel to the coast, you will find more slices (pardon) of golf paradise. At Calabash, there is Pearl Golf Links, (910) 579-8132, designed by Dan Maples. It offers 72 holes of golf and a grand and informal clubhouse. Pearl Golf Links also has one of the best driving ranges in the state. Close by is Marsh Harbour Golf Course, (803) 249-3449. You can enjoy

Calabash-style seafood and then work it off on these courses.

Brandywine Bay Golf and Country Club, (252) 247-2541, west of Morehead City, is set in dense woods and laced with streams and ponds. Originally designed by Bruce Devlin and redesigned by Ellis and Dan Maples, this coastal course plays 6611 yards from the championship tees, 6138 yards from the regular men's tees and 5196 yards from the women's tees. Golfers will find a pro shop, snack bar and putting greens.

Up north, on the Outer Banks, you can get a feel of Scottish moors and winds at The Village of Nags Head course, (252) 441-8073. You're surrounded by history and hang gliders, and, according to *Golf Digest*, perhaps the "longest, strongest and most irritating 6,100 yards you've ever encountered."

Traveling west, there is Tanglewood, (336) 766-5082, in Clemmons, outside Winston-Salem. Tanglewood rivals some of the state's finest courses for championship play and it is among Robert Trent Jones' best known courses. Lee Trevino won the 1974 PGA here and the 1986 Public Links Championship. It's a public course and considered by Insiders to be among the best 25 public courses in the country. The par 5, Hole No. 5, says *Golf* magazine, is one of the "most challenging" in the United States.

Golfers find summertime happiness in the mountains. Grandfather Golf and Country Club, (828) 898-4388, is at the center of the courses around Blowing Rock and Linville, North Carolina, in the northwest mountains. It is a private course designed by Ellis Maples. The championship course at Grandfather is always highly rated in the statewide survey and among the most challenging mountain courses in the country.

One of the newer courses in the northwest mountains is, despite its name, Olde Beau, (800) 752-1634, part of a residential mountain community about 20 minutes north of Elkin. The course is long, 6713 yards, and the signature hole is No. 15, a par 4 that overlooks the scenic Mitchell River Gorge. Play involves mastering the vertical, especially on the back nine, but golfers like its character. Arnold Palmer Course Designs helped with the layout and Curtis Strange was on hand for the opening tee off in 1991.

The second hub of mountain golf is in the Highlands area south of Asheville. You will find a number of private clubs here such as The Cullasaja Club, (828) 526-3531, with a course designed by Arnold Palmer and down the road at Cashiers, there's the Wade Hampton Club, (828) 743-5950, by Tom Fazio, rated No. 8 among the Top 40 in the state in 1998.

Located in Cashiers, North Carolina, the High Hampton Inn & Country Club, (800) 334-2551, offers some of the most dramatic scenery of any of the mountain courses. It is an 18-hole par 71 course designed by George W. Cobb. It features bent grass greens, a practice range with a covered hitting area, two putting greens and, during the season, it offers a series of golf schools. The Inn itself, once the home of Confederate General and Governor Wade Hampton, is in the National Register of Historic Places and the resort offers a variety of activities in addition to golf.

Golf is a natural in North Carolina. See you at the tee!

INSIDERS' TIP

The Jimmy V Celebrity Golf Tournament is played at Prestonwood in Cary. Named after NCSU's late basketball coach, Jim Valvano, the tournament is a good place to catch up on Dick Vitale stories.

North Carolina is a sports state and the Triangle is the center of that interest, especially at the college level.

Spectator Sports

Here's a social tip: If you're new to the Triangle and don't know what to talk about to your new neighbors, fellow employees or church members, ask them about sports. Especially basketball. You'll be accepted immediately. Why, this is the only place in the United States, according to some, where people during basketball season spend more time talking about sports than the weather or sex!

North Carolina is a sports state and the Triangle is the center of that interest, especially at the college level. Charlotte puts on airs with its NBA Hornets and NFL Panthers, but it's the Triangle (not that bluegrass place) that is the capital of college basketball, host to the National Hockey League's Hurricanes (yes, ice hockey in the Tar Heel state) and home to the most celebrated minor league baseball team in the world, the Durham Bulls.

We have world-record sprinters and hold a lock on women's college soccer. The tickets are reasonable and the locations are close. For example, you don't have to drive more than 60 miles round trip to see not one, not two, but three Division I university teams: arch rivals University of North Carolina and North Carolina State University and, if that weren't enough, those famous Duke University teams with their now nationally infamous fans. These teams play to win and, depending on the sport and the year, they bring home national championships. In addition, the Hornets and Panthers sell tickets in the Triangle and the local media treats them like home state if not hometown teams.

The Triangle also has been chosen as the site of the 1999 Special Olympics World Summer Games, an event that will draw an estimated 7,000 athletes from 150 countries.

How serious are we about sports? Consider this true story: Gov. James B. Hunt held an emergency meeting during the state's 1977 energy crisis. It was the first afternoon of the fabled ACC Basketball Tournament and a North Carolina team, the Wake Forest University Deacons, had just been upset by an out-of-state team. The emergency committee gave its report. The Governor sat there pensive, silent. He finally shook his head, looked up and pronounced: "Poor old Wake Forest, they just don't have any luck, do they?" As governor of North Carolina, he knew better than the crisis committee what really bothered his constituents. So, if you want to watch sports, here's where you start.

Collegiate Sports

Raleigh

N.C. State University

Reynolds Coliseum, Box 8503
Tickets: 515-2106
Information: 515-2102

The powerhouse in the Raleigh-Cary corner of Triangle sports is North Carolina State University (also known as State, NCSU or the Pack), the sprawling campus between Hillsborough Street and Western Boulevard in Raleigh. It has a rich sports tradition and when it's winning, you can feel it in Raleigh's mood. Its teams, nicknamed the Wolfpack, have produced such famous athletes as quarterbacks Roman Gabriel and Eric Kramer, receiver Mike Quick, running back Ted

FYI

Unless otherwise noted, the area code for all phone numbers listed in this guide is 919.

After enduring a couple of mediocre football seasons, the Pack came back strong in 1998.

Photo courtesy of N.C. State University

Brown; baseball pitchers Mike Caldwell, Tim Stoddard and Dan Plesac; basketball pros David Thompson, Tom Gugliotta, Thurl Bailey and Spud Webb; and in tennis, John Sadri.

Football

Carter-Finley Stadium
Blue Ridge Rd.

Football gets the academic year off to a pulse-pumping start. Now in his sixth year at the helm, Coach Mike O'Cain led the Pack to the 1994 Hall of Fame Bowl and followed that with a dramatic win in the '95 Peach Bowl over Mississippi State. Over the next two years, the Pack stumbled with back-to-back 3-8 seasons, but bounced back during the 1997-98 season with a 6-5 record, winning its last three games. NCSU continued its winning ways during the 1998-99 season with a stunning 24-7 victory over then second-ranked Florida State in September—one of the biggest upsets in ACC history.

O'Cain's predecessor, Dick Sheridan, took the Pack to the 1988 Peach Bowl, the 1989 Copper Bowl, the 1990 All American Bowl, the 1992 heart-stopping Peach Bowl and the fogged-in 1993 Gator Bowl.

Home games are played at 59,000-seat Carter-Finley Stadium next to the State Fairgrounds, off Blue Ridge Road. Game tickets are $20 to $25 at the gate; season tickets for 1998 are $137. The annual end-of-season matchup between the Wolfpack and the UNC Tar Heels took place at Charlotte's Ericsson Stadium in 1998.

Some consider the ritual tailgate feast before the game the best part of the contest and North Carolinians have raised the custom to culinary heights. Consider yourself a baptized Insider to the Triangle when you attend the home game that plays during State Fair Week. The football crowd and the State Fair crowd combine to create the biggest traffic jam in the state.

Photo by Simon Griffiths, courtesy of N.C. State University

The Lady Wolfpack advanced to the Final Four of the NCAA Tournament during the 1997-98 season.

Basketball
Reynolds Coliseum
Main Campus

NCSU fans are some of the most fervent, especially those who call themselves "ABC" fans—Anybody But Carolina. State fans demonstrated their faith in celebratory bonfires in 1983 when the late Jim Valvano's "Team of Destiny" rallied from a lukewarm season record to first capture the ACC Tournament title and then win the NCAA Championship Game with a heart-stopping shot at the buzzer.

The Pack also won the NCAA championship in 1974 after beating UCLA and Bill Walton in two overtimes in what some consider the best NCAA tournament game ever. In 1996, Coach Herb Sendek, former head coach of Miami (Ohio) University, replaced Les Robinson as head coach, becoming the youngest coach in the ACC.

Sendek's teams are noted as fierce competitors and the Wolfpack surprised everyone by making it to the 1997 ACC Tournament Finals before being knocked off by UNC. During the 1998-99 season, the Pack qualified for the National Invitation Tournament for the third year in a row, falling to Princeton in the second round.

Season tickets for 16 home games cost about $380 and they're only $20 for most non-conference games. Don't expect to get any tickets at the door when other ACC teams are in town.

Reynolds Coliseum holds 12,400 fans and you can see the action from just about any seat. The Wolfpack will move to its new home at the $158 million, 21,600-seat "Entertainment and Sports Arena" near Carter-Finley Stadium and the State Fairgrounds in the fall of 1999. The new arena, which will also be the home of the Carolina Hurricanes as well as a regional entertainment showcase, is scheduled to be completed in September 1999. It is currently priced at $157 million.

Football and men's basketball are the profit producers for State's athletic program, but officials expect that the next program to break through will be women's basketball. The Wolfpack women also play in Reynolds Coliseum and the team's head coach, Kay Yow, is recognized as one of the best in the country. It was Yow's USA basketball team that brought home the Olympic gold medal in 1988 from Seoul when the men couldn't. During the 1997-98 season, the Wolfpack advanced to the Final Four of the NCAA Tournament. Tickets are $5 a game; season tickets run $45 to $60. Youths under age 17 are admitted free.

Other Sports

NCSU's other sports also put championship athletes on the field. The Pack's baseball team finished its 1998 season with a 41-23 overall record and made its 11th NCAA Tournament appearance in the last 13 years. The team plays at Doak Field on Sullivan Drive. The team's coach is alumnus Elliott Avent. The Pack plays about 60 games a year and no admission is charged for non-conference games.

NCSU's swimmers have racked up 14 ACC titles and State boasts about alum David Fox, who wears a 1996 Olympic Gold medal as part of the USA's 4 x 100 freestyle relay contingent. He joins fellow alums Duncan Goodhew ('84 Olympics) and Steve Rerych ('68 Olympics) as Olympic Gold Medalists.

In 1996, NCSU wrestlers once again were the ACC champs. Sylvester Terkay and Scott Turner were NCAA national wrestling champions in '93 and '88, respectively.

In track, the men's team defended its ACC championship throughout most of the 1980s and again won the ACC crown in 1996. Recent NCSU graduate Alvis

Whitted holds the ACC record in the 100-meter dash (10.02 seconds). Meets are held at Derr Field, which NCSU generously shares with the greater Raleigh community as one of the city's favorite jogging and running fields. The Pack's cross country teams also have dominated the ACC and both the men's and women's teams won the 1997 ACC Tournament.

Soccer is another sport where NCSU's women have shared ranking honors with the men. Both teams are usually ranked among the nation's top 20 and the men's team made it to the Final Four in 1990.

If you want to see some rising stars in the universe of golf, don't miss the BellSouth Yellow Pages Invitational at MacGregor Downs Golf Course in Cary. It is held the same week of the Masters Tournament in Georgia. NCSU is a co-sponsor of this college cattlecall of the best young players in the country. The tournament invites 12 teams, including the ACC's Big Four of NCSU, UNC, Duke and Wake Forest, and it's a place where you may see the next golf superstar on his way to the pro tours.

Durham

Duke University
Tickets: 681-2583
Information: 684-2633

A school that's sometimes called the "Harvard of the South" (locals refer to Harvard as the Duke of the North!) isn't supposed to have a big-time sports program. After all, Duke is a small school compared to its Triangle neighbors in Raleigh and Chapel Hill. The undergraduate enrollment is about 6,000. It's a private

INSIDERS' TIP

Some Duke students at the makeshift "Krzyzewski Village" camped out in tents for over a month, waiting to buy tickets to the two Duke-Carolina basketball games in 1998. Remember, these kids' parents are paying over $21,000 for tuition alone to have a warm bed and a roof over their children's heads.

school with high academic standards and SAT scores that average around 1300—a difficult task for coaches recruiting 270-pound tackles or 7-foot basketball centers. Duke has been featured on the cover of *Parade* magazine for its success in promoting good grades and great athletes.

Duke teams soar—like the 1990-91 and 1991-92 Blue Devil basketball teams, which won back-to-back national championships. Duke won it all against UNLV, Kansas, Indiana and Michigan. Duke went to the Final Four five years in a row and was the first team since UCLA to repeat a championship.

Football
Wallace Wade Stadium, Main Campus

Blue Devil teams have been national powers in football since the '30s, when the famous 1938 Iron Dukes under Football Hall of Famer Wallace Wade went undefeated, untied and unscored on but lost the Rose Bowl, 7-3, to Southern California in the last 40 seconds. The Blue Devils are one of only a handful of schools that have played in all four of the major bowl games: Rose, Cotton, Orange and Sugar. Former Blue Devil stars include quarterbacks Sonny Jurgensen, Ben Bennett and Dave Brown and linebackers Mike Curtis, George McAfee and Bob Matheson.

After the dream season of 1989 that included a bowl game and ACC co-championship, Coach Steve Spurrier, Coach of the Year in 1988 and 1989, left for Florida's warmer climes. Coach Fred Goldsmith took the helm in 1994 and led Duke to an 8-4 season and Hall of Fame Bowl game. For that, he was named ACC Coach of the Year and won the Bobby Dodd National Coach of the Year award. However, the Blue Devils have struggled over the past few years, finishing 3-8 in 1995, 0-11 in 1996 and 2-9 in 1997. Goldsmith was fired after the Blue Devils finished with a 4-7 record in 1998. He was replaced by Carl Franks, a former assistant offensive coordinator at the University of Florida.

On almost any autumn Saturday

Photo courtesy of Duke University

Elton Brand led the Duke Blue Devils to the NCAA finals and then opted to enter the NBA draft.

afternoon or evening that the Blue Devils are playing at Wallace Wade Stadium (except the Carolina game), you can get a ticket at the gate. The price is $20 cash ($25 for the UNC game); preferred season tickets in '98 are $90. Other season tickets cost $30 and $60, depending on the seat. Before the game, enjoy food and interactive games at the new Blue Devil Tailgate Terrace.

Basketball
Cameron Indoor Stadium, Main Campus

Duke's basketball teams have been one of the best shows in the nation for more than 20 years. Cameron Indoor Stadium is absolutely one of the best spots to watch college basketball in the country. If you can get a ticket—go! In 1978, 1986, 1990, 1991, 1992 and 1994, the Blue Devils advanced to the NCAA's Championship game. Duke won it all in 1991 and 1992. In 1999, Duke swept the Atlantic Coast Conference regular season, captured the ACC championship and came two points short of winning a third national championship against the University of Connecticut Huskies.

The Lady Blue Devils made it to the 1999 NCAA finals for the first time in school history.

Duke stars who moved into the NBA include Elton Brand, William Avery, Corey Maggette, Grant Hill, Christian Laettner, Bobby Hurley, Danny Ferry, Johnny Dawkins, Mike Gminski, Gene Banks, Jeff Mullins and Jack Marin, with more to come. Recent Duke graduate Roshown McLeod joined the list after being drafted by the Atlanta Hawks in the first round of the 1998 NBA draft.

At Cameron Indoor Stadium (which seats 9,314), you get two shows for the price of one: you get to watch the basketball team and you get to see the notorious Duke fans—The Cameron Crazies. Long before TV broadcasters like Al McGuire and Dick Vitale compared them to Attila's hordes, the students were entertaining visiting teams with all sorts of digs, barbs and sarcasm. For instance, when UNC's basketball uniforms were redesigned to include argyle diamonds, Duke fans greeted the Tar Heels by throwing argyle socks onto the court.

Season tickets have been sold out since the early 1980s. To get basketball tickets, you can join the Iron Dukes, which supports Duke athletics, but that's no guarantee—the allocation of season tickets is based upon contributions to the Iron Duke organization. Single tickets cost $20 for non-conference games and $25 for all home ACC games. Holiday game tickets are sold when the students are away so check the Duke ticket office in September for availability. (No, it's not true that if you can spell Coach Mike Krzyzewski's last name, you get in free.)

Other Sports

Duke's national athletic prowess doesn't stop with basketball and football. For instance, the 1998 U.S. Women's Open Golf Tournament kept Duke students glued to their television sets as they watched Blue Devil golfer Jenny Chuairiporn finish in second place after an exhilarating sudden-death playoff.

Also in 1998, Duke swept the men's and women's ACC Tennis Championships. It was the men's seventh title in eight years and the women's 11th consecutive ACC championship.

Its men's soccer team usually is ranked among the top 20 and it won the 1986 NCAA national championship. In 1995, the team advanced to the NCAA Final Four, finishing second in the nation with a 1-0 loss to Wisconsin. In 1994, the Duke women's team beat the juggernaut UNC women's soccer team, an unheard-of feat since UNC was undefeated at home in a stretch of about 20 years! In 1995 the women's team made it to the first round of the NCAA tournament, finishing with a record of 14-7-1. You can watch some of the best college soccer at the Duke soccer field in the fall. The 1997 men's soccer team placed first in the ACC, while the women's team placed second.

The Blue Devils also are ranked in men's lacrosse and the men's and women's tennis teams are frequent ACC champs. The women's volleyball team has won the ACC championship four times in recent years and the growing women's basketball program put the Blue Devils into the NCAA tournament in '95 and '96. In 1998, the team reached the Sweet Sixteen.

Track teams have included Dave Sime, once one of the world's fastest runners.

North Carolina Central University

1801 Fayetteville St., Durham
• **Tickets: 560-5170**
• **Information: 560-6573**

NCCU is a member of the NCAA Division II Central Intercollegiate Athletic Association and offers a number of sporting events to Triangle residents. The school became known in the '70s for its track teams, coached by now-retired Leroy Walker, who was the United States track coach at the Montreal Olympics. There are 12 schools—including St. Augustine's and Shaw in Raleigh—in the CIAA, a conference that has produced dozens of players in the pro ranks.

Football
O'Kelly-Riddick Stadium, Main Campus

Like the larger ACC schools, football is one of the NCCU Eagles' biggest spectator sports. The team went to the NCAA quarterfinals in 1988 and has been a contender in the conference over the years. In 1997, the Eagles finished with a 4-7 overall record during a rebuilding year.

NFL Hall of Famer Larry Little was the Eagle head coach from 1993-98, compiling a 33-32 record. After three losing seasons in the past four years, NCCU decided not to renew Little's contract. He was replaced by former Livingstone coach Rudy Abrams. Past NCCU stars include John Baker of the Pittsburgh Steelers (now sheriff of Wake County) and John Brown, one of the first black pros, who played for the old Los Angeles Rams.

Season tickets go for about $60 for five home games or $10 per game at the gate. O'Kelly-Riddick Stadium seats about 11,500.

Basketball
McLendon-McDougald Gym, Main Campus

NCCU's basketball history includes John D. McLendon's then-dramatic fast-break teams of the 1930s and one of the game's first 7-foot players. Sam Jones of the Boston Celtics, who is a former Eagle star, was inducted into the NBA Hall of Fame in 1983.

In 1989, when Duke lost the championship to UNLV, Durham did not go without an NCAA national title—the Eagles brought home the NCAA Division II basketball championship title instead! During the 1996-97 season, the Eagles compiled a 20-6 record, which included a fourth CIAA Southern Division Championship in five years and a return to the NCAA South Atlantic Regional playoffs. The Eagles finished with a solid 18-8 record during the 1997-98 season.

Season tickets for NCCU basketball cost about $60, with single game tickets selling for $10. Games are played in the 3,200-seat McLendon-McDougald Gym.

Other Sports

NCCU's track teams under Leroy Walker brought national attention to the Durham school, especially the Eagles' famed "six-pack" of sprinters who helped win the NCAA Division II national championship in the '70s. The team continues to get respect at national meets such as the Penn Relays.

In women's sports, NCCU's volleyball team made it to the NCAA playoffs in 1988 and its basketball team is an annual contender for conference honors.

The 1998 softball team defeated Virginia State to capture the CIAA Championship.

Photo courtesy of N.C. Central University Public Relations

The NCCU Eagles play at 11,500-seat O'Kelly-Riddick Stadium.

March Madness … It All Started Here

We know that CBS has trademarked March Madness and spread it into the national vocabulary, but the craziness started here, in what Triangle residents justifiably call the basketball capital of the United States.

Big time college basketball arrived in the Triangle when Everett Case began recruiting talented athletes from "up north" to play at Raleigh's North Carolina State University during the 1950s. They whipped everybody on Tobacco Road and many teams beyond. At that time, the teams played in the Southern Conference. and believe it or not, the end of season conference tournament was

played in Raleigh's Memorial Auditorium, which was smaller than it is now. (Carolina stopped Case's team in 1957 when the undefeated Heels won the NCAA national championship.)

The conference evolved into the Atlantic Coast Conference (ACC) and the madness took hold in the 1960s when the ACC sent only one team to the annual

Antawn Jamison

NCAA tournament—that team was not the regular season winner, but the take-all winner of the ACC Tournament. By this time, too, the Triangle's ACC sports teams all had acquired a strong sports tradition and thousands of alumni, thanks to the GI Bill and huge college enrollments following World War II. The crowds found themselves squeezed into two small basketball arenas at Duke and Carolina; only State's Reynold's Coliseum, which seats 12,000, was worthy of the name. Going to an ACC basketball game became a mark of social standing as much as sports loyalty. Why, you might even be on TV! Season tickets to Carolina games, in particular, were items that were sometimes listed in wills or divorce settlements.

Add to this insatiable demand and fixed supply the heat of year-long bragging and boasting among fans who lived and worked cheek by jowl in the Triangle, and you have the ingredients for an ACC tournament. Teams that had fought like gladiators all year to post winning seasons, national rankings and often Top 10 listings, buckled on the armor for a grueling contest that began Friday morning and ended Sunday afternoon. Three games in less than three days. Remember, only one team could go to the NCAA. And beware the lowly team that found a rabbit's foot.

Photo courtesy of UNC Sports Information

Imagine rooting and boosting your team through the season to a 19-1 or 18-2 record and then, on a last second shot by some no-name kid from a Clemson team that's 11-9, your team loses by one point. Or worse, after leading the game for 36 minutes, your team falls behind by three points to Carolina, and Dean Smith employs his infamous Four Corners Offense. Like watching a snake squeeze the life out of a struggling dog, you have to endure the tick, tick, tick of the clock while your increasingly gasping, frenzied team tries to recapture the ball, to no avail. Aauuggh! Madness. March Madness. Now you know.

Chapel Hill

University of North Carolina at Chapel Hill

Dean E. Smith Center, Manning Drive
• **Tickets: 962-2296**
• **Information: 962-2123**

UNC-CH is also known as Carolina, the Tar Heels, the Heels and Chapel Hill. Carolina fans are some of the most ardent in the ACC. If you don't believe it, just ask a fan why they say the sky is Carolina blue. Most of all, Carolina's athletic tradition is a winning one—Atlantic Coast Conference championships in a variety of sports every year.

In 1982, the school posted national championships in three different sports: basketball, lacrosse and women's soccer. The 1992-93 men's basketball team won the national NCAA championship and the women's team won it all in the 1993-94 season. UNC women have one of the best all-around sports programs in the country.

Football

Kenan Stadium, Main Campus

You have to act fast to buy season tickets for UNC football games. In 1990, UNC's team kept national champ Georgia Tech from having an unblemished record. Since 1992, the Heels have been "bowling" every year, including the 1994 Sun Bowl, the 1995 CarQuest Bowl and the 1996 Gator Bowl. In 1997, the Heels defeated Virginia Tech 42-3 in the Gator Bowl, capping a stellar 11-1 season and a national Top 10 finish. Long-time head coach Mack Brown resigned at season's end to accept the head coaching position at the University of Texas and defensive coordinator Carl Torbush stepped in and led the team to the Gator Bowl victory.

In 1998, the Heels finished 7-5 and captured a 20-13 victory over San Diego State in the Las Vegas Bowl.

The football tradition is strong at Carolina with the likes of Charlie "Choo Choo" Justice among its great running backs. Some of its most notable graduates include Natrone Means, all-pro linebacker Lawrence Taylor and tailback Kelvin Bryant. Other Carolina greats include Chris Hanburger, "Famous" Amos Lawrence and Super Bowl champion Harris Burton.

If you go to a Carolina football game, plan on making a day of it since pregame parties and tailgating are part of the ritual. Since tickets are retained by families year after year, you may see the same folks at the games, which makes the afternoon a neighborly get together. Don't get alarmed when you start running into bumper-to-bumper traffic as you approach Chapel Hill. It's that way every home game. Finding parking in Chapel Hill on game day is like looking for a lost contact lens in a dark movie theater. Plan ahead. It is illegal to park on the sidewalk, especially during game days. Parking there will result in a ticketed or towed car during the game. A better option would be to park at University Mall and take the shuttle. If you don't know where the stadium is, just follow the crowd. Kenan Stadium, which was recently renovated and expanded, seats

60,000. Individual tickets are $22 and about $110 for season tickets.

Basketball
Dean E. Smith Center, Manning Dr.

Under former head coach Dean Smith—for whom the 21,572-seat arena ("The Dean Dome") is named—Carolina basketball compiled a legendary record, including two NCAA championships ('82 and '93). Smith, a Kansas transplant, once led a U.S. Olympic team—with a number of Carolina players—to the gold medal.

During the 1996-97 season, UNC captured the ACC Tournament title and advanced to the NCAA Final Four. In the fall of 1997, Smith shocked the Tar Heel faithful by retiring after 36 seasons and 879 victories—the most of any coach in NCAA Division I history. Long-time assistant coach Bill Guthridge stepped in during the 1997-98 season, guiding the team to a 34-4 overall record, a second consecutive ACC Tournament Championship and a second consecutive Final Four appearance.

Carolina basketball tickets are so valuable that they sometimes have been mentioned in wills and as part of divorce settlements. UNC box office officials acknowledge that tickets are rarely available. If you go to preseason games, against non-ACC opponents, your chances for tickets aren't that bad. When available, these tickets cost about $18. Joining the alumni's Rams Club improves, but doesn't guarantee, your chances of obtaining basketball tickets.

If you're wondering why there's such a fuss over Carolina basketball, just look at the list of some of the pros who wore Tar Heel blue: James Worthy, Bobby Jones, Mitch Kupchak, Phil Ford, Walter Davis, Brad Daugherty, Sam Perkins and,

of course, Michael Jordan. Tar Heels Antawn Jamison and Vince Carter recently made the list, joining the Golden State Warriors and Toronto Raptors, respectively. Before he left for the NBA, Jamison was honored with just about every national award available, including Associated Press Player of the Year, the John R. Wooden Award and the Naismith Award.

In addition, the Heels are winners and behave accordingly as evident in the 1993 NCAA championships that brought UNC its third national title, defeating the highly touted "fab five" from Michigan. Tar Heel fans will never forget when Michigan's Chris Webber called the last minute "time-out," which sealed the Tar Heel victory.

Finally, Tar Heel teams have one of the highest graduation records among Division I basketball.

Other Sports

Carolina is a championship competitor in a long list of other NCAA sports. In fact, the 1997-98 season included a second-place finish for the Sears Director's Cup, an annual award that is presented to the best overall sports program in the country. Carolina teams regularly capture ACC championships in such sports as women's soccer, field hockey, women's cross country, women's basketball, men's and women's swimming, wrestling, men's and women's indoor track, men's golf and men's and women's outdoor track, among others. These sports always offer an exciting, low-cost entertainment option for families, students and young professionals in the area.

During the past 15 years, the school has become as much a national power in lacrosse—1987 and 1991 NCAA champs—as it is in basketball. In 1996,

INSIDERS' TIP
If you went to school outside of the ACC, keep an eye out for your school's fan club. Several, such as Penn State and Ohio State, have active groups in the Triangle who gather regularly for big football games.

Photo by Bill Richards, courtesy of UNC Sports Information

UNC's women's soccer team is a national powerhouse, capturing 14 NCAA titles since 1981.

the team reached NCAA Tournament quarterfinals. It regularly swaps national championships and number one rankings with such schools as Johns Hopkins and Syracuse.

The field hockey team has won 14 ACC titles since 1983. The team won the 1989 NCAA title.

Likewise, the women's soccer program is the best in the country. After 10 straight NCAA national championships, the unthinkable happened in 1995 when Notre Dame defeated the Tar Heel women on their home field. The team regained the NCAA titles in 1996 and 1997, and captured the 1998 ACC Championship, its 10th straight ACC title. They made it to the NCAA Championship once again, but lost to the University of Florida.

The 1993-94 women's basketball team won the NCAA title in a dramatic, final three-point shot in the final second by Charlotte Smith. The 1997-98 team won the ACC Tournament, its fourth ACC title in five years, and advanced to the NCAA Tournament.

Track and field, wrestling and baseball are the school's other spectator sports. UNC has been the ACC wrestling champion for six of the last seven years and was an NCCA champion in 1993. UNC has won six straight ACC swimming titles. In its first year of competition, the UNC women's rowing team captured third place in the 1998 NCAA National Championships.

Professional Sports

Baseball

Carolina Mudcats Baseball
Five County Stadium, Zebulon
• 269-2287

Steve Bryant is a fellow who heard a voice say, "Build it and they will come." He did and they did. Bryant, who is a billboard advertising executive, wanted Raleigh to have its own baseball team. Since he was kept out of the city by the 30-mile rule (he had to be at least 30 miles from the Durham Bulls, the Triangle's other pro team), Bryant built his stadium in a field outside Zebulon. The stadium opened in mid-season of 1991 and the Mudcats draw some of the largest crowds in the Southern League.

The Mudcats' logo is a grinning catfish and the Mudcat baseball hat is one of the hottest caps in the league among collectors. Now affiliated with the Colorado Rockies, the Mudcats were formerly a farm team of the Pittsburgh Pirates and almost half of the Pirates team in '97 got their training here. They've put graduates such as pitcher Esteban Loaiza, catcher Jason Kendall, infielders Kevin Young, Tony Womack, Kevin Polcovich and Freddy Garcia, and outfielder Jermaine Allensworth into the Big Leagues. In 1995, The Mudcats, a Double A affiliate, won the Southern League championship for the first time with a minor league winning record of "95 games in '95." The Mudcats did not fare as well during the 1998 season, finishing with a 59-80 overall record.

A $15 million renovation of Five County Stadium is underway to eliminate bleacher seating and create box, reserved and general admission seating for 6,200 fans. The renovation will also upgrade the press box, concession areas and rest rooms. Tickets range from $4 to $6.50. You can get the usual baseball fare at the concession stand, or for $3, you can treat yourself to a catfish sandwich!

Durham Braves
Durham Athletic Park • 956-9555

A summer college baseball team that plays its home games at historic Durham Athletic Park, the Durham Braves compete in the Coastal Plain League. The roster includes players from Duke, UNC and N.C. State. The Braves compete against teams like the Wilson Tobs, Rocky Mount Rockfish, Edenton Aces, Florence Red Wolves and Wilmington Sharks. Kids love Bravey the Bear, the team's ubiquitous mascot.

Photo courtesy of Mudcats Baseball

The Carolina Mudcats are the Double-A affiliate of the Colorado Rockies.

Durham Bulls
Durham Bulls Athletic Park, 409 Blackwell St.
• 956-BULL, Information: 687-6500

The Durham Bulls have been a Triangle tradition since the first Bulls' team took the field in 1902. Ninety-six years and several leagues later, the Bulls are a worldwide phenomenon. A good bit of that success is due to the 1988 movie "Bull Durham" in which Kevin Costner and Susan Sarandon brought stardom to the Bulls and their hometown.

The 1994 season was the last in the venerable old Durham Athletic Park—the "DAP"—before the team was moved to the country's best minor league ballpark just off the Durham Freeway. The newly renovated, 10,000-seat Durham Bulls Athletic Park or "DBAP" is a brick stadium that evokes baseball memories even though it offers such modern amenities as corporate skyboxes. The facility is surely one reason the Bulls held the league's attendance record in 1997, drawing a total of 381,589 fans for the season.

From 1980 until 1997, the Bulls were the Class A affiliate for the Atlanta Braves and played a large role in the team's success during the '90s. Steve Avery, Ron Gant, David Justice, Jeff Blauser, Chipper Jones, Mark Lemke, Andruw Jones and Javy Lopez are among players who spent time in a Bulls uniform before advancing to Atlanta.

In 1998, the Bulls embarked on their inaugural season as the Triple-A affiliate of the Tampa Bay Devil Rays, moving from the Carolina League to the International League. Over 2,000 seats were added behind the right field wall to comply with Triple-A requirements and the famous "snorting bull" was moved to left field.

The Bulls won the division championship in 1998 and advanced to the International League Championship Series before losing to the Buffalo Bisons.

At the bargain prices of $5.50 for reserved seats and $4.50 for general

Photo courtesy of Durham Bulls Baseball Club, Inc.

In its inaugural season as the Triple-A affiliate of the Tampa Bay Devil Rays, the Durham Bulls baseball team won the 1998 division championship.

admission, it's no wonder that Bulls' fans return again and again to watch some baseball and partake of ball park *haute cuisine* such as El Toro beer, hot dogs, pizza, popcorn, barbecue sandwiches, burritos and soda pop.

Hockey

Carolina Hurricanes
Season tickets: (888) NHL-TIX1
Information: 467-PUCK

Over the past seven years, Triangle fans of hockey followed the minor league Raleigh IceCaps. However, the IceCaps recently moved to Georgia (as the Augusta Lynx) to make room for the arrival of the National Hockey League Carolina Hurricanes, the Triangle's first major-league franchise. Formerly the Hartford

Whalers, the Carolina Hurricanes moved to North Carolina in 1997 and are taking up temporary residence at the Greensboro Coliseum until the completion of the state-of-the-art "Entertainment and Sports Arena" in September 1999. The new arena, which is located near Carter-Finley Stadium in Raleigh, will also be home to the NCSU Wolfpack men's basketball team and a variety of entertainment events.

Led by head coach Paul Maurice, the Hurricanes compete in the Southeast Division of the Eastern Conference and hope the move to North Carolina will put them on the winning track. During the 1997-98 season, the Canes showed flashes of brilliance, especially with their tenacious defense, which was led by the superb goalkeeping skills of Trevor Kidd. However, the team came a few wins short of making the playoffs.

In July 1998, the Hurricanes signed free agent center Ron Francis, the ninth-leading scorer in NHL history. Other standouts include Sami Kapanan, Gary Roberts, Jeff O'Neill, Glen Wesley and goalie Arturs Irbe, a native of Latvia. Keith Primeau, who led the team with 30 goals during the 1998-1999 season, has not signed a contract and his playing status is still up in the air. The Canes selected rising star David Tanabe in the first round of the 1999 draft. The offensively skilled defensiveman should make an immediate impact on the Canes' squad. The Canes lost goaltender Trevor Kidd to the NHL expansion team, Atlanta Thrashers, who later dealt him to the Florida Panthers during the off-season.

The Canes made the playoffs during the 1998-99 season for the first time since 1992, falling to the Boston Bruins in the first round. The Canes led the Southeast Division (which also includes the Florida Panthers, Washington Capitals and Tampa Bay Lightning) with a 34-30-18 overall record. The team also set a franchise record, giving up only 202 goals during the season. Maurice was rewarded for leading the team to the playoffs with a three-year contract extension. The 32-year-old coach is the youngest head coach in the NHL.

Season ticket packages are available for the 1999-2000 season, which will be played at the new Raleigh Entertainment and Sports Arena. Individual prices run from $22 for general balcony seats to $99 for VIP and Club Ledge seats. Make sure to purchase tickets early for such high-profile opponents as the New York Islanders and the New Jersey Devils. Games can be heard on the Carolina Hurricanes Radio Network, which includes WRBZ-850 "The Buzz" in Raleigh.

Soccer

Raleigh Capital Express
WRAL Soccer Complex
Perry Creek Road, Raleigh • 781-RALX

Started in 1993 as an amateur group, the Capital Express (formerly known as the Raleigh Flyers) are now affiliated with the United States Soccer Federation's 30-team A League. Capital Express soccer is great family fun and a good chance to see some exciting, hard-hitting soccer played by future Major League Soccer stars. The roster is full of standout players from area colleges such as North Carolina State, University of North Carolina and Duke. The team competes against the likes of the Atlanta Silverbacks, Charleston Battery, Hershey Wildcats, Maryland Mania and Richmond Kickers. The team

Photo by Kent Smith, courtesy of Carolina Hurricanes

The Carolina Hurricanes competed at Greensboro Coliseum before moving to their new home, the Raleigh Entertainment and Sports Arena, in the fall of 1999.

struggled during the 1998 season, finishing with an overall record of 5-23. However, it showed dramatic improvement in 1999 under the tutelage of interim coach John Dugan, finishing with a record of 11-17 and winning four of its last seven games.

The season runs from mid-April to mid-September. Most games start at 7:30 PM. Tickets are about $10 for adults, $8 for youth and $12 for VIP seating.

Raleigh Wings
Flyers Stadium, WRAL Soccer Complex Perry Creek Road, Raleigh • 848-3063

The Raleigh Wings, a professional women's soccer team, celebrated its inaugural year in 1998. The team features a lot of home-grown talent, including players from North Carolina State, Duke and the University of North Carolina. For the 1998 season, the Wings achieved a 17-0 overall record and captured the league championship with a 4-3 victory over the Boston Renegades in August. The Wings captured the league championship once again during the 1999 season with a dramatic 3-2 victory over the Chicago Cobras. The game was attended by a record crowd of 2,260 fans at the WRAL Soccer Complex.

The season runs from late May to late July. Tickets are $6 for adults, $4 for youth (18 and under) and $9 for VIP seating.

Stock Car Racing

Orange County Speedway
9740 N.C. 57, Rougemont
• (336) 364-1222

Over the years, Orange County Speedway has seen the likes of Jeff Gordon, Bobby Labonte and a host of other Winston Cup drivers compete on its 3/8-mile, high-banked oval track. The Speedway is located north of Durham on N.C. 57 and offers racing events on most Saturdays from late March to early October. Races usually start at 7:30 PM. Tickets cost $12 for adults, $10 for students, $6 for children 10 to 14 and children under 10 are admitted free. The Speedway is home to the infamous Orange County "Bologna Burger."

Wake County Speedway
2109 Simpkins Rd., Raleigh • 779-2171

Built in 1962 as a dirt track, Wake County Speedway is now a 1/4 mile, semi-banked oval track made of asphalt. Catch the action of exciting track racing every Friday night at 8 PM from mid-April to mid-September. Drivers compete in four divisions: Late Model Sportsman, Modified Four Cylinder, Street and Economy Four Cylinder. The Wake County Speedway is located south of Raleigh off Hwy. 401 South.

Within a few hours, you can be swimming in the Atlantic Ocean or hiking along the Appalachian Mountain range.

Daytrips and Weekend Vacations

One of the great things about living in the Triangle is its proximity to the coast and mountains. Within a few hours of driving time, you can be swimming in the Atlantic Ocean or hiking along the Appalachian Mountain range.

On the coastal side to the north, you'll find beautiful white sandy beaches along the barrier islands of the Outer Banks, each with its own distinct personality. On the southern coast, narrow islands host populated towns. Heading west, there's the Great Smoky Mountains, the Blue Ridge and the Piedmont plateau. Each mountain chain provides spectacular views, beautiful waterfalls, state parks and hiking opportunities for various skill levels. In between, you may enjoy state parks, historic sites and villages, battlegrounds, a native habitat zoo, handmade pottery and a casino.

For more information about visiting North Carolina, contact the N.C. Travel and Tourism Division, N.C. Department of Commerce, 430 N. Salisbury Street, Raleigh, NC 27611, 733-4171, or (800) VISITNC. For information on historic sites, contact the Division of Archives & History, N.C. Department of Cultural Resources, 532 N. Wilmington Street, Raleigh, NC 27604-1147, 733-7862.

Beaches and Ports

North Carolina offers some of the finest beaches on the East Coast. When people in the Triangle talk about the beach, they are usually talking about the area known as the Crystal Coast, the Cape Fear Coast or Wrightsville Beach at Wilmington. The Outer Banks are beautiful and definitely worth a visit, but will take more than a weekend to explore. The port cities of Wilmington, Morehead City, Beaufort and New Bern offer a unique blend of history and modern-day commerce.

The Southern Coast

Some of the more popular Southern beaches of North Carolina include Wrightsville, Carolina, Kure, Holden, Ocean Isle and Sunset. Though intimidating to early European explorers who named the area Cape Fear, today's traveler will enjoy the rugged beauty of the coast, its waters and the gracious hospitality of its people. From the Triangle, Wilmington is an easy 2-hour drive down I-40. To learn more about this area, pick up a copy of *The Insiders' Guide to Wilmington*.

Wilmington

Wilmington, the state's largest port city, sits on the Cape Fear River and is really worth more than a daytrip. This historical city is well known for its growing film industry.

Wilmington is the permanent home of the Battleship North Carolina, a 35,000-ton battleship memorial to the men and women who served in World War II. A

The Cotton Exchange in downtown Wilmington is a complex of former cotton warehouses that has been converted into specialty shops, galleries and restaurants.

fundraising effort, Operation Shipshape, has been launched statewide in an effort to restore the ship to its former glory. In town, Wilmington has a historic homes tour and Chandler's Wharf, which shows the city as it was in the 1800s. The restored Cotton Exchange building is home to a variety of unique shops and restaurants near the Hilton Hotel.

Fort Fisher is located at Kure Beach, site of one of the country's largest land-sea battles in 1865 and a museum of items from Confederate blockade runners. The North Carolina Aquarium is less than 2 miles away. Here you can view live marine life and participate in special aquatic programs.

Kids will enjoy the amusement park atmosphere of Carolina Beach, a short drive down U.S. 421 south.

Wilmington is also home to Screen Gems Studios, one of the largest production studios east of Hollywood, which contains eight sound stages and 100,000 square feet of stage space. *Ironweed, Blue Velvet, Crimes of the Heart* and *The Year of the Dragon* were among the movies filmed here. Studio tours can be arranged by calling (910) 675-8479.

Orton Plantation near Wilmington, (910) 371-6851, is one of North Carolina's best-known Southern plantations and rivals those of Virginia. It was an 18th-century rice plantation and the gardens are now open to the public. The best time to visit is in the spring when the plantation's dazzling azaleas are in full bloom.

Wrightsville Beach

Wrightsville Beach, just over the bridge from Wilmington, is on the barrier islands, which protect the state's Atlantic coast. This is an upscale community with miles of beautiful sandy beaches perfect for long walks, swimming, surf fishing or most any water sport you may enjoy. Accommodations include quality hotels and motels, apartments and cottages, and there are many eating establishments featuring, naturally, seafood.

The Crystal Coast

The name "Crystal Coast" describes the area around Beaufort, Morehead City and the beaches of Bogue Banks. Visitors can choose between the historic preservation area of Beaufort, Morehead City's famous seafood boardwalk, golf courses and shopping or any of the public beaches. From the Triangle, the Crystal Coast is an easy 3 1/2-hour drive down U.S. 70. To learn more about this area, pick up a copy of *The Insiders' Guide to NC's Central Coast & New Bern*.

Beaufort

This quaint seaport has a wide boardwalk along the waterfront and narrow streets lined with white frame houses. It has become a favorite dockage for seagoing yachts. Many of the town's beautiful historic homes have been restored and are nestled among grocery stores, gift shops, a wide variety of restaurants and several of North Carolina's most popular bed and breakfast inns.

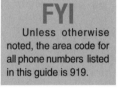

FYI

Unless otherwise noted, the area code for all phone numbers listed in this guide is 919.

Bogue Banks
(Atlantic Beach, Pine Knoll Shores, Salter Path, Emerald Isle)

Bogue Banks is one of 23 barrier islands off the North Carolina coast. Unlike most of the "outer banks," the 27-mile-long Bogue Banks runs from east to west. The Atlantic Ocean drums its southern shore while Bogue Sound laps its beaches to the north. This unusual orientation leads to one of the island's unique features: the sun both rises and sets over the ocean.

Atlantic Beach is the most highly developed of the Bogue Banks beaches. Its surf is mild, the beach is very wide and the sun-warmed shallow water is the most enjoyable of the state's beaches. This beach is traditionally THE BEACH for Triangle teenagers.

The North Carolina Aquarium at Pine Knoll Shores is one of the three nationally accredited aquariums on the North Carolina coast. It is open daily from 9 AM until 5 PM.

Salter Path is a residential community making the transition to a tourist community with new restaurants, motels and campgrounds. West of Salter Path is Emerald Isle, which was incorporated as a resort town in the mid-50s and has been attracting North Carolina's sunlovers ever since. Emerald Isle features houses for rent—beachfront, soundside, modern, rustic, casual, elegant and in every price range. The annual Beach Music Festival is a popular event held in mid-May and features top beach music groups.

Nearby is the Crystal Coast Amphitheatre where *Worthy is the Lamb,* an outdoor drama based on the Passion of Christ, is performed.

Fort Macon State Park

More people visit Fort Macon than any other state park. Fort Macon was built between 1828 and 1835, then restored in 1936. Fort Macon stood guard over Beaufort inlet during the Civil War and World War II. You can fish from the rock jetties, swim at the public beach or enjoy your lunch at the picnic areas.

Morehead City

Morehead City ("Morehead" to everyone at the coast) is an easy town to like. Fill the town with blocks and blocks of seafood restaurants, internationally renowned sport fishing fleets and scuba diving charters that explore the "Graveyard of the Atlantic" and you only have half the story.

The Morehead Waterfront is devoted to commercial fishing, sport fishing, preparing fish and eating fish. Unlike most coastal waterfronts, the Morehead Wharf

Photo by Rich Weidman

Since 1870, the 208-foot Cape Hatteras Lighthouse has warned passing ships of the treacherous Diamond Shoals, the "Graveyard of the Atlantic."

is not devoted entirely to tourism. Shipping and fishing-related commercial activities keep the area bustling.

In addition, the waterfront offers scuba diving charters (Olympus Dive Shop is world famous), sport fishing charters, boat rentals, sailboat excursions, party boat tours, daytrips to Cape Lookout and seafood sold fresh off the boats.

New Bern

Only a little over an hour's drive from the Triangle sits this historic little town of lacy crape myrtle trees. New Bern is located at the confluence of the Neuse and Trent rivers. Union Point Park is where most of the waterfront activity buzzes. It was New Bern's linkage to Pamlico Sound and the Atlantic that made this an ideal port. The town was founded in 1710 and named for Baron Christopher DeGraffenried's home of Bern, Switzerland. It became the first colonial capital of North Carolina.

When Royal Governor William Tryon began building his residence/government capitol offices, they took on the appearance of a palace more than a modest government home with offices. The original palace burned in 1798, but has been completely rebuilt and refurbished to its former splendor. The restoration includes the Tryon Palace, the John Wright Stanly House, the Dixon-Stevenson House that was occupied by Union troops during the Civil War and the Academy Museum.

This daytrip is a must-do on any Insiders' list. In the spring, the Royal English Gardens are abloom with tulips. During the summer, costumed guided tours bring history alive. Actors portray Governor Tryon and his wife and their servants talking about the everyday happenings in the 1700s. By early December, the palace is decorated much as it was during the holidays in 1770 for the Tryon Palace Christmas Celebration, a must-see holiday event.

Outer Banks

There is nothing quite like North Carolina's Outer Banks. These barrier islands are marked with the names of American history—Kitty Hawk, Nags Head, Roanoke Island—and they include the longest stretch of undeveloped beach in the country. Hang glide off Jockey's

Ridge or experience a blue fish blitz; these are just some of the luring pastimes of these beaches.

The Outer Banks are, at minimum, a 4-hour drive from Raleigh—longer to Cape Hatteras and its fabled lighthouse. Enjoy the drama of *The Lost Colony* at the Waterside Theatre near Fort Raleigh. To get to the isolated, quaint village of Ocracoke where Blackbeard was caught and hanged, you take a ferry. To learn more about North Carolina's Outer Banks, pick up a copy of *The Insiders' Guide To The Outer Banks*.

Piedmont

The region located between the coastal areas and the mountains is known as the Piedmont. Business and industry thrive here within North Carolina's richest agricultural region. Food, fiber, manufacturing, education, research and commerce enjoy the resources of the land and its people. The history and culture of the Piedmont is rich and increasingly diverse.

Bentonville Battleground
Newton Grove, N.C. • (910) 594-0789

American history buffs must visit this historic site, which is less than an hour's drive from the Triangle. The Battle of Bentonville was the last, full-scale action in the Civil War, fought over three days, March 19 through 21, 1865. There were over 4,000 casualties in the armies fighting under Union Gen. William T. Sherman and Confederate Gen. Joseph E. Johnston, who surrendered on April 26 at Bennett Place near Durham. The battleground today maintains a picnic area and visitors center. The Harper House, where a field hospital was established, still stands and is outfitted as it might have appeared

during those bloody three days. Maps inside the center and a film presentation tell the history of the battle, the largest ever fought in North Carolina. On occasion, the battle's anniversary is observed by reenactments that give visitors a more realistic idea of conditions of the times. Visiting hours are 10 AM to 4 PM Tuesday through Saturday and 1 PM to 4 PM on Sunday.

Fayetteville

Fayetteville, home of Fort Bragg and Pope Air Force Base, also boasts a variety of other attractions, such as wonderful architecture, several colorful festivals and outstanding regional theater.

For those who are interested in learning more about Fayetteville's place in military history, Fort Bragg is open for individual and group tours. Call (910) 396-5620 or 396-2920 for information. The 82nd Airborne War Memorial Museum (at Ardennes and Gela streets at Fort Bragg) is a great place for a military history buff. Admission is free to the museum, which is open Tuesday through Saturday 10 AM to 4:30 PM and Sunday 11:30 AM to 4 PM. Call (910) 432-5307 for more information.

Not to be missed is the Cape Fear Regional Theatre in Fayetteville. Located on the corner of Hay Street and Highland Avenue, CFRT is housed in a beautifully renovated old movie house that seats 327 people. Not a bad seat is to be found. CFRT consistently receives rave reviews from theatre critics across the state for its innovative productions and is reason enough to visit Fayetteville. Call (910) 323-4233 or 323-4234 for the current schedule and ticket information.

Those interested in historic architecture will want to view Fayetteville's Market House in the center of the downtown area.

INSIDERS' TIP

Take the back roads. There are 44 Scenic Byways that have been identified and marked by the North Carolina Department of Transportation.

When Union General William T. Sherman and his men passed through Fayetteville in 1865, they destroyed the Confederate Arsenal and many other buildings but left the Market House intact, it is said, because of its beauty.

There are many other beautiful old buildings in Fayetteville and you can see some of the oldest homes, churches and other historic places during the Olde Fayetteville by Candlelight Tour held each December. The Dogwood Festival is Fayetteville's welcome to spring. Held over 10 days starting the first weekend in April, this event allows Fayetteville to show off its dogwood trees (more than 100,000) and thousands of blooming flowers. The many activities include parades, tours and street dancing. The International Folk Festival is held on the last Sunday in September. The festival centers around the Market House downtown and features a big parade, international foods and musical entertainment.

For information on Fayetteville, contact the Fayetteville Area Convention and Visitors Bureau, 245 Person Street, Fayetteville, NC 28301, or call (910) 483-5311 or (800) 255-8217.

Kerr Lake, Lake Gaston

These two man-made lakes provide excellent fishing, boating, picnicking and camping. Both are about an hour's drive north of the Triangle near the Virginia state line. Kerr Lake has a shoreline of 800 miles, over 1,000 family campsites and three commercial marinas. For information, call Kerr Reservoir at (919) 438-7791.

Lake Gaston offers at least three access areas: Summit, Henrico and Stonehouse Creek. For more information on Lake Gaston, call the North Carolina Wildlife Resources Commission at 733-3633.

Morrow Mountain State Park
Route 2, Box 430, Albemarle, NC 28001 • (704) 982-4402

Just across Badin Lake from the Uwharrie National Forest is this scenic, 4,600-acre state park in Stanly County. This is a pleasant retreat for swimming,

Photo courtesy of N.C. Zoological Park

About a million people a year travel to the North Carolina Zoological Park, the largest natural habitat zoo in the United States.

camping, boating, hiking or picnicking. For information on vacation cabins and tent/trailer campsites, call or write.

N.C. Zoological Park
Route 4, Box 83, Asheboro, NC 27203
• (800) 488-0444

Like the famous San Diego Zoo in California, North Carolina's zoological park gives visitors the chance to observe animals while they roam in areas similar to their native habitats. This is a perfect outing for the whole family. Here you can observe more than 1,000 wild animals and birds amidst 60,000 exotic plants. This ever-expanding facility is the largest natural habitat zoo in the nation.

You won't want to miss the R.J. Reynolds Forest Aviary, the only one of its kind anywhere. A 55-foot-high glass dome houses exotic plants and birds from all over the world. Walking through the aviary is like exploring a tropical forest, complete with all the sights and sounds. The newest sections in the zoo are the Sonora Desert Habitat and the North American Region, which has everything from polar bears to alligators.

The zoo is located off of N.C. 220, south of Asheboro. The zoo is open from 9 AM to 5 PM April through October and 9 AM to 4 PM November through March. The zoo is not open on Christmas Day. Admission is $5 for senior citizens and children ages 2 to 12 and $8 for adults. Traditionally, the zoo does not charge admission the second Monday of June, July and August and only charges half-price admission December through February.

Pottery Museums

One of our favorite daytrips is a trek through pottery country in Randolph and Moore counties. Here, just about 2 hours from the Triangle, you'll find pottery being made from native clays, just as it was in the 1700s. In fact, some of the local potters belong to the same families that were shaping this native clay two centuries ago.

Stop first at the Seagrove Potters Museum, (336) 873-7887, in Seagrove along N.C. 220, south of Asheboro and the North Carolina Zoo. Here you'll see samples of the area's world-famous pottery from its earliest days to the present. At the museum, which is open free to the public Monday through Saturday, 10 AM to 4 PM, you can also pick up a map to the shops of some 95 local potters. Our personal favorites are Phil Morgan's Pottery, Jugtown and Westmoore Pottery.

Raven Rock State Park
NW of Lillington, N.C.
• (910) 893-4888

Raven Rock is a 2,731-acre state park that makes a pleasant picnic outing for the family. Located on the Cape Fear River, it's about a 1 1/2-hour drive from the Triangle and has hiking trails that aren't too taxing. The rocks along the river are huge and in winter giant icicles 15 to 20 feet in length hang from them. A good time to go to Raven Rock is spring or fall when the climate is temperate. Take along water or something to drink because there are no fountains or facilities once you get down to the river.

Snow Camp
• (336) 376-6948

You'll want to visit this historic Quaker landmark in southwest Alamance County during the summer months when there are plenty of activities. Named by Cornwallis' soldiers following the snowy Battle of Guilford Courthouse, Snow Camp is known today as the site of The Sword of Peace, one of the state's most popular outdoor dramas. From late June through July, *The Sword of Peace* portrays the conflict experienced by peace-loving Quakers confronted by events of the American Revolution. On alternate days, Pathway to Freedom, a drama that premiered in 1994, gives the African-American perspective of this period in our country's history. A children's show, which changes each season, also runs from mid-June through July. Other summer activities at Snow Camp include a traditional Fourth of July celebration complete with a parade and crafts fair and a mid-August molasses festival that has demonstrations of pioneer cooking and crafts. Snow Camp is about a 30-minute drive from Chapel Hill.

Uwharrie National Forest
District Ranger, U.S. Forest Service, Route 1, Box 237, Troy, NC 27371

The Uwharrie National Forest is proof that you don't have to drive 4 hours to reach the mountains. Located on Badin Lake in Montgomery County, this wilderness includes 46,000 acres of piney forests, trails, water sports and more.

Charlotte

Charlotte is a city of commerce and culture. Visitors come for education, entertainment and cultural events. To learn more about the Charlotte Metro area, pick up a copy of *The Insiders' Guide To Charlotte.*

Carolina Renaissance Festival
• (704) 896-5555

The annual Carolina Renaissance Festival was first held in October of 1994. The authentic costumes, music and food are sure to delight the whole family. The festival usually runs for about seven weekends beginning in early October; admission is charged.

Discovery Place
301 N. Tryon St. • (704) 372-6261

Discovery Place is one of America's top science museums. This hands-on science and technology museum in downtown Charlotte welcomes over 400,000 visitors annually and is open every day of the year except Thanksgiving and Christmas. The museum offers an OMNIMAX theatre and planetarium combination that is unique to the United States.

Photo courtesy of N.C. Travel and Tourism

Sid Luck of Luck's Ware Pottery is one of the many craftspeople who display their work in Seagrove.

With a 79-foot dome, the Planetarium is the largest in the nation.

Among the permanent exhibits are the Collections Gallery, the Aquarium and the Knight Rain Forest. "Hands-on" exhibits are also featured with a collection of experiments designed to teach basic principles of science through color, motion and perception.

The Challenger Learning Center simulates a rendezvous with Halley's Comet in the year 2061. Kid's Place, an early childhood learning area, features the Puppet Place stage with shows that delight visitors of all ages. The museum has hosted outstanding traveling exhibits such as Dinosaurs, The Magic School Bus, Bionics and Transplants, Science in Toyland and 1492: Two Worlds of Science.

Open seven days a week, the Exhibit Hall hours are 9 AM until 6 PM Monday through Friday, 9 AM until 6 PM on Saturdays and 1 to 6 PM on Sundays. Reservations for regularly scheduled OMNIMAX and Planetarium shows can be made by calling Scheduling at (704) 372-6261 or (800) 935-0553.

Call for current rates and discounts. Admission is free for everyone on "Wonderful Wednesday," the first Wednesday of each month after 2 PM. Annual family memberships entitle holders to unlimited visits and special benefits, as well as admission to other science museums throughout the country.

Lowe's Motor Speedway

Twelve miles north of Charlotte is the nation's hottest racing facility. The lighted NASCAR track is home to many annual events: Coca-Cola 600, Winston Select 300, UAW-GM 500, Car Quest 300 and Bumper to Bumper 300. Twice a year, in April and September, the AutoFair, one of the nation's largest antique car shows, is hosted on the grounds.

Mint Museum
2730 Randolph Rd. • (704) 337-2000

Originally this branch of the United States Mint served from 1836 until it closed at the outbreak of the Civil War. In 1936, the Mint reopened as North Carolina's first art museum. It is one of the Southeast's finest museums with extensive collections of American and European paintings, furniture and decorative arts. In addition to its own shows, it also mounts larger, nationally prominent exhibits. A small admission is charged. Call for hours and further information.

In early 1999, the Mint Museum of Craft and Design opened at the former Montaldo's building on North Tryon Street, featuring collections of ceramics, glass, wood and fibers. NationsBank provided $8.2 million to donate and renovate the 82,000-square-foot building, the largest bequest in Mint Museum history.

Paramount's Carowinds
Exit 90 off I-77 S. • (800) 888-4386

Paramount's Carowinds, which opened in 1973, is a 100-acre theme park featuring rides, shows, shops and restaurants. More than 1.7 million guests visit Paramount's Carowinds each year. Although the park is generally open daily during the summer and on weekends in the spring and fall, hours and operating dates vary, so before planning a visit, it is a good idea to call.

The Paladium Amphitheatre hosts big-name concerts and special events each season. Attractions range from a variety of thrill rides, like Skycoaster to more easy going attractions, such as Animation Station, a cartoon fantasy land for young children.

INSIDERS' TIP

What is that green vine growing everywhere? It's kudzu. You'll notice some interesting shapes as it takes over trees and shrubs.

Each year, attractions are added or enhanced. In 1996, the new ride was DROP ZONE Stunt Tower, a 56 m.p.h., 100-foot free-fall ride. Try the heart-pounding roller coasters like the Hurler or Thunder Road, Frenzoid and VORTEX, then cool off with Rip Roarin' Rapids and White Water Falls or the wave pool and you're off to a thrilling start. In 1997, in a 7-million-dollar expansion, the park added five new attractions and doubled the size of the Water Works water entertainment complex.

You'll see such characters as Star Trek Klingons, Romulans and Vulcans walking around the park, along with Wayne and Garth. You'll also find scads of movie paraphernalia to buy in the stores. Look for the Paramount Walk of Fame that lists prominent movies and their stars.

Paramount's Carowinds' popular one-price ticket covers all rides and park shows. Palladium concerts, featuring big-name entertainers, are extra. 1998 admission to Paramount's Carowinds for ages 7 to 54 is $29.99 and $17.99 for children ages 4 to 6 and senior citizens 55 and older. Children 3 and younger are admitted free. Groups, family and individual season passes are available. Reduced admission is available after 5 PM. Call (704) 588-2600.

Professional Sports

Charlotte is North Carolina's mecca for professional sports. It is home to the Lowe's Motor Speedway, the Charlotte Hornets, the Charlotte Sting, the Carolina Panthers and the Charlotte Knights. Watch for offers of special travel and ticket arrangements that deliver you directly to the game sites from the Triangle.

Reed Gold Mine
N.C. 24/27 to Reed Mine Rd.
• (704) 786-8337

Long before the California Gold Rush, Reed Gold Mine became the site of the first authenticated gold find in the United States. The site includes a visitors center, mining trails, a mill used to crush ore and a restored section of the underground mine shaft. From April through October, for a small fee, you can try panning for gold.

The Triad

Guilford Courthouse National Military Park
Greensboro • (336) 288-1776

This is the site of the Revolutionary War battle that pitted General Nathanael Greene against British General Lord Charles Cornwallis. In mid-March each year, a mock battle is staged in adjacent Tannenbaum City Park by Redcoats and soldiers of the Revolution in uniform. The battlefield is now a national park with a number of monuments and a visitors center. It is open daily from 8:30 AM to 5 PM and admission is free.

Hanging Rock State Park
P.O. Box 186 Danbury, NC 27016
• (336) 593-8480

This nearly 6,000-acre state park in Stokes County is a great getaway for camping, hiking, swimming, fishing and picnicking. Call or write for more information on vacation cabins and campsites.

Museum Of Early Southern Decorative Arts (MESDA)
Winston-Salem • (336) 721-7360

MESDA is adjacent to Old Salem and features 19 furnished rooms, demonstrating the varied styles and periods of Southern furnishings. It's an antique lover's dream! Admission is charged.

Natural Science Center
Greensboro • (336) 288-3769

Adjacent to the Guilford Battleground, this fine museum for children has reproductions of dinosaur skeletons, rock and mineral exhibits, fish and reptiles and a small petting zoo. The Science Center also

Photo courtesy of Old Salem

Moravian cookies, bread and sugar cakes are still baked daily in wood-burning ovens at the Winkler Bakery in Old Salem.

has a planetarium show. The Center is open Monday through Saturday from 9 AM to 5 PM and Sunday 12:30 PM to 5 PM. There is an admission fee for the museum and the planetarium show. The Science Center is adjacent to Country Park, which has a lake, paddle boats, playground and picnic areas.

Old Salem
Winston-Salem • (336) 721-7300

About 1 1/2 hours west of the Triangle via I-40 is Winston-Salem's restored 18th-century Moravian village. There are almost 100 restored buildings here. Twelve are open to the public, including Winkler Bakery (where you can buy delicious Moravian sugar cake), the Salem Tavern, the Single Brothers' and Sisters' Houses and many other shops and restored homes. Special events are held at Christmas, Easter and July 4th. Old Salem is open Monday through Saturday 9:00 AM to 4:30 PM

and on Sunday from 12:30 to 4:30 PM. Admission is charged.

Reynolda House
Winston-Salem • (336) 725-5325

Reynolda House, former home of R.J. Reynolds of tobacco fame, is now a museum of American art. The collection features paintings by diverse artists ranging from 19th-century landscape painter Frederic Church to Thomas Eakins and Mary Cassatt. The house contains many of its original furnishings and is fascinating in its own right. Admission is charged for the house and gardens. It is open Tuesday through Saturday from 9:30 AM to 4:30 PM and from 1:30 to 4:30 PM on Sunday.

Southeastern Center For Contemporary Art (SECCA)
Winston-Salem • (336) 725-1904

SECCA is just down the road from Reynolda House and well worth a visit. It is a complex of galleries with rotating exhibits by contemporary Southern artists. It is located on the former estate of the Hanes family and many of the galleries are in the Hanes home. It is open Tuesday through Saturday 10 AM to 5 PM and Sunday 2 PM to 5 PM. Admission is free.

Mountains

Just three hours west of the Triangle you begin an ascent into the third distinct region of North Carolina. The mountains are divided into three regions: Northern Mountains, Central Mountains and Southern Mountains. Each area demands at least a weekend to explore. For further reading on this area, order a copy of *The Insiders' Guide To The Mountains*.

Cashiers

Beautiful Cashiers, high in the Blue Ridge Mountains, is a resort town, famous for its waterfalls, including Toxaway Falls (123 feet), High Falls (135 feet) and the beautiful Rainbow Falls, which plunges some 200 feet.

Brevard

Surrounded by the Pisgah National Forest, Brevard offers a variety of activities from rugged outdoor adventures to communing quietly with nature or delving into the magical mountain lore through music, drama or local crafts.

You can spend the day locating a few of the 250 waterfalls in Transylvania County and Brevard. The best way to see them is to take the scenic 79-mile drive that loops through the Pisgah National Forest. You may also hike along the designated trails or explore the Pisgah Forest on horseback.

When you're ready to return to civilization, check out the annual summer Brevard Music Festival that features many well-known musicians. It's held at the Brevard Music Center. Call the Chamber of Commerce, (800) 648-4523, for dates. If you're a bluegrass fan, go to Silvermont on East Main Street for original mountain music and bluegrass. Drive back down U.S. 64 to Flat Rock and take in a play at the Flat Rock Playhouse, the state theater of North Carolina. Flat Rock is also the site of Connemara, the home of poet Carl Sandburg.

Throughout the mountains you'll find handmade quilts, mountain furniture and toys. Insiders like the Curb Market (Farmers Market) in downtown Hendersonville on Tuesday and Saturday mornings. You'll find handmade articles, jellies, fresh vegetables and fruit and the like.

Chimney Rock, Lake Lure

The town of Chimney Rock, with a river running beside it, is a favorite of tourists. You can still enjoy a climb up to the spectacular Chimney Rock Park or ride up in a 26-story elevator inside the mountain. You'll be at the top of the chimney-shaped rock with a panoramic view that is worth the trip all by itself. Below is Hickory Nut Gorge, which includes the French Broad River and Lake Lure. Pack a picnic lunch to enjoy at one of the park's many picnic areas.

Cherokee

The history of the Cherokee Indian Nation can be explored by a stop at the Cherokee Historical Association. Across the street on Darma Road is the Museum of the Cherokee Indian. This is a modern museum displaying over 10,000-year-old

---

INSIDERS' TIP

The Wildflower Program, supported by personalized license plate funds through the North Carolina Department of Transportation, provides beautiful roadside color along many of the state's major highways.

artifacts with explanatory audio/visual programs that chronicle the events of the Cherokee. The museum recently completed a $3.5 million renovation that features new interactive exhibits documenting the history of the Cherokee people. Computer-generated images and special effects re-create events such as the tragic "Trail of Tears" in 1838.

The not-to-be-missed Oconaluftee Indian Village is a reproduction of how the Eastern Band of the Cherokees lived 200 years ago. And the Qualla Arts and Crafts Mutual in the village is a shop that looks more like a museum. This shop of artisans' works is responsible for keeping alive the authentic arts and crafts of the Cherokee. It is also the only place that you'll find these distinct crafts.

Of course, no trip to Cherokee would be complete without attending *Unto These Hills*, now in its 47th season at the newly renovated Mountainside Theatre. The outdoor drama unfolds the tragic story of how the proud Cherokees were driven west on the "Trail of Tears" from their Smoky Mountain homeland.

Maggie Valley

If you like gunfights in a mile-high Ghost Town in the Sky theme park and warm mountain hospitality, go to Maggie Valley. There's also a first-rate zoo in town called Soco Gardens Zoo.

Asheville

Called the "Land of the Sky," this mountain city where wealthy vacationers once came for relief from the summer heat is still drawing visitors.

The centerpiece of the downtown historic district is Pack Place Education, Arts and Science Center. This bustling complex contains four museums, a performing arts theatre, courtyards, permanent exhibitions, a gift shop, restaurant and lobby galleries. Tickets are required for admission to theater events and to each of the four museums: the Asheville Art Museum, The Colburn Gem and Mineral Museum,

Photo by Rich Weidman

The Last of the Mohicans was filmed at Chimney Rock Park, which offers a breathtaking, 75-mile view on a clear day.

Completed in 1895, the 255-room, French Renaissance-style Biltmore Estate took 1,000 men five years to construct and remains the largest private home in the United States.

The Health Adventure and the YMI Cultural Center. You may buy a one-day pass that is good for all four or you can buy single tickets. No admission charge is required for visitors to enter Pack Place and view the historic exhibit "Here is the Square," visit the Craft Gallery that spotlights regional crafts or shop in the Museum Gift Store. The fourth Friday of each month is "Free Day" when no admission fee at the museums is charged. Call (828) 257-4500 for further ticket information and hours.

A landmark in itself, Pack Place also serves as the logical starting point for a number of walking tours of downtown Asheville featuring buildings of architectural and historic significance. For more information, call the Asheville Area Convention and Visitors Bureau at (800) 257-1300.

Biltmore Estate and Winery

One of the best daytrip excursions is to the Biltmore Estate, Gardens and Winery, which remains the largest private residence in the United States. Between

1888 and 1890, George Washington Vanderbilt, grandson of the railroad promoter Cornelius Vanderbilt, purchased a total of 125,000 acres of land for the estate he planned to build. The architectural style was designed by Richard Morris Hunt to resemble a chateau in France's Loire Valley and it rivals the grandest palace abroad. The castle-like house contains 255 rooms, which took 1,000 artisans five years to build for the six residents and their guests (not including the 100 servants). You can tour the main house with its beautiful antique furnishings, priceless paintings and ceiling frescoes that are kept in excellent repair. The servant's quarters, where even the butler had his own servant, are also interesting.

A favorite time is the Christmas season when the house is resplendent with thousands of poinsettias and Christmas trees trimmed with many original ornaments. Concerts fill the magnificent halls. The estate is open from 9 AM to 5 PM year round except Thanksgiving, Christmas

Day and New Year's. For more information call (828) 255-1700 or (800) 543-2961.

Another enjoyable—as well as tasty—tour is that of the estate's winery.

The old dairy barn has been renovated into a lovely open air restaurant, Deerpark, where you may see herds of deer roaming the land. Afterward, stop in Biltmore Village where the houses of the original construction workers have been converted into shops and restaurants.

Blue Ridge Parkway and Mount Mitchell

The scenic Blue Ridge Parkway meanders uninterrupted for 500 miles through three states. Although begun in the early 1900s, construction was halted during WWI. As a public works project during the Depression, the parkway was finally completed and opened in 1935. It is considered to be one of America's most scenic parkways. The frequent overlooks afford breathtaking panoramas of high peaks, waterfalls and lakes tucked into lush valleys.

Spring is alive with color with mountain laurel and red rhododendron in awesome abundance. Fall plays the same game with "leaf-lookers" drinking in every ounce of autumnal beauty. An excellent daytrip is to Mount Mitchell State Park at Milepost 355. At 6,684-feet above sea level, Mount Mitchell is the highest peak east of the Mississippi River and you can hike through the park's many nature trails. To camp here, call (828) 675-4611 to reserve one of the nine campsites.

Linville Falls, Linville Caverns, Old Hampton Store

At Linville Falls and Gorge, there are three hiking trail options, from easy to rugged, depending on your energy and time. The gorge is the deepest slash in the earth's crust east of the Grand Canyon. The river tumbles into the gorge from its head to form a 90-foot fall of water. To reach the falls, you'll walk through a 1/2 mile tunnel of towering trees so dense that spatters of sunlight are rare. Waterfalls, some dramatic, others serene, draw visitors to watch their grand displays.

This is not a picnic area; you'll have to go farther up the parkway for food, but restrooms are available and the park is open year round, depending on the weather.

There are probably undiscovered caves all through the mountains. Linville Caverns, like others, was discovered by accident in 1822 when curious fishermen followed trout disappearing into the side of a mountain. Trout in this 20-million-year-old limestone cave have become blind due to the lack of a light source. Don't expect the splendors of Carlsbad or Luray, but the cavern, on three levels, is an interesting and enjoyable half-hour experience. It's open year round, but check times, (828) 756-4171.

The Old Hampton Store, (828) 733-5213, sits just outside the town of Linville. This neat old 1921 general store offers a wide assortment of notions that you need and some that you probably don't—such as horse hoof medication. Churns and washtubs hang from the ceiling and the back screened door is perpetually in motion. Out back, the stone gristmill grinds cornmeal and grits nearly every afternoon. These products are sold with apple butter, local jams and old fashioned tin cookware. Kids can buy marbles by the pound and sturdy clothes are available upstairs.

Best of all is lunch. The store serves the leanest and most delicious barbecue around and its root beer is excellent. Top this off with a slice of terrific carrot cake or your choice from assorted cheesecakes.

Grandfather Mountain

This famed 6,000-foot mountain can be seen for miles around and looks like a giant sleeping grandfather. It is considered North Carolina's top scenic attraction. You'll want to visit the natural habitats for native black bear, white-tailed deer, cougars and bald and golden eagles. Stop

Photo by Rich Weidman

Linville Falls plunges about 90 feet into Linville Gorge, which is part of Pisgah National Forest.

in at the nature museum that offers state-of-the-art displays along with entertaining movies on native wildlife (especially the film on the red-tailed hawk). For those brave enough to cross it, the Mile High Swinging Bridge, which connects Linville's Peak with the visitors center, rewards you with a spectacular view.

The museum's restaurant is a great place for lunch. You can also picnic on the mountain. Grandfather Mountain is open daily from 8 AM to 7 PM.

An exciting Grandfather Mountain experience is the annual Highland Games, the second weekend in July. You don't have to be a Scot to enjoy the bagpipes, dancing, saber-toss and watch Border Collies return lost sheep to the flock, as well as other games of skill. Another popular

yearly event that comes the fourth Sunday in June is Singing on the Mountain.

Ski Country

Each year thousands of Triangle skiers listen to weather reports, watch the sky, send up snow prayers and wax skis in hope of bringing on the first winter's snow. That's when you'll see packed cars bearing ski racks headed for one of the many North Carolina downhill ski resorts.

Appalachian Ski Mountain, home of the French-Swiss Ski College outside Boone, has one of the best teaching schools for beginners. It has nine slopes and trails with a peak elevation of 4,000 feet. Ski Beech, north of Banner Elk has 14 slopes and trails and a peak elevation of 5,505 feet, making it the highest in the East with a vertical drop of 830 feet. The resort also has a charming Swiss Village-type appearance with an outdoor ice skating rink encircled with shops and restaurants. Sugar Mountain Ski Resort, just to the south of Banner Elk on N.C. 184, boasts 20 slopes and trails, peak elevation of 5,300 feet with a vertical drop of 1,200 feet, and needless to say, fairyland views. Ski Hawksnest is sometimes less crowded and has 12 slopes and trails, a peak of 4,819 feet and a vertical drop of 669 feet, plus night skiing.

All of these resorts have chair lifts, rope tows, lockers and restaurants. Beech and Sugar even have nurseries. You can get a ski report by calling (800) 962-2322. High Country Hosts at (800) 438-7500 is a good source of mountain area information.

You can ski cross-country at Moses Cone Park on the parkway just outside Blowing Rock and at other gated-off areas by calling the Ranger's office at (828) 295-7591.

Blowing Rock

A lot of towns are dressed up to look quaint these days. Blowing Rock is the genuine article. In summer, the main street is lined with pyramid-shaped planters spilling over with pink and white begonias. Since the days the rambling 100-year-old Green Park Inn was built over the center of the Continental Divide, the town has taken on an aristocratic appeal.

Window shopping on Main Street is a favorite pursuit with lots of antiques and Oriental rug houses. Evenings find folks at the auction house, which is a show in itself. The park on Main Street is a gathering place for tennis, people-watching and craft shows.

You may enjoy horseback riding along the trails of Moses Cone Estate on the Blue Ridge Parkway. Make reservations with Blowing Rock Stables, (828) 295-7847. The adventurous will enjoy canoeing and white water rafting through Class 3 (fairly mild) to Class 5 (pretty wild) rapids down the Nolichucky.

Children in North Carolina grow up on trips to Tweetsie Railroad on U.S. 321/221 in Blowing Rock. The drawing card is a 3-mile action-filled train ride on an original mountain train, complete with Indian attacks and settler rescues. The attraction has amusement rides, live entertainment, crafts, shops and picnic tables. It's open daily from May through October and on weekends in November.

Boone

In the heart of Boone lies the beautiful campus of Appalachian State University. Boone is also home to the Appalachian Cultural Museum where the evolving lifestyle of mountain people is displayed with artifacts and information on the abundant variety of rare and unusual herbs and plants.

During the summer (June 21 until August 17), make reservations for the outdoor drama *Horn In The West*, now in its 44th season. The musical drama revolves around life in Appalachia during the days of Daniel Boone. For reservations, call (828) 264-2120. Adjacent to *Horn In The West*, you'll find Hickory Ridge Homestead, which is an interesting tour of five representative homesites of the 1800s.

Glendale Springs

It's a toss-up to know whether people go to Glendale Springs for the wonderful gourmet food at the inn or to see the frescoes. Ben Long's controversial frescoes at Episcopal Holy Trinity Chapel are among the most highly visited in the state. A number of craft shops have sprung up in town, which changes the area's once "hidden away" flavor but does not diminish its overall appeal.

Laurel Springs

Because Tom and Nancy Burgiss' 200-year-old farm yielded enough "Hurricane Hugo" lumber to build a dancing barn, the popular Mountain Music Jamboree took up new residence here. Folks come from near and far to dance the Texas Two-Step and old-time mountain dances. Dance classes are Monday and Tuesday nights; Texas Two-Step dances are on Friday and live Bluegrass and Old Time Music are on alternating Saturdays.

If you're looking for an apartment, you'll have no trouble finding something in the Triangle area to suit your needs.

Apartments and Temporary Housing

If you're looking for an apartment, you'll have no trouble finding something in the Triangle area to suit your needs. From simple studios to three-bedroom apartments with clubhouse, swimming pool and more, you have a wide variety of choices. Rents for apartments should be fairly stable for the rest of 1999, but costs vary depending on location and available amenities. In some apartment complexes, six-month leases are available.

Temporary housing is also abundant. Conveniently located near many of the major highways, rooms and suites are available in many price ranges. Most require a minimum one-week stay and many give deeper discounts the longer you stay. A wide list of services and amenities is included with the cost of the room.

Apartment Publications

Apartment Finder
2626 Glenwood Ave., Suite 120, Raleigh • 782-7819

A free, quarterly, color, digest-sized publication from Haas Publishing Company, the *Apartment Finder*, is available at most large retail centers, banks, hotels and other visitor centers. It's a comprehensive guide serving the Triangle. The magazine has locator maps and gives a detailed description of the larger apartment communities.

The Apartment Book
5561 McNeely Dr., Ste. 203, Raleigh • 571-2787, (800) 849-2787

Veteran publisher Tom Smith started this book and an apartment locator service in 1993. The book can be found at over 850 locations throughout the Triangle, usually at big grocery stores next to newsstands. It's free, as is the locator service.

Newspapers, Real Estate Ads

The local newspapers are always a good source for current rental properties. Also, check the Triangle's weekly publications (see "Media" chapter). If you're looking for a room, house or an apartment in a private home a block from campus and you have the time, you'll find the dailies and weeklies are a good bet.

Corporate Temporary Housing

Campus Arms Motel Apartments
2222 Elba St., Durham • 286-9133
Weekly/Monthly

The Campus Arms is frequented by people using or visiting nearby Duke University, or the Veterans Administration or Durham Regional hospitals and traveling business executives who need to stay in town for more than a week. Each of the 29 furnished apartments contains a living room, kitchen, bedroom and bathroom. Four are efficiencies equipped for the handicapped. Apartments can be rented by the week or month and include a telephone, color cable TV and weekly maid service.

Candlewood Hotel
1020 Buck Jones Rd., Cary
• 468-4222

Candlewood is a relatively new extended-stay hotel with 79 rooms that offer a variety of amenities such as a fully equipped kitchen, microwave, coffee maker, television with VCR and compact disc player. Business guests can take advantage of personalized voice mail, a speaker phone, computer data port and conference calling capabilities. Candlewood also offers a fitness center and free laundry facilities.

Chapel Hill Inntown
609 Hillsborough St., Chapel Hill
• 967-3743 • Weekly Rates

Tucked into a cul-de-sac within walking distance of town are seven townhouses reserved for out-of-town guests needing a place to stay for at least a week. It's perfect for traveling business executives or families visiting for a short time. You can choose between one-bedroom and two-bedroom units, each fully furnished and equipped with washer and dryer, color cable television, central air conditioning, linens, towels, all cooking utensils and appliances. There's even cut firewood for the fireplace.

Crossland Economy Studios
5008 N.C. 55, Durham

Crossland Economy Studios opened in October 1998 and is designed specifically for extended-stay travelers. Each room offers a fully equipped kitchen, cable TV, free local calls, voice mail, computer data port, coffee maker and weekly housekeeping. A 24-hour coin laundry is on the premises.

Duke Tower Residential Suites
807 West Trinity Ave., Durham
• 687-4444

A furnished all-suite hotel for extended stays, Duke Tower Residential Suites is located near Duke University Medical Center and Northgate Mall and 15 minutes from RDU Airport.

Exercise facilities, outdoor pool, laundry room, fully equipped kitchen and office services are available. Pets are permitted for an additional charge.

Execustay, Inc.
308D Millbrook Rd., Raleigh
• 518-1707, (800) 959-7829

This service requires a 30-day minimum stay. It offers fully furnished one-, two- and three-bedroom apartments, townhouses and private homes.

Extended StayAmerica
1701 Regency Pkwy., Cary • 468-5828
3105 Tower Blvd., Durham • 489-8444
2700 Slater Rd., Morrisville • 380-1499
911 Wake Towne Dr., Raleigh • 829-7271

Extended StayAmerica efficiency suites offer fully equipped kitchens; free local calls, voice mail and data port; and laundry service.

FYI

Unless otherwise noted, the area code for all phone numbers listed in this guide is 919.

INSIDERS' TIP

Most city ordinances and apartment complexes prohibit outdoor cooking on barbecue grills within 10 feet of the building.

Extended-stay hotels such as Candlewood are perfect for business travelers staying a day, a week or longer.

Globe Corporate Stay International
• 851-1511, (888) 900-1992

Five locations serve Raleigh, Cary, RTP, Durham and Chapel Hill. No minimum stay is required. Apartments are furnished and have a kitchen with cookware, microwave and a washer/dryer.

Home Suite Home
113 Grosvenor Dr., Raleigh
• 676-1794

Locally owned and professionally managed, this firm advertises that one phone call does it all.

Homestead Village
4515 N.C. 55, Durham • 544-9991
4810 Bluestone Dr., Raleigh • 510-8551
3531 Wake Forest Rd., Raleigh
• 981-7353
1920 Ivy Creek Blvd., Durham • 402-1700

Homestead Village offers extended-stay lodging at an affordable weekly rate. Amenities include a fully equipped kitchen, well-lighted work area, coffee maker, iron and ironing board, personalized voice mail,

telephone with data port, twice weekly housekeeping and free local phone calls.

Marriott Residence Inn
1919 N.C. 54 E., Durham • 361-1266

Conveniently located just outside Research Triangle Park, Residence Inn offers one- and two-bedroom studios with comfortable living room areas and fully equipped kitchens. Other amenities include laundry facilities, pool and whirlpool. Daily maid service is also available.

Meredith Corporate Housing
2603 Village Ct., Raleigh • 787-2800

If you need more amenities than a hotel room, you may want to consider a guest house. The Meredith Guest House offers 43 suites that are nothing less than small, well-furnished apartments. It has one-, two- and three-bedroom units and is conveniently located off the I-440 Beltline at the Lake Boone Trail exit on Wycliff Road. Included is a 24-hour message center and maid service. The units rent by the day or month and many Triangle companies lodge employees on temporary assignments in this facility. Relocating families with children find the guest houses less cramped than motel rooms. Pool and fitness center privileges are available.

Oakwood Corporate Housing
• 460-4550, (800) 520-5288

This temporary housing service has locations in Raleigh, Durham, Chapel Hill and Cary. An economical alternative to hotels, it is ideal for business travelers, transferees and relocating individuals and families. Housing is provided for extended stays of 30 days or more and all accommodations are fully furnished. In addition to the Triangle, Oakwood has 1,000 locations across the nation.

StudioPlus Corporate Suites
921 Wake Towne Dr., Raleigh • 546-0879
600 Weston Pkwy., Cary • 677-9910
2701 Regency Pkwy., Cary • 460-4800
2504 N.C. 54, Durham • 361-1853

Conveniently located throughout the Triangle, StudioPlus features such amenities as a fully equipped kitchen, cable TV, voice mail/data port, weekly housekeeping, on-site laundry facility, fitness center and outdoor pool.

Walden Executive Suites
103 Melville Loop, Chapel Hill
• 929-8634

Walden Executive Suites is located 3 miles from UNC Hospitals and 6 miles from Duke University Medical Center. Suites are fully furnished and have a full kitchen, washer and dryer and free local calls. Maid service is available. A seven-day stay is required.

Wynne Residential Suites
Raleigh • (800) 849-2787

This service offers convenient locations throughout the Triangle and can provide everything from furniture, housewares, washer and dryer, linens and kitchen necessities to optional maid service.

Locator Services

Apartment Book Locator Service
5561 McNeely Dr., Ste. 203, Raleigh
• 571-2787, (800) 849-APTS

Lone Wolf Publishing offers this free apartment locator service offered in conjunction with its *Apartment Book*.

Carolina Apartment Locators
3717 National Dr., Suite 207, Raleigh
• 510-9800 • (800) 365-5755

Carolina Apartment Locators can be very helpful when the market is tight or when you need expert help with your search. The firm can arrange short- and long-term leases, furnished or unfurnished apartments, without a fee.

Corporate Apartments By CORT
1820 New Hope Church Rd., Raleigh
• 876-7550
Durham and Chapel Hill • 493-2563

CORT offers furnished apartments for long- and short-term rentals. CORT can also provide design assistance as well as housewares and electronics.

INSIDERS' TIP
Many apartment complexes are currently offering special concessions, such as one month rent free with a one year lease or reduced security deposits. Ask the property manager about special offers.

Extended StayAmerica features efficiency suites in four locations throughout the Triangle.

Drucker & Falk Welcome Center
7200 Stonehenge Dr., Ste. 106, Raleigh • 870-0777

Drucker & Falk is the largest single owner of apartments in The Triangle. The group is well organized and knows the area and needs of relocating clients. Its locator services are free.

Rental Resources
5540 Centerview Dr., Suite 303, Raleigh • 859-0089, (800) 319-0089

Rental Resources specializes in single family and townhomes, filling a niche left void by apartment communities. Its Ex-ecutive Service includes picking up the prospective client, showing currently available accommodations that meet specific needs, assisting with the leasing process, facilitating school registration for children and more.

A Rental Solution
8541-A Glenwood Ave., Raleigh • 781-9925, (800) 365-5182

This firm offers free information on price, availability and features of Triangle apartment properties, including fully furnished corporate apartments, as well as a roommate listing service.

Triangle real estate in the
'90s has proved to be
a sound investment.

TRIANGLE AREA REALTORS

A REALTOR® committed to providing you with personal service as you move to the Triangle. Let me help make your relocation less stressful and more enjoyable. Call my toll free number for a relocation package and welcome to our fine community.

Francine Taylor
Owner/Broker

F.T. Realty and Company
3117 Poplarwood Court, Suite 202
Cypress Building
Raleigh, North Carolina 27604

Toll Free:	800-265-8750
Direct:	919-872-1098
Fax:	919-872-0198
Pager:	919-857-8015
e-mail:	ftrealty@juno.com

As a Prudential real estate professional, I LISTEN to what you need. Then I DELIVER. Some people call this a WINNING ATTITUDE. I call it BUSINESS AS USUAL.

Roger Sloop
Broker Associate
Crabtree Office

3309 Arrow Drive
Raleigh, NC 27612

Toll Free: 888-782-5502
Voice Mail: 919-783-2373 Ext. 3013
Fax: 919-782-2940

 Prudential
Carolinas Realty

Serving
the
Triangle
since
1988.

Karen Albanese, CRS
Realtor®/Broker

6736 Falls of Neuse Road
Raleigh, NC 27615

Direct: 919-845-5813
Office: 919-847-2222
Fax: 919-870-0144

COLDWELL BANKER ADVANTAGE

Coldwell
Banker
Champion's
Dirt
Lady!

Linda Jacobs, CRS, GRI
Realtor®/Broker

107 Edinburgh South
MacGregor Village Shopping Center
Cary, NC 27511

Office: 919-462-0093
Toll Free: 888-863-1581
Voice Mail: 919-501-2864

COLDWELL BANKER CHAMPION REAL ESTATE

FONVILLE MORISEY

"Real Estate is a relationship business based on integrity, trust and capability. My success comes from maintaining the highest standards of professionalism, service and dedication to my clients.!"

Jayne L. Gregory, CRS, GRI
Office Associate of the Year
Durham/Chapel Hill Office

1304 Highway 54 West
Durham, NC 27707-5506

Direct: 919-402-1248
Fax: 919-402-1209
E-mail: JLG2965@aol.com
www.realtor.com/Triangle
AreaNC/JayneGregory/

You'll Never Need To Know Another Agent.

Specializing in Real Estate In Raleigh, Cary, Apex & other Triangle Communities.

John English, ABR
Office Associate of the Year
Raleigh Office

6301 Creedmoor Road
Raleigh, NC 27612

Office: 919-785-4223
Toll Free: 800-986-9140
Fax: 919-785-4209
E-mail:JohnEnglish@Realtor.com
www.JohnEnglish.com

FONVILLE MORISEY REALTY ™

- One Of The Largest Triangle Real Estate Companies
- 11 Area Offices
- www.fmrealty.com

"One of Raleigh's top REALTORS for 15 years. **Let me show you why!"**

Mella Pool
Executive Associate
Falls Office

5925 Falls of Neuse Road
Raleigh, NC 27609-9500

Direct: 919-874-7531
Mobile: 919-740-0111
Fax: 919-874-7509

" I treat my clients with the respect and high quality of service that I would expect." Named one of the *Triangle Business Journal's* Top 25 Real Estate Agents in the Triangle

Linda Garner, CRS, GRI
Executive Associate
Kildaire Office

1149 Kildaire Farm Road
Cary, NC 27511

Direct: 919-469-4469
Toll-Free: 800-399-7710
Fax: 919-469-4409
E-mail: lindagarn@aol.com

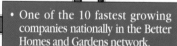

REMAX

"#2 in the Carolinas,

#17 in the United States,

#20 in the World–

Time to Call Pat...

Time's Flying."

Pat Cross
Marketing Associate

RE/MAX Realty 2000
4601 Six Forks Rd., Suite106
Raleigh, NC 27609

Toll Free: 800-727-7281
Direct: 919-786-4148
Fax: 919-571-9881
E-mail: PHCr@aol.com
www.patcross.com

"Call me–
I will care about you. I build relationships one buyer at a time through outstanding personal service– I've been selling homes in Cary and the RTP area since 1972."

Lillian L. Smith, CRS, GRI
Accredited Buyer's Agent

RE/MAX Property Associates
1140 Kildaire Farm Rd.
Suite 101, Cary, NC 27511

Toll Free: 800-326-3562
Mobile: 919-272-2550
Home: 919-467-6592
E-mail: ncrebroker@aol.com
www.lilliansmith.com

**TOP REALTORS®
FROM RE/MAX**

"A seasoned professional... the first ingredient for a good move is my personal commitment to quality service for everyone."

Bill Edwards, CRS, GRI
Broker

RE/MAX Preferred Associates
7340 Creedmoor Road
Raleigh, NC 27613

Toll Free: 800-515-3779
Voice Mail: 919-845-2164
Fax: 919-676-3114
Mobile: 919-649-8200
E-Mail: billed@prodigy.net
www.bedwards.com

Dedicated, Professional Service. Home buying is just that simple. Ask for ML.

ML Johnson
Broker

RE/MAX Southland Realty
5160 NC Hwy 42 West
Garner, NC 27529

Toll Free: 800-325-1845
Office: 919-773–0991
Fax: 919-773-0186
Home: 919-553-7396
E:mail: ml@remax@juno.net

LOCAL WISDOM.

Baseball–**The Bulls**

Pizza–**Lilly's**

Airline–**Midway**

More Information

What you think is important. Please share your ideas.

IN APPRECIATION, WE WILL SEND YOU A COUPON FOR **$10.00 OFF** A COPY OF ONE OF OUR GUIDES.

Name _____

Title _____

Company _____

Address _____

City, State, Zip _____

Phone _____ **Fax:** _____

E-mail _____

Age: ❏ Under 25   ❏ 25-35   ❏ 36-50   ❏ 51-65   ❏ Over 65

Annual Household Income: ❏ Under $25K   ❏ $25 to $35K
❏ $35 to $50K   ❏ $50 to $75K   ❏ $75 to $100K   ❏ Over $100K

Triangle Area: ❏ Newcomer   ❏ Resident   ❏ Student   ❏ Visitor
❏ Planning to Relocate   Date move projected: _____

How did you obtain *The Insiders' Guide To The Triangle?*

❏ Bookstore ❏ Chamber of Commerce ❏ Publisher ❏ *Welcome Home!*

❏ Employer ❏ Friend ❏ REALTOR® ❏ Other _____

Will the book be used by: ❏ Individual   ❏ Family   ❏ Business

How many times do you refer to your guide per month?

❏ 1–3 ❏ 4–6 ❏ 7–9 ❏ 10–15 ❏ 16 and up

Suggestions for future editions: _____

_____

Please send more information on the following:

❏ Cary ❏ Chapel Hill ❏ Durham ❏ Raleigh ❏ Surrounding Areas

   ❏ Accommodations   ❏ Banks in the area   ❏ Chamber of Commerce
   ❏ Child Care   ❏ Private Schools   ❏ Employment Services
   ❏ Health Care   ❏ Retirement   ❏ Shopping
   ❏ Religious Organizations _____
   ❏ Apartments & Temporary Housing—Mo. Rent: _____ to _____
   ❏ REALTOR®   ❏ Builders—Price Range: _____ to _____
   ❏ Development amenities desired: ❏ Pool ❏ Tennis ❏ Golf Course

The Insiders' Guide to The Triangle

Please take a moment to fill out our reader survey and you will receive a coupon good for **$10.00 off** the purchase of your next *Insiders' Guide To The Triangle* or *Charlotte.* Your comments are very important. In appreciation, we will enter your name in our Grand Prize drawing. Thank you!

$500 GRAND PRIZE
In Entertainment and Dining Gift Certificates

$100 SECOND PRIZE
In Entertainment and Dining Gift Certificates

FIVE $25 THIRD PRIZES
In Entertainment and Dining Gift Certificates

UNLIMITED $10.00 FOURTH PRIZES
Coupon good toward purchase of next Insiders' Guide

EVERYONE'S A WINNER!

Real Estate and Neighborhoods

In this chapter you will find the people and services who can help you buy or build a home and information about some of the neighborhoods throughout the Triangle. Since the Triangle residential real estate market is one of the strongest in the country, it's not surprising that the area has some of the best and most experienced sales agents in the country. Many of the companies here offer relocation specialists who can make a move, if not a totally pleasant experience, less painful than a root canal. Triangle real estate in the '90s has proved to be a sound investment. Some neighborhoods have seen their homes more than double in value. Not surprisingly, it's been a seller's market and Christie's Great Estates, the real estate subsidiary of the famed auction house, even has a presence in the Triangle market. The Triangle offers a variety of neotraditional neighborhoods that feature a pedestrian-oriented, village ambience to city living in the downtown areas of Durham and Raleigh.

For more information, check out local publications such as *New Home Guide* and *New Home Builders* that feature new subdivisions and neighborhoods. The local newspapers are also good sources for market information and services.

If you want amenities without the entanglements of home ownership, visit some of the Triangle's new luxury apartment complexes and see our chapter titled "Apartments and Temporary Housing."

Builders

If you are shopping for a house, you may want to know who built it, or maybe you're looking for a custom-built home. Finding that perfect fixer-upper might mean you need a trustworthy remodeler. A great way to get a list of reputable builders is from the Home Builders Association in your chosen area. Association officials will refer you to a short list of builders, depending on location, type of house you want to build and price range. To receive a free copy of *New Home Builders*, call 782-7819.

**Home Builders Association
Raleigh-Wake County
(Includes Cary)**
6510 Chapel Hill Rd. • 233-2033

**Home Builders Association
Durham-Chapel Hill**
20 W. Colony Place, Ste. 180 • 493-8899

Home Inspectors

Before you buy your new home, you will want to be certain everything is in top condition. Due to the widespread damage caused by Hurricane Fran, particular attention ought to be paid to the structural integrity of any home you are considering buying in the Triangle. A qualified home

TRIANGLE CUSTOM BUILDERS

Name	Phone #	$ Range	Areas Served	Homes	Est.
American Heritage Homes, Inc.	233-9666	$250s-$1M	Apex, Cary, Raleigh, Wake Co.	15	1990
W.T Barker Construction Co.	859-0044	$180s-$350s	Apex, Cary, S. Wake Co.	18	1989
D.G. Baron Co.	858-5000	$150s-$500s	Cary, W. Wake Co.	15	1989
Beaman Building and Realty, Inc.	828-8484	$350s-$1M	Cary, Raleigh, Wake Co.	8	1990
Benchmark Homes	847-8924	$370s-$550s	Cary, Raleigh	15	1979
Buildmaster Homes, Inc.	881-4300	$90s-$600s	Cary, N. Raleigh, N. Wake Co.	30	1987
Cady Construction	847-7000	$90s-$400s	Raleigh, Wake Forest	50	1970
J.H. Carter Builder, Inc.	878-6660	$330s-$1M	Raleigh	10	1972
Tom Charnetzky Custom Homes	554-2199	$100s-$180s	Granville, Franklin, Wake Co.	40	1983
Creech Construction Co.	781-2929	$250s-$700s	Apex, Cary, Raleigh, Wake Co.	12	1952
Crist-Chapman Builders, Inc.	848-3030	$250s & up	Triangle	24	1979
Steve Dickson Builders, Inc.	829-0554	$130s-$400s	Cary, Raleigh, W. Wake Co.	21	1974
Stephen Dilger, Inc.	848-0342	$300s-$1M	Wake County	10	1983
W.E. Dixon & Associates	461-0394	$250s-$800s	Wake and Orange Counties	30	1984
T.L.Evans Builders, Inc.	848-9852	$250s-$700s	Wake County	10	1979
Jeff Fike Builders, Inc.	363-4868	$150s-$450s	Wake County	24	1984
Richard Gaylord Homes, Inc.	783-5777	$210s-$280s	Cary, Chapel Hill, N. Raleigh	28	1980
Charles Grantham	562-7027	$200s-$490s	Raleigh	10	1987
Hurst Built, Inc.	460-1192	$400s & up	Cary, Raleigh	12	1985
Isenhour Enterprises, Inc.	932-2821	$250s & up	Orange and Chatham Counties	19	1991
McClure & Associates	878-8006	$100s-$500s	N. Raleigh, Wake Co., Chapel Hill	12	1987
N.C.W. Development, Inc.	467-3927	$300s-$500s	Apex, Cary, Wake Co.	25	1989
Oaks Construction Co.	469-3555	$200s-$700s	Wake County	12	1983
Olde Heritage Builders	269-4555	$130s-$400s	Franklin & Wake Co.	20	1982
John J. Palczuk Builders, Inc.	847-5161	$200s-$600s	N. Raleigh, Wake Co., Chapel Hill	12	1983
Park Homes	876-4788	$90s-$300s	Wake County	125	1988
Premiere Homes, Inc.	781-4177	$200s-$350s	Wake County	35	1980
Prestige Associates	932-5800	$400s-$850s	Chapel Hill	20	1990
Bryant Roberts Builders	383-8518	$125s-$500s	Durham & Orange Counties	50	1973
Rufty Custom Built Homes	460-8550	$475s & up	Cary, Chapel Hill, Raleigh	15	1988
Sheffield Builders, Inc.	510-0011	$150s-$500s	Durham, Orange & Wake Co.	8	1985
Skywater, Inc.	846-7597	$150s-$600s	N. Raleigh, Wake Co.	23	1987
Sparrow Construction Co.	833-7341	$400s-$700s	Wake County	15	1969
Spectrum Homes	848-2041	$200s-$450s	Raleigh, Wake Co.	27	1980
Starmount Realty, Inc.	848-0228	$375-$550s	Cary, Raleigh, Wake County	12	1929
Tall House Building	878-7121	$300s-$3M	Triangle	12	1976
Upright Builders, Inc.	462-8383	$150s-$450s	Wake County	25	1988
Whitney Blair, Inc.	967-7196	$195s-$395s	Chapel Hill, Durham	15	1983
Williams Construction Co.	471-1308	$150s-$1M	Triangle	42	1972
Mason Williams Construction Co.	848-0799	$170s-$500s	Wake County	15	1993
Williams Realty & Building Co.	781-7107	n/a	Raleigh	12	1954
Witt-Banks Homes	851-5111	$250s-$500s	Apex & Cary	40	1973
Woodard Builders	469-8018	$100s-$600s	Wake County	20	1983
Lance Youngquist Construction	460-0047	$400s & up	Apex, Cary, W. Wake Co.	14	1984

inspector can give you peace of mind about the structure of your home. Most of these companies provide full structural and mechanical inspections. Many offer specialized services such as tests for radon, lead, carbon monoxide and gas leaks. The American Society of Home Inspectors is a national certification organization. You can be assured of a home inspector's qualifications if he or she displays the ASHI symbol.

Buyers' Agents

The fastest-growing trend in Triangle real estate now is the use of buyers' agents. These agents represent the buyer in the negotiation and purchase of homes and other real estate. Some companies now provide buyer representation exclusively, while other traditional listing companies offer both buyer and seller services. Buyers' agents are licensed in the full spectrum of real estate transactions and provide multiple listing services as all Realtors do. We have included information on two of the Triangle's best-known buyers' agents.

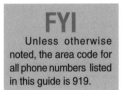

FOR HomeBUYERS
4000 Wake Forest Rd., Raleigh
• 878-1110, (800) 333-2893
Ann Davis, an experienced real estate agent, established FOR HomeBUYERS in 1991 to serve only buyers. All agents exclusively negotiate and close deals for buyers and are certified Buyers Representatives.

Home Buyer's Choice
219 E. Chatham St., Cary
• 481-0116, (800) 444-1442
Home Buyers Choice in Cary was founded in 1993 by Margit Gratzl, a broker with more than 14 years' experience. It provides a truly customer-oriented full-service relocation department.

Realtors

There are over 3,600 Realtors in the Triangle area. Membership in the Triangle MLS allows any Realtor to access information on homes anywhere in the Triangle. The companies listed in this Guide are a sampling of the real estate firms in the Triangle. A good resource for information is the appropriate Board of Realtors listed below.

Raleigh/Wake Board of Realtors
1301 Annapolis Dr. • 834-6739

Durham Board of Realtors
3200 Croasdaile Dr. • 383-2117

Chapel Hill Board of Realtors
501 W. Franklin St.
• 929-4032

Ammons Pittman Realtors
911 Paverstone Dr.,
Raleigh • 847-5555
Relocation: (800) 476-6363
Jud Ammons is one of the more imaginative developers in the Triangle and his partner, George Pittman, is a former president of the Board of Realtors. They have a relocation department that will be glad to send you a personalized Relocation Package.

Arbor Realty
431 W. Franklin St., Chapel Hill
• 942-9937 • Relocation: (800) 849-4422
Arbor Realty is a small but unique real estate company. It donates all its profits to local and state land preservation efforts and offers great service to its customers.

TRIANGLE PRODUCTION BUILDERS

Name	Phone #	$ Range	Areas Served	Homes	Est.
Anderson Homes	828-6030	$ 80s-$140s	Durham & Wake Counties	100	1980
Centex Homes	781-1952	$130s-$300s	Triangle	490	1987
Cimarron Homes	493-0672	$ 90s-$230s	Durham County	100	1982
Bill Clark Homes, Inc.	781-4500	$ 80s-$300s	Wake County	150	1977
Country Lane Development Corp.	783-0095	$ 90s-$150s	Wake County	100	1990
Dave Servoss Homes	828-6015	$120s-$200s	Durham & Wake Counties	100	1994
Engle Homes/NC	387-9016	$130s-$250s	Apex, Cary, Raleigh	100	1974
Fortis Homes/NC	872-5252	$120s-$280s	Durham & Wake Counties	300	1965
Homes by Huff & Co.	544-9880	$120s-$200s	Durham	140	1981
Landwright Homes	383-2121	$ 90s-$275s	Triangle	150	1982
McNeil-Burbank Homes	781-5225	$150s-$220s	Triangle	60	1989
M/I Homes	828-1106	$100s-$250s	Triangle	200	1987
HJ Morris Construction, Inc.	876-9004	$ 90s-$160s	Wake County	150	1988
Pulte Homes	677-0122	$ 90s-$250s	Triangle	600	1985
Robuck Homes	876-9200	$180s-$250s	Wake County	85	1957
Squires Homes	881-9350	$ 90s-$300s	Wake County	300	1991
St. Lawrence Homes	676-8980	$140s-$330s	Triangle	210	1989
Sunstar Homes	469-1316	$100s-$390s	Wake County & Durham	280	1985
Timberline Builders, Inc.	387-7540	$130s-$350s	S. Wake County & Durham	37	1992
Toll Brothers	233-0939	$240s-$400s	Cary	40	1994
Torrey Homes	596-1662	$100s-$300s	Triangle	420	1996
David Weekley Homes	460-8781	$160s-$260s	Wake County	90	1995
Westminster Homes	462-0070	$100s-$250s	Wake County	200	1967
John Wieland Homes	481-3309	$200s-$400s	Triangle	50	1994
Zaring Homes	782-4854	$160s-$300s	Wake County	170	1994

Block & Associates
204-C Colonades Way, Cary • 859-6300

This local company uses innovative technology to meet the needs of its clients. Listings are posted on the Internet.

Century 21

These are independently owned affiliates of Century 21:

Becky Medlin Realty
1233 W. Academy St., Fuquay-Varina
• 552-4517

Haywood Davis Realtors
1011 Broad St., Durham • 286-2121

J.K. Sherron & Associates
4021 Barrett Dr., Raleigh • 510-5000

Park West Realty
1708 N.C. 54E, Durham • 361-5752

Russell Gay & Associates
6817 Falls of Neuse Rd., Raleigh
• 848-5600

Vicki Berry Realty
5312 Six Forks Rd., Raleigh
• 782-9797

Chapel Hill Realty Group, Inc.
151 E. Rosemary St., Chapel Hill
• 942-4149

Another locally owned real estate firm, it specializes in the Chapel Hill area.

Coldwell Banker

These are independently owned affiliates of Coldwell Banker:

Coldwell Banker Realty Center
501 W. Franklin St., Chapel Hill
• 942-4482

Coldwell Banker Advantage

6 Consultant Pl., Ste., 100 • 493-3300
150 Cornerstone Dr., Ste. 101, Cary
• 467-5111
4800 Six Forks Rd. Ste., 150, Raleigh
• 783-6066
6736 Falls of Neuse Rd., Raleigh
• 847-2222

Coldwell Banker Champion Real Estate

107 Edinburgh South, Cary
• 462-0093
6131 Falls of Neuse Rd., Raleigh
• 876-6131

Distinctive Properties

605 Jackson St., Durham • 688-9314
Since 1980, Eugene and Signe Brown have specialized in historic residences in Trinity Park and other older Durham neighborhoods.

Fonville Morisey

Relocation: (800) 846-7356
3600 Glenwood Ave., Raleigh • 781-7731
2395 Kildaire Farm Rd., Cary • 859-0800
1149 Kildaire Farm Rd., Cary • 467-3232
1243 N.W. Maynard Rd., Cary • 469-6300
1738 Hillandale Rd., Durham • 383-1341
1304 N.C. 54W, Durham • 493-4434
1004 Vandora Springs Rd., Garner
• 772-7240
5925 Falls of Neuse Rd., Raleigh
• 872-4450
100 Sawmill Rd., Raleigh • 847-9300
6301 Creedmoor Rd., Raleigh • 781-4452
8100 Creedmoor Rd., Raleigh • 847-2511
Fonville and Morisey are two UNC fraternity brothers who teamed up in the early '70s during a year in which the market dried up. They persevered and today are one of the largest agencies in the Triangle.

They are especially strong in new home developments as Fonville Morisey Builders Marketing Group.

Both Fonville and Morisey are active in the Raleigh real estate community; Fonville, for example, is past president of the Board of Realtors. They kept their company in the forefront and were among the first to offer relocation services, a full-service mortgage company and a training school for agents.

Franklin Street Realty

1525 E. Franklin St., Chapel Hill
• 929-7174 • Relocation: (800) 849-2226
This company is comprised of experienced agents knowledgeable in the Chapel Hill/Carrboro market and is conveniently located one block from the Siena Hotel on Franklin Street. Clients can expect that "hometown" difference with this agency.

FYI

Unless otherwise noted, the area code for all phone numbers listed in this guide is 919.

Hodge & Kittrell Realtors

3200 Wake Forest Rd., Ste.101, Raleigh
• 876-7411
Joe Hodge, a Triangle native, continues building the business started by his mother, Nadine Hodge. In 1991, he was president of the Raleigh Board of Realtors. The company enjoys a loyal following and is considered one of the better agencies in the area.

The Home Team

1721 E. Franklin St., Chapel Hill
• 967-6363 • Relocation: (800) 326-3577
The Home Team opened in late 1989 and its agents pride themselves on selling Chapel Hill's most distinctive homes.

INSIDERS' TIP

The Triangle includes some of the nation's top real estate salespeople: Better Homes and Gardens' No. 1 national producer lives here as well as RE/MAX's No. 2 and No. 5.

Howard Perry and Walston/ Better Homes and Gardens

Relocation: (800) 868-7653
4112 Blue Ridge Rd., Ste. 200, Raleigh
• 782-5600
981 High House Rd., Cary • 467-1882
1130 Kildaire Farm Rd., Ste. 100, Cary
• 380-8585
1600 E. Franklin St., Chapel Hill
• 967-9234
490 N.C. 42W, Clayton • 553-0744
5285 N. Roxboro Rd., Durham • 479-1020
8 Consultant Place, Durham • 490-9000
1002 Vandora Springs Rd., Garner
• 772-9410
112 W. King St., Hillsborough • 732-6101
7048 Hwy. 64 E., Knightdale • 266-5500
7320 Six Forks Rd., Raleigh • 847-6767
5000 Falls of Neuse Rd., Raleigh
• 876-8824
5509 Creedmoor Rd., Raleigh • 781-5556

HP&W/Better Homes and Gardens began in 1973 and is the largest residential real estate company serving the Triangle. HP&W runs a number of on-site sales offices for developers, as well as for its own projects. It maintains a relocation office, real estate school, property management operation and commercial division.

The Prudential Carolinas Realty

Relocation: (800) 334-8161
7500 Six Forks Rd., Raleigh
• 846-8101
1815 Kildaire Farm Rd., Cary
• 859-3300
1407 E. Franklin St., Chapel Hill
• 929-2186
921 Morreene Rd., Durham
• 383-4663
3933 Arrow Dr., Raleigh
• 782-5502
5821 Falls of Neuse Rd., Raleigh
• 876-7030

With 17 offices in North and South Carolina, the company is one of the largest independently owned and operated real estate companies in the Carolinas. The company offers in-house mortgage services and operates a real estate school and a relocation department.

RE/MAX

These real estate companies are independently owned affiliates of RE/MAX.

RE/MAX Preferred Associates
7340 Creedmoor Rd., Raleigh
• 676-9766

RE/MAX Property Associates
1140 Kildaire Farm Rd., Cary
• 469-4700
1230 E. Academy St., Fuquay-Varina
• 557-1522
6801 Falls of Neuse Rd., Raleigh
• 518-8100

RE/MAX Realty 2000
817 N. Smithfield Rd., Knightdale
• 217-9600
4601 Six Forks Rd., Ste. 106, Raleigh
• 571-9822

Photo by Robert Thomason

Residents of Oakwood, one of Raleigh's oldest neighborhoods, show off their restoration handiwork during the annual Christmas tour.

Realty Executives-Triangle
6308 Falls of Neuse Rd., Raleigh
• 872-6660
Hwy. 64E, Knightdale • 266-3666
Hwy. 70, Garner • 772-7574
3713 University Dr., Durham • 490-1944

Owner, Patrick Crawford, has this national franchise on the fast growth track.

Simpson and Underwood
3700 Computer Dr., Raleigh
• 782-6641

Simpson and Underwood is well connected to old Raleigh and knows that market. It has gained a reputation for representing many of the better homes.

Tony Hall & Associates
311 W. Rosemary St., Chapel Hill
• 933-8500 • Relocation: (800) 382-0673

Tony Hall is a very experienced Chapel Hill real estate agent. He and his staff of 10 agents specialize in relocation.

Tripointe Properties
201 Timber Hill Place, Chapel Hill
• 929-7100

This firm is located in the Timberlyne shopping center at the north end of town. There are 13 agents in the office, handling a lot of residential resales and new developments.

Weaver Street Realty
116 E. Main St., Carrboro • 929-5658

Weaver Street founder Gary Phillips and his partners and associates believe that ecologically sound land development also makes good business sense.

Phyllis Wolborsky, CRS
Howard Perry and Walston
Better Homes and Gardens
6504 Falls of Neuse Rd., Raleigh
• 876-2372

As one of the top Triangle Realtors serving clients since 1969, Phyllis has sold over $800 million in residential sales.

York Residential
801 Oberlin Rd., Raleigh • 821-7177
Relocation: (800)-334-3010
1127 Kildaire Farm Rd., Cary • 467-1811
311 Oberlin Rd., Raleigh • 832-8881
8312 Creedmoor Rd., Raleigh • 846-7100

This company is a division of the York companies, a business name that has been in the Triangle building and development market since 1910. As the residential arm of the York companies that include commercial brokerage, property management and construction, it offers relocating companies a full range of real estate services, including Christie's Great Estates sales and auction services.

Neighborhoods

You've probably heard the advice about the three most important things to consider when looking for a new home—location, location, location. While the purveyors of this advice were probably talking about resale value, choosing a location or neighborhood that suits your personality and lifestyle is equally important. Developers today are leaning toward the trend of offering "neighborhood amenities," such as championship golf courses, clubhouses, swim and tennis complexes, jogging trails and private lakes. Here is an overview of some of the area's favorite neighborhoods—old, new, big and small.

Raleigh

Raleigh is a city of neighborhoods, most of them filled with comfortable homes of traditional design. Visitors often are struck by how one lovely neighborhood simply leads to another. The city's steady growth has brought more contemporary styles, such as California cluster homes, and larger, luxury homes that sell for $500,000 and up.

If you divide the city into quarters with the Capitol building at the center, you will find that most of the recent growth has been in the northwest and northeast quadrants. The expected future growth of the city continues to be in these areas.

The median price for a new home in 1998 is $147,000. If you are looking for a new home priced under $100,000 consider the Village at Beacon Hill and Timberidge at Parkside or one of the outlying towns such as Clayton, Knightdale, Wake Forest, Wendell or Zebulon. From $100,000 to $170,000 consider a top builder's new communities or Dominion Park, Durant Trace, North College Park and Winchester, where several builders are available. From $170,000 to $300,000 consider Breckenridge III, Bridgeton Park, LaCrosse Pointe and Umstead Ridge. From $300,000 ask to see Barclay Manor, Bartons Creek Overlook, Boulder Creek, Cross Gate, Macon's Path, Olde Creedmoor and Sheffield Manor IV. This Guide offers an insight into some neighborhoods.

Bent Tree

This development first appeared on the subdivision drawing boards in the 1980s as a neighborhood of mini-estates in North Raleigh. In the '90s the project was given a new name and developed as Bent Tree. It is off Strickland Road in North Raleigh, about a mile east of Six Forks Road. The homes are traditional in looks, but you will find sumptuous modern master suites, bathrooms and grand landscaping. Prices start at $350,000.

Boylan Heights

Boylan Heights is an older neighborhood located within walking distance of the downtown complex. It was part of the Boylan Plantation and, as the name implies, occupies high ground. It has a mixture of low income housing on its periphery and lovely, larger homes at its core. Homes now sell for $120,000 and up, a bargain by Raleigh standards.

Brentwood

This area includes a number of neighborhoods, most of them with Brentwood in their names and located north of the I-440 Beltline and west of U.S. 1. The homes are affordable brick, single-story or split-level, and residents generally have been families with growing children. Homes start at about $100,000.

Brookhaven

Brookhaven is one of the 1940's suburbs outside of the I-440 Beltline and northwest, beyond Crabtree Valley Mall, off Glenwood Avenue.

For years, Brookhaven residents lived outside the city limits, but today it is protected by a neighborhood overlay zoning district reserved for older Raleigh neighborhoods. Its lots are spacious and its conventionally designed homes were well built. Starting prices are around $150,000.

Cameron Park

This is one of the author's favorite Raleigh neighborhoods, but not just because he lives there. It has big, old trees throughout and three neighborhood parks around which streets wind and curve and in which residents play, picnic and walk their dogs. Cameron Park was one of the city's first suburbs, started in 1910. It is located one mile west of the Capitol and is bounded by Hillsborough Street to the south,

The North Raleigh subdivision of Bent Tree is a neighborhood of mini-estates with prices starting at $350,000.

St. Mary's College and St. Mary's Street on the east, Oberlin Road and NCSU on the west, and Clark Avenue and Cameron Village Shopping Center to the north.

Cameron Village is within walking distance, as are Wiley Elementary and Broughton High schools. Homes range from some of the most contemporary in town to traditional, white-columned Southern manses, but most are comfortable structures with plenty of room. Prices run from $200,000 to over $300,000.

Country Club Hills

As its name implies, Country Club Hills surrounds much of the golf course at the Carolina Country Club on Glenwood Avenue. The development is marked by large lots and hilly terrain and has some unconventional designs. It has a 1950's look about it with lower profile, ranch-style homes, although most are large and there are many conventional, two-story homes. The neighborhood has retained a woodland flavor, helped in part by its lack of sidewalks and a street matrix that is winding and

twisting and is as puzzling as a maze. Its location off Glenwood Avenue puts it close to both the I-440 Beltline and Crabtree Valley Mall as well as one of the main thoroughfares downtown. Many of its residents custom-built their homes and it is not a hotbed for sales. Prices range from $275,000 to $450,000.

Eaglechase

Located off Poole Road in east Raleigh, Eaglechase has been very popular with first-time home buyers and, for the money, it's one of the best buys in the Raleigh market. You can find three- and four-bedroom homes with two baths for prices around $105,000. The community is nicely landscaped with protective earthen berms at the entrances and along Poole Road. Amenities include a swim club.

Falls River

You should visit this planned neighborhood even if you don't decide to live here. Falls River is a 1,140-acre community that lies east of Falls of Neuse Road and north of Durant Road in North Raleigh. It is a "neotraditional" community that borrows planning themes from the early 20th century such as grid-like street patterns, sidewalks and village-type living. It offers a diverse mixture of residential homes, from multifamily apartments, condominiums and townhouses, to traditional single-family detached homes. Altogether, 2,975 residences will be built, and a population of 7,500 will live at Falls River at build out. There are extensive conservation and recreational commons—262 acres, much of it along the banks of the Neuse River. Amenities include a swim and tennis club as well as playing fields, jogging and greenway trails. Prices range from $160,000 to $350,000.

Five Points

This "inside the Beltline" community surrounds the five-way intersection of Glenwood Avenue, Fairview Road, Whitaker Mill Road and Glen Avenue. A favorite with artisans, musicians, politicians and writers, this neighborhood's prices range from $100,000 to $250,000.

Foxcroft

Foxcroft is one of the few "equestrian" neighborhoods near Raleigh. The area is located east of the city, but not within the city limits. It is north of U.S. 64 and east of New Hope Church Road. Foxcroft was developed for people who wanted enough room to keep their horses on their property. Homes vary in size and style, going back to the single-story ranch house popular in the 1960s and including some very contemporary designs. Starting prices are about $250,000.

Greystone

Greystone, which lies outside the I-440 Beltline to the northwest, began in 1980 and reflects the trend toward planned communities. Unlike many suburban developments that aim at the young or middle-aged family, Greystone appeals to

the entire market and even includes a retirement village for older residents. It features a child-care center in the middle of the community. Amenities include two recreational lakes stocked with fish and a swim and tennis club. Prices vary, but they are aimed at middle-income buyers, from $100,000 to $200,000.

Harrington Grove

Harrington Grove is a Centex Crosland community located in northwest Raleigh that includes three distinct neighborhoods —The Woods, The Downs and The Oaks and features popular transitional designs. Residents can join a neighborhood swim/ tennis club. Prices start at $140,000.

Hayes-Barton

Named after Sir Walter Raleigh's home place in England, Hayes-Barton has become the home for many of the city's "Establishment" since its development in the 1920s and '30s. The neighborhood is located close to downtown and is roughly bounded by Glenwood Avenue to the east and St. Mary's Street to the west, both of which curve around and intersect in the north. Wade Avenue serves as its southern boundary.

This area is filled with large homes, some on spacious lots, as well as many of modest size. A winding stream runs beside Cowper Drive. It's at the center of a small park that leads to the neighborhood's entrance off Glenwood Avenue. So desirable is a Hayes-Barton address that several builders bought smaller older homes, tore them down and built new, larger ones.

The hub of the Old Raleigh Establishment, the Carolina Country Club, is conveniently located nearby on Glenwood Avenue. Home prices range from $400,000 to over $1 million.

Hedingham

This is a premier, planned community in northeast Raleigh. It sits on 553 acres

TRIANGLE GOLF COURSE COMMUNITIES

Name	Location	$ Range	# of Holes	Opened
Crooked Creek	Fuquay-Varina	$200s-$400s	18	1994
Croasdaile	Durham	$300s-$600s	18	1966
Eagle Ridge	Garner	$130s-$400s	18	1998
Glen Laurel	Clayton	$170s-$500s	18	1993
Governors Club	Chapel Hill	$300s and up	27	1990
Grove Park	Durham	$100s-$200s	18	1997
Hedingham	Raleigh	$90s-$250s	18	1991
Lochmere	Cary	$200s-$1 million	18	1991
MacGregor	Cary	$180s-$600s	18	1968
Mill Creek	Mebane	$160s-$800s	18	1995
North Ridge	Raleigh	$190s-$350s	36	1968
Preston	Cary	$250s-$1 million	54	1988
River Ridge	Raleigh	$190s-$450s	18	1997
Riverwood	Clayton	$150s-$200s	27	1997
Sunset Ridge	Holly Springs	$190s-$700s	18	1991
Treyburn	Durham	$190s-$2 million	18	1989
Wakefield Plantation	Raleigh	$130s-$2 million	18	*
Willowbrook	Clayton	$130s-$175s	18	1997

*To open in fall 1999

between New Hope Road and the Neuse River and has access to U.S. 64 E. It contains a variety of homes and apartments and is expected to have over 2,400 units when completed. The centerpiece is the golf course development, Hedingham on the Neuse, that wraps lots around an 18-hole course. The community has 62 acres of greenways and a riverfront park, plus the usual amenities that go with a golf course, such as a clubhouse, grill room, swim and racquet club, and basketball and volleyball courts. Homes start at the amazingly low price of $90,000 and go up to $250,000.

Hymettus Woods

This inside-the-Beltline neighborhood is a perfect example of residential "infill" where small parcels of property in desirable areas are developed. Fourteen lots are located on less than 5 acres adjacent to Hymettus Park, which occupies the corner of Wade Avenue and Dixie Trail. The homes are custom built with attention to detail. Price tags start at $450,000 and go up to $1,250,000.

Mordecai

Pronounced Mord'e-kee, this downtown neighborhood is within walking distance to state government complex jobs and Peace College. It also contains the restored Mordecai House and Park which, together, are one of the city's historical treasures. Mordecai's sturdy homes are survivors and it's a place for bargain hunting home buyers. Prices range from $90,000 and upward.

North Hills

Although there is a specific neighborhood called North Hills, many Raleigh residents consider North Hills Terrace, North Glen, North Ridge, North Bend and North Clift as part of North Hills. North Hills encompasses the broad stretch of North Raleigh suburbs roughly bounded by Wake Forest Road and Falls of Neuse

Road to the east and North Hills Drive to the west.

Homes in North Hills vary in size and look, although most reflect the conventional styles of the 1960s and '70s. Trees abound and the city's Optimist Park Pool near Six Forks Road and Millbrook Road serves the area. Realtors consider the area a good value for the real estate dollar and homes sell for $125,000 to $220,000.

North Ridge

This North Raleigh neighborhood surrounds North Ridge Country Club, whose members are often connected to the Triangle's corporate establishment. It is also located close to Ravenscroft, a prestigious private school. The homes are big and impressive and many show the touch of an architect, so it's not stamped by any particular style. Some of the older homes may sell for $200,000, but a $300,000 to $400,000 price tag no longer raises eyebrows.

Oakwood

Oakwood is one of the city's oldest neighborhoods—one that has been improved by the efforts of its residents. It is located downtown, behind the Governor's Mansion, roughly bounded by Person, Franklin and Edenton streets and historic Oakwood Cemetery, where some of Raleigh's most famous citizens are buried. Oakwood is where the bankers and burghers and railroad managers who prospered in the years after the Civil War built Victorian homes with spacious rooms and high ceilings. Residents show off their restoration handiwork at the annual Historic Oakwood Christmas Tour. The range of prices go from $150,000 to over $500,000, but bargains still come on the market for those willing to scrape wallpaper, refinish floors and restore supporting beams.

Olde Raleigh

This is anything but old Raleigh. It's one of the most lavish developments in the city, between Duraleigh and Edwards Mill roads in northwest Raleigh, not far from Rex Healthcare. It has 137 single-family lots, three small lakes and guarded, electronic gates. Single family homes sell for $450,000 to $1 million. Empty nesters may want to check out the luxury townhome community, Olde Raleigh Villas, located between Duraleigh and Ebenezer Church roads, which start at $240,000.

Photo by Rich Weidman

Raleigh's Five Points neighborhood is lined with a variety of quaint shops and restaurants.

River Ridge

Located east of Raleigh off of Rock Quarry Road, River Ridge is a brand-new, luxurious golf community that features an 18-hole golf course, clubhouse, pool, tennis and volleyball courts. Prices range from $190,000 to $450,000.

Springdale Estates

Springdale Estates is one of three Springdale neighborhoods in northwest Raleigh, located on either side of Leesville Road on a rolling, wooded countryside. Typical of development in the 1970s, homes in Springdale Estates are built on large, 1-acre lots. It has a lake in the middle and it's one neighborhood where you will find contemporary designs mixed in with traditional and colonial styles. Located close to RDU and RTP, prices in this neighborhood range from $200,000 to $440,000.

Stonebridge

The entrance to this North Raleigh neighborhood is located off Six Forks Road. The houses are traditional in style and are large with three and four bedrooms being the norm. Expect to pay $150,000 to $390,000 for homes in Stonebridge.

Stonehenge

Located on both sides of Creedmoor Road, Stonehenge has been a favorite North Raleigh community among real estate agents. Begun in 1976, Stonehenge has continued to grow and add new neighborhoods, as well as townhouses and apartments. The homes are traditional in appearance and located on acre lots in the older sections. Seven Oaks Recreation Center, part of the Stonehenge community, has 12 acres of lighted tennis, basketball and volleyball courts as well as a competitive-size swimming pool. Prices range from $175,000 to $285,000.

Wakefield Plantation

Wakefield is a 2,260-acre "equestrian" community located adjacent to Falls Lake in northern Wake County on Falls of Neuse Road. It features an 18-hole golf course designed by Hale Irwin, an equestrian facility, 85-acre town park, tennis courts and a pool. Each estate homesite has from 2 to 10 acres. Prices for this new home community range from $130,000 to $2 million.

Wildwood Green

Wildwood Green is a northwest Raleigh community built around one of Raleigh's old private golf courses located off Strickland Road. The amenities include an 18-hole championship golf course, swimming pool and tennis courts. The homes are custom built and the average price is in the upper $200s.

Williamsborough and Drewry Hills

While there are a few contemporary styles in these neighborhoods, traditional and Williamsburg homes prevail. These neighborhoods are within the I-440 Beltline, near North Hills Mall. One of the city's greenways along Crabtree Creek forms the southern boundary. Older parts of Drewry Hills have homes that sell for $200,000, and in Williamsborough, prices go for well over $500,000.

Woods of St. Albans

This neighborhood came on the market in 1994 and is another example of "infill" that extends outside the I-440 Beltline. The neighborhood is located in a pocket of previously undeveloped land between North Hills Mall and Eastgate Shopping Center off St. Albans. Its convenient location close to shopping and employment centers, makes these traditional, Williamsburg-styled homes popular. Prices start at $175,000.

Wyndfield

Wyndfield is a small development featuring expansive homes. Located out of the city limits west of Six Forks Road, it's actually closer to Falls Lake than Raleigh. Many of the original homes were custom built in the '70s and they have a personal touch.

Residents prize their spacious lots, narrow streets and quiet isolation. Swimming pools are not unusual. There are some neighborhood tennis courts and residents are close to the boating, fishing and recreation at Falls Lake. Wyndfield is one of a number of similar subdivisions with names such as Coachman's Trail, Martindale, Trappers Creek and Trotters Ridge. Home prices start at over $200,000 and quickly escalate.

Cary

With 85,000 residents, Cary is currently the seventh-largest city in North Carolina. Many of the neighborhoods are Planned Unit Developments, or PUDs, and they are built as complete communities. They contain a mixture of housing, from apartments to single-family homes on conventional lots. Some even include neighborhood shopping centers and office and industrial sections. Most have their own recreation centers and complexes. These planned communities are designed to help newcomers get to know their neighbors in a hurry. You can meet neighbors on the jogging or walking paths that may run past your back yard. You'll meet others at the homeowners association, community clubhouse, swimming pool or tennis courts.

This Guide lists a number of the established as well as some of the newer neighborhoods of Cary. Our list is not inclusive. It is a sampler and highlights some of the communities that have gained special attention. They are located throughout Cary and are convenient to Research Triangle Park or the I-440 Beltline around Raleigh. Many of the newest neighborhoods are being developed along N.C. 55 and in southwest Cary.

Cary has been the strongest housing market by far for most Triangle real estate companies. Because of Cary's reputation as a prime residential area, prices reflect its popularity. $70,000 homes are rare and most start at $125,000 or more. Community spirit in Cary is high and children, teens, active adults and senior citizens are a vital part of this town's arts, religious, cultural and athletic synergy.

If you are looking for a new home priced from $100,000 to $130,000 you will have to consider a cluster or townhome. For $130,000 to $200,000, consider production builders' communities, such as Fieldstone, Coventry Glen, Brookgreen Forest, Forest Creek, Lochmere Forest, Devereaux and Park Village. Other new home communities to be considered in the area are The Reserve, Cambridge, Camden Forest, Fernwood, Glenridge, Landsdowne, Normandie, Oak Chase, Ashley Woods, Riggsbee Farm, Silverton, Somerset, Tatton Place, Wellsley, Wessex, Whitebridge and Wyndfall. If you can't find the home of your dreams in Cary, many families are now looking at nearby communities in Apex such as Ashley Downs, Beckett Crossing, Haddon Hall, Pearson Farms and Walden Creek.

Braeloch

Braeloch is a Squire's Homes community conveniently located off N.C. 54, one mile west of I-40. These attractive traditional homes have the feel of custom-built houses. New homes are still available with prices starting at $170,000.

Carpenter Village

Carpenter Village is a brand-new 400-acre community located on Morrisville-Carpenter Road across from

Preston. It includes a swim and tennis club. A village center, complete with a dinner theater, is in the planning stages. Eighty homes have been built and a total of 575 townhomes, single family homes and Charleston homes will be constructed over the next 4 to 5 years. Prices range from $140,000 to $500,000.

Downtown

This is the older part of town and it retains much of Cary's small-town flavor. The Town Hall and Chamber of Commerce are nearby, as is Ashworth Drugs on the corner, where you can get a first-rate milkshake. The library and Cary Elementary School are within walking distance, as is Russell Hills, one of the downtown subdivisions. Older homes in downtown's residential area, some in the process of restoration, come in a mixture of styles that one finds in most small towns of the 1950s. Prices vary depending on the house, but although the larger homes with the spacious yards will sell for $200,000, you might find a $75,000 bargain.

Greenwood Forest

Greenwood Forest is one of Cary's first large subdivisions, once on the southeast outskirts of town, but now right in the middle. It is bounded by the slanting Walnut Street from the northeast and the curving East Maynard Street that wraps around its southern border. It is a typical 1950's, early '60s neighborhood (no sidewalks) and has a mixture of home styles. Cary High School is nearby—some would say within walking distance—as are Cary Village Square and Cary Towne Center. Prices on these conventional homes start around $110,000 and go up to $160,000. Other neighborhoods of this vintage and price range are Greenwood

Acres, Pirate's Cove, Tanglewood and Walnut Hills.

Kildaire Farms

Kildaire Farms was Cary's first PUD and was hailed with lavish praise during the 1970s. It was named after the 927-acre farm owned by the Kilgore family. It is located at Kildaire Farm Road and Cary Parkway. About 2,600 residential units fill the PUD. It includes a 230-acre greenway system winding throughout the community, with jogging trails and bike paths. The Kildaire Farms Racquet and Swim Club has 13 lighted tennis courts and an 8,500-square-foot swimming pool. There's a membership fee for Kildaire Farm residents and, unlike most PUDs, nonresidents may also join. The Cary Athletic Club is also located here. Prices vary, depending on the project. For example: homes in Royal Ridge go for over $250,000 and Fox Chase homes start at around $130,000, while some townhouses are being marketed for around $65,000.

Lochmere

The 1,000-acre Lochmere development began in 1981 and became a textbook example of a successful PUD. It offers a variety of neighborhoods and is located on the southern end of Kildaire Farm Road, east of U.S. 1, not far from Regency Park. Lochmere has two man-made lakes big enough for sailing, canoeing and fishing. In the center is its 18-hole golf course—Lochmere Golf Club. A swimming and tennis complex is also available to residents, along with jogging trails, including a path around the larger lake. The Homeowners Association is extremely active in this community. There are several neighborhoods within the development, and they have names such as

Photo by Tim Johnson

More than 20 neighborhoods make up Preston, the Triangle's largest golf course community.

Fairways, Lochwood, Lochview, Windsong, The Greens, Williamsburgh Commons and Lochridge. Homes range from $200,000 to $1 million. Homes located in the Birkhaven neighborhood start at $340,000. Condominium prices start at about $130,000.

The Highlands is a neighborhood within Lochmere that started in 1987. It contains 343 homes, most of which are single-family detached homes. It has its own swim and tennis club, but members have access to Lochmere also. Homes range between $190,000 to $350,000.

MacGregor Downs

MacGregor Downs lit the fuse that led to Cary's growth explosion. It boasts a lake, a championship golf course and private country club and a tournament-caliber tennis complex as well as a swimming pool. Townhouses and condominiums are built on property closer to the club and tennis complex.

An adjacent but separate neighborhood is MacGregor West. It is especially upper-end in price range, averaging around $370,000, and reflects the sumptuous amenities that newer homes offer today, such as extravagant master bedroom suites and elaborate bathrooms. The MacGregor West mini-estates—those homes sitting on 2- to 3-acre lots—go as high as $1.5 million.

Oxxford Hunt

Oxxford Hunt is another residential community with English sounding neighborhoods such as Trafalgar. It is located off West Chatham Street and includes about 450 homes and apartments. Oxxford Hunt has a mix of housing, from single-family homes to condominiums and apartments. Prices are moderate, from $140,000 and up for the single-family homes. This is a family neighborhood. Residents pay modest homeowners dues to maintain common areas such as jogging trails, playground, tennis courts and swimming pool. This development is adjacent to Fred Bond Park.

Park Village

Park Village is a popular new family community built by Sunstar Homes. It is located off Davis Drive, 1.5 miles south of High House Road. Amenities include a swimming pool, clubhouse, mini-parks, walking trails and a children's playground. Prices start at $170,000.

The Parkway

This development stretches along Cary Parkway and has become a popular Cary address. It is located in west Cary and contains 20 separate neighborhoods with names like Arlington Ridge, Candlewood and MacArthur Park. Prices range from $150,000 to $250,000.

Preston

Preston is the Triangle's largest golf course community and one of the state's top-selling country club communities. Located off High House Road and only 10 minutes from the Research Triangle Park and RDU International Airport, Preston is at the heart of the area's booming residential market. Thoughtful planning that emphasizes beauty, privacy and convenience has allowed the community to respond to the tremendous growth of the area.

More than 20 neighborhoods make up this development, offering a diversity of home styles and a variety of price ranges—from $250,000 to $1,000,000. Preston Village boasts a two-acre Great Lawn, athletic field, putting greens, sheltered picnic areas, gazebos overlooking the lake and a huge play area designed for kids.

The centerpiece of the community is Prestonwood Country Club. The clubhouse complex and ballroom includes an expanded Olympic-size pool (with poolside dining), a fitness center and additional composition tennis courts. The championship golf course has expanded to 54 holes and is home to the Jimmy V Celebrity Golf Classic each August.

Regency Park

Regency Park is near the intersection of U.S. 1 South and U.S. 64. Approved in the late '70s, Regency Park did not begin developing until the '80s, but when it did, it established itself as one of the Triangle's classiest developments. It also marked a change from previous PUDs because it did not focus entirely on residential projects. It contains some of the Triangle's best office buildings and has helped change Cary's image from that of a bedroom community to a professional work center. The residential area is made up of single-family detached homes, cluster homes, townhouses and estate houses.

Regency Park Estates is an exclusive enclave of only 55 residences; each homesite is 1-acre or larger.

Weatherstone

Weatherstone is a new upscale community conveniently located off High House Road near Weatherstone Elementary School. It includes a pool, tennis courts, a playground and a 22-acre lake. Prices range from $260,000 to $300,000.

Weston Pointe

Located between Weston Parkway and Cary Parkway, the Weston PUD was first developed as an employment center. Weston Pointe is the residential part of the development and offers new homes built by well-known and respected area builders, North Hill, Inc. and Robuck Homes, Inc. Prices range from $230,000 to $280,000. As with most of the new planned communities, Weston Pointe has walking trails and a swim and tennis club.

Other Wake County Communities

Crooked Creek

Located in Fuquay-Varina, Crooked Creek is a beautiful golf course community that contains an 18-hole course and swim club. Prices range from $200,000 to $400,000.

Eagle Ridge Golf & Country Club

Located south of Raleigh and minutes from downtown, Eagle Ridge features an 18-hole golf course designed by Tom Kite, a clubhouse and a 200-acre nature preserve and park along Swift Creek. Single-family home prices range from $130,000 to $400,000.

Glen Laurel

Home of the 18-hole Neuse Golf Club, Glen Laurel is located off 42 East in Clayton, about a 20-minute drive from Raleigh. Amenities include a swim and tennis club, clubhouse, ball field, playground and walking paths along the Neuse River. About 330 of the 650 planned single-family homes have been built, with prices ranging from $170,000 to $500,000.

Riverwood

Riverwood offers golf course living amidst the countryside of Clayton near the banks of the Neuse River. Home sites average over 3/4 of an acre and home prices range from $150,000 to $200,000.

Sunset Ridge

Sunset Ridge is located about 20 minutes south of Raleigh in Holly Springs. It is home to Devil's Ridge Golf Course and a professionally staffed Swim and Racquet Club. Approximately 575 of 600 homes have been built and a village center with shops and offices is on the planning board. Prices range from $190,000 to $700,000 for single-family homes. Townhomes start at $150,000 and Charleston homes start at $230,000.

Willowbrook

Another new development in Clayton, Willowbrook features an 18-hole golf course, tennis courts and a swimming pool. Prices range from $130,000 to $175,000.

Durham

When the influx of newcomers to the Triangle began in the late 1960s and early '70s, it seemed everybody wanted to live in North Raleigh, even though Durham was a shorter commute to many jobs in Research Triangle Park. Now Durham has been discovered by all sorts of folks, and they've learned what Insiders knew all along—it's a great place to live.

Thanks to Durham's recent popularity, home prices have gone up significantly in recent years, placing the cost of housing here slightly above the national average. The average cost of a home in Durham is now about $136,000, one of the best home values in the Triangle area.

Durham is just 15 minutes from RTP or Chapel Hill, and offers homes, apartments and condominiums to suit just about any lifestyle and budget.

Durham has many new home communities under development. If you are looking for a home priced under $100,000, consider Brighton, Creekside, Greystone, Marbrey Landing, Rolling Hills, Stratton Park, Stone Hill Estates and Twin Lakes. If your price range is from $100,000 to $150,000, you should look at Brittany Woods, Cedar Valley, Crooked Creek, Eastwood Park, Eno Trace, Greycliff, Lenox, Pickett Crossing, Vantage Pointe and Wood Hollow. Between $150,000 and $200,000, ask to see American Village,

Briardale, Dover Ridge, Grandale Forest, Green Mill, Heather Glen II, Sunningdale Wellington Forest and Whitehall. Over $200,000, Coles Pond, Fairfield, Hardscrabble Plantation and Winstead are excellent communities.

Croasdaile

Croasdaile was developed in the '60s around its own 18-hole golf course and country club. Homes in Croasdaile usually sell for $300,000 or more, with some in the $600,000 plus range. Croasdaile Farm offers lots of 1/2 to over 2 acres from $55,000 to $156,000 and luxury townhomes from $275,000.

Dover Ridge

Dover Ridge is a new family community located north of I-85 on Guess Road. About 50 to 60 homes have been built with plans for a total of 214. Dover Ridge offers 27 acres of recreation space, including a soccer field, volleyball court, playground and picnic area. Prices range from $150,000 to $200,000.

Duke Forest

Duke Forest was built in the 1930s adjacent to Duke University's own woodlands in southern Durham to provide comfortable housing for faculty and administration. Today residents include "civilians" as well. Here you'll find architectural styles ranging from the traditional homes of the 1930s to wood-and-glass contemporaries. Prices range from $150,000 to over $350,000.

Duke Park

Duke Park is demographically and architecturally diverse. Located east of Trinity Park and just south of Interstate 85, it features a variety of homes built from the 1940s to '60s that sell for $60,000 to $130,000. Duke Park has an active neighborhood association and baby-sitting co-op. An oak-shaded community park is complete with a swimming pool.

Photo by Tim Johnson

Sunset Ridge in Holly Springs is home to Devil's Ridge Golf Course and a Swim and Racquet Club.

Photo by Tim Johnson

Located about 5 minutes from Duke University, Croasdaile offers homes in the $275,000 to $1 million price range.

Falconbridge

Located midway between Chapel Hill and Durham on N.C. 54, Falconbridge offers townhomes and single-family residences convenient to the cultural, educational and employment opportunities afforded by both towns. Minutes from Jordan Lake and Research Triangle Park, it's within the Durham Public School System.

Falconbridge's traditional and contemporary single-family homes sell for $140,000 to $250,000 and townhomes are in the $80,000 to $100,000 range. There is a private swim and tennis club in the neighborhood.

Fieldstone by the Eno

The charming community is nestled against the Eno River State Park and consists of Buckwater Creek, Ridgestone and Cabes Mill neighborhoods. Prices range from $150,000 to $230,000.

Forest Hills

One of the most exclusive and picturesque of the old city neighborhoods, Forest Hills features gracious homes on winding, tree-shaded lanes adjacent to an expansive park. Large homes constructed in the 1930s and '60s of brick, stone and wood are nestled on carefully landscaped lots up to an acre in size. Homes sell for anywhere from $150,000 for a bungalow a street or two away from the park to $375,000 and more for a stately brick mansion. Forest Hills Park features tennis courts, a swimming pool, softball fields, open fields for frisbee and other weekend sports. A seemingly endless greenway is flanked by gigantic willow oaks.

Garrett Farms

Garrett Farms is a popular neighborhood that contains approximately 300 homesites. Home prices average around $190,000.

Grove Park

Grove Park consists of neighborhoods with names such as Cameron Place, Grove Crossing, Grove Ridge and Nichol's Landing. Amenities include a clubhouse, 18-hole golf course, Junior Olympic-size swimming pool, tennis courts, a lake and children's playground. Very affordable homes range from $130,000 to $200,000.

Hope Valley

Here you will find a variety of residences ranging from nicely landscaped, suburban ranches from $170,000 to $200,000, to some of the most colossal older homes in Durham. Flanking the Hope Valley Country Club's 18-hole golf course, tennis courts and swimming pool are Old English Tudors and Colonial mansions with price tags from $300,000 to $700,000 and up. New homes can still be built in Hope Valley neighborhoods with names such as Arborfield, Carlton Crossings, Eagle Ridge, Greenbriar, Greyfield, Hunter's Forest, Oakbrook, Stonebridge and Windsor Oaks. Conveniently located midway between RTP and Chapel Hill, the area has experienced an unprecedented building boom in recent years. You'll find brick ranches, colonials, split levels and contemporaries in a wide range of prices.

Hope Valley Farms

Located in southwest Durham, Hope Valley Farms contains 750 homes and has plans for a total of 1,000 over the next couple of years. Amenities include a clubhouse, Olympic-size pool, tennis courts, fitness center and playground. Prices range from $100,000 to $250,000.

Lakewood

Of all the neighborhoods that grew up around the turn of the century, Lakewood was the most popular, thanks to the now defunct Lakewood Park, a rollicking amusement park known as "the Coney Island of the South." Today Lakewood is a shopping center surrounded by bungalow homes dating from the 1890s to the 1930s. Prices range from $58,000 to about $90,000.

Marydell and Bent Creek

These 5- to 10-year-old neighborhoods off Garrett Road near Jordan High School have a variety of spacious and attractive homes on wooded lots. Prices range from $185,000 to $300,000.

Milan Woods

Located in northeast Durham, off U.S. 70 at the Geer Street exit, Milan Woods was once described by a panel of Triangle real estate agents as "the most attractive community" and "the best home value" in its price range. Milan Woods offers affordably priced ($85,000 to $130,000) traditional and transitional homes on wooded home sites.

Morehead Hills

In the 1880s, some of Durham's industrialists and financiers began building their homes in a neighborhood developing adjacent to Forest Hills and near the hilltop residence of Eugene Morehead. The construction of the East-West Expressway saw the demolition of many fine homes. To this day, Morehead Hill remains a small island of wide tree-lined boulevards and well-landscaped yards. Its homes date from the turn of the century to more contemporary energy-efficient solar models. Prices range from $75,000 for a small home to $150,000 or more for a newer or restored larger home.

Old North Durham

If you want historic charm at a more reasonable price, North Durham may be your best bet. Built in the early 1900s, some of the city's most elegant and spacious homes, once fallen into disrepair, are now being returned to their former splendor. An active homeowners association in Old North Durham is helping draw new people into the neighborhood to participate in its renaissance.

Parkwood

One of the oldest residential subdivisions in southern Durham, Parkwood offers a range of appealing family homes in a neighborhood setting, priced in the $85,000 to $140,000 range. Located on N.C. 54 near I-40, it's convenient to Durham and Chapel Hill and only minutes from Research Triangle Park. An elementary school and a branch of the Durham Library are located in Parkwood.

Rockwood

Rockwood is a hilly, winding, tree-shaded neighborhood, located just south of Forest Hills. Contemporary homes are interspersed with those built in the 1940s. Residents also enjoy a neighborhood park. Prices start around $125,000.

Treyburn

Situated on 5,300 rustic acres along the Little River north of Durham, Treyburn is the largest development in the Durham area. Treyburn has commercial and industrial tenants, including a medical facility and a satellite campus of Durham Tech. When completed, it will be about the size of RTP. The developers say it will eventually house 10,000 residents in 4,400 condominiums, apartments and single-family homes "oriented to provide golf, waterfront or open-space views." The membership-only Treyburn Country Club features a beautiful clubhouse, a 25 meter Olym-

pic-size pool, a tennis facility and a 72-par golf course designed by Tom Fazio.

Many families already call Treyburn home and a 369-unit residential retirement community and condos adjacent to the clubhouse are planned. Home sites are selling for $75,000 for a half-acre lot to $175,000 for 2 acres on the waterfront. Homes sell from $190,000 to $2 million.

Trinity Park

Durham's older, in-town neighborhoods have enjoyed a comeback. The oldest and one of the most popular locales is Trinity Park. This community was developed at the turn of the century around Trinity College, now Duke University's East Campus.

Here you'll find medium to large homes on small city lots conveniently located between Duke University and downtown. A few homes contain apartments and condominiums, but most remain single-family residences. Prices usually start at over $110,000 for a bungalow in good condition. Larger, restored homes are in the $150,000 to $190,000 range. Homes tend to go quickly for the asking price.

Photo by Evelyn Ward

Trinity Park, Durham's oldest in-town neighborhood, developed at the turn of the century around Trinity College, now Duke University's East Campus.

Watts Hospital

Directly to the north of Trinity Park is an area known as Watts Hospital, named for the facility that was once the focal point of the neighborhood. Today the old Watts Hospital building houses the N.C. School of Science and Mathematics, a special public high school for students from across the state who are gifted in those fields.

Residents include young singles, families and senior citizens. The bungalows and larger houses were built in the 1940s and '50s and the lots are larger than in Trinity Park. The main streets are shaded by some of the most majestic willow oaks in Durham. Oval Park is a pleasant recreational retreat here for kids and adults. Most homes sell for $80,000 to $130,000.

Willowhaven

Located north of downtown, Willowhaven offers a variety of designs, from traditional to contemporary, on family-size lots larger than you'll find in the city. Begun in the 1950s, Willowhaven was developed on 1.5-acre lots around the Willowhaven Country Club. Homes sell for $150,000 and up.

Woodcroft

Perhaps the most successful development in southwest Durham is Woodcroft, an award-winning $300 million planned community and shopping center on 750 acres. Begun in 1981, Woodcroft offers more than 2,500 residential units. The area is almost fully developed, but many homes are available for resale.

Woodcroft features a series of distinct "neighborhoods" offering a variety of housing options from $70,000 condos and $90,000 townhomes to single-family homes selling for $125,000 to $250,000. Each subdivision is surrounded by woods or open space. All residents have access to jogging trails, athletic fields and a community club, complete with a swimming

pool and tennis courts. There is also a shopping center that serves the Woodcroft community and adjacent neighborhoods.

Woodlake

Woodlake is located on Fayetteville Road across from Woodcroft in southwest Durham. Woodlake is a unique community of six neighborhoods, Grayson Ridge, Chesden, Old Hickory, Candlewood, Shannon and Lake Village Townhomes, offering homes in a variety of styles, sizes and price ranges from $130,000 to $300,000. A lakeside swim club is one of the many amenities.

Chapel Hill

Chapel Hill has come a long way from the day in 1793 when an auctioneer offered the first 22 lots for sale in the new university village. Today this growing town of about 45,000 residents and 24,000 students is considered one of the most desirable addresses in the Southeast.

Despite the pressures of new commercial and residential development, Chapel Hill still exudes the charm of a historic university village. Add to that some of the best public schools in the state and access to RTP, Raleigh and Durham, and it is no wonder Chapel Hill has become a haven for young families, professionals and retirees.

The demand for housing translates into some of the highest home prices in the Triangle. The median sales price of a new home in Chapel Hill is $265,000 and a resale home is $185,000. Large older homes or custom-built new homes in some of the finer neighborhoods can easily cost $450,000 or more.

Some folks are choosing to build on land in the rolling countryside to the north and south where an acre sells for anywhere from $7,000 to $40,000 or more.

Both Chapel Hill and Carrboro also offer a wide range of condominiums and townhomes, from $35,000 to $40,000 for a small one-bedroom unit to $175,000 and up for a luxury apartment unit. Townhomes were in generous supply just a few years ago. Today they are a very hot item for retirees, small families, singles and students. In addition to the communities described below, some other home communities you may want to check out with a Realtor include Highland Meadows, Meadow Ridge, Northwoods, Southbridge, Springcrest and Wexford.

East West Properties was recently given the green light to start development on the controversial 435-acre Meadowmont community, which is located off N.C. 54. The project was designed in the "neotraditional" mode and will eventually contain 1,298 housing units and 785,000 square feet of commercial space.

Historic Districts

Chapel Hill has three historic districts. The first, the Franklin-Rosemary District, was established in 1976 and includes sections of the town's main thoroughfares, Franklin Street (Chapel Hill's main business street, named for Ben) and Rosemary Street, a block to the north. (It is said that Rosemary Street was so named to honor a Lady Rose who lived at one end and a Lady Mary who lived at the other.)

The Cameron-McCauley Historic District was established in 1990. It takes in an area ranging from just south of West Franklin Street up to the University Drive area, and includes the area around the landmark Carolina Inn.

The newest historic district, which was established in 1993, is the Gimghoul area. This neighborhood is named for the "medieval and mysterious-looking" Gimghoul Castle, built by Masons as the meeting place of the Secret Order of the Gimghouls, a university society that continues today.

In these neighborhoods, you'll find rambling brick, cedar shake or wood-frame colonials, many built in the 1920s and '30s, as well as smaller homes tucked behind hedges and old stone walls. Expect to pay $200,000 for a home that needs work and from $350,000 to $600,000 for one that's been remodeled and updated. Also close to downtown and campus is a unique neighborhood around Cobb Terrace, a narrow winding circular road. This neighborhood features a mix of larger colonials and more modest wood-frame homes and cottages on smaller lots.

All of the historic districts are within walking distance of the campus and many restaurants and stores. These are three of the most convenient neighborhoods for university faculty and medical center personnel.

Booker Creek

Northeast of Lake Forest is Booker Creek, a 1970's neighborhood featuring one- and two-story traditional homes. Most homes in Booker Creek are 1,800 to 2,500 square feet, and prices range from $185,000 to $250,000.

Cedar Hills and Timberlyne

Farther up the road are two neighborhoods offering traditional and contemporary homes from 1,800 to 3,000 square feet. These neighborhoods are popular with families, and homes here sell from $185,000 to $300,000 and up. This area offers convenient access to I-40 and to shopping at Timberlyne Shopping Center.

Chesley and Chandler's Green

Chesley and Chandler's Green are newer Chapel Hill neighborhoods along Weaver Dairy Road. They feature large, elegant homes in the $300,000 to $500,000 range. Chesley adjoins Cedar Falls Park. Both neighborhoods are a stone's throw from East Chapel Hill High School.

Countryside

Heading north, just above Cedar Falls Park, is Countryside, a neighborhood of one- and two-story homes, mostly in the

1,500 to 2,500 square feet range. These homes sell for about $160,000 to $225,000.

Culbreth Park/Tandler

These two developments in Chapel Hill are designed to provide affordable housing in a marketplace that has very few "starter homes" left. Culbreth Park is next to Culbreth Middle School. Tandler is a bit closer to the UNC campus off Merritt Mill Road. Home prices range from $100,000 to $140,000, depending on whether the buyer is eligible for a subsidy based on family income level. See a Realtor for more information.

Dogwood Acres

A few miles south of town, between U.S. 15-501 and Smith Level Road, is this older neighborhood of small cottages and ranch-style homes, many on lots of almost an acre. One of the more affordable neighborhoods in town, Dogwood Acres is a good place to look for a first home. Homes start at about $120,000.

Downing Creek/Downing Woods

The Downing Creek and Downing Woods neighborhoods are located off N.C. 54, east of Chapel Hill. These neighborhoods offer homeowners home sites amid buffered forests, custom-built transitional homes and a private swim and tennis club. Though the address is Chapel Hill, these neighborhoods are in the Durham Public Schools district. Homes are convenient to Chapel Hill, Research Triangle Park and I-40, and are priced from $195,000 to $300,000.

Falconbridge

Located midway between Chapel Hill and Durham on N.C. 54, Falconbridge offers townhomes and single-family residences convenient to both towns. It's located minutes from Jordan Lake and RTP and is served by Durham Public Schools. Falconbridge offers traditional and contemporary single-family homes

from $175,000 to $325,000 and townhomes starting at about $120,000. There is a private clubhouse with tennis courts and a swimming pool.

Forest Hills

Next to Westwood is another neighborhood of somewhat smaller homes of a similar vintage. Here you'll see a variety of home styles and sizes from modest wood-frame cottages to larger traditionals and a sprinkling of newer homes. Prices are in the $140,000 to $225,000 range.

Franklin Hills

Franklin Hills, which is located off East Franklin Street, boasts stately two- and three-story homes with plenty of custom features: gourmet kitchens, formal dining rooms, whirlpool baths, vaulted ceilings, winding stairwells, porches, upper balconies and more. Expect to pay $300,000 to $400,000.

Glen Lennox

Heading east of Chapel Hill, off the U.S. 15-501 Bypass are two neighborhoods built in the 1950s known as Glen Lennox. In Glen Lennox, you'll find mostly frame and brick ranches selling for $150,000 to $175,000.

Glendale

If you like the idea of owning a home adjacent to Battle Park, but you favor more contemporary architectural styles, Glendale is for you. Located between Franklin Street and the northern perimeter of the park are newer, more contemporary homes, some built into the sides of hardwood-covered bluffs overlooking the woods. You'll see a variety of styles including ranches and split-levels on hillside lots large enough to convey the feeling that you are in the wooded countryside, though Franklin Street is just a minute away. Here homes built in the 1960s sell for $190,000 to $300,000.

Greenwood

Greenwood is just southeast of Glendale and Battle Park and still a pleasant walk to campus. This neighborhood features a mix of traditional and contemporary homes. Prices here are in the $185,000 to $475,000 range for the large custom homes built in the last several years.

Heritage Hills

Like Dogwood Acres, Heritage Hills is south of the town limits but within the Chapel Hill-Carrboro School District. Homes here are 15 to 20 years old and start in the $135,000 to $185,000 range. Heritage Hills offers a private swim and racquet club.

Hidden Hills, Estes Hills, Coker Hills and Coker Hills West

These family neighborhoods are located in the wedge-shaped area between East Franklin Street and Airport Road. They feature a variety of ranch, contemporary and colonial homes on midsize to large lots and are convenient to elemen-

tary and middle schools, downtown and University Mall. Prices range from $155,000 to over $350,000.

Homestead Village

Homestead Village is located off Homestead Road only minutes from downtown Chapel Hill. Built by Landwright Homes, prices start in the $170,000 range.

Ironwoods

Just 2 1/2 miles north of town off Seawell School Road and Estes Drive, this development offers wooded lots and spacious traditional and contemporary homes with custom features. Prices begin around $205,000.

Lake Forest

What's special about this neighborhood is that it has its own private lake, Eastwood Lake, large enough for fishing and boating. Lake Forest offers a variety of housing styles from New England and American colonials to ranches, split levels and other contemporaries, most built

Photo by Tim Johnson

The growing community of Lake Hogan Farms is conveniently located 2 miles from Carrboro and 5 miles from downtown Chapel Hill.

The Mt. Bolus neighborhood off Airport Road in Chapel Hill offers lots of privacy and wooded views.

in the 1960s and '70s. Prices range from about $180,000 to $600,000 or more for a special large property with a pool and perhaps its own dock on the lake.

Lake Hogan Farms

Located off Homestead Road, this development consists of 438 homesites on over 310 acres. Homesites range from estates to townhomes. The Commons includes a Swim and Tennis Club. A 12-acre spring-fed lake will offer light boating and fishing. Single-family homes will be featured in Bolin Ridge, The Woods and Lake Hogan Estates. The Greenfields neighborhood will offer 91 patio homes. Prices range from $199,000 to over $500,000.

Mill Race

Located close to Bolin Creek, but within walking distance of Downtown Chapel Hill, this new home community is in the heart of Chapel Hill. Mill Race offers 25 homesites with prices ranging from $422,000 to $481,000.

Morgan Creek Hills, Farrington Hills and Laurel Hill

These three neighborhoods offer a mix of home styles on large, wooded lots in the rolling countryside off Mount Carmel Church Road south of town. Homes here start at about $185,000 and go as high as $350,000 or more.

Mt. Bolus/Winding Ridge

Heading north of town off Airport Road, you'll turn east into Mt. Bolus. This magnificent hill rising above Bolin Creek was named for Joseph Caldwell, the first official UNC president whom the students affectionately called Diabolus (devil) or Bolus for short. Today Mt. Bolus offers a mixture of traditional, ranch and contemporary homes clinging to the sides of steep hardwood-shaded bluffs.

Just south of Mt. Bolus Road is a neighborhood called Winding Ridge. It features spacious homes with an abundance of custom details such as oak panelling, granite kitchen counters and wine cellars.

These neighborhoods offer lots of privacy and wooded views, all just minutes from UNC and downtown. Prices vary with the size and location of each home, but generally range from $250,000 to $400,000.

The Oaks and The Oaks II and III

East of Glen Lennox is this neighborhood built in the 1980s, surrounding the Chapel Hill Country Club and its golf course. It features a mix of traditional and contemporary homes. In The Oaks II and III, you'll find sprawling custom homes of brick, stone, stucco and wood on spacious lots with greenway views. Most feature large living rooms, spacious master suites, cathedral ceilings, arched windows, detailed woodwork and two- or three-car garages. Some homes in The Oaks II and III are in the Durham County School System. Expect to pay $350,000 and up to $1 million.

Old Forest Creek

Just off Piney Mountain Road, this development runs along Rock Creek within walking distance of Estes Hills Elementary and Phillips Middle schools. Larger traditional and contemporary homes feature wood, stucco and stone exteriors, cathedral ceilings, formal dining rooms and spacious master bedrooms. All are within walking distance of town and UNC. Prices are in the $250,000 to $350,000 range.

Southbridge

Just south of Chapel Hill, across from Culbreth Middle School, is a newer development featuring two-story traditional and transitional homes on hilly terrain. This is a popular neighborhood for university faculty due to its proximity to UNC. Homes sell for $190,000 to $325,000.

Southern Village

Developed by Bryan Properties, Southern Village is located in south Chapel Hill along U.S. 15-50. This "neotraditional" community of 535 homes is being built in the style of a village, where sidewalks, porches, a greenway, a bus stop and a corner store will help bring neighbors together. Houses are designed away from the "cookie-cutter" mode, with styles ranging from long, narrow Charlestons, to Georgetown and "Courtyard" style homes. With the variety of home styles comes a variety in home prices. Homes sell for $200,000 to the $500,000 range.

Stoneridge and Sedgefield

On the northernmost edge of Chapel Hill, on the other side of I-40, are these two developments of gracious contemporary and traditional homes with the privacy afforded by wooded lots of 1-acre or more. Stoneridge also has a private racquet and swim club in the neighborhood. This location provides easy access to Research Triangle Park, Durham, Raleigh and RDU International Airport. Prices range from $300,000 to $600,000 and up.

Westwood

Until 1950, the town of Chapel Hill was composed of 850 acres. Another 289 acres were annexed east of town that year, and in 1951 the town added 61 acres, which today make up the neighborhoods of Westwood and Forest Hills just to its south.

Westwood is located along a winding, hilly drive across Columbia Street from the UNC Hospitals. Here you'll find large two- and three-story traditional homes of brick or wood, many built in the 1950s. They feature hardwood floors, high ceilings, sweeping porches and spacious yards framed by low stone walls. Prices go from about $200,000 for a fixer-upper to $400,000 plus for a recently remodeled home.

Carrboro

Real estate prices in Carrboro are generally somewhat lower than in Chapel Hill. You can still find single-family homes in

The rolling countryside of Chatham County is home to Fearrington, a planned development featuring rustic-contemporary homes and condominiums.

the $115,000 to $175,000 range for a new three- to four-bedroom home. Some other communities are Bel Arbor, Berryhill, Sunset Creek and University Station.

Bolin Forest and Quarterpath Trace

Just off North Greensboro Street are two neighborhoods filled with young families. Bolin Forest is a neighborhood of two and three bedroom homes ranging from about $130,000 to $185,000. Homes in Quarterpath Trace are traditional styles with three to four bedrooms. Prices range from $175,000 to over $200,000.

Cobblestone and Barrington Hills

Travel north out Hillsborough Road and you'll come to Cobblestone and Barrington Hills. In Barrington Hills, you'll find modest contemporary homes built in the late 1970s, starting at over $125,000. Cobblestone's newer homes are in the $120,000 to $160,000 range.

Morgan Glen

Morgan Glen is a pastoral residential development consisting of eleven 10-acre tracts, with restrictions against further sub-

division. A 150-foot swath along Morgan Creek was given to the Triangle Land Conservancy for a perpetual wildlife conservation easement. All property owners have access to the creek that runs through the development and the easement allows wildlife to coexist with people. Resale homes on the large lots are in the $300,000 to $450,000 range.

Plantation Acres

Wedged between North Greensboro Street and Old N.C. 86 is Plantation Acres, a family neighborhood of ranch-style homes built in the 1960s. Most are three-bedroom houses that sell for $120,000 to $150,000.

Spring Valley

If you drive through Webbwood, you will come to a newer development called Spring Valley, featuring two-story rustic-contemporary homes, many with a view of a man-made pond. Homes here start at about $140,000 to $160,000.

Weatherhill Pointe

These award-winning cluster and patio homes are adjacent to the Chapel Hill Tennis Club. In the $125,000 to $160,000 range, these are among the more affordable homes built in Chapel Hill and Carrboro in the last few years.

Webbwood

A bit further from downtown Carrboro is Webbwood, a neighborhood featuring a blend of modest traditional and contemporary homes built in the 1970s. Prices start around $125,000.

Windwood

West of downtown Carrboro is Windwood, another neighborhood of ranch homes built in the 1960s. These are smaller houses in a price range of $100,000 to $150,000.

Chatham County

The lower property taxes and often lower home prices of Chatham County have helped this area prosper. Excellent schools like North Chatham Elementary and Northwoods High School serve these communities. You can find a three-bedroom home in one north Chatham community for under $100,000. There are also still many 2- to 10-acre tracts to build on. For more information on home and land sales in Chatham County, follow the real estate listings in *The Chapel Hill News*, as well as *The Chatham Record* in Pittsboro.

Fearrington

Fearrington is located about 8 miles south of Chapel Hill in rural Chatham County. This planned development features rustic-contemporary homes and condominiums clustered around greenways, tennis courts and a market area. The Fearrington Village Center includes a cafe, bookstore, crafts shop, gardening store and jewelry store. There is also an award-winning country inn and fine restaurant. Fearrington is very popular with retirees but is home to young families as well. Children living here attend Chatham County schools. Prices start at $130,000 and can be more than triple that for the larger homes in the newest phases of the development.

Governors Club

Governors Club is situated on 1,600 rolling acres adjacent to Jordan Lake on scenic Edwards Mountain, about 4 miles south of Chapel Hill. Among its many features are a 27-hole golf course designed by Jack Nicklaus, horse trails and footpaths, a 24-hour security gate entrance and a private country club. Developers of Governors Club have attracted executives with families, professionals and retirees. Plans call for about 1,250 single-family homes, golf villas, townhouses, patio homes and "club cottages," with home prices ranging from $300,000 to $3 million.

Governors Village

Governors Village is a 300-acre community that began development in 1996. It is located across from Governors Club and features a "neotraditional" neighborhood style. Amenities include swimming and tennis facilities and two parks. Home prices start at about $200,000.

It's no surprise that the Triangle has become one of the hot spots for retirement.

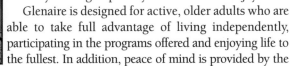

Aging is *Uniquely Personal*

...*So Are Our Residences*

As we grow older, our needs and abilities change. Some older adults are quite self-reliant while others require considerable care. At **Alterra**, we provide a variety of residences to meet your unique needs or those of someone you love. Whether assisted living or memory care, our residences are designed to meet the ever-changing needs of older adults. And though they vary in design and purpose, all **Alterra** residences share a common trait—a caring and dedicated staff committed to preserving the dignity and quality of life of those we serve.

Alterra

AGING WITH CHOICE

Alterra Wynwood
AN ASSISTED LIVING RESIDENCE
2220 Farmington Dr., Chapel Hill
(919) 933-1430

Alterra Clare Bridge
A MEMORY CARE RESIDENCE

7870 Chapel Hill Rd., Cary (919) 852-1355	2230 Farmington Dr. Chapel Hill (919) 929-5850

Retirement living in tune with the lifestyle you've earned.

WOODLAND TERRACE, NESTLED IN THE HEART OF CARY, NC, IS A BRAND NEW, FULL-SERVICE RETIREMENT COMMUNITY IN TUNE WITH THE EXPECTATIONS OF TODAY'S SENIORS. OUR SERVICES AND AMENITIES ARE GEARED TO THOSE WHO WANT MORE OUT OF LIFE THAN A ROCKING CHAIR, AND EXPECT NOTHING SHORT OF THE BEST IN RETIREMENT LIVING.

OUR 22-ACRE CAMPUS FEATURES A CROQUET LAWN, WALKING TRAILS, EXTENSIVE GROUNDS AND A COMMUNITY LAKE WITH A BEAUTIFUL FOUNTAIN. SURROUNDING IT ALL ARE SPACIOUS COTTAGES AND APARTMENT HOMES WITH A VARIETY OF FLOOR PLANS. WE OFFER INDEPENDENT LIVING, ASSISTED LIVING IN OUR VERRASPRING[SM] RESIDENCE AND ALZHEIMER'S CARE IN THE ARBORETUM.[SM] SO IF NEEDS CHANGE, TRANSITIONS CAN BE SEAMLESSLY MADE.

BEST OF ALL, WOODLAND TERRACE DOES NOT REQUIRE AN UP-FRONT FEE. WE'RE SIMPLY A RENTAL COMMUNITY.

OUR INFORMATION CENTER IS NOW OPEN, AND WE ARE CURRENTLY TAKING PRIORITY RESERVATIONS. CALL 919-465-0356, OR COME BY AND GET ACQUAINTED.

LIVING LIFE TO ITS FULLEST IS WHAT WE'RE ALL ABOUT.

WOODLAND TERRACE

300 KILDAIRE WOODS DRIVE
CARY, NC 27511
PHONE 919-465-0356
A KISCO FULL-SERVICE
RENTAL RETIREMENT COMMUNITY
WWW.KISCORETIREMENT.COM

Wouldn't You Like Your Parents to Live Closer To You?

Independence Village, North Carolina's best kept retirement secret, is a wonderful place for your parents to begin a new life. In addition to taking advantage of our warm climate and spending time with you and their grandchildren, your parents can maintain their active, independent lifestyles.

- Independence Village adjoins one of Raleigh's most prestigious and gracious neighborhoods, Olde Raleigh
- Studio, one and two bedroom apartments
- Monthly rental—no entry fee or endowment
- Scheduled transportation
- 3 meals served daily
- 24-hour Emergency Assistance
- Weekly Housekeeping and Linen Service
- Variety of Activities and Social Events
- Beauty/Barber Shop
- Convenient to I-40, Rex Hospital and Crabtree Valley Mall

Assisted Living Opening Soon!

Call Terri Oliver to schedule a personal guided tour and complimentary lunch.

919-781-8226

3113 Charles B. Root Wynd • Raleigh, NC 27612

www.citysearch.com/rdu/independence

Retirement and Senior Services

During the 1990s, North Carolina established itself as one of the most popular states in the country for retirement. At last count, it was in the top five for retirement migration with the population of people age 65 and older estimated to number 980,000 by the year 2000. It's no surprise that the Triangle has become one of the hot spots for such migration. With a youthful demographic base and new jobs attracting young families, the grandparents are not far behind. The presence of two excellent research and teaching hospitals—University of North Carolina's Hospitals and Duke University Medical Center—also appeals to retirement age residents. And all the things that attract other people are magnets for older citizens, too: moderate climate, change of seasons, low crime and tax rates, metropolitan airport, and a vibrant cultural life. Communities and facilities catering to older citizens prosper here, and the Triangle is home to some of the country's best. Many retirees add to their respective community's civic life. So, the Triangle is a great place to kick back, live longer and stay active.

Retirement Communities

As the retirement community has grown, so have the number and levels of services. When choosing a retirement community, be certain that the level of care provided matches your needs:

Independent living is for those who are able and willing to take care of themselves, but don't want the hassle of taking care of a big house. The convenience and activities of a retirement community are attractive to this group. Independent care housing can be a single, detached house, a condominium, a cottage or an apartment.

Assisted living is the next level in retirement and provides assistance with activities of daily living such as preparing food, providing local transportation and housekeeping. Many residents are capable of doing most things for themselves but, from time to time, need assistance. Room and board, activities, administration of medications, medical transportation, assistance with personal hygiene and 24-hour supervision are provided.

Intermediate care is appropriate for persons who may need nursing intervention, but not on a continuous basis. Rehabilitation programs, activities and personal care assistance are available. The care is provided under the direction of a physician.

Nursing care provides full-time, around-the-clock, long-term health care. While many nursing care tenants can do a lot of things for themselves, they need assistance with medication management and other health and comfort issues. Such care is for those who are too ill or impaired to be ambulatory. Some retirement communities even offer on-site physicians and nurses with their nursing care facilities.

The Triangle offers retirement communities in all of these categories and some that offer a combination of all. These continuing care communities are ideal because the level of care is adapted to the needs of the resident. Now, the red flag warning! Some retirement communities offer assisted living care and nursing care only to those tenants who started with the community as independent living tenants. For additional information, contact Resources for Seniors, 872-7933, or the Department of Social Services in your county.

The following communities are listed according to the level of care provided.

Planned Communities

There are a number of neighborhoods and developments that are not exclusively for retirees, but do have a large number of retired people in the community. They include Treyburn in Northern Durham County, Governor's Club in Orange County and Fearrington in Chatham County.

Continuing Care Retirement Communities

Carol Woods
750 Weaver Dairy Rd., Chapel Hill
• 968-4511

Carol Woods opened in 1979 after years of grass roots planning. It is a nonprofit community located on 120 acres on the outskirts of Chapel Hill. It provides a complete range of retirement services, from independent living to assisted living and nursing care and it maintains an on-site, 60-bed health center. A geriatric nurse-practitioner is on-site and physicians are on call at the center's outpatient clinic.

Carol Woods offers a greenhouse,

aquatic center and croquet court. The community is among the area's largest with 140 cottages for independent living and 140 apartments with six different floor plans. The community is close to both Duke University Medical Center and UNC Hospitals. Carol Woods offers a financial package in which a single monthly fee covers all the community's services.

Carolina Meadows
100 Carolina Meadows, Chapel Hill
• 942-4014

Carolina Meadows is an accredited not-for-profit, fee-for-service retirement community located minutes from the charm and cultural activities of Chapel Hill. Floor plans range from studio apartments to 1,800-square-foot villas with garages. Construction was completed in 1997 and there are now 392 homes and 560 residents. The community is located on 160 acres in a beautiful country setting surrounded by a hardwood forest. It provides privacy and security along with dining, health care and recreational facilities.

An Ambulatory Services Clinic is also on site. A 41,000-square-foot assisted living facility called The Fairways. The 90-bed Carolina Health Center provides a residential environment to residents at all levels of care. The design includes a separate Dementia Care (Alzheimer's) Unit.

Croasdaile Village
2600 Croasdaile Farm Pkwy., Durham
• 309-9000

Croasdaile Village, the newest continuing care retirement community of The United Methodist Retirement Homes, Inc., opened in June 1999. Situated in the gently rolling hills north of downtown Durham, Croasdaile Village offers gracious, secure retirement living in a pastoral setting that once was home to a working family farm. The 100-acre site, adjacent to the planned community of Croasdaile Farm, includes walking trails, a scenic lake and expansive green spaces where residents can

enjoy the outdoors. The Village Commons, in the center of Croasdaile Village, houses common areas and amenities.

Croasdaile Village provides a wide selection of apartments, cottages and homes designed to complement residents' pursuit of a carefree, gracious and abundant retirement lifestyle, as well as a health care center that provides assistance and medical care for residents who require it.

The Forest at Duke
2701 Pickett Rd., Durham • 490-8000

The nonprofit Forest at Duke opened in 1992 on a 42-acre campus near Duke University. It offers three levels of care: independent living, assisted care and nursing care. The community contains 80 cottages, 160 apartments and 30 skilled nursing beds. Like other full-service continuing care villages, the Forest has housekeeping, security, transportation and maintenance for residents.

The Forest provides an attractive setting for residents and services such as community and private dining, beauty and barber shops, a library, a bank and even a swimming pool. Moreover, there is an active schedule of events for residents, many of which are offered in the spacious auditorium.

Glenaire
200 W. Cornwall Rd., Cary • 460-8095

This retirement community opened in 1993 in the heart of Cary and has just completed a major expansion of its facilities. Glenaire's 30 acres are beautifully landscaped. Well-designed accommodations and programs are offered for residents in cottages, a range of apartment options, two distinct levels of assisted living and three nursing sections, providing Medicare, Medicaid and dementia care.

Glenaire is home to 275 active adults beyond age 65 living in residential settings and 120 residents in progressive levels of care. The residents have relocated from the local area as well as from some 10 states, and many have family ties in the area. The Community Center is the focal point for activities, from the arts to exercise and educational experiences. Also available are game and craft rooms, library, bank, gift shop, barber and beauty salon, storage spaces and postal service. Among the features provided for all residents are meal plans, housekeeping, maintenance and grounds services.

All residents are members of the Residents Association, which has an active role in the governance of the community and programming of campus life. Glenaire seeks to attract younger residents who look for opportunities for themselves in retirement and who value involvement in community life. The facility is an affiliate of the nonprofit Presbyterian Homes, Inc., which manages two other facilities, River Landing in High Point and Scotia Village in Laurinburg, NC.

Springmoor
1500 Sawmill Rd., Raleigh • 848-7080

Springmoor offers a full range of care, from independent living to nursing care. It is built on 45-wooded acres off Creedmoor Road, 3 miles north of Crabtree Valley Mall. The 600 residents are invited to use the walking and jogging trails as well as the indoor swimming pool in the 500-acre Greystone Village community of which Springmoor is a part.

The complex is a mixture of apartments, villas and private homes. In the apartment complexes, there are dining rooms, health centers and a nursing wing for those who need 24-hour care.

Springmoor maintains a clinic with a physician on duty and has a special wing for Alzheimer's disease victims. Residents have access to a wide variety of amenities, including a store, a bank, post office, beauty salon and library.

Whitaker Glen
501 E. Whitaker Mill Rd., Raleigh • 839-5604

This attractive community is locally owned and conveniently situated not far from Five Points. It offers independent and assisted living as well as nursing care. Whitaker Glen is a complex of four buildings containing 96 units, split between one- and two-bedroom apartments. The support building includes a dining room that serves three meals a day for those residents who cannot or choose not to cook. Scheduled transportation to shopping centers is available. Nurses are on duty.

Apartment Retirement Communities

Abbotswood at Stonehenge
7900 Creedmoor Rd., Raleigh • 847-3202

This retirement community offers independent apartment living. It is designed for the "senior, middle-income adult" and

does not require a large endowment fee. Its monthly membership fee covers the rent for the one- or two-bedroom apartments that includes maid service and all utilities except telephone.

The complex contains 120 units and is located on 10 acres off Creedmoor Road in North Raleigh. The "private quarters" have bedrooms, great rooms, kitchens, storage space and, with the two-bedroom units, two bathrooms. The service at Abbotswood includes a 24-hour security and emergency call system, breakfast and dinner, additional storage space and scheduled transportation. Residents also have access to exercise rooms, activity rooms and a library. There is a Wellness Program that includes a health coordinator who is on duty Monday through Friday and helps residents keep in touch with their family physician, as needed.

Durham Regent
3007 Pickett Rd., Durham • 490-6224
Durham Regent offers apartment living with month-to-month rent and no buy-in fees or leases. It is owned and managed by Holiday Retirement Corporation. Utilities are included in the monthly rent and residents are provided three meals a day, weekly housekeeping and free local transportation.

Apartment Retirement Communities Offering Assisted Living

The Heritage of Raleigh
5950 Falls of Neuse Rd. • 873-2400
Reserve your space at The Heritage, Raleigh's newest luxury rental retirement community, which offers a maintenance-free lifestyle with all the familiar comforts

of home. Spacious studio, and one- and two-bedroom apartments are available for one affordable monthly fee. Amenities include a dining room, indoor swimming pool, on-site health clinic, housekeeping services, scheduled transportation, library, billiards room, full-service bank, 24-hour concierge service, and fitness and exercise programs.

Independence Village
3113 Charles B. Root Wynd, Raleigh • 781-8226

This monthly rental community offers apartments and assisted living facilities. It opened in 1990 and is 1/2 mile from Rex Hospital off Duraleigh Road in Raleigh. Within walking distance of Olde Raleigh Village, it contains 165 units with a choice of studio, one- and two-bedrooms.

Independence Village provides meal service along with a variety of activities. The community also has a crafts room, beauty salon and barber shop, library and a billiard room. Scheduled transportation is included in the monthly rental fee. The fees vary based upon the size of the unit, but in general are very reasonable. Although there is a waiting list, the community usually can accommodate a new resident within a year.

Woodland Terrace
300 Kildaire Woods Dr., Cary • 465-0356

Located in the heart of Cary, Woodland Terrace is a full-service retirement community that provides a variety of amenities geared to today's seniors. Independent living, assisted living and Alzheimer's care are available here. Spacious cottages and apartments surround the community lake, giving the 22-acre campus the appearance of a small Southern town. Amenities include weekly housekeeping, maintenance, scheduled transportation to shopping and medical appointments, an optional laundry service, a beauty salon, a barber shop and coordination of home health services.

Assisted Living Facilities

Brighton Gardens
3101 Duraleigh Rd., Raleigh • 571-1123

A Marriott assisted living community, Brighton Gardens offers 115 residential suites, meals, planned social activities, weekly housekeeping and scheduled transportation. An on-site center provides specialized care for residents with Alzheimer's.

Carolina House of Cary
111 MacArthur Dr., Cary • 460-5959
Carolina House of Chapel Hill
100 Lanark Rd., Chapel Hill • 918-7600
Carolina House of Wake Forest
611 S. Brooks St., Wake Forest • 562-8400

The three Carolina Houses provide assisted living in a comfortable, caring residential atmosphere. Private studios and suites are available. A monthly fee includes all meals, housekeeping and daily assistance. The facilities also offer The Discovery Program, a self-contained, state-of-the-art Alzheimer's and memory-impaired care program. Carolina House is locally owned and operated by Southern Assisted Living, Inc.

Chancellor Gardens of Durham
4434 Ben Franklin Blvd., Durham • 479-9966

Chancellor Gardens is a recently opened assisted living community located near Durham Regional Hospital. The three-story brick building, which encloses a beautiful courtyard, contains 96 studio and one- and two-bedroom apartments. A licensed nurse is on site 24 hours a day. Residents enjoy a state-of-the-art fitness program, nutrition counseling and regular health screenings. Amenities include an elegant dining room, formal living room, gift shop, ice cream parlor and library. Chancellor Gardens also provides customized programs for residents living with Alzheimer's disease or a related memory disorder.

Alterra Clare Bridge of Cary
7870 Chapel Hill Rd., Cary • 852-1355
Alterra Clare Bridge of Chapel Hill
2230 Farmington Dr., Chapel Hill • 929-5850

Clare Bridge provides specialized assisted living for memory impaired residents in a homelike environment. Licensed nurses are available 24 hours a day. Clare Bridge also offers nutritious and well-balanced meals and snacks, ongoing health care monitoring, life enrichment programs, housekeeping and personal laundry and linen services. Both facilities are owned by Alterra Healthcare Corporation.

Heartfields Assisted Living at Cary
1050 Crescent Green Dr. • 852-5757

Heartfields offers assisted living with personalized services in a residential setting. Amenities include 75 spacious suites, transportation, on-site worship, wellness programs and meals. Nurses are on-site 24 hours a day. The separate HeartHaven program serves residents with Alzheimer's and related memory disorders.

Manorhouse
801 Dixie Tr., Raleigh • 828-5557

This facility opened in 1991 in a landscaped, central location at the intersection of Wade Avenue and Dixie Trail. It is close to Rex Hospital, North Carolina State University and the State Fairground complex. Manorhouse offers adult care, including dining, housekeeping, 24-hour-a-day licensed nurses, activity and exercise rooms, as well as scheduled transportation, on-site worship and an active schedule of things to do, from walking tours to bingo to crafts and other classes.

Meadowbrook Manor of Durham
5935 Mt. Sinai Rd., Durham • 489-2361
Meadowbrook Terrace of Raleigh
4510 Duraleigh Rd., Raleigh • 781-6605

Both Triangle Meadowbrook locations offer complete assisted living services, providing peace of mind for seniors and their families. Meadowbrook features affordable monthly rates, private rooms, housekeeping and laundry services, dining, transportation and on-site worship. An on-site Alzheimer's Special Care Program provides specialized care for residents with Alzheimer's or related memory impairment.

Outlook Pointe at Northridge
600 Newton Rd., Raleigh • 848-4906

Outlook Pointe provides assisted living in a comfortable, home-like environment. Amenities include 24-hour assistance, a wellness program, transportation and on-site worship services. Outlook Pointe's "Keepsakes" Program is designed for residents with Alzheimer's and related memory disorders.

Shepherd House Assisted Living
405 Smith Level Rd., Carrboro
• 929-7859

Shepherd House, which opened during the summer of 1998, offers a variety of services for seniors in Orange County. Amenities include well-balanced meals, transportation, shopping trips, daily scheduled activities, housekeeping services and on-site worship.

Alterra Sterling House
1110 Falls River Ave., Raleigh
• 844-9747

Opened in the summer of 1999, Sterling House provides a wide range of specially tailored services to meet the needs of its residents. Amenities include all nutritious meals, personal and medical assistance, emergency call systems, on-site worship, laundry and linen services, and housekeeping. Sterling House is owned by Alterra Healthcare Corporation.

Sunrise
4801 Edwards Mill Rd., Raleigh
• 787-0777

Sunrise is a national company founded in 1981 in Fairfax, Virginia. Its Raleigh facility, which overlooks Crabtree Valley Mall, opened in 1996. The attractive, small-scale complexes continue to win architectural awards and feature billiard rooms, libraries and rocking chairs on the front porch. Sunrise communities provide housekeeping services, dining facilities and nursing care. Sunrise also offers specialized programs for residents with memory disorders.

Willow Springs Rest Home and Retirement Center
624 Jones Ferry Rd., Carrboro
• 968-3072

This 120-bed retirement home offers assisted care for its residents. It provides 24-hour care and offers a range of services and activities: housekeeping, transportation, exercise classes and bingo. There are private and semiprivate rooms.

Alterra Wynwood of Chapel Hill
2220 Farmington Dr., Chapel Hill
• 933-1430

Wynwood offers assisted living through a variety of programs, including customized care programs. Residents receive individualized assistance with their unscheduled needs 24 hours a day, even as their needs change. Meals, housekeeping and personal laundry and linen services are included. Wynwood is equipped with a comprehensive emergency response system. The facility is owned by Alterra Healthcare Corporation.

Nursing Homes

The Brian Center
6000 Fayetteville Rd., Durham
• 544-9021

The Brian Center Health & Retirement Home of Durham provides skilled, intermediate and assisted-living care. It offers rehabilitation services in the areas of physical therapy, occupational therapy and speech therapy.

Carver Living Center
321 E. Carver St., Durham • 471-3558

Carver Living Center is a 120-bed nursing care facility with a solid local reputation. It has private and semiprivate rooms. There is a licensed geriatric nurse practitioner available and primary care physicians from Duke Medical Center on call. It also offers rehabilitation therapy for residents who need only short-term nursing care before returning home.

Rex Convalescent Care Center
4210 Lake Boone Tr., Raleigh • 782-6600

This 140-bed facility is part of Rex Healthcare's total system and opened in 1991. It is located on the Rex campus and provides assisted living and nursing care, including physical, speech and occupational therapy. Its medical director is on call 24 hours a day. While most of the residents are age 65 or older, it does have younger tenants. Proximity to the hospital campus and its various specialities makes Rex Convalescent Care Center especially convenient (see "Rex Healthcare" write-up in our "Health Care" chapter).

Special Services and Activities

As our population grays, the services and activities available for seniors are growing in quality and quantity.

Adult Day Care

Adult day care is a concept that is growing in popularity and provides seniors with supervision, meals and activities Monday through Friday. Call Resources for Seniors at 872-7933 for more information.

Fifty Plus

P.O. Box 51277, Durham, NC 27717
• 493-5900

Fifty Plus is a monthly tabloid produced by AdVenture Publishing, Inc., for the Triangle. As the name suggests, it is aimed at those readers who are 50 years old and counting and it is a good source for information. Fifty Plus features articles on travel, health and wellness, finance and local profiles—plus a monthly calendar of events such as support group meetings, AARP chapter meetings, senior citizen center activities, entertainment and much more.

Home Health Care

Home health care is a fast growing service nationwide because it allows seniors to stay independent and in their own homes longer. In-Home Care, Inc., is a joint venture by Baptist Homes and Presbyterian Homes of North Carolina. For more information, call (888) 446-4663.

Senior Living

P.O. Box 31763, Raleigh, NC 27622
• 254-3603

A resource magazine for seniors, Senior Living contains feature articles, a summary of retirement community types, directories of area retirement communities and other valuable resources and hotline numbers.

Raleigh

As a capital city, Raleigh has a number of statewide services to help retired and senior citizens. Check the Department of Human Resources—Division of Aging, 693 Palmer Drive, 733-3983, for more information. The City of Raleigh also has a very active life for senior citizens, starting with its RSVP program, 831-6295. This is a good way for you to meet some very interesting people and do some good deeds such as reading news accounts over the Radio Reading Service for blind listeners. RSVP also sponsors the Foster Grandparents Program.

If you like dancing and card playing, there's a group that regularly meets at the city's Golden Years Association at Pullen Park's Activity Center. Yes, there's a Meals on Wheels program in Wake County, too, 833-1749.

There are two AARP chapters in Raleigh and the Resources For Seniors is another good place to start for information on services as well as nursing homes. For a listing of community services and telephone numbers of the preceding, check the front of the telephone book under Community Services numbers.

Durham

The Parks and Recreation Department, 560-4355, provides a variety of activities of interest to senior citizens, including exercise classes, square dances, field trips and social clubs. The Durham Council for Senior Citizens can be reached at 688-8247.

The Duke Institute for Learning and Retirement, located at Duke University, offers a variety of senior-oriented courses. Call 684-2703 for more information on class schedules and rates.

Chapel Hill

Both the Chapel Hill Parks and Recreation Department and the Carrboro Recreation and Parks Department sponsor special activities for senior citizens. There is an AARP chapter in Orange County as well as a number of volunteer opportunities including RSVP, 968-2054, and SCORE, 967-7075. Four Senior Centers offer a variety of activities: Chapel Hill Senior Center, 968-2070; South Orange County Senior Center, 968-2080; Carrboro Senior Center, 968-2075; and Hillsborough Senior Center, 732-8181.

Whether it's the trash being picked up on time or fire truck response time, the quality of utilities and services ranks high.

Utilities and Services

The Triangle is a place that works. Whether it's the trash and recycling being picked up on time or the fastest fire truck response time in the state, the quality of utilities and services ranks high. In Raleigh, for example, the garbage is picked up twice a week, yard waste is picked up once a week and the recycling truck stops every other week. This is not a trashy place.

Here is where you will find the information for those things you have to do to set up house: get the water, electricity and gas turned on; take that new, "beautiful you" picture for your North Carolina driver's license; buy tags for the pets and car; and call the cable guy. We also tell you where to go to register to vote. After all, Insiders are always good citizens.

ABC Laws

In North Carolina, the state controlled Alcoholic Beverage Commission operates ABC stores, outlets where liquor is purchased. ABC stores are open from 9 AM to 7 PM Monday through Saturday. You can buy beer and wine at most supermarkets and convenience stores seven days a week, but keep in mind that alcoholic beverages may not be purchased on Sunday until noon. You must be at least 21 years of age to purchase beer, wine and liquor in North Carolina.

Liquor by the drink is available at many restaurants throughout the Triangle. State laws prohibit the establishment of facilities open to the public designed only for imbibing spirits; therefore, places that serve alcohol must also serve food.

Voters in each county and municipality in North Carolina decide if alcoholic beverages will be available and in what fashion. For example, in rural Chatham County just south of Chapel Hill, you can sip beer and wine in several restaurants, but liquor is illegal.

North Carolina has stiff Driving While Impaired (DWI) laws. If your blood alcohol concentration reads 0.08 percent on the Breathalyzer test and you are convicted of DWI, there is a mandatory revocation of your license for one year. You will also spend at least one night in jail, be required to pay a fine and perform community service. Restaurant owners and hosts of private parties can be held liable if someone drinking at their place has an accident involving property damage, personal injury or death.

Automobile Information

Driver's License

If you're moving to North Carolina, you have 30 days in which to get a license after establishing residency. You must apply in person at the nearest driver's license office. Appointments may be made but are not necessary. If you already have a license, you will be asked to take written, road sign recognition and vision tests. A road test may be required. The tests are not difficult, but it helps to first read over the North Carolina DMV Driver's Handbook. It is available at all driver's license offices. Take cash ($10-$20) to the office. In-state personal checks printed with the correct name and address are accepted at most locations, but call first. Licenses are good for five years and expire on your birthday.

FYI

Unless otherwise noted, the area code for all phone numbers listed in this guide is 919.

Cary
211 N. Academy St. • 468-0319
Raleigh
4004 District Dr. • 733-4540
6081 Capital Blvd. • 850-2892
Durham
101 S. Miami Blvd. • 560-6896
Homestead Market Shop. Ctr. • 560-3378
Chapel Hill/Carrboro
Carrboro Plaza Ctr. • 929-4161

The Division of Motor Vehicles provides a 24-hour, seven days a week telephone service, DMV *directAccess*. Just dial 715-7000 for information regarding driver's licenses, vehicle registrations and insurance requirements.

Auto Plates

New residents must register their motor vehicle within 30 days of moving to North Carolina. Plates cost $25. Motorists can obtain plates and renewal decals by mail. For an extra $20, the state also

permits "vanity" plates so you can put your name, message (keep it clean!) or favorite number on your plate.

Newcomers also have to obtain a N.C. title ($35) for their car and registration, which usually ranges from $40 to $150, but can cost more. Before your auto can be registered, you must provide a title to the vehicle, your insurance company's name and a policy number, an odometer reading and photo identification. You must also complete a title transfer application and have it notarized, so don't forget to bring cash for the Notary Public. Applications are available at the plate office. The State Division of Motor Vehicles (DMV) is headquartered in Raleigh at 1100 New Bern Avenue, 733-3025, and there are offices throughout the Triangle where tags can be purchased.

Raleigh
North Hills Shopping Ctr. • 781-4967
Cary
South Hills Mall • 469-1444
Durham
Northgate Shopping Mall • 286-4908
1920 N.C. 55 • 544-6607
Chapel Hill
University Mall • 967-7059

Auto Safety Inspections

Safety inspections are required 10 days after initial plates are purchased and on an annual basis thereafter. Inspections are done at service stations, automobile dealerships and vehicle repair garages licensed by the state. Because of varying

INSIDERS' TIP

When you go to get your driver's license, call ahead to make sure you have the exact documents and method of payment required. The only way to avoid a line is to be at the door when the office opens.

requirements, they should be done in the county in which your vehicle is registered.

Auto Tax

Within a few months of registering the vehicle, owners will receive a personal property tax bill from the county showing an assessment on the vehicle's value. Property tax bills are collected by the county in which your vehicle is registered. Call for more information.

Wake County • 856-5400
Durham County • 560-0380
Orange County • 732-8181

Pet Regulations

Raleigh

Pet owners are required to purchase tags for their dogs and cats. You can obtain these through the mail. The tags are issued once you show evidence that your pet has had a rabies shot. Neutered animals are cheaper than non-neutered to encourage residents to help reduce the stray dog and cat population. The pet tags must be renewed annually and can be obtained at City Hall, 222 W. Hargett Street; call 890-3200. For stray dogs or cats to be picked up, call 831-6311. The city also has a leash law for dogs, although your pooch is not likely to get picked up unless it becomes a nuisance. If your dog does get collared, you can retrieve him from the SPCA kennel on U.S. 70 S. in Garner.

Cary

Cary requires licenses for dogs and cats. The onetime license fee for neutered pets is $10. For non-neutered pets the fee is $20. For information on pet licenses, call the Cary Town Hall at 469-4052.

Durham

When you list your personal and real estate property holdings with the city and county tax offices, you will be asked if you own a dog. If you do, you will be assessed a licensing fee. Dogs are also required to have all the appropriate shots, including a current rabies vaccination. There is a yearly fee for cats as well, which drops dramatically when your cat is neutered. You can call the animal control department at 560-0630.

Chapel Hill

Chapel Hill ordinances require dog leashes, tags and rabies vaccination. All dogs must be leashed, in a vehicle or in an enclosure when off the dog owner's property. Dogs and cats older than 4 months must have a current rabies vaccination. Dogs older than 3 months are required to have current dog tags ($3 for neutered or under 9 months; $5 for all others). For more information, call the Orange County Animal Shelter at 967-7383.

Recycling Information

Raleigh

All Raleigh homeowners have curbside recycling service twice a month. The city collects aluminum, newspapers, glass, and plastic milk jugs and soft drink bottles. Check with your neighbors to learn which week and which day is your pickup day and call the city's Sanitation Division, 831-6522, to obtain your green recycling container.

The city also manages eight drop-off sites for apartment dwellers and those not currently served by curbside pickup. The county maintains additional sites at various schools in the city and county. Reynolds Aluminum also operates a center at which you can take your aluminum cans for reimbursement and BFI operates a recycling facility, The Recyclery, at Eastridge Commerce Park off U.S. 64 E., at which tours are conducted. The city also offers certain days per year when it accepts hazardous wastes such as engine

TRIANGLE SERVICES & UTILITIES

Service	Name	Area Serviced	Telephone #
Electric Power	Carolina Power & Light	Raleigh/Cary	508-5400
	Duke Power Company	Durham	382-3200
	Duke Power Company	Chapel Hill	967-8231
Natural Gas	Public Service Gas Co.	Triangle	877-776-2427
Water and Sewer	City of Raleigh	Raleigh	890-3245
	Town of Cary	Cary	469-4050
	City of Durham	Durham	560-4411
	OWASA	Chapel Hill	968-4421
Telephone	BellSouth	Raleigh/Cary	780-2355
	BellSouth	Chapel Hill	780-2355
	GTE South	Durham	800-483-4300
Cable Television	Time Warner Cable	Raleigh	832-2225
	Time Warner Cable	Cary	467-2800
	Time Warner Cable	Durham	220-4481
	Time Warner Cable	Chapel Hill	968-4631
Cellular Telephone	GTE Wireless	All Areas	800-727-CELL
	ALLTEL	All Areas	233-3000

oil, old paint, pesticides and pet flea collars at designated drop-off sites.

For information about Wake County solid waste reduction programs that promote reuse and/or increase recycling, contact the Wake County Solid Waste Management Division at 831-6522.

Cary

Cary's award-winning recycling program is a leader in recycling rates, participation rates and the variety of materials recycled. Much of the town's solid waste is diverted from landfills through curb-side recycling, yard waste composting, drop-off center recycling and town departmental recycling efforts. The participation rate in the curbside program is estimated to be 99 percent with more than half of all eligible residents setting out recyclable materials each week.

Cary is unique among its Triangle neighbors in the variety of materials collected in its curbside program. These include aluminum cans, steel cans, clear glass, brown glass, green glass, plastic bottles (#1, #2, #5 and #7), newspapers, glossy magazines, corrugated cardboard, milk and juice cartons, drink boxes, six-pack rings, aluminum foil and aluminum pie plates. The town also provides fall leaf collection and weekly yard waste collection for composting.

Cary operates a recycling drop-off center for apartment and condominium residents. Items collected at the Citizens Convenience Center on North Dixon Avenue include aluminum cans, steel cans, newspapers, glossy magazines, corrugated cardboard and #1 and #2 plastic bottles. In addition, the town's Public Works Department collects motor oil, phone books and Christmas trees for recycling. Contact the Town of Cary Recycling Program at 469-4387 for more information.

Durham County

Durham residents recycle newspaper, glass bottles and jars, steel and tin food cans, aluminum beverage cans, soft drink and other #1 plastic bottles, and milk jugs and other #2 plastic bottles at curbside. If you live within the city limits, call Durham's Solid Waste Management Department, 560-4185, to obtain a bin and collection information. Additional recycling services include collections at 30 Durham apartment complexes, Durham Public School System buildings, North Carolina Central University and over 200 area businesses.

Durham County residents have curbside service provided every other week by Tidewater Fiber. If you live in the county, call Tidewater Fiber, 680-4150, to obtain a bin and a collection calendar.

Tidewater Fiber also manages 19 public drop-off sites in Durham that accept the same items recyclable through the curbside service. In addition, glossy magazines are collected at 10 sites, mixed paper at five sites and corrugated cardboard at seven sites.

Orange County

Orange Community Recycling provides weekly curbside recycling of newspapers, glossy magazines, glass bottles and jars, aluminum and steel cans, plastic soda and other #1 bottles and milk and other #2 bottles to all single family residences and most apartment complexes within the town limits of Carrboro, Chapel Hill and Hillsborough. The same service is provided on a bi-weekly basis to roughly one-half of the

homes in the unincorporated area of the county.

There are 13 drop-off recycling locations throughout the county that collect the same materials as curbside, plus corrugated cardboard, aluminum foil and pie plates, paper milk cartons and juice boxes, other plastic bottles and six-pack rings. Six of the drop-off sites are at staffed solid waste centers with restricted hours and seven are unstaffed 24-hour recycling sites. Waste oil, car batteries, latex paint and hazardous waste are handled separately.

For more information from Orange Community Recycling, call 968-2788.

Taxes

No Triangle municipality has an income tax. The state does have an income tax that has a 7 percent cap. The state's sales tax is 4 cents and all counties have the option to tack on an additional 2 cents. All do; so the rate is 6 cents per dollar of merchandise. Local governments raise money primarily through the property tax. This tax is levied against real estate as well as personal property, so renters have to pay personal property taxes (on such items as automobiles) just as homeowners do. If you live in the county, you pay only the county property tax.

Raleigh

If you live in Raleigh, you pay both the city and the county property tax. The tax rate for Wake County (per $100 assessed value) is 0.63 cents; the city rate is 0.5250 cents. A Raleigh resident with a house assessed at $100,000 can expect to pay a combined property tax bill of about $1,155 annually. Property is reevaluated every eight years.

Cary

Cary residents pay Wake County taxes at the 0.63 rate and Cary town taxes at the rate of 0.54 per $100 assessed value.

Understanding Piedmont Political Processes

As North Carolina's Capitol City, politics play a big part of Raleigh's life and by proximity, the Triangle. The late Terry Sanford, for example, was not only governor for one term, but he later served as president of Duke University and then U.S. Senator from Durham. In between, he ran for president. And he was a UNC Law School graduate.

We assume that anyone who reads also wants to be a good citizen, so here's the deal: North Carolina elects its governor in presidential election years, every four years. Until the 1990s, North Carolina was the only state in the union that had not given its governor the veto. Now he has it as well as permission to run for a second term. All state legislators, members of the Senate as well as the House, must run for office every two years and elections are held in even years, e.g. 1998. The power in the House is in the Speaker's office; in the Senate where the Lt. Governor presides, the real power is in the Senate Majority leader's position. The people who run county government, the boards of commissioners, run in partisan elections every four years. Judges are also elected, although the length of their terms differ. The lowest court is the District Court; then Superior Court which takes on serious crimes such as murder and defacing an *Insider's Guide*; then comes the Court of Appeals and best and last, the Supremes. (Incidentally, Insiders know that If you want to see Supreme Court justices at lunch, you can often catch Chief Justice Burley Mitchell holding court at Ms. Leah Levine's Upstairs Restaurant on Wilmington Street.)

Photo by Tim Johnson

State Capitol

Local municipal elections in the Triangle are held in odd years, e.g. 1999, and are nonpartisan, although some candidates have tried to make them partisan in recent years, especially in Raleigh municipal elections. Most cities allow their councillors four year, staggered terms; Raleigh's mayor and councillors, however, must face the voters every two years. School Board elections are also nonpartisan and members serve four year, staggered terms. Wake County has one county-wide district as does Durham. Chapel Hill and Carrboro share one school system. There is a flaw in the system in regard to school boards and county commissioners. School leaders, who generally holler for more money to meet parent demands, cannot levy local taxes for schools; that responsibility falls to the county commissioners who look at tax increases the way Dracula fears daylight. This can make for embarrassing shouting matches between school leaders and county office holders.

If you want to see politics in action, spend a day in the halls of the General Assembly when it's in session. You can also introduce yourself to some of the state's capital press corps who have offices on the first floor. They're the scruffy bunch over in the corner in the House and Senate chambers. The cafeteria serves Southern fare, and the food is cheap. If you want to ask Governor Hunt a question, attend one of his press conferences, usually weekly, in the Administration Building on Jones Street. And if you want to get involved at the grass roots level, show up at your neighborhood's annual party precinct meeting and tell them you're a generous contributor or stop by state party headquarters in Raleigh. Both the Democratic and Republic parties maintain offices on Hillsborough Street.

Durham

If you live anywhere inside the Durham city limits, you have to pay a city property tax in addition to the county property tax. Check with a real estate agent, map or the county tax office to determine exactly what rate applies to you. Current rates for the county, per $100 assessed value, are 0.9497 cents; additional city taxes are assessed at 0.68 cents per $100. The rates are subject to change each summer.

Chapel Hill

If you live within the town limits of Chapel Hill and Carrboro, you will pay property tax to those municipalities in addition to the property tax you pay to the county. Tax rates in 1998 were assessed at 0.9105 cents per $100 value for Orange County; an additional 0.538 cents per $100 for Chapel Hill residents and an additional 0.660 cents per $100 value for Carrboro residents. Hillsborough is an additional 0.50 cents per $100. There is also a school district tax to supplement state funding for the Chapel Hill-Carrboro schools. Motor vehicles are subject to a 3 percent highway use tax, which is billed annually. The minimum tax is $40 and the maximum tax is $1,500.

Voter Registration

Don't forget to register to vote. To register, you must be a U.S. citizen, a non-felon, at least 18 years of age by the date of the upcoming election and a resident of North Carolina and your precinct

for 30 days prior to the next election. You can register at various locations, including your local library, by simply showing some identification that contains your permanent, local address. You may also register at the local board of elections in your community or at any bureau of the Division of Motor Vehicles while doing business there. Once registered, you will receive a postcard from the board confirming that you are a registered voter and the location of your polling place. Call your local board for more information on specific requirements and voter registration sites.

Raleigh and Cary
Wake County Board of Elections
339 S. Salisbury St. • 856-6240

Durham
Durham County Board of Elections
200 E. Main St., 3rd Floor • 560-0700

Chapel Hill and Carrboro
Orange County Board of Elections
110 E. King St., Hillsborough
• 732-8181, Ext. 2350

Human Services Numbers

The current editions of local BellSouth and GTE phone books include comprehensive listings of human services in the front pages. The numbers range from crisis hotlines, family planning, mental and physical health services, to senior citizens', veterans' and women's services.

Preparing Leaders Through Educational Excellence

A Nurturing Environment   Advanced Placement Courses
Excellent Teachers   After-school Care
Small Classes   Honor Code
Arts & Technology   SACS Accreditation
Chapel   Competitive Sports
Convenient Locations   100% College Acceptance Rate

St. Timothy's & Hale
Co-educational Episcopal Day Schools, K-12

St. Timothy's Lower School (K-4)   St. Timothy's-Hale School (5-12)
4523 Six Forks Road   3400 White Oak Road
Raleigh, NC 27609   Raleigh, NC 27609
Mrs. Cathy Clement: (919) 781-0531   Mr. Chris Kelley: (919) 782-3331

Schools and Child Care

The Triangle area offers parents a mixed blessing when it comes to schools for their children. Although the schools are some of the best in the state, many are bulging at the seams with ever-increasing enrollments. With private schools, magnet schools and the new state-sanctioned charter schools supplementing public school, education for children continues to be a popular issue and one that parents need to look at closely.

School construction has been a priority in the area and every effort is being made to include plans for building new schools as new subdivisions are built.

The State Department of Public Instruction sets the curriculum and students are tested at the end of each school year. The state also provides most of the funding for the public schools, with each county contributing a portion of the property taxes collected.

Even though Wake County is the largest school system in the Triangle, a tremendous increase in enrollments forced attendance at several schools to be capped for the 1997-98 school year. Durham and Orange counties have not experienced such an influx of new students, but are keeping a close eye on enrollments.

This chapter gives information on public schools, private schools, after-school programs, preschools and day-care programs, with a town listing under each category.

Public Schools

Wake County Schools

The Wake County Public School System, which was formed in 1976 with the merger of the former City of Raleigh and Wake County School System, serves the entire county, including Raleigh, Cary, Apex, Fuquay-Varina, Garner, Holly Springs, Knightdale, Morrisville, Rolesville, Wake Forest, Wendell and Zebulon. Wake County students consistently score above national norms and individual schools within the system have earned national recognition for their cutting edge programs. In fact, the Wake County School System is the best successfully integrated large city system in the country.

With an enrollment that reached 93,000 students in the fall of 1998, the Wake County School System is the second-largest system in the state and the 37th largest in the nation. The school system contains 107 schools and employs over 6,000 teachers, resulting in a teacher-student ratio of about 1 to 23.

Wake County students averaged 1052 on their 1998 SAT scores, which is 35 points above the national average and 70 points higher than the state average. Of the 4,091 graduates in the class of '97, over 85 percent planned to pursue higher education. The school system also produced

Photo by Tim Johnson

Built in 1929, Needham Broughton High School was the first major work of William Henley Dietrick, one of North Carolina's foremost architects.

61 National Merit semifinalists in 1997. The 1997 end-of-grade tests given to 8th graders statewide also showed Wake students well above the state average: 83.3 in reading and 79.0 in math.

In Wake County, school assignment for most students is based on the home address of the student's parent or legal guardian. The Wake County School System is evaluating redistricting options once again in an effort to accommodate population growth, so expect more changes in the coming year.

The Wake County School System includes 35 magnet schools that draw students from all over the county. Through the magnet program, parents can select schools that emphasize a curriculum that best fits their child's talents. However, you must first register your child at his or her base school and then apply for admission to a more specialized school. For more information about magnet schools, call the Student Assignment Office at 850-1921.

Magnet schools offer a number of options:

1. Gifted and Talented (GT) K-8 schools offer courses in English, math, science, social studies and a variety of electives that emphasize the basics but include computer studies, foreign languages and fine arts. There are 11 Elementary GT and 3 Middle School programs. Enloe High School in east Raleigh is designated as a GT magnet, offering students a chance to concentrate in special fields such as mathematics, biology, chemistry, the humanities, art, music and drama.

2. The Classical Studies program, which emphasizes basic courses and basic education skills, is located at Raleigh's Aldert Root Elementary.

3. International Studies are offered at Wiley Elementary School. In addition to the basic courses, the school offers electives in foreign languages and the study of world cultures.

4. The Language Arts/Communication magnet, which concentrates on skills in language arts, is located at Joyner Elementary.

5. Year-round programs are offered at West Lake, Oak Grove, Durant Road, Green, Jones Dairy, Timber Drive and Morrisville elementary schools and West Lake and Durant Road middle schools. The school system is planning to convert

two additional schools into year-round facilities for the 1999-2000 school year: Adams Elementary in Cary and Lufkin Middle in Apex. Application must be made to attend the year-round schools and slots are filled through a lottery. Year-round schools do not serve a base population, so you can't guarantee attendance by the location of your home. Year-round schools are intended to make better use of the facilities and increase each student's retention.

6. Extended-day magnets are located at Combs, Joyner and Olds elementary schools in Raleigh and provide before- and after-school supervision. Essentially functioning as day care for students, the programs offer instruction in arts, sports, music, industrial arts, etc., rather than baby-sitting. Monthly fees are $130 for a family's first child enrolled, $125 for the second child and $120 for the third child.

7. Creative Arts and Sciences, which is offered at Bugg Elementary, emphasizes instruction in visual arts, music, dance and theater and provides hands-on lab work.

8. The Montessori method of teaching is offered at Poe Elementary.

9. The Community Model magnet at Lincoln Heights Elementary features reduced class sizes. The average K-2 classroom has 15 students and the average 3 to 5 classroom has 18 students.

10. The Pre-International Baccalaureate Program, which is offered at East Millbrook Middle, provides a rigorous and challenging curriculum that focuses on global education, verbal and written communication and intercultural awareness.

11. Accelerated Studies at Southeast Raleigh High features innovative teaching, unique learning opportunities and academic support.

The Wake County School Board requires more credits in the basics such as English, mathematics, science and history. The state requires all students to pass a competency test of basic skills before they are awarded a diploma. The board, however, has attracted national attention with experimental programs such as the Writing to Read Program, which uses computers to help students develop writing skills at an early age and become familiar with computers. All middle schools also have computer labs and courses for students to learn about computers. Students have Internet access through an on-line service donated by the Raleigh *News & Observer*.

The high schools that serve Raleigh and Cary students offer a broad range of courses, including foreign languages and higher mathematics.

As befits a large system, special programs are available for handicapped children, including educable mentally retarded and seriously emotionally and learning-disabled children. Project Enlightenment is an acclaimed service of the system that offers family therapy as well as individual therapy for young children, parents and teachers.

Dr. Jim Surratt is the superintendent of the Wake County School System.

FYI

Unless otherwise noted, the area code for all phone numbers listed in this guide is 919.

**For More Information
Wake County Public School System
850-1600**

Durham

The Durham Public School System, which was created in 1992 through a merger of the former city and county school systems, enrolls approximately 29,000 students in 27 elementary schools (K-5), nine middle schools (6-8), five senior high schools (9-12) and a school program for hospitalized students. Four of the schools operate as year-round programs: Easley, Eastway, Holt and Pearsontown.

The Durham Public Schools offer excellent educational and recreational opportunities and have a reputation for innovative programs and stringent academic standards. Graduation requirements exceed state standards and include computer education and additional math and science courses. The system enforces the state's toughest academic standards on student athletes.

The student-teacher ratio is 26:1 for elementary and middle schools and 28:1 for high schools. Over 40 percent of the system's teachers hold advanced degrees. Approximately 85 percent of Durham high school graduates continue their educational studies.

Strong funding for the school district translates into a variety of innovative programs. For example, the school system expanded the state's definition of "academically gifted" with a local program for elementary students who are gifted in the arts and communication.

In addition, the system employs special academic programs for gifted, handicapped and learning-disabled students in grades K to 12. It also provides advanced courses such as Latin and foreign languages in the middle schools, an extensive cultural arts program and sophisticated audiovisual facilities, including cable television instruction to supplement classroom work.

A vocational education program offers instruction in 65 different courses, one of the most comprehensive in the state. The system also provides one of the best individualized services in the state for students with learning disabilities or with physical, emotional, speech, hearing, visual or mental handicaps. A special developmental reading program is available for grades 1 to 5 followed by a supplemental program in basic skills for grades 6 to 8. A number of other programs, including elementary physical education, computer instruction and cultural arts, have been state and national models.

The school system includes eight magnet schools. Because of the high demand, new students are selected by random lottery. Parents must apply in person beginning in January for the following school year. For more information, call 560-3667.

The magnet school program includes the following study areas:

1. Geoworld and Pre-International Baccalaureate: This pre-IB program located at Burton Elementary is designed to prepare students for Shepard Middle School and focuses on communication and research, speech making, debating, foreign language, global geography and current events.

2. Accelerated Model and Biosphere: C.C. Spaulding Elementary offers this program that enhances the basic curriculum by emphasizing the study of the life sciences through the ecosystems and by observing living environments.

3. Humanities: Club Boulevard Magnet School emphasizes thematic studies in children's literature and the arts, with a comprehensive curriculum in writing and research, reading, mathematics, social studies, science and computers.

4. Montessori: This program at Morehead Elementary promotes the development of social skills, emotional growth, physical coordination and cognitive ability while encouraging students to progress at their own rate in multi-age classrooms.

5. Arts/Core Knowledge: R.N. Harris Elementary offers a combined program of arts integration and a specific core studies system designed to give students the advantage of entering each grade level with a solid common base of knowledge.

INSIDERS' TIP

Over 100 area businesses support Durham Public Schools by providing materials, financial assistance and tutors for students.

6. Science and Technology: Y.E. Smith Elementary emphasizes the study of physical sciences through the use of high technology. Areas of study include geology; astronomy; robotics; matter and energy; and light, heat and sound.

7. International Baccalaureate at Shepard Middle School provides a program with emphasis on foreign languages and law, preparing students for the study of the IB program at the high school level.

8. Durham Magnet Center for Visual and Performing Arts currently serves 1,200 students in grades 6 to 11 and will expand through grade 12 by the year 2000. It offers dance, theater, stage craft, photography, creative writing, vocal and instrumental music, as well as piano, strings and guitar.

The Durham Public School System is led by Dr. Ann Denlinger, who became superintendent in 1996.

For more information
Durham Public School System
560-2000

North Carolina School of Science and Mathematics
1219 Broad St. Durham, NC 27705
• 286-3366

Founded in 1980 as the nation's first statewide residential public high school, this unique facility provides exceptional opportunities for 550 high school students in grades 11 and 12 who have a strong interest and potential in science and mathematics. Students live on the 27-acre campus of the former Watts Hospital and School of Nursing. Admission is extremely competitive and the process begins each November.

Chapel Hill-Carrboro

The Chapel Hill-Carrboro School System consistently ranks among the top

Photo by Evelyn Ward

Formerly the Watts Hospital, the N.C. School of Science and Mathematics was founded in 1980 as the country's first statewide residential public high school.

public school systems in North Carolina and the United States, boasting one of the highest average end-of-course and end-of-grade scores in the state. In addition, the system has the lowest dropout rate in the state.

The system enrolls 8,550 students in seven elementary schools (K-5), three middle schools (6-8), two senior high schools (9-12) and a hospital school at UNC Hospitals for inpatients unable to attend school. One of the elementary schools operates as a year-round program.

Although Chapel Hill and Carrboro are separate towns run by two different mayors and town councils, they share one school system. Keep in mind that the boundaries of the Chapel Hill-Carrboro school district are not the same as the Chapel Hill and Carrboro town limits. Therefore, it's possible to live outside of either town and avoid paying city property taxes but still be within the Chapel Hill-Carrboro school system.

The average combined SAT score for Chapel Hill-Carrboro Schools' class of '98 was 1188, the highest in the state. Over 85 percent of the system's graduates continue their formal education.

It's not surprising that the Chapel Hill-Carrboro School System enjoys such an excellent track record. First of all, the system leads the state in per-pupil expenditure. Chapel Hill and Carrboro Schools also benefit from both the relative wealth and higher-than-usual education levels of local residents. With a public school system heavily populated by the sons and daughters of academics and professionals, many award- and scholarship-winning students emerge from the local school system each year.

A well-endowed tax base and parents who are concerned about excellence means that the system can afford to spend money on special programs. Chapel Hill-Carrboro Schools educate a larger-than-average percentage of "exceptional" students, particularly in programs for the academically gifted and learning-disabled. Enrichment programs augment elementary classroom teaching and classes for the "highly gifted" are offered in grades 4 through 8.

Honors courses are available in the language arts, math and sciences in grades 6 to 8, with advanced placement classes available at the high school level. Phillips Middle School is currently operating a model math and science program using computers and lab experiences to increase both faculty and student achievement in those areas. Both Chapel Hill High and East Chapel Hill High offer an impressive array of athletic and extracurricular activities, including team sports ranging from lacrosse and soccer to tennis, golf, football and basketball. East Chapel Hill High opened in 1996.

Dr. Neil Pedersen is the superintendent of the Chapel Hill-Carrboro School System.

Over 6,150 students in northern Orange County, including Hillsborough, are served by the Orange County School System, which contains six elementary schools, two middle schools and one high school. Randy Bridges has been the superintendent since 1997. Call 732-8126 for more information.

**For more information
Chapel Hill-Carrboro School System
967-8211**

Charter Schools

The North Carolina General Assembly passed the Charter Schools Act of 1996 in an effort to create an avenue for parents, teachers and community members to develop new and innovative methods of educating all children within the public school system. Charter schools are essentially deregulated public schools that operate as autonomous schools of choice within a school district.

The State Board of Education is authorized to grant approval of all charter school proposals. If approved by the state, the charter school must sign a contract with the local school board that describes its educational objectives.

A total of 34 North Carolina charter schools began operation for the 1997-98 school year and approximately 29 more opened in the fall of 1998. Here is a list of some of the Triangle charter schools:

Exploris Middle School, 112 South Blount St., Raleigh • 834-4040
Healthy Start Academy, 515 Dowd St., Durham • 956-5599

Opened in 1997 at a cost of $15 million, Cary Academy's 52-acre campus contains six neo-Georgian buildings.

John H. Baker Jr. High School, P.O. Box 550, Raleigh • 856-5929

Magellan Charter School, 9400 Forum Dr., Raleigh • 844-0277

Maureen Joy Charter School (Formerly Durham Community Charter School) 320 Belvin Ave., Durham • 317-1711

New Century Charter School, N.C. 54, Carrboro • 942-7722

Orange County Charter School, 660 Cornelius St., Hillsborough • 644-1965

Sterling Montessori Academy, 202 Treybrooke Dr., Morrisville • 462-8889

The Village Charter School, 630 Weaver Dairy Rd., Chapel Hill • 967-2606

For more information about charter schools, contact the Office of Charter Schools at 715-1730 or the NC Charter School Resource Center at 461-8824.

Private Schools

Raleigh and Cary

The Triangle's private and parochial school tradition is a long one, dating back to Raleigh's early decades when Saint Mary's College was founded in 1842. Wake County offers a diversity of private and parochial school opportunities. Below is a list of some of the private schools and programs located in Raleigh and Cary. Call each school for current tuition.

The Achievement School
400 Cedarview Ct. • 782-5082

The Achievement School is a local private school founded in 1979 to help children with learning disabilities such as dyslexia and attention deficit disorder. The school offers children in grades 1 through 12 a highly structured program with close personal and positive teaching. With a total enrollment of 110, the school offers a favorable 1:4 teacher-pupil ratio. The accredited school offers half- and full-day instruction in a wide range of courses, including the basics—language and mathematics—as well as computers, art, physical education, science, drama and foreign languages.

Cardinal Gibbons High School
1401 Edwards Mill Rd. • 834-1625

Cardinal Gibbons is Raleigh's only Catholic high school, providing coed

Area High Schools Make Strides

Triangle public high schools have established a tradition of academic and athletic excellence. Magnet schools, vocational programs, advanced placement courses, honors classes and extracurricular activities are just a few of the many options available to students in the Wake, Durham and Chapel Hill-Carrboro school systems.

High schools in the **Wake County Public School System** have made great strides over the past decade and the district's average Scholastic Assessment Test (SAT) scores currently rank second among all state school districts. **Athens Drive** High School (233-4050) has shown the greatest gains: The school's average 1998 SAT score was 1,050, up 52 points since 1993. Athens Drive serves 1,800 students and features a community library, child development center, peer mediation program and courses in English as a Second Language. The Jaguars finished second in the 4A state baseball championships in 1998.

Broughton High School (856-7810), which opened its doors in 1929, is Wake County's oldest high school. The school's 1,600 students can take advantage of a career center, two endowed teaching chairs and one of only two Air Force/Junior ROTC programs in the country. Students scored an average of 1,084 on their 1998 SATs. The Caps were state champions in women's soccer, golf and men's tennis, and captured second place in the 1997-98 4A Wachovia Cup, which honors the best overall interscholastic athletic performance.

Built in the 1960s, **Enloe** High School (856-7918) in east Raleigh is now a "Gifted and Talented" magnet school, offering nearly 2,400 students an opportunity to concentrate in fields such as math, biology, chemistry, the humanities, art, music and drama. The Eagles' average SAT score (1,127 in 1998) consistently ranks at the top of the Wake County School System. The school was ranked among the top 100 high schools in the country in a 1998 *Newsweek* magazine survey.

Leesville Road High School (870-4250) opened its doors in 1993 and currently serves approximately 1,800 students. It is part of the Leesville campus, which includes an elementary and a middle school. The three schools share two gyms, an auditorium and a theater. Leesville Road students averaged 1,083 on their 1998 SAT scores. The school has four networked computer labs, an automated media center and a fully functional television studio. For the second time in three years, the Pride won the 4A Wachovia Cup in 1997-98. They were state champions in men's soccer and track.

Millbrook High School (850-8787), which opened in 1967, offers a strong academic curriculum for its 2,000 students. The school has a career center; new fine arts, science and vocational wings; and a new media center, gym and cafeteria. Students averaged 1,011 on their 1998 SATs. The Wildcats finished second in the 1997-98 state 4A golf championship.

Built in 1968, **Sanderson** High School (881-4800), which is North Raleigh's oldest high school, serves approximately 1,800 students. The school boasts a high percentage of North Carolina scholars. About 82 percent of the graduating class pursues further education. Sanderson also features a 4-year curriculum in Air Force ROTC, a 3-year Academy of Finance program and a career center. The Spartans' average SAT score in 1998 was 1,039.

Southeast High School (856-2800) opened in August 1997 at a cost of $31 million. It is an "Accelerated Studies" magnet school that features innovative teaching, unique learning opportunities, flexible schedules and academic support. Students form an academic team that stays together with the same academic coach for four years. The school's challenging instructional programs emphasize math, science and state-of-the-art technology.

Cary High School (460-3549) has a long history dating back to the town's famous Cary Academy in the late 1800s. In 1907, Cary High became the first state-assisted public high school in North Carolina. The school recently completed a $3.4 million renovation, which included a new career center, and it also has an Accelerated Learning Center. Cary students scored an average of 1,050 on the SAT. The school, which has an enrollment of approximately 2,000 students, is famous for its marching band and has hosted one of the state's noted music events, Cary Band Day, since 1960. In athletics, the Imps brought home 1997-98 state titles in women's cross country and wrestling, and the 1998 men's soccer state championship.

With an enrollment of nearly 2,300 students, **Apex** High School (387-2208) is one of the largest high schools in the state. The school's curriculum includes a full schedule of advanced placement courses, including biology, chemistry, physics, calculus, English, U.S. history, European history, French, Spanish and German. The average SAT score for 1998 was 1,099.

Photo by Tim Johnson

Cary High School

The newest high school in Wake County is $35-million **Green Hope** High School (380-3700), which opened in the fall of 1999 to 850 students in grades nine and 10 (grades 11 and 12 will be added over the next two years). The state-of-the-art school is located off Carpenter-Upchurch Road, convenient for students in Morrisville, Cary and Apex. The school's mascot is the falcon and the school's colors are green and burgundy.

The **Durham Public School System** offers students a variety of educational opportunities. The $26.7 million, 290,000-square-foot **Hillside** High School (560-3925) in southeast Durham opened in August 1995. In addition to the standard curriculum, Hillside offers several special programs, including the International Baccalaureate Program and three centers of specialization (Business and Finance, Health Sciences and Medical Professions in Research and Administration, and Law and Government). The school also features cutting-edge technology and a number of vocational programs. Students scored an average of 883 on their 1998 SATs.

Jordan High School (560-3912), located in southwest Durham County, has a tradition of sending most of its students on to college. Approximately 90 percent of Jordan's graduates pursue further education. Jordan had the highest average SAT score (1,089) in the district for 1998. The school offers a variety of advanced placement and honors courses.

Northern High School (560-3956) offers a strong curriculum balance among academics, vocational and fine arts courses. The school's vocational program has been identified as a Model Program in a curriculum audit. Northern also established the first high school Habitat for Humanity in the world and is a center for International Studies. The average SAT score at Northern for 1998 was 982.

Riverside High School (560-3965) in northern Durham had the second-highest average SAT scores (1,027) in the district for 1998. The school's engineering center is a mini-magnet program. Through the program, students can take on highly technical independent projects. Riverside students publish an arts and literary magazine, *Reveries*, annually. The Pirates claimed the 1998 4-A state championship in volleyball and its wrestling team consistently ranks high in the conference.

Southern High School (560-3968), located just north of Research Triangle Park, provides its students a comprehensive educational program. It also offers classes and programs for the academically gifted, trainable mentally handicapped, behaviorally/emotionally handicapped and hearing impaired. Students can take advantage of the school's health sciences center of specialization. Students averaged 888 on their 1998 SAT scores.

The **Chapel Hill-Carrboro School System** has the highest average SAT scores in the state. Students at **Chapel Hill** High School (929-2106) averaged 1,179 on the 1998 SAT. Chapel Hill High students consistently receive top honors in state competition in math, science and foreign languages.

The newest high school in Orange County, $37.5 million **East Chapel Hill** High School (969-2482) opened its doors in 1996. It offers a variety of advanced placement courses. The 1998 graduating class had a grade-point average of 3.5 on a 4-point scale and averaged 1,202 on their SATs. Over its first two years, the Wildcats won state championships in four sports. The school also boasts of nearly 60 campus clubs.

---

instruction for 600 students in grades 9 through 12. The school provides a college preparatory curriculum and about 98 percent of its seniors go on to college. The average SAT score for seniors is over 1,000, well above the state average of 976.

Uniforms are required and students must take religious instruction in all grade levels. There are about 50 full-time teachers at the school, which is administered by the Franciscan Brothers of Brooklyn.

Construction has been completed on the new Cardinal Gibbons High, which can accommodate 800 students. The new building opened in the fall of 1999.

Cary Academy
1500 N. Harrison Ave., Cary • 677-3873

Founded by leaders of SAS Institute, the Cary Academy opened in August 1997 with 248 students in grades 6 to 10. The facility, which sits on a 52-acre campus

on Harrison Avenue, offers a rigorous college preparatory program to equip students for success in higher education. The school currently has an enrollment of 475 students and added grade 11 during the 1998 school year and grade 12 in 1999. The campus features a state-of-the-art Media and Administration Building, separate Upper and Middle School facilities, a Sports and Fitness Center and a Fine Arts Building.

Cary Country Day School
610 Nottingham Dr. • 467-6991

Nearly 100 children, preschool through kindergarten, enjoy educational experiences that include computer instruction, swimming, summer camp and before- and after-school day-care programs at the school, which is part of Nobel Education Dynamics. The nurturing environment is provided by experienced teachers.

Discover Cary Academy

At Cary Academy, *discovery* means boundless opportunities to explore, uncover, and pursue ideas while building on existing knowledge. This newfound awareness will ignite creative thinking and foster ongoing exchange.

If your student would thrive in this type of learning environment, please call our Admissions Office at **677-3873** to learn more about our academic and extracurricular programs.

We also invite you to visit us at our Web site at **www. caryacademy.pvt.k12.nc.us** for the latest information on Cary Academy, our programs, and student activities.

1500 North Harrison Avenue, Cary, NC 27513   919 677 • 3873

School-day and full-day programs are available. Cary Country Day School is related to Millbrook Country Day School, 787-7568, and North Raleigh Country Day School, 847-3120.

Cathedral School
204 Hillsborough St. • 832-4711

Proud of its tradition of academic excellence, Cathedral School is ideally located in the heart of historic Raleigh, offering its students the opportunity to experience the city's history firsthand with visits to cultural, historical and scientific facilities, which are all within walking distance. The school, a Catholic faith community since 1909, encourages students from all denominations and ethnic backgrounds to pursue academic excellence within the framework of Christian principles. With a current enrollment of 270, Cathedral School offers a 4-year-old program, a K-8 curriculum and a supervised after-school program.

Friendship Christian School
5510 Falls of the Neuse Rd. • 872-2133

Friendship is a Baptist-affiliated school for boys and girls from 4-year-old kindergarten through grade 12. It was started in 1970 as a day care and kindergarten and its current enrollment is 450 with a 20 to 1 student-teacher ratio. The school follows a traditional college preparatory teaching format and the students average over 1,000 on their SAT scores. In addition to advanced-placement courses for college-bound students,

INSIDERS' TIP
Become a mentor. Contact your local school to learn how you can have a positive effect on a student.

the school offers a state-of-the-art computer lab.

Millbrook Country Day School
2215 W. Millbrook Rd. • 787-7568

Millbrook is housed in a relatively new facility with a state-of-the-art pool and playground. Over 160 children, from infants through preschool, are enrolled in the school. This school, along with two other related schools—North Raleigh Country Day School, 847-3120, and Cary Country Day School, 467-6991—are members of Nobel Education Dynamics.

Montessori School of Raleigh
7005 Leadmine Rd. • 848-1545

Started in 1975, the school takes children from 18 months and goes through the 6th grade. Enrollment is about 325 and teachers follow the Montessori method, which emphasizes individual development at the child's own speed and meeting the needs of each child. Parental involvement in the school is expected, though not required. Classes average about 25 students, but have two teachers per class. Day-care service for before- and after-school hours is available.

North Raleigh Country Day School
10200 Strickland Rd. • 847-3120

This school, along with two other related schools—Millbrook Country Day, 787-7568, and Cary Country Day School, 467-6991—are members of Nobel Education Dynamics. All have excellent reputations and are known for providing educational extras such as computer instruction, swim lessons in on-campus pools and complete before- and after-school day-care programs. Summer camp programs are also available at all three locations. The North Raleigh Country Day School, with 230 students, expanded its program in the 1997 school year to offer instruction for children from age 3 through the 6th grade. The 6-acre campus is convenient and offers excellent facilities. It is accredited by the National Association for the Education of Young Children (NAEYC).

Our Lady of Lourdes
2710 Overbrook Dr. • 782-1670

This is the other Catholic elementary-middle school serving the Raleigh and Cary area. It goes through the 8th grade, and many of the students continue at Cardinal Gibbons. The school requires uniforms. Lourdes has about 500 K-8 students and uses lay teachers.

Raleigh Christian Academy
2110 Trawick Rd. • 872-2215

Sponsored by the First Free Will Baptist Church, this school began in 1977. It has all grade levels, from kindergarten to 12th as well as a day-care program that takes infants as young as one year. Enrollment is around 680. At the elementary school level, before-school day care starts at 7 AM and after-school care ends at 6 PM.

The Raleigh School
1100 Edwards Mill Rd. • 546-0788

The Raleigh School began as a preschool when North Carolina had no kindergarten in its public schools. It is a co-op, which means that parents have to help with some of the chores. Beginning in the 1997-98 school year, the Raleigh School opened for students through grade 5. Current enrollment is about 115.

Ravenscroft School
7409 Falls of Neuse Rd. • 847-0900

Ravenscroft School, one of the best known private schools in the Triangle, was founded in 1862 by members of Christ Episcopal Church and named for the first Episcopal bishop of North Carolina. The school offers a coed, college preparatory day school for students from preschool to 12th grade. While the school has no denominational affiliations, it maintains its Judeo-Christian heritage and strives to help students understand basic values and pursue ideals of integrity, service, compassion and sportsmanship.

The school upholds rigorous academic standards in keeping with its college preparatory goals. All graduates go on to colleges or universities. SAT scores average about 1240. The school is located on an attractive, wood-fringed 127-acre campus in North Raleigh and enrolls over 1,000 students with a 16:1 student-teacher ratio.

Saint Mary's High School
900 Hillsborough St. • 839-4100

Saint Mary's School is a four-year preparatory school for girls in grades 9 to 12. The school, which has an enrollment of 240 students, boasts a student-teacher ratio of 10 to 1. The beautiful 23-acre wooded campus, situated between the State Government Complex and North Carolina State University, is listed on the National Register of Historic Places.

St. Timothy's Lower School
4523 Six Forks Rd.
Admissions: 781-0531
School Office: 787-3011
St. Timothy's-Hale School
3400 White Oak Rd.
Admissions & School Office: 782-3331

St. Timothy's Lower School and St. Timothy's-Hale School are fully accredited coeducational Episcopal day schools for students in kindergarten through grade 12. Located in close proximity to the North Hills section of Raleigh, both schools enroll students of all faiths from the Triangle and surrounding areas.

Established in 1958 by St. Timothy's Episcopal Church, St. Timothy's Lower School enrolls 400 students in kindergarten through grade 4. A challenging academic program emphasizes appropriate activities in reading, language arts, math, science, social studies and French. Art, music, drama, physical education and a technology program complement the academic program. A strong cultural arts

program and a week-long creative writing seminar designed to improve the writing skills of fourth grade students are also offered. Low student-to-teacher ratios foster the development of close relationships between faculty and students.

St. Timothy's-Hale School enrolls 385 students in grades 5 to 12. Students pursue an accelerated college-preparatory program in classes small enough to permit individual attention. Graduates must successfully complete a minimum of 24 high school credits, which include four years of English, foreign language, history, math, science and one year of physical education. The curriculum includes a two-year Latin requirement designed to improve reading, writing, grammar and vocabulary skills. Advanced placement courses and electives in music, art, drama and computer science are offered. Students are also encouraged to participate in athletics and extracurricular activities. One hundred percent of St. Timothy's-Hale students attend college.

The schools are engaged in a capital campaign to build a new upper school facility and chapel, to complete renovations at St. Timothy's Lower School and to create a faculty excellence fund at both schools.

Wake Christian Academy Inc.
5500 Wake Academy Dr. • 772-6264

One of the oldest and largest private Christian schools in Wake County, Wake Christian Academy enrolls students from K-12. It offers a curriculum based on Christian values and has a full extracurricular program.

Durham and Chapel Hill

With the relatively short distance between Durham and Chapel Hill, the private schools often attract students from both communities with a wide choice of excellent private and parochial schools. We advise that you visit these facilities, meet

Photo by Tim Johnson

One of more than 600 Waldorf schools worldwide, Emerson Waldorf School offers students a classical education firmly grounded in academics and the arts.

the principals, observe a few classes and activities and compare tuition costs before making a decision.

Carolina Friends School
4809 Friends School Rd., Durham
• 383-6602

This nondenominational school, founded in 1963 by the Quakers, is located on 45 acres of wooded countryside equidistant from Durham, Chapel Hill and Hillsborough. The Friends School features a decidedly open and progressive approach to education: students are grouped by common interests and abilities rather than age or grade level. There are no letter or numerical grades; instead, students receive written evaluations and "credit" or "no credit."

The school enrolls close to 500 students in prekindergarten through grade 12 with a student-teacher ratio of 10 to 1. The lower school is for ages 6 to 10, the middle school for ages 10 to 14 and the upper school for those 14 to 18. CFS offers "early schools" for 3- to 5-year-olds in three locations: 404 Alexander Street in Durham, 531 Raleigh Road in Chapel Hill and at the main campus, 4809 Friends School Road in Durham.

While reading, writing and math are continually stressed, students also focus on annual themes such as "the human body" or "ecology." Independent study, community service projects, field trips and sports are also part of the curriculum. While 90 percent of the students proceed to college, programs are available for the non-college-bound as well.

Cresset Christian Academy
3707 Garrett Rd., Durham • 489-2655

Located on a beautiful 40-acre campus, Cresset Christian Academy provides instruction for nearly 350 students, from preschool through 12th grade. The preschool program includes toddlers through 4-year-olds and classes are

INSIDERS' TIP
If you want to know what your child's school is offering for lunch, check the local newspaper for school menu listings.

small. Affiliated with Cresset Baptist Church, the school bases its instruction on Biblical concepts.

The program uses a mixture of a Beka curriculum and other quality materials to lead students in the development of character and intellectual excellence. The curriculum is college preparatory in nature.

Cresset provides instruction in the arts, drama and music. There is a competitive athletic program for the middle and upper schools and private music instruction is offered. The upper school boasts an award-winning concert choir.

A special program is offered for students with attention deficit disorder and learning disabilities as well as one for intellectually gifted students.

Duke School For Children
1516 Hull Ave., Durham • 286-1866
3716 Old Erwin Rd., Durham • 493-2642

Founded in 1947, the Duke School for Children is run by a parent-owned corporation. The total enrollment of the school is 475 for students from preschool through 8th grade.

Durham Academy
3116 Academy Rd., Durham • 489-9118
(Pre -K thru Grade 8)
3601 Ridge Rd., Durham • 489-6569
(Grades 9 thru 12)

Founded in 1933, Durham Academy is the oldest primary-through-secondary private school in the area, providing instruction from preschool through 12th grade for over 1,000 students. Admission is based on the student's potential to satisfactorily perform college preparatory work. The campus is located in Durham, about a 20-minute drive from Chapel Hill.

Enrichment courses include computers, wind ensemble, chorus, dance, drama, studio art, typing, economics and comparative religions. Independent study, internships and volunteer service conclude the 12th year. Juniors and seniors may take a semester of independent study. Many of these students go on to highly competitive universities and colleges.

The Emerson Waldorf School
6211 New Jericho Rd., Chapel Hill
• 967-1858

The Emerson Waldorf School is located on 25 wooded acres south of I-40 off N.C. 86 and Mt. Sinai Road north of Chapel Hill. As one of more than 600 Waldorf schools worldwide, it is part of the world's fastest-growing independent school movement.

A typical day at Emerson Waldorf begins with a two-hour "main lesson" that focuses on a single theme. The selected subject may remain the same for several weeks. All history, spelling, mathematics and science problems are related to the main lesson subject. In addition to the basics, Waldorf students study foreign languages, music, handwork and other electives. The school has 175 students in kindergarten (ages 4 to 6) through 8th grade.

Hill Learning Development Center
3130 Pickett Rd., Durham • 489-7464

The Hill LDC, affiliated with Durham Academy, offers a remedial program for children with learning disabilities or achievement difficulties in kindergarten through grade 12. The LDC program provides private instruction for children enrolled in schools in Durham and the surrounding counties in conjunction with regular classroom work.

Immaculata School
721 Burch Ave., Durham • 682-5847

Immaculata is a 350-student Catholic school founded in 1909 to provide a unique learning program in a Christian environment. Class instruction, small groups and independent study are geared to meet the needs of both slower and more advanced students. The school enrolls students in prekindergarten through grade 8. Families with more than one child attending the school receive tuition discounts.

The Jewish Community Day School of Durham/Chapel Hill
1935 W. Cornwallis Rd., Durham
• 286-5517

The Jewish Community Day School of Durham/Chapel Hill (JCDS) is a private, independent school offering integrated secular/Judaic studies from preschool through grade 5. JCDS provides an environment where children develop a love of learning, positive Jewish identity and a healthy self-image while achieving the highest standards of academic excellence. Low student/teacher ratios allow for rapid individual progress. All teachers are experienced and certified. Hebrew is taught as a second language and the Judaic component is designed for families of diverse Jewish backgrounds and practices. JCDS is located on a beautiful, wooded site with playing fields and playgrounds.

The Kantner School
7500 Schley Rd., Hillsborough
• 732-7200

The Kantner School was established to provide academic excellence in the basic areas of learning in a college preparatory environment. Named for its founder, Beth McClees Kantner, the school's student body comes from the entire Triangle area. The school has 100 students in prekindergarten through grade 12. As a nonprofit school, Kantner has one of the lowest tuition rates in the area. Tuition is lower for each additional child who is enrolled in the school. Kantner has a rolling enrollment policy, offers before- and after-school programs and provides transportation from Durham and Chapel Hill.

The Writing Center and Computer Lab offer state-of-the-art technology.

Beginning in kindergarten, all students participate in creative writing and technology-based curriculum. Students have Internet and E-mail access to aid them in their research. Kantner has a competitive athletic program in which all students from 5th grade and up can participate without the pressure of tryouts. Each quarter, middle and upper school students select an "X-Block" from a menu of activities. X-Block meets once a week for two hours and activities have included Drama, Wilderness Training, Tutoring, First Aid, Environmental Club, Choral Music, SAT Preparatory Class and Ceramics. Community service is completed during X-Block also. Private violin and guitar lessons are available after school.

Montessori Community School
4512 Pope Rd., Durham • 493-8541

This school is a nonprofit organization directed by parents, promoting child-centered and child-initiated learning. It has a part-time toddler program and an elementary program through grade 6. There are over 200 students enrolled at the school, which is located on nine wooded acres near I-40 and U.S. 15-501.

Montessori School
1165 Weaver Dairy Rd., Chapel Hill
• 929-3339

The Montessori school practices the methods of Marie Montessori, an Italian educator and physician who believed that children learn naturally if placed in an environment consisting of "learning games" suited to their individual abilities and interests.

The 3- and 4-year-olds attend until 11:45 AM, 5-year-olds until 2 PM and ages 6 through 9 until 2:30 PM. There are about 20 students in each of the preschool classes and about 30 students enrolled in the primary program.

St. Thomas More School
920 Carmichael St., Chapel Hill
• 929-1546

St. Thomas More School was built in 1964 as an outgrowth of St. Thomas More Catholic Church parish. The school's 460-student enrollment is open to non-Catholics as well. The school's philosophy is "to help our students to integrate religious truth." Students from prekindergarten to grade 8 are served and there is an after-school program as well.

Triangle Day School
4911 Neal Rd., Durham • 383-8800

Triangle Day School opened in 1991 as a college preparatory day school. It has an enrollment of 110 students in kindergarten through grade 8 and a low student-teacher ratio. The program also emphasizes foreign language, physical education, computers, music and art.

After-School Programs

After-school programs are designed for the older child who is in school, but who needs an activity to keep him or her busy until mom or dad gets home.

Raleigh-Cary

The Raleigh-Cary area offers three primary providers of after-school care: the public schools' extended-day program, the YMCA and YWCA and the diverse city recreation programs. Contact information can be found elsewhere in this chapter or in the "Parks and Recreation" chapter.

TIP Offers Unique Educational Opportunities

Founded in 1980, the Talent Identification Program (TIP) is a nonprofit educational organization that identifies and serves the educational needs of academically talented 7th graders based on standardized test scores. Students must score in the upper 3 percent on the national norm of a standardized test and attend a school within TIP's 16-state region to be eligible for the program.

Through a series of specialized programs, TIP offers supplemental courses in computer, natural and social sciences, engineering, humanities and mathematics to qualified students. The Summer  Residential Programs, open to students in grades 7 to 10, are single-course, three-week terms generally equivalent to a year of high school work or a semester of college-level work. The students live in supervised dorms, frequently eat meals with instructors, receive academic assistance outside of class and attend planned recreational activities. This past summer, courses were offered at Duke University, Davidson College, Appalachian State University, the University of Kansas, Duke University Marine Lab and Harbor Branch Oceanographic Institute (Ft. Pierce, Florida).

The PreCollege Program gives 11th graders the opportunity to attend undergraduate summer session classes at Duke University and earn college credit. During the six-week, two-course session, students live on campus in supervised residence halls and have access to all available campus facilities and services. Drama, yearbook, literary magazine, student government, intramural sports and community service are some of the opportunities available to them.

The Scientific Field Studies Programs provide 10th- to 12th-grade students unique adventures in science through travel to locations in the Western Hemisphere that feature ideal research environments. This past summer, programs in Costa Rica (tropical ecology), the Rocky Mountains (mountain ecology and

Photo courtesy of N.C. Travel and Tourism

Duke University

biology), Mountain Lake in the Appalachian Mountains (aquatic ecology, biology and botany) and the Southwest (archaeology and geology) were offered.

For students seeking to further expand their studies and traveling experiences, the International Program for 8th through 11th graders offers them that opportunity. Each year, several sites are selected based on their importance to European history. This year, England, Italy and Germany were chosen. The typical three-week program provides room and board, and experienced instructors, teaching assistants and resident advisors.

Since courses and programs are limited to a certain number of qualified students, they often fill up early. Eligibility requirements and application dates vary. For more information, contact TIP Educational Programs, Duke University, PO Box 90747, Durham, NC 27708-0747, 684-3847.

Durham

The public schools in the Durham area offer before- and after-school care at many school sites. Call to inquire about the availability of transportation at your child's school. Several private schools also offer earlier and later drop-off and pickup times for students. Local day-care programs also offer transportation from some schools to the centers for after-school care.

After-school care is provided at various neighborhood centers run by the Durham Parks and Recreation Department. For more information on these after-school programs, contact the Durham Parks and Recreation Department, 560-4355.

Chapel Hill-Carrboro

Affordable after-school care is available at all seven public elementary schools and all three middle schools. For more information, contact the Administrative Offices at Lincoln Center, 967-8211.

Some of the private schools we described also offer after-school care. For more information, contact the school.

Preschools and Day-Care Programs

Since North Carolina has the highest percentage of working women in the nation and because many of these women are mothers, adequate day care for children has long been part of the state's social fabric. A higher-than-state average of working women, many in professional ranks, also work in the Triangle area. Therefore, the Triangle has a number of private and quasi-public day-care operations and several Triangle businesses—such as Cary software giant SAS—provide day care for employees' children as part of the company's benefit package.

North Carolina has enacted minimum standards for child-care facilities. All providers must be registered with the North Carolina Division of Child Development, 662-4499, located at 319 Chapanoke Rd., Suite 120. Ask your provider or center for its registration number to verify this registration. If you want to check out a center's record, you can go to this office in Raleigh and look in the state files to see if any complaints have been lodged against the center.

State standards also set the following adult-to-provider ratios: infants up to 1-year-old (1:5), 2 years (1:10), 3 years (1:15), 4 years (1:20) and 5 years and older (1:25). However, these standards allow fewer adults per child than federal standards permit.

Raleigh and Cary

There are several kinds of providers for full day-care service, which usually take infants from 6-weeks-old to kindergarten-aged children. The small mom-and-pop provider is at one end of the spectrum, yet regulations and insurance rates are putting many such programs out of business. At the other end are the national child-care centers such as Kinder-Care, which has 12 locations, La Petite Academy (13 locations) and Young World. They can be found in the Yellow Pages under "Child Care."

In between are single-site providers, many of which, again, are in churches. Two of the best are First Baptist Church in downtown Raleigh and Pullen Memorial Baptist Church's Method Day Care. Some of the other churches with established programs for 2-year-olds and up are West Raleigh Presbyterian, Edenton Street Methodist and First Cosmopolitan Baptist Church.

Learning Together is operated on contract with Wake County School System and Department of Social Services and it serves gifted and learning-disabled children. Tammy Lynn Center is a nonprofit school for the handicapped. Three of the city's housing projects have day-care centers. They are: Chavis Heights, Walnut Terrace and Halifax Court.

The Child Care Resource Center at 3901 Barrett Drive, Suite 104 (832-7175 for referrals), is not a day-care center but rather a nonprofit information center that helps families find day care suitable to them and their budgets.

The Growing Child at 1120 Sawmill Road (846-1164) is a program that supplies community oriented care—most children who attend Impressions live within a 3- to 4-mile radius of the center. Located within the Greystone neighborhood (see the "Raleigh Neighborhoods" section in our "Real Estate and Neighborhoods" chapter), the Center provides full day- and preschool care for infants (6 weeks) through age 2. Hours are from 7 AM until 6 PM. Call for tuition.

Here is a short list of some of the well-established day-care programs in the Raleigh-Cary area:

Edenton Street United Methodist Church, 228 W. Edenton St. • 832-2029
Ernest Myatt Presbyterian Child Development Center, 4926 Fayetteville Rd. • 779-0316
First Baptist Church, 99 N. Salisbury St. • 832-4650
First Cosmopolitan Baptist Church,1515 Cross Link Rd. • 833-3283

Hudson Memorial Children's Ministries, 4921 Six Forks Rd. • 787-1086
It's Academic, 300 S.E. Cary Pkwy., Cary • 481-1744
It's Academic, 580 E. Chatham St., Cary • 388-3024
KinderCare, 12 locations • (877) KinderCare
La Petite Academy, 104 Baines Ct., Cary • 856-5200
La Petite Academy, 955 W. Chatham St., Cary • 467-5875
Learning Together, 568 Lenoir St. • 856-5200
MacGregor Creative School, 203 Gregson Dr., Cary • 469-2046
Method Day Care Center, 1801 Hillsborough St. • 828-2926
New Hope Baptist Learning Center, 4301 Louisburg Rd. • 876-5850
Raleigh Preschool, 1215 Ridge Rd. • 828-5351
Tammy Lynn Center, 739 Chappell Dr. • 832-3909
YWCA, 3 locations • 828-3205

Durham

There are at least 150 child-care centers and preschools and 280 child-care homes in the Durham area. They include Montessori schools, church-affiliated centers, national chains, small independent operators and school-age programs. Day-care centers in Durham usually charge $75 to $175 a week. Child care in private homes usually costs $60 to $150 a week.

To learn more about choosing quality child care and child-care regulations, contact the Durham Day Care Council, a child-care resource and referral agency at 115 Market Street, Suite 300. Or call the TOTLINE at 403-6955 for referrals and information on child-care centers and homes, preschool programs and school age child care in Durham.

The **Asbury Preschool**, 806 Clarendon St. • 286-2668

Beth El Synagogue Preschool, 1004 Watts St. • 682-1238

Bethesda Baptist Child-Care Center, 1914 S. Miami Blvd. • 596-5420

Bryson Christian Montessori School, 2811 University Dr. • 489-5539

Chesterbrook Academy, 117 Woodcroft Pkwy. • 489-8899

Cresset Christian Preschool, 3707 Garrett Rd. • 489-3744

Duke Memorial Week Day School, 504 W. Chapel Hill St. • 688-5130

The Enrichment Center at RTP, 10 T.W. Alexander Dr. • 549-4802

Epworth United Methodist Preschool, 3002 Hope Valley Rd. • 489-6098

First Presbyterian Day School, 305 E. Main St. • 688-8685

Grace Baptist Church Child Development Center, 1004 N. Mangum St. • 682-0671

Hope Valley Preschool, 1600 Chapel Hill-Nelson Hwy. • 493-0326

KIN, Too, 1416 Broad St. • 286-5432

KinderCare, 3 locations • (877) KinderCare

Lakewood Avenue Children's School, 1701 Lakewood Ave. • 493-5882

Montessori Children's House of Durham, 2400 University Dr. • 489-9045

Montessori Community School, 4512 Pope Rd. • 493-8541

Mt. Tabor United Methodist Day Care, 4200 Bahama Rd. • 479-1614

Primary Colors Child Care Center, 3008 Dixon Rd. • 490-1173

Scarborough Nursery School, 309 Queen St. • 682-5037

Triangle Children's Center, 1900 Sedwick Rd. • 544-2815

Westminster Kindergarten, 3639 Chapel Hill Rd. • 489-8432

Yates Baptist Child Care, 2819 Chapel Hill Rd. • 489-5760

Chapel Hill-Carrboro

There are at least two dozen preschools and many more child-care providers in Chapel Hill and Carrboro. One way to learn about which facility or home setting is right for your needs is to ask for recommendations from friends and neighbors, then go observe.

Or you can contact Child Care Networks, a private, nonprofit organization that assists people in matching their child-care needs with the right facility, home setting or provider. For more information, call Child Care Networks at 542-6644.

The following are some of the preschool and full day-care programs in the Chapel Hill-Carrboro area:

Amity United Methodist Nursery School, 825 Estes Dr. • 929-6149

Binkley Preschool, 1712 Willow Dr. • 968-1427

Carrboro United Methodist Day Care, 200 Hillsborough Rd. • 929-5143

Chapel Hill Cooperative Preschool, 106 Purefoy Rd. • 942-3955

Chapel Hill Day Care Center, East Franklin St. • 929-3585

Family Preschool, 632 Laurel Hill Rd. • 967-9684

Holy Family Day Care, 200 Hayes Rd. • 929-5004

Kindercare, 210 S. Elliott Rd. • 942-7223

La Petite Academy, 110 Kingston Dr. • 929-9148

Montessori Day School, 1165 Weaver Dairy Rd. • 929-3339

Preschool of the Arts, Village Plaza • 933-7278

University Methodist Preschool, 150 E. Franklin St. • 967-8867

Wee Care Child Development Center, 1702 Legion Rd. • 942-8957

Colleges and Universities

The Triangle takes its name from the geographical location of the three major universities in Raleigh, Durham and Chapel Hill. Two more universities and five colleges provide educational opportunities unavailable elsewhere.

Associate's, bachelor's, master's and doctoral degrees are offered in a wide choice of curricular and flexible class schedules allow students to attend full-time, part-time, on weekends and even on-line. Credit and non-credit continuing education classes are available, as well as certificate programs in such diversified fields as real estate, nonprofit management and welding, just to name a few.

The universities and colleges offer more than an education on a classroom-learning level. They provide an education through their libraries, museums, gardens, theater and music programs and sports. (See our chapters on "Attractions," "Arts and Culture" and "Spectator Sports" for more details.) They also provide research in medicine, science, technology and business. They are a vital part of the Triangle and the Triangle is part of them.

Raleigh

North Carolina State University
Admissions: 112 Peele Hall, Box 7103
Raleigh, NC 27695 • 515-2011

One of the three corners of the Research Triangle, NCSU is one of the state's and nations's premier research institutions, confirmed in 1994 by Phi Beta Kappa, which conferred chapter status to the University. The campus is on Hillsborough Street about 1.5 miles from the Capitol. With a 1,563-acre campus and nearby research stations and recreational facilities covering another 2,700 acres, NCSU comprises a big chunk of Raleigh's real estate and much of the area's economic, social and artistic life. There are several other schools in the city, but "State," as it's often called, commands the most attention.

Founded in 1887 as a land-grant school for agriculture and the mechanical arts, it was long derided as a "cow college" by fans of arch-rival UNC-Chapel Hill. But NCSU is now known as far more than an "ag and tech school." It is among the nation's leaders in engineering, textiles, forestry, architecture, wood and paper science and biotechnology. NCSU is now the largest school in North Carolina, with over 27,000 students who average 1070 on their SAT scores and earn about a 3.5 GPA in high school.

The 1998-99 tuition for an in-state student at NCSU costs $1,182 a year; out-of state, $5,765. Considering the school's reputation, that's a bargain. Decreases in state funding may cause an increase in tuition prices over the next few years. The school maintains housing for about 7,000 students and tries to place all freshmen who are not commuting in campus housing. The school has about 19,000 undergraduates; it receives about 11,000 applications a year, from which it accepts 3,400 freshmen. Average class size is 35. About 85 percent of the students come from North Carolina. The student body is composed of about 40 percent women and 60 percent men.

In August 1998, Dr. Marye Anne Fox succeeded Larry K. Monteith as NCSU's chancellor. Fox, the first woman to hold the post in the school's history, is a nationally renowned scientist and former vice president for research at the University of Texas.

The university is divided into colleges; the largest is Engineering and the newest is Management. The others are Agriculture and Life Sciences, Education and Psychology, Forest Resources, Humanities and Social Sciences, Textiles, Physical and Mathematical Sciences, and Veterinary Medicine. There is also a School of Design and a Graduate School.

NCSU offers 89 undergraduate, 85 master's and 52 doctoral degree programs. Former chancellor, Larry K.

FYI

Unless otherwise noted, the area code for all phone numbers listed in this guide is 919.

Montieth, put new emphasis on undergraduate programs, proposing a unique Freshman College for NCSU. The result is that undergrads at NCSU have access to world-class research facilities. In the field of engineering, the school maintains a close relationship with a number of Research Triangle companies—over 150 Park employees hold adjunct professorships at NCSU. Its work in signal processing, communication and microchip technology is at the forefront in national research. One of the nation's premier software companies, SAS in Cary, was started by an NCSU professor in the statistics department of mathematical sciences.

NCSU's Centennial Campus, located on 1,000 acres adjacent to the main campus, is a research and advanced technology community where university, industry and government partners interact in programs directed toward technological solutions to problems and the creation of new products. Slated for development over the next 20 years, Centennial Campus will ultimately consist of a dozen or more research clusters made up of university, corporate and government laboratories, a hotel conference center with an 18-hole golf course designed by Tom Fazio, retail stores and housing situated around a central lake. The first cluster, on the north side of Lake Raleigh, has 15 major buildings completed or in the planning/construction stage. About 3,200 people currently work at Centennial Campus, which will eventually employ over 25,000.

Among public universities, NCSU has been ranked eighth nationally in terms of industry-sponsored research and 24th in terms of research expenditures. Its School of Textiles is not only the largest in the country, but is considered the best by many in the industry. Departments at NCSU ranked among the top 10 of their kind in the nation include: plant pathology;

Photo by Tim Johnson

Founded in 1887, North Carolina State University has evolved into one of the nation's premier research institutions.

The famous tunnel leading to the Student Union at North Carolina State University depicts the wisdom of students past and present.

entomology; horticulture; wood and paper science; forestry; parks, recreation and tourism management; statistics; architecture; mathematics and science education; community college and adult education; food science and nuclear engineering.

The main library, D.H. Hill, is especially strong in biological and physical science, engineering, agriculture and forestry. Its Libraries Information System has been selected as one of the nation's six "Libraries of the Future."

What's surprising is NCSU's record in the non-science areas. Its design school is also ranked among the top 10 in the country. In the humanities, NCSU's faculty includes writer Lee Smith, one of the South's best-known authors.

Outreach and continuing education play a major role at NCSU, too. The Jane S. McKimmon Center is one of the largest continuing education centers in the nation, serving more than 110,000 people in about 1,600 different programs annually.

The Japan Center, one of NCSU's institutes, conducts Japanese language programs for business people, as well as courses about Japanese customs for companies interested in doing business in Asia. It also helped establish the Saturday Japanese School at Effie Green Elementary School in Raleigh for Japanese children whose parents are here on assignment with Japanese affiliates. It permits the children to continue their education in native Japanese.

Life at NCSU is not all books. There are 35 social fraternities and sororities and an active intramural athletic program. Plus, there are hundreds of student organizations, including a radio station, a newspaper and the University Theatre. Being in the center of Raleigh gives the school access to the capital city's cultural life, too. The campus becomes one big party when the Wolfpack teams are winning— like in '74 and '83 when the basketball teams captured the national championship. Victory celebrations center around the Brickyard, the historic gathering place for students in the heart of the campus.

There's an unpretentiousness about State students that's quite refreshing. Some are the first in their families to go to college and they tend to be diligent and hard working. NCSU is big, it's a bargain and it's among the best research universities in the nation.

Meredith College
3800 Hillsborough St.
Raleigh, NC 27607 • 829-8600

Meredith College, founded in 1891, is a private, comprehensive college for women and one of the Triangle's best values for a good education at a good price. With an enrollment of over 2,500 students in both undergraduate and graduate programs, Meredith is the largest private four-year women's college in the Southeast. In a 1998 survey of "America's Best Colleges," *U.S. News & World Report* ranked Meredith 15th among Southern colleges.

The school's 225-acre campus in west Raleigh is near the I-440 Beltline and I-40. Meredith provides the city with one of its loveliest architectural settings, complete with a tree-lined drive, columned brick buildings and flowering trees and shrubs and a master plan for future growth. Meredith's beautiful campus is the site of many community events, such as the Labor Day concert by the North Carolina Symphony, weddings, and civic and educational meetings.

For the 1998-99 school year, tuition, room and board cost $12,740 per year. Tuition only for nonresident students is $8,840. The faculty-student ratio is 1 to 17. In the past decade, the college has strengthened its reputation as a resource center for many nontraditional students (over age 23). The Continuing Education Community Programs offer short courses on a wide variety of topics such as computers, creative writing and financial planning. The college also offers a post-baccalaureate certification program for legal assistants.

With over 36 majors and 12 concentrations, Meredith offers bachelor of arts, music and science degrees. Admissions officials consider both SAT and high school records when admitting students. Over 65 percent of incoming freshmen rank in at least the top 25 percent of their class and the median SAT score for freshmen is between 810 to 1,000. The John E. Weems Graduate School (named after Meredith President Weems) offers master's degrees in business administration, education, music and health administration. Over 215 women are currently enrolled in the graduate programs. The MBA program features evening classes year round and is tailored for the demanding schedules of professional women.

Meredith also offers students opportunities to participate in International Programs and in cooperative education and internships in and around Research Triangle Park.

Longtime Meredith President John E. Weems recently announced that he will retire in 1999 and Maureen Hartford has been named as his successor.

Peace College
15 E. Peace St., Raleigh, NC 27604
• 508-2000

Peace College is another of Raleigh's scenic college campuses, located downtown close to the state government complex. It is the second oldest of the city's colleges, founded in 1857 and named for William Peace, who gave the land and $10,000 to help build Main Hall. Until 1995, it was a two-year, liberal arts college for women. While still a women's college, it now offers five baccalaureate degrees in biology, business administration, communication, human resources, liberal studies and psychology. It continues its two-year Associate Degree programs in music, the arts and science.

Peace College is affiliated with the Presbyterian Church (USA) and enjoys a strong relationship with the First Presbyterian Church of Raleigh. However, women of all denominations attend the school.

With an enrollment of 600 students, Peace offers a faculty-student ratio of 1 to 14. The college's size allows young women to become involved in campus and community activities. The students often assume leadership positions not generally available to them at larger schools.

The cost of attending Peace is lower than at many comparable colleges. Tuition, room and board for the 1998-99 academic year is $12,980; for day students, tuition is $8,040. If you reside in North Carolina, you can subtract from that

Founded in 1857, Peace College is the second oldest of Raleigh's colleges.

the $1,300 tuition grant from the state. Peace students receive assistance through scholarships and need-based financial aid, totalling 2.5 million dollars annually. The fiscal strength of the college is based on a $33 million endowment, with no indebtedness.

The college considers both high school rank and SAT scores when admitting students. According to the admissions brochure, an applicant should rank in the top half of her graduating class and SAT scores should be average or above average when compared to the scores of all college-bound students. The college does not release SAT scores. Peace also offers early admission to exceptional students. In addition to its regular programs, Peace is a member of Cooperating Raleigh Colleges, a consortium that allows students from member colleges to take classes at other member colleges. Peace students thereby have the opportunity to attend a larger university while still enrolled at Peace. Students are also offered a summer international-study program in England and Mexico each year.

The new president of Peace College, Laura Carpenter Bingham, is the first alumna and the second woman to hold the post in the college's history.

Peace is known for the tradition of graduating its Associate Degree students in long, white dresses, carrying red roses. As of May 1997, four-year graduates created a new tradition by wearing green caps and gowns and bachelor's hoods. Graduates will agree the oldest tradition at Peace is the lasting friendships that develop among students.

St. Augustine's College
1315 Oakwood Ave., Raleigh, NC 27610
• 516-4000

St. Augustine's was founded two years after the Civil War by the Episcopal Church to educate freed slaves. In 1867, it opened its doors to its first four students. Today St. Augustine's continues its affiliation with the Episcopal Church and its commitment to educate its predominately black student body. In 1995, it installed Dr. Bernard W. Franklin as college president to succeed

Dr. Prezell Robinson, who led the school for almost 30 years. Franklin resigned in 1999 to lead Virginia Union University.

The school's green, wooded campus is located in east Raleigh, near the Governor's Mansion. St. Aug's, as it is called, adds grace and energy to its 125 acres of the capital city.

Tuition, room and board cost about $5,544 a year. There are over 1,700 male and female students—with more men than women—enrolled, drawn from every state in the Union, the District of Columbia, three territories and 28 foreign countries. Many students board in one of the seven dormitories or 24 duplex apartments.

The college is one of two historically black colleges and universities to own and operate both commercial radio and television stations, WAUG 750 AM and WAUG-TV 68, respectively. It is the only historically black college to house a privately held, full-powered commercial television station (WRMY-TV 47) on its campus. The structure of its academic program consists of the following divisions: Business; Education; Liberal and Interdisciplinary Studies; Natural Sciences, Mathematics and Allied Health; Urban, Social and International Studies; and Military Science. Each division has its own faculty and offers a choice of majors leading to either the Bachelor of Arts or the Bachelor of Science degree. There are six Centers of Excellence designed to produce graduates that will be globally sophisticated, analytically adept and personally challenged. The centers focus on urban research and enterprise; mathematics and science; teaching; management science; visual and performing arts; and technological research.

St. Augustine's is considered to be among the top 5 percent of black institutions in the country. It maintains cooperative programs with other Raleigh colleges, including NCSU, where students interested in technical degrees can take engineering courses. It also offers an Army ROTC program and a co-op program that permits students to work in their field while attending college during alternating semesters.

The school considers its small size an advantage, especially to black students who may be the first in their family going

One of the oldest black four-year colleges in the United States,
Shaw University has a current enrollment of about 2,500 students.

to college. Students enjoy an active social life in clubs, fraternities, sororities and intramurals. Its lecture program has brought numerous national and international speakers to the school, including the Rev. Jesse Jackson, former Virginia Gov. Douglas Wilder and the late Arthur Ashe. The school has an envious athletic record and boasts over 250 world-class athletes among its alumni. It has won several national CIAA championships in cross country, track, tennis and volleyball. The men's basketball team were the 1996 CIAA champions. St. Augs student, Jerome Young, and his coach, Antonio Pettigrew, were on the 1,600-meter relay team that set a world record of 2:54.20 at the 1998 Goodwill Games.

Shaw University
118 E. South St., Raleigh, NC 27601 • 546-8200

Shaw is one of the country's oldest black four-year colleges. Shaw traces its beginnings to 1865 when a former Union Army chaplain began teaching theology to young blacks with the financial backing of Massachusetts industrialist Elijah Shaw. Its enrollment is about 2,500 men and women with a faculty to student ratio of 1 to 15. Black Baptist churches helped the University overcome financial difficulties in the 1980s. Under the leadership of President Talbert Shaw and alumni such as Willie Gary of Florida, who made a $10 million gift to Shaw, the school has survived and progressed. Shaw has added many new programs, including the Institute for the Study of Ethics and Values and its $11 million northeast campus that has new residential halls. Dr. Shaw has encouraged more scientific courses and degrees are offered in engineering and computer studies, radio-television, audiology and adaptive physical education.

The campus is located downtown, just east of Memorial Auditorium. Shaw's landmark building, beautiful Estey Hall, is a national historic landmark named after Vermont philanthropist Jacob Estey. It is believed to be the first building in America built to house women on a coed campus. It has been restored as a community building and was reopened in 1993. The school became a source of civil rights activity during the 1960s when Dr. Martin Luther King Jr. visited the campus. The school offers majors in 31 areas of study in the arts and sciences. Tuition, room and board is about $9,192 a year. Financial aid is available to most students.

Wake Technical Community College
9101 Fayetteville Rd., Raleigh, NC 27603 • 662-3500

Wake Tech is part of the state's heralded technical and community college system established in 1958. Its main campus is located south of Raleigh, beyond Garner, on the highway to Fayetteville. The school offers a variety of vocational, technical and continuing education courses. The college transfer program allows students to complete their first two years at Wake Tech and then transfer to a four-year school.

The Wake Tech campus has grown steadily over the years, with many area residents seeking to upgrade skills in fields such as computer programming and nursing. Indeed, the college is challenged to accommodate all comers. Enrollment, including part-time students, is over 44,000!

Associate degrees are offered in a number of programs and graduates in such fields as electronic and computer technology and pharmaceutical technology have been vigorously recruited by Research Triangle companies. It also offers more traditional vocational programs such as auto mechanics and heating and air conditioning. The business administration curriculum is popular with clerical employees anxious to improve their job skills and prepare for supervisory roles.

Other courses include office automation and computer graphics technology.

Its offerings are lifesavers to some and lifechangers to many, with courses such as the GED test (high school equivalency) and, for international students, "English as a Second Language" provided. It's also the best educational bargain in the Triangle. Courses for residents are $20 per credit hour; for nonresidents it's $163 per credit hour, with an additional fee of $10 if the course is taught off campus at one of the participating Wake County public schools.

Durham

Duke University

Box 90586, Duke University
Durham, NC 27708
Undergraduate Admissions • 684-3214

Duke University has long been considered one of the finest private colleges in the nation. In a 1998 nationwide survey by *U.S. News & World Report*, Duke was ranked the sixth-best national university (public or private) in the country. No wonder the *New York Times Magazine* called it one of the nation's "hot" colleges.

It began in 1892 when Trinity College, a Methodist school located in rural Randolph County, was moved to Durham with the help of tobacco magnate Washington Duke. In 1924, James Buchanan Duke endowed the institution and it was renamed in the family's honor.

Today Duke encompasses 575 tree-shaded acres in Durham, including the Georgian architecture of the East campus off Broad Street and the Gothic towers of the Duke Chapel on the West campus a 1.5 miles away. Here you'll find over 11,000 students working toward a variety of graduate and undergraduate degrees.

Duke's admissions criteria are tough— only about 25 percent of the 14,000 students who apply eventually enroll and tuition is steep, about $23,220 a year. Students who make the grade leave with prestigious credentials from one of Duke's highly acclaimed schools: Trinity College of Arts and Sciences, School of Engineering, Graduate School, School of Law, School of Medicine, School of Nursing, Divinity School, Nicholas School of The Environment and Fuqua School of Business.

Many students choose interdisciplinary programs such as Women's Studies, the Institute of the Arts or Technology and Liberal Arts. The Terry Sanford Institute of Public Policy offers graduates and undergraduates a chance to prepare for their chosen careers by studying under federal government officials and nationally respected journalists.

Duke is known for its specialized research in science and medicine. Duke University Medical Center is engaged in highly sophisticated cancer research, among other things, drawing its patients from all over the world (see our "Health Care" chapter). The Center for the Study of Aging and Human Development is the

Photo by Robert Thomason

Duke University's West Campus is known for its distinctive late-Gothic Revival buildings.

first such facility in the country to study what happens biologically, psychologically and socially as people grow older. Duke's Primate Center is an active teaching facility devoted to the preservation and study of humanity's primate relatives.

The 12,500-square-foot Botany Greenhouse holds the most diverse collection of plants under glass in the Southeast, including over 2,500 different species. Visitors may tour the facilities from 10 AM to 4:30 PM every day except Friday.

Finally, there is the F.G. Hall Laboratory for Environmental Research, containing special high-pressure chambers for simulating deep-sea diving experiments. A research dive to 2,250 feet set a new world's record.

You don't have to be a research scientist or student to enjoy having Duke University in the neighborhood. Anyone can take advantage of the resources available at the Perkins Library, considered among the top 10 university libraries in the nation, with over 4.5 million books and 33,000 periodicals.

You also can enroll in one of dozens of stimulating courses offered through Duke's Continuing Education program. A recent schedule included classes in foreign language studies, creative writing, computers, business skills and career counseling. For a schedule, call 684-6259. If you are age 50 or older, you might sign up for Duke's Institute for Learning in Retirement, a program of classes taught by peers and professionals, including history, language, literature, religion, science, current affairs, business and fitness.

Even if you don't want to study anything at all, Duke has something for you. You can hike, jog or picnic in Duke Forest, the 8,300-acre preserve that serves as a laboratory for Duke's School of The Environment.

Other attractions open to the public include the Bryan University Center and Page Auditorium, where more than 500 events are presented each year, including the world-renowned American Dance Festival; the Art Museum and galleries on both the East and West campuses; and the 20-acre Sarah P. Duke Gardens. Of course, there's always Atlantic Coast Conference basketball, football, soccer and baseball brought to you by the Duke Blue Devils. For more information on these, see our chapters on "Arts," "Attractions" and "Sports."

N.C. Central University
1801 Fayetteville St., Durham, NC 27707
• 560-6100

Founded in 1910 by educator Dr. James E. Shephard, N.C. Central University later became the first state-supported liberal arts college for blacks in the United States. Today NCCU is part of the 16-campus University of North Carolina system and continues to provide educational opportunities to students of all races.

The campus is set on 104 acres southeast of downtown Durham. About 6,000 students work toward bachelor's and master's degrees in over 50 fields. Students enroll in one of five schools: the Undergraduate and Graduate Schools of the Arts and Sciences, the School of Education, the School of Business, School of Law and School of Library and Information Sciences. Graduate programs also have been established for careers in criminal justice and public administration.

NCCU's law school is the only one in the state that offers working adults an opportunity to earn their degree through an evening program. NCCU also provides an extensive continuing education program, including courses of study available to many workers at their place of employment.

The school opened its new $12 million Biomedical Biotechnology Research Institute in August 1998.

Durham Technical Community College
P.O. Drawer 11307, Durham, NC 27703
• 686-3333

As a member of the N.C. Community College System, Durham Tech is a

Photo by Tim Johnson

Located southeast of downtown Durham, North Carolina Central University was founded in 1910 by educator Dr. James E. Shepherd.

two-year institution that offers vocational and technical training to residents of Durham and Orange counties, as well as fully transferable credit to four-year colleges and universities. More than 20,000 students attend Durham Tech annually. The school features 37 programs of study, 20 of them leading to an associate's degree. Courses of study include accounting, architectural drafting, automotive mechanics, business administration, computer programming, criminal justice, dental laboratory technology, early childhood development, electronics, general education, light construction, occupational therapy assistant, opticianry, paralegal training, pharmacy technology, practical nursing, respiratory therapy, secretarial science and more.

Day, evening and weekend classes are available. Durham Tech also offers short courses, workshops and seminars for continuing career development. It also customizes training programs for businesses and industries in the area. In addition, Durham Tech provides programs in adult basic education, high school completion and English as a Second Language.

Chapel Hill

University of North Carolina At Chapel Hill
**Morehead Planetarium Bldg.
Franklin St., Chapel Hill, NC 27514
Visitors Services • 962-1630**

For more than 200 years, the University of North Carolina at Chapel Hill has been nationally acclaimed for its teaching, research and public service programs.

INSIDERS' TIP

Most hotels in the area put out the "no vacancy" sign toward the middle of May, when graduations take place. If you plan to visit the area during that time, or if you have a graduate in the family, make reservations early.

Chancellor Michael Hooker says it is his goal to make UNC number one among all public universities.

The nation's oldest state university has been a leader in higher education since it opened its doors in 1795. The first student to register, Hinton James, was the University's only student for several weeks. UNC is consistently ranked as one of the top state universities in the country. In 1997, *Money* magazine named UNC as the best college value in the country and in 1998 *U.S. News & World Report* ranked it third in the nation among public universities. The 1998-99 tuition for state residents is about $2,224 per academic year; for nonresidents, it's about $11,210.

What started in one building with only a handful of students and two professors has mushroomed into a major research university with nearly 200 buildings, more than 24,000 students and nearly 2,400 faculty members, more than 90 percent of whom have a doctorate or their field's terminal degree.

With 14 colleges and schools and more than 70 departments and related centers and programs, UNC offers students a wide choice of curriculums leading to nearly 400 different undergraduate, graduate or professional degrees. You can study in one of eight colleges in the Division of Academic Affairs (General, Arts and Sciences, Business Administration, Education, Journalism, Law, Library Science and Social Work), or one of five schools in the Division of Health Affairs (Dentistry, Medicine, Nursing, Pharmacy and Public Health). More than 1,500 courses are offered through special institutes, seminars and workshops.

In 1997, the Kenan-Flagler Business School moved into the new, $43 million, state-of-the-art McColl Building, which is named for Kenan Flagler alumnus Hugh McColl, chairman and CEO of Bank of America.

Even for nonstudents, UNC is a fantastic resource to have in the neighborhood. With more than four million volumes, its libraries are among the best in the Southeast. You'll enjoy the Rare Book Collection, the North Carolina Collection and the Southern Historical Collection housed in the Wilson Library, as well as the resources in the newer Davis graduate library. North Carolina residents can apply for library cards, which cost $10. For information on applications, call 962-1053.

UNC is also the site of the UNC Hospitals complex, the state's principal referral, diagnostic and treatment center (see our chapter on "Health Care"). UNC and the medical center are the largest employers in Chapel Hill.

What's more, UNC's 729-acre main campus, known as "The Noble Grove," is rich in history, as well as just a nice place to stroll. Among the major attractions offered by UNC are the Coker Arboretum, McCorkle Place, Polk Place, Morehead Planetarium, Ackland Art Museum, Louis Round Wilson Library, N.C. Botanical Garden, PlayMakers Repertory Company, Dean E. Smith Center (the "Dean Dome"), Memorial Hall and, of course, Atlantic Coast Conference Basketball (the Tar Heel men were the national champs in 1993 and made back-to-back Final Four appearances in 1997 and 1998 and the Lady Tar Heels won the NCAA title in 1994), football (UNC-CH was ranked in the top 10 at the end of the 1997 season and enjoyed a victory over Virginia Tech in the Gator Bowl) and soccer. For more information on these attractions, see our chapters on "Arts," "Attractions" and "Sports."

The Triangle area is known for its medical research and technology.

Health Care

The Triangle area is known for its medical research and technology. Durham, the City of Medicine, is recognized throughout the world for the high quality of its medical facilities. The University of North Carolina Hospitals are also recognized as leaders in the fields of primary care and specialized services.

As in other areas throughout the United States, rapid developments and changes in the health care industry are also affecting the Triangle. In the past year, hospitals in the area have expanded or taken over other hospitals and clinics. Wake Medical Center in Raleigh opened its state-of-the-art birthing center in Cary and Rex Healthcare opened Wellness Centers, offering medically sound and professionally supervised fitness and health programs in Raleigh and Cary. Duke University Health System recently purchased Durham Regional Hospital and Raleigh Community Hospital.

This chapter is divided into Hospitals and Medical Care with listing by town under each heading.

FYI

Unless otherwise noted, the area code for all phone numbers listed in this guide is 919.

Hospitals

Raleigh and Cary

As throughout the nation, health care in Raleigh and Cary is changing. Physicians are consolidating practices and health care alliances are forming to offer families and patients lower medical costs. Regardless of changes in the delivery system, citizens' access to high quality medical care has been constant. Even when excluding UNC Hospitals and Duke University Medical Center, Raleigh and Cary residents are served by three general hospitals and three specialty hospitals.

Dorothea Dix
820 S. Boylan Ave. • 733-5540

Dorothea Dix was a crusading Yankee who came South and helped start the state's first programs for the mentally ill. In 1856, the state opened its first hospital for the mentally ill and it was appropriately named after the persistent Dorothea Dix. Today the hospital occupies several hundred acres of rolling historic countryside southwest of downtown Raleigh, surrounded by highways and the Beltline, the Farmers Market and neighborhoods.

Dix Hospital has seen its resident patient load diminish as treatment of the mentally ill has de-emphasized institutionalization. With 596 beds, the hospital remains one of the state's largest psychiatric hospitals for adults and adolescents, and it is accredited by the Joint Commission on Accredited Hospitals (JCAHO). It contains a full hospital staff with surgical and radiology units and a special children's psychiatric outpatient clinic, as well as an adolescent education program and adolescent inpatient services.

The hospital often is the subject of news reports because it also provides forensic services and receives patients who are referred by the courts for one reason or another. As a state hospital, it accepts indigent patients and has a policy of billing patients according to their ability to pay.

Rex Hospital, Raleigh's oldest hospital, recently completed construction of a new Emergency Department.

Photo courtesy of Rex Hospital

Holly Hill/Charter Behavioral Health System
3019 Falstaff Rd. • 250-7000
Outpatient: 250-7206
RESPOND: (800) 242-7837

This system is a joint venture of Columbia/HCA Healthcare Corporation and Charter Medical Services. The combined facility offers a full continuum of mental health and chemical dependency services for adolescents, adults and older adults. The hospital has 193 licensed beds and there are more than 50 psychiatrists who are active staff members.

Outpatient services include individual and group therapy, family therapy, day treatment programs and a chemical dependency intensive outpatient program. Inpatient services are provided for individuals with acute psychiatric or substance abuse problems. There is also a residential treatment center for adolescents, located at the North Raleigh site.

Holly Hill/Charter offers RESPOND, a 24-hour crisis intervention, assessment, information and referral service, free of charge to any individual seeking help for an emotional or chemical dependency problem.

Raleigh Community Hospital
3400 Wake Forest Rd. • 954-3000

Raleigh Community Hospital (RCH) opened its doors in 1978. It is conveniently located a block north of the I-440 Beltline exit onto Wake Forest Road. Formerly an affiliate of Columbia/HCA Healthcare Corporation, RCH was recently purchased by Duke University Health System for an estimated $175 million.

RCH, which admitted 6,400 patients in 1997, has 218 private and semiprivate beds, 15 of which are dedicated to intensive care. The hospital offers general medical and surgical services, and maintains an emergency room 24 hours a day with full-time emergency medicine physicians. The staff includes nearly 500 physicians, many of whom have offices located nearby.

Other services include The Childbirth Center, Same-Day Surgery Center, Diabetes Treatment Center, Rehabilitation Services and Health Plus Wellness and Cardiac Rehab Center. RCH also offers Raleigh's only Psychiatric Unit within a full-service hospital. In addition, the hospital provides radiology, pathology, CT and MRI scanners, respiratory therapy and a sleep-study center. A full-service pharmacy, The Plaza Pharmacist, is located on the RCH campus, as well as Raleigh Sports Medicine and Physical Therapy.

A member of the American Hospital Association, Raleigh Community Hospital earned the distinction of being the only hospital in the Triangle to receive Accreditation with Commendation by the Joint Commission on Accreditation of Healthcare Organizations in 1995. Less than 5 percent of all hospitals in the nation receive this distinction.

Rex Healthcare
4420 Lake Boone Tr. • 784-3100

Rex is the city's oldest hospital and its board of directors always has included the names of Raleigh's power elite. It's more than a city hospital; it is Raleigh history as well, tracing its roots to John Rex, a merchant and property owner who left money and land in 1839 to establish a hospital for the capital city. It took city leaders until 1894, however, before they erected a hospital bearing the Rex name on South Street. Since then, Rex has migrated about town and, in 1980, moved to its current facilities on a 62-acre site at the intersection of Blue Ridge Road and Lake Boone Trail. It is both the city's oldest and newest hospital and takes pride in its history as a not-for-profit institution.

Rex has recently signed a non-binding letter of intent to make Rex Healthcare part of the UNC Healthcare System. The partnership will strengthen Rex's ability to offer high-quality, cost-effective healthcare to the community and benefit from UNC's ability to introduce new treatment capabilities and advances in care.

Rex has 394 beds, all of them in private rooms, and includes a family birthing center with 40 rooms. More importantly, over 3,500 employees at Rex include some of the best physicians in the Triangle and its Cancer Center is as good as you will find, which is reflected in the 40,000 cancer treatments it performs annually. The Family Birth Center delivers over 5,200 babies annually, which is more than any other Triangle hospital. Rex's Wellness Centers, including the new $8.5 million, 62,000-square-foot health and wellness center on Cary Parkway, have become popular with the fitness crowd.

As a full-service integrated health care organization, Rex provides care in obstetrics, pediatrics, surgery and the latest in 24-hour emergency-room care. It also has a same-day surgery unit. Rex's specialized departments include clinical laboratories, intensive care, cardiac care and rehabilitation, nursery, physical therapy, radiation and radiology, respiratory therapy and a telemetry unit. It also has a 140-bed convalescent-care center. Rex is fully accredited with the JCAHO and maintains the Rex Blood Plan, a not-for-profit community blood bank.

Rex recently completed construction of a new Emergency Department and also opened a new adult day care and diabetes education center.

Wake Medical Center
3000 New Bern Ave.
250-8000

WakeMed is the city's largest general hospital, and as a public hospital, it maintains a high standard of care and serves all citizens regardless of their ability to pay. Today it offers the most advanced technology available through its 739-bed, five-hospital system, a 68-bed Rehabilitation Institute and the Medical Education Institute.

The new $21 million, state-of-the-art Wake Heart Center contains all of the latest technology and an experienced staff of cardiologists, cardiovascular surgeons and critical care nurses who perform the most advanced cardiology procedures. The Heart Center also provides a mobile cardiac care fleet, cardiac rehabilitation and an educational resource center. Over 1,000 open heart surgeries are performed annually at the Heart Center, one of the top three centers for the treatment of heart disease in the state.

Changing and growing according to community needs, Wake Medical offers vital services, including the only trauma center in the county, a Maternity Center where more than 3,600 babies are born every year, and a growing pediatric department that includes a children's emergency transport service, all on the central campus on New Bern Avenue just off I-440. A special $2 million Children's Emergency Room, one of only two in the state, opened in the summer of 1997.

In 1991, Wake Medical expanded into western Wake County, opening **Western Wake Medical Center in Cary, 233-2300**. This 80-bed community hospital, located at 1900 Kildaire Farm Road, offers a 24-hour emergency department, an intensive care unit, general medical/surgical and telemetry beds and outpatient diagnostic services. Western Wake is also the site of the new $1.9 million, 10,400-square-foot Women's Pavilion & Birthplace, Cary's only obstetrical center, where 835 babies were delivered during its first year. Wake Radiology Oncology Services, a state-of-the art, 65,000- square-foot cancer radiology center, opened at Western Wake in June of 1998.

Southern Wake in Fuquay-Varina and Eastern Wake in Zebulon are short-term skilled nursing facilities.

At WakeMed's Medical Education Institute are 45 outpatient clinics, the AHEC (Area Health Education Center) for continuing education programs and a full-service Medical Library. The Center features Healthworks, a cardiac rehabilitation center, and two mobile cardiac care units for specialized ground transportation of patients from eastern North Carolina. The 56-bed Wake Rehabilitation Hospital is the county's only inpatient rehab hospital serving patients recuperating from stroke, traumatic brain injury, multiple trauma, arthritis, neurological disorders and orthopedic conditions. After discharge, many patients continue treatment through the Rehabilitation Institute on Wake Forest Road.

The most advanced neonatal intensive care nursery in Wake County is at WakeMed, and a 38-bed maternity center offers family-centered single-room care for women who want to labor, deliver and complete their hospital stay in the same room. In the Neuro-Intensive Care Unit, patients with back and neck problems have access to the area's only endovascular specialist, neuropathologist and neuroradiologist.

WakeMed's team includes more than 4,000 nurses, technologists and support staff, and an affiliated physician staff of over 700. The hospital is proud of its history of delivering quality care and was the first hospital in Wake County to have CAT scan and MRI services.

A teaching hospital, WakeMed is affiliated with the University of North Carolina at Chapel Hill School of Medicine.

Durham

Durham is the City of Medicine. The medical industry is the town's top employer, utilizing almost a fourth of the city's work force. Here there are five major hospitals and a cadre of specialized diagnostic and treatment clinics. There are also a number of well-known weight-loss and fitness programs.

Duke University Medical Center
Erwin Rd. • 684-8111

It all began more than a half century ago when tobacco magnate James Buchanan Duke bequeathed $4 million to the university named for his father for the purpose of constructing a medical school and hospital. Today Duke University Medical Center is rated one of the best private tertiary-care facilities in the world. In July 1998, *U.S. News and World Report* ranked this teaching hospital fourth in the nation on an honor roll of top hospitals. Duke received top marks in the areas of cardiology, geriatrics, cancer treatment, orthopedics and urology.

Duke University Health System has recently expanded throughout the Triangle with acquisitions of Durham Regional Hospital and Raleigh Community Hospital.

With some 3 million square feet of space, DUMC offers patient care, physician training and specialized research into the causes and treatment of disease. To give just one example, Duke is a major research and treatment center for pediatric and adult AIDS patients, one of a few sites in the nation (along with neighboring UNC Hospitals) conducting clinical trials on new drugs used in the treatment of AIDS.

Duke University Hospital is a facility to which doctors and other hospitals refer patients from around the world. At the same time, it is a primary-care hospital for residents of the Durham area.

The original 400-bed facility opened in 1930 and today is licensed for 1,124 beds. The 870-plus bed North Division includes a 39-room operating suite, a burn-and-trauma unit and a helicopter service for the quick transport of critically ill or injured patients. In the Duke Children's Hospital, more than 120 beds are dedicated to children's services, making it one of the largest children's hospitals in the Southeast. Construction of a special Children's Emergency Room is underway, which will make the medical center one of two in the state to provide such a service.

Connected to the North Division is The Duke Eye Center, the only one of its scope between Baltimore and Miami, providing both patient care and research into the causes of eye disease.

The hospital's South Division includes nine buildings housing inpatients in psychiatry, medicine, surgery and obstetrics/gynecology, as well as outpatient clinics, an ambulatory surgery program, a rehabilitation unit and the Comprehensive Cancer Center, one of the only federally supported facilities of its magnitude between Washington, D.C., and Birmingham, Alabama. Other specialty facilities include the Heart Center and the Sports Medicine Program.

Most doctors on the staff at DUMC are also teachers in the School of Medicine here. The faculty of more than 2,000 clinical and research physicians includes many physicians who are world renowned in their fields. Duke University Medical Center's programs in surgery, cardiac care, obstetrics and gynecology, cancer treatment and AIDS research and treatment are among the many medical center services that are well known nationally and beyond.

Durham Regional Hospital
3643 N. Roxboro Rd., North of I-85
• 470-4000

Since opening its doors in 1976, this 451-bed facility has enjoyed a reputation as a fine community hospital. Duke University Health System recently took control of Durham Regional after negotiating a 20-year lease of the facility with Durham County.

In recent years, renovations at Durham Regional have improved access for outpatients and enhanced emergency room services and surgical capacity. A freestanding surgical center across the street from DRH offers outpatient surgical services.

With nearly 400 medical staff members representing virtually all specialties of medicine, Durham Regional Hospital

INSIDERS' TIP

There are 21 managed care companies licensed to operate in the Triangle with a combined membership of over one million people.

offers personalized, quality health care services. Just ask a new mother. Durham Regional delivers almost 3,000 babies each year. Expectant parents are offered an orientation tour of the obstetrics facilities before the birth takes place. Many mothers are able to leave the hospital with their newborns within 24 hours of delivery.

Durham Regional Hospital's outpatient services are equally popular. For example, its day surgery program features a growing list of procedures that do not require an overnight hospital stay. The hospital offers special programs to help patients cope with a variety of problems, from asthma to backaches. There are even wellness classes to help you control your weight and to reduce stress through biofeedback.

Durham Regional Hospital, through its HomeCare health services, provides at-home nursing services for patients of all ages. The hospital also provides the Lifeline program that allows elderly, frail or handicapped patients to signal the hospital through an electronic device when they need emergency medical service.

Some of the other services affiliated with Durham Regional Hospital include:

Lincoln Community Health Center offers a wide variety of outpatient medical services on a sliding fee scale. Oakleigh (309 Crutchfield Street, 470-6600) offers treatment for adults and families suffering from alcoholism and drug dependency. Emergency Medical Services responds to medical emergencies with Advanced Life Support ambulances and can also provide non-emergency, Basic Life Support transportation. Its Wheelchair Van Service is for people confined to wheelchairs, or who do not have their own transportation. DCHC also operates the Watts School of Nursing.

Lenox Baker
Children's Hospital
3000 Erwin Rd. • 684-6669

An integral part of Duke University Hospital, Lenox Baker Children's Hospital provides pediatric rehabilitation services to patients from newborn through 18 years of age. Patients treated here have some type of physical, cognitive or medical disability that impairs their level of function. Services are provided by a multidisciplinary team to coordinate individual medical, surgical, therapeutic and/or psychosocial care. The hospital offers both inpatient and outpatient treatment through its clinics, inpatient units and the physical, occupational and speech therapy departments. Specialized programs for children with brain injuries and physical disabilities are provided.

North Carolina
Eye and Ear Hospital
1110 W. Main St. • 682-9341
911-A Ridge, Rd., Roxboro • 597-2826

North Carolina Eye and Ear Hospital (formerly McPherson Hospital, founded in 1926) is a leading private hospital for treating the eye, ear, nose and throat. Today it serves more than 70,000 patients a year from across the Southeast. A full-service eye clinic and ear, nose and throat clinic provide services ranging from routine eye and ear exams to more advanced treatments. The hospital provides overnight accommodations for patients requiring inpatient care.

Other services include allergy testing and treatment, pediatric eye and ear care, facial reconstructive and cosmetic surgery procedures, speech and hearing services and conveniently located optical centers at both the Durham and Roxboro locations.

Veterans Affairs Medical Center
508 Fulton St. • 286-0411

This 502-bed general medical and surgical hospital shares many services and physicians with nearby Duke University Medical Center. It also operates a 120-bed nursing home unit. Through its affiliation with Duke, the VA Hospital participates in accredited residency training programs in psychiatry, internal medicine,

Founded in 1953, Durham's 502-bed VA Medical Center shares many services and physicians with nearby Duke University Medical Center.

general and thoracic surgery, anesthesiology, neurology, neurosurgery and ophthalmology, among other areas. Specialized treatment for veterans is available in such areas as neurosurgery, plastic surgery, open-heart surgery, home dialysis and nuclear medicine.

Chapel Hill

UNC Hospitals
Manning Dr. • 966-4131

Built in 1952 as a teaching hospital for the UNC School of Medicine, the UNC Hospitals complex has become one of the state's largest medical referral centers, drawing patients each year from throughout the Southeast for specialized diagnostic and treatment services. UNC Hospitals contains 684 beds and serves as the community hospital for residents of Orange and adjacent counties.

The hospital's staff is composed of faculty from the UNC Schools of Medicine and Dentistry. Many are recognized nationally and globally as experts in their fields. There are nearly 900 attending physicians and 500 interns and residents on the medical staff.

UNC Hospitals was the first hospital in the nation to have an intensive care unit, and the present Adult and Pediatric Critical Care Center's services are among the most advanced facilities available. Accident and disaster victims from all over North Carolina use the services provided by the N.C. Jaycee Burn Center, the Trauma Center and Carolina AirCare, the helicopter and ground patient transport service. UNC Hospitals also has the UNC Lineberger Comprehensive Cancer Center and a nationally recognized Comprehensive Hemophilia Diagnosis and Treatment Center and an organ-transplant program.

UNC Hospitals (which includes the main facility, the N.C. Women's Hospital, the N.C. Children's Hospital and the N.C. Neurosciences Hospital) and its medical staff are recognized as leaders in the care of patients with diseases such as arthritis, cancer, digestive diseases, cystic fibrosis, growth disorders, neurological disorders, hemophilia and infertility. UNC Hospitals is a major referral center for the care of premature infants and women with high-risk pregnancies.

In its 1998 survey, *U.S. News & World Report* ranked UNC Hospitals as one of "America's Best Hospitals" in the following categories: gastroenterology, geriatrics, gynecology, neurology, pulmonary care and urology.

UNC Hospitals offers highly specialized care for patients with complex medical problems, as well as a complete range of high-quality, routine services for families. Expectant parents appreciate the family-centered maternal and infant care, including private delivery rooms with comfortable home-style furnishings and a visitation policy that allows siblings to visit as soon as the baby is born.

UNC Hospitals also offered one of the first outpatient surgery programs in the country, making it possible for more patients to avoid the necessity of a costly hospital stay for many types of surgery. The Ambulatory Care Center that opened in 1993 offers an expanded outpatient surgery service, as well as more convenient and accessible acute and preventive medical care for children and adults. Elderly and home-bound patients can participate in the hospital's Lifeline program, which provides them with an electronic device so they can signal the hospital when they need emergency medical assistance.

UNC Hospitals' staff physicians, who specialize in internal medicine, pediatrics, obstetrics and gynecology and family medicine, also provide day-to-day medical care. Call UNC HealthLink (966-7890) for information.

Medical Care

Triangle residents have access to a wide range of primary and specialty care. The medical delivery system here has been changing rapidly during the past several years. In some ways, there is more competition among doctors and dentists than ever before as urgent care centers and Health Maintenance Organizations (HMOs) have proliferated in our area. However, the growth of HMOs has resulted in some consolidation of medical services as practices have merged or been bought by local hospitals or HMOs. There are a large number of doctors, dentists and health care specialists, many of whom trained in the Triangle's nationally recognized teaching hospitals. Among the area hospitals, HMOs and private practitioners, you will easily find quality medical care.

For your family or "primary-care" physician, however, you want to find a family practitioner or an internist for the adults in

Seminars for a Healthier, Happier You

Would you like to learn how to simplify your life, understand why your feet ache or get a cholesterol screening? These are just a few of the many seminars, programs, workshops, screenings and events available through area hospitals. For either a small fee or no fee, you can learn yoga, take a refresher course in driving, find out about facelifts and cosmetic surgery, or attend some of the many other seminars that are held by health-care facilities throughout the Triangle.

Through Duke Healthy Connections, part of the Duke University Health System, Duke University Medical Center sponsors monthly events at various locations in Durham. During the summer of 1998, *Glaucoma: "How Do I Know If I Have It? Is It Inherited? What Can Be Done To Prevent It?"* and *Corneal Diseases & Corneal Transplants: What You Need To Know* were discussed at the Duke Eye Center. The Duke Center for Aesthetic Services offered *Cosmetic Surgery Options for Women "Individual Choices"* and *Facelifts And Cosmetic Surgery Of The Face "Dramatic Subtleties."* Duke Women's Services presented *PMS: New Treatment*

Options and *Oh, My Aching Feet.* The programs were conducted by medical doctors and lasted about two hours. Other programs administered by registered nurses included *Helping Women Cope With Losses, Baby Care Class* and a *Cancer Education Series.* For more information on Duke Healthy connections, call 416-DUKE.

This past summer at Wake Medical Center, WakeMed Star Dates included a *Cholesterol Screening* for a $6 charge and a *55 Alive Refresher Course,* designed for drivers over 50, with topics on safely entering and leaving expressways and how to compensate for hearing and peripheral vision loss. WakeMed also offered a free *Sibling Class,* where children from ages 3 to 12 toured the Women's Pavilion & Birthplace and made a toy for their new baby brother or sister. The popular *Safe Sitter Program* teaches girls and boys from 11 to 13 how to be safe baby-sitters. The two-day class costs $40. WakeMed also offers a *Families First Club,* a free club for parents and children under eight. The club provides free parenting seminars, a quarterly newsletter and a calendar of events and special events just for club members. Call 250-STAR for upcoming events and a free set of "Star Date" calendar stickers.

Rex Healthcare's Wellness Center offered summer programs such as *Simplify Your Life,* a seminar that taught attendees how to find balance and conquer time wasters, opening up new possibilities for living a simple life. *Holistic Health For Women* was another topic discussed, touching on the physiological and psychological hormonal issues that women may encounter. Yoga, Tai Chi and CPR for infants and children were other classes taught during the summer. The Rex Wellness Center also provides a series of aerobic classes from 6 to 8 PM during the week. A variety of choices is available from low impact to super step to aqua aerobics. Some classes are free, but others require a fee or membership in the Wellness Center. For more details, call 783-4490.

Photo by Tim Johnson

Western Wake Medical Center

UNC Hospitals provide community service through UNC HealthLink, UNC HealthScene, UNC HealthTouch and *The Newcomer Guide to Health Care in Chapel Hill.* UNC HealthLink, 966-7890, is a free service staffed by registered nurses. They'll answer questions about your immediate health concerns, help you make an appointment or provide information about faculty physicians at UNC. *UNC HealthScene* is a free bimonthly journal that provides up-to-date health information on the prevention and treatment of diseases, as well as tips to maintain a healthy lifestyle. Call 966-7890 for a free subscription. UNC HealthTouch, 966-0000, is a 24-hour-a-day service that allows callers using a touch-tone phone to enter a four-digit code and hear confidential health information on various topics from Aging to Varicose Veins. *The Newcomer Guide to Health Care* provides tips on allergies and heat exhaustion, a medical center map, advice on how to select a doctor and forms to help you transfer your medical records. To request a copy, call 966-7890.

your family and a pediatrician or family practitioner for the children.

How do you find such a physician? Many people ask a trusted friend or neighbor to recommend a doctor. If you know a staff member at a local hospital, he or she can often be a good, unofficial source. If you call a physician who is not taking new patients, ask his or her office staff to recommend someone else.

Some people may prefer a group practice that includes not only internists or primary care physicians but also specialists in other areas such as heart, lung, digestive and infectious diseases. A group practice can be a good choice for a family who knows it will need such specialty care because of existing medical conditions. If you're middle-aged or younger and healthy, an internist, family practitioner and (if you have kids) a pediatrician should be able to provide any needed care. The local telephone book's Yellow Pages, county medical societies and community hospitals all can provide some information about physicians in your town.

Raleigh and Cary

We have combined Raleigh and Cary medical information since the subject spills over city lines; Cary residents, for example, may use Raleigh-based physicians and vice versa.

The Physician Referral line (a free service) is open from 10 AM until 5 PM Monday through Friday to provide names and phone numbers of local physicians, in different specialties, who have indicated they are taking new patients. Information about a physician's medical school and postgraduate education is available only if the physician is a member of the Wake County Medical Society.

The Wake Dental Society has a similar referral system and you can get that information by calling the state society's office and asking for the number of the current Wake County chapter president. He or she is the one who provides the information.

The Triangle United Way provides First Call, a free information and referral service, at 460-1811 (Wake County) or 688-2316 (Durham County). The Cary Chamber of Commerce also publishes a list of local physicians and dentists.

Meanwhile, if you sprain your ankle moving in or your child runs a fever before you've found a family physician, you may want to try one of the area's urgent care centers. For major emergencies you must go to the Emergency Room at one of Raleigh's three major hospitals.

Below are contact numbers for health care sources.

Wake County Medical Society
800 St. Mary's St., Raleigh • 821-2227

N.C. Dental Society
1600 Evans Rd., Cary • 677-1396

N.C. Chiropractic Association
333 Fayetteville Street Mall, Raleigh
• 832-0611

The Alcoholism Treatment Center
3000 Falstaff Rd.
• 250-1500

A Wake County Human Services agency, the center provides outpatient services and has 34 beds for inpatient services. If you're a member of AA and want to find a local chapter, the center can help you. It is a licensed psychiatric hospital with a full nursing staff and certified alcoholism counselors, and there is a substance abuse day-treatment program. Services also include family counseling for those who live with alcoholics and substance abusers.

Planned Parenthood

100 South Boylan Ave. • 833-7526

Located at the corner of West Morgan Street and South Boylan Avenue near downtown, the local chapter provides family planning programs for individuals as well as organizations such as church youth groups. It also conducts pregnancy tests and gynecological exams, but performs no abortions. It does make referrals.

Carolina Breast Cancer Detection Centers

**300 Ashville Ave., Ste. 100, Cary
• 467-4191**
3821 Merton Dr., Raleigh • 787-7411
4301 Lake Boone Tr., Raleigh • 781-6707
110 S. Estes Dr., Chapel Hill • 942-3196

These centers specialize in the detection of breast cancer. Physicians serving the branches are on staff at Wake Medical.

Wake County Mental Health, Developmental Disabilities and Substance Abuse Services

3010 Falstaff Rd. • 250-3100
401 E. Whitaker Mill Rd. • 856-6400
**Evaluation & Emergency Services:
250-3133**

Services of this public service agency are delivered in many locations throughout Wake County by agency staff or through contract affiliates. Assistance is offered for children, adults and families affected by mental illness, developmental disabilities and/or substance abuse. Services include assessment and treatment, emergency care, case management, brief individual/family therapy, community support services, mobile crisis intervention, services for persons who are deaf or hearing impaired, vocational services, psychiatric services and medication monitoring. Court-ordered evaluation and treatment are offered here as well as an in-home assistance program, intervention services, housing assistance and services for the homeless. Regular hours for out-patient services are Monday through Friday, 8:30 AM until 5:15 PM. Evaluation and emergency services are available 24 hours a day, seven days a week. Fees vary according to the type of service provided.

Durham

There are probably more physicians per capita in Durham than in most major cities: More than 1,500 licensed doctors make the county's physician-to-patient ratio better than five times the national average.

How does a newcomer know where to turn for medical care? Probably the best way is to ask your friends, relatives or coworkers for recommendations. If you're unable to come up with a good referral, try one of the sources listed below.

Durham-Orange County Medical Society
• 383-2602

Durham Regional Hospital Physician Locator Service
• (800) 362-8677

Duke Family Medicine Center
2100 Erwin Rd. (Pickens Bldg.)
• 684-2885

This facility, sponsored by Duke University, offers health care for the entire family, including OB/GYN, family counseling, substance abuse evaluation and nutrition counseling.

Lincoln Community Health Center
1301 Fayetteville St. • 956-4000

Lincoln Community Health Center offers an extensive range of medical services to patients on a sliding-fee basis. Services offered under the sponsorship of Durham County Hospital Corporation

(see "Hospitals" section of this chapter) include medical care for the whole family, mental health counseling, dental care and health education.

Diet and Fitness Centers

Durham has a number of well-known weight-loss and fitness programs, earning Durham an international reputation as the Diet Capital of the World. Here are brief descriptions of three of the best known.

Duke University Diet and Fitness Center
804 W. Trinity Ave. • 684-6331

This program, part of Duke's Department of Community and Family Medicine, offers a comprehensive treatment and education plan for individuals with weight management problems. Long-term lifestyle changes are the goal here, and the center emphasizes nutrition, behavior and fitness. Psychologists and their staff of physicians work with patients to achieve and maintain weight-loss.

Rice Diet Clinic
1821 Green St. • 286-2243

The Rice Diet is the reason that Durham has become a mecca for dieters and a spawning ground for dozens of wildly successful and innovative weight-reduction centers. At the Rice Diet Clinic, patients are put on a strict, six-phase eating plan calling for initial emphasis on rice and fruit, eventually followed by steamed vegetables, chicken, fish, eggs and an average weight loss of 15 to 25 pounds in 2 weeks.

To date, over 20,000 patients have been to the Rice Diet Clinic. And the Rice Diet itself has spawned another major industry for Durham, each year bringing to local weight-loss centers $40 million and 2,000 dieters.

Structure House
3017 Pickett Rd. • 493-4205

Structure House claims to be the first intensive residential weight-control program in the nation to successfully combine psychology and lifestyle counseling with medicine, nutrition and exercise. Started in 1977, Structure House is the brainchild of Dr. Gerard Musante, the first psychologist in the United States to treat obesity as a psychological, rather than a physical problem.

Chapel Hill

Chapel Hill medical care is impressive in both its quality and diversity.

UNC Hospitals Services
Manning Drive • 966-4131

Many Chapel Hill area residents go to the staff and clinics at UNC Hospitals and the UNC School of Medicine for their day-to-day medical care. Just call for an appointment. There are also walk-in clinics for people who do not have a regular doctor and need to see someone right away. If you need more information prior to making an appointment, call UNC Healthlink, 966-7890. Healthlink is staffed by registered nurses who provide health information and easy access to medical services at UNC Hospitals. Here are brief descriptions of some of the services available:

The Ambulatory Care Center is on the corner of Mason Farm Road and South Columbia Street. The ACC features modern treatment and exam rooms and spacious waiting areas with playrooms for children. There is ample on-site parking. Other outpatient services available at UNC Hospitals include the Internal Medicine Clinic, Surgery Clinics, Pediatrics, Outpatient Surgical Services and Pediatric Acute Care Service.

The Family Practice Center, 966-0211, on Manning Drive near U.S. 15-501 Bypass, houses family physicians who can provide general medicine care for every member of the family, including obstetrics, pediatrics and minor surgery.

Fearrington Medical Center, 542-6800, is a UNC Hospitals outpatient center offering internal medicine and physical therapy at the Fearrington Village.

**The Triangle benefits
from a rich media tradition.**

Media

North Carolina has a rich media history and the Journalism School at the University of North Carolina in Chapel Hill is one of the best. If you want to drop some names on your out-of-state relatives, casually work into your conversation that Edward R. Murrow, Charles Kuralt, Charlie Rose and David Brinkley, by the way, came from North Carolina.

The Triangle benefits from this rich tradition. It has three daily newspapers, including the Pulitzer Prize winning *News & Observer*, probably the state's most influential newspaper. The Triangle's television stations are respected way stations on the path to prime time.

Here's where you can pick up some of that history and gain an Insider's savvy about bylines and broadcasts, business news and best personals (ads, that is). Who carries the NCSU Wolfpack's sports? Who's the voice of the Tar Heels? For the Duke Blue Devils? Important, vital stuff. You'll find it here. And yes, for all you Morning Edition and All Things Considered addicts, the Triangle does provide a daily fix.

Raleigh Newspapers

The News and Observer
215 S. McDowell St. • 829-4500

This is the daily morning newspaper in Raleigh and many in Chapel Hill and Durham as well subscribe to the *N&O* in addition to—or instead of—their local newspapers. The paper, which is owned by the California-based McClatchy chain, has a tradition for outspoken opinions dating back to founder Josephus Daniels' campaigns for prohibition and against lynching. A grandson, Frank Daniels Jr., recently retired as publisher and was replaced by Fred Crisp. Former Executive Editor Frank Daniels III pushed the paper into computer technology and the *N&O* is recognized nationally for its use of such wizardry in investigative and general news reporting.

The news coverage, separate from the newspaper's editorial opinions, is tough but fair. Its onetime chief investigative sleuth, Pat Stith, still strikes fear in the hearts of bureaucrats. Former editor Claude Sitton won the Pulitzer Prize for commentary in 1983 and former book editor Michael Skube won it in 1989. The 1996 Pulitzer was awarded to the paper for its series on the environmental threats to the Neuse River. Its prize-winning cartoonist, Dwane Powell, deserves a Pulitzer and his caricatures are coveted trophies even by his victims. Washington correspondent, James Rosen, won a 1998 National Press Club Award.

The *N&O's* outlook has lately become more local and trendy. With veteran reporters and writers such as Rob Christensen, Joe Neff, Ruth Sheehan, Wade Rawlins, Jim Jenkins and columnists Barry Saunders and Dennis Rogers, it is the most influential newspaper in the state with a daily circulation of 160,000.

The Carolinian
610 Maywood Ave. • 834-5558

Published twice a week, *The Carolinian* targets the capital city's southeast black community and has its greatest influence there. It has been a voice for Raleigh blacks for decades and its current principal writer sets his own agenda when reporting the news. Articles are oriented toward African-American issues and personalities, religious commentary and sensational crime.

Cary Newspapers

The Cary News
212 E. Chatham St. • 460-2600

Published on Wednesday and Saturday, this newspaper has grown with the city and keeps its 11,500 readers focused on Cary. It is owned by the California-based McClatchy chain and sometimes serves as a stepping stone for reporters or managers who move up to the *N&O*. It does a good job of covering Cary city news, local school news and sports. "Cary Calling," a feature started in 1991, allows area residents to phone in their opinions on any topic. The responses are printed in the Saturday paper. This has become one of the most controversial features in the newspaper.

Durham Newspapers

The Herald-Sun
2828 Pickett Rd. • 419-6500

It all started back in 1889 when the Durham and Northern Railroad found itself without any editorial support in its right-of-way battle with the Durham and Clarksville line. At the urging of several alarmed aldermen, the *Durham Daily Sun* was established, eventually taking its place as an afternoon paper. In 1929, just before the stock market crashed, Edward Tyler Rollins purchased *The Sun* and merged it with his morning paper, *The Herald*.

Today the paper is headed by publisher David Hughey. *The Herald-Sun* emphasizes local news, with state, national and international news coverage provided by the Associated Press wire. In addition to local editorials, you'll find the opinions of nationally syndicated columnists James J. Kilpatrick, Russell Baker

and George Will. As part of the great Triangle newspaper wars, *The Herald-Sun* also publishes an Orange County daily edition, *The Chapel Hill Herald*.

The Carolina Times
923 Fayetteville St. • 682-2913

The Carolina Times, published weekly on Thursdays, emphasizes local, state and national news affecting the black community. The paper was established in 1926 by long-time civil rights activist Louis Austin, whose goal was to offer a voice to blacks at a time when they clearly had no say in local, state or national politics. Austin died in 1971, but his objectives continue to be carried out today under the leadership of his daughter, Vivian Austin Edmonds, the current editor and publisher. *The Carolina Times* emphasizes local news, sports and features, but provides state, national and international news from the Associated Press wire service.

The Triangle Tribune
119 Market St. • 688-9408

The weekly *Triangle Tribune* made its debut in March 1998, covering the black communities in Chapel Hill, Durham and Raleigh with a focus on business, education, health and politics. It is published on Sundays. The paper's owners also publish *The Charlotte Post* and *The Chronicle* in Winston-Salem.

Chapel Hill Newspapers

The Chapel Hill Herald
106 Mallette St. • 967-6581

Chapel Hill has become a battleground in the great Triangle newspaper wars and the last chapter has yet to be written in the battle for the upscale local readership.

The Chapel Hill Herald is an impressive local edition. If you subscribe to the Durham paper and you live in the Chapel Hill area, you'll get *The Chapel Hill Herald*

The Chapel Hill News keeps local residents informed about the activities in the "Southern Part of Heaven."

edition with front page coverage of local news, including coverage of adjacent Chatham County. Inside are local features, national columnists and plenty of scoop on everything from the courthouse to campus.

The Chapel Hill News
505 W. Franklin St. • 932-2000

Now owned by *The News & Observer*, this local paper in Chapel Hill is on the ascent. *The Chapel Hill News* is published on Wednesdays, Fridays and Sundays to over 25,000 Chapel Hill-Carrboro households. The newspaper got its start as a weekly in 1923 and has undergone numerous changes in both name and format prior to its present status as a thrice-weekly paper.

Under publisher and editor Ted Vaden, the paper keeps readers up to date on local government, university news and town tidbits. You'll find coverage of Chapel Hill, Carrboro, Orange County and UNC, as well as state and regional news. The editorial page features commentary by local, regional and nationally syndicated columnists. Entertainment pages, book reviews and a food and dining column round out the paper.

Triangle Publications

Brightleaf: A Southern Review of Books
P.O. Box 11485, Raleigh • 664-8650

Editor and publisher David Perkins describes *Brightleaf* as "a combination of *The New York Review of Books*, *Publisher's Weekly* and the old *Saturday Evening Post*—with a Southern point of view." The bimonthly publication, which premiered in September 1997, features the work of many acclaimed regional writers, such as Reynolds Price, Doris Betts, Ernest Gaines, Lee Smith, Allan Gurganus, Elizabeth Spencer, Fred Chappell and Clyde Edgerton.

Business Leader
3801 Wake Forest Rd., Ste. 102, Raleigh • 872-7077

Business Leader is a monthly magazine published by Business to Business, Inc. It offers the local business community features on area businesses, marketing strategies, industry trends, business law and commercial real estate.

Carolina Parent
103 W. Main St., Suite. 210, Durham
• 956-2430

This parent and child-oriented publication was begun in 1987 by publishers and editors Barbara Matchar and Gita Schonfeld. In 1993 it was purchased by *The News & Observer,* which sold the monthly publication to Carolina Parenting, Inc., in 1998. The paper features well-written pieces, both humorous and informative, by and for parents. It includes a comprehensive calendar of events of interest to parents and kids in each issue. It is distributed free throughout the Triangle and has a circulation of over 35,000.

Carolina Woman
P.O. Box 52687, Durham
• 852-5900

Founded by Editor and Publisher Debra Simon in 1993, *Carolina Woman* provides feature articles on subjects such as business and health, as well as recipes, a calendar of events and horoscopes. The publication is distributed free throughout the Triangle.

The Independent Weekly
2810 Hillsborough Rd., Durham
• 286-1972

The Independent, which began publishing in 1983, hails itself as the Triangle's "news alternative" and it does, indeed, take on some big assignments that others often miss. It was started by Harvard graduate and Nieman Fellow Katherine Fulton. The weekly has settled into a Triangle niche after first trying to be a state-wide publication. That niche is a newspaper that's long on crusading opinions and politically correct reporting. It publishes the most entertaining "personals" in the Triangle.

The Independent has berated local slumlords, state prisons, highway building and

General Assembly high-handedness. It also publishes a great entertainment calendar and comic review of national cartoonists and zany features. Several national journals have cited it as one of the best of its kind in the country. Godfrey Cheshire, the former film critic for *The Spectator,* recently joined *The Independent.* Its biggest treat is the wild, brilliant writing by award-winning columnist, Hal Crowther, husband of novelist Lee Smith. Crowther is far and away the state's best newspaper columnist—and a big reason 150,000 "Indy" readers pick it up free at newsstands and racks everywhere on Wednesdays.

La Voz de Carolina
P.O. Box 12471, Raleigh • 875-0551

The Hispanic community is a growing, dynamic part of Triangle business and culture. *La Voz de Carolina* is a weekly publication with a circulation of 15,000 that spotlights international, national and North Carolina news of special interest to the Hispanic community. Subscriptions are available for home delivery. Copies of the paper may be picked up at no charge in area businesses.

> **FYI**
> Unless otherwise noted, the area code for all phone numbers listed in this guide is 919.

North Carolina Review of Books
P.O. Box 10443, Raleigh • 508-4183

Pick up this free publication at area bookstores for cutting-edge reviews of contemporary literature.

Philanthropy Journal
5 W. Hargett St., Ste. 805, Raleigh
• 899-3740

Editor Todd Cohen, formerly the business editor at the *N&O,* has taken this Daniels' family publishing venture and developed it into a successful and thoughtful journal covering the growing business of philanthropy. If you are interested in nonprofits, you must subscribe.

The Spectator
1318 Dale St., Raleigh • 828-7393

The Spectator fills an entertainment void that the staid and serious *N&O* misses. The publication was founded in 1978 by R. B. "Bernie" Reeves, who recently sold it to Creative Loafing, an Atlanta-based publisher. Over the years, *The Spectator* has succeeded not so much by competing with the *N&O*, but by going around it. The weekly specializes in a calendar of events, as well as opinions and reviews on the Triangle's nonpolitical life, especially movies, music and art, including architecture.

The Spectator's writers, such as Bill Morrison, have earned a local following and the newspaper's no-holds-barred policy on letters to the editor reflects its indulgence of different points of view.

Triangle Business Journal
1305 Navaho Dr., Suite 401, Raleigh • 878-0010

The weekly *TBJ* works hard and effectively to keep the business community in touch with each other. People, company dynamics, commercial real estate, finance, investments and other aspect of business are reported in an attractive, concise format.

Triangle Lifestyle
P.O. Box 12826, Raleigh • 839-0785

A relative newcomer to the Triangle publishing scene, *Triangle Lifestyle* offers trendy and traditional features on local arts and entertainment, area restaurants and night life, shopping, fashion, health and fitness and gardening. Founder and publisher Margaret Webb introduced this bimonthly magazine in 1997.

Triangle Newcomer Magazine
5000 Falls of the Neuse Rd., Ste. 400, Raleigh • 878-6151

The semiannual *Newcomer Magazine* was previously published by Bond Publishing, which sold it to Signature Publishing, Inc., in 1998. It includes tips on selecting a neighborhood, home buying, building and decorating, utility hookups and pet licensing as well as information on public and private schools, colleges and universities. Health care options, leisure activities, retirement and religious options are included along with a Triangle business perspective. Charts and maps direct the newcomer to utilities, financial services, accommodations and radio and television stations.

Triangle Pointer
88 McClamroch Cr. • Chapel Hill • 968-4801, (800) 400-1901

Triangle Pointer is the Triangle's oldest guide and calendar magazine for lodging, restaurants, entertainment and a number of other items such as art exhibits, church services, museums and TV programs. It is free and distributed at area motels. Published monthly, each issue includes a handy guide map to Chapel Hill, Durham, Raleigh and RTP.

INSIDERS' TIP

The Durham *Herald-Sun* is the largest family owned newspaper in the state. Until 1995, that distinction belonged to the Daniels family (Josephus, Jonathan, Frank, Frank Jr., and Frank III) who dominated North Carolina journalism for 101 years through the *N&O,* sometimes called the Nuisance and Disturber. The paper is now owned by the McClatchy chain from California.

Television

Raleigh-Durham is currently the nation's 29th largest television market. The Triangle's TV stations all see themselves as regional media and have helped foster the idea that the Triangle is one metropolis probably more than any other institution. Cable connections are available in most parts of the Triangle and bring in a number of outside stations, including TBS in Atlanta. The stations based in the Triangle are listed here alphabetically, along with network and channel number. The numbers may be different, however, if you are a cable subscriber.

WKFT-40
131 Wind Chime Ct., Raleigh • 846-7271
Fayetteville • (910) 323-4040

WKFT is an independent affiliate of Charlotte-based Bahakel Communications, which acquired the station in 1997. Some of its most popular shows are reruns of *Matlock*, *The Beverly Hillbillies* and *Gunsmoke*.

WLFL-22, WB
3012 Highwoods Blvd., Raleigh
• 872-9535

Formerly an affiliate of Fox, WLFL became the new Warner Brothers affiliate in August 1998. The station, which is owned by Baltimore's Sinclair Communications, offers a popular 10 PM newscast. It also features a number of popular new shows for the young set, including *Buffy, the Vampire Slayer* and *Dawson's Creek*. Other fare includes movies and popular reruns, such as *The Simpsons*, *Frasier* and *Home Improvement*.

WNCN-17, NBC
1205 Front St., Raleigh • 836-1717

WNCN took up the NBC affiliate that WRDC dropped when it switched to UPN. Highly advertised as "a whole new NBC,"

WNCN features a personable news staff with 3-D weather reports.

WRAL-5, CBS
2619 Western Blvd., Raleigh • 821-8555

WRAL became an affiliate of CBS in 1985 and before that, had established itself as the premier station in the Triangle and one of the best stations in the country. Though finding the airwaves more competitive these days, the station continues to compete for the top spot among Triangle viewers.

The station's news team features co-anchors David Crabtree and Pam Saulsby, chief meteorologist Greg Fishel and sportscaster Tom Suiter. WRAL goes the extra mile to provide coverage on local newsmakers no matter where they go, be it Hurricane Bonnie or the NCAA tournament. Its parent company is Jim Goodmon's Capitol Broadcasting.

WRAZ-50, FOX
2619 Western Blvd., Raleigh • 821-8550

Formerly known as WRAZ-50 WB, this station became the new Fox affiliate in August 1998. Owned by Carolina Broadcasting System, which leases it to Capitol Broadcasting, WRAZ broadcasts from WRAL's facility. Fox 50, as it calls itself, relies on the Fox network's hit shows, such as *Ally McBeal*, *Party of Five*, *The X-Files*, *The Simpsons* and *King of the Hill*. It also has a 10 PM newscast. During the season, Fox airs NFL football.

WRDC-28, UPN
3012 Highwoods Blvd., Raleigh
• 872-2854

This local UPN affiliate runs such high-rated shows as *Star Trek Voyager*, *Xena: Warrior Princess* and popular syndicated reruns. WRDC switched from NBC to UPN in 1995 and no longer sponsors a local newscast. Original programming is limited, as UPN is a

TRIANGLE RADIO STATIONS

Station	Programming Format	Request Line	Special Programming
WAUG 750 AM	Gospel	546-9284	Tom Pope Show
WBBB 96.1 FM	Adult-oriented Rock	860-9600	All Rock All The Time
WCHL 1360 AM	Contemporary Standards	942-8765	Tar Heel Sports, Chapel Hill News
WCLY 1550 AM	Gospel	821-1550	All Gospel All The Time
WCPE 89.7 FM	Classical	556-5178	Opera House, BBC World News, Met. Opera
WDCG 105.1 FM	Contemporary	860-1051	Bob & Madison
WDNC 620 AM	News, Talk, Sports	942-8765	Bulls, Hornets, Duke Sports, G. Gordon Liddy
WKIX 96.9 FM	New Country	860-9549	Mad Dog & Morgan Show
WPTF 680 AM	News, Talk, Sports	878-1724	NCSU Sports, Rush Limbaugh, Dr. Laura
WQDR 94.7 FM	Country	860-9470	Pinecone Blue Grass, Country Countdown USA
WQQK 97.5 FM	Contemporary, R&B	848-9765	Gospel Live
WRAL 101.5 FM	Adult Contemporary	860-1015	Cornerstone, Bill in the Morning
WRBZ 850 AM	Talk, Sports	875-9100	Imus, Mike Solarte Show, Sports Babe
WRDU 106.1 FM	Rock	860-1061	John Boy and Billy, Rock Line
WRSN 93.9 FM	Soft Rock	361-0939	Love Songs After Dark
WRTP 1000 AM	Christian Contemporary	839-1000	Focus on the Family
WTRG 100.7 FM	Oldies	860-1007	Tar Heel Sports, Paul Harvey Commentary
WUNC 91.5 FM	NPR News, Classical	966-5454	Morning Edition, All Things Considered, Back Porch Music
WWND 102.9FM	Jazz	860-1029	All Jazz All The Time

developing network. Like WLFL, WRDC is owned by Sinclair Communications.

WRPX-47, PAX
Gresham Lake Rd., Raleigh • 872-4748

The Triangle's newest television station, WRPX-47, hit the airwaves on August 31, 1998. Owned by Paxson Communications of West Palm Beach, Florida, PAX-TV features family fare such as *Touched by an Angel*, *I'll Fly Away* and *Dr. Quinn, Medicine Woman*.

WTVD-11, ABC
4111 Liberty St., Durham • 683-1111

WTVD has been trading the No. 1 spot with WRAL since it settled on a solid, veteran North Carolina reporter, Larry Stogner, as its news anchor and Miriam Thomas as co-anchor.

The station gives more attention to political coverage than the competition and its veteran reporters have good noses for news and scoops. It broadcasts 90 minutes of local news and

Let's Go Surfin' Now...

It's no secret that the Triangle is a popular place. So where do savvy travelers go to find out about a place that constantly makes the top five in almost every "Best Of ..." list? Well, after they've read all about the Triangle in their *Insider's Guide*, they'll check out the Internet.

One of the most informative web sites is GO, Triangle Guide Online at **www.news-observer.com/ go/go**. Pages include On Campus, Dining Out, Entertainment & Recreation, New In Town?, In School, Find Your Faith, Your Town and Plan Today.

On Campus provides links to all the universities and colleges in the area and also gives you the option to link to North Carolina on the Web and Research Triangle on the Web. From North Carolina on the Web, you can link to several sequenced news articles featured in *The News & Observer* and many official sources such as the North Carolina General Assembly, state demographic profiles, economic trends, city and regional road maps and the overview and history of North Carolina agriculture. The North Carolina Encyclopedia link provides connections to political, geographical, educational and historical web sites.

Dining Out features information and reviews of area restaurants. Entertainment & Recreation provides links to an entertainment calendar, activities for children and parents, articles from the *N&O* on area events, and links to art museums and galleries, plays, children's activities, movies, music and recreation. New In Town? offers information on life in the South; clubs and organizations; real estate; utilities; state, county and city government; and much more.

In School gives links to area school districts, the N.C. Department of Public Instruction, school menus and calendars, and NandoNext, an online newspaper featuring stories and art by students from Triangle high schools. Find Your Faith has a link to the *N&O's* Faith section, which provides information about religion, a calendar of events and a directory of every church, synagogue and mosque in the area.

Your Town allows you to choose any town in the Triangle (it lists 24, including RTP) and access information on just about everything you need to know about a town. Plan Today gives weather forecasts and lists daily events.

Another Triangle area web site is CitySearch at **www.citysearch11.com**. Pages include links to Feature Stories, Arts & Entertainment, Eat & Drink, Community, Shops & Services, Professional Services, Sports & Outdoors, News and Travel & Visitors. This site links to many of the area's commercial establishments with articles about and links to local attractions and events.

Virtual Raleigh at **www.virtualraleigh.com** provides links to Raleigh area information such as maps, real estate and apartment listings, weather, news and radio stations, and even books about North Carolina. Local professional and college sports as well as links to area attractions are also provided. Links to Arts &

Museums and Dining provide a comprehensive listing of just about every gallery, museum and restaurant in the Triangle area. There's information on church events, hospitals, places to stay and local and state government.

The chambers of commerce for each town also have web sites. Contact the Cary Chamber at **www.carychamber.com**, the Chapel Hill-Carrboro Chamber at **www.herald-sun.com/cchamber**, the Durham Chamber at **www.herald-sun.com/dcc** and the Raleigh Chamber of Commerce at **www.raleighchamber.org**. You also can access the Durham Convention & Visitors Bureau at **www.dcvb.durham.nc.us** and the Raleigh CVB at **www.raleighcvb.org**.

You can also reach Apex at **www.apexchamber.com**, Clayton at **www.claytononline.com**, Fuquay-Varina at **www.fuquay-varina.com**, Garner at **www.garnerchamber.org**, Hillsborough at **www.ci.hillsborough.nc.us/Hillsborough**, Holly Springs at **www.ci.holly-springs.nc.us**, Knightdale at **www.ci.knightdale.nc.us/Knightdale** and Wake Forest at **www.citysearch.com/rdu/wfchamber**.

Other informative sites are the State Capitol/Visitors Services Section at **www.ah.dcr.state.nc.us/sections/capitol**, North Carolina—The Tar Heel State at **www.virtualcarolinas.com** and The Official North Carolina Travel Guide at **www.visitnc.com**.

With all this information, pretty soon you'll be an Insider too.

---

sports starting at 5 PM. Its sports coverage team has attracted national notice. WTVD has a bureau in Fayetteville that keeps us updated with operations at Ft. Bragg. The station's coverage of the weather is excellent.

WUNC-4, PBS
10 T.W. Alexander Dr., RTP • 549-7000

The state's university system operates the public television channels in North Carolina. The main studio is in Research Triangle Park. UNC-TV is one of the best PBS affiliates in the country and has a large following. WUNC has launched several programs that have become national PBS shows. Its local coverage of public affairs includes daily reviews when the General Assembly is in session.

Unlike many public television operations, it has a seasoned staff. The station has moved away from local craft shows toward more popular programming such

as *National Geographic, Nova, Frontline* and British mysteries and comedies. The Sesame Street gang also lives here.

Time Warner Cable
Carrboro/Hillsborough • 967-7068
Cary • 467-2800
Chapel Hill • 968-4631
Durham • 220-4481
Garner • 772-2553
Raleigh • 832-2225
Wake Forest • 556-6011
Wendell • 365-9010

Time Warner Cable serves Triangle viewers and offers several levels of service. You can get the networks, ESPN, CNN, TNT, Headline News, USA, BET and some others, including local access for about $32 a month. When Raleigh negotiated a new contract with Time Warner, the cable company agreed to help develop local, public studios for grassroots, community-based productions.

Triangle churches and ministries are responding to the spiritual needs of our growing population.

Worship

Triangle churches and ministries are responding to the spiritual needs of our growing population. The spiritual heritage of North Carolina is rich and deep. And today, in addition to the traditional hymns, sermons and Bible lessons, the seeker can find the timeless Biblical message proclaimed in contemporary music, multimedia and interactive study groups.

Ministries extend to health and fitness training, mission trips and community outreach. Southern Baptists and Roman Catholics, ultraconservatives and moderates all contribute to a healthy community of faith. Most congregations have many newcomers in their membership. They understand the stresses of moving and are happy to extend a welcoming hand.

It's a good idea to call first for time of worship, especially during the summer when many churches change their schedules. During the remainder of the year, most mainline Protestant churches hold at least one Sunday service at 11 AM; Catholic services will vary, but the early mass is normally at 8 AM.

The places of worship in this chapter are organized first by denomination and then by area: Raleigh, Cary, Durham and Chapel Hill.

Assemblies of God

Raleigh

Raleigh Christian Community
7000 Destiny Dr. • 266-7000
Raleigh Christian Community church is one of the most dynamic in the area. RCC meets the needs of its congregation through a variety of ministries and through home growth groups that meet all over the city. Its mission is characterized by powerful praise and worship, practical, relevant teaching from Senior Pastor Robert Spradley and a strong emphasis on relationships.

The northeast Raleigh church also sponsors Raleigh Christian Community School and RCC Little Preschool.

Baptist

Raleigh

First Baptist Church
101 S. Wilmington St. • 832-1649
One of the oldest—over 175 years—and largest of the predominately black churches, First Baptist sits across from the southeast corner of the Capitol, downtown. Its congregation numbers more than 600 members, many of whom are part of the city's civic leadership. The church maintains an active program of youth, music and religious education. A big day in the church year is its anniversary Sunday, which is celebrated the first Sunday in March and usually draws a big crowd.

First Baptist Church
99 North Salisbury St. • 832-4485
This is one of the city's largest Southern Baptist congregations. It is a busy, active church and includes many city leaders among its congregation. First Baptist recently severed its relationship with the Southern Baptist Convention since it is more moderate than the denominational conservatives who now control the SBC. The church provides many needed services, including a popular Infant/Toddler Day Care Center.

Photo by Tim Johnson

Located in downtown Raleigh, First Baptist Church is one of the area's oldest and largest Baptist congregations with more than 1300 members.

First Cosmopolitan Baptist
1515 Cross Link Rd. • 833-3283

Another of the city's large black Baptist churches is First Cosmopolitan, which sits just outside the I-440 Beltline in east Raleigh. The Reverend W. B. Lewis has been active in city affairs and leads a congregation of about 800 members. The church is over 90 years old and operates a day-care program for over 70 preschool children. It also has a special program to help older children with their homework.

Forest Hills Baptist Church
201 Dixie Tr. • 828-6161

Forest Hills is a Southern Baptist Church with a rich heritage for ministering to a wide variety of people. As one of the largest congregations in the city, Forest Hills offers programs for families, single adults, college students, international, senior adults, youth, children and preschoolers. The ministry staff offers many creative programs to meet the demands of such a diverse congregation.

Greystone Baptist Church
7509 Leadmine Rd. • 847-1333

Dr. Gene Watterson is pastor of this Southern Baptist congregation that was founded in 1984 as a mission of First Baptist Church. It numbers about 630, about 25 percent having come from non-Baptist backgrounds. Several Girl Scout troops meet here, as do a number of homeowner associations. There are two Sunday services and a van taxies members from nearby Springmoor retirement complex.

Hayes-Barton Baptist Church
1800 Glenwood Ave. • 833-4617

This is a Southern Baptist congregation and one of the largest in the city with 1,900 members. In the heart of "The Establishment" neighborhood, it has many influential citizens as members; Senator Jesse Helms attends church here when he's home from Washington. Hayes-Barton offers a wide range of Bible study and church programs. The church oversees a mission for the deaf. It also sponsors Girl, Cub and Boy Scout troops.

Mid-Way Baptist Church
6910 Fayetteville Rd. • 772-5864

An independent Baptist church, Mid-Way is one of the largest in the area with over 1,600 members. James L. Upchurch has been the pastor from the beginning. The church considers its preschool and singles classes to be two of its stronger programs. Sunday services start at 9 and 10:30 AM.

Mt. Olivet Baptist Church
3500 Edwards Mill Rd. • 787-1910

Mt. Olivet is in the middle of the city's northwest growth area and has grown with it, especially with Southern Baptist minister Tom Vestal, who has been there since 1978 and has helped double the church's membership, which now totals around 450. Services are broadcast weekly on Raleigh cable channel 22.

Providence Baptist Church
6339 Glenwood Ave. • 571-1171

This Southern Baptist congregation has made a reputation for outgrowing its buildings, and its current home, dedicated in 1992, was once one of the city's largest hotels. It has a strong Bible-study program and a prayer room that is open 24 hours a day. Pastor David Horner preaches in what was once a convention hall, backed up by a choir with full orchestra. Sunday School classes are held in the old barroom.

Pullen Memorial Baptist Church
1801 Hillsborough St.
• 828-0897

Adjacent to the NCSU campus, Pullen Memorial attracts a college crowd, including students and faculty. Characterized by *The News and Observer* as "the city's premier liberal church," it has a diverse congregation of about 900, active outreach programs, a strong music program and a day-care center.

Wake Chapel
4509 Bland Rd. • 872-7776

Led by Senior Pastor John J. Wilkins Jr., Wake Chapel Baptist Church encourages the "full experience of the Holy Spirit through study, prayer, devotion and service." Multiple ministries, including Christian Guidance for Children, Support for Singles and Services for Senior Citizens, address the special needs of the of the membership. In addition, Wake Chapel targets the concerns of the community at large through outreach programs that include AIDS, legal assistance, employment and support services.

Wake Chapel offers two Sunday morning services, Sunday School and a Tuesday night prayer service and Bible study.

Wake Cross Roads Baptist Church
3329 Forestville Rd. • 266-2957

This is the oldest church in Wake County. The church was founded in 1789, a few short months after George Washington was inaugurated as the country's first president. Wake Cross Roads is responsible for starting at least 13 other churches in the Raleigh area. Though over 200 years old, the church is very active and growing. This congregation has just finished a building program to triple the capacity of their worship facilities. The church has been associated with the Southern Baptist Convention since its formation in 1845. Bill Bowyer was called as pastor in February 1998.

FYI

Unless otherwise noted, the area code for all phone numbers listed in this guide is 919.

Cary

Apex Baptist Church
110 S. Salem St., Apex
• 362-6176

Established in 1873, Apex Baptist Church is an evangelical congregation of the Southern Baptist Convention with about 1,200 members. Phillip Qualls is the pastor. Sunday worship services are at 9:15 AM, 10:45 AM and 7 PM. A mid-week prayer session takes place Wednesdays at 6:30 PM.

Bethel Baptist Church
1111 West Chatham St. • 467-6789

Bethel Baptist is one of the larger independent Baptist congregations in Cary. The pastor is Bobby G. Jordan.

Colonial Baptist Church
6750 Tryon Rd. • 363-3500

Committed to Bible exposition, Colonial Baptist Church is one of the fastest growing churches in the area. In order to meet the demand, it currently offers three morning worship services. Programs include Catalyst (Adult Electives), Impact (Teen Discipleship) and Kids' Clubs. Graded Nursery and Children's Programs are provided for all services.

First Baptist Church
218 S. Academy St. • 467-6356

Dr. Steven Rumley is the pastor of First Baptist Church, the oldest and largest Southern Baptist church in Cary. The church offers a variety of programs for its congregation, including weekly Bible study; a music ministry; and ministries for children, youth, singles, families and senior adults.

Greenwood Forest Baptist Church
110 S.E. Maynard Rd. • 467-0481

Greenwood Forest is another large Southern Baptist Church. It, too, maintains a preschool program.

Durham

First Baptist Church
414 Cleveland St. • 688-7308

This large church was established in 1845 and is affiliated with the Southern Baptist Convention. It calls itself "the caring place."

Grey Stone Baptist Church
2601 Hillsborough Rd. • 286-2281

With nearly 3,000 members, this Southern Baptist Church constitutes the largest congregation in Durham. Established in 1894, Grey Stone has been in its present location, near Ninth Street in west Durham, for more than half a century. The Family Life Center includes basketball, volleyball and racquetball courts, a weight room, game room and gymnasium. There are weekly church suppers and activities for senior citizens. In addition, the church operates a year-round child-care center

Photo by Tim Johnson

Established in 1894, Grey Stone Baptist Church has the largest congregation in Durham with nearly 3,000 members.

for ages 2 through 5. Dr. Malbert Smith Jr. leads the congregation.

Homestead Heights Baptist Church
4007 Holt School Rd. • 477-3859

Established in 1962, Homestead Heights offers Sunday services at 8:30 AM, 11 AM and 6 PM. Sunday School starts at 9:30 AM. The church also has a Wednesday worship service at 6:30 PM.

White Rock Baptist Church
3400 Fayetteville St. • 688-8136

Established in 1866, White Rock is one of the largest predominantly black churches in Durham. Sunday worship services begin at 10:45 AM.

Other large Southern Baptist congregations in Durham include those of Bethesda Baptist Church (Miami Boulevard) and Guess Road Baptist Church.

Chapel Hill-Carrboro

Binkley Memorial Baptist Church
1712 Willow Dr. • 942-4964

Binkley's congregation has been known for its progressive outlook. Binkley is affiliated with the American Baptist Church. The church building also houses a highly regarded preschool program.

First Baptist Church
106 N. Roberson St. • 942-2509

Chapel Hill's largest black church was established in 1865. Reverend J. R. Manley has been its pastor for over 50 years. The church is affiliated with the American Baptist Convention. It is the site of one of the school system's Head Start preschool programs, as well as an after-school program for school-aged children.

University Baptist Church
100 S. Columbia St. • 942-2157

University Baptist Church is an imposing building at the corner of Franklin and Columbia in downtown Chapel Hill. This large and rather traditional congregation has Sunday School and a College. Dr. H. Mitchell Simpson is the pastor.

Catholic

Raleigh

Church of St. Joseph
630 Peartree Ln. • 231-6364

Located near Wake Medical Center, St. Joseph celebrates a rich Catholic tradition and enjoys a diversity of ethnic and national cultures. The small, yet growing, parish of about 210 households welcomes newcomers to its parish family. The church has the distinct honor of being the Shrine of Our Lady of Czestochowa, with a unique and beautiful statue of the Virgin Mary.

In addition to its many educational programs, St. Joseph also serves the larger community of the Triangle by providing ministry to people living with AIDS, as well as a tutorial program for needy children. Reverend Thanh Nguyen schedules the sacrament of penance on Wednesday evening at 6:30 PM and on Saturday at 3 PM. The Sunday mass schedule is 9 and 11:30 AM.

Our Lady of Lourdes
2718 Overbrook Dr. • 782-1973

Our Lady of Lourdes began in 1954, and has 1,320 families. It also maintains a K-8 school. The church building, which can be seen off Anderson Drive, was completed in 1976 and is one of the more contemporary in Raleigh with glass and gleaming white exterior. Members are proud of their summer Bible and adult education programs. The parish celebrates the feast of Our Lady of Lourdes every year. The pastor is Reverend Jeffrey A. Ingham, who oversees an assistant, a full-time youth minister and a music minister.

Sacred Heart Cathedral
200 Hillsborough St. • 832-6030

Catholic life has been growing in Raleigh since 1821 and has boomed during the past 25 years when many Catholic families moved into the city from the Northeast. Built in the 1920s, the Cathedral sits on the corner of Hillsborough and McDowell streets and is the parish to about 1,200 households. The Cathedral underwent a major restoration that was completed in fall 1998.

Cathedral School, prekindergarten through grade 8, has a student body of 250. The rector is Father Tim O'Connor. A 5 PM mass is held on Saturday, four masses on Sunday morning and there is also a Spanish mass. Confession is heard in the rectory. The Cathedral is the smallest cathedral in the contiguous United States.

St. Raphael
5801 Falls of the Neuse Rd. • 876-1581

An offshoot of Our Lady of Lourdes, St. Raphael has become the largest Catholic parish in town with 3,200 families and well over 6,000 parishioners. Reverend Robert Curry, S.J., directs a staff that includes an associate pastor, a music director, and religious and youth education directors. Its parish center is used by many groups. The parish also holds an annual Colonial Fair in September to raise money. It celebrates four Sunday masses, the last at 5:30 PM.

Cary

St. Michael's Catholic Church
804 High House Rd. • 468-6100

With nearly 5,000 parishioners, St. Michael's is the largest Catholic church in Cary and its Pastor is Father John A. Wall. Mass is held at 5 PM on Saturday and on Sunday at 7:15 AM, 8:45 AM, 10:30 AM, 12:15 PM and 6 PM. St. Michael's also offers mass in Spanish and Korean. The church operates an early childhood center.

Durham

Immaculate Conception
810 W. Chapel Hill St. • 682-3449

One of Durham's oldest churches, Immaculate Conception was established in the early 1900s. The parish has more than 2,500 members. There are three masses every Sunday morning and one every Saturday evening. In addition, the church operates preschool, after-school and summer camp programs.

The other Catholic churches are Holy Cross (1400 S. Alston Ave.), which serves a predominantly black community located near N.C. Central University; Holy Infant, which has enjoyed a surge in membership thanks to a location near Research Triangle Park, and St. Matthew in northern Durham County.

Chapel Hill-Carrboro

St. Thomas More
740 Gimghoul Rd. • 942-1040

Established in 1930, St. Thomas More has grown dramatically in the last 15 years and is currently building a new, larger church on Carmichael Street. As the only Catholic parish in Chapel Hill, it now has more than 1,700 members. There is a Saturday evening mass, and four Sunday masses. There is also a mass in Spanish on Sunday. During the week, services are held daily at 5:15 PM. The parish is affiliated with St. Thomas More School, Pre-K through 8 (see "Schools and Child Care" chapter). Mass is also celebrated at the Newman Center on Pittsboro Street, adjacent to the UNC campus. It is held at 12:15 PM Tuesday through Friday, at 5:15 PM on Saturday and at 9 and 11 AM on Sunday. Mass is also held at 7 PM Sunday nights for students during the school year. Call 929-3730 for information on the Newman Center.

Episcopal

Raleigh

Christ Episcopal Church
120 E. Edenton St. • 834-6259

This is one of the foundation churches of the city located across the street from the Capitol. Reverend Dr. Winston Charles is the rector. The church building is historic and its stained glass windows are beautiful. The Sunday Schools are lively, the music is some of the best in town and the church's outreach programs include missions to Appalachia, volunteers to help the illiterate, a Wednesday night Alcoholics Anonymous chapter and food distribution through Wake Relief.

St. Mark's
1725 New Hope Rd. • 231-6767

For years, St. Mark's has been one of the smaller Episcopal congregations in the area but one of the most enthusiastic. One member describes the congregation as an "involved" membership of 300 plus.

St. Michael's
1520 Canterbury Rd. • 782-0731

St. Michael's is one of the largest Episcopal parishes in its diocese with 2,400 members. The church's contemporary building displays a high, steep, slate roof that is supported by huge wooden beams, giving the nave a dramatic openness. It has a busy preschool and kindergarten as well as an excellent choir and music director.

Cary

St. Paul's Episcopal Church
221 Union St. • 467-1477

St. Paul's is one of a kind in Cary with a congregation of about 1,100. The Reverend George Adamik is rector.

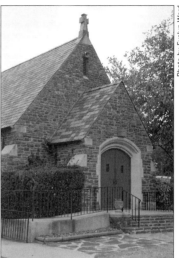

Photo by Evelyn Ward

The picturesque Holy Cross Catholic Church is located next to North Carolina Central University.

Durham

St. Phillips
403 E. Main St. • 682-5708

St. Phillips is the oldest Episcopal church in town, established in 1880. It is a very committed and socially responsible parish, the site of Durham's oldest soup kitchen. There are three Sunday morning services from September through May, and two during the summer months. There is a Wednesday evening communion service at 5:45 PM from September through May.

St. Andrew's (1852 Liberty Street) has a growing Hispanic congregation. St. Joseph's (1902 West Main Street) is the second oldest Episcopal church in Durham. And St. Luke's Episcopal (1737 Hillandale Road) is reputed to have one of the best preschool/kindergarten programs in Durham. St. Titus Episcopal Church (400 Moline Avenue) serves a predominantly black community. St. Stephen's

(82 Kimberly Drive) has services at 8, 9 and 11 AM, with Christian Education classes at 10 AM. It is located in Durham's Hope Valley neighborhood.

Chapel Hill-Carrboro

Chapel of the Cross
304 E. Franklin St. • 929-2193
The Chapel of the Cross has always been a socially conscious church. The church has fostered and housed many service programs, including Habitat for Humanity, Meals on Wheels, Alcoholics and Narcotics Anonymous meetings, and English as a Second Language classes. The church also houses a half-day childcare center. Sunday services are held at 7:30, 9 and 11:15 AM and 5:15 PM. The ministers are Reverend Stephen Elkins-Williams, Rector, Reverend Stephen Stanley, Associate for Campus Ministry and UNC Episcopal Chaplain, Reverend Tambria Lee and Reverend Vicky Jamieson-Drake.
The other Episcopal church in Chapel Hill, Church of the Holy Family, is located at 200 Hayes Road, off U.S. 15-501, and features a day-care program.

Evangelical

Cary

Redeemer Covenant
P.O. Box 4414, Cary, NC 27519 • 460-0702
The vision of this relatively new church is "to help people reach their God-given potential in Jesus Christ." The congregation consists of about 150 members. The priority the membership places on children is reflected in the exciting programs provided for the young people of the church. There is a distinctive "family" feeling here, ministering to the needs of the

church community and beyond. The church meets at the Cary Family YMCA on Cary Parkway. Sunday worship service and programs for all ages begin at 9:30 AM.

Interdenominational

Raleigh

Crossroads Fellowship
2721 Millbrook Rd. • 981-0222
Crossroads is an interdenominational Christian church established in 1988. It draws approximately 1,500 people on a typical Sunday. Worship services and Sunday school are held at 9:15 AM and 11 AM.

Jewish

Raleigh

Beth Meyer Synagogue
504 Newton Rd. • 848-1420
This synagogue is the oldest of the three Jewish congregations in Raleigh. Beth Meyer serves about 340 families. Rabbi David Bockman assumed responsibilities in 1999. The congregation is conservative in practice. Beth Meyer worship service is held at 8 PM Friday and 9:15 AM Saturdays.

Temple Beth Or
5315 Creedmoor Rd. • 781-4895
Like Beth Meyer, Temple Beth Or was downtown before it moved to the present location on Creedmoor Road. The synagogue is very contemporary and it is worth a visit just to see the award-winning architectural design. The Bema (altar) was rescued from a temple in Chicago that was being torn down. Beth Or is a reformed congregation of about 450 families

under the leadership of Rabbi Lucy Dinner. Worship service is held on Friday at 8 PM.

Cary

Synagogue Beth Shalom
P.O. Box 5161, Cary, NC • 481-1880

This synagogue is Cary's one and only and members meet in a temporary space until a new synagogue is built next year. The young, vibrant congregation, which is under the leadership of Rabbi Deborah Bodin Cohen, consists of over 70 families who are members of the reformed movement. Started in 1983, it has an active Sunday School.

Durham

Beth-El Conservative and Orthodox Synagogue
1004 Watts St. • 682-1238

Though over 100 years old, this synagogue is strong and growing under the leadership of Rabbi Steven Sager. Services are 8 PM on Friday (6 PM on the first Friday of each month) and 9:45 AM on Saturday. Beth-El also operates a religious school.

Judea Reform Congregation
1955 West Cornwallis Rd. • 489-7062

The Judea Reform Congregation is led by Rabbi John S. Friedman. Services are held on Friday evening with a monthly family service at 7:30 PM.

Chapel Hill-Carrboro

Hillel Foundation (Jewish Student Center)
210 W. Cameron Ave. • 942-4057

The Hillel Foundation is the only Jewish center in Chapel Hill. It serves the needs of members of the UNC community, with High Holy Day services, Shabbat, Jewish university classes, parties, dances, discussion groups and occasional dinners and breakfasts. Call for information.

Lutheran

Raleigh

Holy Trinity
2723 Clark Ave. • 828-1687

This is a congregation of the Lutheran Church of America and numbers about 1,000 members, making it one of the largest in the Triangle. It was organized in 1912 and has helped start St. Philip's and Christ the King Lutheran as well as two new missions. Close to NCSU, it considers itself a "home congregation away from home" for Lutheran students. Pastor Royall A. Yount Jr. has help from Associate Pastor Lawrence F. Holmes and the Reverend Beverly D. Alexander, who serves as the church's campus pastor. There are two services on Sunday as well as Sunday School.

Cary

Christ The King Lutheran
600 Walnut St. • 467-8989

The dean of the Lutheran congregations, this church has a preschool, too. Its pastor is the Reverend John Nagle.

Another large Lutheran Church in the area is Resurrection Lutheran Church-LCMS at 100 Lochmere Drive, 851-7248.

Durham

St. Paul's Lutheran Church ELCA
1200 W. Cornwallis Rd. • 489-3214

The largest Lutheran church in Durham, St. Paul's congregation continues to grow. There are two Sunday morning services and Sunday School at 9:45 AM during the school year; in the summer, there is only one service at 9:30 AM.

Another ELCA congregation in the area is Christus Victor located at 1615 N.C. 54 East. Grace Lutheran at 824 N. Buchanan Boulevard belongs to the Missouri Synod.

Chapel Hill-Carrboro

Holy Trinity
300 E. Rosemary St. • 942-2678

Holy Trinity, the first Lutheran church in town, was established in 1946. It is located in the Historic District, one block from downtown. Services are held at 8:30 and 11 AM (10 AM during the summer). The pastor is Reverend Terry Morgan.

Nondenominational

Raleigh

Brooks Avenue
Church of Christ
700 Brooks Ave. • 821-2400

Lindsey Garmon, the new minister at Brooks Avenue, leads the church in its mission "to speak where the Bible speaks, to be silent where the Bible is silent and to emphasize what the Bible emphasizes." Special ministries include programs for youth, leadership, singles, young married couples and families. Sunday worship services are at 8:15 AM, 10:30 AM and 6 PM.

Cary

Crosspointe Church at Cary
Imperial Theater, Cary Towne Center • 469-9111

Founding and preaching Pastor Steve Larson's goal was to start a "real church for real people." Larson came from Michigan to Cary in the spring of 1996. The church was launched in October 1997 in the Imperial Theater. Nurseries, children's worship and an upbeat, multimedia, contemporary worship service are conducted in the various theaters. Small groups meet for study and service projects.

Durham

Duke University Chapel
Main Campus • 684-2572

Though some tourists have been directed toward the basketball stadium when inquiring as to where Duke students worship, Duke Chapel's reputation as the most stunning church facility in Durham is well deserved. The 1,800-seat Gothic Revival structure was built to fulfill James B. Duke's dream of "a great towering church which will dominate all the surrounding buildings." The 210-foot tower, patterned after Canterbury Cathedral, contains a 50-bell, four-octave carillon. Inside, the double doors are flanked by portal figures of churchmen Savonarola, Martin Luther, Thomas Cooke and John Wesley, as well as Thomas Jefferson and fellow Virginian Robert E. Lee. The vaulted interior is lighted with 77 stained-glass windows.

INSIDERS' TIP

The Triangle religious community has grown very diverse. For instance, the area includes such places of worship as the Buddhist Kadampa Center in Raleigh, 7404 Chapel Hill Road, 859-3433; the Hindu Society of North Carolina in Morrisville, 309 Aviation Parkway, 481-2574; the Islamic Center of Durham, 2806 Carver Street, 477-7623; and the Islamic Center of Raleigh, 3020 Ligon Street, 834-9572.

Chapel Hill-Carrboro

Chapel Hill Bible Church
1200 Mason Farm Rd. • 968-4754
Founded in 1971, the nondenominational and evangelical Bible Church has grown to over 1,200 adults attending on a regular basis. The children's and youth ministries are strong and there is also an international students program. Services are held at 8:30, 9:45 and 11:15 AM; service times change for the summer.

Orthodox

Raleigh

All Saints Orthodox Church
520 Buck Jones Rd. • 859-1332
Raleigh has a growing Orthodox community and can boast four Orthodox congregations within its municipal borders. All Saints is the newest of these four congregations and is home to about 70 member families. A goal of the church is to provide the area a completely English-speaking, pan-Orthodox parish with an emphasis on evangelism. The congregation is under the jurisdiction of the Antiochian Orthodox Christian Archdiocese of North America. Worship is conducted each Sunday at 10 AM.

Presbyterian

Raleigh

Davie Street Presbyterian
300 E. Davie St. • 834-8855
This Presbyterian church is a downtown congregation that contains some of the city's prominent black families. It was founded in 1872 and numbers about 140 members. Its minister is Byron Wade, who cites the church's outreach programs for youth and older parishioners as strong points.

First Presbyterian
111 W. Morgan St. • 821-5750
This oldest Presbyterian church in town continues to have a lively role in the city's life. Its pastor, Dr. Edwin W. Stock Jr., preaches the church's Sunday sermon at 11 AM. The church began in 1816 and today counts a membership that is slightly over 1,700. The church has a special program for elderly members and attracts 60 men to a Wednesday 6:30 AM breakfast and Bible study. Despite its age, the church, according to one member, "baptizes a lot of babies."

Hudson Memorial Presbyterian
4921 Six Forks Rd. • 787-1086
Started in 1957, this North Raleigh congregation met first in nearby schools and has grown and expanded to 1,400 members. The church is strategically located one mile north of the I-440 Beltline on a major thoroughfare connecting the northwest quadrant of Raleigh to the downtown area. Hudson Memorial has several Sunday services and supports a preschool program. It also provides a mother's day out, Monday through Friday, an active music program and after-school care from 3 to 6 PM.

West Raleigh Presbyterian
27 Horne St. • 828-5468
This is a university church, a block away from the NCSU campus, whose 350 members include many faculty and students from not only NCSU but also Peace College and Meredith. Dr. P. Joseph Ward is the minister. The church has many outreach programs serving the community. It has an active junior and senior high youth program.

White Memorial Presbyterian
1704 Oberlin Rd. • 834-3424
White Memorial has the largest Presbyterian membership in the city—over

4,000 members. Located on the edge of Hayes-Barton, an important part of its mission centers on community ministry. Minister Art Ross leads this influential congregation. The church maintains a full range of programs, including a well-known preschool and kindergarten with veteran teachers for children 2 to 5.

Cary

Cary Presbyterian
614 Griffis St. • 467-8700

This is the oldest of the mainline Presbyterian congregations and one of the largest. It also operates a preschool. The Reverend J. David Wiseman is minister.

Cornerstone Presbyterian Church
Davis Drive Elementary, 2151 Davis Dr., Apex • 303-9200

Formerly called Davis Drive Fellowship, Cornerstone is a church development of the Presbytery of New Hope. The church currently meets at Davis Drive Elementary in Apex. Newcomers are welcome to experience worship, education, fellowship and service to others. Sunday worship is held at 11 AM and Sunday school begins at 9:45 AM.

Kirk of Kildaire Presbyterian Church
200 High Meadow Dr. • 467-4944

Established in 1979, Kirk of Kildaire has a congregation of about 700 families. Sunday worship is held at 8:30 AM and 11 AM. Sunday school classes are offered during both services. Tom Spence is the pastor.

Peace Presbyterian Church
2850 S.W. Cary Pkwy. • 467-5977

Associated with the Presbyterian Church of America, this congregation of 175 families started in Cary in 1979. The church has an active Bible study program and a number of its members are "home schoolers."

Built in 1916, the First Presbyterian Church in downtown Durham contains stained glass windows from Germany.

Photo by Tim Johnson

Durham

First Presbyterian
305 E. Main St. • 682-5511

Durham's oldest and largest Presbyterian church is located downtown. More than a century old, First Presbyterian has an active, growing congregation today. There are youth and adult fellowship programs.

Chapel Hill-Carrboro

Church of the Reconciliation
110 N. Elliott Rd. • 929-2127

This Presbyterian community is characterized by its progressive congregation, described as "inclusive, diverse and committed to social justice." The Chapel Hill Cooperative Preschool is located at the church. Reverend Mark Davidson is the pastor.

University Presbyterian
209 E. Franklin St. • 929-2102

The largest Presbyterian church in town, University Presbyterian has more than 1,000 members. The church also is the site of a parent's morning out program and a well-respected preschool and half-day kindergarten. Reverend Dr. Bob Dunham is the pastor, Lynn Stall is the associate pastor and Ollie Wagner is the pastor for campus ministry.

Quaker

Durham

Friends Meeting House
404 Alexander Dr. • 286-4958

Associated with the Carolina Friends School, this is the only Friends Meeting in Durham. It is located near Duke Gardens.

Unitarian Universalist

Chapel Hill-Carrboro

Community Church of Chapel Hill
106 Purefoy Rd. • 942-2050

Founded in 1953 as an interfaith congregation, this church continues leadership in areas of peace, justice and spirituality. Sunday services and religious education are held at 11 AM. The Reverend Charles Kast is the pastor. The church

is located just off Mason Farm Road south of the UNC hospitals.

United Church of Christ

Chapel Hill-Carrboro

United Church of Chapel Hill
205 Wilson St. • 942-3540

United Church was the founder of the Inter-Faith Council and has been a strong participant in its activities. In fact, the Family Assistance program and the administrative offices of this group are housed at the church. The United Church has participated in numerous exchanges with citizens from other countries and has been very active in the Habitat home-building program. Services take place Sunday at 9 and 11 AM. The church is led by clergy couple, Jill and Richard Edens.

United Methodist

Raleigh

Asbury United Methodist
6612 Creedmoor Rd. • 847-2818

One of the fastest growing Methodist churches in the state, Asbury is located along one of the city's growth arteries outside the I-440 Beltline. Started in 1979, its minister is Marshall Old, who pastors along with a full-time staff of four, to over a 1,000 members. It caters to young families and operates a preschool program as well as an after-school program for working families. It also has a day camp in the summer

INSIDERS' TIP

Many area churches offer "Mother's Time Out" programs, which give mothers a daytime respite from their children for a reasonable fee. Most programs provide care for a few hours and serve the children some kind of refreshment.

and a School of Music year round for preschoolers to adults.

Edenton Street United Methodist
228 W. Edenton St. • 832-7535

Considered the "mother" church for Raleigh's Methodists, Edenton Street traces its history back to 1811, and with a membership of nearly 3,000, it is one of the city's largest congregations of any faith. Dr. Roger V. Elliott is the senior minister and has carried on the church's leadership in such fields as urban ministries. Music lovers throughout the city also have long enjoyed the church's tradition in music. As one church official noted about church members, many of whom live in the suburbs, "They all have to drive past other churches to get here, so they must want to come here."

Hayes-Barton United Methodist
2209 Fairview Rd. • 832-6435

Founded in 1936, Hayes Barton has approximately 2,145 members. The Reverend Doug Jessee is the pastor. The church is known for its mission work and it contains a preschool program and a youth service-oriented group.

Highland United Methodist
1901 Ridge Rd. • 787-4240

Started in 1954, Highland has over 2,000 members and a congregation that is filled with many of the people who work in Research Triangle Park and NCSU, giving it a definite "high tech" flavor. Minister Dr. Jim H. Bailey has an associate pastor, Reverend Jonathan Jeffries. The church attracts many members because of its music program, which includes a handbell choir. There's a large preschool program for children from 2 to 5 years old and an after-school program for grades K-5, along with a church softball and basketball team.

Cary

Disciple United Methodist Church
Morrisville Elementary School
• 363-5700

Disciple United Methodist is one of the newest churches in Cary. The church, which is currently meeting at Morrisville Elementary on Morrisville Parkway, is known for its friendly people and unique blend of contemporary and traditional worship. Worship begins at 10 AM and everyone receives a hearty welcome and friendly smile.

First United Methodist Church
117 S. Academy St. • 467-1861

This the oldest of Cary's United Methodist congregations. As one of the town's largest congregations, with 3,500 members, it has recently completed a highly celebrated renovation and expansion. Its minister is the Reverend Woody Wells. It operates a preschool and kindergarten. First United has an informal service at 5:30 PM on Saturday. Sunday services are at 8:25, 9:45 and 11:05 AM.

White Plains United Methodist
313 S.E. Maynard Rd. • 467-9394

White Plains was founded in 1961 and has become home to nearly 900 families. The church offers two traditional services at 8:30 and 11 AM and a contemporary worship service at 9:45 AM. On the second Sunday of each month, the service is broadcast on WACN TV throughout the Triangle. It has active music program, including a full church orchestra and handbell program. Each summer, church members participate in an Appalachian service project. It also is the only church in the area to offer a Christian bookstore named "The Carpenter's Shop." In its "children's center," it has one of the Triangle's few preschool programs that includes handicapped and "special needs" children with other children.

Durham

Trinity United Methodist Church
215 N. Church St. • 683-1386

This was the first Methodist church in Durham, built in 1832 in a school house in Orange Grove about a mile east of town. The current Gothic stone building, located across the street from City Hall, was reconstructed following a fire in 1923. It is among the largest Methodist congregations in Durham. There are two services on Sunday morning: 8:45 and 11 AM.

Duke Memorial United Methodist Church
504 W. Chapel Hill St. • 683-3467

Duke Memorial was established over 100 years ago. Today it is the largest of the 24 Methodist churches in Durham. Duke Memorial also operates a preschool.

Chapel Hill-Carrboro

Carrboro United Methodist
200 Hillsborough Rd. • 942-1223

Established in 1910, Carrboro United Methodist has a growing congregation, presided over by the Reverend Daniel T. Earnhardt. It also houses a daycare center that includes an after-school care program and a full-day toddler-care program, 929-5143.

University United Methodist
150 E. Franklin St. • 929-7191

The Reverend William Gattis and the Reverend Ronald Gonia preside over this large congregation, which has 1,800 members. Services are held at 8:45 and 11 AM, with Sunday School at 9:45 AM. There is a half-day preschool at the church, 967-8867.

Index

Index of Advertisers